Thirty Years On

Is Comprehensive Education Alive and Well or Struggling to Survive?

Caroline Benn and
Clyde Chitty

David Fulton Publishers
London

David Fulton Publishers Ltd
2 Barbon Close, London WC1N 3JX

First published in Great Britain by David Fulton Publishers 1996

Note: The right of Caroline Benn and Clyde Chitty to be identified as
the authors of this work has been asserted by them in accordance with
the Copyright, Design and Patents Act 1988.

Copyright © David Fulton Publishers Ltd

British Library Cataloguing in Publication Data

A catalogue record for this book is available from the British Library

ISBN 1-85346-353-1

Typeset by The Harrington Consultancy Ltd
Printed in Great Britain by BPC Books and Journals, Exeter

Contents

Acknowledgements

The authors would like to express their gratitude to the Board of RICE (Right to a Comprehensive Education), the Standing Conference on Studies in Education and The Esmée Fairbairn Charitable Trust for their generous financial contributions towards the carrying out of this research project.

The authors owe a special debt to Ian Campbell, Lecturer in Professional Studies and Information Technology at East Birmingham College, who played a major role in the project throughout. Not only did he coordinate all aspects of the collation and analysis of the data, but he also provided many crucial insights which were invaluable in the authors' interpretation of the findings.

Special mention should also be made of Paul Button, who played a key role in the design of the database, undertook a considerable amount of the data entry and prepared many of the tables in the text.

Special thanks are also due to the following, starting with John Owens, Editorial Director at David Fulton Publishers, who supported and encouraged the authors throughout. Those who helped with advice and assistance at various points during the project were: Charles Bell, Hilary Benn, Joshua Benn, Shane Blackman, Frances Burgess, Alison Bullock, Graham Butt, Sue Butterfield, Ray Campbell, Willie Campbell, Peter Carter, Tony Cobb, Tom Crompton, Robert Crone, Nasrin Daryani, Margaret Doran, John Fairley, David Fulton, Pam Fulton, Jan Fletcher, Derek Gillard, Lyndon Godsall, John Harkin, Andy Johnson, Gordon Kirkpatrick, Denis Lawton, Mairtin mac an Ghaill, George Mardle, Sandra Mecdonnell, Anthony Mor O'Brien, Guy Neave, Jenny Neave, Peter Newsam, Audrey Osler, Lindsay Paterson, Frank Pignatelli, Maurice Plaskow, Stewart Ranson, Peter Ribbins, John Rigg, Martin Rogers, Derek Rushworth, Roger Seckington, Linda Stewart, Jim Thawley, David Watts, Ruth Watts and Keith Wymer.

Last but not least, the authors would like to thank the Copy Editor, Alan Taman, for all the time and energy he has spent in preparing this book for publication.

Foreword

This book celebrates the thirtieth anniversary of the publication of the famous Circular 10/65 which established comprehensive education as 'official' government policy in 1965.

Five years later Caroline Benn and I published the first independent inquiry, *Half Way There: Report on the British Comprehensive School Reform.* At that time just over a third of pupils in maintained schools in Great Britain were in comprehensive schools. Today over 90% of pupils of secondary school age are in comprehensive schools, although the selective system of the past still retains a foothold in some areas of England.

Over the last 30 years the country as a whole has, then, voted with its feet, establishing systems of comprehensive education in almost every area. This is in sharp contrast to the situation that existed in 1965, when 90% of pupils were in grammar, technical and modern schools that comprised the tripartite system, based on selection at the age of 11.

Comprehensive education, over the recent period, has been strikingly successful in gaining loyal support from local communities and parents throughout the country. An immense debt of gratitude is due to the teachers, who, in spite of almost unbelievable difficulties and persistent criticism, have believed in the system, given it their loyalty and energies, and carried through this historic transformation successfully.

Comprehensive schools have not been popular with governments over the last 16 years. From Prime Ministerial level downwards, obloquy has been heaped on them, with the national press and media playing their part. Attempts have been made to destroy specific local systems and revert to selection, all of which have failed.

The persistent and unprincipled attacks on local authorities, which brought comprehensive education into being and supported it, have sought to destabilise comprehensive education's base and infrastructure. New types of schools have been created by the government, including opted-out schools, directly financed by the state, with the aim of outflanking the comprehensive system. Despite all this – indeed, paradoxically, perhaps because of it – comprehensive systems still cover the country and still provide secondary education for the majority of the nation's children in the state system. The crucial problem remaining, then, is that of establishing a truly national system of education, catering for all. Compared with most other advanced industrial countries, Britain has lagged behind in achieving this objective, and does so at its peril.

In this book, Caroline Benn and Clyde Chitty report the results of their survey into comprehensive education in Great Britain today. They have done this as a result of their own initiative and relying on resources they organised themselves. It is remarkable that no government, over the last 25 years, despite disposing of massive research moneys, has considered it worthwhile to launch a serious inquiry into the progress of comprehensive schooling, even though most young people now attend such schools and colleges. The huge gap thus created has now been filled by the authors of this book who have taken it upon themselves to do a job so clearly needed, and indeed so very important for the nation as a whole. We must all be grateful for their initiative and determination.

Both authors are highly qualified to undertake this task, having been closely identified with comprehensive education for over 30 years. For 25 years Caroline Benn, now a lecturer in further education, was the editor of *Comprehensive Education*, the journal of the comprehensive movement, and information officer of the Comprehensive Schools Committee set up in the 1960s to monitor the reform nationally. Clyde Chitty, now lecturing at Birmingham University, who assisted with *Half Way There*, has had long experience as a teacher, head of department, and finally as Vice-Principal and Principal of a large Leicestershire comprehensive school.

Both have worked energetically, and with great efficiency, to carry through the survey on which this book is based, and to present its findings to the public. There is, to my mind, no question that this book will make a major contribution not only to our knowledge and understanding of our existing school system, but also to clarifying the road to the future.

Brian Simon
December, 1995

Introduction

This book marks 30 years of comprehensive education – by any standard, a landmark in British education reform. This seems a good point at which to take stock of the achievements of comprehensive education to date – and to define the problems that still remain.

Although 1965 was the year when reorganisation of secondary education became national policy, comprehensive education reform itself began many years earlier. Looking back, we can see this initiative as the final stage in the long drive to secondary education for all which has concerned Britain from the start of the twentieth century, just as the nineteenth century was concerned with a drive for elementary education for all. All the signs are that the twenty-first century will see increasing pressure to make learning available to everyone throughout their working lives and beyond. Indeed, this third drive, long discussed, has flourished anew in the last 30 years.

We speak broadly in terms of comprehensive education, rather than narrowly in terms of comprehensive schools, to concentrate discussion on the array of forms comprehensive education has taken and the range of ages to which it applies. It is time to move on from sterile debate pegged to one or two past institutional embodiments of the comprehensive principle, which for one reason or another have come to narrow the debate, even to caricature it. A good deal of comment, particularly in the mass media, is still concerned with parrying positions nobody holds, and in many cases, never did!

But myths flourish readily in conditions where a particular type of education is discussed so widely. Yet practically no information at all is being provided about the practices which characterise it or about the institutions in which it is developing – that is, information particular to comprehensive education as a system and to its institutions as a class, however diverse. In the absence of such knowledge, it is only to be expected that many will elevate anecdote to universal truth, or encourage developments without knowledge of their practical implications.

Absence of knowledge and information also abets attempts to ignore, diminish, downgrade and ease comprehensive education out of the public frame. Of course, comprehensive institutions at secondary level share features with grammar schools or secondary modern schools or special schools or private schools. But to pretend that they are the same as other schools – and may simply be classed, analysed and judged in the same 'secondary' system by the same criteria as comparable institutions – raises barriers to understanding any of them, and is positively harmful for comprehensive education.

Comprehensive education, precisely because it does aim to encompass everyone, needs its own documentation, its own analysis, its own monitoring, its own pedagogy and its own development plans. Those devised for schooling on behalf of particular social groups or schools directed by law to concentrate upon a limited range of attainment – be it high or low – are not appropriate. Yet all too often the needs of these minorities dominate the needs and practices of the majority, particularly when they are institutions limited to those who are already high attainers or to those from backgrounds of more than modest means and more than modest knowledge of the system. To impose blanket prescriptions on the majority dictated by the welfare of non-comprehensive institutions – as a consequence of not recognising comprehensive education's own unique needs – after so many years of heated debate about this one principle in particular, seems almost perverse.

Yet since 1979 plans specifically for comprehensive education – for its structure, its curriculum or its assessment – have not really been on the agenda. Even before this, there was a marked lack of support, including effective legislation, for the development of the comprehensive education that was supposedly being supported by the governments of that day. Indeed, very little official pacing of its progress overall has ever been undertaken. In 1965 the National Foundation for Educational Research (NFER) was commissioned to provide information about comprehensive reorganisation, a detailed but essentially limited exercise that ended in 1972 (Monks, 1968; 1970; Ross et al., 1972). Nothing comparable ever followed, though a Centre for the Study of Comprehensive Schools was started in 1980. Owing to restricted funding, it never developed a full research programme and became instead a cheerful cheering section for good practice, its true potential neglected.

Official yearly statistics relating to the numbers of comprehensive schools and data related to their work were sometimes published in the 1970s by governments or HMI, but since 1979, with governments actively hostile to the comprehensive principle, official information has dwindled almost to nothing. In the education statistics for Britain in the year of the survey only one table gives any information on such schools and this is minimal (see *Education Statistics for the United Kingdom*, HMSO, 1993, Table 18). In most DfE statistical bulletins no information is given about comprehensive schools as a class – that is, relating to participation in the system or to staffing or special needs[1]. In official handbooks – such as OFSTED's manual of practice – comprehensive schools are not mentioned as such. The *Parents' Charter*, sent in 1993 at a cost of £3 million to every household, told citizens about grant maintained schools, city technology colleges, assisted places, voluntary schools, training credits, 'selective schools for the academically able', and even about 'the important role' of private education. It completely failed to mention comprehensive schools or colleges. Yet in this same year another government publication claimed that 'over 90%' of pupils during the secondary years owe their education to comprehensive schools (*Education Statistics for the United Kingdom*, HMSO, 1993, p. 95).

In the external examination results, however, comprehensives are singled out, with no additional information provided to show the way these schools differ in their intakes and objectives from others with which they are compared on a one-to-one basis (as in 'league tables'); and in several sets of DfE statistics comprehensive schools are distinguished only after grant maintained comprehensive schools, sixth form colleges and tertiary colleges have been removed from comprehensive totals where some of the first and almost all of the last two belong.

At the heart of the national education service there seem to be two contradictory policies operating: one accepting comprehensive education, another actively undermining it. Yet nowhere is there information presented to permit an analysis of just how these policies are working through the system and the effects they are having on teachers and learners, institutions and communities.

At the start of official reorganisation, there was no shortage of analysis and writing on comprehensive education's development, including its problems. There were many books and research projects relevant to comprehensive education, many of them essential reading for all involved in education in the late twentieth century; but more recently such analysis and writing has become a rarity. The journal *Comprehensive Education*, which chronicled the reform from 1965, now appears only sporadically, though the independent publication *FORUM* is still a consistent provider of discussion and research specifically orientated to comprehensive education from 3 to 19. Information is available school-by-school and occasional individual research projects cover small groups of comprehensive schools, but in the last 20 years there has been nothing giving a full profile of comprehensive education for the country as a whole and the stage of development it has reached.

After 30 years there is undoubtedly a great deal to discover that official statistics have left untouched, but because official support for successfully developing comprehensive education has diminished, no plans exist to undertake this work. Yet any future direction of the education system has to take the development of comprehensive schools and colleges into account, if only because nine out of every ten of those in secondary education in Britain are in comprehensive education of one kind or another.

At the very simplest level, a general profile of those schools and colleges would seem essential reading for everyone involved in teaching in such schools and colleges, for parents of students attending them and for officials planning their future. Defining more clearly the nature of comprehensive education, and the variety of ways in which it is now being practised, may not make value judgements easier where there is disagreement, but it could make us better able to concentrate on the several routes that comprehensive education could take over the next 30 years. These are by no means fixed. If everyone's energy is subsumed with unreal discussion about which route back to the past is preferred, the real choices might never be discussed. Decisions will be taken by special interest groups or political people with temporary mandates, or – worst of all, and much the most likely – by default.

The Second National Independent Enquiry

For all these reasons – and because the future always offers a possibility of governments more sympathetic to the comprehensive principle – it seemed a good time to look broadly at the state of comprehensive education from 9 to 19 in the United Kingdom. Accordingly, we undertook an independent enquiry into all comprehensive schools and colleges in the academic year 1993–94.

We called it the Second Independent Enquiry because it was in the same mould as the first such Enquiry conducted in 1968 (and followed up later in 1970), published under the title *Half Way There, A Report on the British Comprehensive School Reform* written by Caroline Benn and Brian Simon, with Clyde Chitty as a research assistant. It provided a whole generation with a profile of the kind of comprehensive education Britain was developing in response to national policy requirements at that time.

Most of the research for the Second Independent Enquiry was conducted from March to May in 1994 (see Appendix I for full details). Like the first it took the form of a questionnaire. In 1968 this was sent to all comprehensive schools on a list that was available from the DES, supplemented by a fuller one from the Comprehensive Schools Committee, the main voluntary body supporting the reform. In 1994, with no such lists, there were problems relating to definitions both for schools and colleges – these are fully discussed in Appendix I.

The 1994 survey therefore used its own definition and its first objective was to make sure contact was made with all categories of secondary schools and general education colleges likely to qualify under these definitions as 'schools for all levels of attainment where admission is without academic selection, or open access colleges acting as one of the main providers of education for the 16–19 age range in the area'. The questionnaire was sent to all schools and further education colleges in the United Kingdom, making it clear that only those meeting these definitions should respond. The 1994 questionnaire was much longer than that used in 1968. A few of the questions were in the same form, and these have provided some interesting comparative insights. Most of the questions were new, however, and related to developments which have occurred in education since 1970. Some of these related to colleges, which had not been included in the first Enquiry.

We were well aware that surveying the total population of schools, adding all the colleges, covering every region of the United Kingdom, and devising a questionnaire of such length and complexity (moreover at a period when schools and colleges were daily bombarded with research questionnaires) risked a drastically lower response rate than the 81% obtained in the first Independent Enquiry. But the chance to collect information on a wide range of comprehensive experience and practice for the whole of the UK – in the certain absence of any government initiatives to undertake this work – overrode any inclination to reduce the numbers of questions, to use smaller samples, or to confine our work to one region or age range. We were interested in establishing the widest ranging data base possible, to be used for this report as well as for further research, available to comprehensive schools and colleges and those working in their interests. In the end over 5000 schools and colleges were mailed with 148 questions, some having 30 or 40 additional sections.

A few of those replying complained about the length, but none queried the survey's definitions of 'comprehensive' and many were supportive of the exercise and grateful that an interest was being taken in such an important aspect of British education, which thousands, as we discovered, believed was being neglected. We also discovered a fair number of schools, colleges, staffs and parent groups that were profoundly depressed by official attitudes to their comprehensive commitment. Several schools and colleges phoned before replying, almost always to ask if we were independent as claimed, and most wanting assurance we were nothing to do with the government, or were not an agency commissioned by any government department or quango.

A few Scottish respondents pointed out the way some of the questions assumed 'English' answers, but on the whole most Scots were kindly uncritical of any bias of this kind. Several further education principals were less than happy about the restricted nature of the enquiry for not asking in more detail about the work of colleges as a whole. Some were also disappointed with the restricted space allowed for writing in the additional courses or qualifications they were providing. All such comment was quite justifiable, including a larger observation occasionally made that the survey was more orientated towards schools than colleges. We accepted that our information about further education colleges would be incomplete because we looked at their work only up to the age of 19. But to have left them out of this survey would have been to exclude institutions we believe will be at the heart of the future development of comprehensive education.

We were very grateful to all who replied in full, including those few with misgivings. We would have been happy with a final response rate of one in four; as it was, we achieved an overall 35% return – 41% in respect of the largest group, schools in the English counties. Most pleasing of all was that among the 1560 institutions included in the final data base that provides the information for the chapters that follow, every single Local Education Authority in England and Wales is represented , as is every single Educational Region of Scotland[2] and every single Education and Library Board in Northern Ireland. Represented also are the Channel Islands, the Isle of Man and the majority of schools run by the Services Children's Education Authority (SCEA).

We are satisfied that the information we make available, while it must be read in certain parts with caution (for reasons given in the Appendix and at a few points in the text), gives a reliable general picture of comprehensive education in Britain from 9 to 19 years in this thirtieth anniversary year of the official start of secondary comprehensive education.

The future

The research presented here was undertaken for the purpose of providing information for all who are interested in comprehensive education, but particularly for those who will be working for its future development. It is the first book to look at comprehensive institutions in the UK overall for more than two decades. Inevitably it has several shortcomings, of which we are only too well aware. But we believe it also provides a great deal of valuable information not available elsewhere.

Because we believe the needs of comprehensive education have been neglected in practice for years (however much the idea is still debated) , our primary focus in this research when examining both the context within which schools and colleges work, and the practices of individual schools and colleges, was on those aspects most closely related to the fundamental aims, principles and values of comprehensive education. Our purpose is to review the last 30 years, to present a broad outline of current practices and to give general indicators of comparative differences within the population of comprehensive schools and colleges. It would have been impossible to set out detailed comparative findings on every aspect of comprehensive education.

Inevitably what we present in this book is a first recording of the major data that was made available. To have subjected some of it to more sophisticated analysis (as is needed in some places) would have required at least another book. In time, possibly a second volume will take shape, for several further objectives appeared as we worked through the data, including the need to set out the areas where further research and information might be required; and where alternatives policies could be developed within schools and colleges; where communities could effect change themselves, as against those areas where government initiatives might be required. Throughout the book these are signposted and at the end are some recommendations. For the best form of anniversary congratulations we can offer is to set out as clearly as possible the work that still needs to be done, in the hope of engaging those who have the greatest interest in doing so – namely the great mass of citizens whose education is now underwritten by the comprehensive principle, and those who have the responsibility for translating it into reality.

Throughout the book we have tried to show the positive changes that are taking place, including the organic connections that are growing between ostensibly segregated sectors of education and their institutions. We have also highlighted some negative changes that have grown inside comprehensive education, some without our realising. We believe the most serious problem is that the main principle of comprehensive education – giving equal value to all learners and all forms of learning – has been and is being seriously compromised.

We look forward to:

- learners and teachers achieving more academic freedom, more self-management and more responsibility for how and what they learn and teach;
- education communities asserting their democratic rights against central government and its unrepresentative agencies;
- employers, large and small, taking their part within the wider community as just one voice, not the dominant voice;
- local and regional governments being given the chance to rationalise, plan and monitor the education service in the public interest through the process of democratic consultation, as well as taking on new roles in relation to the provision of services.

Taking hold of the comprehensive principle to ensure individual, group and community development through all these means, will flow from renewed democratic activity, but nobody can prescribe the direction this should take. No outsiders can undertake the work communities have to do for themselves in deciding between alternatives and then taking responsibility for developing them. Some minimal changes in national legislation and some specific guidance from government are essential in key areas, but the last 30 years have demonstrated that it is not safe to rely on governments, even if nominally pro-comprehensive – because it is never a good idea to wait for someone 'up there' , be it a kind minister or a progressive local administrator, to hand down solutions or opportunities. It is certainly not wise to let a centralised state continue to dictate so much of what takes places in our minds, workshops and classrooms.

As for achieving equality in education, for over a century we have seen the severe limitations of achieving change through paternalistic public programmes and centralised direction that relied on simplistic market mechanisms that favour most those who are already well-favoured. Millions of hours have been spent on equality and the system is still markedly unequal; billions of pounds have gone on excessive administrative, curricular and assessment change that leaves the system still with many basic faults. Internationally, Britain 'keeps up', but always belatedly.

Governments – whether local, national or international – can be enlisted in the drive for improved and extended comprehensive education, but they should not be handed total power to do it on behalf of the people. Part of the challenge of implementing the comprehensive principle should be the development of awareness of individual and community interests and how they interact in any one locality or region. Needed simultaneously is the capacity to appreciate the needs and interests of those whose lives and needs and cultures are quite different, locally, nationally and internationally. These can be accepted as part of our own wider interest rather than as some rival claimant. In Britain ultimately all have a common dependence on the same public education service.

The comprehensive principle of equal educational rights is one that teachers and parents in the majority of schools and staff and students in the majority of further education colleges support. This does not mean they agree on all aspects of implementation or even on most of them. But if we join with others, apply our skills of critical enquiry, and put all decisions to the democratic test, the next 30 years might benefit a great deal from the last 30.

Throughout our work and visits, we could not help but be impressed by the competence and dedication of those who work in Britain's comprehensive schools and colleges, and the enthusiasm of so many who are learning there. These are the principle persons to whom our work is dedicated.

Notes

1 See, for example, DfE, *Statistical Bulletins* 8/94 or 10/94.
2 Our survey took place before local government changed in Scotland, replacing the old regions with new district authorities.

1

History and the International Context

The modern version of a common education emerged after the Reformation at a time of quarrels and competition among Protestants' learned groups, who also found themselves pitted against established and segregated monastic orders. The European scholar, Comenius, suggested that teachers and learners should desert closed sects and unite instead in common institutions of learning. From there he went on to develop the idea of human learning as an orderly arrangement from younger years to older, and from elementary to advanced knowledge. These three elements of commonality, community and progression have characterised most education systems developed since.

As the industrial age approached, it was realised that the learning may have been in common for scholars gathered in universities or for artisans in guilds – and possibly in some of the early schools that fed them candidates – but that no such centres were open to common humanity. Spreading learning at this level was a much more prolonged task – and although in earlier centuries a few schools gave free education to local children, for far larger numbers the churches and private benefactors were the main providers of elementary instruction.

The Industrial Revolution required much more than limited reading skills acquired through moral catechism. In the first half of the nineteenth century much of Europe moved to establish public elementary schools and in some areas also secondary *lycées* and *gymnasia* . In England and Wales at this time several attempts to establish public education failed owing to antagonism between religious and social groups (Morrish, 1970; Walford, 1990). Instead, public funds were given by the state to the main religious bodies to continue their work of establishing schools for the poor, with governments, as far as they could, regulating the education of the more prosperous citizens.

The USA, by contrast, was building a public education system based on common education for all citizens. By 1837 it was established in the north-eastern states and the movement had its own journal, sent free to all teachers. *The Common School Advocate's* pages discussed the three Rs which, along with spelling, history and geography, had been agreed as the common curriculum on the grounds that everyone needed these 'to perform the common business and common duties of life' – both boys and girls, rich and poor (*The Common School Advocate*, 1838, 1(2)). Within the *Advocate's* pages the arguments of today also appeared, with, for example, some teachers favouring the introduction of additional subjects like chemistry, geometry and trigonometry for all pupils and others claiming that parents were far more interested in the 'fundamentals' of education so that all their children would have work when they left school, thus 'procuring (the) subsistence...necessary to securing their future happiness' (1838, 1(1)). There were also arguments about whether common education was about pupils' discipline, the 'regulation of their social actions' or about improving the conditions of their society.

Two propositions commanded agreement in the *Advocate*. First, that America was well ahead of Britain in the education of the poor, as it 'has been observed by gentlemen who have visited England, that the articulation...of words among the English peasantry is...hardly intelligible' and that the 'superiority of our youth' in learning is 'obvious'[1]. The second was a universal insistence that 'from every member of the community' should come 'earnest support for our common schools'. Common schools meant common public funding (1838, 1(1)).

Britain chooses divided education

Those who made best use of the public system in America, as later in Europe, were the professional and moneyed classes, but enough of the rest were involved to distinguish the system from that in Britain, where the Industrial Revolution was creating a society divided into those with land or capital or profession and those with no wealth, no possessions and no privileges. Richard Cobden, the political reformer, having visited the USA, spoke of the 'great gulf that separates the middle from the working classes and the middle from the higher classes' in Britain, advocating a common education system 'which would tend...to break down that barrier' (quoted in Rubinstein and Simon, 1973:4). His vision was of 'the common school...of so superior a quality that people should find nowhere in their vicinity...whatever their class might be...a better opportunity' for their children.

But common education did not find much favour in Britain during the period. Three national education commissions got to work, each 'largely concentrating on provision for a particular social class' (Walford, 1990: 21). There was Clarendon on the 'great' public schools; Taunton and the Act which followed in 1869 dealing with separate institutions for the 'upper middle class... middle middle class... (and) lower middle class'; (see Shrosbree, 1988; Simon, 1994:177) while Newcastle (1861) concentrated on 'sound and cheap elementary instruction to all classes of the people' (Introduction to the Newcastle Commission quoted in Walford, 1990:21). The Education Acts of 1870 in England and 1872 in Scotland finally required the state to provide elementary schools for the working class wherever voluntary schools had left gaps in the provision.

It was not until the end of the nineteenth century and the formation of many new radical political movements, that common education was advocated widely in Britain. At an international conference of socialists in 1896 delegates from all over Europe and the USA pressed for a full education for all working people[2]. Britain's Keir Hardie spelled out what kind it had to be: free at all stages, open to everyone without any tests of prior attainment at any age – in effect, a comprehensive 'broad highway' that all could travel (Reported in the *Westminster Gazette* (1 August 1896) and quoted in Benn, 1992:135). The emerging labour movement was not united on this issue, however. Many in the Fabian Society took an élitist position – Sydney Webb, for example, favouring specialised and differentiated schooling – in effect, a 'ladder' by means of which the clever working-class child would rise (see Webb, 1908:288). He strongly backed the new fee-paying grammar schools introduced in the 1902 Act which provided a few free scholarship places.

Nor did Conservatives or Liberals always agree among themselves. Many from both sides opposed the expansion of popular education because of the cost to the large landowners and industrialists, the main taxpayers; but others among them, more aware of the world outside Britain, knew state expenditure was urgently necessary to enhance Britain's trading and military edge. Thus during the debate on the 1902 Act, Balfour warned that 'England is behind all continental rivals in education' (quoted in Green, 1990:10). In both Europe and the USA publicly financed elementary schools, fuelling rival industrialisation, had forged ahead in the second half of nineteenth century. Now the USA was starting common secondary high schools as well. Many schools on the continent were giving a special place to engineering and science, so conspicuously downgraded in England's classical model of education, the one preferred by gentlemen. Historians today looking back at the start of the twentieth century's public education for the majority, can say confidently that the development of a national public system of education in England and Wales lagged behind much of Europe and the USA 'by a good half a century' (see, for example, Green, 1990:6).

During the twentieth century this gap has continued, retained by the same forces: a natural reluctance to disturb the alliance of schools with particular social groups, and a continuing indifference to technological, technical and vocational education. The First World War produced change in many areas. The USA decided democracy required a break with the segregated secondary education common in the countries of Europe (Bureau of Education, Department of the Interior, 1918)[3]. The newly formed Soviet Union (whose education system was comprehensive from the start[4]) made a similar break. But the war failed to produce much change in Britain's support for a divided system that tolerated a high level of early leaving. To be sure, secondary education for all became the campaign of much of the labour movement from the early 1920s but even its strongest advocate, R. H. Tawney, assumed there would be different types of school (see Tawney, 1922). Those who began arguing for the common school again were largely groups of workers or teachers in their several organisations (see Rubinstein and Simon, 1973:15–18), followed by a few locally elected governments, like that in London in the 1930s. Arguments for common schooling also continued in Europe in the 1930s and plans were being made for more common schools in both France and Germany when the Second World War began (Rubinstein and Simon, 1973:15–18).

It is also noteworthy that during the inter-war period, in a number of foreign countries, a higher percentage of students was gaining access to higher education than was the case in Britain: almost twice as many in Germany, more than twice as many in France, over three times as many in Switzerland, and almost ten times more in the USA. What also stood out was how well Scotland scored (almost on a level with France). It was clear that Scotland's education system, based on a widespread respect for learning and a more traditionally egalitarian social outlook, was making particular advances of its own.

But there were, of course, those pushing hard in England and Wales as well. Many in the trade unions and the Labour party endorsed a more equal system and at their conferences in the early 1940s voted specifically for a unified education system when, at last, secondary education for all should be introduced[5]. They were reacting to suggestions from the Spens Commission of 1938 that the new system should be divided into three types of school: grammar schools for some, technical schools for a few others, with the large majority in new 'modern' secondary schools. In 1942 several chief executives in local government, concerned with planning a more rational system, also asked for an end to plans for a differentiated education at the secondary stage, but it was plain the decision-makers at the Ministry of Education were determined on the divided system. A year later the Norwood Commission reinforced the idea of three types of schools by coming up with a novel theory that children naturally had three 'types of mind'. One type liked learning; another liked applied science or art; while the majority did not like 'ideas' and was 'generally... slow' (SSEC, 1943:2–3).

With all Britain's citizens now fighting another world war together, even a public school teacher was concerned at the dangerous detachment of Britain's ruling élite, criticising them for failure to 'face the possibility of real progress at home' in social change or education (T.C. Worsley, quoted in Simon, 1991:42). Another with the same fears was the new principal of the London University Institute of Education, Fred Clarke. In 1940 he wrote that the new tripartite system being proposed would be 'hardly intelligible... in... any British dominion or in the United States', warning that failure to change will 'weaken the power of Britain to cooperate with the other free peoples of the world' and simply 'intensify social conflict' at home (Clarke, 1940:44, 57).

1945 and after

Such critics were right to suspect that the British selective system was going to be hard to shift: even a newly elected Labour government after a major war, with a mandate for radical change, made little headway. Despite the clear wishes of its rank and file and a new Education Act of 1944 that had specifically left the door open for common education, Labour did not propose common schools (nor any change in the private sector). Instead it issued a circular (No. 73, 12 December 1945) to tell local authorities to 'think in terms of three types' of state school for the new secondary education, accompanied by a booklet to explain that the new 'modern' schools would be for working-class children 'whose future employment will not demand any measure of technical skill or knowledge' (*The Nation's*

Schools, 1945). The Labour party, as distinct from the Labour government, objected strenuously to this document and it was withdrawn by the Education Minister, Ellen Wilkinson. But the policy was not withdrawn; it was merely re-issued in a new form (*The New Secondary Education*, 1947) after intense pressure from education officials, the latter a far more formidable force in the first half of the twentieth century than the DfE has now become in the second.

Once again, Britain contented itself with a move others had taken a generation before, simply making secondary education free and available to all. It put right the failure to move between the two world wars but it did little to establish a system that would be appropriate for life after the second, when the education system had to prepare for the internationalisation of every aspect of culture, work and production. Although the 1944 Act was hailed as a great step forward, those who implemented its several important changes failed to grasp the opportunity it presented to move the necessary two steps rather than just one (for a fuller discussion, see Benn, 1980.) Instead of reforming education radically (as the medical system was being reformed into a new National Health Service at the same time), the Labour government proposed instead the well-rehearsed divided system, newly cloaked in spurious educational thinking about children's minds, backed by supposedly scientific methods of measuring intelligence which would make all the necessary decisions about selecting children for different types of school.

Just as Britain thought it was moving forward quickly, inevitably within a few years other countries started overtaking it again, for immediately after the Second World War many began widening the entry to their academic courses or schools, anticipating the demand for qualifications that shortly materialised; but few politicians and officials in Britain seemed aware of the likelihood of this demand. Instead of widening grammar school entry, they proposed to restrict it; they also refused to accede to the request of secondary modern schools, taking 80% of the age group, to give qualifications themselves. In fact, secondary modern schools were not allowed to run exam courses until Labour had left office and Conservatives began a 13-year occupation of government in 1951(see Simon, 1991: 111–112).

By now the alternative common school had acquired a new name, first used when a British educator in 1929, lately returned from teaching in America, commended the 'comprehensive high school' (Thomson, 1929:274; see Rubinstein and Simon, 1973:16). Between 1945 and 1951 several local authorities sent in plans to introduce comprehensive high schools in Britain but the Labour government rejected most of them[6]. Yet after Labour left office in 1951 the weight of support for the change to comprehensive education, coming from all sections of the labour movement, put such pressure on the leadership that within 5 years the party had officially adopted a policy of promoting comprehensive schools and opposing the 11-plus examination. Not all of the leadership was always convinced (including Hugh Gaitskell and Harold Wilson) but the party's own members and affiliates had made a commitment which would not be changed.

Now it was the turn of Conservatives not to notice what comparable countries were doing, when the post-war period after World War II saw deeply rooted selective systems reoriented in country after country. Scandinavian countries started reforms almost as soon as the war ended and so did Japan, where almost overnight an élitist system of imperial secondary schools was transformed into a uniform comprehensive system; while commonwealth countries like New Zealand or Canada further extended systems they had already started before the war. Throughout northern Europe, although there were pauses and there were arguments, common schools for the years up to 15 or 16 were established within two decades, and plans for the older secondary years laid down for development thereafter. After some delay the same changes began taking place in European countries bordering the Mediterranean; as well as in Israel, where welding disparate cultures into one 'new' nation could be achieved only by providing a common education. All eastern European countries reorganised on the common school model of the Soviet union, including East Germany.

In some countries the change was only partial. In China, for example, reorganisation was delayed and began only during the Cultural Revolution (King, 1991). In West Germany popular opposition to the divided system of 'high road and low road' (as Germany's system is sometimes called) did not materialise as it did elsewhere because Germany's vocational and technical education offered a rigorous and well-developed alternative path to advancement, and its limited numbers of comprehensive schools were oversubscribed from the start (Neave, 1970). Even partially reformed, such a system was in advance of a country like Britain, where vocational education and training were rudimentary and technical schools had completely failed to take off. Conservatives in office in Britain during the 1950s and early 1960s, while not averse to a few comprehensive experiments here and there in remote areas, especially during the reign of the pragmatic Education Minister, Edward Boyle, continued to support the divided system and the 11 plus that Labour had introduced.

This refusal to change fuelled an ever-growing popular reaction against Britain's divided system. The middle class was expanding and grammar schools were not. The 11-plus exam was perceived as riddled with failure for the following reasons:

- one research project after another delivered the undermining message that intelligence testing was fallible and intelligence very probably not inherited, after all (see Simon, 1953; Vernon,1957);
- errors in school placements were high (NFER, 1957);
- there was a great deal of inequality in outcome (Floud, Halsey and Martin, 1956);
- talent was wasted and many young people left far too early (see the Crowther Report, 1959).

When all these findings were put together they revealed a vast 'interlocking network of inequalities' (Douglas, 1964:xviii). Meanwhile, several local authorities had started comprehensive schools and many people were happy with the work they were doing. Society did not fall apart because pupils of all levels of attainment were now being educated together; some argued such schools brought greater social cohesion. Whether that was true or not, one thing such schools undeniably brought was an end to the 11-plus examination.

Almost all these arguments for change were internal to Britain. Few people promoted comprehensive education in the 1960s on the grounds that Britain was still far behind other countries in updating its secondary system as well as its technical and vocational education. Indeed the Conservatives' staple argument for years was that Britain's grammar schools and public schools were the envy of the world, and that it was other countries that were meeting problems in their education systems. They failed to read reality and could explain the burgeoning movement for the abolition of selection only as the politics of envy or the expression of doctrinaire socialism. Labour compared Britain's manufacturing and industrial technology internationally but not in the context of schools or the nature of secondary systems. Its secondary education policy was content to capitalise on widespread social discontent and Labour went into the 1964 general election with a promise to abolish the 11-plus and develop the system on comprehensive lines – without any clear idea of what this really meant. Conservatives went into the 1964 election, as in to all other elections between 1946 and 1979, committed to holding the political line exactly where it was at any given time.

The official start of comprehensive reform

After winning the 1964 election the Labour government did not come out with a plan for gradual development of the system towards full comprehensive education – as so many other countries had done. Instead, it concentrated upon the structural framework of schooling, gathering together reorganisation schemes which local authorities were using at the time to obviate the 11-plus process. It issued them in the form of Circular 10/65 in England and Wales, and Circular 600 in Scotland. Local authorities were not given any legal duty to change; they were simply invited to choose a scheme and start the planning process.

Although dates for submission of schemes were given, they were never enforced. In effect, it was left to the local authorities to move at their own pace, an approach that prolonged the reform by at least a decade because, while some approved of the national policy and moved ahead quickly to implement it, others were opposed and took very little action. Fatally, it was made clear that partial plans would be accepted – in the hope that the rest would follow. In some cases plans were approved and then overturned when local councils changed hands politically; or hastily cobbled together when the change was the other way around. It was usually Conservative controlled local authorities that refused; although occasionally it was Labour areas that balked and Conservative ones that co-operated (Batley *et al.*, 1970). But the constitutional issue was clear – whose electoral will was to prevail: the national electorate's or the local ratepayers? Was this a national reform or not?

The question could be left undecided while Labour had a small majority between 1964 and 1966, but when the general election of 1966 gave it a large majority and a clear mandate on this specific issue, it was time for an education act to reorient the system and plan the reform's development. Yet 4 more years passed before Labour finally started drafting such an act, intended for presentation after the general election of 1970. In the event the Conservatives won the election and the act died. In all its years of government from 1924 to 1979 Labour has never implemented a major education act – nor introduced any major new academic qualifications. All such changes have been implemented under coalition or Conservative governments.

Nevertheless, there was some progress because the Labour government continued to support the change. But development was uneven. Most schools were already non-selective and it was clear that no one objected to secondary modern schools developing as comprehensive schools. Planning here went ahead well. Resistance took place around many of the grammar schools, soon supported by the powerful public schools, themselves subject to a Public Schools Commission's intention in the late 1960s to try to 'integrate' them into the national system, as Labour had pledged. The boarding side of the Commission's costly and prolonged exercise came to nought because proposals were based on the continuation of selection (Public Schools Commission, Report No. 1, 1968). Proposals for the direct grant grammar schools – that they should either become comprehensive or go fully private (Public Schools Commission, Report No. 2, 1970) – brought over 50 to comprehensive status. But the change was not accomplished until 6 years after the Commission reported and also resulted in over 100 of these schools becoming private.

In Scotland the picture was more positive. Circular 600 started official reorganisation in 1965 but the door was already half open; for immediately after World War II Scotland's Advisory Council on Education had recommended a comprehensive system for all its secondary pupils from 12 to 16 as 'the natural way for a democracy to order the post-primary schooling of a given area' (SED, 1947, para 164). It also recommended a new curriculum with a largely common core and a new common leaving exam for all. In the event Scotland fell in with the national Labour government's plans after 1945; but was keener than most when called to end selection 20 years later. There was controversy, of course; some of the academies were very ancient and divisions inside schools between pupils were quite entrenched. But on the whole Scotland's reorganisation went along more purposefully – and with greater local support – than was the case in England.

The Conservative government of 1970 had Margaret Thatcher as its Education Secretary from 1970 to 1974. All pressure to implement comprehensive change was promptly withdrawn and local authorities were told that if they still wanted comprehensive schools the new government would look at them but only on a one-by-one individual school basis. No more schemes for whole areas. Yet schemes continued to pour in, presented as individual changes. More schools were sanctioned to change to comprehensive status by Margaret Thatcher as Education Secretary than by any other minister, Labour or Conservative, either before or since.

During this period the half-way mark in reorganising the total population was passed and still the figures moving to comprehensive education continued to rise; so that when Labour was returned in 1974 there seemed no reason at all why the new government, especially after its second election win in 1974, could not finally bring in a new education act. During its years out of office, at least one official Labour party education committee had published a truly radical set of proposals for extended comprehensive education development[7].

It was not just ending selection, now undermining the capacity of a substantial number of comprehensive schools; it was also the pressing need to develop a curriculum and assessment system compatible with comprehensive education. After all, in 10 years all that had happened was that age groups had been rearranged under one roof rather than two. Innovative schools were pressing ahead to create a new sort of education out of the old, spurred by new groups urging comprehensive curriculum and assessment change – like the Programme for Reform in Secondary Education (PRISE). But other schools simply pasted the two traditions together and waited for national directives to develop further. Instead of a major act, however, came a two paragraph bill giving the Secretary of State the power to ask LEAs to plan non-selective systems. There was no legal requirement to end selection, and the Act produced no visible effect (Bellaby, 1977). Nevertheless, many Conservatives called it 'jackboot legislation'.

Up to this point official Conservative policy was to be 'against the 11-plus but not in favour of turning grammar schools into comprehensives' (Conservative Central Office, 1979). But much more aggressive policies were being formed in that other Tory tradition sometimes opposed to the old élitist top. It demanded consumer-oriented education, an end to the Schools Council, more national testing, a return of the school-leaving age back to 15, and the holding of national 'enquiries' into everything progressive – from streaming and large comprehensive schools to sixth form colleges – and even into RE, to make sure that 'communism' was not being taught therein (see, for example, Rhodes Boyson, *The Times Educational Supplement*, 21–28 January, 1977). The type of populist Tory, backed by an influential section of the media, soon overshadowed both the Conservatives' élitist centre as well as those moderate Conservatives from the local authorities (or often teaching in comprehensive schools), who favoured a measured continuation of the reform and who argued, rightly, that comprehensive education was as much the property of the Right as of the Left.

1976 and after

The proposals of the groups constituting the New Right got an even wider hearing after Labour had declared open season on its own reform in 1976. In a dramatic right turn the Labour government announced a sudden halt to the forward march of comprehensive change. First, there was extensive media briefing, which included a secret memorandum (known as the Yellow Book) leaked to selected newspaper and media editors but not released to the public. This 1976 document promoted the imposition of a new 'agreed' core curriculum and claimed that the reorganisation of secondary education was now complete – though 11-plus selection still existed in whole or in part of over half the local education authorities in England and Wales. It was followed by a speech by the Prime Minister, James Callaghan, delivered at Ruskin College, Oxford, and widely perceived as 'a major political attack on Britain's Schools' (O'Connor, 1987:2); and this was itself followed by an orchestrated great debate to argue the case for subordinating the secondary curriculum (at least for those pupils thought to be 'non-academic') to the 'needs' of the economy (see Chitty, 1989, 1993).

During the last years of Labour's term of office the cause of comprehensive education slipped progressively from view. In 1979 the Conservatives returned to power and although their anti-comprehensive measures were high profile, very little was achieved initially with the exception of the funding of private schools through the Assisted Places Scheme. The repeal of the 1976 Act made little difference since the Act itself had been ineffective. Far more important was underwriting selection for grammar schools and certain voluntary schools in the 1980 Act, the first time the 11-plus had ever been enshrined formally in law (Section 6(3) (B) and (C)). The comprehensive schools were beleaguered by such changes and by constant denigration but not mortally threatened because several areas were still trying to go comprehensive and almost all local authorities that attempted to reintroduce grammar schools met strong opposition and failed at the first fence[8]. More recent attempts have met the same response[9].

But after the middle of the 1980s, when ministers had been bombarded with the work of an ever-growing number of right-wing think-tanks with small but interlocking memberships, the Thatcher government began planning more fundamental change. Ideologically driven by commitment to the market and to privatisation, the reforms were designed to deal with the problems of society by blaming spending on public services, including on an education system where it believed emphasis on equality had got out of hand through comprehensive development that encouraged too many to want to go too far in society. As a senior civil servant had already explained behind the scenes: 'there has to be selection because we are beginning to create aspirations which increasingly society cannot match', in part because of the very success of the education system 'in contrast to the public mythology which has been created'. 'When young people cannot find work at all...or work which meets their abilities or expectations...then we are only creating frustration with perhaps disturbing social consequences...people must be educated once more to know their place' (Ranson, 1984:241).

Thus began a long series of changes in education to meet the needs of a society where 'young people cannot find work'. What characterised all the changes was the absence of any popular demand for them from any section of the education community nationally or locally, nor even from the populist media. One by one all had to be imposed by means of a parliamentary majority against continuing opposition from all other political parties and from much of the educational establishment. The changes included a succession of education acts giving the Secretary of State sweeping new powers to issue regulations to control almost every aspect of the education system, including power to create appointed bodies to take over elected bodies' work. As part of the reorientation of education to 'national' goals, all learning in schools was to be devised and administered from the centre through a single, hastily devised 'national' curriculum, since much modified. Classroom activity was also to be more intensively policed from the same centre. Tests were to be administered in addition to national examinations. Consumer 'league tables' would be constructed where every education institution could be viewed in an anti-comprehensive hierarchy, designed to shame those in its bottom half to respond to 'customer' demands by immediately improving – or so it was argued.

The Government also decided to curtail the educational partnership of local and national governments by removing many powers from local authorities (and in certain cases abolishing authorities altogether). At the same time – to control expenditure far more finely (and eventually start to cut it down) – it appeared to give away powers, particularly budget making, to governors of schools and colleges to manage through privatised 'independence' and Local Management of Schools (LMS). What looked like a popular democratic move was actually a constriction of local democracy in terms of the accountability of the system to the community that paid for it. It also had a deeper purpose: to make schools and colleges themselves undertake the cutting of public services that were planned to follow, a task thousands of schools and colleges were forced to engage upon in time. Opposition to this task,which grew rapidly, was not apparently foreseen.

Another objective, discussed at educational planning meetings in

Downing Street in 1986 and 1987, was to break up the comprehensive system some way other than by returning to the 11-plus. A set of legal changes was thus put in train to allow selection to return naturally, starting with subjecting intakes to comprehensive schools (but not others) to engineered enrolment, 'open' up to a government-fixed ceiling and regulated by 'choice', where, once 'chosen' up to maximum numbers, schools would be able to select if they wished (by doing the 'choosing' themselves). To ensure institutions could develop in this way outside the remit of local education authorities (LEAs) (who might try to continue administering fair admissions systems), a whole new sector of 'private' schools was also proposed – made up of newly created technology colleges and a sector of LEA schools that was induced to opt out of their partnerships with democratically elected authorities. Both types of school were to be run entirely with public money, at first at funding levels higher than those earmarked for schools remaining with the locally accountable system.

To further break up the comprehensive system, the Education Act of 1992 removed all local colleges from their partnerships with democratically elected authorities and subjected them to quango-funding and control through a privatised market. Their government was reoriented in the direction of employer control and away from community accountability. All this made it harder to plan comprehensive systems, particularly those involving all-through arrangements between secondary schools and sixth form, tertiary and further education colleges. But that was the whole point: there were to be no local systems, only individual education 'businesses' competing with one another for 'customers' within the centrally controlled legislative framework.

The declared purpose was to 'free' schools and colleges for exciting development but the cumulative effect of 16 Education Acts between 1979 and 1993, combined with hundreds of attendant regulation changes and additional 'corrective' legislation (to remedy unworkable aspects of previous, over-hasty legislation) left many schools and colleges feeling oppressed and deluged rather than liberated. Many teachers and lecturers also felt increasingly devalued by the constant sniping at their capacities and the persistent downgrading of their professional work and conditions of service.

Comprehensive schools particularly mistrusted the new national testing arrangements (SATS) introduced for ages 7, 11 and 14, not because they were against testing (at least for diagnostic purposes and under their own control) but because they resented the huge bureaucratic load imposed and suspected the exercise was being introduced chiefly for comparative purposes rather than to help schools improve their education. Resistance was widespread, and only ostensibly overcome when the workload associated with the tests was vastly reduced and promises made that tests would not be misused for selection (though without legal changes such a promise was hollow). In Scotland resistance to both testing and the National Curriculum was much stronger, and was not entirely overcome.

Many in schools and colleges and local authorities began looking towards opposition parties for some sign of rescue from the chaos, especially as Labour had so vigorously opposed every one of the changes in parliament. But one by one each change was tolerated by oppositions – not just those changes which were gaining public acceptance (like some aspects of local management or some information publication) but also those (like retaining selection) which continued to bear condemnation. Although Labour's policies for the future, outlined in a series of publications in the 1990s, were generally positive and supportive of schools and colleges, they were often short of specific commitments, particularly in respect of comprehensive education, which was rarely mentioned in most of them.

1988 and after – The UK seen internationally

Far more positive and radical proposals came during the late 1980s and 1990s from national bodies and think-tanks of the centre-right, the centre, the centre-left and the left – as far apart ideologically as the National Commission, the RSA, the IPPR, the Hillcole Group and independent groups of teachers from schools and further education colleges. (See for example Allen and Waugh, 1995; Chitty, 1991; CBI, 1989; IPPR, 1990, 1993; National Commission on Education, 1993; Teachers' and Lecturers' Group, 1995.) There seemed a possibility that if a few of the key proposals common to all of them were adopted, at one bound Britain might make up that distance it had lost over the twentieth century and pull level with the rest of the world. For what characterised them all, however different their analysis or solution, were specific proposals for unifying the curriculum and assessment of the later years of secondary education and ending the segregation of vocational and academic education. All were based on an awareness of how far Britain had fallen behind internationally – not just in educational attainment but for some, in cultural understanding and positive social development as well.

Central to most of these proposals was Britain's failure to compete with the rest of the world industrially. This was a failing regularly cited in the policies and programmes of political parties from the late 1970s onwards too – but only in relation to work-related education, particularly training. Instead of attending to the 'basic purpose and curriculum of the comprehensive' as a whole during the 1980s, as so many at the time knew to be required (see, for example, Hargreaves, 1982:218), change involved a succession of training initiatives for 16-year-old school leavers alone. These were organised through the Manpower Services Commission (MSC) of the Department of Employment with little reference to mainstream education. Driven by the knowledge that most competitor countries had training systems far in advance of Britain's, few governments or officials made the connection that most of these countries also had comprehensive education systems far in advance as well.

From 1977 to 1989 change was breathtaking in this area and so was expenditure: £89 billion spent on introducing 25 training schemes, of which 22 were subsequently cancelled, some after only a year or two in existence. Each new programme for school leavers was widely publicised as providing the missing training the country needed and the missing education youth would want to take up, but repeatedly schemes were undermined by governments' misusing them for social and economic engineering – to mask rising unemployment, cut back on public spending for the disadvantaged, or meet employers' short-term needs. The Youth Opportunities Programme (YOP) started in April 1978 with a passable allowance and high hopes for the development of vocational education but gave way to successive versions of the Youth Training Scheme (YTS), each offering lower allowances, fewer benefits, worse conditions, and greater coercion (see Benn and Fairley, 1986). Although some schemes pioneered new work-related education of quality, by the mid-1980s it was clear that most were patchy or poor, offering few qualifications and little permanent work. Many employers remained unmoved by the necessity to train but were not in the least averse to using young people on schemes as temporary free labour or as replacements for older permanent workers. In 1985 YTS was made a 2-year 'course' with much fanfare; 2 years later it was all but dead.

The Government then changed tack. It began reducing the funding for training schemes in the hopes that employers would participate by doing the work of training themselves. To induce them to do so, it privatised the MSC's Area Boards into regional Training and Enterprise Councils (TECs, LECs in Scotland) modelled after American training and industry councils (TICs). But the Government did not propose the American model of comprehensive education that underpinned these Councils. Throughout the years when opponents of comprehensive education in Britain tried to claim that the USA was abandoning comprehensive education, it had actually been extending it to the age of 20. Beyond the comprehensive high schools were the comprehensive Community Colleges, now the largest branch of higher education in the USA, serving over half of Americans who enter higher education for the first time, even more of black or other ethnic groups or of women (Deegan, 1991:46). In addition to the first 2 years of degree courses, literacy and adult education, these colleges also offer the vocational courses that local industry needs – at last count, training for over 1400 occupations (Deegan, 1991:46). British Governments of the 1980s might have had greater success importing these developments than focusing on the idea of trendy 'magnet' schools that ministers brought back from visits to America, one of the many evanescent American experiments now rapidly losing ground there as a solution for inner city ills.

A much more important British initiative began with the announcement in 1989 that schools in future would be able to run vocational courses like those from BTEC, followed by vigorous government action to hack some paths through Britain's renowned jungle of vocational qualifications with a view to reorganising them into a single new system of vocational qualifications: GNVQ for educational qualifications and NVQ for qualifications gained through work (GSVQ and SVQ for Scotland). Some courses were fashioned from scratch, others by conversion of existing vocational courses. They were made roughly equivalent to existing academic qualifications; targets for the year 2000 were set; and the Government even talked about an all-purpose single diploma at 18 for everyone.

For a brief moment it looked as if at last a British government was going to catapult the country into a position where it could compete with other industrialised countries which had already made all these changes through comprehensive education reform and an integration of vocational and academic education. But this was not the plan, for the Government made clear it would not be changing the segregated academic education of the 16–19 group. It would stick to the separate 'A' level examinations in England and Higher Certificate in Scotland (or some new version of these). The qualifications system itself was not being unified; academic and vocational courses were not being integrated; and institutions were not being reorganised into a coherent system – though government initiatives hoped to make it look as though this was happening, particularly those conducted by the curriculum review team led by Sir Ron Dearing.

18

Once again the fear was that Britain would rush to catch up with the rest of the world by another separate-but-equal operation that would be outdated before it even began, only remarkable for showing that 'capacity of the English system to absorb change by simply adding initiatives and thereby increasing complexity and confusion' (Spours, 1993). Instead of clearing the jungle, more trees were planted.

As the twenty-first century approached, curriculum, assessment, institutions, and system were still divided after 16, with selection increasing in some areas before 16. There was much doubt about the 'equivalence' of vocational paths to academic education; as well as about the standards of some vocational courses. There was continued dismay that the narrow and over-specialised 'A' levels and Highers would only be tampered with, not integrated with vocational education. Technological education was not yet firmly and widely established for all. A common core for 16–19 was not yet on the agenda. Nor were those in part-time education or training after 16 yet accepted as part of mainstream education. There was no longer even a guaranteed place on a training scheme. Early leaving continued. Dropping out remained high from all types of courses. The gap between Britain and most of the industrial world with which the twentieth century started is still there at its end (Table 1.1).

Table 1.1 Full-time education and training in 10 leading industrial countries, 1990. Results are given as percentages of age group

16 years			17 years
Canada	100	Japan	90
Germany	99	Germany	89
USA	96	USA	89
Japan	93	France	85
Denmark	92	Canada	80
France	90	Denmark	78
Australia	76	Spain	63
Spain	71	Australia	54
United Kingdom	57	Italy	47
Italy	54	United Kingdom	42

(From DfE (1993) *Statistical Bulletin* No. 19/93).

Britain did not stand still, however. The numbers in full-time education staying on after 16 began to rise after common assessment for the earlier years of secondary education was introduced in 1986 with the common GCSE – just as percentages rose in Scotland when SCOTVEC reforms were introduced in 1984. The vocational drive of the 1990s also contributed to rising numbers staying on full time (along with the

Equality

realisation that good jobs were unlikely to be available at 16). In 1994, for example, England had 73% in full-time education at 16 (DfE, *Statistical Bulletin* 10/94,1994).

Nevertheless, other countries also continued to develop their systems. In 1995 the French reorganised their comprehensive curriculum yet again for the older secondary years, further integrating academic and vocational baccalaureate pathways. In 1992 far eastern countries like South Korea had already overtaken Britain in percentages proceeding to university with percentages higher than the target Britain later set for university entry for the year 2000, having doubled its university population by converting polytechnics into universities. Far from being too drastic, even supposedly fundamental changes in Britain would undoubtedly turn out once again not to have been anything like fundamental enough.

The world picture

League tables of national participation do not give a full picture, particularly in relation to which parts of the population within any country are enjoying the education being provided; or how quality compares. In the USA, for example, always with excellent comparative figures, and more opportunities than most, black and other ethnic minorities and poorer citizens were not enjoying the same rights in terms of basic provision and quality of learning in the 1990s. In a few troubled and economically deprived areas their chances of a full comprehensive education of quality were low. To the extent that this is so, the American system is less than fully comprehensive in operation, however so in structure. And the same is true for most comprehensive systems throughout the industrialised world. Dealing with increasing social polarisation in all these countries, particularly in their large cities, is an urgent world task.

At least in many of these countries the deprived citizens in areas of urban decay or social blight do not have to argue for basic rights in principle; their struggle is to make sure of them in practice. Struggling upwards is twice as hard in countries without comprehensive systems, where unequal rights of access, standards of accommodation and funding, or unequal facilities and teaching time and curricula are embedded in the system as part of its normal operation.

Comprehensive education also has its special characteristics according to the way it is put into practice. It took a highly libertarian, democratic and individualistic form in a country like Denmark (often criticised for being over-liberal); while in a country like Japan, it was highly regulated, pitting everyone in fierce competition almost from birth (often criticised as illiberal and over-controlled). Yet both countries provide models that others advocate; as do the USA and China and Russia. Pacific-rim countries, south east Asian countries and industrialising countries in Africa and South America thus have competing systems from which to choose and often debate the merits of each. Study of the differing characteristics and their appropriateness for different cultures or economies – along with alternatives which developing countries themselves have promoted[10] would seem to be a better use of research or world support than pouring effort into the retention of selective systems.

In several parts of the world which had colonial regimes the systems of the colonising European county have been inherited. South Africa, for example, has developed much of its organisation from Britain and soon its new citizens will be demanding greater rights of access to institutions previously reserved for a privileged few. The demand to set up more racially integrated grammar schools will be overtaken by the question of whether education for all citizens should not be in common. In most of the world this question does not yet arise, including South Africa, for it is comprehensive primary education that has to be established first.

Secondary education in most of the world is still very limited in supply and therefore selective, as it was in Britain in the nineteenth century. If we construct a league table for the world for the ages 12 to 17 (as we can through the UN's figures processed by the World Bank)[11], Britain scores up at the top with the rest of the industrialised world: with 82% of this age group in education, along with 96% in Japan, 97% in Germany and over 100% in Canada (because some students are enrolled in two institutions). But figures are also high for countries we are not always used to thinking of as advanced or that have only lately became so – like Kuwait at 90%, Cuba at 89% and Egypt at 82%. Most people in the world are in countries where just under a half receive secondary education: Brazil at 39%, India 44%, China 48%, Iraq 47%, and Nicaragua 38%. Some of these will move quickly up to 'advanced world' level; China plans to do so by the year 2049 (King, 1991:49). Others will take longer, and a few longer still: like Haiti now at 19%, Afghanistan at 8% and Rwanda at 7%.

There may well be individual exceptions that prove the rule, but in general most countries start off with highly selective systems and gradually translate to comprehensive ones as they move up the industrialising scale, particularly if they wish to compete at the top. It does not mean that:

- some do not single out certain groups for specialised education at times;
- remoter areas do not have to concentrate selectively;
- inside many schools divisions are not apparent;
- many countries do not also have exclusive, private schools for a tiny international clientele (although Britain is 'the only advanced industrial nation in the world that boasts two systems: one for the wealthier and more privileged, and the other for the rest' (Simon, 1994:66).

It means only that where public money is financing education for the majority, the long-term aim is organisation up to the age of adult specialisation without institutionalising social or attainment selection.

It is also clear that comprehensive education is not a principle practised exclusively by societies governed by the Left. It is equally at home with capitalism, a fact that the Right in Britain still finds it difficult to accept. So much of their argument since 1965 has depended upon ritual references to 'the mad, doctrinaire socialist ideas of comprehensivisation', words that ring strangely hollow when still spoken, as these were by a Member of Parliament in 1995[12]. The continuing failure to read world reality hampers any party or government within a world where implementation of the comprehensive principle in some form or other is an integral part of modernising an industrialised society, capable of adaptation by capitalist, socialist, authoritarian, and liberal regimes alike. This principle is incompatible only with hierarchically organised tribal or feudal societies, which seek to regulate themselves by inherited social or economic authority, or with societies where cultural, social or racial segregation is practised within a rule of one dominant culture rather than within a diversity of equally valued groups.

In the long run, however, full comprehensive education is probably impossible in conditions where democracy does not also exist. This follows from its defining social inclusiveness, its place in the community, its rationality, and its belief in the inherent educability of everyone. Authoritarian societies that run comprehensive systems, and fail to appreciate the democratic essence of the comprehensive principle, can find the system will not service certain modernising requirements as well as it should, and could even confound them, along with such regimes themselves. Comprehensive education's basic nature is to accommodate change, not to preserve a political status quo; to make use of new technologies, particularly those in electronic communications, but not to be controlled by them.

Comprehensive education cannot produce its best results where it is only half developed, as it is in Britain. For comprehensive education to work well, every citizen without exception has to have equal rights within the education system. These rights have to be held in common and agreed in common. A bill of rights for education is thus more appropriate than citizens' and parents' charters based on constricted commercial models of customer–provider. Comprehensive systems are not at their best when education is reduced to a consumer business turning out qualified human products as if they were commodities; or when used exclusively as a sorting shop to service employers' short-term needs; or as a game board for special interest groups or utopian blueprints, both of which eventually bring restrictions of academic freedom.

Comprehensive education is not even designed to improve the economy, though it may do so indirectly. In the long run it is the other way around. Economies are there to support education, and to provide for all our other human rights to be exercised. Education is a fundamental human activity. How far it will be exercised within a comprehensive context is an issue almost every community in the world will be considering in some form during the coming century.

Notes

1 Ascribed to two books: Noah Webster's *Dictionary* and McGuffey's *Reader*, two of the most widely used textbooks in early American school systems.
2 The Second International, four yearly conference, held in Queens Hall, Langham Place, London.
3 The USA's view on its new universal comprehensive secondary system was set out in Bulletin No 35, Bureau of Education, the Department of the Interior, 1918, stating that 'common interest and solidarity' made it necessary to have academic, vocational, full- and part-time education in the same comprehensive high school and not in 'separate continuation schools which is the custom in less democratic societies'.
4 The decree setting out the education system – 'an uninterrupted educational ladder' – was issued 4 days after the Revolution in 1917 and is printed in Reed (1961) *Ten Days that Shook the World*, pp.297–99.
5 The first resolutions calling for comprehensive education from both the Labour party and the TUC were at their yearly conferences in 1942. Labour Party conferences passed similar resolutions in most subsequent yearly conferences.
6 London, Middlesex and West Riding plans were returned, though some individual schools allowed in rural Anglesey and the Isle of Man, and in parts of London. In each case only if no grammar schools were affected.
7 *Higher and Further Education* (1973). Report of a Labour Party Study Group, chaired by Geoffry Rhodes, MP, sometimes known as the Rhodes Report.
8 The area of Stroud was still trying to go comprehensive in 1982, supported by the local Conservative MP, Anthony Kershaw. Other councils either voting for

comprehensive schools or refusing to reinstate grammar schools and selection included Hereford,Worcester, Salisbury, Solihull, Redbridge, and Cheltenham.

9 In Buckinghamshire and the London Borough of Kensington and Chelsea in 1995; also in Barnet, where the return of Queen Elizabeth School to grammar status was opposed formally by every other local secondary school in the authority.

10 One example is the education plan developed in Burkina Faso by the government of Thomas Sankara in the 1980s, ended after a military coup and his assassination.

11 World Bank (1993) *Social Indicators of Development, 1993*, Baltimore, Md.: Johns Hopkins Press. Figures taken from information the UN collects are but crude indicators and some countries are unable to provide statistics at all – South Africa being one.

12 N. Hawkins, MP, recorded in Parliamentary Report, *Hansard,* Education Debate, 7 February 1995, p.152.

2

The Debates About Comprehensive Education

Common schooling has always been at the centre of educational debate because societies alternate between support for education as a cohesive force in the community and support for education organised separately for distinct groups within it. A community's commitment to the extension of mass education is always contending with pressure at each stage to invest more in the education of distinct groups.

Although comprehensive schools got caught in the party political net in the UK after the Second World War (see Chapter 1), party lines are not clearly drawn on this issue; and each major party's educational tradition houses contradictory strains.

Conservatives are committed both to maintaining an academic and economic élite as well as advancing a competitive learning society for everyone that can support a highly developed capitalist economy – aims which are not always compatible. Nationally, Conservative leaders have always maintained a hard face against comprehensive education but locally there is support for it among Conservative voters,teachers, and local councillors. A recent gratuitous reference in the DfE White Paper *Choice and Diversity* (published in July, 1992) caricatured comprehensive education as a system for those who believe 'children are all basically the same' and that 'all local communities have essentially the same educational needs' (DfE, 1992:3); and the prime minister has promised to 'reverse' comprehensive school development[1]. But no overt action to return the 11-plus has ever been proposed in practice because from the start there has been support from the public, including the Conservative voting public, and those few Conservative controlled authorities which have tried have always been defeated, usually by their own political supporters. This is one reason why policy to return selection to the system over the last 15 years has had to be indirect, complex, and continual – not through a single education act but through at least a dozen; not through a few straightforward changes but by means of hundreds and hundreds of pages of new regulations.

Labour has always given more support to comprehensive education locally and nationally, and until the 1990s, through party policy statements. But its policy also has its contradictions. One section of Labour has always supported the principle of the 'broad highway' where all could travel as far as they wished through the education system, while others have supported the concept of the ladder of opportunity by means of which the clever working-class child could rise, making use of what Sidney Webb once called the 'progressive differentiation of the publicly provided school into a number of specialised schools each more accurately fitting the needs of a particular section of children' (Webb, 1908:288–9). This contest between universalists and meritocrats started a hundred years ago (see Chapter 1) and has characterised discussion in every generation since[2].

Although the creation of municipal grammar schools in the 1902 Act caused the elementary system to begin the process of 'winnowing out' the educationally successful from the rest (Simon, 1991:27),there was no real debate nationally about secondary education during the first half of the twentieth century. After the First World War there was growing agitation to extend it to greater numbers in the population – either in the form of more free places in grammar schools (which Labour governments oversaw) or further development of the upper years of elementary education (which Conservatives oversaw). But governments of the 1920s and 1930s – of all political hues – did not so much oppose secondary education for all (recommended by two national commissions during this time) as keep postponing it. Debate was always headed off.

During this time there was no national debate either around IQ testing, the new science of the mind, which claimed that intelligence was largely fixed at birth. In the age of eugenics, separation by IQ was not really challenged until 11-plus testing came under fire after World War II (see, for example, Simon, 1953). And although there were always critics of the divisions caused by Britain's unique 'two nations' practice of private and 'public' schools for the better-off and state schools for the rest, there was never a national debate about it until the 1960s – and even then this was hard to disentangle from the comprehensive debate.

Only one educational debate could qualify for national status in the first part of the twentieth century and that was the debate over religious schooling, which dominated party political and public life from the start of the century and raged for years afterwards.It grew from old religious rivalries and took the form of disagreement about whether the ratepayer and the taxpayer should have to pay for denominational schools (which had previously paid their own way), on top of having to pay for the community's own schools. The fact that most denominational schools 'belonged to' the Church of England, promoted by the Conservative party, deeply offended the large non-conformist population and the Liberal Party; later, similar support for Catholic schools offended others. Those positively supporting a secular education (including the early Labour party until reluctantly persuaded otherwise by its Catholic members) objected in addition to any religious teaching in schools.

This conflict had been inevitable after the state took over responsibility for educating the nation from 'voluntary' bodies and it was replicated in many European countries in the nineteenth and twentieth centuries. The USA avoided it through its constitutional separation of state and religion, requiring religious schools to pay for themselves (as they still must), and banning all religious instruction from the public school system.

Levels of passion, bitterness and tractarian activity over the issue of religious schooling in Britain exceeded those reached over comprehensive education, which became the second national debate of the twentieth century, flaring up when the first was supposedly resolved by the 1944 Act's 'religious settlement' with its (still existing) mêlée of legal status and funding arrangements. The religious issue did not die, however, not only because funding changed and new religious groups demanded new schools, but also because it is still part of the continuing debate about educating people in common. This debate has been central to education discussion in Britain since the early nineteenth century – whether separation was along lines of attainment, gender, social class, religion, race, culture or wealth.

This debate is complicated by the fact that society's manifold differences can combine in so many different ways, not all combinations incompatible with the common educational process that is differentiated enough to provide for everyone.It is easy to see that many of the aspects of the old religious debate (and the social class one before that) are involved in the ever-continuing debates about comprehensive education today.

Definition

The definition of a comprehensive education has always been elusive. During the 1930s schools of this nature were known as 'multilateral', 'unified' or (later) 'all-in'. After the Second World War the Ministry of Education firmed this up as schools '... intended to cater for all the secondary education of all the children in a given area without organisation into three sides' (Ministry of Education, 1947). Although clearer about the context, it was essentially a negative definition, as was the legal definition used 30 years later in legislation defining a comprehensive system for the purposes of planning the 1976 Education Act: one where no schools were entered by selection. Gone was the commitment to serving everyone, or a given area, or providing all that was normally provided for the age group (which had been added in the early 1960s); and absent still was any positive definition about the nature of the system or any positive statement about the aims, objectives and practices of comprehensive education itself.

Today's DfE definition reflects this same negative approach and is even more minimal: the 'structure of secondary education' in England and Wales varies from one local authority to another and there is a division between selective schools on the one hand – 'modern, grammar, and technical' – and, on the other, comprehensive schools, the latter defined as 'schools which cater for all children irrespective of ability' (DfE, *Statistics of Education,* 1993:95). Thus 30 years after Circular 10/65 in many areas it is still a matter of schools named comprehensive in and amongst a selective system of schooling. Comprehensive education is also seen as applying to schools alone and children only rather than also to young adults and to those in colleges. Despite the fact that in large areas of Britain the selective school has gone and comprehensive education has established itself as the *de facto* system, developing upwards through the colleges, it is still a system without any clear definition, officially or otherwise.

1965

Possibly the most fateful interim definition of comprehensive education, which many later came to regret, was made in 1964 when Labour was attempting to reconcile its two traditions during the general election that brought it back to power after 13 years. It claimed comprehensive education was 'grammar education for all' (Election Manifesto, 1964). Circular 10/65 reiterated this by declaring that the chief object of comprehensive education was to preserve 'all that is valuable in grammar school education' for those who now receive it and to 'make it available to more children' (DES, 1965:1). This left unanswered the main question of whether early specialisation was still the best course, even for the grammar few; much less what was going to be enjoyed by those beyond the 'more' for whom such education would still not be 'available' – both questions which 30 years later have still not been fully answered.

Shortly after this the NFER, directed by the Labour Government to undertake research on the new schools, came up with a good workaday definition from the point of view of administrators (Monks, 1968:xi):

- 'to eliminate separatism';
- 'to collect pupils representing a... cross section of society in one school' and thus contribute to 'an integrated community beyond the school'; and
- 'to concentrate' teachers, accommodation and equipment economically.

The last objective means that there were savings to be made by organising comprehensively, one of the reasons that has always commended the system to many Conservatives and most administrators. The first was the explicit promise to end selection, expected because it had wide popular support. It was the second that was unexpected and proved the most controversial, widening the debate considerably into how much – or even whether – schools should be used for social engineering.

There was still little, however, about what kind of education should go on inside such schools, how they would meet the needs of pupils with all levels of attainment, or what implications the changeover had for curriculum, grouping or assessment policy. For all anyone could tell, it looked as if it was going to be acceptable for the old education in two or more schools (albeit with the new CSE exam Conservatives had proposed in their last hours of office) to continue as before under one roof, a course few of those working in the field were prepared to accept. Thus the definition of comprehensive education in a positive sense in terms of detailing what constituted an 'undivided' educational experience was a task left to those who supported the reform in practice.

There was no shortage of teachers, parents, learners, academics and citizens ready to oblige with goals – for the reform carried a heavy load of hopes in the community at large, in respect of social and economic, as well as educational, change. To many, therefore, its main goal was equality. But 'equality' – like 'freedom', 'choice' and 'standards' – can have many definitions, and those put forward in these early years were certainly various, as many have since pointed out (Ball, 1981:6–10; 1984:2–3; Reynolds et al., 1987:4–28; Weeks, 1986:5–7). Equality could be about upward mobility (Ford, 1969); developing talent wherever it was; or making a wide variety of achievement possible (Miles, 1968; Ross et al.,

1972). To some it was about the collective advance of the working class, long denied the same opportunities in education as the middle and upper classes; while others saw it as individuals developing themselves to the full (Pedley, 1963); or as an economic necessity 'to close the wide gap…in the life experience and especially the educational experience of management and men' (Peston, 1971). Possibly, Pat Daunt, head of Thomas Bennet School in Sussex, expressed the principle at its simplest: 'The education of all children is held to be of equal worth' (Daunt, 1975:10), thus updating the old principle of 'parity of esteem' between types of school – and applying it to all types of pupils and all types of learning within a single school.

But what did this mean in practice in schools that were trying to reconcile equality with individual difference, one of the central tasks of comprehensive education? Was it, as so many began to assume, really about the social and economic context of education and the way it related to schooling practices and policies? Or, important as this context was to the development of comprehensive education, was it primarily an educational task: about the 'opportunity to try out what secondary education can do to develop human powers, as opposed to channelling them in segregated ways' (Simon, 1970:7)? Was it about promoting the cognitive and general development of all human beings by successively removing the barriers that impede this development; and not primarily about social mixing? The first independent Enquiry put this second view more explicitly still: 'A comprehensive school is not a social experiment it is an educational reform' (Benn and Simon, 1970:64).

The grammar and national media backlash

To a determined group of citizens in 1965, however, comprehensive education was seen very much as new social mixing, and thus as an attack upon their privilege as well as upon the 'poorer working class pupils' who, they believed, had benefited from the selective system in the past. Within months of the Circular, a group opposed to comprehensive education met at Hampton Grammar School in October 1965 and formed The National Educational Association, one of the first of many organisations and think-tanks set up to 'fight' comprehensive education and preserve the grammar school. No association was ever formed to save the secondary modern school, where most of the country's teachers, parents and pupils were centred. The movement to save selection was thus no mass movement. It was rather the work of an organised minority with supporters in positions of influence in many sectors of education, particularly in higher education, in the media and throughout the upper ranks of society.

Proliferating pro-grammar groups and their supporters were very vociferous. Despite the fact that no legislation had been introduced, there was constant complaint about government coercion, and in the years that followed 1965 comparison to commissars and storm-troopers, along with cartoons showing comprehensive pupils in identical uniforms walking obediently to school in serried ranks[3]. These objections were answered by supporters of the new comprehensive system, in this case a tertiary college head, that it was precisely 'because humans are individuals, because each one is different that we should have one school for all', a school that avoided classification according to wealth or class or race or attainment level (Janes, 1985:6).

Charges of uniformity continued even while comprehensive schools began to diversify, a few experimenting with new forms of school organisation or teaching styles. Others assembled together as many of the old trademarks of excellence as possible, including formality and uniforms, in order, as one comprehensive school said recently, to be 'as much like Manchester Grammar School as dammit' (*The Sunday Times*, 10 April 1994). Observing the outer ends of such multiple development led one supporter in the early days to claim that there were two competing models of the comprehensive school – one egalitarian and the other meritocratic – and to list in detail the characteristics of each (Marsden,1969:2-5). It is a distinction educationists and others have subsequently made much of (Ball, 1981:6–10; Reynolds *et al.*, 1987:4–18; Weeks, 1986:66–68), suggesting two distinct approaches could be seen in practice (some regretting the fact that only the meritocratic seemed to be surviving).

The existence of such a division was immediately called into question by those working in the field. One headteacher (Rowe, 1970:8–10) claimed such a distinction did not exist because 'different schools...combine different points from...(the)...two lists and rank them differently in order of priority'. In any case, it was folly to suggest a school must aim to produce a single type of human being; or that if you believed in equality, you would give lower priority to science (as was claimed), or that if your approach was meritocratic, you would discourage out of school activities (also claimed). Brian Simon found the division equally unhelpful, pointing out the danger of providing 'meritocrats with "egalitarians" to knock down for their lack of concern about standards' (Simon, 1970:6–8). Simon argued that the real division was between those who believed in the comprehensive school because it mixed social classes, thereby bringing about a more harmonious society, and those who rejected bipartism on *educational* and *psychological* grounds.

Although in the early days the national media and educational press were willing to print non-judgemental profiles of new comprehensive schools or show the wide variety of approaches being tried, they were more concerned with relaying news about 'progress': how many LEAs had submitted reorganisation plans or 'gone comprehensive' and how many were holding out. Some decided to take the government's line that all was going well (what one Labour MP characterised as a policy of 'kidology'; Chris Price, *New Statesman*, 25 October 1986); while others decided to voice the fears of comprehensive campaign groups that the pace was unacceptably slow and needed legislative support. On the date final submissions for reorganisation were due in 1966, two veteran correspondents, Colin Chapman (*The Sunday Times*) and Stuart McLure (*Observer*), each commented on the same set of figures; one claiming the reform was galloping along, the other that it was seriously stuck.

However, the media honeymoon did not last long and fascination at progress soon wore off. When the Black Papers burst on the scene in 1969 – with colourful articles by Tory politicians, academics and journalists denigrating comprehensive education – much of the mass media became instant converts to their bad news and apocalyptic warnings, undoubtedly sensing that this more controversial turn to the 'debate' was much better copy and far more beneficial to circulation. They were right. Public appetite for clashes on this issue could not be assuaged. Since the matter touched the life chances of most of the population, coverage increased in local, national and regional papers. Indeed, one local paper claimed more column inches had been given to comprehensive education reform than had been used to cover the whole of the Second World War (*Bristol Evening Post*, 12 May, 1965).

The Black Papers did not develop the debate; they just raised the temperature by claims that requiring grammar schools to admit pupils of all levels of attainment was a left-wing conspiracy, a 'sinister attack on excellence' (Pedley, 1969:47); or that the whole reform was 'too much attempted too fast', an ironic comment in view of the rate at which reforms have moved in recent years. Viewed years later, the Black Papers were seen as a colourful collection of 'diatribes' with 'no substantial relationship to the realities of comprehensive schooling' (Ball, 1984:6; Wright, 1977). All the same, they revealed the depth of feeling against equality that existed in certain circles, and a dominant concern for the 'able' pupil. The class-based nature of education was defended because 'social divisions' in education were a 'product of human society' which schools 'merely reflect' (Szamuely, 1969:49); and a Conservative MP opposed equality as 'harmful' because meeting the needs of able pupils 'could be achieved only by keeping those élite schools which made 'special efforts to bring out the best in talented children' (Maude, 1969:7).

The coverage given to these contributions was generous and continuing and ensured that Black Paper concerns monopolised the debate for years, not just in respect of comprehensive schools but also of 'progressive' education generally. This too came under the right-wing hammer, activists defining as progressive any informal seating arrangements in classrooms, any learning of reading from books other than reading schemes, any form of organisation other than streaming, any form of dress other than uniform, any form of assessment other than externally set GCE examinations, and any form of student democracy at all.

But the comprehensive school was the irresistible target – particularly the stereotype of the large, urban comprehensive school. Such schools were charged with levelling down, setting the lowest common denominator, the destruction of good schools, the undermining of discipline in society, and a decline in standards of writing, reading, speaking, manners, and civilisation. The charge that standards were declining continued to be made, though there was no statistical or other evidence of such a decline by any of the accepted indicators (Wright, 1977), with the possible exception of standards of reporting.

Over the years the bias in national press coverage has been well documented with, for example, Martyn Denscombe's description in 1984 of 'alarmist reports of violence, vandalism and truancy of crisis proportions' (Denscombe, 1984:133; see also Docking, 1980; Galloway et al., 1982; Jones-Davies and Cave, 1976; Laslett, 1977); and Ball's mention of the 'ritual quotation of extreme and atypical examples' (Ball, 1984:18–21). All types of newspapers and broadcasting outlets were criticised, including the BBC's Panorama, although most complaints (including those upheld by the Press Commission) were against the Daily Mail (Denscombe, 1984:134)[4].

Seeing Britain's situation in relation to the rest of the world became increasingly difficult as defence of selection frequently involved distorted information about other countries. This included regular reporting that the USA was abandoning comprehensive education (whenever an education initiative in the USA occurred designed to improve its system). Such events were flagged by confident titles – e.g. 'Comprehensives: A system that Failed', in the case of a report on Scandinavia (where incorrect information in *The Telegraph Magazine* was never corrected)[5]. At other times it was the human interest angle, the story of heroic parents who quit work to teach their own children rather than have them enter a comprehensive school – a story based on a comprehensive experience that never took place. The ordinary citizen only had to read the headline to get the dark message: 'How the Middle Class Cope with Falling Standards' (*Daily Mail*, 6 May, 1977).

A decade later academic observers could conclude laconically that the comprehensive debate was taken over by a 'strident minority of élitists... supported overwhelmingly. . . by the national and local media' with plenty of 'financial backing' (Weeks,1986:41), but at the time many thoughtful people assumed (and many have gone on assuming) that some kind of national disaster was unfolding in the schools. Meanwhile, out in the real world, the reform was slowly making progress, as thousands of communities, thankful that the ordeal of the 11-plus was ending, accepted the new pattern of schooling in area after area. As most were prepared to give it a chance, and support for individual institutions grew, a split in media coverage took place. While the national media remained generally anti-comprehensive and committed to an élitist position – maintained after Conservatives came to power in 1979, when much attention was given to the critiques of right-wing think-tanks (ignoring the activity of mainstream groups supportive of comprehensive education like the Council for Educational Advance or the Campaign for the Advancement of State Education) – the local press began to realise it was in its interests to take a positive view of its local schools and colleges. A national paper like the *Daily Mail* could resist a mass demonstration at its doors to protest at questionable reporting[6], but a local or regional newspaper would not be able to ignore the event (or its repercussions). The relationship between local media and the new comprehensive schools and colleges had to be different. Most of their advertisers' children were students in these institutions.

Many local papers and radio and TV programmes therefore became cheerleaders for local schools and colleges, always ready to report the good news of the good things going on in their midst. This was immensely welcome but it was still an approach that left the popular media unable to air the real problems that were arising in the education system or in the world of occupational training, and conduct public discussions about them in an open, balanced and non-threatening way. In the case of training, only specialist journals or campaign groups even charted the stormy course of successive new training 'schemes' for school leavers during the late 1970s and early 1980s. The mainstream media both nationally and locally virtually ignored this field, which, incredible as it may seem, spawned as much professional comment, as many political discussion documents and as much academic argument in 10 years as the comprehensive school reform had produced in 20. Of the 2000 items published between the mid-1970s and the mid-1980s on training, fewer than 1% are from the mass media, heavy or light, written or spoken (LMNI, 1987:8). This is despite the fact that the numbers of young people in training schemes like the YTS were roughly the same as the numbers in the nation's sixth forms.

In work-related education, the uncritical media acted as a conduit for public relations material put out by government departments or agencies because they were also carrying their advertisements for each new training initiative (financed by colossal increases in government spending in this field) (LMNI, 1987: Section II:37). There was occasional specialist reporting but very little popular criticism (of the kind going on about education in schools) and very little awareness in educational circles of the debates taking place in training and vocational circles about the standards, allowances, conditions, and quality of programmes of successive youth training schemes, where few young people gained qualifications and half regularly failed to find work. Many young people were working in conditions where safety regulations had been waived, accidents were common, and private providers could go bankrupt (LMNI, 1987, Section II:47–53). In some of these cases, young people's training could end altogether with no redress to any forum in the way school students had recourse to governing bodies or local authorities if they believed they had been ill-served. The educational fate of these young people was never as important nationally as that of the sons and daughters of the educationally minded.

The 'neighbourhood' debate

There was even a sense in which there was hostility to these young people, particularly in the ongoing debate about neighbourhood schools, for 'neighbourhood' was a word that turned from benign to sinister during the comprehensive era.

Eric James, editor of the *Times Educational Supplement* (TES) in 1965, when the paper was a leading anti-comprehensive force, was one of several who wrote much earlier (James, 1951:45) that educational standards would decline if there was ever a system of 'comprehensive schools drawing on a limited locality where... tone and prestige (were) coloured by the social status of the particular neighbourhood, as American experience shows'. In Britain there was some of the same fear about social integration as there was in America with respect to racial integration, and fears arose that those previously able to escape 'bad' schools would now have to attend them. Unrealised by most British commentators, however, was the fact that 'neighbourhood' was the commitment of conservatives in the USA, who disliked bussing of poor blacks to white areas, while in Britain Conservatives opposed the neighbourhood idea and approved of bussing in selected pupils to the grammar school.

Circular 10/65 reflected the negative British view of 'neighbourhood' by mentioning some schools where 'stimulus and variety' might be lacking and advocating as full a 'social and intellectual' balance as possible for each. Most local authorities wanted to have mixed intakes but at the same time they also wanted to maintain commitment to the locality. This meant most tried to balance several factors when arranging admissions systems – registering parental preferences for schools as well as drawing up admissions policies relating to nearness, zoning or feeder school arrangements. Some local authorities, usually Labour, were slow to understand the importance of allowing siblings to attend the same school, or friends to move up with each other. But the period before authorities began making allowances for preference was very short, mostly confined to the years between 1965 and 1968. Sometimes change occurred when Conservatives made parental preferences a local election issue (as in Newcastle upon Tyne in 1967); at other times it was Labour that took the lead. Manchester, for example, went over to 'parental choice' as the only method of transfer after 1968 with interesting consequences (see page 51).

The Inner London Education Authority (ILEA) carried balancing furthest with an entry system that tried to combine 'parental choice' with giving each comprehensive school the same percentage of high-, medium- and low-attaining pupils to obviate a 'one class' effect and get a spread of attainment. It never fully worked because certain schools never filled the top attainment band and because many voluntary schools, which went comprehensive only slowly, regularly reneged on their agreements, as their aided status permitted them to do in law. Confidential but carefully recorded transfer figures from the time show this clearly (Williams and Murphy, 1979, 1984)[7].

The balancing process also required testing at 11-plus, which led some to criticise the method for prolonging rather than ending selection, such criticism coming especially from those who were developing a highly positive view of 'neighbourhood' as an asset to a comprehensive school or college. One such head in the north derided the ILEA's approach as 'egg grading' (Bullivant, 1971), claiming it was a school's job to accept its intake and set itself to 'generate success in (and)...raise the standing of the neighbourhood', a view earlier expressed by Brian Simon (Simon, 1966:4–8) arguing that in any area with restricted opportunity – say, an inner city – it was the school that should give a cultural lead, in order to widen opportunity for local people – much as the community colleges had already done in rural areas. The comprehensive should 'accept and reflect its outlook and culture and build on this to...develop new aspirations in its pupils'.

Later the consumer group, the Advisory Centre for Education, also supported the idea of neighbourhood schooling, defined in terms of its own commitment to as close a connection as possible between a school and its parents; while several educationists continued to make impassioned defences of neighbourhood, especially in cities at the time when old neighbourhoods were being dispersed (Hargreaves, 1982).

Increasingly, however, anti-comprehensive campaigners, particularly in the media, used the idea of 'neighbourhood' as a peg on which to hang questionable images of schooling, especially relating to discipline and poor attendance. Even the most benign of the consumer lobby felt obliged to articulate the doubts of 'many educationists' who 'object to neighbourhood comprehensive schools in the big cities because of the way neighbourhoods tend to become dominated by a single class or racial group' or 'by children with housing problems... unfair to the minority... who could be expected to perform well'.

Unchallenged assumptions were hiding in these articulations (as much as in any of the deliberate scaremongering of the grammar school lobby): that only a 'minority' were ever going to 'perform well'; that those who were non-white or had housing difficulties could not succeed (and would always damage the education of whites and/or those in decent housing); again the same fears that whites were raising in the USA about plans for racial integration.

Superimposing 'the market'

'Neighbourhood' was thus a displaced discussion of the long-standing problems of poverty, urban decay and segregated housing in certain cities, as well as the even longer-standing issue of social class mixing. Although there are some cases of notable success and some areas where balance between schools was maintained, 'inner city' problems overall have not always been dealt with any more successfully by comprehensive education than they were addressed by the selective system earlier or by the socially segregated education of the nineteenth century. Today such problems are being rapidly accelerated by the new market approach which encourages 'successful' comprehensive schools to choose pupils from a wide area, leaving 'unsuccessful' schools to pick up the pieces and run down or close – the long-standing remedy of advocates of 'parental choice', today augmented by 'hit squad' proposals where governments send in businessmen and 'experts' to take over.

Situations produced by engineered enrolment and other measures that prevent local authorities from organising balanced intakes are increasingly being described. Several came out in the House of Commons Education Committee's investigation into inner city schools, which heard a roll-call of the fallout, including the tendency of some grant maintained and voluntary schools to take in from ever wider areas, leaving maintained schools as the local school to serve a high proportion of disadvantaged and rejects from 'the prestigious schools as well as new arrivals to the locality' such as immigrants, and more recently, refugee populations (Education Committee, House of Commons, 1994, 16 March, p.15).

The next stage in this process is to close 'unpopular' – or 'failing' – schools and disperse pupils, another of the demands of the 'parental choice' lobby. This can then deprive a poor neighbourhood of any school at all (a process that would have gone faster had there not been a need to keep unfilled schools – see Chapter 4). Certain inner city areas first began to experience these losses in the 1980s at a time of falling numbers and some reacted vigorously. When an attempt was made to shut down a comprehensive school in the Croxteth area by a Liberal and Conservative majority in Liverpool, there was an unexpected occupation of the building not just for 2 days but for 2 years, while education was carried on by local people, unpaid teachers and outside volunteers (Carspecken, 1985:107–36; Carspecken and Miller, 1983:154–61; *Comprehensive Education*, 1983).

Their case was that every neighbourhood deserves its own educational centre and that removing a school from a poor area was a special form of social discrimination. But under the present market approach the process is likely to continue and to include further education colleges as well. According to one study (from the Director of Education Services, Peat Marwick, 1995), 20% of further education colleges will disappear in the next few years. This is serious for the future of comprehensive education because every area should have a 'serving' further education centre as well as its local schools.

Through pressures of the kind described, the market mechanism can replace neighbourhood schools and colleges in some areas by no school or college at all. In a few places it now means poorer children travel miles to find schools (which often do not wish to admit them), again suggesting a parallel with some bussing experiences in the USA – except that in Britain it is a 'punishment', while in America it is supposed to have been a reward. Accumulating evidence in the USA, however, suggests that bussing has made little difference to attainment and that black communities in several cities are advocating spending the money instead on the inner city schools where students live. But time is running out for certain inner city neighbourhoods in advanced industrial countries now that better-off black and other ethnic minorities are themselves attempting to move out, and new poor and disadvantaged populations take their place. According to one civic leader in the USA, 'It isn't about race now, it's about class', about escaping the inner city, the 'poorhouse' of the future with crime, drugs, gangs and declining schools: 'Nobody wants to be around poor people' (De Witt, 1994).

At least the American debate is still based on reality, acknowledging the fact that most neighbourhoods are not poor. In Britain until recently the neighbourhood argument assumed all comprehensive schools were in bad neighbourhoods, failing to register the fact that most neighbourhoods are not slums but places people like living in, and some very pleasant indeed. Later pages show that 'neighbourhood' in 1994 was a popular concept. The recent resistance of the middle classes to market forces and cuts in local education spending is very much a campaign to preserve neighbourhood education in the shires, as several local all-party campaigns in these areas show very clearly (*Guardian*, 27 March 1995). As one CEO in a shire county said in 1995, try to take away local comprehensives here and 'there will be blood in the streets' (Maden, 1995).

When the anti-comprehensive argument condemned 'one class' schools or Eric James decried schools of 'limited social status' so threatening to standards, these were not schools with middle-class intakes, about whom no defender of the grammar schools has ever complained, but schools with working-class intakes. This is what 'neighbourhood' has always meant. Comprehensive schools were assumed to be schools used by the working-class because when the official reform began 30 years ago they had fewer middle-class pupils than they would have had in a fully comprehensive system. The NFER gave evidence on this point in all three of its reports in the late 1960s and early 1970s (Monks, 1968, 1970; Ross *et al.*, 1972) and so later did Steedman's report of the National Child Development Survey (Steedman, 1980). Comprehensive schools had much the same social class composition as did the early secondary modern schools.

At the same time, the NCB research showed that grammar schools, which always claimed to be schools for the poor or working class, had become very much schools for the middle class. Their progress to this intake had been well documented in any case in earlier statistics. For these reasons, those supporting the comprehensive reform had always argued that it was only in the comprehensive schools that working-class pupils as a whole were going to get any educational opportunity. But instead of looking to see what forms of education or practices might increase the attainment levels of working-class pupils in comprehensive schools (while continuing to support the attainment of middle-class pupils) commentators in the national debate speculated repeatedly about whether that middle-class minority and those few 'able' working-class pupils would have done better in the old selective school system. Very few on either side argued that the majority would be better off if they were still in secondary modern schools – just as today few argue they are better off in situations where the new market polarisation is creating schools specifically for the disadvantaged.

There were few disadvantaged schools at the start of the reform – just as there were few comprehensive schools in leafy suburbs serving students drawn mainly from private housing. Today, as the 1994 Survey shows, neighbourhood comprehensive schools of both kinds exist in increasing numbers. In particular, there are many comprehensive schools where the majority of the intake is middle class. Possibly this is why we are hearing less about neighbourhood schools and why – in time – we can expect to see Britain move in the American direction where it is the better-off who battle for the neighbourhood concept. It is also clear that there are very few areas where mixed intakes are an absolute impossibility. Where they are not possible, the intake that exists should be firmly assumed to be one as capable of achievement as any other, to be provided with the same full means of showing this.

Polls and creaming

Whether the working class and black and other ethnic minorities will rally around their own schools in sufficient numbers – rather than seeking to escape them and the areas in which they stand – remains to be seen. Opinion polls in the 1960s showed that the concept of comprehensive education had its strongest support in the skilled working class (C2) and least support in the middle class (A/B)[8]. But opinion polling since has been less reliable because the way the question was asked so often conditioned the outcome, and because the question was so often framed in relation to selective schools rather than all schools. Thus when people were asked if they wanted grammar schools 'abolished', high percentages naturally said no. Even though comprehensive schools were not mentioned, this response was often reported as showing that people were opposed to comprehensive reform. Responses might have been different if the question had been put: 'Rather than abolish grammar schools, would you like to see them developed into comprehensive schools?' At any rate, when questions were asked separately about whether people thought comprehensives were a good idea most polls showed majorities saying yes (though this was rarely interpreted to mean they thought grammar schools were a bad idea).

The tactic was often to couple questions with a 'some-say' link to comprehensive education. Thus in 1983: 'Some say academic standards have declined as a result of comprehensive education, do you agree?'. A small majority said yes. But it was only the barest majority that still said grammar schools had the best education. By then 27% thought comprehensive schools did and only 12% wanted comprehensives replaced. Earlier, 54% of teachers had opposed repeal of the legislation requiring comprehensive education; and almost always, when people were asked if they supported 11-plus selection, most said no, even those in the most politically Conservative areas (Passmore and Durham, 1984; Weeks,1986:176).

Lately, polling has been popularised and often comes through non-scientific phone-ins or write-ins. A Manchester freesheet in October 1994 claimed 99% support for the 11-plus after asking voters to consider whether 'race horses and shire horses' can be taught together when shire horses often 'misbehave', preventing others getting 'a decent education'. Thus, by sleight of question, selection by attainment has become selection by behaviour, pandering to the very real concerns people have about levels of violence and emotional disturbance in society.

During the 1970s, the idea most regularly winning support in polling was the proposal that both comprehensive and grammar schools should be developed side by side. To the comprehensive schools and colleges, however, this coexistence 'solution' was seen as requiring them to perform as comprehensives when systematically denied high attaining pupils. Even

Black Paper contributor Rhodes Boyson agreed that if the two schools are run side-by-side, comprehensives are nothing but 'misnamed secondary modern schools' (Boyson, 1969:60).

Whenever the question was asked, however, it appealed to a majority of the general public, which was one reason why it went on being asked by commissioning editors of public opinion polls. Eventually the word 'coexistence' was dropped in favour of 'creaming', a concept more easily understood: a school missing that part of its local intake required to perform comprehensively across the attainment range. This was one point on which all comprehensive schools protagonists, assembled by the government in 1977 at its comprehensive conference in York, were agreed: 'at one in their opposition to the creaming... of the academically most able pupils... (considering it) demoralising... and not necessarily beneficial to the pupil' (DES, 1978: Introduction).

Comprehensive schools had experience of the problem because just as they lacked as yet their share of middle-class support, they also lacked the full range of attainment. Evidence came from the NFER research (Monks, 1968:227, 1970; Ross et al., 1972:107, 109, 117). In 1968 the Benn/Simon survey showed the significant difference made when comprehensive schools were not creamed by grammar schools: more balanced intakes, much bigger sixth forms (Benn and Simon, 1970: Table 18.3, page 303). It also showed that in 1968 just over half the comprehensives were being creamed by grammar schools. Five years later an NUT survey found that although there was almost double the number of comprehensive schools, almost exactly the same percentage was still being creamed by grammar schools.

There was argument over whether a lower percentage of the age group actually going to grammar schools by this time meant less creaming, but researchers showed that if the very top of the attainment range was creamed off, there need be only a small percentage creamed for the effect to be disproportionately high on any comprehensives in the vicinity (King, 1970; Little, 1973; Public Schools Commission, Second Report, 1970, Vol. 1:118; TES, 30 June 1972). A little later the HMI analysed intakes to 384 comprehensive schools and found in terms of the top 20% of the attainment range that 21% of ('restricted' and 'transitional') schools had no pupils at all from this top 20%, and that some of the remainder (called 'full range') also lacked a large part of the top 20% (HMI, 1979: 6–7). In addition, less than one-third were both fully comprehensive and with a sixth form. After 10 years of reorganisation this seemed a bleak commentary on the lack of action by three successive Labour governments.

As well as evidence gathered nationally, there was also a great mass of evidence of the damaging effects of creaming from local authorities and from individual comprehensive schools (McCarthy, 1968; NUT, 1993). This led to the creation of another synthetic division in comprehensive education: between 'genuine' comprehensive schools and those that were comprehensive 'in name only'. In fact, there was and still is no such division, but rather a continuum. Moreover, some schools could lack a perfect balance and be highly successful, while others with the same imbalance spiralled downwards because in both cases other important factors were involved, including social mix. No one aspect of education is all-important. It is the way the factors interact that tells, an aspect of this complex debate that could never be fully explored while the contest was so simplistically dominated by the 'grammar' issue.

Standards

Nevertheless, 'genuine' comprehensives became important when the debate concentrated on standards. Not the wide view of standards many of those working in comprehensive education were debating at the time, which was whether standards should go beyond passes in external exams to include such criteria as the capacity to think critically, to be tolerant, to work co-operatively, to succeed in an enterprise, or to use knowledge practically. But standards as the anti-comprehensive lobby defined them, strictly limited to external examinations; moreover, at the level that would qualify a student for eventual entry to a university or the professions. Those achieving outside this level were never of the same interest to the selective lobby, and those with demonstrable competence in any field that was not subject to external examination were of even less interest.

Thus the activity of more than half of those in comprehensive schools was not really relevant to the standards debate, which is why comprehensive education needs its own definition of standards that is wide enough and sensitive enough to display a full range of achievement relating to all the many forms of intelligence that characterise human learning at any age range; and to ensure that the education of everyone is being monitored in the same way, and compared fairly. While league tables last, however, none of this is likely to develop, for such tables are simply the 1990s version of the 'grammar tests' that have been applied from the start of reorganisation, evaluating a comprehensive system from a selective perspective rather than from a comprehensive one.

In the 1960s it was assumed comprehensive education's standards could never be as high as those of the old system and that no evidence was needed beyond pointing out the harm such a change could bring. Thus, in 1967, 25 university vice-chancellors wrote to *The Times* protesting at the threat to sixth form standards resulting from comprehensive reform (3 June, 1967). They claimed 'diffusion' and 'inadequate preparation'. Yet when contacted individually by letter afterwards, none chose to give evidence of either threat or offer any proof that university standards would be adversely affected (*Comprehensive Education*, No. 7, Autumn, 1967).

The anti-comprehensive campaign soon realised it had to have more than just opinion, and so the energies and finances of researchers and organisations for nearly 20 years were given over to trying to prove the old system better than the new. Most of it was taken up trying to find some acceptable basis on which to do so through external exam statistics, only to have the search founder at the end on the same rock it met at the start, summed up by one researcher in one sentence: it was 'impossible to obtain comparable children in terms of ability and background in the two contrasting systems' (Barker Lunn, 1969:66).

Sweden had been able to do this in the 1950s because the government divided Stockholm in half, matched pupils and schools in both halves, set one on the course to comprehensive education and kept the others in the old system, and monitored outcomes according to agreed criteria. Not until it found that the new system matched traditional standards at most levels and raised them at some, did it commit the whole country to the changeover (see Husen and Boalt, 1968; Svensson, 1962). The Swedish work was one piece of evidence in place to support the improvements that might be expected from changing to a comprehensive system. There was also data collected for years from surveys that compared standards in different countries (International Studies in Evaluation, 1973-1974; UNESCO, 1962). These almost always found little difference in the performance of top ability pupils in selective and non-selective systems in the countries surveyed, but (depending upon the subject examined) often some improvement at lower or intermediate levels in non-selective systems. There was no evidence to show that comprehensive education was going to lower academic attainment.

A repeat of Sweden's experiment was not undertaken in Britain, so those supporting comprehensive schools had to produce examination results from comprehensive schools individually or in groups. This was done by schools comparing comprehensives' exam results with the results in their previous incarnation or to statistics overall (Pedley 1969; Ross, *et al.*, 1972; Simmons, 1971). Most showed comprehensive schools slightly ahead of the selective system, or holding their own.

More interesting was a follow-up study by a member of the NFER team (after the project team had disbanded) to look at the progress of a small sample of pupils through 'O' levels and 'A' levels (Robertson, 1977). It divided pupils into five levels of attainment and was able to show that those at each level had done as well as or better than students of the same measured ability in the system overall; and when the top 2% of measured ability was tracked, all performed well in 'A' levels and achieved university entry 'with able working class pupils... particularly successful'. This report received almost no comment in the national press, though it contained more new research than all the original Black Papers put together.

Nevertheless, some of the comprehensive research remained less than fully convincing for the same reason subsequent research on grammar schools did: how were these schools chosen and were they representative enough to mean comparison was on a fully like-for-like basis? The other type of evidence comprehensive supporters could give – and it was important enough – was to show the way examination passes had increased in comprehensive schools after reorganisation (Benn and Simon, 1972). The reason this was not enough was because more examinations were being passed by pupils in all types of schools. The most that could be said was that the comprehensive schools were keeping pace.

Few studies in Britain were likely to make valid comparison between comprehensive and selective systems because few had records of the attainment and socio-economic background of all pupils being studied. Two that did were based on the Scottish Education Data Archive (Gray, McPherson and Raffe, 1983; McPherson and Willms, 1987) and showed that in Scotland the comprehensive change had indeed accounted for a rise in pupil attainment overall as well as a discernible narrowing of the gap between working- and middle-class performance – the result of a levelling-up in working-class attainment, and not a levelling-down in middle-class attainment, which also rose (McPherson and Willms, 1988:39).

The National Children's Bureau study (Steedman, 1980) was also able to take individual pupil differences in attainment and social background into account; and, after adjusting like-for-like, found that able pupils did as well in comprehensive schools as in grammar schools. Needless to say, the selective lobby expressed loud doubts but a second such study of the same data (Steedman, 1983) reconfirmed the earlier findings and added more, including those which showed that comprehensive schools did as well for working-class pupils as did grammar schools.

The reassurance was still not good enough. After the Black Papers' teams disbanded, a string of projects, often undertaken by former contributors, did the same piece of research – over and over and over again. By using official statistics of comprehensive schools on the one hand, comparing them with the combined results of grammar schools and secondary modern schools on the other, they aimed to show the latter 'system' was better. Their measure of better was external exam results, mostly GCE. As each of these comparisons was published it received the kind of attention accorded to a major scientific breakthrough, accompanied by articles in every paper and often by a specially prepared TV programme 'explaining' the findings. At first sight reports seemed sensational but the old bugbear of failure to establish a fair basis for comparison rose up to haunt each in turn.

The first research exercise to be given national acclaim was by the chairperson of the governors of Manchester Grammar School (Baldwin, 1976), but Baldwin's 1976 pamphlet, *The Great Comprehensive Gamble*, was discounted for making no allowances for creaming as was his later research. (For critical comments see Venning, 1980; Weeks, 1986:74.) When other researchers re-calculated the same figures, one showed that 'the person who would have passed A-levels at grammar school is now passing them in a comprehensive' (Woodley, 1976:13) and another that the figures 'show a greater rate of improvement of performance for comprehensives than for the grammar/modern sector' (Travers, 1976).

Still undeterred, 'graduates' of the Black Paper circle persevered even after a Conservative government was returned in 1979 and it was clear there would be no returning to the 11-plus system. First to be hit was the ILEA (Cox and Marks, 1981), which Conservative politicians always disliked and later abolished. Selected sixth forms were found wanting in exam passes compared with London Examination Board statistics for the region as a whole. The research was again criticised for failing to allow for creaming. Much more serious, however, was the failure to include any voluntary comprehensives in the totals, a crucial omission in London where most of the grammar schools had been voluntary. This failure left comprehensive education represented almost entirely by comprehensives developed from secondary moderns or those that were purpose built – to be compared against overall statistics. Our own research suggests that comprehensive schools developed from grammar schools even decades later still show differences in examination results from those developed from secondary modern schools (see pages 117–118). How much greater the differences might have been at that earlier time. Information on this was available at the time in the records of intakes to all comprehensive schools in the ILEA. It showed that overall voluntary comprehensive schools had 26% of their intakes in the top attainment band compared with county comprehensives with only 12%. To have left all voluntary comprehensives out of the analysis casts real doubt upon the study's conclusions.

The critics were on surer grounds when pointing out disparity between comprehensive schools, a point which they could have stuck to that might have been useful for the developing system: how poor some of the individual comprehensive schools were in what they were able to offer and how low were the numbers in some sixth forms. This problem had already been highlighted in work showing the deleterious effect of voluntary school creaming on comprehensive school development. These studies and responses to them show that the same data can be used to support both sides of the debate.

The next two publications from old Black Paper colleagues and new recruits went back again to national statistics in the elusive hunt for total system superiority with criteria, as always, limited to standards in passing certain external examinations (Marks *et al.*, 1983). The first project at once ran into the standard trouble: it had failed to allow adequately for attainment creaming and social class differences. The DES believed these points were so important that it issued a public statement to say the exercise was 'flawed' (*TES*, 15 July 1983). When others re-analysed the same data, allowing for attainment and socio-economic differences at the rates most researchers agreed should be observed, comprehensives did as well as selective system schools (Gray and Jones, *TES*, 15 July 1983).

Incredibly, instead of calling it a day (nearly 20 years after the reform started officially and 30 years after it started unofficially) the researchers (with a slightly altered team) tried again 2 years later, this time making finer adjustments to allow for attainment and social differences. Their published conclusions were as before, the selective system was best on number and quality of passes in external examinations – although the systems comparison this time did not occupy the pride of place as it had earlier. More space was given to a wide-ranging look at differences between different types and classes of schools and different subjects – a far more promising and useful line of enquiry, which one of the authors has followed up since in relation to GCSE results within the comprehensive sector (Marks, c.1993).

As for the 'systems' comparison, once again it did not pass the like-for-like test. Allowances made for differences in both social class and attainment intakes were not adequate or convincing, even if elaborate. The words used in respect of attainment make the point: 'we attempt to make an adjustment to allow for those comprehensive schools which do not have many pupils in the top ability group' (p. 65). How 'many' is 'many'? This crucial information was missing[9].

Other researchers undertook comparisons, and although their work too yielded valuable insights, most suffered problems of 'local atypically', the absence of precise information about comparative intakes ; or showed that once intake differences had been taken into account, there was little difference between the two types of schooling (Ford, 1969; Hood, 1983; Stevens, 1980, reviewed in Weeks, 1986:68–80). In 1984 the *Oxford Review of Education* carried a series of articles by veteran researchers on this one topic, generally concluding that as yet no effective base existed for comparing selective and non-selective systems (Clifford, 1984; Goldstein, 1984; Heath, 1984; Lacey, 1984). It did not exist because the nature of selection in 1985 had changed. Gone was a national selective 'system' – which the researchers were postulating still existed. Comprehensive reorganisation had changed secondary education irrevocably.

Finally the hunt to prove that the past was better was called off, and we are quite entitled to ask whether it was worth all the effort; or whether it might not have been better to argue about what kind of a comprehensive system we wanted instead, so that there could have been a debate about standards that was appropriate for the system that was developing rather than the one being left further and further behind. But the drive to test comprehensive education by grammar standards had not been dropped, nor the willingness to compare like with unlike. In the event it was the Government, using 'right to know' as a pretext, that chose to compare 'raw' figures in the form of 'league tables' without any attempt to make fair allowances – a method so crude and destructive that even the Black Paper writers themselves had disowned it (Marks *et al.*, 1981:2). They were, after all, serious researchers, not necessarily opposed to all comprehensive schools.

Right to information – league tables and beyond

The public provision of information through league tables was manifestly politically driven – characterised by one teachers' representative as that 'sickening parade of the poor and disadvantaged in rank order behind the ... prosperous... leafy, gin-and-tonic belts' (Nigel de Gruchy, quoted in the *Observer*, 20 March 1994). Scotland's system was more resilient, which is why Scotland's education system has been able to avoid the worst excesses in operation in England and Wales, and is trying to find more acceptable ways of recording comparison (Munn, 1995).

What is worrying about the hostility to league tables is that it gives provision of information a bad name, and tempts people to advocate an end to the exercise, when what should be sought is its extension. We need more information about schools and colleges and the education and training system as a whole, not less; and it is an even greater pity that information practices have never been devised – and insisted upon by those implementing comprehensive education – that regularly provide information about comprehensive education in a form that is compatible with the promotion of its own development.

The present league tables are not fair, they do not provide full information and they are not genuinely comparative. They are selective tables based on partial information used to produce a hierarchical ranking of all schools by indicators that exclude the achievements of half the students in the country from consideration: number of pupils with five GCSE A-C grades and 'A' level point scores. In present form they are 'grammar' formulations, being used to characterise a comprehensive system, when what is needed is a comprehensive formulation about the performance of a comprehensive public education service and everyone in it. To establish such comprehensive formulations is an urgent task, and devising them may force us to think a great deal more radically about comprehensive education's own goals for development and the information that needs to be made available to compare schools or areas.

But information about performance in schools is not the only information needed by individuals and communities. Data are also needed from nursery education, from colleges, from universities and from governments. For example, there should be full information about admissions and what characterises good practice. The 1994 Enquiry came across practices that no one outside the school or college (sometimes not outside the headteacher's office) knew about, and certainly not parents and students. Possibly schools and colleges should be asked to give information about the pupils who have not been admitted as well as about those that have.

At local authority and government level, information has long been required (but regularly denied) about all forms of public expenditure going into private schools and colleges. This is not just in the form of charity status tax concessions or assisted places, but also the Assisted Places Scheme (see page 148), expenditure by local authorities, and the central government payment of school fees for the children of top civil servants and for military personnel. What is the exact expenditure year-on-year, what does it include, what is each group's profile, and on what grounds are individuals chosen? While they last, we need more information from Training and Enterprise Councils (TECs) about which employers, local institutions or agencies, public or private, get their funding, how much they get, and what their records are in providing qualifications and training.

Nor is it only parents who need information. Adults and other groups need it as well. For example, students at 16, as independent learners, need full information about what courses exist and where they are run in each area. All adults should have full information about their local colleges and universities and those schools which admit adults – not in the form of the largely meaningless percentages (now mandatory for further education, for example) but in terms of what is available, course-by-course in the area, with availability comparisons to other areas of the country. The names of all private firms that are contracted by each publicly-funded school or college or university for any service should be posted publicly and made available to all working and studying in the institution. Information about charges, conditions of work and payment of employees and management should be given, with comparisons nationally and locally.

With information likely to be increasingly generated, it is folly to imagine that its use and nature should continue to be proscribed and prescribed by central governments on ideological grounds rather than made the subject of careful and accountable democratic decision-making at every level. We cannot predict the outcome of making available some of the information held now by governments and local authorities and contracted agencies and quangos, even that held by governors and educational management, but at least we can undertake our discussions – and make our decisions – within a system that has a chance of real public accountability.

Choice in education

Choice was originally a positive idea that went naturally with the comprehensive change. Having people learn what they want to learn (as well as what they must) is the heart of comprehensive philosophy. However, when we look back at the 1960s and 1970s, we can see that there were already signs of the way choice could be used as a substitute for selection (as elsewhere in the world it was being used at the same time as a cover for retaining all-white schools). Since then choice as a concept has got ever further away from being about the means by which individuals – parents, other interested adults or students – as well as groups within the community, can express a preference not only for institutions but for different types of learning or courses within schools and colleges, or for options within courses, or different ways to develop activities in the community or individuals within their jobs. It has become, instead, a limited exercise restricted to entry arrangements to compulsory education and relevant only to parents.

The first use of 'choice' in this context came in a pamphlet issued after the 1944 Act had been operating for a few years, *Choice of Schools* (Ministry of Education, 1950). Its main purpose was to inform parents of the complex arrangements for denominational schools with a few paragraphs about single-sex schools. Arbitration of admissions, otherwise, was by the rule of shortest distance between school and home. There was no mention of the real arbiter of entry to secondary education at the time, the 11-plus examination. That was not a matter of choice at all.

As a force, 'parental choice' developed only after 1965 and the introduction of comprehensive education, spurred by two educational movements originally assumed to be opposed. One spoke for the Conservative Right, through such figures as Rhodes Boyson, while the other was centred in the liberal Advisory Centre for Education with large support from middle-class parents. The Centre's publications expressed the Centre's views (Young, 1970) while the political right's views were set out regularly in the national media and educational journals (Boyson, 1969b). Both sides wanted parents to be able to shop around and schools to adopt sales tactics, with parents as consumers. The difference was that ACE assumed parental choice went naturally with commitment to neighbourhood schooling and comprehensive education, where parents could be closely involved with the education of their children; while the Right opposed comprehensive schools and found the idea of neighbourhood 'a pattern dreadful to contemplate' (Boyson, 1969b).

The national body supporting state education, AASE (later CASE) started out originally in line with ACE; as did the Haringey Council for Educational Advance. A leaflet from the latter stated boldly (and incorrectly) in 1970: 'You have the legal right to choose whichever secondary school you want for your child'. ACE (1969) advised parents who did not get the comprehensive school they wanted always to 'make a fuss'. Pro-selection groups advised much the same (about the grammar school).In time within the comprehensive system there was pressure on LEAs from discerning parents to introduce some element of parental preference into admissions, especially in areas where some LEAs had rigid by-the-book policies that took no account of parents at all.

At this time teachers, while not opposed to parents expressing preferences, were already opposed to parental choice used as the sole arbiter of admissions; so too were most education officers. Thus the Deputy Officer for Hampshire saw 'parental choice', used on its own, as leading to polarisation, with ill effects on those children 'not lucky enough to have articulate and discerning parents' (Potter, 1969).

Figures from LEAs using different systems showed that LEAs whose parents' preferences were met but not widely advertised, experienced least parental dissatisfaction. Those that made parental choice a prime feature had the highest levels of dissatisfaction, as was to be expected when choice was artificially stimulated. In most such areas it was regularly about 20% that chose schools other than the one 'for the area'. In an area with a high-profile for choice, like Newcastle, fewer eventually got the school of their choice than parents choosing in areas with a low-profile for choice like Rotherman or Oldham (Benn, 1970a, 1971b; Lewis, 1971; Taylor, 1971).

These were all areas where 'choice' was balanced with other factors, as was the case in most LEAs. In an area where choice was the only factor, however, problems of polarisation rapidly developed. Manchester was one that chose this direction. Manchester's CEO, Dudley Fiske, spoke and wrote about the consequences over several years. In a paper to a DES conference he warned that 'parents who are less aspirant, less articulate or less competent in handling an appeal, would allow their children to attend less popular schools' (DES, 1978:134). Without balancing factors in admissions, a worrying hierarchy resulted. He talked of the need for children to transfer with established friends, for parents to have the certainty of a place at a known school, of the need for schools to have balanced intakes and teachers high morale. He concluded that 'there is evidence from Manchester that an urban system of comprehensive schools based on parental choice does not meet these needs effectively' (DES, 1978:134). Later he gave chapter and verse as to what had happened to the polarisation of individual schools.

Even earlier, parents themselves began to be suspicious of admissions systems using 'choice' as the only method, especially if they took any interest in the system as a whole. In 1970 a parents' group in Surrey was forced to conclude that 'on balance…a system where transfer is based ENTIRELY on parental choice is likely to produce its own inequalities' (Merton AASE, 1970). Five years later the national president of the Confederation of Associations of State Education (CASE) warned that 'parental choice' would lead to polarised schools, correctly predicting as well that it would also lead to the use of league tables. She even foresaw the subsequent vain attempts to mitigate their damage by 'value-added' data (Bullivant, 1978). She concluded that 'Parental choice' as an admissions system was 'even less fair than the old 11-plus system with "snob" schools for those whose parents know how to choose and "sink" schools for those whose parents don't...know, or don't care'.

Government policy

The Labour Government with Shirley Williams as Secretary of State for Education, expressed continuing partiality for 'parental choice' and in 1978 introduced a Bill to require all LEAs to run admissions systems based on it. The Bill did not lay down balancing factors but at least it substituted the words 'parental preference' for 'parental choice', words that had to remain in the law when a similar provision was introduced by Conservatives in their Education Act in 1980.

No system can give every parent the right to choose in law, only the right to express a preference. Such a right is perfectly compatible with comprehensive education since every parent can exercise it equally. What is dishonest is to promote 'choice' with the clear implication that everyone can have the choices mentioned – as is implied in most campaigning literature issued on 'parental choice', including that from political parties. It is also dishonest to use 'parental choice' to justify retaining fee-paying education or grammar schools. Fee-paying is based on having sufficient means to pay for education outside the public service and is supported by law; entry to grammar schools is based on selection and is promoted by another law. All laws are politically determined. Depending on ideology, therefore, some see entry to these schools as a protected right, others as a protected privilege. It is not a matter of adopting a system where all parents have all these choices against a system where they will be denied any of them, as the debate so often implies; it is a matter of deciding whether the choices that are developed in the public service are those that are open to a minority or those that could be available to everyone.

Over the years there have been sporadic research projects that have showed that parental choice systems linked to parental knowledge led to inequalities for pupils. The best recent evidence on the use of 'parental choice' for admissions in systems comes from the large-scale research project carried out by the OECD into several western countries where similar drives for 'parental choice' were taking place, including new market-managed education systems,where public resources followed children to favoured schools, including, in some cases, private schools (OECD,1994)[10].

Where choice had been encouraged, the positive feature was that parents identified more with schools, a development which could make schools more effective in the long run. The negative features included 'social segregation... because... more privileged groups are more active in choosing "desired schools" and have more access to schools in "prosperous neighbourhoods"'. Choice also increased competition. However, there was no evidence that institutional competition improved performance of pupils.

The main conclusion drawn was that since societies cannot afford to build more 'favoured' schools and shut down 'unfavoured' ones, they will have to provide a greater variety of schools if they want to satisfy choice. The Report warned, however, that this will always fail if choice and diversity are based on either social or academic status – that is, if schools are selective by attainment or by class. Only where choices are about differences in pedagogical style, subject balance, and possibly organisation and ethos, can a 'parental choice' system succeed.

These conclusions confirm several different beliefs held by all sides in the 'parental choice' debate, and illustrate the complexity of the issue. They offer far wiser guidance than the platitudes of the DfE publication *Choice and Diversity* of 1992 and alert us to the need to balance choice with other factors if we are to avoid polarisation. Certain areas in England already experience the result of social polarisation caused by choice uninfluenced by any other factor and there is increasing public awareness of their yearly nightmare of trying to find schools for unplaced pupils. One such acknowledgement (made on the BBC 2 programme *Newsnight* on 14 June 1994) concluded that some believe UK legislation makes ' promises that cannot be fulfilled' and instead of extending choice reduces it significantly. There is a need to cut through the political rhetoric (obligatory on all parties now) to solve the parental choice problem by (a) making sure balance is included in all admissions systems; and (b) that every child is assured of a place in a local school. This issue will have to be faced sooner or later in the United Kingdom, as it has been in almost all other countries.

Just as important is the need to widen discussion of choice. Choice in education in the UK over-concentrates on the single institutional choice of parents at the time of secondary transfer at the expense of choice elsewhere in the system. Increasingly, as courses are modularised and learning becomes more flexible, a great deal more will depend upon the counselling people receive and the freedom to choose widely within the system, especially after the age of 15. Yet it is precisely at this age that the competitive system set up by the market is reducing choice for so many. In recent years the choice of adults,too,has been diminished, as courses in adult education have been curtailed. Choice in education is too important for us to continue to misuse the concept as a substitute for selection.

Choice as a substitute for selection

Conservative policy from 1979 to 1986 failed to stop more areas going comprehensive; and LEAs did not choose to return to selection. Selection through democratic means did not look possible. Tougher and more subtle measures were needed to return selection to the system as well as to open the way to privatisation of the education service. One way used was to formalise 'parental choice' within a market-driven education system as the arbiter of all differences, backed by a complex network of interlocking legislative controls exercised by central government, so that the majority acting through local democracy could not challenge the use of 'parental choice' in its new selective form.

There is no better place to see the ultimate dynamic of the use of 'choice' to retain selection than in Northern Ireland's current arrangements for transfer to secondary schools. Combined with new legislation on engineered open enrolment, the universal 11-plus test is made to look as if it is no longer the Government's imposed policy but instead a means to assist parents to 'choose' the schools they want (see pages 160–162).

The central government devises and marks the 11-plus examination and oversees its administration, but then washes its hands of responsibility by delegating the actual choosing of pupils (both those who pass and those who fail) to secondary school governors instead. The local authority's job is reduced to handing out instructions and explaining the complex web of regulations that directs governors to admit in the strictest hierarchy: grammar schools to choose children who got an A on their 11-plus test, followed by those who got a B if there is space (the cut-off point is usually midway through the Bs, in the process compounding academic selection with social). Those with C and D are filtered into non-selective schools arranged in their own mini-hierarchies. The system is portrayed as the natural outcome of 'parental choice' rather than a tightly policed process of child-batching, requiring a yearly circular of laws and rules far longer than the circulars that introduced comprehensive reform to England, Wales or Scotland (DENI, 11 plus procedure, 1994).

In time, the selective exam may be dropped, for the system is now in place in Northern Ireland for engineered enrolment and 'parental choice' to maintain selection if local schools choose to do so. This is the way 'choice' already operates in parts of England and it is the basis upon which the present Government plans to increase selection, as has already been made clear by Government education ministers in the House of Commons. When asked about its plans for more selection, the Government's answer as late as 1995 was that:

> schools which select by ability or which specialise in particular subjects, have an important part to play in giving parents a choice of schooling for their children ... we believe it is up to local authorities, controlled (voluntary) schools and ... grant maintained schools to make proposals for selective education if they believe that it meets the demands of the parents in the area.
>
> (*Hansard*, 21 March 1995:col. 131)

Parents who want their schools to stay selective can choose this option, regardless of the choices of other parents. That is the policy. Requests from individual schools and LEAs to be selective will be sent to ministers in the way requests to go comprehensive used to be submitted. The views of the majority who oppose such developments have no status, nor indeed any right to be heard.

The policy has already begun to operate. Already several comprehensive schools have been granted permission to become selective or partially selective. In the case of the opted out Queen Elizabeth School in Barnet, objections came from every other secondary school in the LEA. The political party supporting the policy was overturned in the local elections. Neither fact affected the decision. In the case of a few Hertfordshire schools declaring for selection, some of the remaining comprehensive schools said such a development would end their role as comprehensives without their situation ever being considered. Nor are the objections of primary schools forced to sit their children for the 11-plus exams in Essex or Surrey because one or two secondary schools in the area have 'opted' to become (or remain) selective, ever considered. Thus schools and the teachers in them are forced to act against what they believe are in children's best interests and nothing can be done about it because the 'parental choice' of a few parents in a few secondary schools, has precedence[11]. The web of legislation put in place so painstakingly over so many years, is now about to start operating in full.

Changes of this kind represent the second stage of the opt-out school's journey away from democratic accountability: first opting out of its local authority, and then out of comprehensive education. But it is a policy that does not merely apply to opt-out schools; the new selection enables all kinds of secondary schools, if they so choose, to return their locality to selection. Not every GM school will demand to go this way. Nor will most voluntary schools or LEA county schools. Most authorities will not send in plans. But where any school or authorities do so choose (and some will) in the present system nobody else has any say about it because a market model – arbitrated by a single, all-powerful, Secretary of State – has replaced democratic decision-making. Although education is supposed still to be a public service, legislation has taken away the right of citizens locally to have their wishes about their local systems taken into account, or recorded. Yet whether there is an 11-plus or not is the kind of question that societies and communities should be able to discuss. In a market system of education people not only lose their power to change things collectively but also the right to talk about them.

The same 'market' policy forces schools and colleges to work in competitive isolation so that they face many difficulties in building networks of provision that enable them to meet the needs of all levels of attainment during the secondary stage – within affordable spending limits. The polarisation of institutions can lead to unequal distribution of financial and other resources, a 'sharpening of class differences can be expected' with 'continued restriction on the choices of those least able to compete' and 'deepening fissures in social fabric' (Ball, 1981:21). Every year the fissures are widening and without the introduction of new legislation to restore fair and equitable treatment of all parents, schools and colleges within the community of education, the process will continue.

Yet the process could easily be reversed by requirements on all schools to admit as full an attainment range as possible and to agree locally (under the auspices of each LEA) how this might be done. With the changes since 1965 including a national curriculum and a single assessment system, and the increases in numbers of pupils staying on after 16, great schemes of 'reorganisation', as were needed in 1965, are no longer required to end selection. Schools that are capable of moving from comprehensive to selective can now move the other way just as well, as several have already pointed out (see, for example, *TES,* 20 January 1995). Were this requirement enacted, ironically every school would be open for 'parental choice' by every parent. It is not giving parents rights to have their preferences considered that is the problem, it is the misuse of this right to favour one group of parents over another. Equality in the administration of preferences is just as important as equality anywhere else in comprehensive education.

Debates within the comprehensive system

One of the problems faced by comprehensive education in Britain is that its own internal arguments, the ones likely to be most constructive in the long run, have so often had to take second place behind arguments from those opposed to the comprehensive system in principle, or determined to retain selection within the system. Perhaps it is no wonder that Britain has taken so much longer than have comparable industrial countries to make the change.

In the last 15 years, however, that has begun to change. While the hunt to prove the selective system best was being played out in its last form, another type of hunt was proving more positive, the quest for school or college effectiveness. Whereas the hunt for systems comparison has often involved hundreds of schools and thousands of pupils, this research concentrated upon relatively small groups of schools, but looked in great depth over time at everything that went on inside them. It looked at different ways schools were run, including exams and the outcomes from them, as well as their teaching and social organisation, in relation to what they aimed to teach and accomplish. The schools chosen were usually comprehensive, though the research was not specifically directed to proving anything one way or the other about comprehensive education.

Several projects showed that even if some schools did draw from similar areas or have similar intakes, the way they organised and educated made a difference; outcomes were not determined entirely by parental occupation or living conditions, though these factors were still the most significant determinants of educational outcome. The positive outcome of work on school effectiveness was to challenge a depressed view about the capacities of children in certain areas or from certain backgrounds – a view that had grown up in certain types of schools (partly as a result of the grammar school lobby's own concentration on the depressed nature of schools' performance without middle-class and high-attaining pupils).

The effective schools movement provided an antidote to neighbourhood pessimism, just as much as it provided a jolt to schools that were failing to make efforts or make changes or take educational common sense on board. It also provided a much-needed warning to those who might be expecting far too little from those they taught, assuming they were likely to produce little. It concluded that the most effective schools were those where staff agreed on goals and on policies pursued, and were consistent, organised, fair, and active in promoting learning and rewarding achievement.

In other important respects, however, this research was of limited value for comprehensive education because it ignored the overall system within which schools were operating. In other words, even adopting all the practices revealed as effective could only take a school so far if it was locked into a national or local system where selection and polarisation were taking place. Eventually some of the researchers in this field were forced to conclude that, although every school should strive to be effective, 'below certain levels of intake quality... it may be very difficult to be an "effective educational institution"' (Reynolds and Reid, 1985: 194).

Some of this research combined both effective schools and systems comparison. A small area of Wales changing over to comprehensive education provided a chance to compare the old selective system and the new comprehensive one in terms of institutional effectiveness (Reynolds *et al.*, 1987). The researchers, while not drawing particularly favourable conclusions relating to the selective system, drew several unfavourable conclusions relating to the two comprehensives. Although results for the 'higher attaining' pupils were good, the schools overall were found to have poor management, lack of pupil involvement, inadequate pastoral care, distant relations with parents, over-strict rule enforcement, and over-emphasis on academic attainment and streaming at the expense of social and personal development, particularly of the majority of pupils.

As usual, it was reported in the press in an anti-comprehensive spirit, causing one of the authors to complain that press coverage had provided a 'selective mis-reading' of this research since the main argument had not been given: that comprehensives were failing because they were not comprehensive enough (Reynolds *et al.*, 1987). This work had brought the debate on definition full circle, for central to the researchers' conclusions was that the comprehensives they had studied were less successful than they could have been because they were trying to be good 'grammar' schools-for-some rather than good comprehensive-schools-for-all. What should be happening, the letter continued, was comprehensive education giving 'the same experience to all children' while ensuring that this would 'also... be selective... giving different children and different ability ranges a different experience' (Reynolds *et al.*, 1987). The same, yet different; another example of that continuing struggle to reconcile equality and difference that characterises the task of comprehensive education.

But were these Welsh schools typical of anything other than themselves? In the absence of large-scale research no one knew. The same could be said about other studies where even fewer comprehensive schools were examined. Ball (1981), for example, looked at only one comprehensive school. He too found much to criticise in the lack of direction and inadequacy of practice, though the middle-class pupils and high attainers did well enough. As in the Reynolds study, there was the feeling that there should have been more to show for the change than what was being achieved.

The real significance of research of this kind (missed in much of the popular media comment) was that it was criticising comprehensive education from the point of view of supporters of the reform rather than that of opponents. Their object was to drive education forward rather than send it back into an era that had been rejected. Ironically, the research of supporters was far more influential in its criticism than that of the pro-selective lobby. Such studies sparked much more enduring and thoughtful professional and academic debate. It received less coverage in the popular media, where the suggestion still remained – even during the 1980s – that comprehensive change had been far too drastic. In practice, most of the research showed that the change had not been great enough.

The development of the philosophical critique of comprehensive education
The hypothesis of too little change has been central to most of the important writing on education during the last 30 years, but since 1965 the continuing critique of comprehensive education from its supporters has gone through distinct stages, involving several broad groupings of academics and practitioners nationally and internationally, each one ready with a different prescription for success or a new explanation for education's shortcomings. All have contributed constructively to the continuing debate, but their influence has not been as great as it could have been because the continuing critique from opponents has monopolised popular critical space.

Thirty years ago many saw the comprehensive reform as primarily about social harmony and cohesiveness, and the production of a new type of society. There were echoes of this goal in other countries during the 1960s – in the USA with the opposition to Vietnam and Martin Luther's 'dream' for ending the segregation of black from white. Perhaps it could be summed up in Tony Crosland's words: 'The central... argument against the 11-plus lies in the denial of social justice'. Comprehensive education was meant to make society better in some way.

When it was slow to do this in the face of the system's mounting economic crises, the same Tony Crosland turned around and said, 'The party's over' (see Simon, 1991:436). Looking back now, many are critical of earlier advocates of comprehensive education for their naive assumption that it is 'only access which is a problem'. These critics have developed a critique of the social democratic tradition as a whole for its 'failure... to achieve justice and equality for the working class through... the education and spirit of... comprehensivisation' and through other measures (Thewlis, 1988:249). Widespread criticism of this kind was shaped and preceded by several hard analyses of education and society from an impressive range of scholars and practitioners in several western countries (Althuser, 1971; Bordieu and Passeron, 1977; Bowles and Gintis, 1976; Carnoy, 1974) who argued that all education systems are there to reproduce the relationships of capitalism and prepare those going through them for their allotted occupational posts. Such systems, even if 'reformed', could not possibly deliver the social improvements expected of them. These neo-Marxists' arguments were powerful and influential, well-documented and stimulating, but at bottom their outlook was highly pessimistic. They offered only analysis, not a basis upon which those inside education could take action on their own behalf, including those working in comprehensive education in Britain.

In Britain an important response in the 1970s and 1980s came from teachers and educators working in units like the Centre for Contemporary Cultural Studies (CCCS) at the University of Birmingham. They offered a similar critique of the comprehensive system as it was developing within the UK, for mainly replicating the old, divided system within a single set of new walls. Inequality still prevailed; improvements had not taken place; the same gang got the same prizes as before; the same large, alienated groups fled education and abandoned further learning the moment they could. Popular education was fundamentally unpopular and lacking in any understanding of the lives and aspirations and culture of so many of those it sought to reach (CCCS, 1981; Clarke and Willis, 1984; Finn, 1987; Robins and Cohen, 1978; Willis, 1977).

They argued that instead of seeking to drag this population into a world that was alien to them, it was better to start in their world and identify with their needs and aspirations, and make education serve them by operating more closely within the pupils' and students' own cultures. While frequently positive and successful in practice, this approach too had its ceiling, and met objections that some sections of this targeted population could be restricted by this approach. There was then a splintering of the hitherto loosely united supporters of the comprehensive reform, not so much into antagonistic ranks, as into separate examinations of its neglected aspects. Some became increasingly committed to gender equality in education, while others concentrated on anti-racist education and equality in relation to black and other ethnic minority groups. Individual cultures became important; wider social equality became less important (Chitty and mac an Ghaill, 1995).

Others who had earlier developed their own argument about alienation within the system (Hargreaves, 1982, 1994) also began to change tack. They now thought there was far too much concern with structure (form, organisation, selection) and far too little interest in the content of education or the way learning proceeded. They supported new types of schools, greater variety of schooling, more parental control, more 'choice' – in short, the revival of differences both between and within schooling, but without returning to a divided system (Hargreaves, 1994). To some, such arguments represented an invitation to walk an old tightrope over a new chasm.

Another group developed post-modern critiques which de-constructed the reform by approaching education from the point of view of a rapidly changing society – both locally and globally. They saw old social and cultural alignments being disturbed, and new ones gaining adherents, where the essentially single nature of society, however stratified socially, was being challenged by a multiplicity of beliefs and lifestyles, whose cultural relativism characterised people and groups, claiming their allegiance in many new ways. In this view of the world we needed a raft of alternative educational institutions, to match the needs of society as it changed (Aronowitz and Giroux, 1991; Donald, 1990; 1992).

A last group might be called the futurists – those who see the entire education system breaking down in its institutional integrity, with the prospect of individuals and groups forming and reforming around various centres of learning. Their vision encompasses the use of facilities and teachers in different ways at different periods of their lives, with universal access to a vast range of learning materials and information sources in a variety of venues, where learning programmes are negotiated and work is much more self-directed. This is seen as matching a pattern where:

- learning alternates with work throughout life;
- where occupations shift and training develops individuals in different ways, to meet changing economic requirements;
- education may not even any longer be compulsory to 16;

- everyone may have available the same 'catalogue' from which programmes,courses or learning packages can be chosen as required, according to qualifications needed or learning desired – by parents for children, by children for themselves, by adults, by groups, by communities, or by workers working together (see, for example, Harber, 1995; Meighan, 1988).

All these educational stances have windows of truth where, in a single glance, we can see our world anew; but many look at only one aspect of the system, possibly overlooking the chance of a new synthesis; or they start from where they wish to end, rather than where the education system is now. What is required now are practical proposals that continue the development of the comprehensive schools and colleges towards a system in which unification can continue, ownership of learning can be made more complete, and decision-making more accountable. Once this begins to take place, the means by which the system moves forward should be for people themselves to decide. This should apply equally to schools and colleges and universities and to the comprehensive education of the whole community for all age groups. In historical terms, comprehensive education as an educational principle is still very much in its developmental phase.

Curriculum and assessment for a single age group: The same, different, or integrated?

Just as significant for the development of the comprehensive principle has been the debate about the way the curriculum is organised, or the way pupils and students are grouped for teaching. In schools this has meant debates about common courses and about streaming pupils supposedly with the 'same' attainment, as against mixing abilities in the teaching groups, or through the half-way house of 'setting', where streaming takes place within a single subject rather than across the board. A full discussion of this issue in relation to the curriculum and the establishment of a common course, is set out in Chapters 6 and 7. Here it is looked at as part of the continuing debate about practices to ensure social and cognitive development for people of all levels of attainment in common rather than in separated spheres.

Studies on intra-school grouping have almost always relied on public examination criteria. In the early years of comprehensive reorganisation these studies repeatedly proved inconclusive in terms of academic results from selective or comprehensive systems (see Barker Lunn, 1969:167).

Current evidence as to the advantages and disadvantages, both social and academic, of mixed ability as against streamed and setted grouping is also inconclusive.

Yet early comprehensive schools that abandoned streaming gave enthusiastic reports of their improved performances. In 1970, Colin Lacey produced *Hightown Grammar*, which looked at the effects of streaming in an academically selective secondary school. And in a follow-up study of the same school after a changeover to mixed ability groupings (Lacey, 1974), it was found that the 'less able' boys (by comparison with other boys in that particular school) improved their exam performance, whereas the change made little or no difference to the pass rate of the 'most able'. Much the same was shown with respect to the long-term effects of early streamed or mixed ability teaching in the Postlethwaite and Denton enquiry carried out at Banbury School in Oxfordshire in the 1970s. The pupils' public examination results at 16 showed only minor differences between those who had been taught in streamed groups and those who had been taught in mixed-ability classes in the early years of the secondary school (all the pupils being streamed or setted in the later years).

Although there was some evidence of better overall performance on the part of the less able boys in the mixed ability classes, without any lowering of the standards reached by the more able, few differences were found for girls (Postlethwaite and Denton, 1978). And the HMI survey of mixed ability teaching (DES, 1978) found nothing to indicate that one system was necessarily better than the other, but came to the conclusion that, to be successful, non-streaming had to have the full support of the teachers and be properly resourced (see Simon, 1979). *Fifteen Thousand Hours* (Rutter *et al.*, 1979) found little evidence that school effectiveness was related to streaming or mixed-ability teaching. Work on school effectiveness generally has yielded the same inconclusive results that have attended comparisons between selective and non-selective systems, in terms of the limited measures used to judge: external exam results in both cases.

But are these kinds of academic exam results (or exam results themselves) the only measure of success in schooling? Possibly the research has been looking too narrowly and that it is not in academic results (and norm-referenced exams at that) that the effects will be seen, but in institutional ethos and social organisation or in other types of attainment. Research results have shown that streaming in comprehensive schools both highlights and divides on social as well as attainment lines (Ball, 1981; Ford, 1969). In some countries internal divisions are regarded as likely to prejudice education of certain groups and have been made illegal.

Tracking, for example (streaming by separate courses), has been banned in many areas of the USA for many years[12]. In many areas of Britain anecdotal evidence suggests a positive effect on social and general attainment grounds for mixed ability, but little research has ever been undertaken to see whether unstreamed schools are less likely to engender hostility and internal segregation. We are unlikely to have answers to this question in the immediate future, for the introduction of the national curriculum tests and the publication of test results has meant increased pressure on schools to adopt traditional methods of grouping pupils, particularly in the later years of the secondary school. Just at the point where so many schools and colleges were beginning to realise that strategies for individual differentiation within an unstreamed organisation might prove most effective, the doors to this future have been temporarily closed.

16 Plus – the big divide

After the age of 16, and increasingly between 14 and 16 in some schools, the British system is still bedevilled by the three-way split between academic, vocational and work-related education. Although the drive is on to close these gaps, there are three barriers in the way. The first is a structure that is divided; the second is a curriculum that is divided; and the third is a qualifications system that is divided.

Britain's post-16 tracking system has its origins in the divided system of the earlier secondary years, which was there when comprehensive reform began in 1965. The new reform embraced the old system. The GCE 'O' level and 'A' level (which formed the battlefield for the subsequent war over 'results') were exams that were put in place to serve a selective system in 1951: 'A' level was designed originally for about 10% of the age group, 'O' level for 20% (though when it ended some 35% were passing it). The CSE was added in 1965 for the next 40%, leaving 40% with no attainment target in terms of assessment.

For almost two decades after 1965, this non-comprehensive tripartite assessment structure was left in place: a traditional academic route to 'O' level; a CSE route for the middle group; and a third route giving no qualifications, offering the option of leaving at 15, the legal leaving age at the time. Scotland's system was even more stark after 1965. It introduced no CSE equivalent, leaving its only qualification the traditional certificate course. A far larger percentage of pupils had no option but to leave. Looking back, this was hardly the best way to start off a system designed to be comprehensive in either country (as Scotland realised sooner than England).

Nor was it appropriate for the second half of the twentieth century in an advanced industrial nation. Countries that already had comprehensive education had also established unified assessment systems where a wide range of subjects or courses could be provided for almost all levels of achievement and interest within the single school or college complex for the age group up to 17 or 18. James Conant characterised the version operating in the USA in contrast to the 'European idea' of separate schools or courses as 'an *elective* system as contrasted to a *selective* system' (Conant, 1967:4).

Debate over examinations reform

Many of the earliest supporters of comprehensive education, as well as wanting an undivided system, also wanted less obsession with external examining itself, with more emphasis on internal assessment or testing under the control of schools themselves – as well as forms of assessment other than end-of-course or norm referenced examinations which Britain still retained at both 16 and 18.

As early as 1973 several comprehensive school protagonists were trying to promote 16-plus examination reform. John Sayer, headteacher of Banbury School, spoke for many in expressing fears that the 'energies directed into the external examination system are now preventing schools from realising the objectives which that (comprehensive) system is now trying to promote' (Sayer, 1973:13).

Inevitably, in the next 15 years the developing comprehensive system became increasingly frustrated not only by external examinations but by the divided assessment system at 16-plus, especially after the leaving age was raised to 16 in 1972. More and more schools began ignoring the official guidelines and sitting all their pupils for one or the other of the two exams, so that all their pupils were at least aiming for a qualification, even if they were of different status. An enterprising school or two – like Sutton Centre in Ashfield – even tried to beat the system by using CSE only for all pupils. The Schools Council recommended a single assessment system at 16-plus in 1974; pilot schemes testing one out were taking place throughout the 1970s; and in 1978 a national body (The Waddell Commission) recommended national change. All Labour Secretaries of State were regularly lobbied on this specific issue, but all refused to act throughout the late 1960s and right up to the end of the 1970s.

Ironically, it was left to Conservatives to bring in the 'unifying' examination of GCSE in 1986, but not in a form which so many were hoping for – compatible with 'through-assessment' from 14 to 18 and an integrated curriculum. Instead it was an examination which was again external, again at 16-plus, again subject based, again depending on a 2-year course, and, if anything, more finely graded than before. In fact, its grades A–C were soon established as the grades that universities were to look for, while the informal 'requirement' to have at least five of these replicated the long disused school certificate of the 1930s. Like so many reforms which Conservatives undertook, the change had nothing to do with assisting comprehensive education but had a deeper purpose on another agenda. As one external examiner commented at the time, 'the examination tail is wagging the curriculum dog' (MacIntosh, 1983:7).

Nevertheless, the change was real enough and comprehensive schools welcomed the single system enthusiastically, taking advantage of it to unify courses and to innovate – particularly by the development of course work (where the experience of Mode III on the CSE had been particularly positive). This meant assessment could extend to work done throughout the year rather than be based entirely on one sudden-death exam at the end of a 2-year course. But soon this popular and successful initiative was curtailed by arbitrary fiat of the Government. It was dictated by fears of reduced 'standards' although experience in experiments like the Wessex Project showed standards were significantly improved for many by coursework (Rainbow, 1993; Spours, 1993). This was in the wake of a new National Curriculum and mass testing where the central government took control from teachers in classrooms. 'Teaching to the test' was now back on the agenda, forcing the mothballing or diminution of several creative ways to promote learning, including many other forms of assessment which had long been discussed and tried in developing comprehensive schools. These included work in profiles, in developing Records of Achievement, and project work of all kinds – as well as other ways of recording skills, knowledge and ability in practice, some arising from the ever-greater interest in vocational education. Whenever unemployment grows, interest in vocational education grows. For comprehensive education's development, this interest was highly productive. It allowed alternative forms of assessment like criterion referenced testing to be considered as an alternative to the norm referenced 'O' and 'A' levels. It allowed work to take place to shorten the long length of courses, taking years to complete. The modules of 40 hours each devised for Scotland's SCOTVEC courses were a great breakthrough in 1984 (see pages 167–168).

Sometimes new departures were sparked by government programmes intended for other purposes. TVEI, for example, was funded to boost the technological and vocational skills of pupils, which some schools used in pedestrian or selective ways in order to provide segregated courses for pupils of 'lesser ability'. The introduction of TVEI sparked a big debate within comprehensive education because of its segregating potential (Chitty, 1986) – until some enterprising comprehensives used TVEI money in order to extend developments in learning for the entire range of attainment instead. Some schools put into action plans that they had ready but just needed funds to develop. Some used the money more widely than on technology education. In Scotland TVEI was used across the board for academic subjects, including technology in the teaching of English or history. The Wessex Project of modular learning was the most outstanding example of a new development: where all courses of learning between 14 and 18 were reorganised in modules, to be tackled one at a time before moving on. A coherent progression was established right through the later years of secondary education for the first time in Britain, giving 'A national framework for credit accumulation and transfer', true parity of esteem, and the promotion of continuous assessment and autonomous learning (Rainbow, 1993:99).

The debate over 'A' level

All such work was fuelling demand for change in the assessment system but all of it was meeting a major obstacle: the retention of 'A' level, a narrow specialist examination that had been in place for over 40 years by the start of the 1990s. During the 1960s and 1970s there had been two proposals to modify its narrow scope[13]. However, all that could be agreed was another 'parallel' exam from 16 to 18, the Certificate of Extended Education (CEE) which was started in the 1970s and abandoned in the 1980s. Believing 'A'-level to be some sort of talismanic 'gold standard', Conservative governments of the 1980s ignored recommendations for modest change from two more committees (Higginson, 1988; MacFarlane, 1980), ending up introducing only miniaturised versions in A/S levels. The Labour party (1982) had already advocated change (in its fullest policy document on post-16 education over the last 30 years, *Learning for Life*) and so, in time, did almost every other political party and many influential bodies in the country, including the National Education Commission (1993).

By the early 1990s there was widespread support for some form of assessment into which 'A' levels could be incorporated. Though not all those proposing a new system agreed on all points, common ideas emerged, including the integration of academic and vocational learning in a single system of accreditation, the modularisation of courses, and the accumulation and transfer of credits. Most proposed a single qualification, available to the whole age group at 17 or 18; and several proposed scrapping a first exam at 16 altogether. None of the proposals was particularly original, most being adaptions of curriculum and assessment systems already in operation in Commonwealth countries, the USA or in one or other of the countries of Europe.

Throughout the 1980s and into the 1990s the Conservative Government was as deaf to all of these proposals as Labour had been to that for a common 16-plus examination in the 1970s. One of Margaret Thatcher's last acts before her resignation in 1990 was to decide yet again A level would stay. As is now known, one body favoured retention and at a crucial time it called at Downing Street to make its case: the powerful HMC which represented the major public schools (Richardson, 1993; Kerr, 1992:47). Schools representing a very small number of students overall still had the major say in the way the majority's system would develop.

This meant that the impressive and determined drive the Government subsequently undertook to reform vocational education, was carried on in a vacuum. It was another tracked development, not an integration of academic and vocational education, revealing one of the areas where contradictions within the Conservative party were at their sharpest and where those party political (and intra-party) debates which Richardson (1993:29) found were so 'debilitating... for coherent modernisation of education and training practice' were most obvious.

The debate over Highers in Scotland

In Scotland assessment reform has gone a great deal further because Scotland was first in the field with modular courses through its introduction of criterion-referenced SCOTVEC in 1984, covering learning in a wide range of vocational and academic areas. It proved immediately popular and highly versatile. But it had one drawback: it accentuated the separation between a vocational track and the academic education in certificate courses, especially in the upper years (S5/S6). The more successful it became, the more acute the problem. More than one observer concluded that 'The failure in 1984 to include Highers in the modular reform limited the ability of the NC framework to impose coherence on the system'. There was parallelism but 'not on equal terms' (Raffe, 1993:63).

This led to pressure to develop assessment in ways that overcame this division and eventually to a rejection of proposals that would have kept them separate (Howie Report, 1992). In 1994 new proposals were made by the Government (*Higher Still*, 1994). They appeared to respond to wishes for credit transfer and more coherence and integration, suggesting a structure that aggregated modules into subject courses. But on closer inspection it was seen they did nothing to remove the split; in many ways they strengthened it by extending both vocational and academic courses into new 'advanced' levels, based on one route for vocational and another for academic.

The main teachers' union, the EIS, strongly criticised the proposals in these respects (EIS, 1994) as well as registering its suspicions about new changes proposed for lower down the schools, seen as an attempt by the Conservative Government to 'ensure that certain knowledge and skills are inculcated uncritically in school' as they were 'south of the border' in the National Curriculum (which Scotland has so far resisted). They also criticised the omission from the new system of students on Skillstart work (training courses). In effect, the Government's proposals, while appearing to solve the main problem, would institutionalise three separate sides. In Scotland educationists were making the running in defending their comprehensive system from changes that the Government was at that same time manoeuvring into place in England and Wales.

The debate about vocational and work-related education

The origins of the vocational and work-related education debate can be traced back to the Great Debate of 1976 which, in fact, contained little real debate. It represented a prior agreement to move forward in respect of lower attaining school leavers in terms of basic skills at school and training schemes afterwards. In the 1980s governments began using youth training as part of their plans for privatisation, undermining the unions and disciplining youth. There were some useful initiatives for older years and some innovation and good work in youth training, especially where input came from the respected tradition of general education, the mainstay of young workers' education in most day-release programmes. But as the 1980s wore on 'transferable skills' soon deteriorated into a euphemism for no skills, suitable for a low-wage, low-skill economy matched by what continued to be described as 'an early selection/low participation education system' (IPPR, 1990:4).

The weakest point in the new training initiatives lay in the relationship of training to education. At one point David Young, a businessman accelerated into ministerial office and given charge of training, illustrated the detachment by telling an audience of London teachers and education officials that the new 2-year Youth Training Scheme (YTS) would be the equivalent of two 'A' levels. None believed him and possibly he did not believe it himself. Within a few years YTS had ended, its place taken by YT with yet another extravagant promise that could not be kept: that everyone leaving school would be guaranteed a place on the scheme. This promise was broken because of cuts to the funding for youth training. Many young people had to choose for the meagre allowance attached to it rather than because they were committed to the training or education provided. Disillusioned, some also resisted participation in schemes that were perceived as exploitative and from which no benefits appeared to accrue.

The YTS scheme had accomplished its mission, expressed when the White Paper outlining it was placed before Parliament on 15 December, 1981, 'to bring about a change in attitude of young people to the value of training and the acceptance of relatively lower wages' (Paragraph 58).

By the mid-1980s there was pressure to extend the training drive into a wider vocational drive that could introduce work-related education in a more positive light, not as a dead end but as another route upwards. At last the Conservative Government seemed to realise that education was the key to competing in the global economy and that more had to be done to increase the take-up of advanced education courses. Others could see potential benefits to individuals in preparing them for living, learning and earning in more flexible ways, as seemed likely to be demanded by their future lives. Schools had been developing closer links with employers since the early 1980s through projects like that run by the Schools Council and other measures promoted by industry to link schools and the workplace. The clear message was that regardless of employment prospects, our urgent need was 'to increase the supply of occupationally, technically and otherwise qualified young workers' (see Holland, 1986).

A key decision in 1989, akin to lifting the ban on public examinations in the old secondary modern schools, was the licensing of schools to offer Business and Technical Education Courses (BTEC) to their students. For decades, the technical and business courses offered by bodies like BTEC, City and Guilds and the RSA had maintained their reputation for worth but were not considered appropriate for schools. Although one and a quarter million students had already taken such courses by 1985 (Farley,

1986:145), there were huge gaps in the provision for various occupational fields. At lightning speed the task began of filling the gaps and converting existing vocational qualifications to GNVQ and NVQ. Students flocked to the courses. By the year of the 1994 survey 82,000 were already taking GNVQ courses in 1400 institutions.

The vocational backlash

At first sight, the whole exercise had the appearance of a stunning success story, a model reform. But from the start there was almost as much criticism of the new system as greeted proposals for testing, the National Curriculum, or the earlier stages of comprehensive reorganisation.

Staff in schools and colleges, not having been sufficiently consulted or prepared, were inundated with repeatedly changing regulations and directives, adding to already full workloads. One lecturer called the exercise of starting courses 'a monster of bureaucracy and form-filling'. There were rumours that BTEC was dissatisfied with the quality of many conversions and considered them to have diluted the standards of the original courses. There were problems with wholly inadequate funding for some qualifications, particularly in the workplace. Many schools' facilities were inadequate for the new courses (Huddlestone, 1993). There was slow take-up and high drop-out (FEFC, 1994a). Core skills were not yet developed fully. On top of it all, education funding levels were being cut at the same time as it was hoped and expected that more students would take the courses and follow through into higher education.

Some of these criticisms could be dismissed as teething problems, but not the fundamental one that the new reforms did not meet the need for a unified education system for the 14–19 year-olds, being no more than an elaboration of the vocational track of the old tripartite system, merely demonstrating 'the capacity of the English system to absorb change by commonly adding initiatives and thereby increasing complexity and confusion'. Real change in the 16–19 area 'involves a commitment to institutional collaboration', which was not there, and to 'common learning', which was not there. What was there was competition to meet low level demands from a weakened labour market and some predicted that students would 'continue to fail in droves' (Spours, 1993:147, 168).

In anticipation of such criticism the Government had already devised equivalence measures for the new exams: where the various levels of the NVQ and GNVQ were to match levels of GCSE and 'A' levels (and Highers in Scotland). The Prime Minister had even suggested a single new diploma for all at 18 to render all work 'equal', though no one was exactly sure what was yet equivalent to what – for example, was GNVQ level 2 the same as five GCSEs or only 4, and were they A–C or A–G? Would employers and universities and colleges accept them as equivalent? Much was made of universities already accepting GNVQ students for entry, but this was at a period when universities were expanding and secondary population was at its lowest.

Nor did any of this solve one of the biggest problems of all, the large numbers of students – possibly most after 16 – who wanted a system where both academic and vocational study, and work-related education, could be more easily combined in any individual student's programme. It certainly did not meet the demands of those who wanted every student at 16 to take some part of their study in common, the possibility that had been discussed for years. Nor of the growing number who wanted full integration of academic and vocational education.

The Black Paper of vocational reform

These fundamental criticisms had to be distinguished from the backlash that came from those specifically concerned with vocational education, many of whom believed the new courses were inadequate and lacking in rigour. Some saw low standards coming from the domination of course material by employers and lead bodies rather than those skilled in teaching. Others were concerned because the qualifications involved a move to competence testing and had abandoned the principles of norm-referenced testing on the basis of knowledge, the standard measure for academic examinations. Vocational élitists even generated their own 'Black Paper' in the form of a critique from Professor Alan Smithers, *All our Future*, preceded by a half hour television programme in the style of the old Black Paper campaigns (Channel 4, *Class Action*, 7 October, 1994).

Training officers from Fords in Dagenham, along with others from European colleges, argued on the screen that the NVQ and GNVQ compared badly both with the old BTEC courses and with qualifications in other countries. The level of mathematics was far lower than applied in France, Germany or Holland. There was no syllabus of what should be learned; no structured learning or progression, no written exams, no theory, no understanding, no knowledge and inadequate assessment. Rumours began to circulate that the qualifications would be strengthened with the inclusion of more 'knowledge'. As this began to happen, others saw work-related education being divided into high- and low-level vocational programmes.

Further public debate followed about the market-led way in which the new qualifications were introduced, where a 'dysfunctional proliferation of certification for the system is rapidly emerging' as bodies vied with each other to market courses (Spours, 1993:161). The competition was lowering standards, for in colleges (already teaching NVQs by the early 1990s) the Government's system was to pay only for students that passed. Inevitably pressure from college managements grew to pass everyone who entered because the college's income depended upon it. Eventually several college assessors found themselves pressed by management to pass more students than their conscience allowed. When one spoke out to say that only 30% would have passed if he had stuck 'strictly to specifications', he faced dismissal (*Class Action*, 7 October, 1994; see also *THES*, 18 November, 1994). Management backed down, but rumours persisted about similar situations elsewhere, which the FEFC did its best to minimise in its annual report (FEFC, 1994, para. 142). Those with an urgent interest in a well-trained workforce, including the trade unions, urged external assessment if credibility was to be maintained.

The backlash was summarised by Article 26, the monitoring group which takes its name from the UN article guaranteeing educational rights to all. Low standards were being allowed to develop in vocational education and training because both 'are regarded as...second-class...by the professional middle-class educational establishment for whom...lax standards of vocational education and training are quite acceptable, convenient and justifiable' (*Observer*, 27 March and 3 April 1994). This had a certain symmetry with complaints about the early days of comprehensive reform: low standards arising from a mistaken ideology.

The debates on the integration of learning and competence

The true picture was much more complex because many of the changes taking place, albeit lacking rigour, were required for a genuine comprehensive education reform. The problem was not that they were going too far. But, as with earlier change, that they were not going far enough.

When examined from the vantage point of comprehensive education's principles and historical development, the temporary difficulties (including market-led implementation) were not the main problem. The real difficulty was that all the work, including 'improvements', were taking place in a sphere that separated vocational courses from academic. In curriculum and assessment, 'can do' competence-based learning was separated from academic and fact-tested learning instead of being integrated in new ways of assessment suitable for the whole age group using a modular curriculum that was itself the product of the integration of vocational and academic education.

Debate on this integration had been at the heart of one section of comprehensive education from the end of the 1970s, if not before. It rarely featured in popular discussion (which remained fixated on 'parental choice' and 'standards' in compulsory schooling and academic selection at the age of transfer to secondary education). In a symposium called in 1984 to encourage integration of teaching and learning from 16 to 19 in schools and colleges, Fred Flower, the Principal of Kingsway College in London, pointed out that from a student's point of view, there was no real distinction between education and training (Flower, 1984). A comprehensive education system was needed for students in work-related education in the same way as for those who remained in full-time academic study. Comprehensive education after 16 meant providing education full-time or part-time to meet all learners' needs and continue their personal educational development. For those in work-related education, it meant they and their teachers working in co-operation with employers, not leaving it solely to employers (Flower, 1983:18–21).

Integration also meant that the education of the 'academic' students in the age group would change, as would their courses. Here the work of the Further Education Unit was central (embodied in *A Basis for Choice*, 1979 and later documents). During the 1980s the complaint was that the principles which had been laid out for the whole age group by the FEU's work were being destroyed by applying them only to that section of the age group involved in work-related training.

The drive to reorganise vocational education in schools and colleges was to draw together teachers in schools and those working in vocational and work-related education and pit them against those who worked only on academic courses. Teachers need to understand work-related education and the way it can be integrated into other forms of learning.

Trainers in work-related education have the same urgent need: to understand the way the work in schools' and colleges' full-time courses can augment work-based education.

The competence debate

Part of this deeper debate within the comprehensive movement was about the relationship between norm-referenced assessment (as used in external exams in schools) and criterion-referenced assessment (as used in vocational courses),with special reference to the concept of competence. For it had long been argued by those in the colleges that competence should have an honoured place in common assessment along with norm-referenced learning – for all learners. Others went even further. Flower and his colleagues argued that norm-referenced graded exams could be replaced by 'a series of goals progressively attainable by all' through a concept of competences that ran across the curriculum and across the attainment range – providing for all a 'combination of skills, knowledge, attitudes and experiences which are acquired in the achievement of a capability' (Flower, 1984:14). These interpreters of comprehensive education were advocating a much more fundamental reform, expressed through commitment to assessment that would replace traditional norm referenced exams by criterion referenced testing in all three areas of learning: academic, vocational and that related to work – as a way of integrating learning itself.

All integration work was put at risk with a new vocational drive in which narrowly designed vocational courses would bring the concept of competence into disrepute. This forced many who supported comprehensive education to see it as a straight case of opposing competence in order to oppose dilution of standards for work-related courses as well as to preserve 'academic' standards in comprehensives. Others looked deeper and saw that it was the corruption of the concept of competence that was the problem.

The social context debate

Some of those professional groups for whom NVQs have been devised opposed them vehemently. One was a section of Community and Youth Workers who found the NVQ's version of competence to be 'pseudo-objective, mechanistic and narrowly task-centred', 'run through with Positivist and Behaviourist assumptions' (Norton *et al.*, 1994:22, 29). They argued that people may be trained to do the work of a youth and community worker but they 'are not *educated* about how to be a youth and community worker' through NVQ (p. 28). Some of this criticism paralleled Smithers' complaint about lack of 'knowledge' ; but it was much more about the stunting of competence by the complete failure to include 'cognitive competence' in the course (Norton *et al.*, 1994:30). The Youth Workers' own earlier version of competence had included this 'critical knowledge', so necessary 'to understand and change the prevailing social, cultural and political conditions which limit and oppress the young people and adults they work alongside' (Norton *et al.*, 1994:29).

As training of all the major professions and occupations is renewed, competence and its interpretation will be to the fore, as it already is in the new approach to teacher education. The narrow and limited way in which the new teacher education is being implemented (Hill, 1991, 1995) should not obscure the fact that competence as a criterion for teacher education in other areas of the world – in Europe or Australia, for example – has a far wider interpretation, involving a 'relational' mixture 'of knowledge, skills and understanding' (Lucas, 1995).

The underlying debate is thus one about the narrow way competence is being interpreted in the vocational education being developed, a criticism also coming from those teaching in the General Education tradition, who have found the GNVQ and NVQ courses often narrow, over-prescriptive, squeezing out the skills of observation, critical enquiry, problem solving, the capacity to deal with ideas, and the chance to value one's own work in relation to wider society. In one occupational area after another, claimed one GNVQ teacher in 1995, the new vocational courses take out 'all the imagination and the fun stuff' (Waugh, 1995). If you are teaching joinery, you are only allowed to teach them to 'cost up how much wood is needed'. You cannot talk about the art of joinery, or about manufacturing, or working life, much less about why unemployment exists.

The fault is the de-contextualisation of so much of the new vocational education, whether in business or health or art and design. The spread of subject areas covered by the new courses may be wide, relevant and on the face of it, exciting. But learning is based on current practices, with no knowledge encouraged about their historical development or their place in any social or economic context. Business students are trained to perform in up-to-date ways, even though many will work in organisations that will be dated, inefficient, and ill-organised. Where in the training is the education to challenge what they will meet? A course on good health 'practice', to take another example, is restricted to the student's own personal habits, providing no chance to consider factors affecting health in society like toxic dumping or pollution or the stress of not finding work (*GNVQ Handbook*, 1994). Practical and vocational skills are 'apparently devoid of values or social context' (Robinson, 1994).

Behind it is a denial to those who are training or working in vocational areas of those general academic skills of critical enquiry or scientific method, those 'conceptual and critical skills which would enable them to understand their situation and its causes and possibly generate some alternative futures not envisaged within present government policy'

(Evans, 1991:60). In reforming vocational education, the Government has gone only half way. It has devised qualifications that imparted partial independence only – through skill ownership and enterprise attitudes, but denied the full independence that would come from the ability to exercise the responsibility that should go with a full education, and backed off from building in the skills of critical enquiry that any education requires. Academic freedom is a comprehensive education issue: the right to exercise it cannot remain confined to those bound for universities, and denied to those in work-related learning.

The debate over TECs and LECs

There is little likelihood of the integration of either curriculum or structure while learning for those in part-time education from 16 to 19 remains segregated under the control of the TEC and LEC structure, and when so much vocational education depends upon their auspices. Work-related learning at this age is not just about meeting employers' needs; it is about the continuing education and personal development of students of secondary age. Their education (and the funding that goes with it) belongs within the same education structure that oversees the education of their peers. Privatised quangos indirectly accountable to a distant auditor general, run by 'top business people', were always likely to fall short of what was demanded of them in this sphere.

Employers' needs are not synonymous with learners' needs. Each takes account of the other but ultimately individuals are independent learners. The education and training of many 16–19 year olds may need to be assisted by employers for work placement and possibly provided through employers' own training programmes, but oversight of the qualifications and progression of learning should be overseen by the educational service. Now that the training work of the old Department of Employment has integrated with the Department for Education, this should be a much easier step to take.

The debate about credits and vouchers

The concept of giving people the cash equivalent of what governments would otherwise be spending on their education – rather than devising an education service to meet their needs – is an idea regularly discussed in education systems that think of themselves as market-led. It has been spurred by such developments as standard spending assessments based on pupil numbers, and in 1995 was introduced for nursery education by diverting money intended for nursery schools into individual payments to parents.

This decision was made despite a pilot programme of vouchers conducted in 1977 in one area of Kent, which showed the scheme to be impractical, not necessarily responsive to parental choice, and prohibitively costly to run (Kent County Council, 1978). A similar experiment conducted in Alum Rock in California at the end of the 1970s was also a failure and was discontinued (see Chitty, 1989).

But not only did the Conservative Government introduce nursery vouchers in 1995, it also introduced 'credits' for certain young school leavers from the early 1990s onwards. These were cash sums given to 'buy' training within each TEC or LEC. The credit system varies, however, in the amounts given, the ages where it applies and the training for which it can be cashed. In any scheme, however, credits merely substitute for the education which these same young people would receive free as of right if they were enrolled on a full-time college course or were attending a school's sixth form. Trainees are not receiving any special gift.

So far the take-up has been slow and where credits are 'cashed in', it can often mean just handing them over *en bloc* to the further education college or a training agency. Their main virtue is that they could well raise awareness of training opportunities and generate interest in the ownership of skills – but only so long as there are opportunities available. Whether the credit system will persuade employers to train is another matter. Even if it did, the amounts that are available for the actual training in some cases are so low that no effective training might follow.

Vouchers for compulsory schooling would be a different matter. If every parent received the basic minimum cost of their child's education, those attending private schools would use the voucher as part-payment of the school fees. In effect, vouchers would represent a large increase in public funding subsidy for private education. For this reason private schools are among the strongest supporters of vouchers.

How the other 93% of parents would fare would depend upon just what the money given was supposed to cover and just how much the Government would continue to fund in the public education service. If it was simply a matter of the service staying exactly as it is, governed by its present laws, where voucher holders could be refused if the school was selective or 'full' or preferred another type of student, there would not be much visible difference at first – other than even less public accountability from individual schools and colleges.

Eventually, most pretence of democratic control of, and access to, education would evaporate, for the system would be market-led from first to last. Vouchers would simply be devices to regulate selection by 'parental choice' and formalise competition for entry to all schools and colleges. Over time polarisation would increase (as happened in the American experiment that was abandoned). Under the present system the schools with richer parents or in richer areas would be likely to be those with more Government funding. They would also be able to 'top up' their vouchers to improve their own services and so withstand the cuts in voucher levels which would inevitably follow any wide-scale introduction of the system. The use of vouchers to reduce expenditure on public services (by cutting them systematically, forcing people to pay privately instead) has always been one of the main attractions of the system to the political right.

In a full voucher system of a radical kind, however, where the Government did not continue to run the schools or run an education service at all, but allowed citizens to vote on levels of funding, and allowed parents and teachers to organise their own education, the outcome could be different. Vouchers as an alternative to state education was one of the central ideas of the de-schooling movement (Illich, 1971), appealing to many who would like a system where it would be made easier for like-minded teachers and parents to get together and set up their own schools, colleges and networks. This would include teachers and parents opposed to many of the conventional practices and forms of education; or wanting schools for their own religions or political points of view. Vouchers could in certain circumstances lead to a radicalisation of education, providing ways for people to control their own education that do not exist now — the very opposite result from that intended by some of the proposers of vouchers today. It could also lead to schools segregated on racial and ethnic lines in ways that could be very socially divisive.

It is unlikely that any government would relinquish so completely its hold upon the education system as to permit the free system suggested. An agency would need to be created to undertake the administration. This would eventually be overlaid with its own powers to direct and control, and would inevitably be very costly. But it is useless to speculate. For most people, vouchers represent a system not yet sufficiently experienced for opinion to be formed.

The democratic debate

All the issues raised in previous sections are legitimate questions that communities should be empowered and free to discuss. This includes 11-plus selection in primary schools or course choices at 16 anywhere in the system. It includes asking whether schools can opt out of local responsibilities or whether universities should be undertaking more local education. All are issues for a democracy to decide. Yet those affected by such issues are being left out of the key discussions, and decisions are increasingly being taken by self-perpetuating groups accountable to no one.

Over the last two decades people have been encouraged to influence education by the exercise of choices which often prove illusory or by participating in a market-led system which is not designed to be responsive to the community's control. Democratic control of education has been threatened by the weakening of the LEAs, the strengthening of central controls over curriculum, assessment and funding and the removal of power to smaller interest groups like governors and management teams. Important though their work is, their own increased power is no substitute for the loss of so much control of local and regional and national education policy and practice through the ballot box.

A fair and integrated comprehensive system up to 19 is unlikely to develop without oversight and guidance from bodies answerable to local or regional electorates. Market forces are not an adequate substitute, which is why most advanced industrialising countries do not make this mistake of thinking they are. After a recent trip to look at American school boards, a British local government officer reported the prevailing view in that country, certainly one fully committed to an enterprise economy, that when it comes to education, 'public education is far too important to be left to the market; it is under democratic control' (Bell, 1994).

At what point does competition cease to be healthy and become polarisation driven by narrow interests and privilege? Competition is healthy only if it is in the control of individuals and institutions; and only where the necessary co-operation between them is not impeded by it. At present, co-operation is frequently blocked, and competition harms certain institutions and individuals, situations best addressed by an elected body accountable to the whole community, which can develop a system that protects rights, while assisting co-operation in sharing resources and responsibilities equitably.

Democracy is the only antidote to market destruction, the only route to the balance of conflicting interests, the means by which decisions can be taken where all the parties to the process of education are consulted and can influence the system's working. At the root of the quest for accountability in education is the obligation on all those spending public money to answer to the public as a whole for their decisions. Equitable planning and funding of public services, fairly distributed between areas and institutions, can be secured only by these means. Power given to government appointees, funding that is arbitrarily dispensed, boards and bodies that replace themselves without reference to electorates, or even to qualified individual professionals whose commitment is to commercial contracts, will not secure the fair, high-quality and democratically directed education service that society has a right to expect.

The system has also to be intelligible, impossible at present where cumbersome arrangements for schools and colleges involve eight separate bodies for funding and the issue of directives for the education of those from 9 to 19: LEAs, foundation trustees, the Funding Agency for Schools, the FEFC, the HEFC, the TECs, informal business sponsorships and voluntary donors. This is no formula for coherence.

Nor for accountability to the community, as funding quangos combined with market control turn ever more schools and colleges 'into increasingly closed societies that are not democratically responsible either to the public or their staff' (Article 26, Press Release, 28 November 1994). Yet can this long continue in a system where the chance to pursue comprehensive opportunity beyond the age of 18 and into adulthood, will be advocated by increasing numbers of this same public?

There is an urgent need to explore new, democratic forms of government and to revive the democratic management of institutions. Amid the welter of jargon about value for money, customer choice and performance indicators, attention has wandered from the many ways of organising democratic accountability locally or regionally. Care has also lapsed in planning, whether it be pre-school or post-school provision for our localities and regions. Yet planning of these next two stages of comprehensive education is one of the most important tasks communities should be undertaking as they approach the twenty-first century. For comprehensive education, therefore, the debate about encouraging higher levels of democratic activity is the most important debate of all.

Notes

1 John Major, letter to former NUT president, Fred Jarvis, and speech to 1992 Conservative Party Conference, reproduced in Chitty and Simon (1993:144–52).
2 See Benn, 1980; Fenwick, 1976; Rubinstein, 1979; and Simon, 1991.
3 See *Worcestor Evening News*, 5 January, 1969.
4 *Panorama*, 21 March 1977; later admitted to have destroyed a school, *Butler to Baker*, BBC 2, 3 January 1993. *The London Programme*, 16 March 1984, also

demonstrated the hostility of the press to comprehensive education, including the *London Evening Standard*. For further coverage of several arguments involving misrepresentation of research or work, including the NFER's complaint against the *Daily Mail*, see *Comprehensive Education*, Issue 31, 1975. See also Issue 28, 1974, for report of press council judgement against the *Daily Mail* for imbalance and failure to give a right of reply. Recent examples of writing which still bears the hallmarks of Black Paper indoctrination include a ritual 'unattributed' comment that the problems of the school being discussed could be attributed to staff 'too influenced by Marxist thinking'.

5   *The Telegraph Magazine*, 2 April 1971. Several readers in Britain took the matter up and there developed a long correspondence between the editor, the Swedish Embassy in the UK, and the The Swedish Board of Education in Stockholm. The latter denied the figures the article contained, which had been attributed to them. For a full report see *Comprehensive Education*, No 21, 1972, which reproduced the correspondence.

6   Elliott School, Wandsworth, marched to the *Mail*'s offices to protest at a *Mail* reporter (who had once been a teacher) joining the staff claiming to be a teacher wanting to teach the most difficult pupils, then leaving it and writing a series of articles attacking the school.

7   The differences between voluntary comprehensive schools and maintained ones were greatest in the 1970s but narrowed in the 1980s. For the full figures, see page 158, note 10.

8   For example, Gallup, June 65: 54% thought comprehensives a good idea, 17% disliked, 16% did not know and 13% had never heard of them. Reported in, *Comprehensive Education*, Issue 1, 1965. See also New Society/Research Services National Survey, *New Society*, 26 October, 1967, showing rise in support for comprehensive education where such schools had been introduced.

9   If adjustment was made solely on the basis of the percentage of comprehensive schools HMI found to have a 'restricted range' (HMI, 1979) as appears to be claimed, this is a small percentage of comprehensive schools. Only 12%, in fact. What is more, they appear to be contrasted here to 'full range' comprehensives identified by HMI, leading readers to assume this NCES study rated all comprehensive schools outside the restricted range as full-range schools. Yet all remaining comprehensives in the HMI study were not full-range; many were simply less restricted. Where is the adjustment in the NCES research for those many schools 'not restricted' but also not 'full range'? If it is made, this is not made clear.

But this is the least of the difficulties. Also to be queried are the assignments of social class to schools based on figures which apply to LEAs as a whole (which the authors themselves divide arbitrarily into three classes of LEA). A class rating to an LEA as a whole, no matter how many types of LEA are designated, is never going to be exact enough for the use this kind of research will make of these indicators. As the NUT had already said in respect of other research using this method, to have taken 'just one of the indicators...and used that to represent the social class of every child in the LEA...the end result is that children from wildly dissimilar areas are treated as identical'.

What is particularly dubious, given what we know about social class intake differences in the middle of the 1970s, is giving grammar schools the same class intake rating as comprehensives inside the same LEAs. Even schools fairly near geographically would have large class differences in intake, greater than the LEA-effect would cover – e.g. grammar schools given higher working-class intakes because they were situated in working-class LEAs (and given predictions for performance on this basis) which would in fact have been drawing many of their pupils from middle-class areas of these LEAs or, if aided schools, some from outside the LEA altogether.

Comprehensive schools, where they were situated in middle-class LEAs, would have been given more middle-class intakes than they had (and be predicted to perform better), when they would have been drawing far more working-class intakes from within those LEAs than were the local grammar schools because the rate of middle-class intakes to grammar schools was rising disproportionately faster (as such schools declined in overall number) than it was in comprehensive schools.

Even if just a small percentage of such schools were given incorrect attainment or SEG ratings for the several reasons given above, it could have accounted for almost all the difference Marks found between predictions for the two systems.

There is also the difficulty presented by the LEAs chosen for the research (for these were not figures related to total populations in England, only to certain areas, many of them those used already in the 1983 research). They are not named. We cannot see how many were those which the DES at the time claimed had 100% comprehensive schooling and where this 100% was in dispute locally. This would have been where the LEA or the national government was paying for local pupils to go to direct grant and private selective schools in the LEA rather than to LEA schools. These could be substantial percentages, all creamed from comprehensives. In 1978, in Bedford, for example, 1050 pupils out of the total of 4148 secondary pupils still went to four schools run by a single trust (2 direct grant and 2 private); the LEA paid for what amounted to 12% of the pupils in Bedford (on top of which would come the fee-paying creaming). For years local campaigners for comprehensive reform in Bedford had disputed the LEA's claim to be 100% comprehensive, and had even appealed to the Ombudsman (Bedford CASE, 1978). Other towns had similar situations. Nowhere are these creaming percentages allowed for in the NCES research, especially in their conclusion that LEAs which were fully comprehensive had 5% poorer results (p.113) than overall.

Lastly, there is the question of being unable to register the results which pupils in the comprehensive system would have obtained at further education colleges – in several local areas where all post-16 exams were in colleges and not in schools. Earlier projects on comprehensive academic results (Ross et al., 1972) pointed out that a larger proportion of comprehensive leavers qualified in this way than did those leaving other schools at 16, and warned that their own comprehensive school examination findings were an underestimate because it was impossible to include the college results. There is no evidence the NCES project of 1985 found a way to include these results or make these allowances. If so, results for a comprehensive system would have been further under-estimated.

10 The countries (or parts of countries) studied included the UK, The Netherlands, Austria, the USA, and Sweden.

11 *TES*, 26 August 1993: Queen Elizabeth Boys in north London; Queen Elizabeth in Penrith; Archbishop Tenison in Lambeth. In Hertfordshire nine schools have indicated they wish to select.

12 Legislation against tracking was first passed in 1936; since then lawsuits brought against tracking have been upheld in several communities, including Washington,

DC, and most recently Rockford, Illinois. The grounds against it are that it discriminates against specific groups of citizens in practice.

13 Q and A proposals in the 1960s; and N and F proposals in the 1970s.

3

Development and Types

Those who say that comprehensive education leads to uniformity have only to look at the variety spanned by our 1994 survey – from a well-established middle school with 10 pupils in a remote area to a general further education college with over 5,000 full-time students. There are schools with boarding and colleges that have on-the-job training as well as the first years of degree courses. It is very hard to wean people away from the limited image many still carry, and get them to look at comprehensive education rather than comprehensive schools.

Concentrating on a single type of secondary school misses the essential point that we are looking at a system which includes primary and nursery education; schools that serve one sex or one religion, and colleges where people attend part-time as well as full-time. What it does not have is selection by attainment. There is no formal attainment test to enter any of its many doors; and each school or college aims to provide a full range of learning – not every course or subject that could be studied, but, as the earlier definitions put it, 'all that is normally provided for the age range'. Over and above this basic provision, colleges and schools stamp their hallmark of special traditions and facilities – and co-operate together to extend comprehensive opportunity in their local areas.

Progress to a comprehensive system

The question often asked over the last 30 years is, 'How far has the comprehensive change gone?' Some are assuming it was completed long ago, while others fear that it is gradually dissolving. Both conclusions would be wrong. It has made substantial progress but there is still some way to go, though judging how far depends a good deal on which statistics are used and which areas of Britain are examined in relation to state education.

In Scotland and Wales, over 99% of pupils are in comprehensive schools. In Northern Ireland it seems equally straightforward: the '11 plus' still divides the secondary system (see pages 160–62). In England the picture is patchier with only 82.9% of schools comprehensive in 1993 (DfE, 1994: Table 4). The table included all grant maintained schools but it excluded both middle schools deemed secondary and sixth form colleges. When sixth form colleges were added, the 1993 percentage rose to 86%; adding middle schools pushed it up to 91.7%. On the other hand, some grant maintained schools are selective and should be removed, which would lower the percentage considerably.

In some recent statistical tables, particularly those relating to academic results, *all* grant maintained schools and sixth form colleges are shown separately from comprehensive schools (see, for example, *Statistical Bulletin*, 7/94, Tables 9 and 10), thus removing from comprehensive totals many institutions that belong within the comprehensive system. General further education colleges have always occupied separate sections in statistical tables. Tertiary colleges, another important part of comprehensive education in many areas, are sometimes shown on their own, at other times subsumed within general further education statistics. All this makes it difficult to look at comprehensive education as a whole, quite apart from being able to compare it accurately to years gone by.

There is also the question of whether private education, which includes City Technology Colleges, should be counted as part of the national 'progress' picture of comprehensive education. It never is in government statistics, which stopped showing numbers of private secondary schools in 1973. Yet private schools are shown in 'league tables' alongside comprehensive schools.When fee-paying schooling is included as part of the national total, the percentage in state sponsored comprehensive schooling is obviously lower.

Table 3.1 puts together some of the ways by which national progress can be viewed. Although these present intriguing differences, they should not obscure the main fact that, with the exception of Northern Ireland, the last 30 years have witnessed sustained and substantial progress in secondary schooling, along with significant progress in further education. In 1965 when the reform began officially, less than 10% of the secondary age group was in a comprehensive school in England and Wales. And even though there will be disagreement about exact percentages now, the overwhelming majority of primary school children proceed unimpeded to a similarly comprehensive school at secondary level.

Table 3.1(a) does not reveal the fact that in England comprehensive percentages have gone down from the high point in 1987 before grant maintained schools and engineered enrolment were introduced. The slippage is not dramatic at just under a percentage point but over time this trend could matter, since percentages in grammar and technical schools are starting to creep up as well. The only form of selective schools shown in government statistics are grammar schools and technical schools but some aided, controlled or 'Other' schools (classed as comprehensive) are selective or partially selective. They are not shown separately. The main area to watch, however, is the bulk of grant maintained secondary schools. Official statistics show them by legal status in most tables, giving no indication of the percentages that are selective, leaving us unable to determine whether selection on a much larger scale may be returning without our knowledge.

In Table 3.1(b) we try to allow for this reality in the figures for the year of the survey in England, based on research relating to grant maintained school admissions practices which suggested one in three were already operating selectively. Adding these selective percentages to continuing grammar school/secondary modern selection and to the private schools' percentage, lowers comprehensive progress to 74% (79% if middle schools are included). These percentages are only a little higher than similar calculations made for England and Wales in 1977[1]. This trend-in-reverse would not have to continue at the present rate for many years more to restore the picture for selective versus non-selective schooling to that of 1965.

Such a return is highly unlikely, however, because the degree of selection is not uniform and because the changes that are taking place within and between schools and colleges and in the curriculum and assessment systems, particularly after 16, are 'on the ground' changes that are unlikely to be reversed, no matter how much manipulation goes on through the complex web of legislation now in place to encourage selection. Comprehensive education is not in danger of breaking up; but it is in danger of becoming far less effective than many might have expected.

Changes in patterns of comprehensive education

Just as important as progress overall is the way the structure of the comprehensive system itself has changed over 30 years. At the start it was based on local arrangements to end 11-plus selection adopted by LEAs over 20 years, imposed on top of the residual effects of education planning since the 1930s.

Table 3.1 Progress to comprehensive education

(A) Secondary schools, England and Wales, 1950–1994. Results as percentages with numbers in parentheses

Year	Pupils		Schools	
1950	0.4	(7988)	0.2	(10)
1965	8.5	(239,619)	4.5	(262)
1977	78.6	(2,982,441)	70	(3083)
1994	86.9	(2,715,013)	80	(3095)

1950 figures from DES, 1969: Vol. 1, Table 3(3).
1965 and 1977 figures from DES, Vol I: 1977, Table 3(3).
1994 figures from HMSO, 1994: Table 128. They include GM schools for both England and Wales. Statistics for Wales relate to one year earlier and are taken from *Statistics of Education and Training in Wales: Schools* (Welsh Office, 1993: Table 1.02).
Figures for 1950–1977 are for maintained schools only. Middle schools are not included for any year and sixth-form colleges are not included in 1994.

(B) Secondary Education, 1994. England. Results as percentages with numbers in parentheses

Types of School		Overall
Comprehensive		79.0
Comprehensive secondary	(2399445)	73.9
Middle deemed secondary	(161056)	5.0
Selective, non-comprehensive, and		
private		21.0
Grammar	(116193)	3.6
GM selective*	(128214)	3.9
Technical	(2198)	0.1
Other	(35820)	1.0
Modern	(90672)	2.8
Private[†]	(312502)	9.6
Total	(3246100)	100.0

Based on DfE, 1994b, Tables 128 and 127a.
* GM school numbers are approximate only and are based on research estimates that one-third of GM schools are using selective entry methods (Bush *et al.*, 1993:95). All other GM comprehensive schools are included in the comprehensive total.
[†]Private schools (from Table 127a; Independent Schools, including City Technology Colleges) only include pupils between ages 11 and 19, not all of whom will be in schools selective by attainment.[2]

Chapters 1 and 2 have already mentioned the slow progress of comprehensive reform in Britain, including the resistance of two powerful educational interests: the lobbies campaigning for the preservation of grammar schools and fee-paying schools, particularly the HMC schools. Other countries found it easier to develop their state grammar schools to comprehensive status, but none had such powerful private sectors. Though many countries have their élite sectors of education, they are usually at the post-secondary stage. The existence in Britain of strong élitist secondary schools has rendered resistance to secondary comprehensive education particularly acute and destructive.

There were, however, other causes of Britain's slow progress. Unlike reforms made in recent years by Conservative governments in relation to grant maintained, CTC or specialist schools, no extra money was ever given to LEAs or schools to effect the comprehensive changeover – apart from one grant in 1975 of £25m to speed reorganisation building. All change had to be accomplished within normally planned expenditure; and although new building (to accommodate growing populations) was supposed to be compatible with comprehensive change (as requested in Circular 10/66), some of it was not. Extra money for raising the school leaving age in the early 1970s was not officially co-ordinated because these years coincided with an interim spell of Conservative rule when the Heath Government (1970–74) cancelled Circulars 10/65 and 10/66 as one of its first acts. As a result, much of this money went on buildings which were not necessarily compatible with the changeover to comprehensive education.

A further cause of the slow pace was Labour's deference to the autonomy of local authorities, which Labour governments sometimes overplayed to avoid taking the difficult decisions required to secure continuing comprehensive development. By contrast, recent Conservative-led reforms have been both abrupt and directed against local authorities. Both are possible ways to promote policy changes and only time will tell which was really the most successful. It could be that gradual change coming from the ground up is more well-rooted than change imposed hastily from the top. On the other hand, it may be that 'action is action' and that those governments that are the most active achieve the greatest measure of change.

Which forms of comprehensive reorganisation have been the most popular?
Another feature of Labour governments in the 1960s and 1970s was that Labour set up no special government agency to co-ordinate the comprehensive reform. Although there were occasional teams of officials working on scheme approvals, all such vetting was accomplished within the normal workings of the Department of Education (DES). It had its own agenda from the start. Of the six different schemes suggested in Circular 10/65, only one really counted: the 11–18 all-through 'orthodox' comprehensive. All other arrangements were viewed as temporary until

new building could convert them to all-through schools or staying-on rates had increased to the point where every school could grow its own sixth form.

Thus a number of areas which pioneered other age 'breaks', many with strikingly successful records both in terms of innovation within the schools and negotiation of smooth and early transition, were never given the full support required to develop in large numbers. Any success they had – as in Leicestershire (towards which the DES was particularly hostile) or in Yorkshire – was due to the local authorities' own officers, locally elected councillors (of all parties), and those who worked in the schools and colleges themselves (Benn and Simon, 1970; Fairbairn, 1980; Pedley, 1963).

Little conscious control over the process of structural change was ever exercised either, though all plans had to obtain approval from the DES. Vetting was supposed to be strict on sixth forms, calculated on the basis of grammar school sixth form numbers. Between the ages of 9 and 16, however, all kinds of age ranges were allowed, including two-year schools. By the end of the 1960s there were 23 different types of comprehensive school in terms of age-range. However, these were soon identified as falling into three main schemes (as set out in Table 3.2):

1. The 'all-through' scheme, with a self-contained single school taking pupils from 11 (or 12) through to 18.

2. The 'tiered' scheme, sometimes called a 'middle school' scheme, which had a break at 13 or 14 with upper schools going on to 18.

3. Schemes with a break at 16 where schools had no sixth form or S5/S6 years. Students moved out either to colleges or to the upper sections of other schools.

In 1965, the government also put forward some extra 'interim' schemes, which were tiered arrangements where long-course and short-course schools ran parallel up to 13 or 14 and those wanting to enter the sixth form transferred from the short-course, the rest remaining behind until leaving at 15. It was through these schemes that 'parental choice' first got a bad name, for this was the device that replaced '11 plus' selection for those transferring to the academic schools, some parents getting the choice, others 'guided' not to make it. Although such schemes had initial support from some LEAs and survived for a long time in some Conservative areas (like Kent) – where they were particularly unpopular with teachers, parents and education officers (see Benn and Simon, 1970:107) – most had been developed into total transfer schemes by 1976.

In Scotland almost all agitation over structural reform was on this point of parallelism because the Scottish school system had institutionalised it in many areas – with only the certificate-course pupils moving up to the local academy. Several Scottish areas had local parent groups organising in protest during the 1970s against such parallel schemes. These protests, backing a strong commitment everywhere in Scotland to the all-through school, ensured that Scotland's secondary education became not only 99% comprehensive but is housed almost entirely in all-through schools.

Table 3.2 The main types of comprehensive education in Britain, aged 9–19 (schools and colleges). Results as percentages, with numbers of establishments in parentheses

	1968*		1994 survey	
All-through schemes	56	(420)	40	(626)
Tiered schemes	21	(149)	15	(233)
16 plus transfer schemes	22	(156)	45	(703)
Total	100	(725)	100	(1560)

* Based on Table 6.2, Benn and Simon, 1970. The 1968 enquiry did not include further education colleges.

All-through schools

The first trend to stand out is that over 30 years all-through schools have steadily declined as a proportion of the total. In 1965 they were nearly 79% of all comprehensives in England and Wales (Monks, 1968:229)[3]. By 1968 this was already down to 56% (Benn and Simon, 1970: Table A.1, p.372) and by 1977 to 51% (DES, 1978: Appendix I). Table 3.2 shows that by 1994 all-through schools were only 40% of the total schools and colleges (44% of all schools). Actual percentages may be somewhat higher since the survey had proportionately fewer respondents from the larger cities (which have higher numbers of all-through schools). Overall, because all-through schools are larger schools, they contain a larger share of all pupils. But the all-through school cannot any longer claim to be the 'orthodox' model, as was the case 30 years ago.

Even so, it still sets the pace and commands the allegiance of many communities, particularly in Scotland. Whatever else groups have disagreed about, both between and among themselves, it has rarely been about the desirability of having a 'sixth form' (or upper standard years in Scotland), believed to provide the academic continuity and prestige favoured by parents, and the career opportunities that teachers prefer. At a conference on comprehensive education convened by the Secretary of State for Education in December, 1977, a DES spokesperson was able to record 'passionate local support for sixth forms... especially of those parents whose children expect to stay on at school after 16' (DES, 1978:vi). The all-through school is the model on which most books and records of development, or research relating to comprehensive schools, have concentrated. It seems quintessential, the school that matches the grammar school, except that it is there for everyone. Yet its dominance continues to decline.

1994 findings

Tables A5 and A6 give information about the all-through schools in the 1994 survey. Their average size (974) was larger than the survey average (893) and slightly larger than their average in 1968 (Benn and Simon, 1970: Table 5.2, p.72 when it was 950). Their intake of the top 20% of attainment in 1994 was, at 18.6%, roughly the same as the survey average of 18.0%. In terms of social class composition, its proportion with predominantly middle-class intakes (31%) was higher than the survey average (of 26%) and it also had a higher average percentage (41.9%) passing GCSE (five grades A–C or Standard Grade 1–3 in Scotland) compared with the survey average of 39.3%. It had higher percentages of its 17 year olds entering for two or more 'A' levels than schools of other age ranges; but its 'A' level point score was only very slightly above the survey average and lower than the score for 14–18 upper schools (see Table A6; see also Appendix II for further information about survey figures for examinations).

Although overall figures suggest that the all-through comprehensive is above average for many criteria, these global figures hide considerable differences. Some of the most prestigious comprehensive schools (albeit defined narrowly in 'league table' terms) are of this age range but so too are some of the most problematic. Anxieties about size remain – both large size and small. So too misgivings about the long age-span and retaining students after 16, when some 16 year olds wish to transfer to a college (or leave altogether) because they have become disenchanted with school uniforms and the company of 11 year olds. In other cases, the good relationships built up in earlier years persuade students to stay on who might otherwise have left education altogether.

The cost of the 16–19 year olds inside the all-through school is also high – compared with spending on the school lower down. The smaller teaching groups and the small overall size of many comprehensive school sixth forms (see Chapter 9) has always tended to make them a relatively uneconomical way of providing for the sixth year of comprehensive education. Those advocating concentrated post-16 systems once commented that 'teachers battling in the Lower School with over-large classes of D streamers may be forgiven if they feel they are paying too high a price for the status symbol of the sixth' (Janes *et al.*, 1985:10). Today the price is even higher, as resources and time are directed to the minority of students with a chance of increasing league table scores.

Thus the sixth form is both the source of the all-through's prestige, as well as its one real liability, having had to struggle since 1965 against a selective examination system, building itself around 'A' level which was designed for only 10% of the age group. It is no wonder that many came to view its sixth form as a 'grammar school' sitting on top of a comprehensive school and 'not in the least comprehensive' (Terry, 1987:5). This was despite its equally long struggle to create a 'new sixth form' that welcomed a far wider percentage of the age group and encouraged students overall to continue with education during the 1970s.

More have been encouraged to stay since then through the combined effects of unemployment, the futility of years of 'training schemes' and the introduction of a common assessment system at 16. The long-postponed decision to allow popular vocational qualifications into schools is encouraging more staying on but changing matters in ways that add new problems for the sixth form of the comprehensive school. Such schools are having to consider for the first time the possibility of education for the whole age group rather than focusing their work mainly on 'academic' courses. Vocational education is very different and not necessarily congenial to all the staff in many all-through schools. It is also difficult to see how a full range of vocational courses can be offered in most sixth forms. Thus another split threatens: between those comprehensives that run 'grammar' sixth forms with academic courses only, and those that extend to include vocational courses like the General National Vocational Qualification (GNVQ).

But that is not the end of the likely divisions. Many sixth forms can manage GNVQ courses for level 1 and 2 in a few vocational fields but for a wide range of fields and for level 3 as well, it soon becomes a question of making contact with the further education colleges in the area. Some all-through schools are already moving in this direction (see Chapter 9). Those that are not do not always offer a full range of courses. Disparities in the all-through school after 16 are growing and will have to be addressed. Thus its future is destined to see many more changes yet.

Tiered and middle schools

Tiered schemes enabled many local authorities to reorganise without waiting for new buildings – by using the old secondary modern schools as lower schools and the grammar schools as upper schools, as well as by extending junior schools or small secondary moderns into 'middle' schools to feed directly into upper schools.

In many ways this was the obvious solution to going comprehensive in the shortest possible time, matching the orthodox structural pattern of many other countries with their system of junior and senior high schools. Had tiered schemes been given equal encouragement in Britain in 1965, structural reorganisation could have been complete within 10 years. Tiered schemes were initially popular too – one in five of all comprehensives by 1968 (see Table 3.2), but they have steadily declined since. Even with the introduction of 9–13 middle schools to this category, by 1977 they were down to 18% (DES, 1978: Appendix I). In the 1994 survey it was 15%.

Few LEAs adopted tiered schemes after the initial phase of the reform, and over time some that did began turning them back into one of the other two schemes. One (Gateshead) said tiered schemes were always only temporary until all-through schools could be organised (DES, 1978:48–54). Others thought such schools suffered because of the discredited 'parental choice' transfer process associated with earlier interim schemes (Weeks, 1986; Whalley, 1970), though these views never held sway in areas like Leicestershire (Eggleston, 1965). In the 1980s, reasons for changing back included the falling rolls in primary years and, after competitive entry legislation was introduced in the late 1980s, the need to have transfer ages compatible with schools in other areas.

The new competitive 'market' also renewed fears about the upper years of middle schools not having the same advantages as the lower years of all-through schools. Particularly evident has been the drop in the number of 'middle' schools themselves (both 9–13 and 8–12), schools started with high hopes in the wake of the Plowden findings in 1967 about new approaches to this age range, including child-centred learning, preparing well in the basics and promoting innovation in teaching. From the early 1970s, the Black Paper assault on various aspects of the progressive approach at the primary stage began to be felt. At regular intervals new evidence was produced to claim that schools can be divided into those that are 'good' (rigorous, in rows, in uniforms, and streamed) and those that are 'bad' (child centred, informal and grouped around different tables), another one of those damaging illusions foisted on comprehensive education. The truth is that most middle schools (and primary schools) combine methods, materials and practices from several educational traditions in choosing their own unique approach to learning.

The drop in middle-school numbers was not about the quality of the children's education, nor about the buildings. In our 1994 survey, middle schools had the highest rate of purpose building for all school types – at 46% – as well as the highest attendance rates (Table A5). It was basically about subject specialisation and the resources this required (Taylor and Garson, 1982); or, as one editorial writer put it when yet another LEA changed back, 'A good teacher is not the same as a specialist' (*Guardian*, 2 June, 1993).

Upper schools

The move away from upper schools was also about competing in the market of an exclusively British system where first examinations were taken at 16 rather than at 17 or 18 (as in most other countries). Despite the role model of private education, upper schools of 13–18 or 14–18 were queried on the grounds of not having enough 'time' after pupils transferred to prepare for this first examination. In 1968 these schools were just under 7% of the survey total; in 1994 this was down to 5% (Benn and Simon, 1970: Table 5.2, p.72; Table A2).

Yet many upper schools have been successful, and those in Leicestershire pioneered a special brand of community education, commanding great local loyalty. In 1968 upper schools had higher percentages of pupils in the top 20% of the ability range than any other type of comprehensive, higher percentages staying on after the leaving age than any other, and larger sixth forms able to offer more 'A' levels (Benn and Simon, 1970, Tables 5.2, p.72 and 8.6, p.133).

In the 1994 survey they maintained some advantages. For example, they had higher than average rates of purpose-building, and the 13–18 school was the comprehensive type most likely to offer single-sex education (see also Weeks, 1986:63). Although upper schools' five GCSE grade A–C pass rates were average or slightly below, 'A' level point scores for the 14–18 schools were higher than for any other type of comprehensive school. Their sixth forms were larger too (see Tables A5 and A6) and they had the highest average number of students entering BTEC or City and Guilds national examinations. This is a set of indicators with much potential for success, particularly as vocational education spreads; yet the trend away from this form of organisation with such potential has been very little discussed. It needs attention since neither middle schools nor upper schools are going to disappear. This pattern of reorganisation may well resume popularity when the current age of cut-throat competition becomes more co-operative and a 14–18 curriculum and assessment system is at last in place.

Schemes where there is a break at 16

The last type of scheme comprises schools which end at 16 – together with the sixth forms and the colleges to which learners intending to stay on move. In 1994 this was the most popular of the schemes in terms of numbers of institutions: 45% of the total, almost double the percentage (21%) in 1968 (Benn and Simon, 1970: Table 5.2, p.72).

This development has not only made comprehensive colleges more important, it has also made the 11/12–16 schools prominent, for in 1994 two out of every five comprehensive schools ended at the age of 16. These schools deserve a lot more attention than they have ever received, particularly an understanding of the differences between the comprehensive systems in which they exist locally.

For 'short-course' comprehensive schools divide into those that coexist with all-through schools (students sometimes moving at 16-plus to the all-through school in what used to be called a 'mushroom' system) and those where schooling leads directly to a college. In 1968 just over 4% of all-through schools were formally constituted as 'mushroom' sixth forms. Today almost any all-through school would welcome such students from other schools, but more and more who might once have sought to transfer to another school probably prefer to go directly to a college – if there is one near enough.

If there is not, this can sometimes leave the 11–16 school isolated by contrast to the one that is directly tied to a sixth form or a tertiary college and which is, in effect, in an 'all-through' arrangement, where considerable effort goes into maintaining continuity and informing students of their choices at 16. This continuity took time to build up, but after 1979 such schemes were not favoured by governments. Ministers with particularly élitist outlooks – like Keith Joseph – actively discouraged schemes involving tertiary colleges (see Chapter 9) and competitive 'market' changes since have made it even harder to organise all-through linked schemes of this kind. Thus many 11–16 schools exist on their own, dotted in between schools with other age ranges, or forming loose links with several colleges or schools but none at a formal level.

In its last long look at comprehensive education (DES, 1978), the DES was much concerned with the age of transfer to various institutions and concluded tactfully that 'no single pattern has the monopoly of advantage', adding that all schemes could work well provided good liaison was maintained. But between the lines the DES expressed concern about the 11–16 comprehensive school in particular and mentioned its 'pecking order problem' as 'a pattern with a built-in tendency towards self-perpetuation' (DES, 1978:150). Later, a researching academic concluded that the 11–16 school was the 'strongest reason we have for feeling pessimistic about the comprehensive system' (Weeks, 1986:177). In his view 'an ideology for them is desperately required' (p.61).

But any 'ideology' these schools lacked was because the ideology of the comprehensive school had not yet broken from that of the grammar school. This was why a comprehensive without a sixth was assumed to be a lesser sort of school. It had (and still has) less favourable staffing and funding (because it did not have its own sixth form). If, in addition, its intakes were unbalanced or its curriculum and range of courses not equal to those for the same age range in schools nearby, disadvantage multiplied. Since the advent of GCSE and the National Curriculum, many of these problems have been eased. What still remains to be done, however, is to secure for all such schools formal tertiary links with a local college, followed by the funding and staffing that could go with an 'all-through' arrangement of this kind. Such an arrangement is presently not possible owing to the new competitive 'market' and to the fact that 'schemes' of comprehensive education are no longer recognised, let alone organised.

To the 'triple disadvantage' short-course comprehensive schools endured – inferior status, poorer staffing allowances and difficulty for pupils in transferring to other schools or colleges on equal terms (DES, 1978:161) – have to be added drawbacks others have named like the loss of leadership of older pupils and difficulty in recruiting specialist staff because of the lack of an 'academic top'.

Yet many 11–16 schools do well, and have always had defenders who were prepared to look at the way this age group could be approached in positive terms of enjoying its own full education. They saw advantages, including smaller size, and the ability to offer leadership and 'personal and social responsibility' to 15 year olds. They saw far greater choice with transfer to a tertiary or sixth form or FE college than most students in all-through schools could ever get. And although some found the 'academic atmosphere poorer' (Terry, 1987:27), others found it well up to standard provided there were no competing selective schools (King, 1970).

1994 findings

In 1968 short-course schools were found to have lower intakes of the top 20% of the attainment range than other comprehensive schools, and far lower than average staying-on rates (Benn and Simon, 1970: Table 5.2, p.72). But the same survey also showed that the greatest disadvantages came from situations where they were working 'in parallel' with all-through schools which had sixth forms designated to 'serve' them as outside entrants. However, when all schools in an area were 11–16 and all students could transfer to a college, the situation could be very different.

In recent years, few researchers have concentrated on this age range despite the fact that the numbers of such schools have grown. The 1994 survey (see Table A5) showed that short-course comprehensives are still not receiving the full intake of the top 20% of attainment: their 15% was below the survey average of 18%. A far higher proportion than the survey overall had predominantly working-class intakes as well as a significantly lower percentage with middle-class intakes (see Table A5). They were less likely to be full at intake than institutions overall (only 27% compared with 40%) and they were also less likely to have grown from grammar schools.

So far the disadvantages are those related to less social and attainment selectivity overall. With an average size of 763, the short-course school was smaller than the all-through school by about 200 pupils but nearly 200 higher than their average in 1968 (Benn and Simon, 1970: Table 5.2, p.72). To some, their smaller size always constituted an advantage, perhaps accounting for the fact that some have found discipline easier in such schools, and their pupils better adjusted. (Benn, 1971a; Dean *et al.*, 1979; Terry, 1987).

In addition, their average for five GCSE A–C passes in 1994, though below the survey average, was on a par with the 14–18 upper schools (see Table A5); and their percentage for pupils transferring on to continuing education at 16 was higher at 64% than the survey average for staying on within the all-through schools (56%; see Table A6), although the two figures were not strictly comparable. 'Going on' rates in short-course schools can take into account students transferring on both to further education and sixth forms elsewhere, while all-through schools can measure only those staying on within their own walls (see Chapter 9). Nevertheless, it was encouraging that the going-on rate for short-course comprehensive schools was very nearly the same as the percentage of the 16-year-old age group in full-time education in Great Britain in the same year.

We cannot help but conclude that educational opinion has not yet caught up with the changes that have occurred in the short-course comprehensive, for certainly the 'academic' differences the 1994 survey found were not great enough to account for their perceived second-class status in so many observers' eyes. Nor are 11–16 schools the only schools where there is a 'pecking order problem', as suggested by the DES. Such problems can just as easily be experienced among 11–18 schools. Thus what is required is not so much a new ideology as an attack upon pecking-order problems and their causes; as well as making sure 11–16 and 12–16 schools are no longer required to accept inferior staffing levels because they do not have sixth forms, or more than their share of educational burdens for the same reason.

Although some short-course schools co-operate with all through schools up to 16, their most significant relationships in respect of transfer upwards in future are likely to be with the colleges. In 1971 the head of one such school commented prophetically, 'I...only warn that an 11–16 school which does not forge continuous and strong links between itself and the 16–18 establishment it feeds, both at staff and pupil level, is doing itself a great disservice' (Benn, 1971a:14). Twenty-five years later and all too many such schools are still being done a disservice by a system that has stopped evolving its comprehensive education. Each and every short-course comprehensive should be brought into a formal working partnership with 16–19 education in its area, preferably with a single tertiary college – a priority for the next stage of comprehensive development.

The comprehensive colleges
Barely envisaged in Circular 10/65, which only touched in passing on the sixth form college, the development of the comprehensive colleges – sixth form, tertiary and general colleges of further education – was very much a product of the 1970s. The colleges make up only 9% of the institutions in the survey, but the numbers of students over 16 are higher than those in the schools (see Chapter 9).

The colleges have come a long way as partners in comprehensive education since the start of formal reorganisation, when almost none was involved in any comprehensive scheme. Their percentage in the first independent enquiry was less than 0.5% (Benn and Simon, 1970: Table 5.2, p.72), representing a few sixth form colleges, the first begun in 1966, pioneered in authorities like Luton (which had sent a working party to America to study community colleges and comprehensive high schools). By the mid- 1970s, there were over 100. Today it is 116, rather less than there would have been had not so many evolved formally into tertiary colleges in the late 1970s and early 1980s. Before being segregated under FEFC control, they educated a quarter of the maintained sector's students over 16.

The original rationale was to concentrate academic classes in a viable way, which meant sixth form colleges were often known as 'A level academies'. One early brochure from Stoke-on-Trent claimed its college was designed 'specifically for young adults preparing for university'. As time went on, they began opening their gates more widely, intent on developing their own identities rather than remain clones of grammar school sixth forms.

From the start, sixth-form colleges were well supported and the subject of much well-informed writing. They were popular with students and got good academic results (printed up separately today in government league tables, thus withdrawing their contribution to the totals representing compre-hensive education nationally). Like all 'sixth forms' they are well provided for relative to the lower age groups, with an average class size at 13.7 compared with all secondary schools (21.4); and almost negligible numbers of classes with numbers over 30 (DfE, *Statistical Bulletin* 9/94: Table 7).

They retain many features of the school rather than college. In our 1994 survey their average size, 887, was much smaller than the average for comprehensive colleges overall (1587), and smaller than the average all-through school. They enjoy close links with their feeder schools and provide a wide range of extra-curricular activities for students as well as a very wide range of 'A' level subjects – and, in some, selected vocational courses as well, increasingly provided in co-operation with further education colleges (see Chapter 9).

Their greatest drawback is their greatest asset: they concentrate the post-16 students on academic courses to such a degree that by default they are in danger of becoming selective schools all over again (see Chapter 9). Try as they will to be more generalist and to widen their doors to the whole attainment range, the continuation of 'A' level and their concentration upon it sets a limit to their comprehensiveness. This has been reinforced by the fact that 73% of sixth-form colleges in the 1994 survey grew physically out of grammar schools (question 9A and D) – compared with only 16% of tertiary colleges and 2% of further education colleges (which is why far fewer sixth form colleges – only 16% – were purpose built than is the case with other types of comprehensive institution – Table A5).

Sixth-form colleges were much the most selective of all comprehensive institutions in the 1994 survey with 58% of their intake in the top 20% of the attainment range (Table A5). In addition, they were the only type of comprehensive where the majority had predominantly middle-class intakes (questions 36 B and D). As might be deduced from these two findings, their 'A' level results were better than those of any other type of comprehensive institution in the survey. However, their percentages offering vocational education to 18, or with high levels entering higher education by means of such qualifications, were particularly low. So far they are not enlarging to include vocational education even on a par with many all-through and upper-school sixth forms (see Table A6 and Chapter 9).

In the absence of any co-ordinated post-16 planning, as vocational courses take their place in the comprehensive curriculum, sixth-form colleges and school sixth forms will encounter many potential students who want vocational preparation or part-time enrolment, and who may try to bypass the sixth forms of comprehensive schools or sixth form colleges (or be directed past by those 'full' enough to relinquish the funding they would bring) and head instead for a tertiary college or a general further education college, where a wider curriculum is provided. Such a development threatens a new post-16 split into selective and vocational institutions unless there is a decision to integrate academic and vocational courses in a new post-16 curriculum, as proposed by so many educators today (see page 15). With integration sixth-form colleges would be drawn into more formal co-operation with further education and with employers, providing a model of development for existing sixth forms of both comprehensive and grammar schools to follow, as they too widen their intakes in the years to come. In all but a small number of cases, the selective tendencies of the sixth-form college have been structural rather than any purposeful form of development, but they do show how easily the system can drift backwards when the next stage of development is delayed.

There is a danger that a few highly selective sixth-form colleges could possibly switch to the private sector but they would be certain to be offset by some private schools coming the other way, anxious to undertake work beyond the bounds of the old 'A' level. Whether state or private, institutions intending to stay in business for the 16–19 age group in the long run will have to understand the comprehensive educational needs of that age group as a whole and the variety of ways in which these can be met. The days of 'A' level domination are drawing to a close.

The general further education college

The general further education college is in many ways a key to the next stage of comprehensive education's development. Yet the work of such colleges is a closed book to many who work in schools, particularly to those who concentrate upon 'A' level students after 16. In the education of the 16–19 age group there has always been more discussion and information about the work that goes on in schools than about the provision for 16 year olds who are in further education. Only very recently has full information begun to be collected about the patterns of learning of those in the colleges: their attendance profile, the length of their courses, their qualifying percentages, the various way they combine learning or the opinions they have formed about their education or training.

Now that vocational education is being reorganised with qualifications like NVQ and GNVQ being widely developed in so many work-related fields, the colleges will be taking them on and developing them furthest – because they are already skilled at this work and have connections with industry and local employers. So far, they are carrying the greater share of GNVQ work and increasing their provision of NVQ, despite the fact that many of their 'workshop' facilities need updating.

In time, all schools with sixth forms and all sixth-form colleges will need to look to them for assistance and collaboration in a way that has never been necessary in the past. As we see later, informal networks are common and formal ones increasing (Chapter 9). Further education colleges carry on with the work they have been doing for the last 20 years, accommodating an ever-wider age and attainment range from 16 onwards, open to full-timers and part-timers, flexible in providing what the local community needs. What is different today is that fewer and fewer are content (or will be allowed) to remain humdrum, work-a-day institutions with limited offerings, specialising in one small type of work-related education. More and more are developing into comprehensive general colleges, adding constantly to their work-related education by piecing together grants and funding from both government and industry. Most are building up a good range of GCSE and 'A' level work and as wide a range as possible of vocational qualifications at several levels. In addition, more and more are developing connections with local universities, running franchised degree courses for 1 or 2 years.

Although there are huge gaps and much imbalance in college provision – with some areas far better served than others – the further education colleges, including the tertiary colleges, constitute a network already in place throughout the country upon which to base a unified 16–19 system. With sixth-form colleges there is more homogeneity across the country but their education is limited when it comes to vocational provision for the age group as a whole.

Much more important, there are thousands of individual sixth forms in the schools with their own uneven provision. They are half the equation. That is why the goal should be a 16–19 network in each area which gradually unifies the work of all schools and all colleges (see Chapter 9). The reorganisation of the 16–19 system is one of the major tasks of the next stage of comprehensive education, now made easier by the unification of education and training within one government department.

Tertiary colleges

Tertiary colleges were not envisaged in Circular 10/65 at all and their pioneers did not appear on the scene until 1970. Among them were far-sighted administrators like Jocelyn Owen, Chief Education Officer for Devon, spurred into action by the chance to resolve several dilemmas that all-through schools and further education colleges were contending with in trying to sort out which students were suitable for school and which for college (Owen, 1970). The idea of combining them was first suggested by another administrator, William Alexander (Terry, 1987:13) and the first tertiary colleges were in Barnstaple and Exeter where the local further education colleges were extended to incorporate the sixth-form work of local schools. Today there are nearly 60 tertiary colleges with their own Association, declaring that 'they combine elements from both Sixth Form Colleges and Sixth Forms with Further Education Colleges' (*Education Yearbook*, 1994:383). In a word, as their advocates never tire of telling the world, the tertiary college 'is more comprehensive than an 11–18 sixth form could ever be' (Gane, 1985:186).

Nevertheless, tertiary colleges are not the rivals of the sixth form or FE college; they simply represent those areas where the tertiary synthesis has gone furthest. All three college types (as well as the sixth forms of schools) have had to grapple with the same educational problem of providing education to young adults between 16 and 19 who were no longer compelled by law to study, negotiating with them what was to be learned, consulting them directly rather than their parents. In fact, the issue of parental involvement is a clue to the differences between colleges as well as between colleges and schools. Parents of sixth formers in schools are often totally involved in their children's education and influential in choosing their courses. Sixth form colleges are likely to have structures that recognise parental interests and although some further education college brochures now include invitations to parents to visit and discuss their children's studies (usually only for students under 19 and often only in relation to 'A' level courses), this has not always been their habit. Tertiary colleges started the work of drawing parents into further education, though not as fully as in schools or sixth form colleges. After all, one of the advantages of the college is that it allows young people many of the freedoms that are not given to them in schools. One of them is to decide matters themselves.

The cultural tradition from which so many further education students come is also apparent inside the comprehensive schools. Ball, for example, recorded that middle-class children consulted their parents about options at 13-plus, while working-class children were far more often left to make the choice on their own (Ball, 1981:153). Because of this, counselling is very much a part of practice in comprehensive colleges, as it should be throughout the educational experience in the later secondary years. Not every parent is an educational expert and it is an ill-directed system that favours the children of those who are. On the other hand, as one astute further education lecturer wrote in the 1980s, care should be taken not to abuse the counselling function by pressuring students to opt for courses that schools or colleges themselves happen to offer and wish to fill (Pratley, 1983), an endemic danger that has increased in recent years in the market-driven system.

Historically, the major obstacle to joint school and college development in a tertiary system was the existence of different and conflicting legal 'regulations'. The biggest obstacle now is legislation that directs each college (sixth form, tertiary or further education) to operate solely in its own interests rather than in the interests of students. Instead of devising the best possible education and training programme for each young person within a common 16–19 system that pools the local options (and allows young people themselves to decide), the objective has been to increase institutional competition at 16 by driving colleges and schools into closed, competitive isolation. Selectivity at 16 has increased as a result but more than this, within both selective and non-selective institutions the aim is to recruit or retain the greatest number of students, convincing them they 'need' what happens to be on offer (often denying them access to information about what is offered elsewhere). In increasing numbers of schools and colleges this has led to an unbalanced and limited education for large numbers of young people.

Providing open choice at 15-plus is one of the most urgent tasks for the next stage of comprehensive reorganisation, which only a fully developed tertiary system would be able to provide by making all the courses on offer in all the institutions in any given area available to all students without financial loss to their 'home' institutions (see Chapter 9).

Tertiary colleges do more than provide a bridge or even a structural model for a system educating the whole of the 12th and 13th years of secondary education in a unified way. They provide the educational principle that could be used within a variety of forms of organisation, for they aim to offer vocational and general education, learning for its own sake as well as for a purpose, and learning related to work. Many in the early tertiary college movement wanted to develop a full continuity from 14 to 18 in co-operation with feeder schools (Janes, 1895), a challenge still to be met.

The educational principle behind tertiary college development was curriculum unification. They were not originally established as rationalising and concentrating devices, as were sixth form colleges; nor as a means to go comprehensive quickly, as tiered schemes were. They did not intend to become shadow grammar schools, as all too many sixth forms of 11–18 schools have had to become. Their supporters viewed them as a positive advance in realising comprehensive principles after 16 by bringing together the whole age group. The long-term objective was not the achievement of a social mix, though that would be a welcome by-product, but the avoidance of any split between academic and vocational education. Integrating academic and vocational education was the guiding principle.

Meanwhile, they try to provide a full 'A' level range – often keeping incorporated sixth forms in tact within the tertiary complex, with the advantage that they are more expandable than sixth form colleges or sixth forms – with the same range of vocational courses usually available in the further education colleges: City and Guilds, RSA, and BTEC courses and the growing range of GNVQ and NVQ at all their levels. They accommodate part-timers as well as full-timers, adults as well as young people. Tertiary colleges, like so many FE colleges, also offer specialised courses, for they are large enough to act as centres for the rarer types of study or training for certain occupations. This is the level at which specialisation makes sense – not the years before 16 when young people are laying down that broad base for lifelong learning.

Where they are part of an all-through comprehensive system and where they have set their sights on serving as community colleges – as at Bilston College in Wolverhampton – they have scope for continuous development. Where tertiary colleges are not yet successful, the cause of the problem is usually rooted in confusion about their goals and the fact that they are working in areas where too many sixth forms already exist (both comprehensive or grammar) to make their work coherent. To this extent tertiary colleges and many further education colleges are like the old secondary modern schools, seeking to improve their work and revolutionise their education, but within a divided system that makes their full development difficult. The key to all their futures is comprehensive reorganisation, where their relationship to the sixth forms of schools in their areas can be transformed within a unified system.

Some 1994 survey findings for the comprehensive colleges

The comprehensive colleges were the largest institutions in the survey on average (1587), with the further education colleges largest (1891). Several colleges had sizes between 2,000 and 5,000 full-time students, occasionally with 15,000–30,000 additional students attending part-time. Each further education college was unique, having beginnings in relation to the different needs for work-related and adult education in each area. Small or large, they hummed with activity all day and often into the evening, whether their work was in a central campus or an outlying annexe.

The comprehensive colleges offered a greater diversity of education and training and overall had a mix of those with vocational and academic study. There was a lower percentage overall of students age 17/18 entering for two or more 'A' levels (44%) than in the all-through schools (89%), but a far higher average number entering 'A' levels' vocational equivalent, the City and Guilds and BTEC national qualifications – 315 per college – against the all-through schools with only 11 students per school (Table A6)[4]. Most comprehensive colleges also had direct relationships with their local TECs, while less than half of all-through comprehensive schools had them (Table A6).

Another common feature of the three types of comprehensive colleges was that significantly higher percentages had more than 5% of their students who did not have English as a first language than was the case with schools (tertiary colleges, 29%; sixth-form colleges, 25%; survey average, 16%; see Table A5). All three of the colleges also had very high turnover rates – students enrolling or leaving during the academic year. For example, 82% of tertiary colleges enrolled at least one new student a week compared with a survey average of 22% enrolling at this rate.

But there were differences between the three types of colleges. Those who view the further education college as the 'secondary modern' and the sixth form college as the 'grammar' school of 16–19 might initially have their opinion confirmed in the finding that the further education college's intake of students with attainment in the top 20% of the attainment range was estimated well below that of all other survey schools and colleges: at only 13% against a survey average of 18% and a sixth-form college average of 58%. The further education colleges' social class profile is much less middle class than the survey average as well, only 17% having predominantly middle-class intakes compared with the average of 26%, and very much less than the sixth-form college with 57% (Table A5). This strongly suggests that the sixth forms of some all-through comprehensive schools themselves are more middle class than the earlier years in such schools – as sixth form colleges are in relation to the 11–16 schools from which they draw their intakes.

Table A6 shows how very much nearer the sixth form college is to the schools than to the other two colleges in the figures for some important aspects of vocational education. For example, its average student number entering for BTEC or City and Guilds national qualifications was only 10 per college, one below that for the all-through schools (while the tertiary college had 279 and the further education college 435 average per institution). The sixth form colleges' percentage of the 16–17 age group on day release or working part time (6%) was half that of the all-through schools and 15 times lower than that for tertiary colleges. However, the percentage of sixth-form-college students entering for two or more 'A' levels (78%) is far higher than the other two colleges, much nearer that of the schools with sixth forms.

Those who claim that the tertiary college amalgamates both traditions might have their opinion supported by the figures showing tertiary colleges' percentage of the top 20% of the attainment range at intake (26%), which lay between that of the further education college and sixth-form college. The tertiary colleges' percentage entering for two or more 'A' levels (37%) also lay between the other two colleges. On the other hand, its percentage with working-class intakes was much the same as the further education college and for middle-class intakes only slightly higher.

The tertiary colleges' overall average size was not much different from the general further education college but, as Table A6 shows, its numbers in the 16–19 age group are significantly higher and several general further education colleges are *de facto* tertiary colleges for surrounding schools. Were it not for the constraints being laid on them, the pivotal role of the further education college and its future potential would be far more widely recognised, as would a growing, informal comprehensive tertiary education culture.

For governments charged with reorganising the structure of education for the twenty-first century, promoting the integration of vocational, academic and work-related education, and boosting the numbers getting qualifications in the system, the tertiary approach to reorganisation for 16–19 is likely to be the most cost-effective way forward as well as the model most likely to keep the commitment to excellence within the sixth year that always prevailed in the sixth form.

Over the last 30 years much headway has been made in pioneering sixth-form colleges, in translating so many into tertiary colleges, in organising so many tertiary colleges out of further education colleges, and in developing so many further education colleges themselves as general colleges serving their areas. Most important of all is the work that remains: to draw the sixth forms of the schools into tertiary networks as part of their own growth towards fully comprehensive status (see Chapter 9).

Physical and educational foundation of comprehensive schools and colleges

Size

Size was a matter of great controversy in the early years of the comprehensive reform, always cited as one of the main drawbacks of a comprehensive system. Popular fear was fuelled that such schools were too large. Professional fears, on the other hand, were that they were too small, for DES thinking was calculated not on the size required for education in the years of 11 to 16, when the majority of the age group was in school, but on the size of the sixth form which only a small minority entered (Ministry of Education, 1947). The Ministry had concluded early on that if it required 255 grammar school pupils to yield a sixth form of 90, there had to be 1800 in the comprehensive from 11 to 16 to produce a comparable size of sixth form.

Conservative government ministers regularly used this as an argument against the comprehensive. In 1952, for example, a former Conservative education minister, R.A. Butler, dismissed comprehensive schools as 'soulless, educational factories' (Butler, 1952:35). The caricature was repeated endlessly, especially as the early comprehensive schools were nearly all large. When the national reform began officially in 1965, average size was 915 and several schools were over 2000. Yet 2000 was the size Conservative education ministers, including Quentin Hogg as late as 1965, were still insisting was the proper size for all of them (*Hansard*, House of Commons, Vol. 705, Cols. 423–4, 21 January, 1965). Even as late as 1977, at a conference chaired by Labour's Secretary of State, Shirley Williams, it was declared that there were 'no insuperable objections to...a school with...3000 pupils' (DES, 1978:11).

The problem was not that larger schools could not be successful – for they could – but that Britain had practically no very large schools. It quickly became apparent that existing smaller schools had to be used. This meant that argument about the viable size of comprehensive schools had to be reconsidered. Circular 10/65 talked in terms of six- or seven-form entry (about 1000–1200 for all-through schools), but even that was larger than most existing schools.

One solution was tiered schools. The introduction of several such schemes brought the average size down somewhat: by 1968 it was 789 in England and Wales and 703 in Scotland (Benn and Simon, 1970: Table 5.4, p.79)[5], but the pressure for large all-through schools continued. Despite this pressure, the same survey found that 30% of practising 11–18 comprehensive schools were below six-form entry, the minimum size the government had by then decreed; and so were 60% of 11–16 comprehensives (Benn and Simon, 1970: Table 5.3, p.78). Yet the policy of the Government remained obdurate. No plan to go comprehensive was returned because schools were too big; but many because they were considered too small.

But how small was too small? The DES itself regularly turned down schools from one area on the grounds of being too small, while accepting ones of the the same size elsewhere (Benn and Simon, 1970:76–77). It was obvious that there was little consistency on this point in practice, however much there was in DES policy. When Labour returned to office in 1974 there was a softer line, and the new circular(10/74) claimed 'there is no ideal size'; but in London during this period, ILEA reorganisation was held up for several years because many selective schools had only five-form entry and the government was still insisting on six or seven.

Meanwhile, the anti-comprehensive campaign, as well as much of the education press, regularly maintained that large size was the comprehensive reform's greatest problem (O'Connor, 1977:35). Although there were continuing proposals to reduce the impact of large size through schemes of internal organisation and in the arrangements of buildings, including imaginative proposals like the concept of the mini-school, which divided schools into 'bases' where groups of staff and pupils did all their teaching and learning (Toogood, 1984), the main campaign on size from those supporting comprehensive education for the first 20 years was to prove that existing smaller schools could become viable providers of comprehensive education in practice.

Schools that were always going to be small because of their remote situation started the challenge and provided some pointers. Solutions of bussing, boarding or boating pupils off to larger schools often involved selecting those who went and those who stayed, failing to offer full access to secondary education to the age group as a whole within reach of where they lived. A small group interested in the subject began working on the ways this could be provided by staffing adjustments (made by some LEAs in the days when they could respond to differing needs). This permitted some schools to have more specialist teachers than were allowed in other schools. Another approach was to organise '2-year' timetabling to maximise the work of existing staff, and a third was to make use of peripatetic teaching in co-operative schemes. Today, of course, there is distance learning, including on-line classrooms, connecting students in the remotest areas with classrooms and teachers in the larger centres.

The small group of experts specialising in making the small school work were very influential and their writing spread the word – as well as practical advice, particularly in relation to the 14–16 year olds (see, for example, Halsall, 1968, 1973). It soon transpired that the most effective solution for the very small comprehensive school lay in restricting the excessive range of subjects offered, a decision that cut across what many early advocates of comprehensive education had stressed was the unique asset of the new schools: a wide offering of many languages, different types of science, a big variety of practical and cultural subjects (see, for example, Pedley, 1963). In certain schools this offering had to give way to a basic curriculum centring on 'O' level subjects that 80% of the age group regularly chose – with no exotic extras – and occasionally only one foreign language. Teaching these basic academic combinations well to all pupils was deemed more consistent with the comprehensive principle than continuing to offer a wide choice to some.

By the 1980s comprehensive schools had discovered that any school with more than 500 could provide a choice wide enough to still most criticism over restricted choice internally. A single examination through the GCSE was the turning point; and by the time the strait-jacket of the National Curriculum was clamped upon schools, the problem had virtually disappeared as an issue of whole-school viability, becoming instead a curriculum or timetable issue for everyone, irrespective of school size.

Meanwhile, large size was ceasing to be discussed, especially after engineered enrolment legislation after 1986 introduced the concept of the 'chosen' school, and funding changed so that higher numbers meant higher funding. Grammar school size was rising too and some grammar schools were reaching sizes over 1300 by the 1980s (Bridges, 1987). Ironically, because of this rise and the GCSE reform, most remaining grammar schools could now convert quite easily to comprehensive intakes in structural terms, as even they themselves recognise.

1994 findings

As far as overall size goes, the 1994 survey showed more homogeneity in size as a result of 30 years development: slightly larger average sizes but a reduction of the extremes at either end.

All-through 11–12 to 18 schools averaged just over 1000 in England; in Wales the average was 972, in Scotland 732, and in Northern Ireland 650 (questions 25, 7 and 6A). Although institutions in villages or the countryside were much smaller than those in towns, large cities or suburbs (Table A5), and short-course comprehensive schools smaller than all-throughs, the average size of all-through schools in the English shire counties (1022) was virtually identical with that for greater London (1021) – with the other metropolitan boroughs only very slightly larger at 1086.

The grant maintained school had a larger average size than LEA schools or than any of the voluntary sector schools (Table A5) and because of this it is unlikely that complaints about 'soulless educational factories' will be heard much today. Though the average size of a comprehensive school may be slightly larger than it was 30 years ago, in 1994 there were smaller percentages of very large schools as well as far smaller percentages of very small ones compared with the late 1960s. At that time 38% of all schools in Britain taught 600 pupils or less (Benn and Simon, 1970: Table 5.5, p.79); in 1994 only 6% of all-through schools did so (question 6A) and only 27% of schools overall. In 1968 14% of all schools were over 1200 (Benn and Simon, 1970: Table 5.5, p.79); it was 12% in 1994, with only two schools at 2000 or over.

Purpose-building – Necessary or not?

Closely related to size was the issue of purpose-building, another big debating point in 1965. Even those who supported the reform believed at that time that the purpose-built comprehensive school was far superior to the school that had been adapted from an existing school.

Few would deny that starting off with a new school is a great advantage in any system, and in many cases this proves to be so. But the first independent enquiry revealed that the main advantage for comprehensives was that purpose-recruited staff went with such buildings, an advantage that ceased as the system developed and original staff moved on. In any case, not everything was perfect in the purpose-built school, where bad design could present as many difficulties as adapted schools. The design of a few early comprehensives was unrealistic, with too many floors, corridors unable to accommodate the traffic using them, or layouts requiring long walking time from end to end (Benn and Simon, 1970:95–102; Dawson, 1981; Weeks, 1986:119). The original inspiration provided by Impington Village College, designed by Walter Gropius and Maxwell Fry at the end of the 1930s, 'crystallised for many progressive architects and educationists alike the ideal of what a modern school should both look and be like' (Weston, 1991). But by the late 1960s this 'modern vision' was being used unimaginatively in many local authorities, translating into too many large blocks.

This phase did not last long. Very quickly, spurred by a new generation of architects, large blocks began being broken up into smaller manageable units, using cantilevered half-floors, buildings arranged around courtyards like the Wyndham School in Cumbria, or radiating from an administrative centre (Benn and Simon, 1970:95–102; Sharp, 1973). In one case, Sutton Centre, the school was designed as a series of separate buildings embedded at various sites in the town centre. Comprehensive schools in other countries had already moved in these directions: the Walter Gropius School in Berlin was an all-age all-through school formed from inter-locking stellar units grouped in various combinations within a large park-like area.

There was also no substitute for design being undertaken after consultation with those who worked in comprehensive schools and colleges, and architects were told about the importance of finding out what went on in the schools before designing them. Ironically, such close collaboration was more often possible when existing schools were enlarged to become comprehensive schools because the staff were available to be consulted. The adapted school was not always inferior, especially if there was room to enlarge on the same site; it could be much more closely tailored to the wishes of those who worked within. New schools borrowed from this lesson: thus, when the Stantonbury Campus in Milton Keynes was being planned and built in the early 1980s, there was a head on site 3 years before it opened (Makins, 1985; Weeks, 1986:119).

All school building, whether adaptation or building from new, led to discussion about the balance between specialist and general-purpose areas. As soon as the latest advances – such as language laboratories – were discarded, along came problems of integrating information technology facilities in schools and colleges. Today planning is more likely to be in the accommodation of large learning resource centres incorporating multimedia and technology facilities with existing library services; or providing increasing numbers of teaching areas with computer facilities.

The conclusion reached by many who designed for schools and colleges, some earlier rather than later, was that unless it was absolutely necessary to have it fixed, built accommodation for every age and stage should be flexible – capable of being adapted as purposes and needs changed. One signal failure seems never to have been addressed: anyone responsible for approving building plans for schools or colleges should never pass any without directing that the amount of storage space allowed for be doubled, even trebled. It is quite astounding how complaints of too little storage space are heard in every generation about every type of educational building. That applies especially to secure storage areas and other security measures which have now become essential.

Most comprehensive schools and colleges, however built, served their purpose well enough but still the issue of purpose-building continued to be raised in relation to the reform. The Conservative party in the late 1960s announced that no comprehensive school should be allowed to open unless it was purpose built and on one site. Had this ever become government policy it would have held reorganisation up forever (which might have been one of the motives). For in 1965 the NFER found only 25% of comprehensives were 'new' (Monks, 1968:22). In 1968 the first independent enquiry found 28% were purpose-built; with higher percentages in those areas already well ahead with planning. Thus Scotland had 43.5% in this category, and the ILEA 46% (Benn and Simon, 1970: Table 5.10, p.96). The second enquiry in 1994 found that Scotland still led the league table with two-thirds of all its comprehensive schools purpose built (Table A5).

For the majority of areas that reorganised, however, the argument soon became academic. Adaptations and amalgamations had to be tried if the 11-plus was to be ended within a generation. LEAs set about looking at their schools to decide which arrangements were best, with sporadic help from the DES Building Bulletins giving advice on conversion techniques; and, as time with on, with economies and cuts the order of the day, with particular local authorities taking the lead in continuing to produce imaginative new designs for both buildings and grounds from nursery years up to college level.

Differences between purpose-building and adaptation
Other than being slightly larger if purpose built, there was little difference detected in 1968 between the nature of the intakes to purpose built as

against adapted schools, nor of percentages staying on (Benn and Simon, 1970). The purpose built tended to offer more subjects to exam level ('O' and 'A' level) but the non-purpose built schools had larger sixth forms. Educationally speaking, it seemed to be a draw (Benn and Simon, 1970).

By 1994, however, quite a few differences could be detected. First, the percentage of purpose-built comprehensives had increased to nearly one in three (Table 3.3), as might be expected after three decades of replacement building. Colleges averaged slightly less (29% for tertiary and 30 % for further education).

There was only a small difference in the GCSE (five A–C)/Standard Grade (five 1–3) results in 1994 that favoured the adapted schools (40% against 38%), and the same with 'A' level average point scores (13% against 12%). There was more of a difference in the nature of the intake, the adapted schools having nearly comprehensive intakes at 19% of the top 20% of the attainment range compared with the purpose built at only 13%. Purpose-built schools had slightly more of their number with predominantly working-class intakes than those that were not purpose built. Schools drawing most of their pupils from council housing had the highest levels of purpose-building at 46%, while those drawing from the single category of substandard housing had the lowest (11%). Despite this last finding, it looked in 1994 as if the change over 30 years has tended marginally to favour the adapted school more than the purpose-built in several important ways – owing to their intakes and situations rather than their architecture.

Table 3.3 Origins of comprehensive schools and colleges, 1994. Results in percentages, with numbers in parentheses

Purpose built	32.7	(511)
Adapted with a grammar/senior secondary in the base	25.0	(391)
Adapted with a secondary modern/ junior secondary in base	38.0	(594)
Purpose built as/or adapted from adult or FE college	3.3	(52)
No response	0.7	(12)
Total	100	(1560)

It would seem that this once-raging battle that assumed bricks and mortar were the key to educational success can be settled by common sense. It is exciting to have a new building and it is essential to have good upkeep, but the context of a school within the school system, and the policy determining use and organisation of a building, are always going to be more important for educational outcome than its architectural pedigree. A lot of the negative comment about purpose-building was meant to increase the chances of grammar schools being left untouched, while a lot of the positive comment was over-optimistic investment in the magic of new premises continuing forever.

Even so, a school or college that is well designed for a comprehensive purpose or with special architectural integrity (e.g. Pimlico School in London, Farnborough College in Hampshire, Queens Middle School and Alton Tertiary College in Hampshire, Cleator Moor School in Cumbria, and Northampton's Sixth Form Centre) will always contribute an indefinable extra to the education that goes on inside. At best such schools and colleges will be part of that ongoing tradition that transcends design movements and is characterised by the belief that 'architecture can contribute to a society that seeks to be more open and less formal', providing settings that help people 'to know and claim their social rights' (Weston, 1991:53).

A split site

A split site was another characteristic that was supposed to be one of the great liabilities of going comprehensive, such schools being regularly called 'botched' schemes.

There were great protests if amalgamating schools were not on one site or directly adjacent to each other, even though purpose-built comprehensives after the 1960s were being deliberately designed as buildings scattered more widely. Some complaints came from those determined to keep grammar schools from combining or enlarging, others from those who feared administrative and logistical burdens that could come with awkward physical arrangements. Although in time distinctions became evident between positive and negative splits (some being decidedly negative), from the start the situation of those working in schools was approached in the positive spirit typified by one head in the late 1960s: 'Being split is difficult; it is, however, more tolerable than selection at 11-plus' (Benn and Simon, 1970:93).

The first independent enquiry found that 24% of comprehensives were on split sites; in Scotland the figure was 31% (Benn and Simon, 1970: Table 5.9, p.91). The NFER survey of 1965 found 22% of comprehensives split, with half having sites separated by more than half a mile (Monks, 1968: Table 7, p.91). From the first, it was obvious that much depended on how far apart the sites were and what the liaison was like. Those splits that were most difficult were those with much traffic between, where times of travel could differ dramatically according to the time of day; while those where journeys always took the same time, even if sites were more widely separated, were far easier to run. In most split-site schools, the aim was for students to stay where they were for most of the time (moving only for blocked half days) and for staff to do the commuting.

Most split-site schools chose to separate by years, with earlier years – frequently the 11–13 age range – on the smaller sites. Ironically, this arrangement was soon seen to offer advantages because it enabled new entrants to be taught in their own smaller quarters rather than being thrown at once into the larger school (see Chapter 6). These divisions were often retained even when schools moved to one site, or were borrowed by one-site schools that had never been split. In some cases (e.g. Brent) this led to running the two sites as two separate schools for a time.

But most such schools always planned to organise on one site eventually, even if not in one building. After 30 years it looked as if most had succeeded, for the 1994 survey showed that the percentage of schools and colleges still on two sites had declined to 16.6% (question 37) and of sixth form colleges to 8%. Most of the splits in 1994 were in further education, with 71% of tertiary colleges and 85% of further education colleges on split sites. A good number were on three or four, and one college had 13. Far from regarding this as a weakness, colleges regarded their multiplying work and satellite stations as one of their greatest strengths.

Because they are so often organised over a wide area in several locations, tertiary colleges and schools with two or more sites often organise more efficiently than do other schools and colleges (O'Connell, 1970). They are forced to work harder on timetables, communications and liaison to make sure their separation does not hold them back. Rutter found fewer behaviour problems in such schools (Rutter, 1979:102), while others found better examination results (Monks, 1970). The 1994 survey found no difference in academic results (at either GCSE A–C or at 'A' level) between schools and colleges on one site and those on more than one. As for staying on, so often assumed to be adversely affected by being on two sites, there was also no difference – 56. 4% for all-through schools on two sites against 55.9% for those on one (questions 37 and 115). So much for the harbingers of doom who argued that a generation would be blighted for attending schools and colleges organised in two buildings instead of one. Possibly there were so few actual problems in the long run because the complaints forced attention to be paid to the potential difficulties and helped solve them.

Grammar versus secondary modern origin

A quarter of all comprehensive schools and colleges were formed from a single grammar school (Table 3.3). These (question 9A) were more likely to be full in the September of our survey year – 46.8% compared with 32.4% for schools formed from a single secondary modern school (question 9B), while it was only 21.3% where the school had been formed from two secondary modern schools (question 9D).

Comprehensive schools formed from a single grammar school had a five GCSE A-C/ordinary grade 1–3 pass rate percentage of 42% while those formed from two secondary modern schools (question 9D) had one of 35%. Their staying-on rate was not much higher at 57% than a school formed from two secondary modern schools at 54% but their intake of the top 20% of attainment at 24% was higher than intakes to institutions with other forms of foundations – like a grammar and secondary modern at 19% (question 9C), a single secondary modern at 18% (question 9B); and two or more secondary modern schools at 14% (question 9D). The ex-single grammar school category also had a higher proportion with predominantly middle-class intakes (at 37%) than the survey average of 26% or than the 22% for comprehensive schools formed from two secondary moderns.

At first sight it looked like a straightforward scale of attainment and class differences from top to bottom, starting with comprehensive schools formed from a single grammar through those formed from a grammar and secondary modern combined, then a single secondary modern, and, lastly, two secondary moderns combined. This seemed especially likely when we knew that the two types most likely to be grammar based were the sixth-form college and the grant maintained school, while the type least likely was the short-course comprehensive of 11/12–16.

But it was not quite so simple. The staying-on rates of comprehensive schools with secondary modern schools in their base were not significantly different from those with grammar schools in their base (question 9 – B and D as against A and C). As for social class, a higher percentage of comprehensive schools formed from a single secondary modern (39%) had a predominantly middle-class intake in 1994 than had schools with both a grammar and a secondary modern in the base (24%).

On examination performance, to take another example, schools formed from a single secondary modern school (question 9B) had a five GCSE A–C level average of 41%, which was above the survey average and very near those of schools formerly a single grammar school (42%), higher than the percentage from schools where a grammar school and a secondary modern had combined in the foundation (38%) or where two secondary modern schools had combined (35%). At 'A' level the comprehensive formed from a single secondary modern school actually had a higher score (at 13.5) than the comprehensive formed from a single grammar school (at 13.4) with a grammar and secondary modern at 12.6 points, and that from two secondary moderns at 12.4.

What this seems to show is that schools formed from single schools (either grammar or secondary modern) showed differences from schools which had been formed from 'new' combinations. More sophisticated analysis would be required to see if these were significant, and, if so, what other causative factors might be related. But our indications are of interest in view of the debate about shutting schools down and re-starting them with new heads and new names. The whole issue of 'folk memory' is important to schools and colleges and to their success. On the other hand, where a school has made great changes, it is often discouraging that the 'old' image cannot be shaken off; while some with a reputation that was once high, might coast without making the necessary changes.

A pessimistic view was taken by several earlier researchers (e.g. Bellaby, 1977) about the likelihood of significant benefits arising from comprehensivisation when the cultures of the existing schools were so different. The findings of 1994, although showing some of the differences that confirmed these earlier predictions, also showed that not all outcomes were predictable from the origins of schools. In other words, context does make a difference.

Different types of comprehensive schools

Mixed and single-sex schools

The great majority of comprehensive schools and colleges are mixed – 94% in our 1994 survey. All the middle schools were mixed and so were all three types of colleges – as well as all comprehensive schools in Scotland, and most of them in Wales. In England 93% were mixed, with just over 4% single-sex girls and just under 3% single-sex boys. For girls this was much the same percentage as applies nationally in the comprehensive sector, for boys slightly less[6].

Elementary schools of the nineteenth century were mixed, even if boys went in by one door and girls by another; but schools for the middle class were segregated by sex. The early municipal grammar schools were often single sex and the Hadow Report of 1926, considering secondary education for all, recommended separate schools for the sexes, combining the middle-class tradition with that of many denominational schools. In 1945 the main Ministry pamphlet on schooling continued to encourage single-sex schools in the post-war era (Ministry of Education, 1945).

So many of the older, more prestigious (and denominational) schools were single sex that people came to believe that 'single-sexness' was somehow necessary for academic attainment or the maintenance of moral discipline. Yet today in Britain single-sex education is rare in primary schools and in institutions starting after the age of 15, as well as in nursery education. Even in those middle years from 11 to 16 it is becoming rarer.

It has often been said that comprehensive reorganisation caused the decline of single sex education by rationalising provision. In fact the decline began immediately after World War II when educators were already predicting that by 1965 Britain's secondary schools would be largely mixed. One said that 70% of schools in cities and 57% of schools in the counties would be mixed by 1965. This was not a bad prediction: by 1968, England and Wales was 60% mixed and in the comprehensive sector by this time, 77% (DES, 1970: Vol. I, p.2). In the Benn and Simon enquiry of 1968 81% of all comprehensive schools were mixed, with 9% girls and 10% boys (Benn and Simon, 1970:284); and much the same percentages had applied in the NFER survey relating to 3 years earlier (Monks,1968:236).

In the 1970s and 1980s the trend to mixed education continued, and not just in the comprehensive sector. In the private sector, both day and boarding, where single-sex schools had been in the majority, by 1994 65.4% of all private schools were mixed (DfE, 1994a: Table 5B) – with single-sex private schools down by a third since 1984 alone (DfE, 1994a: Para. 17).

Gender-related changes in education in recent years
Sex differences in educational attainment also narrowed considerably during the 1980s with girls taking the lead in several key fields: passing exams, staying on to the sixth form in greater numbers, and obtaining an ever-enlarging share of higher education places (Reid, 1981:10; *Social Trends*, 1985, 1990). In England in 1993 46% of girls got five good GCSE A–C passes compared with only 37% of boys (DfE, 1994a). One cannot say these improvements for girls have been caused by the increase in mixed

education; only that they have coincided with it. Nor can we say that working-class girls have benefited in the same way as middle-class girls.

Those researching the differences of performance of the sexes in single-sex and mixed education, have gone quite some way to destroying the belief that 'single-sexness' is necessary for academic excellence in either gender. R. R. Dale's work is particularly interesting, since he looked only at grammar schools and after exhaustive research concluded that boys' progress 'is improved by co-education' and girls 'not harmed' (Dale, 1974: Vol. III, p.267). His main conclusion was that 'the question of comparative progress in academic work should never again be raised as an obstacle to a policy of co-education'.

There are those who have always argued strongly that no single-sex school can be really comprehensive – 'All comprehensive schools should be mixed. Families are' was a typical view at the start of comprehensive reorganisation (Benn and Simon, 1970:291). However, the women's movement has made comprehensive educators less hostile to separate consideration of girls. It has not acted to prevent the move to mixed schools, but it has directed more attention to girls' and women's equal treatment within mixed classes, lecture halls and training workshops. To some this meant separation of girls for certain subjects, to ensure they were not overlooked in the teaching process. Others, however, believed such separate teaching, while it gives an immediate boost, does not have long-lasting results (Measor and Woods, 1984:169). Better to make sure mixed classes were as girl-oriented as could be than separate girls out. In certain fields and subjects it is now considered necessary to do the same for boys who can also be overlooked in some fields and whose curriculum can also become unbalanced. Only a few mixed schools in our 1994 survey arranged separate teaching for either sex (see Chapter 5), although one school had divided all teaching by gender.

At secondary level others concerned with girls' educational equality saw improvement coming not from separate teaching but from insisting on a compulsory core for everyone that included science and maths up to 16, a policy that had already been followed with success in other comprehensive systems of the world (Davies, 1984). Later it was realised that neither sex should be allowed to drop subjects that are essential during the compulsory years. This raised consciousness about equal opportunities over 30 years has succeeded in wiping out the common practice of subjects specific to one gender only, a hangover from pre-comprehensive schooling. About half the mixed comprehensives in 1968 had such practices (Benn and Simon, 1970:292): for girls in 11 subjects, including catering and child care, which were not open to boys; and for boys, 10 subjects, including engineering and woodwork, which were not open to girls. Although there is hidden bias still, open subject restriction by gender in comprehensive schools and colleges has been virtually eliminated in the last 30 years.

This was not always the case with work-related education where, during the training schemes of the 1980s, young women were often 'frozen out' of male training fields like design and engineering and herded into 'caring, service and commercial occupations' (Brown et al., 1985). Several school-based, work-related projects, including some introduced under TVEI, were designed in ways that also pushed girls into stereotypical occupations. In 1984, for example, a 'staggering 64% of girls on YTS were in administrative/clerical or sales/personnel service work' (Marsh, 1986:161).

Despite pressure to organise separate women-only training in many occupational areas and to encourage more girls to train in a wider variety of occupations, gender bias is still common in work-related education. For example, it would be instructive to discover what percentages of young women in the later years of secondary education today are on GNVQ business courses, as against percentages studying engineering, manu-facturing, or design. Or later, within business occupations, to see how many make it through to management, that area 'where capitalist authority fuses most completely with masculinity' (Cornell, 1982:97) and so often excludes women. In this respect, to cite one recent set of changes in Britain, it is worrying that the membership of most TEC and LEC boards, as well as of the governing bodies of most further education colleges, is almost entirely male (see Chapter 8) – not the best omen for the develop-ment of comprehensive education from 16 to 19.

Single-sex comprehensives compared with mixed

In those early years in the 1960s single-sex comprehensive schools made a lot of the running in comprehensive education, particularly boys' schools. In 1965 boys' comprehensives were significantly larger than mixed schools; they also had the largest sixth forms (Monks, 1968:20) and higher percentages staying to the sixth form. Mixed schools, however, offered slightly more subjects per school (Benn and Simon, 1970: Table 17.3, p.287).

In the great comprehensive debate of those times mixed schools had to prove themselves with opinion formers and with those who cared about the welfare of girls. There was particular concern over the fate of girls in mixed schools lest they should find it hard to survive in the academic scrum, when parents cared more about boys' results and careers, and when heavy-handed discipline was usually meted out to boys. For this reason many girls' schools were thought of as gender refuges; and many mixed comprehensive schools in the late 1960s had special posts with responsibility for girls' welfare (Benn and Simon, 1970:286).

It was soon evident that these fears were unfounded and that girls could survive in mixed schools, as they had elsewhere in the world for generations, including in Scotland, which was 99% mixed in its comprehensive schools by 1968. There girls' welfare posts were being phased out by the early 1970s (SED, 1971) with England and Wales following somewhat later.

Comprehensives most likely to be single sex in 1968 were the 11–18 schools and the denominational schools (Benn and Simon, 1970: Table 17.4). In 1994 those most likely to be single sex were upper schools; also aided schools and those that were grant maintained (17% and 15% respectively). In 1968 it was the single-sex comprehensive schools that were largest, but in 1994 it was the mixed that were largest (see Table A5).

In 1994 single-sex comprehensives were much more likely to have developed from grammar schools: 59% of girls' and 57% of boys' comprehensive schools, compared with 23% of mixed ones. Even so, the estimated intakes of the top 20% of attainment in single-sex schools were slightly lower than for mixed: 16% for girls and 17% for boys with mixed at 18%. Mixed and boys' comprehensive schools in 1994 had social class intakes roughly comparable with the survey average, but girls' comprehensive schools had a significantly larger proportion with working-class intakes (and smaller with middle-class intakes), while both boys' and girls' comprehensives had significantly higher percentages of schools where more than 30% were receiving free meals, with a very high percentage indeed for girls' comprehensive schools (see Table A5).

Despite these differences relative to mixed schools, the results at GCSE (five A–C passes) were highest at girls' comprehensives (40.7%), followed by mixed schools (39.3%) with boys' some way behind (33.8%). Single-sex schools also had higher percentages staying after the leaving age than mixed schools (see Table A5). At 'A' level, however, girls' average point score (11.6) was lower than both boys' and mixed schools, though only marginally behind the latter (Table A6). At 'A' level boys' comprehensives had the highest point score at 13.8. One explanation for this can be found in Table A6 where it is evident that boys' comprehensive schools from 16 to 19 had far smaller percentages of students entering for BTEC national qualifications or studying on day release than either girls' or mixed schools, as well as a far smaller average number qualifying for degree level courses through the vocational route of GNVQ or BTEC.

Why it should be girls' schools with a more 'comprehensive' policy of including vocational as well as academic work, with boys' schools appearing to concentrate more on straight 'A' level work, was hard to explain without more investigation. The average size of single-sex comprehensive schools' sixth form at 137 is smaller than the average 11–18 all-through school figure of 152. Without more sophisticated analysis the various factors that might illuminate further these before-and-after differences at 16, we can only conclude that the single-sex comprehensive is holding its own but, like all other schools and colleges, will have to anticipate major changes after 16.

In some big cities, including London, having a 'choice' of single-sex comprehensives has always been expected – just as in the private school world. Elsewhere in the UK and in other countries, school gender segregation is not an item for the 'choice' menu. This should not be a difficulty provided the work of serving the special needs of both continues inside mixed schools. When we come later to consider practice in equal opportunities in 1994 (Chapter 5), there is not much evidence that comprehensive schools were tackling issues related to gender, race or social class equality as thoroughly as they were 10 or 15 years earlier. Possibly competitive 'league table' concerns (plus wearying struggles over the National Curriculum and testing) have dominated teachers' time and energy, with very much less left over for tackling equality issues.

Up to 16, the years of puberty when parents care most about keeping the sexes separate, the girls' comprehensives are setting the pace in some respects, no longer needing special support. After 16 the picture is cloudier, but history shows that activity on behalf of girls' and women's education has pronounced cycles and that, after bursts of progress pressure for equality can flag, allowing new forms of discrimination to build up. Many boys' schools are only just coming to realise the ways in which boys need special support (and the ways in which boys' comprehensive schools also need this, judging by several comments made to us from those teaching in boys' schools). Just as crucial, many schools have been slow to realise that boys and girls from working-class backgrounds need their own special attention – as do students of either gender where race discrimination adds to the likely barriers. In some ways it may be easier to give all these forms of attention in the single-sex schools but there is evidence that it isn't always given there and none that it cannot also be given as well in mixed settings.

With the vast majority of schools mixed and with evidence that increasingly after 16 students of both sexes vote with their feet for mixing, the vast majority of pupils and students in comprehensive education will remain in mixed settings. It is thus to education in this context that the majority of our attention will inevitably be directed when it comes to serving gender need, though the experience of single-sex comprehensive schools and, on occasion, of women-only work-related education, will always have something to teach us.

Comprehensive schools of different legal status

Legal differences between schools are always hard to understand, especially when all of them are comprehensive. Though almost all the comprehensive schools and colleges in our 1994 survey knew their age range, about one in 10 either did not know or chose not to give their legal status in response to question 4; and many citizens find the same difficulty distinguishing between different forms of foundation, ownership, management, governing and financing. It is even less clear now after so many quangos have been created to run separate sectors of education and when new school types have been introduced, some with their own quangos, and each more controversial than the last.

The legal status of comprehensive schools and colleges in the 1994 survey is set out in Table A1.

Most schools are publicly owned and maintained and under LEA oversight. We called them LEA-county schools in the 1994 survey where they made up 65% of the total (and 75% of survey schools). Just under 10% of the total survey were colleges, now funded separately from schools by a variety of quangos in different parts of the UK. Just over 10% of the survey total were voluntary schools set up originally by foundations but now under the overall auspices of local authorities. Some 13% of survey schools were denominational (see Table 3.4); some have diocesan boards as well as LEAs to account to; others are answerable to the opted-out schools' quango. Opted-out grant maintained schools were about 11% of comprehensive secondary and middle schools in England in the 1994 survey.

Voluntary and denominational schools
As was seen in Chapter 2, voluntary status has been controversial in the twentieth century. Today's three types of school in England and Wales date from the 1944 Act's attempt to settle the matter by giving such schools a

choice of different funding arrangements, based on the principle that the more foundation governors paid of their own costs the more control they got. As the years have passed, however, the state has gradually taken over the running costs of all such schools and all capital costs except for 15% from voluntary aided schools. Yet successive education acts have given voluntary school governors ever more control, not less.

Aided schools control their own admissions; and the 1980 Act additionally exempted both aided schools and selective schools from having to accept 'parental choice' of their schools, even if they had the places, where other schools have had to accept it. Engineered enrolment legislation of 1986 and 1988 increased differences, particularly between aided schools and others; and denominational bodies have had concessions more recently on school transport and in matters like consultation over appointments to funding agencies.

The position is further complicated by the fact that so many voluntary schools have taken advantage of grant maintained status – the proportion of voluntary schools opting out being far greater than the proportion of county-LEA schools. In the case of aided schools taking grant maintained status, the advantage is that for the first time they get 100% of capital funding which means they no longer have to find that 15% themselves.

With all these changes, but especially GM status, currently dissolving the old 'settlement' of the 1994 Act, perhaps it is time that all schools funded publicly for 100% of running costs, should also have the same rights of capital funding – along with the same legal relationship to the democratically elected local authority. With ever-increasing 'independence' for all schools (through such changes as LMS and through changes in governing body composition giving more places to the schools themselves), the need to safeguard certain schools to ensure ethos is maintained, has ended. All schools can now control their own ethos, the reason so often given in the past to support a system of segregated legal status for certain schools, particularly voluntary status.

The current proliferation of legal status and funding arrangements is unnecessary and in some cases unfair, as a deluge of comment and research has made clear since the middle of the 1980s, if not before. Harmonisation will be needed sooner rather than later, in a new 'settlement' for the whole school system. Although the task has been made particularly urgent by the continuing controversy over grant maintained status, long before grant maintained schools were introduced there was disquiet over misuse of voluntary status within the comprehensive system. Because of it the Labour Party had stressed 'the need to come to a new agreement with voluntary schools to secure greater harmony with county schools', emphasising the need to avoid admissions 'through testing or interviews employed as devices for selection' (Labour Party, 1982). In 1995 the Labour Party suggested a new settlement made up of three types of schools (Labour Party, 1995), a simplification of the complexity reached by the mid-1990s, but still a divided system. Discussion on the matter can be expected to continue.

Voluntary comprehensive schools, 1994 survey

Comprehensive schools of differing voluntary status are shown in Table A1. Voluntary aided comprehensive schools were slightly under-represented and voluntary controlled slightly over-represented. Table 3.4 sets out the denominational numbers.

Table 3.4 Numbers (%) of denominational and non-denominational voluntary schools (based on question 22)

Non-denominational	25	(11)
Roman Catholic Schools	122	(56)
Church of England Schools	66	(30)
Dual denominational Schools	6	(3)
Total	219	(100)

The large difference in the number of schools having voluntary status (160, set out in Table A1, based on question 4) and the number having denominational/voluntary status in this table (219) is because 59 denominational schools answering question 22 (12 Church of England and 47 Roman Catholic) did not name any voluntary status in question 4. Many were denominational schools naming grant maintained status instead; others, including most Roman Catholic schools in Scotland, gave no status in question 4.

Non-denominational voluntary schools

Most but not all voluntary schools were denominational. Those that are non-denominational, particularly those with aided status, have often been very selective. When reorganisation began in 1965 many refused to take part as comprehensive schools. Throughout the 1960s and 1970s the rate at which these schools became comprehensive lagged far behind schools overall and far behind denominational voluntary schools generally. In time many – like those of the King Edward Foundation in Birmingham – subsequently became private schools.

In the 1994 survey non-denominational voluntary schools had 21.7% of their intakes in the top 20% of the attainment range, higher than percentages for denominational schools over all: 15 of the 25 schools were former grammar schools, including six of the seven that were also aided schools. They were more likely to be full than survey schools as a whole at 48% (as against 40%) and less likely to be mixed (at 84%). The numbers were small and not too many conclusions can be drawn other than to say that this sector did not appear to have many disadvantaged comprehensive schools among its number.

Denominational schools

The majority of voluntary schools in our 1994 survey were denominational schools (see Table 3.4).

Together voluntary and grant maintained denominational schools were 13.4% of the survey total in England, a smaller percentage than denominational comprehensive schools were overall in England in the same year at 16.6% (DfE, 1994b: Table 128). In the survey 86.6% were non-denominational compared with 83.4% for England as a whole, another way of showing that denominational schools were slightly under-represented, though not significantly so for Church of England schools; nor for Catholic schools in Scotland[7].

Denominational schools have always aroused some of the same objections as single-sex comprehensive schools, on the grounds that no school can be considered comprehensive if it selects by religion. That said, it is sometimes hard to distinguish between those who oppose compulsory religious teaching in schools, those who oppose denominational schools *per se* and those who object to denominational schools being classed as comprehensives. Some of those who oppose religious schools are members of religious organisations themselves, of course; their argument is that the world is multi-cultural and multi-faith and that churches should put their support into their communities rather than into maintaining segregated education for their own groups.

In recent decades the debate has got more heated as additional religious groups have asked that taxpayers fund their schools, although there have also been occasions when members of other world faiths, even when occupying most of the places in a given school, have indicated a preference for the school to remain with the LEA[8]. They believed that becoming a religious school further divided young people in a supposedly multi-cultural society.

Others argue that it is inherently unfair to fund comprehensive schools for Jews but not Muslims (the main major world religion making regular demands), even though there are only four state-funded Jewish secondary schools in the UK and even though repeated requests for more Jewish schools have not been met in recent years. Almost all denominational schools remain Church of England and Roman Catholic, and the majority of these are primary schools. The issue is still delicate enough for most governments to aim to keep the proportions much as they are.

Earlier history

After the conflagration over religious schooling at the start of the twentieth century (see Chapter 1) and the 'settlement' of the 1944 Act that formalised the 'dual' system, finding a place for aided schools in early comprehensive school plans was always a problem. When comprehensive reform began officially in 1965, in some cases there was genuine denominational enthusiasm for reorganisation, but in others it was more a recognition that if the churches failed to change, parents of children in Roman Catholic or Church of England secondary modern schools would desert to go to LEA-county comprehensives[9]. In some areas, especially for Church of England schools, the issue was funding[9]. In several areas the church was keen but the individual schools, run by orders and often selective, were not; and clashes occurred within the denominations (Benn and Simon, 1970:279).

During the early years Diocesan Boards often operated at arm's length from LEA education committees and there were problems when denominational schools went comprehensive with different schemes in the same areas. This was particularly the case with Catholic planning: all-through schools when the LEA had a sixth-form college; a sixth-form college where the LEA had all-through schools. Over the last 30 years, however, Catholic schools have been drawing closer to their LEAs and in areas of post-16 co-operation are taking part in consortia work in the same way as other schools (Hainsworth, 1986:16). Many Catholic schools answering the 1994 survey reported collaborative work with LEA schools and those in Scotland seemed particularly optimistic, one writing in the margin, 'Catholic Comprehensive Schools in Scotland are a great success'.

In the 1970s the Roman Catholic comprehensive sector was enlarged by the conversion of 48 former direct grant schools to aided status comprehensive schools, rewarded in some cases by writing off their debts to the state. Since then Roman Catholic private schools have occasionally been accepted for aided status as comprehensive schools, usually at primary stage; our 1994 survey had two which had been accepted as secondary comprehensive schools.

Conversions were nothing like as controversial as take-overs, however, practised for a short period in the late 1970s and early 1980s when the Church of England acted in co-operation with Conservative controlled LEAs, to 'buy' well-established LEA comprehensive schools and turn them into aided schools under Church of England control. There was little evidence of local demand for such schools in the areas concerned; and opposition in nearly all of them. In West London this included all opposition parties, all teachers' unions, all ethnic and minority groups represented on the local community council, the majority of parents and teachers in the school concerned, and local members of the Church of England clergy and laity. Opposition was on the grounds that such a school would be divisive in the community and no longer open to the many minority groups, including children from Jewish, Muslim, and Sikh families, or to those who had no religious affiliation. There was also fear expressed that entry would be dominated by white, middle-class families.

Their greatest resentment was over the fact that the taxpayer had to pay 85% of the Church's bill for these take-overs, showing that the embers of the argument that raged in the early part of the twentieth century have only to be lightly fanned, for the fire to flame high again. In the event, only a few such schools changed hands in this way and the policy was dropped as a Church-related project. Its significance, however, was that within a few years many of its key features returned in the Conservative Government's policy of 'opting out' (see pages 139–140).

Voluntary school admissions

Occasionally there have been one-off criticisms of individual denominational comprehensive schools for the authoritarian way they are run, with one researcher questioning whether the positive aspirations of comprehensivisation could flourish in such schools (Green, 1988). But such criticism has been rare. From the 1970s onwards the issue of greatest controversy has been admissions to voluntary comprehensive schools and how these affected county-LEA schools in the vicinity. The problem arose because after comprehensive reorganisation began, some voluntary schools – far from being the least favoured schools, as was often the case at the start of the century – became favoured in certain areas. Some put this down to their more disciplined ways or better academic results, but others saw the change arising out of hidden selection – academic, social and racial.

Complaints centred inevitably on legal concessions made to foundation governors, the most important and long standing being the right to run unilateral admissions, including the right to interview for 'religious' suitability in aided schools. It was claimed the interview was being used to select by attainment, a claim given substance by the fact that such a procedure was being actively advocated as a device for preserving selectivity in voluntary grammar schools by those who opposed comprehensive education.

Complaints that such rights were being misused by voluntary comprehensive schools to secure greater shares of high attaining pupils were frequently heard in the 1970s, and in London partly confirmed by the ILEA's own figures[10]. There were additional complaints that some voluntary comprehensive admissions policies favoured middle-class applications, and also white pupils[11], seemingly confirmed by the media, including the education correspondent of *The Times* who noted that 'voluntary aided schools are favoured by parents for the simple reason that they are less likely to have West Indian pupils in them'[12]. By the early 1980s there were specific complaints that church schools were 'faking' admissions numbers and misusing the 'practising Christian' criterion (Ball, 1984b:239). The parents' group, The Campaign for State Education (CASE), had passed a resolution at its annual conference in 1979 asking for a change in admissions powers for voluntary comprehensive schools because these could be used 'to undermine the comprehensive principle and the objective of multi-racial harmony'.

In 1981 the Runnymede Trust published evidence gathered nationally that showed that voluntary schools admissions arrangements were prejudicial to racial balance in several areas of the country and concluded that unless changes were made in admissions policies, voluntary schools 'will continue to remove a lot of white children, and a corps of children with a favourable distribution of ability, from other schools' (Dummett and McNeal, 1981).

Throughout the period the churches were responding with vigour and a great variety of publications (Catholic Commission for Racial Justice, *Catholic Education in a Multi-Racial Society*, 1981; Church of England National Society, *A Future in Partnership*, 1984; Gay, 1983; Catholic Media Office, *Learning From Diversity*, 1984). Some explained their unique position and in particular refuted any suggestion that their schools could be in any way racially biased. Other publications admitted that racial imbalances in their own schools were worrying them too. Or that covert selection for aided schools does sometimes go on ('Voluntary Schools', Digest series *Education*, 1985).

It soon became clear that the practices complained of were few and far between, and that there were active groups in both the Church of England and the Roman Catholic communities anxious to develop first-class comprehensive education in their schools and colleges, as well as to take hold of the opportunity to serve the areas where the schools were, including pupils of every background and race. Proof of the denominations' endeavour to fulfil the comprehensive principle is that although they made a slow beginning in going comprehensive in the 1970s, by the middle of the 1990s they had higher percentages of their schools in England with comprehensive status (94.9%) than applied in the county-LEA sector (92.8%) (DfE, 1994: Table 128[13]).

Denominational schools faced the same problems as non-denominational comprehensive schools, and gained the same successes. They were also as varied: some strict and formal and streamed, others pioneers in mixed ability teaching and open styles of learning; some working hard in the inner cities, others working hard in leafy suburbs. A great deal more unites denominational and non-denominational comprehensive schools than separates them.

Nevertheless, problems still continue in respect of certain practices in both denominational and voluntary comprehensive schools, made yet more complex by 'opting out'. Despite several government guidelines on admissions, a few denominational schools that became grant maintained continued to have their practices questioned. In 1994 one was criticised for its interview practices to see if the 'aims, attitudes, values and expectation of the parents and the boy are in harmony with those of the school' (*TES*, 9 December 1994). This practice could be (and probably was) used for social or attainment selection or both; on the other hand, the school could say it was doing no more than many education acts passed since 1979 have encouraged schools with aided (and now grant maintained) status to do, or that other schools with aided or grant maintained status were not also doing.

Although these practices are not seen in the great majority of schools and are certainly not confined to schools of denominational status, and often have developed inadvertently rather than by design, they are the inevitable outcome of a system where some schools have a legal status that gives them advantages denied to schools of a different legal status. The inherent instability of the situation is why so many in the community now argue that it is in the interests of all that basic legal rights should be harmonised across all schools as quickly as possible.

Denominational schools in 1994 – some findings

In the independent enquiry of 1968, denominational comprehensives, although they reported higher attainment levels on intake than non-denominational schools, nevertheless had fewer staying on after the leaving age, and were smaller schools overall, with smaller sixth forms. When it came to entering pupils for examinations at GCE and SCE O grade, both Church of England and Roman Catholic comprehensives had significantly lower percentages of pupils taking these examinations in almost every subject than was the case in non-denominational comprehensive schools (Benn and Simon, 1970: Table 5.6, p.84).

In 1994 findings show a few similarities, but a lot of differences. Still similar is the fact that voluntary schools and denominational schools are smaller than others. This applies particularly to the average size of Catholic schools and to the special agreement and voluntary aided categories. Church of England schools and voluntary controlled schools are larger but they are still smaller than the survey average (Table A5). In Table A6 we can see that the voluntary controlled schools also had the largest average first-year sixth form (113) compared with that of the special agreement schools at 77, the voluntary aided at 88 and the LEA county school of 96. The same differences continued into the seventh year (see Chapter 9).

As for attainment at intake, there were not many significant differences between denominational and non-denominational or between voluntary and county LEA schools. Voluntary attainment percentages were a little higher but none of the differences appeared to be significant (Table A5) except in the case of the six dual denominational schools – mostly Roman Catholic and Church of England working together – which had 22.4% of intake in the top 20% and a far higher staying-on rate (65%) than other denominational schools (Table A5).The staying-on rates inside all-through schools between Roman Catholic, Church of England and non-denominational comprehensive schools, however, showed almost no difference (55.6, 55.7 and 56.1, respectively).

Denominational voluntary schools as a whole were less likely to be grammar-based (only 22.9% of Roman Catholic and 18.1% of Church of England) compared with survey schools as a whole at 26% (question 9 A and C). The exception was voluntary controlled comprehensive schools which were more likely to be grammar-based, at 49%.

When it came to examination results at five GCSE A–C level, as Table

A5 shows, aided and controlled schools had higher performance percentages than the survey average of 40%, and so did both Roman Catholic and Church of England schools – with the Church of England at 42% and the dual denominational schools higher still with 57%. The situation for 'A' level point scores was not quite the same, however. Again, the Church of England schools (13.5) were highest, with county-LEA schools next (13.1), followed by Roman Catholic schools (11.9) and the dual denominational schools (10.0, but only two gave results).

One factor that might have a bearing on the Church of England comprehensive schools' academic scores is the fact that they had a very much higher proportion of schools with predominantly middle-class intakes than almost all other types of comprehensive school: 42% against a survey average of 26% (see Table A5). Only comprehensive schools drawing predominantly from areas of private housing had higher middle-class percentages. Roman Catholic schools, on the other hand, had lower percentages of schools drawing predominantly middle-class intakes: 17%. Even allowing for the social class intakes being estimates and the necessity (as with attainment intakes) of treating them as rough guides only, the difference between Catholic and Anglican intakes in respect of social class was one of the most striking findings of the survey.

Serving the community: changes in denominational schooling

Early on in reorganisation, when denominational schools were asked to talk about their comprehensive task, they spoke about serving their own faiths. Thus one Roman Catholic comprehensive school headteacher in 1972 spoke of teaching of the Catholic doctrine 'as central to the life of the school' and as the purpose of this comprehensive school (Cavanagh, 1972). Yet only 12 years later in the document, *Learning from Diversity*, published by the Catholic Bishops Conference, the suggestion was made that some Roman Catholic schools might 'define themselves ... as a service to the community which embodies the Catholic ethos without being ... denominational' (Catholic Media Office, 1984:21). Many Church of England comprehensive schools had been defining themselves in this way for some time.

Between these dates, Roman Catholic schools experienced falls in school population in line with reduced pupil numbers both nationally and in the Roman Catholic community, whose birthrate began moving closer to that of the population as a whole. A few Catholic comprehensives began adopting the practice of many Church of England schools by taking in pupils from outside their own denominations. Filling available places became even more necessary with formula funding and engineered enrolment in the later 1980s. Some from both denominations may also have been spurred by a general wish to show denominational schools responding to the needs of minority groups in the community, inside or outside their faith.

Some denominational schools therefore began admitting those of other world religions, conscious that other faiths wanted their own schools and could not have them. Becoming schools for 'those with faith' was more common in Church of England schools, which had a much longer tradition of serving as the 'local' school. It was the more regrettable, therefore, that a group of white parents refused to allow their children to attend a Church of England comprehensive school on the grounds that so many of the pupils were non-Christian, and that these parents became media heroes for insisting on another school. It was equally worrying that the Christian Brothers in Birmingham in 1995 voted to close St Philips Sixth Form College because the numbers of Asian students were so high. For after the age of 16, most sixth form, tertiary and further education colleges have been particularly concerned to operate without any religious bias or segregation – even to the point where one of the early tertiary colleges suggested that it should avoid even having a specifically Christian carol service so as not to discourage non-whites or non-Christians from coming to the college (Janes *et al.*, 1985:95–96).

Nowadays the accent in colleges – as in many schools – is one of celebrating society's diversity of religions, life stances and cultures, whether they are represented in the college or not. In a few colleges this tolerance is abused by aggressive proselytising campaigns on behalf of certain sectarian religious interests from both Christian and other world faiths, which can be as destructive as similar campaigns from organised racist groups.

In view of the growing general interest in cultural accommodation (despite a National Curriculum that has tried to play on a mono-cultural theme), the 1994 Survey tried to discover how closely denominational comprehensive schools stuck to intakes from their own faiths (as is usually assumed) and the extent to which they were open to others. The 180 respondents to questions 23 and 24 replied as follows:

(a) reserves places mostly for school's own denomination: 108 (60%);
(b) welcomes practising Christians outside school's denomination: 109 (61%);
(c) welcomes pupils of other word faiths: 53 (29%);
(d) welcomes pupils regardless of beliefs: 60 (33%);

(e) welcomes pupils from the immediate area: 63 (35%).

Only 15 schools used denominational membership as their sole criterion for admission (question 19J), although 40 reserved places mostly for members of the school's own denomination ((a) above) and had no other admissions criterion. At the other end of the scale, 16 schools had entirely open entry regardless of belief – (d) above – and no other admissions criterion.

The vast majority, however, had more than one criterion, including 61% willing to accept practising Christians from outside the denomination, plus a third willing to accept pupils regardless of their beliefs, and the same percentage accepting them from the neighbourhood. Well over a quarter also welcomed pupils from other world faiths.

However, there were considerable differences between the two main denominations: 76% of Roman Catholic comprehensives reserved places mainly for pupils of their own faith, compared with only 15% of Church of England schools. Church of England schools were also more likely to welcome other practising Christians (52%) and other world faiths (one-third compared with just over one-fifth of Roman Catholic schools). As for welcoming those with no declared faith, over half the Church of England comprehensive schools did so (52%), compared with only 17% of Catholic schools. And in serving the immediate area, only a quarter of Catholic schools had such a policy compared with a third of Church of England schools. How far these differences were because the Church of England was more open to non-members rather than because membership of the Church of England is harder to determine (or because more Church of England comprehensives were selecting on some other grounds), is hard to say.

Denominational schools were much more likely to be full at entry in September of our survey than non-denominational schools: Catholic schools at 58.0% and Church of England at 57.6% compared with a survey average of 39.8%. Again, how closely were these figures related to policies of welcoming in those from other denominations and faiths?

A higher percentage of Roman Catholic schools that were full reserved themselves for Roman Catholic pupils only than those not full (80–70%); while a higher percentage of those that were not full admitted regardless of faith than those that were full (24% compared with only 12%) – with much the same percentages applying to admitting pupils who lived locally. Church of England comprehensives that were full also admitted smaller percentages of pupils from other faiths than those that were not full (29% as against 39%), and smaller percentages of those living locally (42% as against 61%).

It is easy to be cynical and see the changes as a result of having too many empty places and deciding to relax entry rules in order to remain full, but this would be to miss an important change that appears to have taken place in the willingness of denominational schools to take in pupils both from other Christian faiths and those of other world faiths: Jews, Sikhs, Muslims, not to mention taking in those regardless of faith or those who live locally. To find so many denominational schools welcoming pupils from outside their denomination, even when full, is relatively new. To find Roman Catholic comprehensives taking pupils regardless of religious views (17%) and welcoming those of non-Christian faiths (22%) would have been very unusual 30 years ago.

It points to an important change in denominational schools in relation to their role in the community. At the same time, it would be unwise to pretend it is a change that has gone very far. There is a willingness to accept others in principle, but not necessarily always in great numbers: 53% took fewer than 5% from outside their denomination; on the other hand, 28% took over 50%. As is to be expected for the official 'state' religion, Church of England comprehensives had higher percentages of schools taking in pupils from outside its own denomination: 51% took in 35% or more, compared with only 9% of Catholic schools taking this high a percentage. Three-quarters of all Roman Catholic comprehensives had intakes where at least 85% were Roman Catholic; but only 30% of Church of England did.

The opening up of denominational education is an interesting idea in an age of diversity and could be a significant trend, where denominations run schools in the spirit and practice of their own religion but are not necessarily only for those of that religion (the way many American denominational schools have been run in the last 30 years). In many cases it will be members of the school's faith who choose to go, but increasingly the way will be open to respond to community needs as they present themselves, including the needs of those of other faiths with no 'schools' of their own, not to mention the needs of the school's own neighbourhood. Although Rutter found that voluntary status was not a factor in school effectiveness (Rutter *et al.*, 1979), many parents have positive views of voluntary schools as socially well-ordered.

What would kill off such developments as well as prolong the old voluntary argument well into the twenty-first century, would be using denominational choice as a cover for social and attainment selection. This is still a danger in some voluntary and denominational schools, particularly where religious tests are applied that go beyond the religion.

In the long run it does no denomination any good to have it suggested so often that parents regularly pretend to a religion they do not believe to enter their child in a school it runs. Pretending religious belief was a practice particularly deplored by a group of Anglican, non-conformist and Catholic educators who met in the early 1980s, united by a common commitment to comprehensive education. They wrote, 'we... repudiate selection on grounds of class, ability, race or income' (including private denominational education). At the same time they expressed support for the view that within the operation of the comprehensive principle, 'people ... have a right to full enjoyment of education within their own culture'. It is not a view shared by all but put in this way perhaps it is a view that can be respected by all.

CTC and grant maintained comprehensive schools

Although City Technology Colleges (CTCs) have sometimes claimed to be comprehensive, none chose to participate in the survey.

The creation of yet another legal status for CTC schools was originally announced in 1986, when the Government planned for 300 such schools to be established all over Britain. However, only 15 have ever been started largely because funding was not forthcoming from the 1800 business firms approached by the Government to pay their capital costs. Most large (and many small) corporations had already chosen to forge links with local comprehensive schools and to make any funding available to them (see Chapters 5 and 8).

CTC schools are classed as private schools, which means loyalty to sponsors and clients and none to local communities. Yet 100% of CTC running costs are paid by the taxpayer, and now these schools are back on the taxpayer's payroll for most of their capital funding as well. The spending inequalities their creation has caused have been spectacular in many areas. Avon saw £8m of taxpayers money spent on a single CTC in a single year with only £ 4.5m given to serve the capital needs of *all* the rest of its local schools, working out at a mere few hundred pounds a school. An editorial in the *Times Educational Supplement* (27 May 1988) was especially critical of the extent of state support for the Djanogly CTC in Nottingham: 'just what sort of priorities are being pursued when one... private school gets £9.05 million and the county of Nottinghamshire's entire capital allocation is less than £2.5 million?' Expenditure on funding their controlling bureaucracy has been even more spectacular. Just three CTCs had more money spent on them by the Government in 1988–89 than was spent on introducing the National Curriculum to 30,000 schools (Chitty, 1989a:40).

Entrants to CTCs are supposed to agree to stay to the age of 18 and thus the schools are sometimes seen as progressive alternatives to the old selective schools (Edwards *et al.*, 1993), designed to give the UK a network of élite technical schools to provide the new 'clerkly' class to fill the middle positions in the new technologically oriented industries. They have also been given legal prerogatives like powers to select admissions and to disregard strict implementation of the National Curriculum. They can adopt such measures as extended days. Some of these concessions are a licence to innovate that might have been beneficial to many LEA comprehensive schools.

There is widespread support to return CTC schools to the public domain, if only to ensure that their facilities are available as widely as possible in their local areas, and that their work – for example, on the Technological Baccalaureate, a 14–18 learning programme – is integrated with the rest of secondary development. Another British generation cannot afford yet another failure with its 'technical' schools. While CTC schools remain isolated enclaves, perpetually cited as examples of a policy that never took off, this is the risk.

Grant maintained schools

Currently the most controversial of the schools with new legal status are the grant maintained (GM) schools, a sector created by encouraging existing LEA county and voluntary schools to operate outside their local school communities (in the manner of the old direct grant schools) and 'bid' for the schools on behalf of those parents currently using them. Many schools were given extra funding as a reward (or inducement) for taking themselves out of community provision. In fact, in the 3 years between 1989 and 1992, more in 'ear marked funding' was spent on helping a few hundred schools to opt out than had been spent on helping thousands of schools to go comprehensive from 1965 to 1979 (LSI, *Newsletters*, 1993)[14].

The GM schools' legal status provided other privileges too, such as running their own admissions systems without having to take account of the system used by the rest of the local school community (the same prerogative that had been causing so many problems for comprehensive education in the voluntary sector). Not unexpectedly, Margaret Thatcher cited this specific admissions advantage and related it to the choice such opted-out comprehensive schools could make later, if they wished, which was to become selective schools. The long-term purpose of reviving selection by giving such schools separate legal status was thus made clear from the start.

Laws were soon in place to permit GM schools to ask the Secretary of State to change their admissions arrangements from comprehensive to selective; or, less directly, to permit them to use the admissions privileges relating to interviewing and reserving special places, to choose parents and children of higher attainments (or 'better' backgrounds), or, when full, to choose increasingly selectively. Selection could start the moment applicants began exceeding places under new engineered enrolment legislation, another change that took place at much the same time.

GM schools are like voluntary aided schools in relation to admissions privileges, but with this difference: most voluntary aided schools are denominational and first among their several commitments is to educate their own community, whatever the attainment, class, or background. This is especially true of most Roman Catholic schools and those Church of England schools which have committed themselves to serving their local communities as comprehensive schools, as so many have. There is thus a built-in protection in the way of many such schools becoming selective; though there are notorious exceptions.

Among GM schools there is no such built-in protection because there is no loyalty other than to self-interest, the 'new' GM tradition. The most reliable research to date suggests that nearly a third of the comprehensives to opt out of local authority control by 1991 took advantage of their position and were operating some form of selective admissions system (Bush *et al.,* 1993:95)[15].

The introduction of GM schools aroused passions and argument beyond what might rationally have been expected, which even the national media, never particularly partial to comprehensive education, has had to reflect. The roots of this opposition were not merely because such schools could assist 11-plus selection to return, they were much deeper. They could be traced back through the hostility to Church take-overs of local schools in the early 1980s (see page 129) to the original 'dual system' introduced in the early part of the twentieth century; even, ultimately, to the Endowed Schools Commission's decision in the nineteenth century to convert schools originally set up to serve the poor without payment, into a 'new' legal status of schools for the fee-paying middle classes.

There was the same deep outrage that schools have been given over to unaccountable oligarchies who could convert them into privileged enclaves, compounded by the knowledge that the community must still pay, for, as in earlier controversies, there was particular opposition to the fact that taxpayers' support would be required for schools which were not to be accessible in the way local LEA schools were. What made the new GM schools even more controversial was that none of their operations was open and above ground in the local community; no GM school had to account to anyone other than itself for its intake policy, expenditure, or use of national resources. None had any obligation to take any local child, no matter how near the child may live to the school; and no one in any area has any right to call upon any GM schools for education. They were entirely unaccountable in a supposedly democratic system.

There would have been a great deal more opposition if the government had not – at the same time as ushering in GM status to undermine local authorities and introduce privatisation within the system – also acted to give LEA schools themselves a greater measure of 'independence' through Local Management of Schools (LMS). Not the same amount of it as GM schools; but enough to give LEA schools more control over their own finances and ethos and freedom from petty restrictions, even if this was at the cost of losing the larger protection of the LEA in some areas, the planning of the LEA, and some of the key services of the LEA. These losses were promoted as increased freedom for all. In reality, changes meant less democracy for all within the education service as a whole, as many LEA schools soon discovered; and as the community as a whole has slowly come to realise.

GM comprehensive schools

But not all GM schools wanted to leave their obligations to their local community behind. Not all wanted to become selective schools; after all, a few opted out in order to retain their comprehensive character in those local authorities trying to force local schools back into selective arrangements. Others were trying to escape the consequences of long overdue attempts to rationalise numbers in a system with many unfilled places, where they were threatened with amalgamation because their numbers were low. Others have opted out, it is said, simply to get a bit more money than is available to the school down the road. They have no wish to leave comprehensive education behind.

Whatever the reasons they chose grant maintained status, the GM schools that took part in the 1994 Survey positively wished to identify themselves as comprehensive schools and many made this plain in written statements attached to their returns. They were almost certainly less selective than GMs overall, as is suggested by their academic results in this survey, which were markedly different from those for GM schools as a whole in national figures (see Appendix II, note B).

As can also be seen, survey comprehensive schools overall had higher scores than comprehensives did nationally, a difference largely accounted for by the fact that many survey figures included Scotland, probably did not include a full share of inner city schools, but did include GM schools that were comprehensive, which national statistics no longer do. Because of these and other differences, comparisons of survey and national figures were not meaningful, however useful survey figures were for comparison between different types of comprehensive schools within the survey itself (see Tables A5 and A6).

For some, however, league table figures are discredited even for these purposes, since they can just as easily be seen not as indicators of how good a school is but of how selective a school is. This conclusion was drawn by the *Times Educational Supplement* (9 December 1994) when discussing a controversial GM school by citing its five GCSE A–C percentage of 54% (high for a comprehensive school in an inner city) and calling the school 'as selective and élitist as you can get while still being officially a state comprehensive'. This percentage was higher than schools of the same legal status in its general area and suggested a good degree of selectivity; but it was not a fully selective school. In the 1994 survey 204 of the participating schools (14%) had higher percentages for 5 GCSE A–C or Standard Grade 1–3 and eight had percentages greater than 90%; the majority were GM or aided, but a few were LEA schools.

The position for GM schools was different at 'A' level in the 1994 survey. Despite individual high results, overall figures were less favourable with a grade point average of 11.9 compared with 12.7 for comprehensive schools and colleges as a whole, lower than the figure in national statistics for GM schools that same year (see Appendix II). Two explanations have been offered for this from the schools themselves:

1. That the GM schools identifying themselves as comprehensives for the survey were likely to include a large number of schools due to close because of small sixth forms (which were reprieved through granting of GM status).
2. A fair number of sixth forms newly added to former 11–16 schools and not yet fully established, since a greater proportion of GM schools receive permission to add sixth forms than do LEA schools.

These factors might well explain some of the difference at 'A' level between

GM and LEA performance in the 1994 survey, but not all of it. A gap this wide also suggested that among the GM schools not represented in the 1994 survey were some very selective schools indeed. This can be confirmed in part by official statistics showing the GM sector with a far larger proportion of official grammar schools than the LEA sector: 13.7% compared with 4.7% (DfE, 1994b: Table 128)[16]; and this is before we start counting GM schools that are still officially comprehensive but with varying degrees of selectivity.

The GM system is not a grammar sector, as is so often assumed; it is a duplicate secondary system with its own continuum of selectivity, much more heavily weighted toward the selective end than the continuum of the LEA sector. In the 1994 survey we saw its less selective end.

Other differences

GM schools are a parallel educational universe and their comprehensive sector was probably fairly accurately represented in the 1994 survey (because it excluded all official grammar schools and possibly a good proportion of schools that were highly selective but still officially comprehensive). At first sight, therefore, GM comprehensive schools in the 1994 survey did not stand out as so very different from LEA schools that they must be ruled out of the comprehensive category. Yet overall they had a great many special features that differentiated them from schools in the survey's LEA sector. Individually each difference was not definitive; but when put all together, the character of the GM comprehensive sector emerged in a different light.

At first sight, many features of the two sectors were the same. GM schools' sixth form years were the same size as LEA schools and so was their average for the percentage of students entered for two or more 'A' levels (56% GMs and 57% LEA schools) (Table A6). Their staying-on rate to the sixth form in all-through schools was not much different either (57.5% compared with 55.5% for LEA schools). Overall their examination results (see above) could not be said to be better or worse.

Some of the differences that did exist were rather slight, but possibly in time significant. For example, the percentage of their intake in the top 20% of the attainment range was higher at 18.5% than the average for LEA schools of 16.6% – not a great deal higher, but higher. Their social class composition was different in that a greater proportion of GM schools had predominantly middle-class compositions than did the survey's schools and colleges as a whole (33.9% as against 26.4%) – as well as significantly lower percentages of working-class intakes (49.6% as against 61.0%). Nevertheless, voluntary controlled and Church of England comprehensive schools both had higher percentages with middle-class intakes, and so, by a much larger margin, did sixth-form colleges (see Tables A5 and A6). GM schools were not the most middle class, though they were near the top.

It was not in these more usually mentioned indicators that we see differences so much as in those that are less noticed. For example, a smaller proportion of GM school's (34.6%) were of the 11–16 age range compared with LEA schools (41.3%); theirs were more likely to be the prestigious all-through schools and for this reason their average size of 910 was larger than comprehensive schools of every other legal status, even larger than sixth-form colleges. Then too a larger percentage of GM comprehensives (30.7%) were formerly grammar schools (question 9A–C) than LEA schools (24.2%). GM comprehensive schools were in better physical shape than LEA comprehensive schools with 39% in the 'good repair' category (question 67 A) compared with 30% of LEA schools.

Possibly even more significant were the next group of differences – not just because the gap between GM and LEA schools was large but because of the nature of the categories. GM schools had far fewer poor entrants than LEA schools, e.g. 46% of LEA schools had intakes where at least 16% were taking free dinners, compared with only 28% of GM comprehensive schools. In fact, GM schools had the lowest percentage of any legal status in the survey for free dinners (Table A5). A smaller percentage of GM schools than the survey average had high percentages of pupils from other cultures and nationalities, like Afro-Caribbean or Pakistani pupils; and a very much smaller percentage of GM schools than overall offered places to pupils coming from schools for those with SEN and other special needs. GM schools were also much less likely to share school premises with the community than other types of comprehensive school.

Some of the many differences cited stem from decisions made in day-to-day practice or school policy and some arise from engineered enrolment legislation which means that when oversubscription is reached, selection may begin in a GM school much more easily than in an LEA one. It does not have to, but the way is open. How many GM comprehensive schools will be taking this road in future, driven to compete without wishing to do so or forced to use this advantage against neighbouring schools in the present 'competitive' market system, and how many will simply drift into selection or greater exclusiveness without design, we cannot know. There are no regular statistics about GM admissions and intakes – any more than

144

there are for private schools. Yet GM schools are fully funded by public money. Some would thus see publication of such figures – or those for free dinners – as having the same importance as 'league table' figures, another example of information required in the public domain (see pages 48–49).

The GM differences revealed in the 1994 survey were not yet great enough for us to conclude that such schools were undermining the comprehensive principle in ways that other types of comprehensive schools might not also have been doing. If the line were held at 1994, and involved only that sector of GM schools that are comprehensive (such as those responding to our survey), there could be a case for accepting GM status and seeking improvements and equalisation by persuasion and practice and regulation changes. But we have not seen the full GM picture in this survey. Nor can we be sure that the same factors that have pushed other GM schools into ever greater academic and social selectivity will not also push these 1994 survey schools in the same direction over time.

Taking the long-term view, therefore, there are enough important differences between GM and other comprehensive schools overall within the survey to suggest that many of these schools are very likely to become increasingly selective over a wide range of grounds. We thus conclude that GM status is probably not compatible with comprehensive education in the long run. On the other hand, with effective (and relatively simple) legislation, most existing GM schools themselves could easily become so (see Chapter 10).

Comprehensive boarding – the line between private and state

Boarding accommodation within state education was well established long before comprehensive reorganisation began (Lambert, 1966) and from the start was included in the comprehensive reform – if only because certain of the earliest comprehensive schools, such as Crown Woods in London or King Edward VI in Devon, had boarding wings. Boarding was being discussed widely during the early years of comprehensive reorganisation because the Public Schools Commission was deliberating about integrating private education, including boarding, with the new comprehensive education system.

In 1968 the first independent enquiry found several comprehensive boarding facilities under-used (Benn and Simon, 1970:294). At the same time many examples of what was called 'unmet' boarding need were reported and some comprehensive school heads estimated that 2% of their pupils needed boarding at some time in their school lives. Using traditional boarding education was difficult because the basis upon which private schools had always encouraged state-supported pupils was almost always related to selection by attainment. This applied to private boarding and day schools as well as to most state boarding facilities.

From the start, therefore, apart from trying to get more boarding establishments (both state and private) to offer places related to boarding need – or a wish for boarding – regardless of academic attainment, those working in comprehensive education encouraged comprehensive schools to expand their own boarding facilities. They also worked to diversify boarding itself, for boarding needs in the population as a whole were recognised to be incredibly diverse. Sometimes boarding was needed for a year when family problems loomed, round-the-clock care at particular stages of development; or for purposes of intensive study at key points in a secondary course when the home could not provide the support required. There was no reason why all boarding education had to be 5 or 6 long years full-time far away from home in a traditional public school regime (which state boarding all too often imitated), when some boarding need was for short-term boarding or weekly boarding, or simply occasional boarding and might easily be provided in the area where the pupil lived; attached to a day school or through the co-operation of several schools.

This is when experiments began in smaller units attached to comprehensive schools. The Owl House in the Abraham Moss Community Education Centre in the middle of Manchester was an example: 12 students, 2 staff, 'family style' living (see *Comprehensive Education* No. 41, 1980). Young people with varying needs were accommodated, staying for varying periods of time. Many were pupils in local schools.

Other sorts of boarding accommodation involved facilities purchased by LEAs outside towns where pupils from the towns requiring a short spell of study free from the distractions of inner city life could be accommodated (Newcastle upon Tyne experiment). Then there was the boarding involving field study centres owned by LEAs or individual schools, where everyone in the school went for short periods to study or to take part in outdoor activities. There were hundreds of such centres at one time, many now likely to have become commercial establishments selling leisure facilities, sold off as part of the first line of spending cuts in the late 1970s.

A last category of need (met much more frequently in other countries) was boarding for students living in really remote areas like off-shore islands, where travel to the nearest large secondary school was impossible on a daily basis, and hostel accommodation was required. Several areas of Scotland, for example, had and still have, such arrangements and at the time of our first survey nearly 2000 Scots pupils were boarding in this way (Benn and Simon, 1970:295).

In 1968 the Public Schools Commission recommended an enlarged version of selective boarding, which involved private schools selecting suitable state pupils for the entire length of their secondary lives (Public Schools Commission, First Report 1968). Once again Britain was a generation too late, for it was a plan that might have survived in 1944. In 1968, however, with the system becoming comprehensive, any boarding offer – indeed, any offer to co-operate with state education on the part of private schools – had to be compatible with the comprehensive principle. The proposals (also unpopular with many private schools) fell to the ground. Only the Second Report of 1970 produced any result, the authors having grasped the point that private day schools wishing to retain a connection to the state, as many did, had to adjust to the comprehensive principle in some form.

During this time many state boarding units, which had their own association (STABIS) formed for the purpose of accommodating boarders for whom the taxpayer paid (like the children of military officers), had to make decisions themselves about whether to end selection, whether to have more mixed boarding, and whether to encourage more units attached to comprehensive day schools. These were changes to meet the wishes of what many called 'the newer type of parent' (Governing Bodies Association/ Headmasters Conference, 1969:3), who wanted their children boarding in schools that were part of a local community rather than locked away in a 'hothouse' or in the sometimes alien atmosphere of the 'public school' (Benn and Simon, 1970:295).

Just at this point in the development of state boarding, the axe of spending cuts descended on public services and state boarding capacity was the first LEA asset to go. In 1978 there were 108 state boarding facilities; today there are just 41 left (STABIS, 1993), several of which were included in the 1994 survey. After a period of about a dozen years, boarding within the private sector also began to fall. Since 1990 it has dropped by 20% (ISIS, 1995). What remains includes much traditional boarding in both state and private sectors. STABIS puts out a market-oriented brochure that claims most of its schools are for the 'usual boarding customer', making no secret about who these are: those who want a 'high quality alternative to independent' education or those 'who wish to find an alternative to their local school' (STABIS, 1993).

All signs point to the old objective of providing state facilities that mirror private ones, and few to that flexible and wide-ranging boarding service comprehensive schools previously hoped might be established. Certainly little points in the direction of some of the boarding experiments in other comprehensive systems – like the 1-year-away Eftersckole movement in Denmark[17]. Nor has the percentage of publicly financed boarding units which are comprehensive changed much in the last 20 years. In 1978, 57% of LEA boarding was comprehensive while the rest was grammar school boarding; 17 years later state boarding is only 68% comprehensive.

Nevertheless, there have been some changes over 30 years ago. Almost all the schools are mixed sex and most are operating as wings or sections of day schools. Few are full LEA schools any more, being mostly grant maintained or voluntary aided. Almost all are in shire counties or pleasant towns, with almost none in the middle of large conurbations. Access to facilities for that old 'unmet need', which if anything has grown in the meantime, is still unlikely to be provided for any more than a fraction of those who might benefit.

With state boarding fees of £3,000 to £4,000, such schools are, of course, unaffordable by the majority unless taxpayers pay the bills, which in many cases they do. Thus many of these schools (as well as private boarding schools) survive on state and LEA money subsidising boarding education for particular groups of society. Just who these groups are is anything but a comprehensive story, as countless previous accounts have already shown (*Comprehensive Education*, No. 41, 1980; Pring, 1983; Walford, 1990:76).

LEAs had long-standing traditions of fee-paying for certain privileged categories of pupils – compatible with a system that was selective but not with one that became comprehensive. Yet many such practices continued in the 1970s with most people knowing very little about those who benefited. The grounds were fairly restricted and based on old customs: e.g. they were children of Church of England chaplains or Army officers, or in need of denominational education (provided they passed selective tests), or 'good' at music, or with parents who travelled in their work (except, of course, those whose parents were travellers). Some LEAs paid over £1m for boarding fees or for placing pupils in private schools. Most were Conservative authorities but some were Labour, including the ILEA. Most had spare places in their schools and therefore the buying represented places twice paid for. All the places were more costly than state education and the bill for LEA place-buying ran to over £40 million a year by 1979. We have this information because at that time LEAs were required to send returns to central government. After 1979 the Government dropped this requirement (another of those pieces of information the public have a right to know).

Other public payments are national – direct from central government to private or STABIS secondary schools or to the parents of children chosen to attend such schools. First, the controversial Assisted Places Scheme started in 1980, entirely based on selection. This now involves about 30,000 and costs over £100m per year. The Scheme was supposed to benefit poorer and working-class children but research has shown that most of those benefiting are middle class (even if some are cash strapped) and at least half have siblings who are feepayers in private education already (those that are not cash strapped). Fewer than 10% of places go to children of manual workers (Edwards *et al.*, 1989:161). It was followed by another government scheme started in 1981 called Aided Places, paying fees averaging £4,000 per pupil in private schools specialising in the arts. There are no published figures about what kind of pupils get these places. The cost to the taxpayer was £2.9m in 1986 and would be well over £3m now (Walford, 1990:76).

A far larger taxpayers' bill has to be met paying fees for the children of senior government civil servants (like those in the Foreign Office) for private or boarding education in the UK (regardless of whether the parent is serving in the UK or outside it); and for private day-school education abroad (regardless of type of public education provision the country has). In recent decades there has been no consideration of education for these children by other less costly means, including attendance at state schools in the UK, while boarding with relatives; much less whether the parents, who are well paid, might pay for their children's education themselves. At last count almost every one of the 400 plus HMC public schools in Britain was on the list of those getting public payments for the 2000 separate full fees involved[18].

The largest taxpayer sums, however, are reserved for subsidies for military families' children. There are several small programmes for selected pupils who will embark on a military career but the largest spending is for allowances to military personnel to pay the boarding education fees for their children, some in the state boarding schools, including some which are comprehensive, but also in those which are private: 22,000 such payments were made in 1978, 75% going to the officer class (who constituted about 15% of military personnel).

These payments were (and are) made despite the fact that there were comprehensive schools in the areas where such personnel worked in military bases in Britain; and comprehensive schools provided by the Services Children Education Authority (SCEA) at several bases overseas. These SCEA secondary schools were some of the most enthusiastic recruits to comprehensive education in the 1960s and 1970s, and were hoping for the participation of the officer class, as they developed. They did not get it: 'We should be honest and say that in most BFES schools...the officer class is missing' (*SCEA Journal*, No. 13, 1977). They are still missing and the cost of their separate boarding education in Britain is currently £113 million a year (*Hansard*, 23 February 1995:567).

Some of those being subsidised in the many ways mentioned so far will have genuine need, but those who have studied private education and its subsidies regard the majority of such payments as 'highly controversial' privileges for those who can either afford to pay their own fees or for those who have excellent schools, state and private, available to them locally or abroad. They have expressed surprise that year on year these taxpayers' payments 'have largely gone unquestioned' by the British public (Walford, 1990:75). That these practices undermine comprehensive education is almost the least of it; they are absorbing millions which might be spent on schools overall, or on boarding for more of those who really need it. They represent old social perks devised for situations that no longer exist; as one MP commented in 1995 when Parliament was discussing the escalating boarding payments to military children at a time when the military numbers were being cut back, they are simply a 'hangover from the days of empire'[19].

Hangovers too are the tax exemptions that go to so many fee-paying schools on the grounds that they are charities, a perennial point of complaint that many forget has already been put to a Parliamentary Committee on Charities. Sitting under the late Lord Goodman, the Committee produced a unanimous Report in 1976 recommending that charity status be withdrawn from any school which was unable to show itself as meeting the 'need of the community as a whole'. This then is a proposal waiting to be acted upon, possibly providing a new *modus vivendi* for bridging private and state sectors in the future. It would have to be on a new basis of mutual benefit rather than on the old basis of private education undermining the state sector by taking both its funding and its high attaining pupils, while offering these few students only one option: fully signed-up life in private education for the whole of the secondary span.

It is unlikely that a single new solution could be devised of the type that the Public Schools Commission tried to organise. The schools on both sides are too diverse. If fruitful collaboration is ever to occur, the arrangements will have to stem from successful individual experiments, out of which practice could be constructed. They might mean private schools which wish to earn their charity status competing to provide programmes that state comprehensive schools might wish to take up on terms that state schools and their LEAs could afford; such as:

- short periods with or without boarding for academic, sporting or cultural activity, using facilities or expertise available;
- intensive study-courses just prior to public examinations;
- holiday or half-term boarding for a comprehensive school's own purposes, using its own programmes and staff;
- post-school sessions during the week.

The possibilities are many. Nor need the traffic be one way.

The capacity for arrangements of mutual benefit is as large as it suits schools to undertake, given needs that comprehensive schools might identify and a general requirement for schools enjoying 'charity' status to earn it by providing for the 'whole community' as recommended by the Report. Whatever forms of co-operation are mooted (and many will be in the coming years) criteria for considering them are what matters. For they would have to include meeting a genuine need identified by comprehensive schools, making sure pupils benefited across the board and across the attainment range, and ensuring that comprehensive schools choose the pupils themselves. Any scheme that smacked of the traditional forms of co-operation where the state's role was to subsidise the private sector while it augments academic or social selection within the system, and undermines the public service, would not survive.

Most schemes would have to seek compromises between those who favour state support for independent schools and those who support the full development of comprehensive state education, many of whom from both sides would disown most such schemes. Yet compromise becomes easier as anger continues to mount over the decline in state support for schools in the public sector and over the continuing contempt shown for teachers' collective professional activity. There is anger too at the 'league table' mechanism, which, after all, is forced on private schools as well, where many that give a caring education with its own type of excellence, whether in special schools or other kinds, are downgraded publicly by the same partial exam criteria as downgrade certain caring, hard-working comprehensive schools with so many other types of achievement to record.

As for the more prestigious private schools, including the public schools, their orientation has changed in recent years. Not long ago such schools saw themselves, and were seen by many, as institutions with a mission of public service, valuable social assets with a national role (Lambert, 1966). Imperceptibly over the last 30 years that old mission and role has sometimes been abandoned under commercial and competitive pressure, as those who study such schools have been quick to point out, one commenting that nowadays some top schools are seen (and see themselves) simply as 'exam mills' (Walford, 1990:55). Many comprehensives are struggling against becoming such themselves. Who knows what common commitment to education as something beyond statistical grading – to do with individuals developing themselves as human beings and communities developing themselves collectively – might not unite a few institutions so many assume to be irreconcilable.

Community education

From the start comprehensive education has been about serving the community – not just a school's or college's own parents or students but the area in which they all live and the democratic community more widely.

In most areas comprehensive schools and colleges have been well accepted and enjoy good relations with their wider communities, including their local media. Anti-comprehensive reporting on comprehensive education has been confined largely to certain sections of the national media and, as has often been observed, most comprehensive schools and colleges do not relate such negative comment to themselves.

Local media coverage, as we saw earlier, has been quite different (see pages 29–34) and in general the 1994 survey bore this out when it asked schools and colleges whether they had received any special publicity in the media over the previous year (question 88): 87% of schools and colleges said they had, almost all of it in the local or regional press, or in local broadcasting; 82% of those who had had attention, said reporting had been 'supportive' of their efforts.

Not that schools and colleges had no negative feelings about the media in 1994. Only 57% believed the media reports had been informative about them, while 17% had had a mixed experience, sometimes helpful, sometimes misleading. However, only 10% had experienced the media as wholly misleading and only 8% found them wholly unhelpful.

As was suggested earlier, local reporting of comprehensive education, while largely supportive, has not allowed real space to discuss some of the important issues that arise – in a rational and non-threatening way – any more than the national media has. Both have been dominated by thinking from the political right – as if this corner was the only one producing new ideas. Thus both national and local reporting need the same injection of genuine critical enquiry that reflects the range of opinions and experiences of education within communities. Britain is a long way from achieving this.

Types of community education

When comprehensive reorganisation began, the use of the word 'community' for a comprehensive school was almost axiomatic and often meant little more than making its premises available occasionally to others, or organising pupils for community activity in the area (Daunt, 1975). Over the years community practices and experiments have grown, and with them an increasingly sophisticated philosophy of community and its relationship to the concept of social and educational change (Fairbairn, 1980; Fletcher *et al.*, 1985; Midwinter, 1971; Moon, 1983). Inevitably, some of this thinking has laid on comprehensive education tasks that were not always easy to fulfil. Hargreaves, for example (Hargreaves, 1982), looked to comprehensive education to reverse the culture of competitive individualism and revitalise inner-city communities being destroyed by commercial redevelopment, the kind of task that takes a little longer than a school generation and even then depends upon the type of education system being developed and the policies used within schools and colleges.

Over the 30 years a wide variety of models for 'community' education have been developed within comprehensive education, the word having even more meanings than the word 'comprehensive'. In the 1994 survey our question on community was in the section on legal status (question 4) and most gave their legal status but failed to add whether they were also community schools or colleges. Those that did were largely purpose built 11–16 schools in countryside areas but they were only a small percentage of those who claimed to be community schools or colleges in the survey, demonstrated by the use of 'community' in their names and by identifying themselves as such in written answers to questions. Some assumed their version of community was everyone else's; thus one, listing groups using the school – like the scouts and pensioners – added, 'the sharing you would expect in a Community School'. But this school's sharing was little different from hundreds of schools that did not regard themselves as community schools.

Recent legal changes have added some versions of community that are fundamentally opposed to traditional views of schools and their relationship to the community in terms of 'ownership'. In the traditional view, seeing that a school or college is used by the local community is one version of 'community'. Many feel strongly that educational premises should be made available to the public because the buildings are a publicly provided resource. This attitude clashes fundamentally with the new 'opted out' philosophy that the premises and buildings belong to the current governors, and that no-one else has any rights respecting them. It also clashes with the 'market' view that premises and facilities are there to be used for money-making by the school or college currently occupying them – to supplement the failing state.

To see how much of the traditional view of community remained the 1994 survey asked all schools and colleges to what extent they shared their premises with others (not counting any sharing that was commercial letting) (question 86): 68.9% of schools and colleges were involved in sharing facilities or premises with the community. The largest sharing was for sporting or cultural or civic activity (48%), followed closely by sharing with adult education users (46%), a relationship not without its problems. When two sets of users of classrooms or sports facilities, who might rarely meet, have to co-operate all the same, much more attention should go to the division of finance for cleaning and catering and managing double-used sites – with decisions made by both sets of users acting jointly instead of just one (as is often the case). This would include the next most likely co-users, who were the Youth Service (sharing accommodation in 27% of the survey's schools and colleges), followed by pensioners with user rights in 10%; while percentages under 5% were chalked up for careers services, disabled groups, local libraries and medical services.

Colleges were much less likely to be sharing sites than schools: only 23% of them shared anything, hardly a welcome figure but understandable in view of their removal from community accountability through 'independence' and quango funding. LEA schools were the most likely to share, twice as likely as GM schools in respect of the Youth Service and half again as likely in respect of adult education. In no category of users did GM schools have over 50% of its schools in sharing arrangements.

Is it the community's wish that some schools are less available than others; that colleges are less available than schools, and that universities are less available than all the rest – when all are built and maintained largely at the community's expense? Does the community accept that charging for use (to get more money for schools and colleges whose funding is being cut) means that only the richer taxpayer or the better-off community groups get to enjoy the use of publicly provided facilities? None of these questions has answers yet because none is really being put to the community.

Possibly they should be; possibly a certain percentage of all use in all publicly provided educational premises should be without charge to local users – with commercial activities restricted to the remaining periods, or arranged as local communities vote to do so. The trouble is today that local communities are getting less and less say, another of the consequences of reduced democratic accountability in the system.

History

Yet the concept of community education remains strong, and looking back over the last 30 years we can identify the way the rise of comprehensive education has contributed to its growth. One strand developed from the thinking behind the network of village colleges developed by Henry Morris in Cambridgeshire in the 1930s, with the object that people of all ages should be using these colleges for educational and recreational activities of all kinds. Many such colleges developed into secondary schools after comprehensive education began, usually continuing to some degree to provide centres of learning and local culture for the surrounding area.

The Morris model was essentially rural (and was particularly influential in Leicestershire where the development of a comprehensive system was in the hands of two Morris disciples,Stewart Mason and Andrew Fairbairn). After 1965 an equivalent urban model developed in the cities, where comprehensive schools and colleges were designed to promote educational 'equity' rather than mere 'equal opportunity' and in the process, often becoming centres for the local area's education as well as its 'constructive discontent' (Midwinter, 1971).

Many schools and colleges wish to keep up a commitment to community use because the community paid for the premises in the first place and therefore should have some right of access. Sutton Centre in Sutton in Ashfield in Nottinghamshire was one of the most adventurous in this respect, where the education buildings were located within the town and open to the town all the time. But there have been many others as well (Robbins and Williams,1977; Wilson, 1981). However, by the start of the 1980s many of those trying to keep up a community commitment saw that funding cuts were starting to destroy the community part of their schools.

Those keeping up the commitment today have to work at it, and in some respects use their work and premises to demonstrate commitment to the area – in effect, becoming a resource run by the community for its own development. Earl Marshall School in Sheffield, for example, has Urdu and Koranic Schools every evening; a weekend Arabic School run by the local Yemeni community and a Cricket Centre organised by enthusiasts from the local Caribbean community – a use consciously resulting from a policy that makes the school a 'centre of local democratic education and activity' by both children and adults, not a facility run by 'us' for 'them' (Searle, 1994b).

Another kind of community development started in those comprehensive colleges, particularly tertiary colleges, which sought from the first to 'utilise resources primarily designed for the fairly narrow base of 16–19... on behalf of the wider population' by exporting their education to the area: adult classes in small village halls or centres, morning afternoon and evening classes, including basic education for minority groups. The object was to build up a college's 'user community' of learners (Blezard, 1985). How many of these imaginative early outreach programmes have survived the age of market constriction is hard to say.

In many colleges today the community remit is much narrowed, defined by those employers serviced by the college and by those consumers who can afford to 'buy' the learning packages. Identifying and meeting wider needs have had to struggle to survive in an era when schools and colleges are forced to operate as 'education businesses' rather than education centres run by the community. Some can combine the two but others can lose sight of their work as catalysts to learning more widely when programmes survive only if they fit in with the business plan, or can attract those with funds. And everywhere post-16 education for its own sake rather than for a specific qualification, is having to wage a rearguard action.

Increasingly, schools and colleges hire out leisure facilities or theatres or dining capacity – for leisure or commercial activity rather than educational use. Some have found this worrying (CEA, 1995; Weeks, 1986:125–26) for nowadays community can mean subtly moving from being about education for local people to being about making money out of them (see Chapter 8). Ultimately, it means being increasingly about education and public facilities for those who can pay rather than for those who have needs.

Educational community

Yet within schools and colleges other interpretations of community education are alive and well. These are where schools and colleges promote education about their local communities, encouraging students and pupils to learn about them and to use them as they develop their own learning. The geography course for Years 7–9 in a Welsh comprehensive school studies the geography of its own local area (Bailey, 1994). In many schools or colleges students undertake projects that take them out into the community to work – like the comprehensive in Sandwell where students offered a cleaning service for the elderly, entertainment in hospital wards, and activities in a local council estate. In Rotherham local community comprehensive schools take responsibility for derelict land in the area. To some 'community' means developing links with schools or colleges in other countries – like the middle school paired with a school in Poitiers; and the Oxfordshire upper school with a sibling school in southern Tanzania.

Quite another version of community education related to the way a local comprehensive system planned the provision of community resources for learning. From the start a local authority like Coventry decided to make all its all-through comprehensive schools into community institutions rather than self-contained schools, venues where courses and programmes for both adults and part-time students were developed in co-operation with local further education colleges (Janes *et al.*, 1985; McHugh, 1976). This was a far seeing plan in view of the way 16–19 education is now developing.

Lastly, community education can also be about defining the relationship of schools or colleges to their parents and students – in particular, breaking consciously with the old objective of comprehensive education as 'grammar education for all' and developing its own distinctive characteristics. As one community school in Derbyshire explained in its prospectus for 1995:

> In the past, schools would aim to take young people from their homes for 7 hours a day, well away from the influence of their family or neighbourhood, to fill them with abstract knowledge. Nowadays, parents and teachers alike recognise the importance of close links between the home and the school, and the need to offer a broader education which takes account of the student's own experiences in the family and the neighbourhood. The need for an effective partnership between home, school, and community has never been greater.
> (Hasland Hall Community School Prospectus, 1995–96)

Thus does 'community' combine the school–parent partnership required by the educationally conscious parent or student in a comprehensive system today with work that builds on the neighbourhood's potential, another of the commitments of so much comprehensive education. It is a definition that 'recognises that access to the fruits of society is not distributed equally... and... that comprehensive education has a part to play in redressing this inequality, at least partially'. It also recalls the common-school past with aims related to 'strengthening the bonds of commonality and solidarity within the local, national and international communities'. Comprehensive education is international as well as national and local.

But the common is composed of the individual, so the same school will differentiate its learning and respect 'individual and cultural differences' – that central task of comprehensive education: to treat everyone equally yet differently. In this particular school this was done by providing extended homework programmes in every subject, differentially planned for students who learn quickly, slowly, or who choose to go at a medium pace, undertaken in co-operation with parents. It is a definition that additionally aims to protect individual difference, offering 'a pervasive climate in which expressions of prejudice and unfair discrimination are challenged at every occurrence'. Lastly, it remembers who has provided its facilities and pays for its work: in a 'comprehensive community school access...should be full and irrespective of age, gender, physical capability, race, culture or circumstance' (Hasland Hall Community School Prospectus, 1995–96).

This is but one prospectus from one comprehensive school sent to the 1994 survey. Its message was unique but could have been replicated thousands of times over, particularly in the many comprehensive schools and colleges that defined themselves with the word 'community'. As these definitions multiply, they help to complete that essential definition of 'comprehensive' that has been missing for so long.

Yet there is nothing inevitable about a comprehensive system having one particular relationship with the community it serves; or even a particularly close one. Community does not come about automatically, even when the school or college is comprehensive or has the name 'community'. It comes about because those who teach and work in schools and colleges, and those who are learning there, acknowledge the social context in which education operates and work positively to be part of it, and accountable to it.

Notes

1 Although official figures showed 83% of pupils in comprehensive schools in the maintained sector in England and Wales by 1977, tables including all pupils in all schools for ages 12 through 18, based on DES Statistics, 1977, showed the percentage to be only 71% (*Comprehensive Education*, 1981).

2 Although fee-paying and socially selective, a large number of private schools are generally non-selective in attainment terms. The Director of the Independent Schools Information Service (ISIS), David Woodhead, estimated that it might well be that a majority of the 2,400 independent schools in Britain accepted the 'wide range of abilities' that often characterises a comprehensive intake, although possibly a smaller proportion at secondary stage. Personal communication to the authors, 2 June, 1995.

3 Overall it was 74%, but this included some not yet fully comprehensive (NFER, 1968:13).

4 Although Table A5 does not give percentages in the colleges passing five GCSE A–C because the number answering this question (112–3) was low, the average for all three colleges (41%) was much the same as that for all-through schools (42%); for further education colleges alone the average was 47%.

5 Sizes in the NFER survey for 1965 (Monks, 1968:88) showed the average size for 1965 to be 865. This was smaller than DES average figures because the research project had lower response rates from inner cities, where the larger schools were concentrated. The same was true of the Benn/Simon survey of 1968. The second independent enquiry of 1994 also had lower response rates from large cities and its sizes will also be less than DfE averages for certain types of comprehensive school.

6 The total number of comprehensive schools in 1994 in England was 2868, of which 118 were for boys(3.5%) and 151 for girls (4.5%) (DfE, 1994b,Tables 112B and C, Table 128). In the 1994 enquiry the girls' comprehensive schools were 4.3% of English comprehensive schools and the boys' were 2.9%. Single sex schools were also under-represented in the first independent enquiry (Benn and Simon, 1972: Appendix 1, note 1, p.515). They were also under-represented in the NFER survey of 1965 (Monks, 1968:236).

7 Roman Catholic schools were 7.6% of 1994 Survey schools in England and 10.7% of comprehensive and middle schools in England overall (DfE, 1994b: Table 128). Church of England schools in the 1994 survey were 5.1% of the total comprehensive and middle schools in England compared with 5.7% of the same total in England as a whole (HMSO, 1994: Table 128); 20% of the Roman Catholic schools in the 1994 survey were outside of England, however (in Scotland, Wales and Northern Ireland).The representation of the two denominations was thus probably comparable overall.

8 Villiers School in Southall with a large Sikh community voted on the matter in 1980; 95% voted to remain an LEA school (result reported in the *Times Educational Supplement*, 12 September 1980).

9 See Nottinghamshire LEA (1966:iv) for discussion of Church of England plans for secondary education.

10 See Williams and Murphy (1979, 1984). In the first piece of research (1979) the ILEA transfer figures for 1974 were analysed for each division showing that voluntary comprehensive schools had 27% in Band I compared with 12% in Band I for county comprehensive schools within a transfer system where each was supposed to have 25%. In a second article (Williams and Murphy, 1984) transfer figures for 1983 were analysed, showing voluntary schools had 24% and county schools 19%, a significant improvement.

11 Evidence presented in a television documentary, *The London Programme*, 23 February 1979.

12 *The Times* 14 August, 1978. The same point is made in relation to private education by Walford, who commented on the almost complete absence of West Indian pupils and working-class children in most private schools, though parents were often

reluctant to admit to this as the reason for their choice (Walford, 1990:55).

13 These percentages include middle schools but exclude private schools and sixth form colleges. The figure for County-LEA schools excludes all grant maintained schools.

14 The amount spent was £30 million; compare this with the £25 million spent on comprehensives over and above normal funding.

15 See also Chitty, 1992:85; *TES*, 3 July, 1992.

16 Note that Table 128's figures relate to the school year 1993–94, while the academic results for Survey schools (and for national figures where these are compared) were for 1992–93.

17 See 'Meet the Danish Efterskole', Copenhagen, 1992

18 For full information see answers to parliamentary questions 26 October 1976; 25 May 1978; and 26 July 1979; and CIPF figures in these and subsequent years.

19 Andrew MacKinlay, who added that even though 'we are downsizing our armed forces, the money spent on boarding school fees for officers' children has gone up' from £85m in 1986 to £113m.

4

Context and Intakes

The distribution of the 1994 survey's schools and colleges for all parts of the United Kingdom is set out in Table A1. The comprehensive institutions of England are slightly over-represented by comparison with national figures[1]. But returns were good enough from Wales, Scotland and Northern Ireland to start by a special look at their distinguishing features.

Northern Ireland

In the late 1960s there was pressure from parents' organisations and the teaching profession to follow the UK towards comprehensive reorganisation. The Association of Head Teachers of Secondary Schools in Northern Ireland reported a 'growing disillusion with selection'. County Armagh and County Tyrone were experimenting with comprehensive schools; and one university researcher from Queens University identified 12 already operating by 1971 (Donaghy, 1971).

But the political troubles soon froze the old education system in place, as almost all schools were denominationally based. Leaders of both denominations were resistant to change and Labour governments found it hard going getting reorganisation off the ground in the 1970s; Conservative governments after 1979 were content to leave matters where they were as far as selection went, but at the same time they wanted to move forward with 'market' changes and privatisation.

In 1994 the Government set and marked the 11-plus test nationally, and announced the scores to schools. Governors then chose the pupils, grammar school governors required by law to choose them in order of marks awarded (see pages 54–55). Academically, the system is no less rigid than the old system in England and Wales, but it is far more dependent on parental knowledge of the system and upon governors' subjective views about 'suitability' of entrants when there is oversubscription within the A and B bands of applicants. A report from the Association for Comprehensive Education (ACE), *The Transfer Market*, comments (1991:22):

> unfettered parental choice...has simply made worse the two tier system, creating socially selective grammar schools....with less able and socially disadvantaged in the secondary intermediate sector.

However, change is on the way; 30% of the school population opted out of the 11-plus in the year of the 1994 survey[2] some spurred by the lately formed Northern Ireland Council for Integrated Education (NICIE) which is setting up schools to receive both Protestant and Catholic pupils. The movement is warily treated by both main denominations, most of whom believe that religious schooling merely reflects, rather than creates, differences. But already it has set up several primary schools and over half a dozen secondary schools and colleges. Existing schools can opt out and become integrated, leading to claims (as yet unfounded) that the new schools are for middle class parents who oppose (or fail to gain entry to) grammar schools (Boycott and MacCann, 1992; Croall, 1993). Ironically, the government is fostering their growth by paying the running costs (while parents find capital costs) even though performance on the hated 11-plus test is not taken into account for entry. In effect, most integrated schools (in areas like Derry, Omagh and Enniskillen) are non-selective, and would qualify as comprehensive under the terms of the 1994 survey.

More important, however, is the movement within existing schools, based on national hostility to the 11-plus system where 39% enter grammar schools and the remaining schools, educating the majority, have to cope with the other side of this destructive division (HMSO, *Education Statistics for the UK,* 1993: Table 18). Opposition has been reflected in long-standing campaigns for comprehensive education, led by the Association for Comprehensive Education (ACE), which has members from both religions as well as from neither. Its objective is not just to end the 11-plus but to get teachers, parents, pupils and communities to focus on an education suitable to 'ALL children in northern Ireland', one that can also defend itself from pressures of underfunding, centralised control and marketisation (ACE, 1988); just as earlier publications had argued not just for the structure to change but also the processes and content of education, using research from the Northern Ireland Council for Educational Research, to demolish the argument that non-selective schools would threaten academic standards (ACE, 1985). The Association's latest campaign against the marketisation of the 11-plus, embodied in *The Transfer Market* (1991), was supported by a formidable array of professional teaching groups from all sectors and all sections of secondary education[3].

Public opinion polling also shows massive support for ending the selective system (McAdam, 1994), where there has long been evidence of disparity between the education of those inside and outside of grammar schools, confirmed in 1995 by a report from the Northern Ireland Economic Council (McAdam, 1995). Although acknowledging rises in attainment in recent years, the Report also recorded 'disturbing' differences between social classes, boys and girls, and denominations, with Roman Catholic students having a higher proportion leaving with no qualifications and fewer 'A' levels. As in the rest of the UK, middle-class children are more likely to get chosen for grammar schools – 2.6 times more likely in Northern Ireland. Since all these separate separatisms are costing £35m a year to maintain, while stunting overall levels of attainment, the Economic Council's recommendation was that comprehensive education be developed after 11, and a single administrative agency set up for all schools.

In late 1994 the Government responded reluctantly to such pressure by announcing itself willing to consider comprehensive plans from a few local areas – in the same way that the Conservative governments had to respond between 1970 and 1974 to similar pressure in England and Wales and Scotland. It also announced that the Craigavon area of Armagh was developing some comprehensive education; but the scheme is in a small area, may only extend to age 14, and is surrounded by accessible grammar schools for which 'parental choice' in the form of the 11-plus will, of course, remain. The Association for Comprehensive Education thus fears:

> The role of grammars now in Northern Ireland are more like opted-out schools in UK... the public image becomes more important than the reality of school life with grammar schools simply taking on a new mission as socially selective comprehensive schools.
>
> (Association for Comprehensive Education, 1991:22, 8)

The 1994 findings

Although official UK statistics for the year of our 1994 survey showed no comprehensive schools in Northern Ireland, 77 schools and colleges replied, including several grammar schools that claimed to be 'almost comprehensive' by taking '60%' of the area; as well as several junior intermediate schools that said they retained large numbers who might otherwise have gone to grammar schools. Unfortunately, most failed to meet the survey's definition of comprehensive.

Those included in the survey were 12 schools and colleges that were able to declare themselves comprehensive within our definition (see Appendix I). This made them 4.6% of the total of Northern Ireland's secondary schools and further education colleges (HMSO, 1993: Table 2); but this total was likely to be an underestimate, since it did not include several of the schools operating as comprehensives by the early 1970s, most of which still exist (Donaghy, 1971).

The comprehensive schools and colleges in our 1994 survey were from both sides of the religious divide. Three were lower schools of 11–14, two were short-course comprehensives to 16, three were further education colleges and four were all-through 11–18 schools, the latter's average at 650 far smaller than the average size for all-through schools in the UK as a whole of 974. The overall average of 689 (against the survey's 893) was smaller too.

Three of these schools and colleges drew from mostly working-class areas and the rest from socially mixed areas; none, however, had a predominantly middle-class intake. Nor did any draw from an area where most of the pupils or students came from private housing. One drew from a council estate and the rest from areas of mixed private and council housing. All but one were in towns and suburbs rather than countryside or large city.

The percentages with social class intake predominantly from the middle class were much the smallest for any area of the UK – 9% against the survey average of 26% (Table A5). At the same time, the overall average intake from the top 20% of the attainment range was not significantly lower than the survey average. At 17.7% it was the same as Scotland's figure.

The average percentage in Northern Ireland's comprehensive schools for five GCSE A–C passes was 36.7%, slightly higher than the averages from London and the English metropolitan boroughs and only one point below Wales' national average, an exceptional achievement in a country where two out of five go to grammar schools.

However, the going-on and staying-on rates of the schools were well below survey averages (Table A5) and as too few made returns for 'A' level scores or vocational courses, these were omitted from the table. The schools' 6th and 7th years were not yet fully developed, the average size of the former as yet only 27.

On the other hand, Northern Ireland's comprehensive schools included a very high percentage of schools with much better attendance rates than those of similar schools in England, Wales or Scotland, and its schools and colleges had higher rates for collaboration in order to provide a full range of courses (see Tables A5 and A6). Schools and colleges serving the 16–17 year group had a higher percentage than did other areas of the UK for students on day release; and two of the colleges providing for 16–19 had over 30% of the 17–18 year olds winning places on degree courses.

Scotland

Survey findings for Scotland in 1994 showed that its secondary system was 100% comprehensive and 100% mixed sex. Its schools, which were the most neighbourhood based (question 33A) of any part of the UK, also had the best academic results (in league table terms) of percentages passing five O grade 1–3 (five GCSE A–C) – with 52.0% compared with a survey average of 39.3.% – some 10% higher than GM schools in England and Wales (and almost the same as Scotland's official national average for the same year; see Appendix II).

In addition, Scotland's schools in the 1994 survey had a large percentage of the age group receiving qualifications in vocational subjects – as well as the highest percentage staying on beyond leaving age in all-through schools of any region in the UK: 70.5% (against a survey average of 56.1%[4]) – a far cry from the picture in the first independent enquiry of 1968 when Scotland had the lowest levels of staying on of any country in the UK (Benn and Simon, 1970:396).

We set out some of the differences that characterise Scotland's education tradition and its recent history elsewhere (see pages 10, 68 and 69; and Tables A5 and A6) and there is additional information for older years in Chapter 9. Set out below are its educational community's differences with the Government over curriculum and assessment reform for the older years of comprehensive education in 1994. At the time threats to Scotland's comprehensive system were widely perceived, not from popular opinion, but from the Conservative Government's dogmatic attempts to impose the market, 'parental choice', and privatisation on the Scottish system. Systemic changes had already begun, including the break-up of regional councils to smaller LEAS. With their commercial restrictions and no requirements to have education committees, the change obviously risked reduction of democratic accountability (Fairley, 1995; Fairley and Paterson, 1995).

At the end of 1994 the president of the Education Institute of Scotland (EIS), the main teachers' organisation, spoke at a national conference held in Ayr of a 'consistent attempt by the government to undermine comprehensive education without directly challenging it' – by the introduction of magnet schools, opting out, league tables, assisted places and the 'placing request legislation' ('parental choice'), aiming to destroy the Scots neighbourhood tradition and bring 'institutionalised classism' from England to Scotland (Norma Watson, speech reprinted in *Education*, 18 November 1994). Dr Lindsay Paterson, from the Centre for Educational Sociology at Edinburgh University at the same conference, said comprehensive education was too rooted and too popular in Scotland to dislodge, but Brian Boyd of Glasgow University's Centre for Research and Consultancy warned that streaming, setting, fast tracking and worse were on their way back, while teachers, so honoured in Scots educational history for their lively independence, were now moving down the 'slippery slope towards teacher-as-technician', the passive teaching role being forced on teachers in England and Wales.

There was particular dissatisfaction with Government attempts to slip in its changes under the guise of reform of the upper years of secondary education through its proposal for *Higher Still*, proposals which the EIS in 1994 condemned for showing the same 'contempt for equality' and the same 'dogma' as evident in earlier government proposals (e.g., the Howie Report), proposing what sounded like narrow 'A' levels, with 'fast-tracks' for some, 'likely to be used...for streaming...at the expense of the great majority'. It was equally worried by changes smacking of the National Curriculum by the 'back door' imposed 'top down...to ensure that certain knowledge and skills are inculcated uncritically in school' as already happens 'south of the Border'. Lastly, proposals for different assessment boards for vocational and academic qualifications (and the lowly position offered Skillstart training) ensures old splits remain 'despite the rhetoric of a new unified system' – and all to be achieved with no new resources by 1997 (EIS, 1994).

It was quite clear that many in Scotland's educational community were locked into a struggle to retain momentum for comprehensive education and that this had got bound up with a struggle to preserve their own educational tradition, particularly to defend it against wider politically inspired changes that had been imposed on England during the previous decade.

History

Earlier chapters discussed the ways Scotland has differed in its approach to education and to social inclusiveness in schooling. Of particular interest was its early declaration after World War II that comprehensive education was the best way to educate all children in all schools (see page 10), even though the policy subsequently followed was to accept selection at 12 plus and in the early 1960s to introduce an O grade examination to precede the existing Higher Grade examination (for those going on to universities and the professions) – the pathway through these two grades known as the 'certificate' course.

By the time Circular 600 was issued in 1965 to start comprehensive reform, pupils in Scotland had for some time stood a greater chance of entering a certificate course than pupils of the same measured ability stood of entering a grammar school south of the border (Douglas, 1964). But therein lay the rub: divisions in Scottish secondary education were often as much related to the 'course' upon which a student embarked inside a school than upon the selectivity of the school. There was a long tradition, especially in villages, of the single school taking in all local pupils – but once inside, those comparing English and Scots schools could say that Scotland had 'rather more inflexible parallelism' than England (Osborne, 1966:203). This was allied to what some educational historians have seen as an oppressive tradition in Scotland where the fact that so many 'afford established authority and tradition an exaggerated respect' precludes real reform (Smout, 1986:229).

Nevertheless, within that Scots tradition comprehensive reform set about changing secondary education by progressively lifting restrictions that prevented pupils developing. In lifting these restrictions Scotland was more radical than England, especially in relation to schools of 12–16 which had no H grade courses, and where, even if transfer was made to a school with H grade, pupils had to study longer than those already there, in order to qualify for Highers. Circular 600 made clear that the mark of going comprehensive was that internal divisions would have to go, a stipulation not made in England.

At the time of the first independent enquiry in 1968, however, one in five Scottish comprehensives were still short-course schools of 12–16 (Benn and Simon, 1970: Table 17.2, p.281). Much more important, the common course in the earlier years was still not provided universally – 21% of comprehensive schools in 1968 were still unable to provide one to those who entered at age 12, whether the school was long-course or short course (Benn and Simon, 1970: Table A4, p.375). But the SED persisted with its definition of comprehensive schools as those with 'all courses including H grade to SV and SVI' (SED,1971:7). No others were properly comprehensive.

The result was a strong drive in the 1970s to convert as many schools as possible into 12–18 all-through schools and, secondly, to introduce common schooling inside the earlier years of secondary schools, where certificate and non-certificate pupils took a common course. This went ahead well but met a problem in the later years of secondary education, for unlike England, Scotland had not introduced a parallel CSE examination to its O grade. The only choice in Scottish comprehensive schools was whether to take the traditional academic course.

More and more did choose this 'academic' route, of course. As a result there was an increased percentage of the age group getting O and H grade passes. 10 years after reorganisation began 17% of Scots students were achieving three or more SCE H-grade passes compared with only 9% achieving the equivalent three 'A' levels in England and Wales. This seemed to make Scottish comprehensive schools much more successful (in 'league table' terms) but at the other end of the scale it was less successful. For, whereas only 17% left English schools without any qualifications at this same time, two in five were still doing so in Scotland (Gray, McPherson, and Raffe, 1983:24).

The defects of a 'grammar education for all' were thus apparent earlier on in Scotland, where there was precious little for those whose intelligence lay in other directions than the narrow certificate route. Scottish teachers' organisations had been discussing this since the 1960s, and pioneering schoolteachers like R. F. MacKenzie of Braehead School had long been warning of the domination of education by certification and the neglect of the majority. Their concerns were very much like those of comprehensive school teachers in England and Wales at the time, who warned about concentrating too much attention on 'expanding grammar education' rather than broadening education itself for the whole age group (Palmer, 1974). Scotland's critics also anticipated the criticisms of many in the 1980s and 1990s in England who realised that competitive individualism was being nurtured in a destructive way (MacKenzie, 1970).

Scotland faced this problem of the majority in the middle of the 1970s, when it set up two committees to tackle curriculum and assessment across the attainment range (known as Munn and Dunning after the names of those who chaired the work). As acknowledged by educationists looking on, 'it had taken some 30 years for the wheel to turn full circle' back to the original 1947 impulse not just for common schools but also for a common curriculum and assessment system to go with them (Gray, McPherson, and Raffe, 1983:32). Instead of setting up a 'shadow' academic examination in the form of a Scottish CSE, Scotland pioneered modular, vocationally oriented courses for the whole attainment range through a new Scottish

Vocational Education Council (SCOTVEC). The trouble was that these courses were separate from the certificate course, so by the start of the 1990s, when Scotland had virtually completed its first stage of structural reorganisation for secondary schooling, it was plunged into a new struggle to try to integrate vocational and academic education and thus once again put itself ahead of the rest of the United Kingdom, where that struggle still lay ahead.

Integrating the world of the school and college will be more difficult in Scotland, however, as the two sectors are not as close as they are in the rest of the UK where very few students at the leaving age choose a college rather than a school. Colleges are mainly for those over 17. For this reason the average sizes of the 16–17 and 17–18 year groups in Scotland in the 1994 survey (97 and 57, Table A6), though comparable with all-through schools elsewhere in the UK, are much smaller than the rest of the UK, where the figures include further education colleges as well.

Scotland also differed from the rest of the UK in keeping a far better record of the change to comprehensive reorganisation over 30 years. In particular, it mounted research that was able to show the difference that comprehensive change had made to pupils' attainment. Much of it came from the Centre for Educational Sociology at the University of Edinburgh, where one study mid-way through the 30 years found that 'comprehensive reorganisation caused an improvement at national level' for working-class pupils relative to middle-class, an improvement in the attainment of girls, and 'in a mere 8 years...significantly reduced social class inequalities ...that had been established over six decades' (McPherson and Wilmms, 1987:19, 27).

Survey results, 1994

Of institutions participating in the 1994 survey in Scotland, 98% were all-through schools. Tables A5 and A6 summarise their characteristics, showing Scottish comprehensive schools continue to be smaller than those in England and Wales. In fact, the Scots average of 718 (against a survey average of 893) was almost the same as it was 30 years ago (703).

Three-quarters of Scots schools were not full (question 12) – 78% in the September of 1993 – partly due to population fall, partly due to the informal 'excess places' policy operating in the UK in 1994 (see page 200 *et seq.*). Seventeen per cent of Scots comprehensives in the survey were denominational (all Catholic Schools, question 22B), a higher percentage than for denominational schools in the survey as a whole. At 68.1%

Scotland's intakes were more working class than the survey as a whole (61%) and the proportion that were predominantly middle-class schools (18%) was lower than the survey average of 26%. Scotland's social intakes were similar to those in Wales (Table A5).

A greater proportion of Scotland's schools and colleges drew from areas of mixed housing than elsewhere in the UK – 61%, for example, from a mix of private and council (question 27 C and E) compared with a survey average of 54% for private/council mix, and fewer of Scotland's schools and colleges were in suburban areas (18% compared with 36%). As would be expected, many more were in the countryside and villages (29% against a survey average of 14%).

H grade differences

As already noted, Scotland's results for Standard Grade with five passes at 1-3 (equivalent to five GCSE A–C) were the highest for any region in the Survey (Table A5) and slightly higher than figures for Scotland nationally (see Appendix II, note B). Table A6 shows the percentage of S4 roll obtaining three or more Higher grade passes at grades 1–3 (question 141b). Scotland's average was 24.1%[5], a figure that hid a very wide range, just as in England and Wales. On the one hand, some schools had percentages as high as 75%, but several had them as low as 5%.

Table A6 shows percentages were higher than the Scots average for schools in towns (question 26B) at 27.4% but lower for schools in the cities (question 26A) with 14.7% or even in the suburbs (question 26C) at 20.4%. This lower percentage for cities was similar to the survey overall but the highest percentage for towns was unique to Scotland. Neither was there the same disadvantage in Scotland as in the survey overall for schools where some of the housing was substandard (question 27E). The figure of 27.0% was only very little lower than schools where the intake was mainly from private housing (29.5%); there were no schools in Scotland in the survey that drew entirely from substandard housing. Schools drawing from council estates had the lowest percentage in Scotland for three or more H grade passes (15.9%).

Further analysis of Scotland's H grade figures (not shown in Table A6) shows that as in England schools drawing intakes from the two most middle-class categories had higher averages at 34.4% (question 36B) and 28.2% (question 36D) than the Survey average for Scotland of 24%. There was also a relationship between results in Highers and school numbers receiving free dinners. Overall in Scotland 18.9% of the schools had intakes where over 30%

qualified for free dinners (question 40D and E), much the same as the survey average of 18.1%. Of Scots schools with free dinners at this high level, however, only 17.4% had three or more passes at Higher grade, compared with 31.2% with such passes in schools where free dinner taking was at the lowest level (question 40A). Poverty made as big a difference as in England, possibly even a greater one.

There was also a relationship between percentages passing three or more Highers and attendance. Schools having rates at 95% and over had 28.5% passing compared with only 16.1% passing where attendance was below 90%. That said, 30% of schools in Scotland overall had percentages of attendance less than 90%, higher than the survey average of 21.4% ; and Scotland's rates of high attendance (over 95%) were the lowest for any region of the UK.

A smaller proportion of schools in Scotland had Compacts with employers or universities (Table A6) than applied elsewhere in the UK, possibly because more schools take responsibility themselves for work experience rather than organise it externally. Schools with Compacts in Scotland (question 136) had lower results for three or more H grades (16.0%) than those without (24.9%).

Over two in five schools (41.6%) overall sent at least 31% or over of their S6 year to university – a figure that is not comparable with that in the rest of the UK because some entrants to universities in Scotland would have left for university after the S5 year. Differences for university entrance between comprehensive schools in Scotland were much like H grade patterns.

Vocational education record

What was most interesting about Scotland were its results in vocational education. These were often the reverse of those for O Grade and Highers in relation to social or demographic factors. Thus when it came to percentage of S5/6 rolls achieving at least three SCOTVEC certificates, schools serving council estates and mixed housing areas with some substandard housing had the highest scores (43.7% and 46.4%) while schools drawing from private housing or a mix of private and council had lower scores (35.3% and 34.2%, respectively). Schools drawing from working-class areas (question 36A and C) had higher scores with 43.4% and 35.6% than those where the majority of the intake was middle class (question 36B and question 36D) with 30.3% and 22.7% respectively; and schools with the highest percentages of free meals quoted above scored

36.6% compared with 26.8% for schools with the lowest level of free meals.

Such figures point to the success of the SCOTVEC in providing high-quality qualifications for those whose intelligence, competence and capacity for attainment are different from those drawn to traditional certificate studies. Scotland has allowed their talents to show. Ironically, it is this very success that now causes so many problems because so many see the need to integrate vocational and academic education instead of continuing to keep them separate to avoid splits in schools between vocational and academic study, as well as splits in students' own programmes – which increasing numbers believe to be divisive. Unifying the curriculum structure is more urgent in Scotland for its own curricular developments have shown that almost all students benefit from having *both* academic and vocational education.

Wales

Wales, like Scotland, traditionally was known for the respect which education enjoyed and for the higher percentages entering grammar schools than elsewhere in the UK. There was less obstruction from such schools to comprehensive education on account of this and today comprehensive education is nearly complete at 99%; but it has had to endure some criticism too, one of its severer critics in the mid-1980s saying that while England had 'been able to develop an authentic comprehensive tradition' Wales was only just starting to do so (Reynolds *et al.*, 1987:328).

Welsh comprehensive schools took most literally Labour's 1994 election sales pitch about comprehensives being 'grammar schools for all'. From the earliest days their comprehensive schools were more internally selective; for example, more than three times as many as in England required 'O' level passes to enter their own sixth forms (as against being open entry) in 1968 (Benn and Simon, 1970:119). When researchers analysed a small Welsh community changing over from selective to comprehensive education in the late 1970s (Reynolds *et al.*, 1987), they concluded that the attempt to retain the grammar tradition intact within the comprehensive school was a brake upon progress.

The grammar pupils were doing all right, but pupils in the middle ranges were not being well enough served; overall the schools had lower scores in areas like reading age levels than was the case nationally. The researchers stressed these were schools in an 'atypical disadvantaged ... Welsh community' and left open the possibility that schools elsewhere in Wales might have been different, but nevertheless felt able to be critical about Welsh comprehensives' conventionality and inflexibility. Other researchers at this time also confirmed a general view that Wales had a tendency to concentrate on the more able.

By the 1990s the general impression of Welsh comprehensive schools was that they were slightly more formal than English (but so were Scots) but otherwise no longer so very different. In any case, the complaints made by Reynolds were also made about schools in England (e.g. Ball, 1984) and it is more than possible to show that Wales has its share of innovative and pioneering comprehensive schools and colleges. Nor do the 1994 survey tables show many fundamental differences between Wales and the rest of the UK.

As Tables A5 and A6 show, however, there are some. For example, the intake of the top 20% of the attainment range makes Welsh comprehensives the most comprehensive of any area of the UK at 20.5%. Their average size is also larger than anywhere else. Their five GCSE A–C scores are slightly lower than the survey average but their 'A' level point score is the same and so is their staying-on rate after 16 in the all-through schools. They have a higher percentage of schools where pupils do not have English as a first language and the highest percentage of schools for all UK regions with attendance rates below 90%. On the other hand, they had the highest percentage of schools of any UK region where more than 30% went on to degree courses.

England – London, Metropolitan Boroughs and the Shires

Each of the three areas of England had its own special characteristics. Tables A5 and A6 show that London and the metropolitan areas had higher average sizes of schools and colleges as well as higher size averages for the 12th and 13th years of education than did schools and colleges in the English counties (though the average size of the all-through comprehensive was very much alike in all three). Intakes of the top 20% of the ability range were higher in the counties than in the two 'mets' – for example, 19.1% in counties compared with 14.5% for intakes to metropolitan boroughs and 16.0% for schools and colleges in London. The percentage of comprehensive schools and colleges having predominantly middle-class intakes was twice as high in the English counties as in either the metropolitan boroughs or London (Table A5). The percentages for English counties' schools with attendance rates over 95% was also twice as high (Table A5).

On only very few measures was it a case where London and the metropolitan boroughs did not differ from the counties. Their turnover was higher, and particularly high in the London boroughs. Their percentages of schools with predominantly working-class intakes was higher, particularly so in the case of the metropolitan boroughs. Their percentages of schools with pupils eligible for free dinners was three times that of the English counties' comprehensive schools (Table A5).

One area of difference was on collaboration with other institutions, where London had a smaller percentage of its schools and colleges collaborating with one another than was the case in the metropolitan boroughs and the counties (and of those that did, far more were only able to offer their courses through such collaboration – questions 83 and 129). Another difference was on percentages of schools and colleges with Compact schemes, where London's rate was very much lower than that of other metropolitan districts. Far fewer London schools and colleges had students who were combining different types of courses (academic and vocational). Such figures suggest that London's traditional separation of school and further education, much greater than in other areas, is taking longer to overcome.

The metropolitan boroughs had the lowest five GCSE A–C passes percentage of 31.8% and the English counties the highest (41.3%) as against a survey average of 39.3% – with London in between, as was the case with national statistics (see Appendix II, Note B).

Although the shire counties had higher percentages sending over 30% to degree courses at 86.3%, compared with London's at 78.6% and the metropolitan boroughs at 81.4%, the metropolitan districts had the highest average number of students per institution accepted on university courses having BTEC or GNVQ qualifications. The English counties had slightly lower percentages for students entering BTEC or City and Guilds national qualifications than did London or the metropolitan boroughs.

Although the comparisons show superiority for the counties over the boroughs in the single GCSE examination, there is less of a gap in the older years and at 'A' level no gap at all in vocational measures. Considering the far greater difficulties faced in cities, and the very large differences the 1994 survey found in housing, social class and attainment intakes between urban and countryside areas, the differences are less than might have been expected.

Additional diversity: Black, Asian and other minority groups

Comprehensive education not only contained the full range of regional diversity in the UK in 1994, including its world-wide outposts under the Service Children's Education Authority (SCEA), it also had much the most culturally diverse population of any school or college sector in the UK, and possibly the most international. Even in a university with a large world population, it would be surprising if the number of world languages spoken every day by students came anywhere near the range that several comprehensive schools regularly achieved of over 40 and occasionally up to 60.

Schools and colleges were asked to give the percentages in their intakes belonging to different ethnic and minority national groups.Each group had to account for at least 5% of the total pupil or student population (question 30), so as to cut out schools and colleges with only a few such students. Since the object was to examine cultural diversity, estimates were asked for regardless of where such pupils and students might have been born; 519 had at least one significant ethnic or national group as defined in question 30 – a third of all the schools and colleges in the Survey (Table 4.1).

Table 4.1 Black, ethnic and national groups in comprehensive education, 1994. Results are given as a percentage, with numbers of schools and colleges in parentheses

Groups making up 5% or more of the school/college population	Percentage of survey	Percentage of all schools with groups (n = 519)
Indian/Pakistani/Bangladeshi	21 (323)	62
Afro-Caribbean	12 (185)	36
European (East and West)	12 (184)	36
Irish	7 (102)	20
Chinese and Asian	3 (47)	9
Middle Eastern and North African	2 (35)	7
South American	0.03 (6)	1
North American/Australian/ Canadian	0.02 (4)	0.7

These groups were not spread one to a school or college, as is obvious from the numbers. More than one in three of the 519 schools and colleges had more than one group. For example, 31 of the 35 schools which had Middle Eastern and North African groups also had either Indian/ Pakistani/Bangladeshi or Afro-Caribbean groups; 150 schools had both Afro-Caribbean and Indian/Bangladeshi groups; 28 had both of these and Irish groups.

In Scotland, to give another example, although 19 comprehensive schools had higher than 5% of at least one ethnic or national group, four of these (Afro-Caribbean, Indian, Chinese and Middle Eastern) were concentrated very largely in only four schools – in contrast to schools taking significant groups of European or Irish pupils, most of whom were the only additional cultural group within any one school.

There were big differences between those schools with ethnic and black groups and those without such groups. For example, their working-class intakes were much higher and their middle-class intakes much lower than survey averages. Thus 81% of schools with West Indian groups had predominantly working-class intakes – as did 71% of schools with Indian, 76% with Chinese and 72% with Irish concentrations. The only schools where this did not apply were those with North American and European groups, where social class figures were at the survey average (though the numbers were small and should be treated with caution, particularly as one school at least returned a form where the European category was misinterpreted to include British pupils). Several schools and colleges in Northern Ireland were amused to find 'Irish' listed as a minority group.

Schools with concentrations of black, other ethnic and national groups were much more likely to have high levels with free dinners than those without. Thus 71.1% of schools with Afro-Caribbean groups and 71.4% of those with middle eastern groups had 16% or more taking free dinners (question 40 C, D and E) compared with the survey average for this level of 43.2%; schools with Indian/Pakistani/Bangladeshi and Chinese groups scored 61% and 60% respectively. Out of the four schools with North American/Australian groups, there was only one school at this level.

Schools which have significant groups from other cultures can be immeasurably enriched and it is important that the opportunity to use their presence be taken – by tapping their special skills and capabilities, including their expertise in languages or other world cultures. However, making use of these extra dimensions often means extra work, particularly because some of these groups will come from families that wish them to assimilate rapidly into British culture without regard to their own, while others will come from families anxious to preserve their own culture in parallel. Schools and colleges have to be sensitive to this major division likely to show itself within almost every group.

Where there is only one minority group within a school, most schools can manage to deal with these sometimes conflicting factors. But where there are more than one, and certainly where there are three or more, the extra work should be recognised by extra support. In any case, some arrangement should be made for schools with any group of this kind present at significant levels, to have staff, even if only part-time, who are purpose-recruited for them, aware of the group's particular – and sometimes different – educational needs and aspirations. This is particularly so where the group's first language is not English.

English as a second language

Closely related to cultural groups is the question of mother tongue languages. In schools with many different languages, the cultural enrichment can be great. It is important to look on such groups for their positive contribution in this respect; as well as to encourage the pupils and students themselves to build on their own cultural skills and knowledge, and to help those that wish to do so to continue the study of their own languages.

But comprehensive schools where large proportions do not have English as a first language face far greater academic tasks teaching a national curriculum or any examination course, where almost all of the teaching is in the English language. This task is even harder now that the accustomed financing of English language teaching to many such pupils under Section 11 funding from the Home Office has been stopped. This has been one of the most damaging of the cuts to education in recent years, and it falls almost entirely on comprehensive schools. There are very few grammar schools, if any, that take in large groups whose English language skills are not yet perfect.

Just as significant, not all comprehensive schools shoulder this task in the same degree. For example, only 2% of voluntary controlled comprehensive schools and 3% of sixth-form colleges had over 15% (question 31C,D,E) without English as a first language compared with one in ten LEA county schools, 12% of FE colleges and 17% of tertiary colleges.

Table 4.2 Numbers (%) of schools and colleges with over 5% not having English as a first language

All schools and colleges	245	(16)
of which:		
having over 30% without English	40	(2.6)
having over 50% without English	39	(2.6)

Schools with levels over 5% without English (Table 4.2) have problems enough teaching a curriculum that requires English to learn it, but those schools and colleges with really large percentages would have more than just a difficulty. They are being asked to do two jobs: be language schools and secondary comprehensive schools at one and the same time. A few extra teachers for English is not an adequate 'additional support', especially since many of these pupils or students will be refugees as well, for whom there is no recognised extra funding in the education system. Such pupils are often highly motivated but at the same time can present extra work for schools because of their problematic legal status, the trauma they will have undergone, and the separation from their families that is common.

Difficult enough from the social point of view for schools, but when we consider that many will be schools where language teaching support has been progressively withdrawn over the last decade, meaning real educational deprivation for so many young people, it is easy to see why so many schools with these groups believe governments – as well as certain sections of society – have decided that certain schools should be asked to bear far larger loads than others in this respect. Often, these same schools are simultaneously singled out for 'low' academic attainment because 'league table' criteria demand a full knowledge of the English language for high scores.

The 1994 survey further confirmed the difficulties of all these schools with over 5% not having English by asking whether they considered the resources they had for teaching English to these students was adequate for the educational task (question 32); 62% said resources allowed them were not adequate[6].

But the difficulties for such schools did not stop here because many were situated in areas of social deprivation as well. Nearly half drawing from substandard housing, for example, were schools that also had 31% or over of their pupils without English; while at the other end of the scale only 2.5% of schools drawing from private housing had intakes lacking English at this level. A quarter of the schools with concentrations at 31% or over level were also in the middle of large cities compared with averages of less than 3% for the three other geographical areas (town, suburb, and countryside). And 91% of the intakes were predominantly working class.

Once again, when viewed overall, the costly aspects of educational provision – in terms of care and staff time required – are loaded on to a relatively small number of comprehensive schools, usually of county-LEA status, often in insalubrious areas. How can 'standard' spending assessments which give each school the same support and staffing across the land deal with these situations? We know that just a few extra staff, recruited possibly part-time from the community of those with the language spoken, would make all the difference. Yet for many such schools there is as yet no adequate mechanism to recognise them as schools with a distinct educational need.

In years to come we will look back on this period as singularly heartless, with its ruthless 'market control' specifically designed to isolate such schools and even close them down rather than grant them the modest extra educational support they need and set seriously about the task of educating all their pupils.

Intakes to comprehensive schools and colleges and some of their characteristics

Attainment

One of the key measures of comprehensive schools and colleges is what percentage of the intake is in the top 20% of the attainment range (question 34). Table 4.3 shows the distribution of attainment intake in the schools in the 1994 survey.

Table 4. 3 Distribution of attainment intake to schools and colleges (as percentage of top 20% in intake, 1993–4). Results are given as percentages of survey total, with numbers of schools given in parentheses

Percentage of school's intake falling in the top 20% of the attainment range	Percentage (No.) of survey total
0–5	16 (225)
6–10	22 (316)
11–15	17.5 (250)
16–25	26.1 (368)
26–40	12.7 (179)
41–60	4 (50)
61–80	1 (15)
81–100	0.5 (6)
Total giving information	100 (1409)

In a comprehensive system the full range of attainment found in the local population should be found in the intakes to individual schools and colleges. This will not always be uniform for there are natural differences from area to area. The argument is not about these; it is about the unnatural differences that arise when selection is retained within the system, and some schools or colleges have artificial concentrations of lower or higher attainment at one end of the attainment range.

Few debates have gone on longer than the debate over creaming (see pages 39–42) for if the full range of attainment is absent, this has an effect on the achievements of the school, particularly where it is the top levels that are missing. Today this has added consequences in view of the limited measures used to construct 'league tables' and because ranking of schools takes no account at all of attainment intake. What it means is that schools and colleges are being rated on their intakes rather than their achievements.

In the first days of reorganisation many comprehensive schools lacked percentages at the top end of the attainment range. Several research projects gave levels for the 'loss' whether through retention of grammar schooling and other forms of selection, or simply the characteristics of the area served (Benn and Simon, 1970; HMI, 1979; Monks, 1968, 1970; NUT, 1973; Ross *et al.*, 1972; Steedman, 1980, 1983; Weeks, 1968, summarises some of these: p.104).

Some researchers have set percentages below which they believe comprehensive schools cease to function if deprived of high attainers. Most put it between 5% and 15% of the top attainers (DES, 1979; King, 1970; Little, 1973). Less attention has gone to the loss of lower levels of attainment and the point at which schools cease to be comprehensive when these are missing, but several schools in the 1994 Survey (Table 4.3) might certainly be queried on this point in the same way as some comprehensive schools have always been queried about loss of percentages from the top end.

To measure either effect, the extent to which the top 20% of the intake range is present in any school has often been used. Table 4.3 reveals a situation today where schools are more polarised than they were 30 years ago, significant numbers missing percentages at both the lower and the higher ends of the attainment range. But the polarisation is not uniform, for numbers missing from the top attainment are greater.

Direct comparisons can be made with the past, for question 34 was the same question asked by the NFER in their comprehensive research project of 1965 as well as in the first independent enquiry in 1968 (Benn and Simon, 1970; Monks, 1968). The findings in 1968 from both projects showed that on average the comprehensive schools contained only 15% of the top 20% of ability (Benn and Simon, 1970:301). Overall, in other words, comprehensive schools were missing the top 5% of ability. What was most interesting about the NFER's research, however, was that it later tested the pupils' VRQ scores in the schools where the original estimates had been made and discovered that their actual ability was 3% lower than the heads had estimated (Monks, 1970:187). Researchers concluded that heads tend to overestimate ability in their intakes (Monks, 1970:106). It could mean that comprehensive schools at this early period received only 12% of the top

20% of the attainment range and were more disadvantaged than assumed.

1994 findings

In the 1994 survey the same question that was asked earlier (question 34) was answered again by almost all schools and colleges, although one or two were gratifyingly bemused – e.g. 'surely 20%?'. The overall average for the 1994 survey was 18.0, which shows an improvement in the intervening years at the rate of 1% a decade. However, if the same 'over-estimating' effect applies still, the top 5% is still missing.

Table 4.3, however, shows that this is not a uniform finding across most comprehensive schools and colleges. What we see here is a continuum of comprehensive schools and colleges characterised by top-attainment intake from 16% of schools and colleges having no more than 5% in the top 20% across to 1.5% having over 60% in this range. The percentage of schools and colleges falling within the range of 15–25% – where in a comprehensive system we would expect most of them to fall – was only 26.1% (Table 4.3). It is not so much a polarised picture as one of a majority 'less than comprehensive', a quarter more or less comprehensive, and a significant minority 'more than comprehensive' – more a three-tier system than a two-tier one.

But attainment at intake is not a full defining figure for comprehensive education for it is dealing with only one type of intelligence. Nowadays – despite attempts to revive the science of IQ (Simon, 1996) – there is more interest in the wide variety of types of intelligence people have – not merely in the type that IQ tests measure. Thus the balance of different forms of intelligence within a school or college is just as important as minimum levels of the one (IQ) kind. So too is there interest in 'academic' attainment as tested through criterion-referenced assessment in addition to norm-referenced public examinations as measures of achievement. The view grows that there are several ways to measure achievement. Comprehensive education's task is to develop all types of intelligence and in doing so to make use of as many forms of assessment as help to do this.

Nevertheless, in 1994 the limited measure of attainment suggested in question 34 was still important to many of those within the school and college system, and differences between schools and colleges in different circumstances (provided in Tables A5 and A6) provide material for a great deal of further investigation.

Colleges overall have higher attainment intakes than do schools, although within the college sector the difference between sixth form colleges on the one hand and FE colleges on the other is one of the widest in the survey at 57.8% to 13.1% of the top 20%. The same table shows other types of comprehensive schools or colleges with higher percentages of attainment than the survey average, including 14–18 upper schools and voluntary controlled schools.

It shows differences too – between intakes to schools in the middle of big cities with 14% of the top 20% compared with schools and colleges in the countryside and villages at 21%. But is this because country pupils are higher attainers or because greater numbers of them come from more settled or more middle-class homes where almost everyone has English as their first language? Or because housing differs? For schools drawing from areas where most of the housing is substandard, only 5.5% of the schools and colleges give estimates of their top 20% that are above the survey average of 18.0. However, if their intakes are mainly from private housing, 70.8% estimate their attainment intakes to be above the survey average (question 27D and B). This suggests perception of attainment is related to opinion about living conditions.

There is also a difference in perceived attainment between schools with predominantly middle-class intakes as against those with working-class intakes (question 36B and D as against question 36 A and C). For example, of the quarter or so comprehensive schools that had attainment intakes over 20% (and were 'more' than comprehensive) 58% were drawing predominantly middle-class intakes (question 36B and D). Only 10% were drawing working-class intakes (question 36A and C). Again, a reader might well wonder how much being perceived was natural intelligence and how much social or cultural background instead.

Intake differences where selection is retained

The first independent enquiry in 1968 was able to show the difference in attainment intakes to schools in areas where selection was retained and those where it was not (Benn and Simon, 1970, summarised in Chapter 18). The 1994 survey carried the comparison a stage further, and presented clearer evidence on this point (although it is important to remember that this situation applied to far fewer schools and colleges in 1994 than it did in 1968).

What was compared in 1994 were not just comprehensives from areas where grammar schools were present as against those where grammar schools were absent (which previous research has studied) but 208 schools divided between those where respondents specifically stated that one of the reasons for their school failing to fill in September of the survey year was because there were grammar schools in the area compared with schools which said they were full specifically because there were no grammar schools in the area.

Table 4.4 Comprehensive schools with/without grammar schools, 1994 (based on question 14A and question 17A)

	Grammar schools present in the area	Grammar schools absent from the area
Average size	801	1052
Percentage:		
In top 20% of attainment	12	24
Going on in 11–16 schools	57	69
Staying on in 11–18 schools	49	60
Gaining five GCSE A–C	29	48
'A' level point score average	10.6	13.4

As can be seen, the difference was quite marked on attainment at intake – as well as on every other marker, including exam results.

The same differences applied when comprehensive schools attributed their being full or not to the presence or absence of comprehensive schools specially favoured in some way – through grant maintained, CTC, selective voluntary, or 'magnet' status (questions 14B and 17B). Those without such schools in their vicinity had an average pass rate for five GCSE A–C of 44.4%; those with them had one of only 27.8%. At 'A' level the difference was not as great (12.3 as against 10.7) as in the case of grammar schools, but differences in the rates of staying on were almost identical.

What was particularly striking about the opt-out/magnet comparison, however, was the difference in social class composition of intakes. Only a very small percentage of comprehensive schools where there were opt-outs or other favoured comprehensives in the area had predominantly middle-class intakes (8.7%) compared with 38.5% where there were no 'favoured' comprehensives in the local system.

These comparisons suggest that where grammar schools (or other specially favoured schools) continue in an area, comprehensive schools whose intakes are affected have much less chance of achieving well in terms of the league-table markers; and that pupils within such schools tend to leave education earlier.

Social class distribution in intakes

The distribution of social classes in the intakes to comprehensive education has been a matter of much discussion in the last 30 years – as has the subject of social class divisions within comprehensive schooling, particularly related to issues of streaming or course choices.

When looking at the six levels of socio-economic grouping often used to measure social class, comprehensive schools at the start of the reform in 1965 were found to have all social classes reasonably represented except for many in the top professional class and some from the clerical class (Benn, 1975; Monks, 1968:30, 92; Reid, 1990:306). At this time grammar schools had the reputation of being the most socially mixed schools and many people went on believing this to be true even though research showed clearly that by the end of the 1960s grammar school intakes had become predominantly middle class with percentages varying from 57% to 82% according to the type of grammar school being measured (Public Schools Commission, Second Report, 1970; Steedman, 1980).

As grammar schools came into comprehensive reorganisation, the middle-class percentages in comprehensive schools began to rise. While Steedman (1980) had found middle-class intakes to comprehensives at 28% (and only 1% higher than intakes to secondary modern schools) for the cohort that entered secondary education in 1968, she also found that in those comprehensive schools most recently formed (she called them 'transitional') the figure was 30%. Later reports from the ongoing NFER project recorded a significant rise in middle-class intakes in the sample studied in the last report, for example, up to 31% (Ross *et al.*, 1972:194) and another NFER researcher, later studying another sample from the survey, found 32% (Robertson, 1977). By 1973 government statistics looking at social class distribution in schools (based on the 1971 census) showed comprehensive schools with 35% of their total as middle class (HMSO, *Household Survey*, 1973:233) as against 39% for Britain as a whole (page 63); and pronounced comprehensive schools 'fairly evenly representative of most socio-economic groups, comparing them with grammar schools (59% middle-class) and private schools (84%) which were not by then 'representative' (HMSO, *Household Survey*, 1973:233–34).

It may seem a small matter that comprehensive schools were short of what was really a very small percentage of middle-class intake overall – by the mid-1970s only about 5% in Britain as a whole – but when so large a proportion of academic attainment (by which the system has always been judged) came from this small percentage, it was important to many people that comprehensive schools have their full share. One figure from the time illustrated its monopoly on national attainment in that two-thirds of the top of the six socio-economic groups had degrees, compared with less than 1% of those in the lowest of the six (Reid, 1990). Steedman (1980) illustrated the same kind of difference in terms of attainment in secondary education: at the level of five 'good' 'O' levels, only 12% of pupils from the working class got them compared with 39% of pupils from the middle class.

Little investigation of the class composition of schools overall has taken place since this period (Reid, 1990); and not only has social class been neglected in favour of gender and race studies, but there has also been a 'neglect of class within ethnicity and sex' studies themselves (Reid, 1990). There have been certain exceptions, one of which is the work of the Centre for Educational Sociology at Edinburgh University, which has monitored school leavers for nearly 20 years (McPherson and Willms, 1988:88).

But class composition relating to occupational or economic status was not the only factor to study in education, and occasional attempts have been made to look at others that might be associated with attainment in education. For example, in one study the DES also looked at population density, overcrowding, supplementary benefit, infant mortality, and overall expenditure in schools to try to see what might lie behind differences. In another study (of the 16–19 age range) the factors examined were level of unemployment in the family, presence of a new commonwealth or Pakistani head of family, homes lacking basic amenities, families with one parent, and families with four or more children. Most of these other factors showed some relationship to educational attainment or advantage in education, but none was as good at calling the outcome as socio-economic background, which most studies have estimated will account for between 60% and 80% of the differences in educational attainment, including examination results.

Thus, once social background was taken into account, there has always been little difference found between grammar schools or comprehensive schools in terms of academic outcomes for pupils individually (see Chapter 2). Although it is generally agreed that social class differences are the major factor in accounting for differences in academic outcome, there is no agreement about exactly what the mechanism is that accounts for this. It is not directly related to intelligence levels, for even where the measured intelligence of students is the same class still makes a difference. For example, even where all students in a group of sixth forms had high IQ scores at the same level, 86% of the middle class got two 'A' levels compared with only 60% of the working-class students (Reid, 1990:294).

It is thus also about the way differences were perceived and about the way factors interacted with each other. In a comprehensive context there may be a further factor to take into account One study, for example, found that while parental occupation related to exam performance, the overall social mix of intakes was important as well (Rutter, 1979). In fact, a school's balance of ability at intake was a crucial factor in relation to gaining qualifications, more important than whether the parental choice had been satisfied,and irrespective of school process (Rutter, 1979:155, 160, 169). Although this suggested academic balance and social mix were strongly associated with exam success, neither Rutter and his team nor anyone else could say academic balance brought success (p.174). The interrelationship of factors held the key, and thus could be more important in comprehensive education than in selective systems. In several places in the 1994 survey (as will be pointed out) the nature of the social mix between working- and middle-class pupils seemed to have an important relationship to what was being measured.

Class inside comprehensives

The value to pupils of education within a mixed social group has not had much attention in recent times, although early studies comparing comprehensive pupils and others in terms of social values and attitudes showed positive gains for comprehensive pupils in social class attitudes and social resilience through being at school with a greater social mix (Currie, 1962; Miller, 1961). But, later, when the studies related to streaming in comprehensive schools, the results were not so positive. Several research studies have shown the way that streaming limited social interaction and reinforced class differences (Ford, 1969; Johannson and Magnusson, 1960), as other studies had shown in the grammar schools (Lacey, 1970). Later some found this also applied to setting pupils for subjects, where allocations to classes and sets internally were not always explained by reference to ability. Very often 'differentiating perceptions are socially constructed' (Ball, 1981:38) or, as had been put more directly a few years earlier, 'Streaming means social and racial segregation with the bottom classes often developing a ghetto mentality' (Wilby, 1979:150).

Ball concluded that comprehensive education cannot change inequalities because it does not take into account differentially distributed resources in society, including knowledge of the school system and parents' own educational qualifications, not to mention 'teachers' conceptualisation of pupils and the effects of streaming' (Ball, 1981:31). Others may have accepted this but they still argued for mixed-ability classes all the same on the grounds that 'teachers in unstreamed schools are virtually unanimous that mixed-ability teaching reduces discipline problems' (Wilby, 1979:150).

By the mid-1990s there were few still arguing that streaming and grammar schools were necessary for the sake of the working class, as had been persistently argued for years. Instead, advocates were making demands on behalf of the middle class in the state system when they argued for more streaming and more grammar schools, apparently willing to accept relegation of the working-class as a whole to lower streams or lesser schools (Gray, 1995; Hutton, 1995).

Such arguments harked back to the very early years when the middle classes were conspicuously absent from comprehensive education (which, except for a few large cities, was no longer the case by the mid-1990s) as well as to the days when grammar school advocates represented comprehensive schools as those where middle-class children were likely to be short changed. In fact, it has been middle-class children whom studies have always shown doing well in comprehensive schooling (Ball, 1981; Reynolds et al., 1987); and, overall, just as well as they had done in selective systems (Steedman, 1980, 1983). The question we should have been asking was this: was the understandable desire to produce good outcomes for pupils from certain articulate and well-informed families allowed to impede the progress of pupils whose families were less knowledgeable? Are grammar schools or forms of internal organisation – like streaming and setting – always the best ones in relation to attainment overall, or only the best in relation to the attainment of pupils who occupy the 'upper' levels of the divisions they create?

Valuing pupils and students equally inside schools and colleges is difficult in a society which does not value their parents and families equally outside it, but it has not deterred most comprehensive schools from making the effort to educate their intakes equitably, using a wide range of grouping strategies (see Chapters 6 and 7). Once grammar schools have started taking all attainments themselves, a comprehensive system will have to try to see that each school receives as mixed an intake socially as is possible within its own general area. However, there will always be a few areas where imbalances will prevail. Although knowledge of the imbalance might be used in judging the achievements of the schools, imbalance in itself should not affect a school's or college's capacity to function as a comprehensive. Every student in every intake to every comprehensive school or college deserves the whole-hearted commitment of its staff and community to ensure as full an education as would be received anywhere else. That is the only possible basis upon which a comprehensive system can operate.

Survey 1994

Our questions on social class were directed to discovering the mix of working- and middle-class intakes that characterised comprehensive education in 1994.

Those filling in the survey questionnaires were asked to call upon their knowledge of the occupations of parents (or students) to give us a class profile of their individual intake. Schools and colleges know the background of their intakes very well indeed and almost all were able to give such information within the classifications named in question 36. Only 18 did not wish to reply. One wrote, 'We do not recognise social class'; and another, 'I don't want to stress lower class. I was myself'. Many more, however, wrote next to this question that there should have been an additional space for the percentages of parents or students who were *un*employed. After all, this is very much part of 'occupational' status upon which class is based.

Five broad categories were given (question 36) and the results are in Table 4.5(a). (Repeated in collapsed form in Table 4.5(b), the basis of statistics shown in Appendix Table A5. References to class difference in the text also are to the collapsed version unless noted otherwise.)

Table 4.5 (a) Social class composition of comprehensive schools and colleges, 1994. Results are given as numbers with percentages in parentheses

(A) mostly working class	415	(26.9)
(B) mostly middle class	91	(5.9)
(C) a mix but probably more working class than middle class	526	(34.1)
(D) a mix but probably more middle class than working class	316	(20.4)
(E) drawn equally from both middle and working class	194	(12.5)
Total	1542	(100)

(b) Collapsed class table (a) (see Table A5)

Working class (question 36A and C)	(61)
Middle class (question 36B and D)	(26)
Drawn equally from working and middle class (question 36E)	(13)
	(100)

What stands out from Table 4.5(a) was that two-thirds of the comprehensive schools and colleges were socially mixed. This is many more than would have been the case 30 years ago. Of those that were 'one class', one out of five was middle class. 30 years ago there would have been no mostly middle-class comprehensive schools.

In looking further at the relationship of class to such factors as attendance or attainment in external examinations – set out in Table 4.6 – we can see how closely social class differences (question 36 A–E) are related to outcomes.

Table 4.6 Interrelationship of intake and outcome, comprehensive schools and colleges, 1994. Results are given as percentages

	Full in September	Five GCSE A–C	Percentage staying on*	'A' level point score†	Attendance below 90%‡	Percentage attainment in the top 20%
Average for survey	39.8	39.3	56.2	12.7	21.2	18.0
Intakes by social grouping:						
Mostly working class	22.9	26.3	49.7	9.6	49.8	10.4
A mix but probably more working class	32.8	37.9	54.6	12.2	14.5	15.7
Mostly middle class	67.1	54.6	64.5	14.2	1.0	30.4
A mix but probably more middle class	59.7	51.2	60.2	14.3	5.1	26.9
Equal mix of social groups	44.4	46.5	58.0	13.8	9.5	21.5

*All-through schools only.
†England only.
‡Schools only.

A first glance might seem to confirm that examination, attendance or staying-on figures so closely parallel the five class categories that each indicator proceeds in five similarly spaced 'steps' according to class. But while the 1994 survey confirms social class as a major factor in most outcomes, it is not quite that simple, for we can also see that the distances between steps are not equidistant. Thus the scores for schools with mixed intakes almost always lie nearer the higher scoring end of whatever is being measured than they do the lower (e.g., for GCSE and 'A' level results).

Mixing – or academic balance, if you like – might produce its own positive effect, greater than the sum of the parts mixed, and is an effect seen in several other tables in the 1994 survey.

Entitlement to free meals – A social needs index

Another indicator that tells us a lot about a school's intake is the level of free meals that its pupils are eligible to receive. This does not apply in the same way to the colleges (other than the sixth-form colleges), although some 60% of them felt able to answer the question making estimates from their knowledge of the social welfare system; tertiary and further education colleges have been omitted from the statistics in Table A5 but are included in Table 4.7.

The measure is accepted by many as a poverty index for a school. For this reason, the free dinner figure is a popular candidate for the 'value added' exercises to make 'league table' comparisons fairer. For others, interest relates more to what the figures show about the extent and nature of poverty within the education system, and where, possibly, extra resources need to be concentrated.

Statistics nationally at the time of our survey showed the variations there can be for this indicator in relation to various areas of the country. Thus the proportion getting free meals in inner London was 31% in the year before the survey while in the English counties it was only 10% (CIPFA, *Educational Statistics*, 1993). Parliamentary questions have also elicited replies on this question, one in particular showing low levels of free dinners taken up in schools that have opted out.

Table 4.7 Eligibility for free meals, schools and colleges (n=1464), 1994

Categories having free meals	Percentages (number) in each category
A 5% or less	17.0 (249)
B 6–15%	39.7 (582)
C 16–30%	25.1 (368)
D 31–50%	13.4 (197)
E Over 50%	4.6 (68)

Our 1994 survey asked schools to give figures of levels of free dinners from their records, set out in the five categories, shown in Table 4.7; 83% of comprehensive schools and colleges had more than 5% taking free meals; 43% (633) had over 15% of pupils qualifying for free meals. For our indicator of high poverty we used categories D and E collapsed, where 31% or over were eligible (18.1% of all schools and colleges replying). Using this same measure throughout (Table A5), we were also able to compare comprehensive schools and sixth-form colleges in relation to 'poverty' at intake.

As Table A5 shows, those school types with low percentages (question 40A) – the more advantaged – were voluntary controlled, grant maintained, upper tier schools, Church of England Schools, schools drawing from private housing, schools in villages and the countryside, and most advantaged of all, the sixth-form colleges.

Those with percentages that were higher than the survey average – the less advantaged – were LEA schools, 11–16 schools, single-sex schools, inner city schools, council estate schools and those drawing intakes from the two housing categories that included substandard housing.

The first category in question 40 – those below the 5% level, which were 17% of those replying – would include schools with both low levels of pupils taking free dinners and those where there were virtually none. They had strikingly different profiles compared with the survey average in terms of intakes and also results, suggesting their relative lack of poorer pupils was a strong factor in outcome. For example, their five GCSE A–C pass rate of 56.1% and 'A' level point score of 14.5 were well above the survey average (of 39.3% and 12.7 respectively). In Scotland the figures for schools in this 'low free dinner' category, though higher, did not show the same marked difference as in England: 56.1% for Standard grade 1–3 (as against 52% for Scots schools overall).

Overall in the survey, the majority of schools that had these 'low free dinner' levels (question 40A) also drew predominantly from the middle class for their intakes (66%). Only 20% drew from predominantly working-class intakes. Such findings suggest that statistics relating to free-dinner take-up in any school – figures which all schools have to hand already – would be useful not just for value-added calculations in relation to 'league tables' but also for setting fair admissions and funding criteria within the school system.

Geographical location

The stereotype of a comprehensive school in countless media profiles and even in popular fiction and drama, is of a school in an inner city, despite the fact that the first independent enquiry of 1968 found that less than one in five were so located; 30 years later it is almost down to 1 in 10 (Table

4.8). Even given the fact that representation of inner city schools in the survey was probably less than for other categories in 1994, this was a considerable drop. Only 11 schools and colleges were unable to answer where they were located.

Table 4.8 Location of schools and colleges, 1968 and 1994 surveys. Results are given as percentages, with numbers in parentheses

	1994		1968*
In large cities	11	(169)	19
In towns	40	(619)	27
In suburbs or outskirts of towns or cities	34	(534)	30
In villages or countryside	14	(224)	10
Other/unknown	1	(14)	4
Total	100	(1560)	100

*Based on Benn and Simon, 1970: Table 16.3, page 275. Unlike other tables in the 1994 survey percentages for 1994 are calculated from the total numbers in the survey rather than from the total number replying (to enable direct comparison with 1968).

The main difference over nearly 30 years ago is decline of the total in the large cities and the growth of comprehensive schools and colleges in the towns, suburbs and countryside areas. Towns now constitute the most numerous category.

Disadvantage has shifted too over time. At the start of this century it was greatest in the countryside and lowest in the suburbs and towns. Today countryside and villages are advantaged areas, with schools and colleges becoming less and less advantaged as we move through the towns and then suburbs, to many of the least advantaged in the middle of larger cities.

For example, schools in villages had higher percentages in the top 20% of the attainment range (21.5%) compared with schools in the cities (13.6%). Put another way, less than a quarter of large city schools had ability intakes above the survey average of 18%, while over half those in the countryside had them, and over one-third of those in towns and suburbs. Only 17% of village schools reported they were in poor state of repair compared with 40% of schools in the cities (question 67A) (and 29% in suburbs and only 19% in towns).

Some examination results showed the same difference. For example, for five GCSE A–C, schools in the large cities averaged 24.2% – well below the survey average of 39.3% – while those in towns and suburbs (the great bulk of the schools) were almost at the average 39.9% and 39.8% respectively. The figure for schools in the countryside and villages was 47.5%, well above the survey average. The same was true for 'A' level grade point average: 10.1 for cities and 15.0 for village and countryside schools (with towns and suburbs near the survey average 12.7 and 12.8, respectively). Staying on into the sixth form in all-through schools was higher in villages too at 62.6%, while for the other three categories, all were at or just below the survey average of 56.1%. There was one advantage village schools did not have, however: they had lower percentages enrolled on GNVQ or GSVQ (Table A6).

But while there may be a contrast to be pointed up between schools in villages and those in the middle of large cities, together these two categories only represented a quarter of the schools and colleges in the survey. Most of the population were in schools and colleges in towns and suburbs and the differences were very few between the two. Scores at five GCSE A–C, and 'A' level and staying-on were not only virtually identical but in both cases were at or near the survey average. Except for a slightly higher proportion of suburban schools with middle-class intakes, it was very hard to see real differences between these two categories; and certainly no polarisation.

The city schools had the highest levels of poverty in their intakes. In 1994, 65.5% of city comprehensives had pupils taking free dinners at the level of 31% or over compared with only 2.8% of schools from the villages or countryside. In the towns it was 12.1% and in the suburbs 14.8%. Again, where the majority are, little polarisation; but at the two geographical ends, quite a lot.

It was the same with the participation of the middle classes. Their proportions in the schools in the large cities were markedly lower than in the other locations. Only 5.4% of city comprehensives drew predominantly from the middle classes compared with percentages nearly five times higher in towns and nearly eight times higher in the countryside (Table A5). Possibly this explains the distorted views of some education writers and media editors, so many of whom live in large cities, particularly London.

Housing: the flexible factor

Schools serving different types of housing areas also show some very stark differences; more, in fact, than between geographical locations, for it is just as much the pattern and quality of the housing that characterises school and college intakes as it is geographical location. In a sense, housing areas define neighbourhood; and with few exceptions few neighbourhoods in Britain fail to contain a mix of housing. Within the large city are enclaves of high-quality housing as well as poor; in the countryside or in the suburbs are enclaves of substandard housing. The exceptions are the large swathes of estates, both council and private. It is these that preclude mixing far more than geographical 'neighbourhoods'.

Schools and colleges have a good knowledge of the housing patterns in their intake areas (and almost every school and college in the survey was able to give one of five housing types to characterise their own). This knowledge is a reason why all schools and colleges should be consulted about the way admissions rules are drawn up in any area – and why no publicly supported schools should be allowed to operate their own separate system, as happens now. In any public service the object should be to achieve intakes to schools that are as balanced as they can be without forcing any institution to serve an 'unnatural' geographical configuration – or any parents or students to make unnecessarily prolonged or inconvenient journeys.

The 1994 survey question on housing was quite similar to the one in the enquiry of 1968, allowing some comparison to be drawn across the intervening years (Table 4.9). Even allowing for the likelihood that those answering from the two substandard categories in 1994 today are under-represented, the 'neighbourhood' changes since the 1960s can be clearly seen: a smaller proportion from council and substandard housing and nearly a fourfold increase in schools drawing from private housing areas. The difference is even starker when we compare the 1994 picture with that for comprehensive schools founded in the 1950s (Benn and Simon, 1972: Table 21.2), when 62% of those founded in 1958 drew from either council housing or mixed housing with a substandard element. Today that figure is 31%.

Table 4.9 Housing patterns and comprehensive education, 1968 and 1994. Results are given as percentages, with numbers in parentheses

	1994	1968*
Council housing	13 (196)	15
Private housing	15 (237)	4
A mix of private and council	54 (839)	42
Substandard housing	1 (18)	4
Mix of all previous, including substandard	17 (256)	35
Total	100 (1546)	100

*Benn and Simon, 1970: Table 20.1, page 335 – subsuming eight schools in last category that had not answered and calculated as percentage of survey total. The 1994 column was calculated on total answering, omitting 14 schools or colleges not replying.

In 1994, 71% drew from mixed housing of one kind or other. It does not mean poor housing has disappeared (indeed, it could be higher today). It means that instead of drawing the bulk of their pupils from relatively restricted housing areas, comprehensive schools now draw more frequently from areas where housing is mixed.

Extremes still exist, as with geographical location; and they can illustrate educational differences more eloquently than many other factors. For example, as Table A5 shows, 88.9% of comprehensive schools drawing from substandard housing and 63.1% drawing from council estates had 31% or more of their pupils entitled to free dinners, compared with only 1.3% of the comprehensive schools drawing from private residential or owner-occupied housing areas in 1994. But what was interesting about the percentages having free dinners at this level from the two mixed categories of housing (at 6.3% – and even the second, which included an element of substandard housing, at 31.8%) was that their percentages were not midway between substandard and private housing but situated towards the advantaged end. Once again, where the category is mixed, there is a benefit in outcome.

Polarisation was evident, however, in some housing comparisons, including considerable differences in their attainment levels at intake. The proportion for private housing is 26.4% in the top 20% of attainment, 'more' than comprehensive; while it was only 9.8% for schools drawing from substandard housing, and 8.6% for council housing schools, a great deal 'less' than average. But for at least one of the categories of mixed housing (council and private, question 27C), again the mix was not midway but towards the higher end at 19.5% – just above the survey average.

Whether the leavening effect of the mix was due to the effect on the school once the pupils had entered or whether it was the effect of mixed housing patterns having characterised intakes before they got to the school, is hard to say.

Academic results at the five GCSE A–C level show polarisation by housing in 1994 but only at the extremes: schools drawing from substandard housing had a pass rate of 18.2% and for those drawing from council estates 23.2%, while those drawing mainly from private housing had double this percentage at 52.1%. Again, what was interesting was that the majority of schools drawing from a mix of council and private housing did not have results half way between these extremes, but towards the higher level at 42.2%.

For 'A' level grade point averages substandard schools had 8.0 and council estate schools 9.2 – with the schools drawing on the private housing having 14.2. Those drawing from the mixed housing have scores towards the upper end at 13.4. Once again, it was only where the housing included an element of substandard housing that averages and scores were towards the lower end rather than the higher at 10.5.

The same effect was replicated in Scotland where for three or more Highers as a percentage of those on roll in S4, council estate schools had 15.9% and private estate schools 29.5%. The two mixed housing categories (from which 65% of Scottish comprehensive schools drew; question 27C and E) were both towards the higher end rather than midway between. Scotland had no schools drawing only from substandard housing but 24% of its schools drew from council housing, almost twice as high as the survey average (question 27A), while its number drawing from private housing was a third less than the survey average (question 27C), at 1 in 10.

To a certain extent mixed housing intakes to schools and colleges can be more easily organised in cities; and sometimes too in towns and suburbs. From the start areas have tried to balance intakes by balancing housing in order – without distorting zones – to include all types of housing in any one catchment area for any one school. But some 'market' oriented schools today look at housing in a competitive way, trying to maximise imbalance for their own advantage by concentrating their recruiting attempts in private housing areas and avoiding those where there is council housing or substandard older housing, a strategy which naturally increases imbalance in neighbouring schools[7].

Table 4.10 illustrates mixing in relation to housing and social class. It collapses the class figures differently from the appendix tables in order to maximise the mixed intakes and one-class schools.

Table 4.10 Percentage of one-class and mixed-class schools and colleges related to location, 1994

	Total survey	City	Town	Suburban	Village	Mixed housing (question 27C)
Mostly working class (question 36A)	27	62	24	23	15	13
Mostly middle class (question 36C)	6	0.5	4	8	10	2
Mixed working class and middle class or drawn equally from working class and middle class (questions 36 B, D and E)	67	37.5	71	69	75	85

Table 4.10 shows cities to be the only area with more one-class schools than mixed schools. Cities have only a third of their schools with a mix compared with all other areas where mixed percentages lie between two-thirds and three-quarters. The villages have the greatest mixing, but at the far right column is a single figure from the housing category – for housing that mixes both private and council patterns. As we can see, it is the equally mixed housing that produces the greatest social mixing of all: 85%.

It has always been claimed that if you want genuine mixing – not just for social reasons but for livelier teaching and learning – it was not specially manipulated admissions systems that would do it, it is a long-term investment in mixed housing patterns – and in particular, avoiding huge enclaves of socially monochromatic housing.

Neighbourhood

As we saw earlier, the word 'neighbourhood' has been distorted by some of the debates around comprehensive education, and in some circles (particularly national ones) it has changed from a positive word to yet another euphemistic description of a working-class school (see pages 34–39). In other circles it retains its positive meaning.

Since so much fuss has been made for decades about the desirability of drawing from outside the neighbourhood to get a mix (rather than drawing from as varied a range as possible within it, which is the alternative), and since the introduction of so much legislation in the 1980s and 1990s was to facilitate avoidance of neighbourhood (including a court judgment that no LEA could dedicate even a small proportion of its own schools to its own residents)[8], we wanted to know just how schools and colleges perceived their commitment to those who lived locally as against those who lived further away.

We defined neighbourhood as students and pupils coming from the LEA, the 'local area' or the local 'neighbourhood'. Each school and college was asked from which one of four patterns based on distance it drew the majority of its intake (question 33); 90% were able to give information (Table 4.11).

Table 4.11 Intakes related to neighbourhood, comprehensive schools and colleges, 1994. Results are given as percentages with number of schools or colleges in parentheses

Intake pattern		
Pupils/students drawn:		
(a) From the local area or within the LEA	73.4	(1030)
(b) From the local area but with a substantial minority from outside the LEA or neighbourhood	21.3	(300)
(c) From inside and outside the local area in equal measure	4.1	(58)
(d) Mostly from outside the local area or LEA	0.9	(14)
Total	100	(1402)

Surprisingly, after almost a decade of urging schools to compete for custom far and wide, and after an even longer period of attrition against LEA-based education, including policies pushing schools to opt out with rights to refuse entry to local pupils, making it harder for LEAs to draw up common admissions agreements for all schools by consultation, a remarkably high percentage of comprehensive schools and colleges is still neighbourhood based. If schools are looked at separately from colleges (question 6A–E), the percentage is even higher: at 76.9%.

Colleges are obviously likely to draw from much further away and to be more regionally based, especially those that have many thousands of students. Thus only 27% of further education colleges draw from the neighbourhood (question 33A), though sixth-form colleges (question 4G) are more neighbourhood based at 41% and tertiary colleges (question 4H) the most neighbourhood based of the colleges with 54% drawing from the LEA or the immediate area.

Neighbourhood has also been negatively applied to the inner city, where it has always been assumed comprehensive schools will have their most locally restricted intakes. The 1994 survey found just the reverse. Large city schools were the least neighbourhood based (question 33A by question 27) at only just 56.2% compared with those drawing from the villages at 72% and towns at 71.2%. Even schools drawing from private housing were more neighbourhood based at 61.4% than comprehensive schools in large cities.

Schools drawing most of the pupils from substandard housing were those most likely to be neighbourhood based at 88% (question 27), but these were only a small number of schools and they were not necessarily in large cities. Council estate schools and those with working-class intakes were both 84% neighbourhood (question 33A) but even 63% of the category of comprehensive drawing mainly from middle-class intakes was neighbourhood based. This was more than aided and special agreement schools (only 49% and 46% respectively), many of which were denominational and designed to serve larger areas, especially if Catholic schools. The other category with low levels of neighbourhood schools was the grant maintained school. Even so, the majority (52.7%) were still neighbourhood based in 1994.

Admissions to comprehensive schools

The 1994 survey asked many questions about admissions, always a crucial issue for any system and particularly so for comprehensive education. In this section we deal mostly with schools (unless otherwise noted) while admissions to colleges is covered in Chapter 9. Issues of 'parental choice' were discussed in Chapter 2 (pages 49–57).

Over the 30 years of comprehensive reform much discussion has taken place about the difference between open and hidden selection; about the balance between the rights of those who live near schools against those who live further away; and about schools that opt out of responsibilities other local schools have agreed to shoulder in relation to admissions agreements. The latter have always included some voluntary schools; now they include in addition many which are grant maintained.

In many areas over the last 30 years admissions policies were decided by party political voting in local elections (see Chapter 2). In this respect the British comprehensive system is different from that of other countries where admissions matters are much more straightforward and not tied to party political views either nationally or locally. Much more influential in some countries – like the USA, for example – have been court decisions, particularly laws affecting the rights of black minorities.

The main reason admissions is still party politically based in Britain is because one of the fundamental rights in other comprehensive systems is not yet available in British law: the right to enter a named local school or college at each stage of the educational process throughout primary and secondary years. A formidable list of educators and administrators have suggested such a fundamental right be introduced in Britain and several local authorities have operated such systems successfully (see Chapter 2). But the right to enter has never been introduced nationally in Britain because selection has never been officially ended, and indeed, still continues.

Nevertheless, during the last 30 years comprehensive-compatible admissions arrangements have been established in many areas and in whole regions where selection has been ended. Admissions in these areas are usually based on nearness to schools (sometimes including zoning) or upon arrangements where lower schools 'feed' upper schools. Parental preference is a feature in them all, exercised by those who prefer a school other than the one named as their local school, a feature present in the law since 1944, made firmer in the early 1980s.

In primary education, which is 99% comprehensive, the rationale of entry is usually fairly clear and not many pupils are refused entry to their nearest school. In addition, few parents want children to travel long distances during these early years. At the secondary stage it can be very different – with some parents willing to send (or being able to afford to take or send) children miles each day to secure the education 'of their choice'.

'Parental choice' is in quotation marks because no system of education could ever operate on the principle that each parent can have a legal right to choose a school (see Chapter 2). Even when the law (as at present) has been widely and somewhat dishonestly described as guaranteeing parental choice of schooling, all it does is provide that parents may express a preference. It does not require that the preference be met. Everyone knows it is met for only certain parents, not others. The question is: do present arrangements meet a higher percentage of preferences as well as benefit a larger number of schools than some of the other systems that might be tried? This is what we do not know.

Most comprehensive-compatible admissions systems will always want to accommodate as much 'parental choice' as they can. What characterises comprehensive-compatible systems as against those based solely on 'choice', however, is that the 'parental choice' factor is only one of the factors used. When 'parental choice' is the only factor and is used in place of an agreed admissions system, experience shows that sooner or later it leads to hierarchy and polarisation (see pages 50–54).

This was what was happening in 1994 because admissions were ostensibly based solely on 'choice' but within a system where, legally, not all parents and schools were equal. Numerous changes to the law in respect of different types of schools (grammar, opted out, CTC, voluntary or specialising) have put a complex hierarchy of 'choice' into operation that is as good as selection in many areas. It means not only have some parents greater rights of choice than others but that some schools have greater rights to select than others. This is not because in life things turn out that way; it is because the present admissions laws have been set up to produce this outcome. To secure a different outcome requires a different system. Not a big change to legislation, but a change all the same (see Chapter 10).

Admissions selection by keeping schools 'empty'

Until 1988 it was usually possible to contact an LEA and discover what admissions policy operated in its area. Since the 1988 Act, however, when admissions policies, like so much else, were thrown to 'the market' through engineered open enrolment, there are many areas where almost no one can tell you the policy that prevails with any certainty, even for the school down the road.

Some schools can admit (or turn down) whoever they wish, while others must admit a child to a school which is not 'full' – unless, of course, the school is a grammar school, an aided school, a school specialising in a particular academic subject, a CTC school, a school offering assisted or aided places or a grant maintained or LEA school given special permission to select; or any school which is 'full'. As can be seen, there are many exceptions to the rule that it is 'parental choice' that decides, and an equally large number of exceptions to the law that requires schools that are not full to admit those who apply.

The 1994 survey illustrated one of the most important features of the system that is required to 'juggle' all these factors and retain this complex selective system in place: many extra empty places. In other words, it showed clearly that most secondary schools must fail to fill. It was not the odd 'unpopular' school, as myth had it; it was the majority: 60.2% of all schools and colleges had empty places at the end of September in the year of the 1994 survey.

The emptiness of schools was probably most striking at this time because the secondary population was at a low point in many areas. It will enjoy a slow rise from now until the end of the century. Several schools said they were normally full and this was just a 'blip year'. For some – even a substantial proportion – this may have been true; but for many more it was clear that being unable to fill came about because an artificial number limit had been put upon their school that had no real relationship to the population of the area likely to come to the school. The limit applied no matter how 'good' their school or how hard they did or didn't work to make it effective. In these circumstances schools readily tend to lose heart, for the prevailing myth is that an 'undersubscribed' school is a shunned school, unchosen by parents, a situation that causes governing bodies to spend long hours discussing this 'failing' as if it were the school's fault. In a substantial number of cases it was clear that being unable to fill bore no relation to the school's policies or record.

Overcrowdedness was associated 30 years ago with poor schools in poor areas, but after the late 1970s when the bulge had passed and numbers began to fall, being 'full' began to be associated with success. Early in the 1980s Ball already cited the new association of overcrowded schools with lower delinquency and higher attainment (Ball, 1984:101). There was the other side as well: funding limitations, staff redeployment, poorer working conditions, loss of morale and the huge weight of government-inspired sniping at comprehensive schooling – even before the onslaught of testing and a detailed national curriculum. Falling numbers was just one more burden.

Why the surplus is required

But surely schools were full in 1994 because parents chose them; and parents chose them because they were the best schools (likely to attract middle-class parents, for example)? At first sight it looked as if this might be the case, for middle-class schools at 67.1% and 59.7% (question 36B and D) were far more likely to be full than were working-class schools at 22.9% and 32.8% (question 36A and C).

A closer look, however, showed the matter was more complex, for the 1994 survey also showed that certain types of comprehensive – with high middle-class intakes and above-average examination results – also have high percentages failing to fill, far above the survey average. These include village and countryside comprehensives (Table A5), the least likely of all the geographical area schools to be full but the ones with the best academic results and most middle-class intakes. Making it even more complex, a larger proportion of schools in the cities were full than in the shires. Could this be because the percentages of parents concerned with 'parental choice' is thought to be greater in the shires and more empty places allowed for the necessary manipulation? Or was it that more city schools were being closed down?

Other discrepancies are that over two-fifths of all schools and colleges that have very high percentages in the top 20% of the attainment range (between 20% and 100%) were also unable to fill in 1993; as were nearly half (48%) of the schools with the lowest levels having free dinners (under 5%). If being full or empty related to desirable features of comprehensive schools that make them chosen, we would not expect many of these findings.

Obviously, some of the reasons for being full relate to the quality of schools and some will fail to fill because they are uninviting or educationally flawed, but it is obvious that all too many are assuming they are 'failing' when what is really at fault is a system that requires empty places in every neighbourhood far in excess of reasonable requirements – for one reason only, to meet the likely effects of 'parental choice' for certain schools.

This finding should not surprise us. Having a surplus of empty places is a well-known (and very controversial) requirement of 'parental choice' systems. It is no coincidence that a huge over-supply of unused secondary school places has been kept in place in schools for nearly 15 years and that governments have colluded with the wasteful expenditure because any national system (selective or comprehensive) that is claiming to operate by 'parental choice' cannot operate unless it has this wasteful reserve. Nearly 20 years ago Alex Clegg, the Chief Education Officer for Yorkshire, spelled it out:

> The only way of meeting parental choice that I can think of is to make all the schools twice as big as we need them and at the same time shut half of them down or keep them only partially filled.
>
> (Clegg, 1969)

As predicted by Clegg, using 'parental choice' as a method of entry unbalanced by any other factor, meant having half or more comprehensive schools 'partially filled' in 1994. It was not an accident. The present situation has been carefully engineered by means of a complex web of legislative changes involving admissions law, 'choice' rules, enrolment rules, differentiated legal rights to 'choose' entrants related to different legal status of school, and graduated exemptions from both 'choice' and enrolment rules for selective schools, aided schools, grant maintained schools and LEA schools 'oversubscribed' or specialising – along with draconian centralised control, leaving LEAs with less and less opportunity to organise fair and agreed admissions systems locally. Never has a system claiming to be merely the free operation of 'the market' been so heavily controlled by government, so policed in law and so remote from democratic oversight.

The risk of polarisation

The problem is that such an admissions system has in-built laws tending to foster increasing polarisation. Another Chief Officer, Dudley Fiske, warned of this outcome earlier after he had experienced a local authority that had tried to use 'parental choice' balanced by no other factors. In several publications he gave chapter and verse for the polarisation that followed (for example, Fiske, 1979; see also Chapter 2). In 1979 he was warning the Government about leaving so many surplus places in the system and urging it to implement a system of planned admissions limits 'to avoid the unacceptable alternative of too few children chasing too many places which makes neither educational nor economic sense' (Fiske, 1979:17).

Fiske's prophecy came true by the 1990s with a system plagued by too few children chasing too many places. It came true as well in that it made no economic sense, since the taxpayer was paying at least £250 million a year for the thousands and thousands of provided-places no one was using (Audit Commission, reported in *Hansard*, 19 July 1994; 7 February 1995). Some make this over-expenditure even higher[9].

Periodically, the Government has blamed empty places on the LEAs and the LEAs have blamed the Government, but, secretly, it suited them both – at least, it suited certain LEAs. If the number of places matched the number of pupils, a system accommodating the 'parental choice' of the favoured could not be organised. On the other hand, if the surplus were reduced it would be much easier to organise fairer entry systems where parental preference was one of the factors and another was a duty on local authorities to balance the needs of schools fairly in respect of admissions.

As Fiske noted, the present system makes sense only in the context of increasing privatisation as the goal for public education. In a private system the schools have no responsibility for anything or anyone outside their feepayers and that was the situation in the state system in 1994 with regard to selective and opted out and CTC schools – as well as some that were 'full' and chose to select thereafter. They had no responsibility to the education service as a whole or to the majority of other schools. Market forces were their guide. To quote Dudley Fiske again:

> market forces may be...acceptable...for the...independent schools...(a system which has) no responsibility for pupils it declines to accept. By contrast, maintained schools must operate as part of a system with responsibility for all pupils.
>
> (Fiske, 1979:17–18)

In the public education service someone has to take responsibility for the service; yet under present legislation no one body has this responsibility. LEA administrators who try to take on the task of seeing to it that every child has a place find it increasingly hard in areas where, for example, the

Schools Funding Agency is sharing the work or is wholly 'in charge', for no funding agency can do the work of an LEA. The end result is that it is not possible to be fair to all schools. It is not possible to treat all parents equitably and, above all, it is not possible to be fair to all children and students.

It is increasingly difficult to be fair to all pupils and students. Every year hundreds of pupils have no schools to attend and no rights at all in respect of any of their local schools. Eventually – and often long after school has started – the hard-pressed LEA finds these pupils a school miles across town where there is an 'empty' place, although very often there are empty places in the schools that are in these children's very streets. The schools concerned, however, do not want these children, for whatever reason, and have the legal right not to take them. The LEA is left to pick up the pieces of this irrational market year on year.

The chance to become selective: one of the objectives of 'parental choice' and 'full' schools

Meanwhile, those schools that are full are the ones that are able to be selective if they wish to be so, another objective of the web of legislation. The findings from the 1994 survey showed polarisation was materialising not just between grammar schools and comprehensive schools, but within the comprehensive system. For 'full' comprehensive schools were more likely to be those whose legal status gives governors rights to select pupils. Thus, for example, we found only 34% of LEA schools were full compared with 63% of aided schools and 61% of grant maintained schools (see admissions systems below).

But even this is too simplistic an analysis. Some 'full' schools are undoubtedly schools that have wonderful images as successful schools because of their middle-class intakes or their academic results. Many that are aided and full have a denominational dimension chosen for a different reason. Some are schools built on their former legal status – for example, 47% of schools based on former grammar schools (question 9A and C) were full compared with only 36% based on former secondary modern schools (question 9 B and D). On the other hand, some schools are full by chance: they happen to be in areas of population growth (question 17H).

The point is that when 'full' (for whatever reason) all schools are given the chance to select. Where there is no fair admissions policy in place to which they subscribe, or where their legal status permits them to 'opt out' of the local system used by other schools, some start selecting from the next year. Over time they subtly change in the direction of increasing selectivity, which is what leads to the polarisation predicted in the past, demonstrated in recent research (OECD, 1994) or evident in the figures of the 1994 survey. This polarisation was evident in examination results. For example, those full had 45% for five GCSE A–C, while those undersubscribed averaged only 35%.

Again, those supporting engineered enrolment will argue that such schools are full because they are 'good'; and being 'good' attract more 'good' parents. Yet oversubscribed schools are 'chosen' by all kinds of parents, not just those who are middle class or whose children are already high attainers. Even if it were true that nearly two-thirds of all British schools are not 'good' because not oversubscribed – which no one can accept – nothing compels schools that are oversubscribed to select on the basis of attainment or class. Their selection of these 'good' parents is their own decision, made in order to stay 'selective' – the outcome Margaret Thatcher intended with her legislation on 'full' schools, as she made clear at the time.

Many oversubscribed comprehensive schools, however, do not select by attainment and social background; they have strict admissions rules relating to the procedure for admitting and they apply these in full public view. But there is no law compelling schools to act in this way; and many schools have very imprecise rules or rules that they hide from public view. Some select by interview, or by addresses, or by primary school reports. They are choosing to be selective – a little or a lot, it is up to them.

In every one of these situations some parents are refused. How do they compare with the ones that were chosen? In a fair admissions system this is information that would be published (like 'league tables' are). But there is no law to compel publication of any school's selection and rejection figures. The selective process, which used to take place in town halls by objective rules which could be checked, can now take place in headteachers' offices, or using governors' prerogative, and cannot be checked.

The worst of it is that so much of this selectivity may be inadvertent, simply failing to recognise the effects exerted by the web of legislation constructed around engineered open enrolment, 'parental choice', opting out, and granting of 'admissions' prerogatives to choose between applicants. The Government could not reintroduce selection openly; it was too unpopular. It chose instead to engineer its return by means of parental choice (see page 54). It is slower but in the end it could mean an even more polarised system than prevailed when selection was open because it includes selection on social grounds as well as attainment; and possibly in some cases on grounds of behaviour and even race.

What characterised full and not-full schools?

The 1994 survey asked in detail why some schools were 'full' and others not. All schools in both groups were given a full range of reasons that might account for their differing situations (questions 14 and 17) and if none applied, space to give additional reasons[10].

Schools that were not full ticked the full range of reasons. Some related their undersubscription to 'creaming' operating in their area, including loss of pupils to grammar schools (15%), to opted-out schools (17%) and to private schools (with assisted places, 17%; and 9% where it was private schools without such places): 14% cited unfavourable placing in league tables. Another set of reasons related to situation: the school was located in a run-down or inaccessible area (14%).

In the section for writing in additional reasons (question 15) undersubscribed schools added such features as 'aggressive' sales work from a neighbouring comprehensive; loss to a local comprehensive better provided for; loss to comprehensives that had sixth forms (from those without); preference for schools with 'social' cachet miles away; loss to local grammar schools, magnet schools and local private schools where the LEA still paid for places for local pupils. Most of these could roughly be characterised as more of the 'creaming' complaints logged earlier.

None of these accounted for the two reasons given by the majority of schools for undersubscription, however, both logged earlier in reply to question 14. These were closely related to each other and were (question 14E) falling population and (question 14L) excess places in the area; 45% and 36% respectively of schools that had failed to fill gave one or both of these two reasons. Some of these schools will become full as population begins to rise again, especially those where undersubscription was by fewer than five pupils (19% of those undersubscribed in the 1994 survey). But it is hardly likely to help the remainder, especially the 41% that were short more than 30 pupils, much less the quarter missing more than 50.

Over-supply of places was re-confirmed in the written-in replies (question 15) where the majority of those answering were on this point. About a third were quite specific, the intake number for their school was fixed too high. A school with a standard number fixed at 150 each year when there were only 130 coming up to secondary school age in the area each year, would never be full. Everyone knew it, yet assigned numbers remained unchanged.Versions of this comment were repeated over and over again: assigned standard numbers were 'inappropriately high' or 'unrealistic' or 'totally unrealistic'.

Others complaining on this point claimed reorganisation should continue in their area, where all schools had excess capacity because of demographic changes, but they recognised that little account is taken by anyone of population levels and planning for the future (now that LEAs were being moved out of the picture). In a few areas reorganisation was still continuing with schools being built, shut, enlarged, moved, or entry year numbers changed, but only at a minimal pace. These latter are changes that any system keeping abreast of change should display. The problem is that there were not enough areas displaying them. Instead there were Government plans to increase the imbalance by giving 'full' schools even greater numbers, thus leaving ever more schools undersubscribed.

A last large group of written-in complaints concerned the 'open enrolment' legislation which permitted so many parents to go on what one school called 'a merry-go-round of personal choices', entering children in several schools and accepting places from them all (without letting any school know where else the child was entered). After 'choosing' one, some schools not chosen suddenly found they had empty places after having refused entry to other children whose parents had not applied four or five times over elsewhere. Schools complained bitterly of not being able to fill places at this point because by then the rejected pupils had been sent somewhere else. As one school put it, 'we are not full due to an incoherent transfer system'; or more succinctly, 'we are not full owing to government policy'.

It is necessary to disentangle reasons given for undersubscription that relate to a failure of Government to manage the system and those that related to schools' own imperfections or deep-seated problems, which were also reported: like expenditure woes, social policy, 'poor decor', 'bad HMI inspection', council estate location with bad image, or the school 'where all the refugees get put'. Some of these might be Government failure as well, but not every school that failed to fill could 'off-load' the problem on to the system. A few were schools that given a choice, most parents would avoid. But all too many were not. It is the *variety* of schools that were undersubscribed, as revealed by the 1994 survey, which showed how unreliable undersubscription is as a measure of a school's worth.

Why schools were full

This conclusion is further confirmed by looking at the minority of schools that were full. For there were a variety of reasons given by schools for being full, not all of which could be linked to their performance, demonstrated in the reasons schools gave for being full both from the list given in the questionnaire (question 17) and in their added written-in replies (question 18).

Some reasons given from the list were mirror images of the those given for undersubscription. They were full because they had no grammar schools in the area (11%), or no-opted out school (8%),or no private schools with LEA-paid-for places (3%) or no schools with assisted places (9%). A small percentage (8%) said they were full simply because there was a shortage of places in that particular area, where population was growing. A higher percentage put their oversubscription down to being in a pleasant neighbourhood (34%). But by far the largest number (87%) said it was their 'good image' (question 17E). This reason had no equivalent among undersubscribed schools (where only 14% thought undersubscription was due to a bad image). Five schools also objected to the word 'image'. Said one, 'Image is transitory, reputation is hard won'.

What might have contributed to this good reputation? Certainly being full itself did but those adding written reasons (question 18) suggested a variety of further explanations. Not all related to success in the market. For example, the most often occurring was that 'we are the only school serving the area' or had now become so since the only other school had closed. Sometimes there was a variant: the 'only mixed RC school in this area'; or the only non-denominational girls' school in area; or we are full 'because we are mixed and the local boys' school is unpopular'.

The remainder of reasons in the written-in section showed great variety: it was 'good primary liaison' that kept one school full; another gave 'thanks to recent LEA expenditure of £5 million' on its buildings. A third spoke of having good discipline, a fourth of having 'good music and games', and a fifth modestly mentioned it was 'the most prominent ecumenical school in mainland Britain'. Then were was 'loyalty to local school' or 'we provide a child-centred education' or 'we are in a feeder system' or 'we are a neighbourhood school'. Had they not been full, these same reasons, we felt, might have been used to explain that as well. Lastly, there were those who cited, often in the language of salespersons, their 'active marketing strategy', which in some cases included marketing their 'Christian ethos'.

Selection is not mandatory
Whatever the reasons for being full, the result, as intended, was to polarise schools, for, once full, a school could start to select. Figures from the 1994

survey showed the result of this process in some of the significant differences between full and undersubscribed schools. Full schools had 21.6% in the top 20% of their attainment intake; schools not full had 15.3%. In terms of social intakes, there were even greater differences. Only 29.3% of schools with predominantly working-class intakes were full but 61.3% of schools with predominantly middle-class intakes were full (question 36). Full and undersubscribed were also related to income since the greater the percentages having free dinners in a school the less likely the school was to be full. Thus only 20.5% of those with the highest level of free dinners (question 40E) were full compared with 51.9% of those with the lowest level (question 40A). As we know, when schools are not full, they lose funding. Thus in the 'market' system of admissions to those with greatest need goes least funding.

In a few areas of England and in Northern Ireland, all children leaving primary schools are still subjected to the damaging 11-plus testing process to determine grammar school entry for the few (and what most see as relegation for the majority). There are many more areas where selective schools exist and set tests for entry; they damage the system locally for the majority, including primary schools, where some parents intending to put their children in for the tests now insist their children be coached specially, but the testing itself is only for those seeking entry. These are two damaging forms of selection which any government supporting comprehensive education would take steps to prevent by asking all schools to accept all levels of attainment.

However, this still leaves the great majority of areas where all schools are comprehensive but some practice forms of hidden selection, discussed elsewhere. One of these is selection on the basis of being 'full', whether schools are full because they have good images or full because of demographic accident. In these cases of hidden selection no law compels schools to select either by attainment or by class background, and especially not just because they are full. A large number that are full do not do so, remaining committed to taking in all levels of attainment and all social backgrounds without selection. Usually they have admissions policies that are open, agreed locally and by which they are seen to abide in the same way as other local schools. Others either do not agree to policy locally or circumvent it by using forms of selection that are not open for scrutiny. These will include schools that are not really aware of the fact that they are 'selecting', since there is no public oversight keeping track of the process.

There was enough evidence in the 1994 survey, however, that a policy giving a minority of 'full' schools an advantage that comes with 'choosing' their own pupils, was a process that could advance polarisation and encourage selection, and, as presently operated, depressed many surrounding schools unnecessarily. The inevitability of more polarisation, therefore, requires the admissions process to be further regulated in the interests of all schools and all parents. Parents have a right to know what methods are being used to decide school admissions.

Admissions systems in use, 1994

One of the keys to a successfully regulated comprehensive system is an admissions system under the oversight of a democratically accountable local or regional body. Whether such a system operates today under the legislative changes since 1986 is a matter of controversy, as more and more schools are encouraged to disregard democratically elected authorities and operate by 'the market'.

To find out the scale of this disregard, we asked the schools and colleges how closely they shared admissions arrangements with their elected authority. The choices ranged from leaving admissions entirely to the LEA across to undertaking admissions entirely on their own with no reference to the LEA (question 10).

Table 4.12 Admissions policy in relation to local authorities, schools and colleges, 1994. Results are given in percentages, with numbers in parentheses

Policy of the school or college		
A – leave admissions to the LEA	42.4	(644)
B – share admissions with the LEA	23.4	(355)
C – do their own admissions, but have regard to LEA system	14.8	(224)
D – do their own, using their own criteria with no regard to the LEA	19.4	(295)
No reply		(42)
Total	100	(1518)

Table 4.12 shows that most schools and colleges have not opted out from co-operation with the local authority on admissions – even though some undertake only to bear LEA admissions policies in mind. Almost two-thirds (66%) co-operate in the process with their LEA, including over two out of five that leave admissions entirely up to the LEA.

There was little difference between age ranges of schools in terms of admissions relationships with local authorities; differences arose almost entirely in respect of the legal status. Namely, where the law gives governing bodies the right to choose pupils, schools were more likely to opt out of arrangements with LEAs.

Only just over 19% of survey schools and colleges undertook admissions entirely on their own, and some of these were the colleges, as would have been expected. Thus 95% of further education, tertiary and sixth-form colleges admitted students without reference to local authorities. By contrast, only 1% of LEA county or voluntary controlled comprehensive schools did so. The categories with the highest percentages admitting pupils without any reference to any elected authority were grant maintained schools (69% of whom did so), followed by aided comprehensives (55%) and special agreement schools (50%).

It is also worth noting that half the schools doing their own choosing were still not full. Such a policy was by no means a guarantee of oversubscription.

This is not the picture some might have expected to find, given the policy of putting schools and colleges under their own local 'management'. Possibly it shows that while schools welcome autonomy in some areas, most still retain a strong impulse to co-operate – with each other and with their local authorities. Indeed, one of the reasons schools are known to wish to stay with local authorities is the help they receive over admissions and the knowledge that they are sharing the area's intakes fairly, and being protected from polarisation themselves. The resentment felt towards opted out schools often occurs because they have opted out of this democratic sharing, threatening other local schools with polarisation.

Although schools doing their own admitting were most likely to be full (49.6% were), the next category most likely to be full were those letting the LEA do all the admissions (38.0% of which were full). The schools and colleges which used either of the half-way measures were less likely to be full (35% and 31% for Table 4.12B and C respectively).

There was some difference in academic attainment between schools where LEAs organised admissions (38% having five GCSE passes A–C) and those where the schools admitted with no reference to the LEA (at 42%) but it was not great. At 'A' level there was no difference.

There was a difference in the percentage of the top 20% of the attainment range between those letting the LEA admit, where it was 16.2%, and schools doing their own admitting, where it was 23.6%; and an especially large difference in the free dinner index: 48% of LEA schools with free dinners at the highest levels (question 40 CD and E) let LEAs undertake admissions compared with only 24% with free dinners at the lowest level (question 40A).

The potential for division is there, even if the differences are still those that could be accounted for by the autonomy of the colleges or the more selective nature of the grant maintained and aided voluntary schools by comparison with LEA county comprehensive schools. It is a division (where it involves voluntary schools) that is long standing, and where harmonisation of admissions arrangements was long overdue even before the opted out schools were created. With the addition of grant maintained schools the issue of harmonising practice in respect of admissions has become more pressing.

Admissions criteria

Although a few schools wrote that having admissions criteria was pointless while the 'false-full' national policy denied them any chance to use them, most schools, whether full or not, had admissions policies. The majority devised them after some form of consultation with their local authorities.

Question 19 set out 11 different criteria often used in admissions and 95% of schools and colleges answered. Only 110 used a single criterion only, that most often used being zoning (used by 34 schools).

The great majority combined one or more of the criteria and the one most often combined was priority to siblings of those already in the school (55.6% using it). Tests – either of attainment, behaviour, or staff opinion as to suitability – were the least often used, by only 3.8%; 13.8% had a policy of first come, first served.

In 1994 most schools of all kinds used one of three traditional criteria, chosen in various combinations: the first was nearness to the school used by 63.5%; followed by feeder school systems at 54.6% and zoning at 54.0%. There were larger percentages of comprehensive schools using these methods in 1994 than had used them in 1970, when only 48% used nearness or zoning, and only 15% used feeder systems (Benn and Simon, 1970: Table 19.1, p.316). The two years are not strictly comparable, however, because 'parental choice' was a separate method at that time (where it was most often used to decide who got the choice of the selective school). Today parental preference is part of the system whatever the other methods used.

Nearness is still the criterion used by most schools (as it was 50 years ago; see page 50) because it is the most ostensibly fair. It is favoured both by schools which operate neighbourhood policies as well as by institutions drawing from much further afield, which nevertheless need some criterion to decide entry when they are oversubscribed after they have met all their admissions obligations. Schools (or sixth-form colleges), for example, that have specific sets of feeder schools often said they needed a criterion for decision-making once all had been accommodated. One such, a church school, advised, 'measure door to door in a straight line'.

Feeder systems have more than trebled since 1968 in popularity: being a system where clusters of primary schools transfer automatically to particular upper schools; or where secondary schools (usually of 11–16) have priority of entry to a local sixth form or tertiary college; and occasionally a further education college. The assurance that goes with knowing where everyone goes 'next' is increasingly valued.

Zoning too is still popular, a method long used in many areas (both rural and urban), its use not curtailed even by the court judgment (see page 196) in the early 1980s that ruled an LEA's own schools had to be open to all pupils, no matter how far away, and regardless of whether local pupils could find a place or not. The combination of the law which ignores nearness, plus this ruling, is not always regarded as fair, and was referred to by Labour's education spokesperson in 1995, when he criticised as 'partial selection' the use of admissions criteria 'blocking entry to those living near a school, or to those who form part of the school's religious catchment area, in order to give preference to those chosen on the basis of selection'. This was on the grounds that such methods blocked 'rights to families in the community the school serves'[11]. There is still a strong commitment in the culture to 'nearness' rights, the system used universally in most other countries.

In 1994 among the additional criteria schools cited when writing in extra answers (question 20) was transport: the pupil had to be on the bus line, or the school's own transport had to pick up in the pupil's area for them to be accepted. A good number also said one of their criteria was whether the applicant had any other school he or she could attend locally that was nearer; if not, this pupil had priority. In effect, a nearness criterion.

A method the 1994 survey did not ask about (and which few cited) but which has been used occasionally in times past, particularly as a way of resolving oversubscription, is the lottery: putting all names in the hat and drawing the places to be filled. It was used in the 1970s for a single girls school in a town with mixed schools; and more recently in Burnley, where a parent challenged it in court in respect of Habergham High School in 1994 (it was declared legal)[12]. Some educationists even recommend it as the system of admissions most likely to prevent selection returning in the system as a whole (Walford, 1990:120). It may be fair but it is rather impersonal and the anomalies that could result are formidable.

New criteria, including 'governors' selection', 'interviewing' and 'giving reasons'

As well as the three most often used methods, some criteria used raised questions marks. The schools most likely to be full in September of the 1994 survey (apart from those with denominational criteria) were those using 'medical or personal' criteria for admissions (51% compared with the survey average of 40%). In the past medical criteria were reserved for only a tiny percentage of pupils (e.g. a pupil in delicate health who could not stand a long journey) but hardly to the extent it was being used in 1994 by about a third of the schools. Only a small proportion of LEA schools used it (3.4%) compared with a large proportion of grant maintained schools (51.9%) and voluntary controlled schools (42.2%). In the latter cases it is more likely that it was the 'personal' rather than the 'medical' factor that counted, possibly in relation to the 'governors' places', another new category of admissions which the 1994 survey did not include but which many schools mentioned as additional methods used (question 20).

A whole raft of criteria related to this new category of 'governors' special places' was revealed in answers to question 20, especially in grant maintained comprehensive schools. The most common-place reservation was for someone with a 'family connection' to the school. This entitlement appeared over and over, sometimes in respect of governors' own children, sometimes children of old pupils of the school in a previous incarnation, sometimes the children of staff who work and teach in the school at the moment, but also in relation to previous staff or other people with a school 'connection' (not always clearly stated).

Grant maintained schools were also distinguished from other comprehensives over admissions in that they were the only comprehensive type with a majority having special governors' subcommittees dealing solely with admissions (question 71F). Only 19% of schools and colleges in the survey overall had such subcommittees, including less than 10% of LEA schools or colleges (including sixth-form colleges) or voluntary controlled schools. But Special Agreement schools (54%) and aided schools (70%) and grant maintained schools (79%) had such sub-committees of governors. In the aided schools admissions matters revolved around religious suitability, not always clear in the case of some denominational schools, but almost always unclear in the case of grant maintained schools.

Another unexplained practice was asking parents who applied to write giving their reasons. Some single-sex schools, for example, said they would give priority to those who expressed a preference for a single-sex school (although it would seem that any parent applying could be assumed to have such a preference without the need to submit it additionally in writing). Requiring 'written reasons' over and above stating a preference has been a matter of controversy for some time. One area of Hertfordshire was cited by the Commission for Racial Equality (CRE) for this practice, where it was claimed the method was used to screen out ethnic minority parents. In some schools using this method it was policy to accept only those who gave certain answers. Obviously parents in the know had a great advantage here.

Interviews are a step beyond the written answer, though sometimes the two are combined. There has always been suspicion attached to the interview (given before selection, not the one after a place has been offered) because interviewing was the policy first suggested in the 1970s as a strategy for retaining grammar schools. A pamphlet issued in the 1970s advised voluntary grammar schools to use their rights to interview for religious reasons as a cover to keep selection going (Maynard Potts, c.1970). Today, interviews given before selection are widely assumed to be for selective purposes, particularly in the case of grant maintained schools. Again, the trouble is that parents do not know for sure and have no way of knowing why they have been rejected in those cases where the schools say they are comprehensive.

Other forms of selection relate to specialisation, which can also involve special admissions procedures, including interviews. This is where some comprehensive schools are given permission to select part of their intake from those who are 'good at' some special study: like music, games, mathematics, bilingual studies or technology. Several schools in the 1994 survey had such admissions procedures, but whether they involved attainment selection is unknown. Legally, however, the question is academic, since it is often forgotten that the 1980 Act gave schools that were partially selective for specialised study the same admissions rights in law as enjoyed by grammar schools. This is part of what is meant by the complex 'web' of legal changes that is engineering a return to selection. It is even more complex still, since the same Act gave selective rights to all aided schools. As one Catholic comprehensive school in the 1994 survey put it, 'being voluntary aided creates selective admissions criteria'. As we know, most religious schools do not use such criteria for selective purposes and not all are aided in any case. But the possibility is there, especially for those that are aided but not denominational.

In the case of denominational schools in the 1994 survey it was not always clear what criteria were applied. Some schools writing their criteria in answer to question 11 or question 20 were very straightforward. They required baptismal certificates or evidence of involvement with the parish – e.g. church attendance at least once a month. On the other hand, there were those whose 'Christianity' criterion was much vaguer, particularly those where it was left to the governors to judge the matter, admitting only those 'governors think would benefit by a Christian education'. Not all requiring a commitment to Christianity were denominational schools. What the legal position is for a religious requirement applied in a non-denominational school is an interesting point.

Even this short examination of the laws that laced the admissions system to comprehensive schools in the UK in 1994 should be enough to show that the system was faced with a formidably complex set of practices that need to be re-examined in the light of any commitment to equal education for all, or to fair treatment for all parents and students alike. In a public education service these matters should not just be fair but be seen to be fair. The evidence from the 1994 survey suggests this criterion is not always met.

Transfer

The move from primary to secondary education, or from lower secondary years to upper secondary schools or colleges, is a major move. How closely were upper schools or colleges related to lower or primary schools in 1994? The answer was, a great deal more closely than in the early days of reorganisation when it was sometimes assumed that pupils could be sent into 'new' schools with little or no preparation beyond a new school uniform.

The traditional British school had up to then prided itself on being a self-contained ship with its captain and crew on board from first to last, the model set by the private and grammar school. Not only was everyone expected to stay on in the same school once arrived, but everyone was expected to know the form before they came. No elaborate induction was required. Over the years comprehensive schools and colleges have had to learn the hard way that transfer arrangements are crucial to comprehensive education – whether taken from the point of view of the pupil or student moving up to a new learning environment or from the point of view of liaison between the institutions concerned. For comprehensive schools and colleges there was no prior 'form'.

At that earlier time most secondary schools would have been unlikely to know (or to record) such a statistic as the numbers of primary schools sending them at least 10 pupils every year, one of the questions the 1994 survey asked (question 25). In 1994 only very few schools and colleges did not know the answer to this, and 99% of those replying had at least one such school attached to them: 50.3% had between five and ten such schools and 18% had at least 16 or more. There were 50 schools and colleges that had over 25 feeder schools sending at least 10 pupils each year.

A number of schools would have higher numbers still but these would have been sending fewer than 10, especially to colleges and schools in the middle of large cities, where ease of transport can mean some institutions have over 60 feeding schools. This can mean liaison is particularly difficult, for almost invariably secondary schools and colleges choose to concentrate on the few feeding schools which send greater numbers or on those that may be nearby. This can create a split between those pupils who already have close links with the schools or colleges they enter, and those coming from far away who are sometimes not seen until they arrive.

Occasionally schools were chosen outside the home area because the student wanted to leave the area or because parents wanted to encourage a new start for a child. But far more pupils came from far away because no local school was open to them. They were directed elsewhere because they had failed in all their other choices or because their local school was closing; because they were newcomers to the area or late applicants or refugees. In almost all cases there were schools nearer but these schools were either 'full' or closed to such students (because they were selective, voluntary, grant maintained, specialising or 'full'). Ironically, as we have already seen, admissions conditioned by new laws to accommodate 'parental choice' as well as schools of different legal status, are contributing to making city schools less 'neighbourhood' based than schools elsewhere, the opposite of what so many assumed was the case (see page 197). Since comprehensive schools in the large cities are also likely to have greater working-class concentrations, this may be one reason why the transfer process between schools was found to be more likely to affect working-class pupils adversely than middle-class (Measor and Woods, 1984).

For the majority of schools and colleges in Britain, the picture is different. Transfer involves only about half a dozen primary or lower schools and in many of these arrangements there is a *de facto* 'all-through' comprehensive education from primary years through to 18, whether in school or college. Organising liaison was much more easily arranged in these areas than where schools or colleges had many dozens of feeder schools. Yet in both cases in the 1970s work in comprehensive schools began to make sure formal induction was well organised: pupils shown around on their first day and given a full explanation of new school life.

Soon it was realised that while formal induction was well handled, it was the informal passage that was crucial (Measor and Woods, 1984). Secondary schools began setting aside a whole day for new pupils to be seen on their own, often before the rest of the school started; or they arranged for each new pupil to be sponsored by an older pupil during the first weeks (Measor and Woods, 1984:166). Induction was not just about locating classrooms but also about answering questions on a whole host of practices unique to that particular school or college.

The next step was to arrange familiarisation visits by pupils the previous term, a practice that particularly far-sighted comprehensive schools had begun in the 1960s, especially in systems where transfer was along feeder-school lines. These visits had nothing to do with 'selling' the school (an objective later overlaid). They were about making sure the transfer process was easy, so that pupils settled in more quickly and learning was co-ordinated. Today such pre-term familiarisation visits are routine – with 89% of the survey schools and colleges organising them in 1994 (question 29B).

However, in 1994 in some schools both liaison and familiarisation were extended only to the lower or primary schools within the school's own authority, not to those outside it; or only to those schools sending large numbers of pupils, not to every pupil or student likely to be coming; and not for those who entered late. Ideally, every entering student needs the same attention.

So does liaison between staff in these schools, which is why liaison meetings between staff in lower and upper comprehensive schools or colleges also began to be organised in the 1970s, making sure schools co-ordinated their curricula planning so that pupils were not immediately repeating work they had just tackled. Only 7% of the schools and colleges in the 1994 survey did not have standing arrangements for meetings with their contributory schools; and 89% claimed to be meeting them at least once a term, with 17% meeting every week. These latter were more likely to be schools in tiered schemes with transfers at 13 or 14, or those that were 11/12–16 schools (feeding sixth form and tertiary colleges).

Forty-six per cent of schools and colleges in the 1994 survey exchanged staff with their contributory schools (or sent them upwards into schools or colleges into which students were due to transfer). The grant maintained schools were most likely to exchange staff, aided schools the least likely. So many and varied were the particular arrangements scribbled in the margin of question 29 that it was evident that this was a question which should have been followed by an open-ended 'write in' section so that comment could have been accommodated more fully on this point. This included staff teaching for a time in the 'other' school (rather than just attending meetings), where several comments confirmed earlier research about the value of such practices (Measor and Woods, 1984:169).

Progression and liaison were always key features in sixth-form college and tertiary reorganisation schemes (Janes *et al.*, 1985; Terry, 1987) and many comprehensive colleges had co-ordinators of liaison as permanent posts, organising regular meetings with their feeder schools throughout the year. In one arrangement, the chair of these liaison meetings rotated between headteachers of feeder schools, to ensure equity and emphasise that although the college called the meetings the business was equally that of the schools (Terry, 1987:4). Some tertiary colleges in the 1980s even spoke of the need to start liaison arrangements with all feeder schools as early as the third year.

Whether all such earlier development in the direction of maintaining 'all-through' liaison has been able to be sustained since the drive to privatisation and its attendant legal changes after the mid-1980s, is hard to say. Schools and colleges have been made into mini-businesses. They have become more market-oriented and they produce glossier booklets about themselves. Some of the lazier ones may have been driven into making contact with their feeder or primary schools for the first time, which is no bad thing. But many of the changes will have been in the direction of sprucing up sales activities rather than improving liaison; about having more open evenings before 'choosing', more 'pre-choice' talks, and more 'pre-choice' research on selected local areas, which some schools or colleges now target for leafleting or marketing – rather than continuing to develop the 'all-through' educational experience. It may be that only the renewed commitment to continuing comprehensive education will permit educational liaison to develop fully.

Attendance

Figures of attendance – and after 16, figures of dropping out – are important in any education system. Some see them as indicators of good discipline in schools or care in matching students to courses; others see them as indicators of the relevance of what education has to offer, as perceived by the students or pupils.

There have been many surveys of attendance figures, drives to better attendance, various analyses of the relationship of attendance to types of schools and attempts to link poor attendance figures with comprehensive reform. Research, however, has found no link between rates of attendance and types of school. It was not the type of school a pupil attended that accounted for differences in attendance – whether grammar, private or comprehensive made no difference – it was the social background of the pupils involved (Chitty and mac an Ghaill, 1995; Steedman, 1980).

No relationship between delinquency and school type has been found either, though delinquency rates overall have been found to have gone up since the 1950s (Rutter, 1979). Instead researchers have found a strong relationship of attendance to academic attainment and to the social class background of the pupil or student. In addition, researchers found that unemployment in the home was associated with absence from school.

In the 1990s a more refined look at attendance was taken with studies emphasising the difference between authorised and unauthorised absence (see, for example, HMSO, *Social Focus on Children*, 1994). Around about the same time the phenomenon of post-registration absence was discovered and occasionally there were attempts to look at absence in relation to the quality of the curriculum, deteriorating funding and stress on teachers. Or at absence in large cities, found to have rates higher than national averages (Rutter, 1979).

Evidence on this issue was brought by several Local Authorities to the House of Commons Education Committee's investigation into Performance in City Schools (O'Keefe, 1992). Manchester, for example, spoke of lower attendance rates but it also gave evidence on other factors like high turnover rates, low parental awareness of schooling, low literacy levels when starting secondary schooling, lack of home-based support and opportunity for homework, and two further factors hitherto less researched but well known to schools, the requirement of pupils at home to act 'in the role of carers for siblings', and secondly, increasingly in the 1980s and after, the need to have children in casual employment in the black economy. A report from the MP, Ann Clwyd, in the mid-1990s suggests up to two million school children are now working (though not all on the black economy), and shows how this affects school attendance and attainment (Clwyd, 1995).

Such activities can be interpreted as 'lack of interest' by parents in their children's education; or it can be viewed as lack of interest in the lives of children and young people by Government, public services or the law, the kind of interest the Select Committee earlier noted was taken of children from homes with 'well educated parents in professional work who have supported children's learning'. Nearly 20 years ago the Chief Education Officer for Manchester, warning of the problems to come from over-fixation on parental choice, suggested it was time to 'talk more of the needs of children than the rights of parents' (Fiske, 1979). Whether children or young people have supportive parents or not should make no difference to their rights in education; yet, increasingly, the system allows this to make a difference.

1994 findings

Schools in our 1994 survey were given attendance rates in three bands – high, medium, and low – and asked to cite that which characterised their school. Tertiary and further education colleges did not give figures in sufficient numbers to be meaningful, and are omitted from the findings given in Table 4.13.

There are some very wide variations in reported figures, as can be seen. For example, 50% of schools drawing mainly from working-class homes (question 36A) registered attendance at below 90%, compared with only 1% where the intakes were mainly middle class (question 36B). Where intakes were socially mixed, however – whether the mix was predominantly working class or predominantly middle class – the low attendance figure dramatically improved and was much nearer the higher end than the lower – another example of a balanced 'mix' producing a leavening effect.

There were poorer attendance rates in the metropolitan boroughs than in the shire counties; and lower than survey average rates in Scotland and Wales – the latter already found earlier. The figures also tended to bear out previous findings that rates decrease as we move north in the UK (Fogelman and Richardson, 1974).

Differences also showed up between LEA schools and those that were aided or grant maintained (Tables 4.13 and A5) – with higher attendance rates for the latter two than LEA schools but neither as high as rates in voluntary controlled schools. There were also higher rates in 11–18 schools than in those catering for the 11–16 age range. In all these cases the differences could be related to schools or they could be related to social class differences.

Table 4.13 Attendance rates in comprehensive schools and sixth-form colleges, 1994. Results are given as percentages

Institution	Rate		
	Over 95%	90–95%	Under 90%
All	30	50	20
County	26	52	22
Aided	37	50	13
VC	49	40	11
SA	23	69	8
Grant maintained	41	52	7
Sixth-form college	19	59	22
11–18	29	54	17
11–16	25	49	26
13/14/18	17	61	22
Middle	56	43	0.5
Working class	9	40	50
Middle class	56	42	1
Mixed, mainly working class	24	61	15
Mixed, mainly middle class	48	47	5
Equally mixed	35	55	10
London	19	48	33
Metropolitan boroughs	15	50	35
Shires	34	52	14
Wales	29	68	38
Scotland	13	57	30
City	8	34	58
Town	27	53	20
Suburban	28	53	19
Village and countryside	46	50	4
Council housing	7	31	62
Private housing	56	41	3
Council and private mixed	31	59	10
Substandard housing	6	29	65
Mixed and substandard	11	49	40

(Based on questions 39 and 4, 6, 36, 35, 26 and 27, excluding tertiary and further education colleges.) Differences between figures in this table and those in Table A5 are due to rounding up of percentages, collapsing of certain school categories and omission of tertiary and FE colleges from the total.

Some figures, however, show that high rates of attendance did not automatically go together with high middle-class intakes, with former grammar school status, and with 'independence' – or, on the other hand, lower rates with LEA schools. Middle schools had good attendance records and these were mostly LEA schools; while sixth-form colleges (with very high percentages having middle-class intakes) had relatively poor attendance figures. This seems to be recording a drop as students move from younger to later years of adolescence (and might possibly apply to sixth forms in schools as well). Also important was the social setting, including the housing. The great difference in figures between schools with intakes mainly from council housing, with low attendance compared with survey averages, and figures from schools drawing from villages and the countryside, with higher attendance than average, cannot be only about poverty as opposed to affluence.

Turnover

Turnover relates to students who enter a school or college after it has started work for the year, an event that every school might experience a few times a year – in contrast to high turnover, a phenomenon unnoticed by the majority of schools because they never experience it.

It is well known that high turnover rates are very disruptive to any school – both educationally and administratively. This applies whether it is turnover of staff or of students (Thornbury, 1978; Weeks, 1986:99), often a feature of schools and colleges in areas where there is much moving in and out of the area, social disruption, and mass movements of groups like refugees or immigrant pupils.

Although high turnover is often associated with some of the situations and conditions that can characterise schools with attendance problems, schools with high turnover can also have good attendance. Turnover figures are not the result of a school's organisation or policies (which attendance rates can be). Turnover rates reflect community stability.

Those who believe 'value added' should accompany all schools' academic results often cite the need to add turnover rates for every school when analysing any 'league table' figures – just as they argue that attainment levels on intake should be added. The House of Commons Select Committee on City Schools showed the reason why when citing the case of one school being judged on its Year 11 GCSE results even though 'one in six taking GCSE in year 11...had not been on the school role at the beginning of year 10' (HMSO, Minutes of Evidence, 16 March, 1994:16).

1994 findings
The 1994 survey defined high turnover as schools or colleges where new pupils entered at a rate of at least one a week (question 38A, B, C). Low turnover was defined as fewer than 10 a year (question 38E). Turnover in

relation to various types of comprehensive schools is given in Table A5.

The table shows that 45.9% of all schools in large cities had turnovers at the high rate – compared with only 5.4% for schools in villages and countryside; that 28.6% of schools with predominantly working-class intakes had turnovers at the high rate (question 36A and C) compared with only 9.8% of those with middle-class intakes (question 36B and D). Turnover was high too in comprehensives schools having high levels of cultural or national groups (question 38): 37.7% of those with Indian and Pakistani/Bangladeshi groups were at this high level; with Afro-Caribbean groups even higher (43.7%) and highest of all schools with Chinese or other South-East Asian pupils, where nearly half were operating turnovers at this level (48.9%). By contrast, the percentage of schools with European concentrations with this level (25.5%) was near the survey average.

The type of housing most often associated with schools having the high level of turnover was not council housing, which had only a slightly elevated turnover percentage at this level (29.2%), and certainly not private housing which had a very low proportion (10.2%). It was comprehensive schools drawing pupils from either of the categories of housing with substandard housing (question 27 D or E), including 58.8% of schools where most of the housing was substandard. These figures suggest turnover relates to the areas in the UK where newcomers and refugees and inflowing poor are directed, or where they congregate because of depressed property prices.

Schools that experience heavy turnover find it very unsettling. A new pupil a day or three times a week involves a great deal of administrative time. Teaching time is taken up inducting new pupils into individual classes, and work in the classes held up to introduce these newcomers to the work and to other pupils. It also means that pupils and students will leave the school as well as enter it, necessitating another load of work related to preparing records to send on after them.

Over one in five comprehensive schools or colleges in the survey (21.4%) had a new pupil at least once a week. At the other end of the scale 28% of comprehensives had fewer than 10 new pupils each year to deal with. This polarisation was compounded by other factors related to housing, social class and poverty, as already suggested. For example, schools with mostly working-class intakes (question 36A) had 28.6% having turnover at the high rate compared with 9.8% of those with mostly middle-class intakes (question 36B). There were also educational differences, for schools and colleges with high turnovers (question 38 A,B, and C) had only 13.5% in the top 20% of their attainment intakes compared with schools with turnovers of less than 10 a term where it was 17.2%. Their five GCSE A–C score was 32.4% as against 39.4% for schools with less than 10 a term.

Just over 2% of comprehensive schools in the survey (32 schools) had turnovers of at least one new pupil every school day throughout the year. A turnover at this high rate means the equivalent of a whole new year's intake between each new year's intake (between 100 and 200 pupils a year). It is schools in this situation that require extra support. Yet no account of turnover is ever kept in terms of 'needs' some schools have that others do not, so that recognition of the work is made and appropriate support or resources allocated. 'Standard' spending assessment policy assumes all schools have 'standard' rates of turnover just as they have standard rates of everything else.

The total number of schools in these uniquely difficult situations is not large but if we use performance indicators for improving standards and judging results, so we should also use indicators for judging needs and improving support where it seems to be justified. It is hard to think that those at the less sharp end would begrudge resources for the heavy extra workload that goes with this level of high turnover (and with many other burdens this survey has shown are carried by a small number of schools but not carried by the vast majority).

Yet this is just the principle which at present is lacking in the British education system: recognition of the differing contexts in which different schools are operating. The government's criticism of comprehensive education made in its 1992 White Paper, *Choice and Diversity*, was that it assumed all schools were the same and the needs of all areas were the same, a criticism far more appropriate to the Government's own egalitarian, market-dominated formula-funding system, which fails to recognise the acute needs some comprehensive schools have that others do not.

As we go through the 1994 survey it becomes clear that several factors interact with each other to produce clusters of schools at one end of several 'disadvantaged' scales, while at the 'advantaged' end of most scales are another cluster of schools. Very often it is the same schools at the two ends, regardless of the scale. The majority of comprehensive schools and colleges are not at either end, a finding that is important to underline, since it is so often assumed that comprehensive schools are almost all disadvantaged. But polarisation was there and could be increasing, and it seemed to many to be important to deal with it.

Policy operating in 1994, however, was unable to deal with this problem; indeed, it was fuelling polarisation rather than solving it, for extra resources and extra spending were to go on principle to schools that were 'doing well' – often in favoured conditions and favoured contexts, protected by laws that advance their development over other schools (at the same time permitting a pile-up of problems to be concentrated in a small number of dis-favoured schools or colleges). This was a policy that resulted from gradually abandoning the comprehensive principle for nearly two decades.

The system's continued failure to recognise and safeguard the needs of an ever-growing number of schools and colleges in less favoured circumstances – few though they are overall – amounts to denying equal educational rights to many parents and students in our schools. The best way to deal with the problem is to renew the process of developing comprehensive education.

Notes

1   About 90% of UK comprehensive institutions in the 1994 survey were in England and Wales; in the UK nationally the percentage is about 87%.
2   This was the percentage in 1994–95 given in a letter from the Department of Education in Northern Ireland (DENI), dated 25 April 1995.
3   Listed as contributing to the publication were the Association of Head Teachers in Secondary Schools, the Education Alliance, The Irish National Teachers' Organisation, The National Association of Schoolmasters and Women Teachers, and the Ulster Teachers' Union
4   The 1994 Survey's staying-on rates cannot be strictly compared with those for Scotland's schools in the same year because official statistics give two rates: 76% for the total staying to S5 and 67% for those staying beyond Christmas in S5. Those answering the 1994 survey were asked about staying on in March and April of the school year and would have been more likely to give the post-Christmas figure, making the 1994 survey figure higher by 3% (but lower than the pre-Christmas figure by just over 5%).
5   This was less than the national average for Scotland in the same year (in the same way 'A' level results were lower than national averages in England; but not because schools did not give results, as was the case in England). In Scotland 91 of the 95 institutions participating gave percentages for Highers. The difference could be partly explained because the 1994 survey asked for figures as a percentage of the S4 roll rather than as a percentage of leavers, the basis of official statistics. In these the average of three or more Highers A–C was 30%. Another explanation might be that those comprehensive schools not participating in the Survey in 1994 included quite a few that must have been more favoured/more selective at this stage than those that did participate.
6   305 answered question 32, being 60 more than the number ringing percentages in the previous question (question 31). It was assumed these schools had not answered question 31 because they were unable to say exactly what percentages they had.

7   Information relating to this tactic was presented to the AMA Academic Panel by the Geographical Information Systems in Education (GIS) whose pilot project had been undertaken in collaboration with Bedfordshire LEA and the Local Government Management Board. Minutes, AMA Academic Panel, 16 December, 1994.

8   Delivered in relation to schools in Greenwich (R. *v.* Greenwich London Borough Council ex p. Governors of the John Ball Primary School).

9   *Newsnight* made the estimate £300 million (14 June, 1994).

10 265 schools or colleges added additional reasons under question 15; 106 added them under question 18.

11 From a speech by David Blunkett, MP, prepared for Saturday, 15 April, 1995, NUT Conference, Blackpool. Although circulated as an advance press release, and widely reported, the passage was actually omitted from the speech as delivered.

12 R. *v.* Lancs County Council ex p. West, 1994. The Government, however, discourages its use (DfE Circular 6/93/Annex C, para. 18).

5

Social and Pastoral Policy and Issues in the Welfare of Pupils

Horizontal and vertical groupings: the background

Comprehensive schools have pioneered new forms of pastoral organisation to ensure that the needs of all their pupils are catered for in a caring and systematic fashion. Since the early days of the reform, there have been two main ways of breaking down large schools into smaller and more manageable units: horizontally – into lower and upper or lower, middle and upper 'schools' (or, more finely, into individual years); and vertically – into house units, each containing a cross-section of pupils from all the years in the school. Over the past 40 years, schools have experimented with various versions or combinations of these broad-based systems, but when comprehensive reorganisation was in its infancy, many believed that only one form of grouping was capable of creating a number of meaningful communities within the larger school. It cannot be gainsaid that the most widely discussed and described form of pastoral organisation in the British comprehensive school in the late 1950s and early 1960s was the house system.

The establishment of the house system as a physical entity was, in fact, Coventry's unique contribution to the evolution of the comprehensive school in this country (see Firth, 1963:111–30). Each of the eight comprehensive schools which Coventry built between 1953 and 1959 was organised on a house basis, the system being designed as the day school's equivalent of the residential houses in independent schools. The houses were built in pairs, the aim being for each school eventually to have five pairs – 10 houses of 150 pupils each. The house provision consisted of an assembly room (which was also to be used as the house dining-room), a study room, a small staffroom, a room for the Head of House, and cloakrooms and toilets for staff and pupils. Much depended on the calibre of the House Heads whose duties were indeed onerous: besides the day-to-day business of house administration, they were responsible for the welfare and progress of each child in their house and for maintaining good relations between the school and the parents.

During the late 1950s and early 1960s, many teachers and administrators stressed the advantages accruing from a fully-developed house system, with each house being encouraged to function as a microcosm of the wider school community. Coventry's example was followed, together with the provision of actual house blocks, in other areas, notably in parts of London, West Bromwich, Walsall and Nottingham. And the system was commended even where it was not possible to provide actual physical bases. One London headteacher, writing in 1958, described the house system as 'the best feature of the English public school', which, when transferred to the state comprehensive school, solves, among other things, 'the vexed problem of continuity' (NUT, 1958:29). And in his book *Comprehensive Schools in Action*, published in 1964, Roger Cole wrote that 'parents whose children attend a comprehensive school which has a house system should realise that the houses are a *sine qua non* of the life of the school.' A house organisation, he asserted, 'is in practice effective, as a means of giving each child a place within a unit smaller than the school as a whole' (Cole, 1964:89, 91).

Of the 331 comprehensive schools participating in the survey undertaken by the National Foundation for Educational Research (NFER) in 1965, 299 used houses, either as their sole means of decentralising the school or in conjunction with some other system. This was 90% of the comprehensive schools investigated in 1965 (Monks, 1968:41). And as late as October 1968, a sociologist writing in *New Society* could talk of a London school with a house organisation as being 'typical of English comprehensives' (Ford, 1968).

Yet all this serves to present a somewhat misleading picture of what was actually happening in comprehensive schools in the 1960s. It was already clear, by the time the Benn/Simon survey was carried out in 1968, that the house system had begun to lose its popularity. Not only were many new comprehensive schools reluctant to inaugurate a house system, but, at the same time, a number of established comprehensives had actually abandoned the system in favour of some other form of social organisation (Benn and Simon, 1970:278; Chitty, 1970:7).

As can be seen in Table 5.1, of the 728 schools which were included in the Benn/Simon survey (81% of the total number of comprehensive schools in 1968), only 122 (or 17%) used the house system as their sole form of pastoral organisation, compared with 291 (or 40%) opting for the year system. Even if we add on the number of schools which worked a house system in conjunction with some other form of organisation, we have a total of only 267, or 37% of the responding schools. In Scotland, only seven schools (10.5%) used the house system as their sole form of internal organisation; and only 20 schools (30%) had any form of house system.

Interestingly the second NFER report (Monks, 1970) modified the 1965 findings a good deal and described a pastoral situation very similar to that depicted in *Half Way There*. The second report now showed only one in five schools with strong house systems and only 36% of schools with any form of house system. Even a majority of larger schools included in the survey, which previously favoured the house system, now used horizontal forms of grouping (Monks, 1970:37).

There are a number of important reasons why the house system steadily lost its popularity in the course of the late 1960s. For one thing, in a number of schools it was wrongly anticipated that it could take care *by itself* of all social and educational guidance. It was often left to the Head of House or senior house staff to deal with all the many day-to-day difficulties faced by pupils — be they academic, social, vocational or medical — and these were pressures that were simply too onerous for many conscientious teachers. An important factor here was the question of time: Benn and Simon found that many schools were reluctant to give teachers with heavy pastoral duties a lighter teaching load than that accorded to the majority of staff (Benn and Simon, 1970:222).

Then again, the house system was undermined by the growing tendency to divide up the large school into horizontal sections, each with its own set of rules and expectations. There was early recognition that sixth-formers should have their own separate quarters and a separate social life; and at the other end of the age range, it was often considered desirable to treat the first year as a separate section or unit, to ease the transfer from the small primary to the large secondary school. For obvious reasons, it was also very difficult for split-site schools to operate successful house systems.

Table 5.1 Internal social organisation of British comprehensive schools, 1968

Method used	All Schools		Scotland		Percentage of each type of school with each method							
	No.	%	No	%	11/12 to 18 Type 1	11/12 to 18 Type 2*	11/12 to 16	11 to 13	11 to 14/13	13 to 18	14 to 18	16 to 18
1 Houses	122	17	7	10.5	20	3	19	14	10	6	19	0
2 Lower and upper school or lower, middle and upper school	86	12	0		17	16	9	0	1.5	0	0	0
3 Years	291	40	44	65.5	28	26	47	79	64	65	56	0
4 Houses and 'schools'	111	15	7	10.5	18	35.5	14	0	4	11	19	0
5 Years and 'schools'	34	5	2	3	7	10	0.5	0	1.5	3	0	0
6 Houses and years	34	5	6	9	4	3	3	3.5	11.5	6	6	0
7 Others and unknown	50	7	1	1.5	6	6.5	7	3.5	7	9	0	0
	100		100	100	100	100	100	100	100	100	100	
Totals	728		67		389	31	154	29	70	34	16	2

* Type 2 = with regular transfer of pupils for sixth-form work.
This table is taken from Table 13.1 in *Half Way There: Report on the British Comprehensive School Reform*, p. 219.

Above all, it needs to be emphasised that only a minority of comprehensive schools enjoyed the 'luxury' of having physical house bases incorporated into their design, and without these, the system could easily acquire an air of artificiality. This important point was made by the late Margaret Miles, first headteacher of Mayfield Comprehensive School in south London, which developed out of a three-form-entry grammar school in 1955:

> House responsibility for discipline, social education and extra-curricular activity can, of course, be properly carried out if a school's buildings have been appropriately planned. Where there are house rooms, small halls, house dining-rooms and cloakrooms, it is possible for the group of people who fortuitously form the house within a large day school to develop a feeling of belonging. Without such physical bases, the development of a house feeling is very difficult; makeshift meeting places instead of house rooms or house blocks simply emphasise the unrealistic side of the house system.
>
> (Miles, 1968:27)

And a similar observation was made by Harriet Chetwynd, headteacher of Woodberry Down School in North London, writing in 1959:

> The house system can mean a very great deal to a school, or it can mean very little indeed. In the day-school, it has tended to be a weak, artificial imitation of the real purposeful organisation of the public school, and is often allowed to degenerate into a convenient channel through which to collect conduct marks or to stimulate enthusiasm for competitions on sports day.
>
> (Chetwynd, 1960:90)

It seems clear from the research carried out by Benn and Simon in 1968 that most schools that abandoned house systems went over to year systems, and that horizontal groupings were seen to have distinct social and educational advantages. Heads of year and tutors could move up with their groups year after year, maintaining a pastoral continuity; and important issues could be dealt with, in morning assemblies and tutor group periods, when it became appropriate to discuss them with the age group as a whole. Extra-curricular activities and experiments in democracy could be organised on a year basis, ensuring a high level of pupil participation and avoiding the automatic dominance by older pupils and sixth-formers associated with many vertical systems. As far as Margaret Miles was concerned, the great advantage of the year system was that pupils could automatically graduate from one year to the next without the need for 'immature' competitiveness:

> In the house system, there is a tendency to encourage the sense of belonging by making all the pupils want to make their house the 'best' house; house

competitions, whether for games or drama or for a system of house points for school work, encourages this rather artificial idea of 'our house' being the 'best house', an idea that has always struck me as being immature and unfruitful of real educational and social development.

(Miles, 1968:31)

The year system appeared to retain its popularity throughout the 1970s and 1980s while, at the same time, the very notion of pastoral care was being broadened in many schools to encompass new areas and commitments (see Lang, 1994:26–41; Weeks, 1986:129–45). Not that the widespread use of the year system was based on research evidence that this particular form of pastoral organisation was *superior* to the house system in terms of its impact on pupil motivation and achievement. Indeed the research carried out by Professor Rutter and his colleagues in the 1970s into secondary schools and their effects on children found that there were no differences between the two systems with respect to any of the team's four outcome measures: attendance, pupil behaviour, examination success and delinquency. In the words of their final report, 'it appeared that either system could be operated successfully as a general framework; and neither appeared to have any particular over-riding advantages' (Rutter *et al.*, 1979:66, 104).

Nor should the impression be created that the schools were necessarily happy to opt for just *one* system of pastoral care, to be used to cope with all eventualities. One comprehensive school located in the London commuter-belt that was the subject of an in-depth 2-year study undertaken at the end of the 1970s operated *four* distinct though often over-lapping structures of authority and task-differentiation:

- a curricular structure of faculties and departments,
- a system of separate 'schools' – lower, upper and sixth form,
- a vertical system of houses,
- a horizontal system of years.

Each was seen as catering for a particular type of pupil need and dealing with a particular type of problem. In this complex structure, problems of the organisation and provision of learning situations were the responsibility of the faculties and departments, problems of a 'pastoral' nature were the province of houses, problems concerned with 'academic progress' were the responsibility of the year heads, and problems of general order and control the responsibility of the heads of 'school' and their assistants. Any problems that proved intractable for the class teacher or form tutor were to be referred upwards to the appropriate layer of middle-management. In the case of referrals for discipline problems, for example, a single chain was established, as shown in Figure 5.1, although there were often considerable and understandable difficulties in distinguishing between different types of pupil 'problem'.

Figure 5.1 System of referral for 'discipline' problems

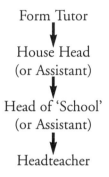

As the authors of the study commented in their report published in 1983:

> It is fairly easy to think of a justification for such a complex and highly sophisticated set of structures. It can be argued that, together, they represent all the major aspects of the teacher's role: as an imparter of knowledge, a supporter and counsellor of children with personal and academic problems, a disciplinarian and custodian of children, a monitor of educational progress and, finally, as an administrator. The rationale for the system, as more than one teacher remarked, was that it constituted a 'net through which no problem will fall'. This has some rhetorical force, but there were also some indications in the comments of many teachers that all was not well with the 'net', particularly with regard to the 'dual' structure of Years and Houses.
>
> (Best *et al.*, 1983:46)

Pastoral systems in the modern comprehensive school

The findings of our own survey depicted in Table 5.2 show that the year system has consolidated its position as the most favoured form of pastoral organisation in *all* types of comprehensive school in Britain. By itself, it is used in 622 schools (46.3% of the 1343 schools responding to question 54). It is the sole form of pastoral organisation in 240 (41%) of the 586 11–18 schools and in 247 (45.6%) of the 542 11–16 schools. If we add on the number of schools where it is used in conjunction with various

Table 5.2 Internal social organisation of British comprehensive schools, 1993–94

	Number of schools												
	11 to 18	%	11 to 16	%	13 to 16/18	%	14 to 18	%	9 to 13	%	11 to 14	%	All schools	%
1 Sites	0	0.0	0	0.0	1	1.4	0	0.0	0	0.0	0	0.0	1	0.0
2 Schools	25	4.3	55	10.1	0	0.0	0	0.0	1	0.8	1	7.1	82	6.1
3 Houses	64	10.9	37	6.8	7	10.0	1	12.5	2	1.6	2	14.3	113	8.4
4 Years	240	41.0	247	45.6	44	62.9	7	87.5	75	61.0	9	64.3	622	46.3
5 Sites and houses	2	0.3	1	0.2	0	0.0	0	0.0	0	0.0	0	0.0	3	0.2
6 Sites and years	9	1.5	10	1.8	2	2.9	0	0.0	0	0.0	0	0.0	21	1.6
7 Schools and houses	12	2.0	7	1.3	0	0.0	0	0.0	0	0.0	0	0.0	19	1.4
8 Schools and years	134	22.9	123	22.7	9	12.9	0	0.0	6	4.9	1	7.1	273	20.3
9 Houses and years	35	6.0	29	5.4	5	7.1	0	0.0	37	30.1	1	7.1	107	8.0
10 Schools, houses and years	26	4.4	18	3.3	2	2.9	0	0.0	2	1.6	0	0.0	48	3.6
11 Sites, schools and houses	3	0.5	0	0.0	0	0.0	0	0.0	0	0.0	0	0.0	3	0.2
12 Sites, schools and years	35	6.0	15	2.8	0	0.0	0	0.0	0	0.0	0	0.0	50	3.7
13 Sites, schools, houses and years	1	0.2	0	0.0	0	0.0	0	0.0	0	0.0	0	0.0	1	0.0
Totals	586		542		70		8		123		14		1343	100.0

combinations of sites, 'schools' and houses, the total rises to 1122 or 83.5% of the 1343 schools. In one out of five schools (273) it is used in conjunction with a horizontal division of the school into lower and upper or lower, middle and upper schools, with the figure rising to 323 if split-site schools are included. In 8% of schools (107) it is used in conjunction with houses, and here, according to the interview data, it is likely that the year system is the main form of pastoral organisation, while the houses are used mainly for competitive purposes. Interestingly mixed forms of internal organisation figure prominently in the table (39% of all responding schools).

By contrast, the house system is the sole form of pastoral organisation in only 113 schools (or 8.4% of the total) – a very different situation from that depicted by the NFER in 1968. When we add on the number of schools using houses in conjunction with some other form of pastoral system, the total still comes to only 294 (21.9% of the responding schools). There is an understandable reluctance to use the house system in split-site schools; and only 19 single-site schools use houses in conjunction with a horizontal system of lower and upper or lower, middle and upper schools. Sadly, a number of comprehensives with physical house bases have been forced to abandon a house structure because of falling rolls.

Uniform policy

In their 1979 review of studies into school effectiveness, Professor Rutter and his team noted that a combination of strict enforcement of uniforms, good and effective discipline (in terms of rule enforcement), the involvement of pupils in discipline (as shown by the use of a prefect system) and a low use of corporal punishment were all associated with good attendance and a happy school atmosphere (Rutter *et al.*, 1979:9, 17).

Table 5.3 shows that of the 1417 schools which responded to question 41 in our survey, a total of 603 (42.5%) said they require full uniform with or without named suppliers. But a further 117 schools (8.25%), while insisting on a full uniform for the majority of pupils, do not require the older pupils to be governed by this policy. Of the 590 11–18 schools responding to this question, roughly a third (201) insist on full uniform for all, while just under one in five (107) have a policy which does not embrace older pupils.

Table 5.3 Uniform policy in all types of comprehensive school. Results are given as numbers, with percentages in parentheses

	Uniform policy	11 to 18	11 to 16	13 to 16/18	14 to 18	9 to 13	11 to 14	Totals all schools
A	Full uniform required	201 (34.1)	314 (56.5)	11 (17.2)	1 (12.5)	72 (53.3)	4 (21)	603 (42.5)
A+C	Full uniform with older pupils excused	107 (18.1)	1 (0.2)	9 (14.1)	0	0	0	117 (8.25)
B	School uniform for main garments only	116 (19.7)	139 (34)	10 (15.6)	2 (25)	55 (40.7)	7 (36.8)	379 (26.7)
B+C	Uniform for main garments with older pupils excused	96 (16.3)	6 (1.1)	28 (43.7)	1 (12.5)	0	0	131 (9.25)
D	No uniform but an agreed dress code	48 (8.1)	35 (6.5)	5 (7.8)	0	7 (5.2)	6 (31.6)	102 (7.2)
E	Free choice of dress	22 (3.7)	10 (1.8)	1 (1.6)	4 (50)	1 (0.8)	2 (10.6)	40 (2.8)
	Other							45 (3.2)
	Totals	590	556	64	8	135	19	1417 (99.9)

A total of 379 schools (26.7%) have a uniform for main garments only and again a further 131 schools (9.25%) do not include older pupils in this policy. A total of 102 schools (7.2%) do not have a uniform as such but expect pupils to abide by an agreed dress code; and just 40 schools (2.8%) have no uniform policy at all and permit 'free choice of dress'. This comparatively small number of schools (142) circling either D or E in answer to our question would appear to indicate that comprehensive schools see the adoption of a school uniform as an important part of projecting a favourable image to the outside world. It is also true, of course, that a strict uniform policy has long been associated with the majority of establishments in the independent and grammar school sectors.

Aspects of discipline and exclusion policies

With the 1419 schools responding to question 42 in our survey, the most common forms of punishment appear to be: placing pupils on report (1385 schools), keeping pupils in detention during break-times or after school has finished (1362 schools) and seeking interviews with the offending pupils' parents or guardians (1405 schools).

Headteachers often indicate a marked reluctance to exclude 'troublesome' pupils for any length of time, but the answers to question 43 show that with all types of exclusion – temporary, indefinite and permanent – the number of schools employing this sanction actually grew between 1991–92 and 1992–93. There were 1078 schools in our survey that excluded at least one pupil temporarily during the academic year 1991–92 and this number had risen to 1187 by 1992–93, showing an increase of 9.1% over the two periods. Similarly, there were 459 schools that excluded at least one pupil indefinitely pending enquiry in 1991–92 and this had risen to 549 by the following academic year, showing an increase of 16.4% over the two periods. And there were 692 schools that expelled at least one pupil permanently in 1991–92, rising to 867 in 1992–93, thereby showing an increase by 20.2% over the 2 years.

In answer to question 44 in our survey, 72% of schools said that they had taken in excluded pupils from other schools in the previous academic year (1992–93); and in answer to question 45, 39% of these schools reported that the number of such incoming pupils was higher than the number of pupils removed; 24% said it was lower and 37% said it was roughly the same.

The rate of exclusions from state secondary schools has recently acquired the status of an important and controversial issue. The 1993 Education Act abolished the category of 'indefinite exclusions'; brought in new procedures whereby LEAs or the new funding agency for grant-maintained schools will now have the legal power to direct alternative schools (but not City Technology Colleges) to admit excluded pupils on their rolls; and introduced a new duty on LEAs to provide education for excluded pupils 'otherwise than at school'. Headteachers will now be empowered to exclude pupils on a 'fixed term' basis for up to 15 days in each school term. This may sound very reasonable, but as Lee Bridges points out in *Outcast England*, a report published by the Institute of Race Relations in 1994, it is a procedure that is open to abuse:

> There is a danger that headteachers may seek to use a series of extended 'fixed term' exclusions (which can amount in total to a quarter of the school year) as a means of circumventing the clear scrutiny of their decisions that would result from permanent exclusions and in order to keep 'difficult' children out of school for long periods and thereby 'persuade' parents to remove them 'voluntarily' from the school.
>
> (Bridges, 1994:14)

There is also genuine concern that the exclusion of pupils from school very often means the exclusion of *black* pupils from school. In 1992 the Department for Education published figures which revealed that there were as many as 3,000 permanent exclusions in the academic year 1990–91. Those in the secondary sector accounted for 87% of the total, with boys four times more likely than girls to be excluded from school. And Afro-Caribbean children made up 8.1% of the total while comprising only 2% of the total school population (see Lovey, Docking and Evans, 1993:3, 8). All over the country, as is shown in Table 5.4, there is a pattern of high exclusion rates of black children from both primary and secondary schools.

It is a worrying fact that comprehensive schools must account for the vast majority of schools from which black youngsters are excluded. According to Chris Searle, headteacher of Earl Marshal Comprehensive School in Sheffield, the ignorance of teachers and of the school system generally about the communities which they serve is a vital factor promoting conflict and misunderstanding between teachers and pupils. In Searle's view:

> Schools have a responsibility to make their codes of discipline and accepted conduct clear, setting them down unambiguously. These must include exclusions procedures, offering guidelines to parents for consultations, advice and independent appeals.
>
> (Searle, 1994:26)

There have been no expulsions from Earl Marshal School since Chris Searle became headteacher in 1990.

Table 5.4 The exclusion of black pupils from school

Location	Date(s)	Percentages of exclusions	Percentages of school population
Birmingham	1990–91	31	9
	1993–94	33	9
London Borough of Brent	1991	85	17
Sheffield	1990	6.7	2

(Sources: Bourne, Bridges and Searle, 1994:39–42; Grosvenor, 1995)

Democratic arrangements and parental involvement

Of the 1192 schools responding to question 59 in our questionnaire, 653 (54.8%) have a prefect system; 435 (36.5%) have societies run by the pupils themselves; and 750 (62.9%) have various forms of elected council also run by the pupils, though it is not clear from our survey what part these bodies actually play in the overall decision-making process of the school.

With regard to parental involvement in the day-to-day life of schools, we have had 1402 responses to question 61, and, of these, only 71 schools (or just over 5% of the total) say they have *no* form of parents' organisation. A total of 268 schools (just over 19%) do have an organisation for parents; 1019 (73%) have a parent/teacher organisation; and 98 (or just under 7%) have a parent/teacher/pupil organisation. A total of 242 schools have a school/community liaison body; 462 schools have a fund-raising committee; and in 444 schools parents have a role to play in classroom support. There is a tendency for fund-raising committees to be associated with schools drawing their pupils mainly from private residential or owner-occupied housing; but parent/teacher organisations are common to schools serving all types of catchment area. It is, of course, true that some communities are in an advantageous position when it comes to compensating for government and LEA economies; and this is a point we shall return to below.

It seems clear that a large number of parents are anxious to be involved with one or other of a wide range of school activities; and from the 400 or so responses to question 62, certain activities stand out as being popular areas of involvement. In 38 cases, parental assistance is available to the PE and sports staff. This apparently involves coaching various school sports teams; refereeing sports matches; providing transport for away games; and taking part in fund-raising activities for the purchase of new equipment. And prominent among the other areas of involvement highlighted by the schools are:

- helping to staff the school library (70 responses);
- helping to run the school bookshop and/or the school tuckshop (8 responses in both cases);
- accompanying staff on school trips (54);
- helping with the school reading scheme (22);
- assisting with musical and theatrical productions (12).

It is commonly held that the now statutory annual meeting of parents and governors is invariably poorly attended by parents, and our own findings would tend to support this. Table 5.5 shows that 30% of schools report that they are not able to attract more than 10 parents to the meeting, with only just over 8% of schools reporting attendances of more than 50.

Table 5.5 Number of parents attending the 1993 statutory meeting of parents and governors

Number of parents attending	Number of schools	Percentage of schools
0–10	367	30.1
11–20	286	23.4
21–30	226	18.5
31–40	138	11.3
41–50	102	8.4
51–70	94	7.7
71–100	3	0.2
Over 100	5	0.4
Total	1221	100.0

The number of parents attending was found to be clearly related to the catchment area of the school. Where the school served mainly council or housing association accommodation, the average figure was 16; in areas of predominantly residential or owner-occupied housing it was 45; and in areas of mainly substandard accommodation it was 9.

Reporting on progress and Records of Achievement

Of the 1399 schools responding to question 89 in Section Five of the questionnaire, 27 (just under 2% of the total) provide parents with a written report on each pupil twice a term; 93 (6.6%) once a term; 609 (43.5%) twice a year; and 670 (48%) once a year. Evidence suggests that reports sent out by schools at very short intervals are comparatively brief documents, with the main comprehensive report being completed at the end of the academic year.

In the vast majority of cases, the report provides a written comment on the pupil's progress in each subject, along with a number of numerical or letter grades to indicate attainment and effort in each course. Only 85 schools provide evidence of each pupil's numerical standing in the class or group. It is customary for distribution of the reports to be followed by an opportunity for parents to visit the school to meet the appropriate form tutor and subject teachers.

A total of 1330 schools have a system of Records of Achievement (just over 95% of the 1394 schools responding to question 91). In over half the cases (703 schools), this is a nationally based system, with local systems accounting for 28% of the total and school-based systems just under 20%.

Special arrangements for pupils

The Warnock Report published in 1978 estimated that around 20% of children might at some time in their schooling have 'special educational needs' (rather than the 2% covered by the existing official definition of 'special education'). Given the wider concept of special education, it was obvious that most of the provision would occur in ordinary schools and that careful planning was therefore required to ensure that the needs of *all* children were being met. Three years later, the 1981 Education Act decreed that, wherever possible, children with special educational needs of whatever kind should be entitled to receive their education within a mainstream school. Each LEA would be required to maintain a 'statement' in the case of those children whose 'needs' were such as to necessitate separate educational provision. Yet despite widespread official support for the concept of integration, research carried out in the 1980s showed that the percentage of pupils being educated in a segregated setting was being reduced only minimally – with the figure actually rising in some parts of the country. And this, despite the fact that the experience of disabled children being educated in mainstream schools was that they did better both educationally and socially, as long as the school was able to respond in a positive way to their 'special needs'. Able-bodied children and teachers also reported that it was a positive and rewarding experience for them (see Rieser and Mason, 1990: 147–8).

Micheline Mason has argued that the widely-used phrase 'special educational needs' actually came about as an attempt to demedicalise the labelling of children with disabilities; in other words, to replace offensive terms such as 'retarded', 'sub-normal', 'crippled', and 'maladjusted' with what was hoped to be less negative labelling based on educational need. Disabled people, she says, welcome the spirit in which this was done, but she suggests that it overlooks the *political* dimension. In her words:

> We do *not* consider ourselves to be special. We consider disability to be a norm within every society, borne out by statistics, and we want our needs to be taken into account as normal human needs. It seems questionable that 20% of young people can have 'special needs'. It seems ridiculous that 45% of young people within inner-city areas can have 'special needs'. Surely the question is: how does the education system fail to answer the needs of 45% of its users?

(Mason, 1990:88)

Of the 1413 schools responding to question 55 in our survey, 1382 (or nearly 98%) indicate that they have pupils with special educational needs *with* statements. And in answer to question 56, 1384 out of 1404 schools (98.6%) indicate that they have pupils with special educational needs but *without* statements. Only just over 30% of schools (440 out of 1398 responding) feel that the resources are adequate to meet these pupils' needs; and this is an area where there is considerable anxiety about the way the Warnock recommendations have been interpreted.

Table 5.6 Percentage of school population estimated to have special educational needs, by type of comprehensive school

Percentage	11–18	11–16	13–16/18	14–18	9–13	11–14	Totals	%
0–20	475	349	55	7	102	16	1004	(76.0)
21–50	105	158	7	1	22	2	295	(22.3)
51–70	2	12	0	0	0	0	14	(1.0)
71–100	3	5	1	0	0	0	9	(0.7)
Total							1322	(100.0)

In answer to question 58, 76% of schools (1004 out of 1322) estimate that they have up to 20% of pupils with special educational needs, with the remaining 24% claiming a higher (and, in a minority of cases, a considerably higher) percentage (see Table 5.6). When the perceived extent of special educational need is cross-referenced with the percentage of pupils qualifying for a free school meal (responses to question 40), the correlation is quite striking (see Table 5.7). Schools with the highest percentage of pupils estimated to have special educational needs are those with the highest percentage of pupils qualifying for free school meals. It is, of course, true that eligibility for a free meal is a somewhat inexact measure of social deprivation, but it is widely used by LEAs and researchers and is the only truly objective indicator in our survey.

Table 5.7 Estimation of percentage of pupils with special educational needs cross-referenced with eligibility for free school meals

Percentage of pupils eligible for free school meals	Percentage of pupils (with and without statements) estimated to have special educational needs
A less than 5	10.7
B between 6 and 15	13.5
C between 16 and 30	18.2
D between 31 and 50	25.9
E over 50	34.2
Average for survey:	16.6

When we come on to arrangements for pupils of exceptional attainment, it is not always clear what is meant by the term. It is often equated with the concept of giftedness which can have a wide array of meanings. Indeed, the late Edward Boyle, writing in the Newsletter of the National Association for Gifted Children, published in the Spring of 1972, said he personally knew of 167 definitions of a 'gifted child'. Some are so hopelessly generalised as to be almost meaningless: for example, one of the definitions from the NAGC–sponsored research carried out by the Schools Council in the early 1970s referred to 'any child who is outstanding in either general or specific ability in a relatively broad or narrow field'. Yet the giftedness movement, which began life in the 1960s, has certainly been successful in winning public support for the idea that a substantial minority of children 'need' extra provision: extra teacher attention, extra facilities, extra programmes, even some separation socially. And this point was highlighted in an article published in *Forum* in early 1982:

> The gifted child is a very difficult concept to challenge, since it now enjoys a fine public image (one reason it has been misused so easily) and because most of us accept willingly that some children are possessed of extra-ordinary talent. It is only when we look behind the scenes that we see quite clearly the way 'giftedness' has taken the place of the old 'ability at eleven' as the justification for continuing with some form of academic selection.
>
> (Benn, 1982:51)

Of the 1386 schools responding to question 93 in our survey, 815

(59%) say that they make special arrangements for pupils with exceptional ability. These 'special arrangements' seem to consist largely of extra assistance in the mainstream classroom; but 306 schools (37% of those responding) provide support for extra tuition or coaching in some subjects; 260 (32%) operate 'express' sets in some subjects; and 22 (just under 3%) have an 'express' stream for all subjects. Of these 22 schools, exactly half are establishments where the catchment area is socially mixed (in terms of housing), with a further seven serving areas with predominantly council or housing association accommodation. Only two schools in areas where housing is predominantly private and owner occupied have such streams.

Equal Opportunities policies

see p234. lack of interest?

Of the 1399 schools responding to question 46, 1314 (94%) say that they have an Equal Opportunities policy. And of those 618 schools admitting pupils from ethnic groups, 280 (45.3%) have a policy for monitoring these pupils in relation to attainment and examinations; 172 schools (27.8%) have a policy for monitoring grouping; and 357 (57.8%) have policies for dealing with racial harassment. There was a comparatively poor response to question 48 asking for details of specific policies in relation to ethnic groups not already highlighted in the questionnaire. Many schools claim that the whole issue is currently under review. One school argues that special policies for particular groups would be 'counter-productive' since they would serve to undermine the school's policy of 'equality for all'. Another argues that there is 'no time to consider equal opportunities policies'; and a third claims that developing specific policies for pupils from certain ethnic minorities would result in their acquiring a privileged status within the school. Five schools are keeping a special watch on the racist aspects of bullying; and two are monitoring exclusions. A number of schools are anxious that racism awareness material should be included in PSE and RE sessions.

In responding to question 49, a total of 1184 schools say that they have a policy for enabling pupils from lower income homes to participate in those activities where financial contributions are required, but only 95 schools have a policy for monitoring socio-economic groups in relation to course choices and options and only 128 schools with reference to grouping policies. Few schools provide examples of other specific policies for equalising opportunity. Typical of a large proportion of the responses to question 50 are: 'all our children have the same opportunities' and 'all

Same for WC so much

our pupils are the same socio-economic group'. One school argues that there is 'insufficient funding for this sort of policy'; and another says that it would be necessary to get 'financial support from local industries' in order to 'compensate for economic hardship'. A number of schools provide uniform support; and three schools emphasise that 'extra music lessons for instrumentalists are free for all pupils'.

Policies for monitoring gender inequality seem to be more popular than those relating to either race or social class. A total of 901 schools have a policy for monitoring gender in relation to examination performance; 807 express a concern about gender in relation to course options; and 557 monitor gender in connection with grouping policies. PE, computer studies and science are the three main curriculum areas where monitoring is in progress; and a number of schools indicate that they are working towards 'a total entitlement curriculum'. Only 120 schools operate classes or courses restricted to one sex only. Much concern is expressed by the 'under-performance of boys at GCSE'; and five schools are developing policies 'to counteract general under-achievement by boys'. This appears to be a comparatively recent development and supports the basic premise of a BBC *Panorama* programme broadcast in October 1994 with the title 'The Future is Female'.

Sex education

Of the 1408 schools responding to question 96 in our questionnaire, 1394 (or 99%) report that they have provided a programme of sex education for their pupils in the years since 1986.

It was 1986 that saw the passing of an education act (the 1986 Education (No. 2) Act: Chapter 61) which contained a number of important provisions relating to the organisation of sex education in schools. By the terms of the Act, governors now had the power of deciding whether or not a school should provide a programme of sex education for its pupils; and it was also the responsibility of school governing bodies (Clause 18) to 'make and keep up to date' a written statement with regard to their school's policy on sex education. One of the more controversial clauses in the Act (Clause 46) specified that governing bodies and headteachers should 'take such steps as are reasonably practicable to secure that where sex education is given to any registered pupils in a school, it is given in such a manner as to encourage those pupils to have due regard to moral considerations and the value of family life'. This was seen as being part of the Government's campaign to ensure that teachers were not preparing sex education lessons based on such dangerous concepts as: respect for different lifestyles, refusal to denigrate minorities and concern to develop new and sensitive definitions of the family (see Chitty, 1994, 1995).

Among the schools providing information for question 97 in our survey (some 1397 in total), the most popular means of providing sex education are within National Curriculum subjects, especially science (1154 schools or 82.6%) and within a structured programme of personal and social education (1187 schools or 85%). Clearly a large number of schools (actually 982) use a combination of the two. Only 588 schools (42.1% of the total) expect tutors to provide sex education in tutorial time. A total of 612 schools (44%) make use of outside specialist staff; and the remainder rely on 'in-house' teachers, a large proportion of whom have had no special training for the task. Evidence from interviews with teachers suggests that like other aspects of the so-called pastoral curriculum, sex education in schools is not always given the priority it deserves.

In the academic year in which the vast majority of our questionnaires were completed, secondary-school teachers were coming to terms with the worrying implications of new regulations concerning sex education enshrined within the 1993 Education Act. As a result of Section 241 of the Act, consideration of AIDS, HIV, sexually transmitted diseases and aspects of human sexual behaviour other than *biological* aspects can no longer form part of the syllabus for National Curriculum science. Governors of secondary schools will no longer have the power, granted them by the 1986 Act, of deciding that a school should not provide sex education for its pupils; though governors will continue to be required to develop a policy explaining how and where sex education will be taught and to make that policy available to parents. Finally, and perhaps most controversially, parents now have the right to withdraw their children from all or part of the 'compulsory' sex education programme. Parents do not have to give the reasons for their decision; nor do they have to indicate what other arrangements they intend to make for providing sex education for their children. Once a request for withdrawal has been made, that request must be observed until the parent changes or revokes it. Clearly teachers are to be censured for not providing sex education in the context of traditional moral values and respect for family life. According to Valerie Riches, Director of Family and Youth Concern, writing to *The Times* in July 1993:

The headteacher's somewhat guarded optimism was, of course, to prove unfounded, but it is true that the period from 1965 to 1970 was one of intense interest in the whole question of pupil grouping. The journals *Forum* and *Comprehensive Education* contained many articles by classroom teachers describing successful experiments in non-streaming; and conferences and workshops focusing on this issue were well-attended and lively affairs. No longer was it taken for granted that secondary pupils should be streamed or setted for academic subjects; and a 1965 *Forum* editorial made the important point that the issue of grouping lay at the heart of the debate about the structure and purpose of schooling:

> One of the key matters in English education today, which touches on every other of moment, is streaming. It raises directly questions of aim and purpose, psychological problems concerning the nature of learning, pedagogical interests in the content and methods of education, and issues surrounding pupil–teacher relationships. The current discussion about secondary reorganisation is, equally, concerned with this underlying issue.
>
> (*Forum*, 1965, 7(3), 79)

By the time the survey for *Half Way There* was carried out in 1968 (Benn and Simon, 1970), a number of schools had moved over to mixed-ability groupings for both academic and non-academic subjects for their first year pupils (see Table 6.1). Of 673 responding schools, 472 (or 70% of the total) were using various forms of banding, streaming and setting in the first year (now known as Year 7). Yet, at the same time, 151 schools (22% of the total) were using mixed-ability groupings for all or the vast majority of their pupils and in all or most of the subjects on the timetable[2]. And if the 30 schools using mixed-ability groupings but setting in *three* subjects (which were among the 43 which answered in category 8 of the Table) were added to the total (making it 181), the percentage rose from 22% to 27%, or just over one school in four. A number of schools maintained these mixed-ability groupings in the second year; and 42 schools (most of them all-through 11–18 comprehensives) for 3 full years (Benn and Simon, 1970:146–53).

Table 6.1 First-year grouping in comprehensive schools in Britain, 1968. Results are given as numbers of schools, with percentages in parentheses

Method of grouping	Total number of schools	(%)
1 In streams	130	(19.5)
2 In broad ability bands	210	(3.0)
3 In sets	36	(5.5)
4 Combination of streams and sets	96	(14.5)
5 Mixed ability (1) (no more than two subjects setted)	42	(6.0)
6 Mixed ability (2) (remedial pupils separated)	80	(12)
7 Mixed ability (3) (for all subjects and pupils)	29	(4.0)
8 Other methods (including no more than three subjects setted)	43	(6.5)
Unknown	7	(1.0)
Totals	673	(100)

Adapted from Table 9.2 in Benn and Simon (1970:147).

There are obvious reasons why schools should have been re-thinking their streaming policies in a period of rapid comprehensive reorganisation (some of them touched upon in the *Forum* editorial quoted above). The very establishment of comprehensive schools was, after all, the result of growing dissatisfaction with the early selection of children for different types of secondary school. This being the case, rigid streaming policies could not be adopted without many teachers being fearful of the potentially harmful consequences. As Brian Simon has argued:

> The comprehensive school was essentially a means by which the need for early selection (and so differentiation) could be overcome. It seemed to many, therefore, to be a contradiction in terms to establish comprehensive schools, but then to continue to differentiate between children in a fundamental way *within* these schools through streaming. Indeed this carried the danger of putting into practice even more precise differentiation of pupils than was attempted under the old bi-partite system. What was in danger of happening was that the main feature of the divided system – and precisely the one that comprehensive schools were established to overcome – would become, with 'prismatic' streaming, the main feature of the comprehensive system itself – a paradoxical situation.
>
> (Simon, 1970:3–4)

It is true that much of the research evidence published in the 1960s tended to emphasise the educational and social *disadvantages* of streaming, rather than the *advantages* of non-streaming. For example: J.W.B. Douglas, in his pioneering study of ability and attainment in the primary school,

The Home and the School, published in 1964, showed that the segregation of young children into separate streams was both a process of social selection and to a large extent self-verifying:

> Children who come from well-kept homes and who are themselves clean, well-clothed and shod, stand a greater chance of being put in the upper streams than their measured ability would seem to justify. Once there, they are likely to stay and to improve in performance in succeeding years. This is in striking contrast to the deterioration noted in those children of similar initial measured ability who were placed in the lower streams. In this way, the validity of the initial selection appears to be confirmed by the subsequent performance of the children, and an element of rigidity is introduced early into the primary school system.
>
> (Douglas, 1964:118)

And in his 1967 study *Social Relations in a Secondary School*, David Hargreaves showed how streaming processes worked to the disadvantage of large numbers of working-class pupils in the lower streams of the secondary modern school, leading to the creation of a 'deliquescent subculture'. According to Hargreaves, the polarisation of pupil subcultures was the direct result of the hierarchical ordering of pupils which the adolescent understood as representing a corresponding hierarchy of social worth. Within such a régime, pupils allocated to the lower streams experienced both failure and rejection, for which the development of an anti-school subculture offered a degree of compensation:

> When the school system is viewed in the setting of societal values, the upper stream members are successful and their efforts and values are rewarded by the status they derive. The lower stream pupils are 'failures'; they are status-deprived both in school and in society; their efforts meet with little success. Their problem of adjustment is 'solved' by rejection of societal and teacher values, for which are substituted a set of peer group values and status derived from conformity to a reversal of societal and teacher values.
>
> (Hargreaves, 1967:176)

On the other hand, a number of headteachers and classroom practitioners contributing articles to *Forum* in the 1960s wrote of the positive advantages of moving over to a non-streamed situation (for a review of the literature, see Chitty, 1969). It was reported in these accounts that mixed-ability teaching resulted in higher levels of motivation among the pupils – along with improved standards of behaviour and a greater willingness to participate in the life of the school. At the same time, it was emphasised that non-streamed schools were *educational* establishments and must be defended in these terms rather than on social or psychological grounds. Above all, it was important to move away from discredited notions of 'innate ability'. In the words of a headteacher outlining his conclusions after conducting an experiment in non-streaming in one of the large Coventry comprehensive schools in the early 1960s.

> The concept of 'innate ability' is not a valid one. That there are hierarchical boundaries between groups of pupils of different abilities is an epistemological concept which we define as an 'a priori' element in our thinking about education. We then set up various criteria in order to 'discover' who those different groups of pupils are, and the groups we form reflect not so much natural differences in ability as the nature of the methods we have adopted in choosing the groups.... The untapped source of ability in our schools... will not be fully revealed until there is a general relaxation of streaming during the first 3 years in the secondary school and all subjects are taught during at least the first two of these within a system of parallel forms.
>
> (Thompson, 1965:89)[3]

Yet despite the campaigning zeal of a number of heads and teachers, all the evidence suggests that the movement to challenge traditional forms of pupil grouping began to lose its momentum in the 1970s as attention shifted to the nature and content of the school curriculum (to be discussed later in this chapter) and government concern about discipline and standards ensured that the majority of schools were reluctant to experiment with new (and largely unproven) methods of organising learning[4]. It seems clear that many comprehensive schools continued (and still continue) to adopt a largely mixed-ability situation in the first year (Year 7), but that there was little inclination to persist with non-streamed groupings for both academic and non-academic subjects further up the school.

An investigation into the use of mixed-ability groupings in comprehensive schools in England carried out by Her Majesty's Inspectorate between 1975 and 1978 found that 35% of schools used mixed-ability groupings 'in most subjects' in the first year, 23% in both Years 1 and 2, 11% in the first 3 years and only 2% in all 5 years (DES, 1978:11)[5]. And a study of London comprehensive schools carried out in 1982 found that 39% of first years relied solely on mixed-ability groupings, with a further 32.5% combining mixed-ability arrangements with setting. Only 12% of second years were fully mixed-ability, with a further 50% combining mixed-ability arrangements with setting. In the third year, only 7% of schools were fully mixed-ability, with a further 46% combining the two systems (Weeks, 1983, 1986:85). More recently, in early 1995, a report in *The Times Educational Supplement* (Burstall, 1995) asserted (though without providing any supporting evidence) that very few comprehensive schools use mixed-ability groupings from Year 7 through to Year 11, with most introducing setting for key subjects in Year 8.

The findings from our survey go some way towards supporting the confident assertion in the recent *TES* article; and it seems clear that, at least where England and Wales are concerned, mixed-ability groupings for *all* pupils and in *all* subjects are indeed largely confined to Year 7[6]. Three tables in this chapter make possible a detailed understanding of the grouping arrangements of each of the years that constitute Key Stage 3; and a fourth looks at the significantly different picture that emerges from an analysis of the situation in Scotland where secondary pupils are recruited at the age of 12.

Table 6.2 shows that of the 1220 schools of all types which responded to question 99 for Year 7, 616, or just over 50%, use mixed-ability arrangements for *all* subjects and pupils. This form of grouping is particularly pronounced in all-through 11 to 18 schools where it is used by just over 57% of the schools surveyed. The only exception to the general pattern is, somewhat surprisingly, the 9–13 middle school where setting in no more than *two* subjects is more popular.

For a more complete picture of mixed ability teaching in Year 7, the 616 schools responding in category 1 of the table should be augmented by the 299 schools using mixed-ability groupings with no more than *two* subjects setted and 107 schools where no more than *four* subjects are setted – making a grand total of 1022 schools (83.8% of all schools responding to the question). This leaves just over 16% of schools (198 in total) using various forms of setting, streaming or banding with little or no scope for mixed-ability arrangements.

Viewed in conjunction with the results of earlier enquiries referred to in this chapter, the figure of 50.5 for the percentage of schools using mixed ability groupings for all subjects in Year 7 is remarkably high. (The percentage in 1968 was, after all, only 4, though rising to 27, if schools using only a limited amount of setting were also included.) What is equally remarkable, however, is that Year 7 is clearly viewed by many 11–16 and 11–18 schools as a transition year – and that, therefore, the use of mixed-ability classes for this age group should not be taken to denote a total commitment to non-streaming as such. Interviews with teachers have confirmed[7] that with many comprehensive schools taking pupils from a wide range of primary schools, there is felt to be the need for a period of assessment by subject teachers in the secondary school before final (or even tentative) decisions are made about 'appropriate' sets or streams. In many comprehensive schools, the use of setting in at least two subjects then begins in the second year (Year 8).

Table 6.2 Year 7/first-year grouping by the type of comprehensive schools in Britain, 1993–94. Results are given in numbers of schools, with percentages in parentheses

This table does not include details for Scotland where the transfer age is 12

Method of grouping	11/12 to 18	11/12 to 16	9 to 13	11 to 14	Total number of schools	(%)
1 Mixed ability for all subjects	316 (57.2)	254 (48.6)	38 (29.7)	8 (47.1)	616	(50.5)
2 Mixed ability, with no more than TWO subjects setted	128 (23.2)	124 (23.7)	44 (34.4)	3 (17.6)	299	(24.5)
3 Mixed ability, with no more than FOUR subjects setted	31 (5.6)	41 (7.8)	31 (24.2)	4 (23.5)	107	(8.8)
4 Ability sets for most or all academic courses	33 (6.0)	50 (9.6)	7 (5.5)	1 (5.9)	91	(7.5)
5 TWO or THREE ability bands with parallel classes	40 (7.2)	44 (8.4)	7 (5.5)	0 (0.0)	91	(7.5)
6 Streaming for all academic subjects but NOT for sport or drama	2 (0.4)	8 (1.5)	0 (0.0)	1 (5.9)	11	(0.9)
7 Streaming for all classes and courses	2 (0.4)	2 (0.4)	1 (0.8)	0 (0.0)	5	(0.4)
Total number of schools	552	553	128	17	1220	(100.0)

Table 6.3 shows that of the 1283 schools of all four types[8] responding to question 99 for Year 8, only 216, or nearly 17%, now use mixed-ability groupings for *all* subjects. This clearly represents a considerable drop from the 50.5% recorded for Year 7. A total of 125 11/12–18 schools, or 21%, operate mixed-ability classes throughout, but only 10.6% of 11/12–16 schools. The most popular category is now that of mixed-ability classes with no more than *two* subjects setted: a total of 423 schools, or 33%. And a further 305 schools, or 23.8%, use mixed-ability classes with no more than *four* subjects setted. This means that the total of schools using either mixed-ability groupings alone or with a limited degree of settings is now 944 (73.6%), compared with 1022 (83.8%) for Year 7. This leaves only 26.4% of schools (339 in total) using various forms of setting, streaming or banding with little or no commitment to mixed-ability arrangements, compared with just over 16% of schools (198) for Year 7. Viewed in this

256

light, and modifying what has already been said, it can perhaps be argued that at this stage, the majority of schools have not totally abandoned the principle of mixed-ability teaching for more rigid systems of streaming and banding.

Table 6.3 Year 8/second-year* grouping by type of comprehensive school in Britain, 1993–94. Results are given in numbers of schools, with percentages in parentheses

Method of grouping	11/12 to 18	11/12 to 16	9 to 13	11 to 14	Total number of schools	(%)
1 Mixed ability for all subjects	125 (21)	57 (10.6)	28 (21.9)	6 (31.6)	216	(16.8)
2 Mixed ability, with no more than TWO subjects setted	201 (33.7)	177 (32.8)	42 (32.8)	7 (36.8)	423	(33.0)
3 Mixed ability, with no more than FOUR subjects setted	127 (21.3)	131 (29.3)	40 (31.3)	7 (36.8)	305	(23.8)
4 Ability sets for most or all academic courses	92 (15.4)	102 (18.9)	8 (6.3)	2 (10.5)	204	(15.9)
5 TWO or THREE ability bands with parallel classes	47 (7.9)	60 (11.1)	8 (6.3)	0 (0.0)	115	(9.0)
6 Streaming for all academic subjects but NOT for sport or drama	2 (0.3)	9 (1.7)	0 (0.0)	1 (5.3)	12	(0.9)
7 Streaming for all classes and courses	2 (0.3)	4 (1.7)	2 (1.6)	0 (0.0)	8	(0.6)
Total number of schools	596	540	128	19	1283	(100.0)

* This is Year 1 for schools in Scotland.

Table 6.4 shows that the trend towards homogeneous groupings continues in Year 9, the year when, traditionally, pupils have been asked to make choices in connection with their upper-school courses. Of the 1230 schools of all four types responding to this part of question 99, only 80, (6.5%) now operate mixed-ability classes in all subjects and for all pupils. A further 225 schools (18.3% of the total) use mixed-ability groupings with no more than *two* subjects setted; and the most popular category is now that of mixed ability classes with no more than *four* subjects setted: a total of 432 schools, or 35.1%. The percentage of schools falling into this category is remarkably consistent across the three main types of comprehensive school: 34.5% for 11/12–18 schools; 35.6% for 11/12–16 schools; and 32.8% for 13–16/18 schools.

The total of schools using either mixed-ability groupings alone or with a limited amount of setting is now 737 (59.9%), compared with 944

(73.6%) for Year 8 and 1022 (83.8%) for Year 7. This leaves 40.1% of schools (493 in total) using either ability sets, streaming or banding, compared with 26.4% (339 schools) in Year 8 and only 16.3% (or 198 schools) in Year 7. A large number of schools (342 or 27.8%) now use ability sets for most or all academic courses. And, once again, the percentage of schools falling into this category is remarkably consistent across the three main types of comprehensive school: 28.8% for 11/12–18 schools; 27.0% for 11/12–16 schools; and 28.4% for 13–16/18 schools. Clearly a number of schools are now beginning to prepare their pupils for the more stratified arrangements of upper-school courses (to be discussed in the next chapter).

As indicated earlier, Scotland has its own idiosyncratic pattern of pupil groupings for Years 8 and 9 (Years 1 and 2 in Scotland). Table 6.5 shows that, whereas in Britain as a whole, only 216 schools, or 16.8% of the total, use mixed-ability groupings for all subjects in Year 8, the figure for Scotland is 73.3%, or 66 schools out of 90. Indeed the percentage for Scotland for Year 8 is higher than that for the whole of Britain for Year 7. And this also serves to underline the marked shift away from complete non-streaming to some form of setting in England and Wales at the end of Year 7, for the 66 schools in Scotland make up a third of all schools using mixed-ability groupings in Britain in Year 8. By comparison, the Year 9 (S2) figures for Scotland do not lend themselves to such easy comparisons. Whereas just over 25% of schools are still committed to a policy of complete non-streaming (compared with only 6.5% for the whole of Britain), a slightly higher percentage (27.5%) has moved over to a situation where there are ability sets for most or all academic subjects and this accurately reflects the percentage for Britain as a whole (27.8%).

In light of the above findings, it seems clear that non-streaming continues to occupy an important place in the culture of many comprehensive schools, but largely as an arrangement thought appropriate for the younger pupils in the school. At the same time, from our own interviews with classroom teachers – and taking into account comments by headteachers in interviews conducted in 1994 for a separate publication

Table 6.4 Year 9/third-year grouping by the type of comprehensive schools in Britain, 1993–94. Results are given in numbers of schools, with percentages in parentheses

Method of grouping	11/12 to 18	11/12 to 16	9 to 13	11 to 14	Total number of schools	(%)
1 Mixed ability for all subjects	46 (7.7)	29 (5.3)	3 (4.5)	2 (11.1)	80	(6.5)
2 Mixed ability, with no more than TWO subjects setted	111 (18.5)	97 (17.8)	14 (20.9)	3 (16.7)	225	(18.3)
3 Mixed ability, with no more than FOUR subjects setted	207 (34.5)	194 (35.6)	22 (32.8)	9 (50.0)	432	(35.1)
4 Ability sets for most or all academic courses	173 (28.8)	147 (27.0)	19 (28.4)	3 (16.7)	342	(27.8)
5 TWO or THREE ability bands with parallel classes	56 (9.3)	65 (11.9)	9 (13.4)	0 (0.0)	130	(10.6)
6 Streaming for all academic subjects but NOT for sport or drama	6 (1.0)	9 (1.7)	0 (0.0)	1 (5.6)	16	(1.3)
7 Streaming for all classes and courses	1 (0.2)	4 (0.7)	0 (0.0)	0 (0.0)	5	(0.4)
Total number of schools	600	545	67	18	1230	(100.0)

(see Hustler, Brighouse and Rudduck, 1995) – there are indications that mixed-ability teaching is an issue which no longer arouses much enthusiasm or excitement. In this respect, the 1990s are very different from the pioneering days of the 1960s. And this observation is endorsed in recent work by Judith Baxter (1995:28–46) which argues that the use of mixed-ability groupings has become a relatively neglected and uninspiring issue in recent years. Baxter is here talking principally about the teaching of English, but her shrewd and perceptive comments could equally apply to many other areas of the secondary-school curriculum. Once the subject of impassioned debate and a catch-all slogan for a radical new paradigm of teaching, the mixed-ability philosophy has gradually become naturalised into routine practice in many schools, with little real awareness of the issues at stake. In Judith Baxter's words:

> The implications of operating it [mixed-ability] effectively are rarely considered on conferences or courses; and a periodical and literature search has revealed that research writing on it is indeed both scanty and uninspiring.

> (Baxter, 1995:26)

Table 6.5 Pupil grouping by type of comprehensive school in Scotland: S1 (Year 8; n=90) and S2 (Year 9; n=91). Results given as numbers, with percentages in parentheses

Method of grouping	12–18		12–16		Total number of schools		Percentage	
	S1	S2	S1	S2	S1	S2	S1	S2
1 Mixed ability for all subjects	64(72.7)	21(23.6)	2(100)	2(100)	66	23	73.3	25.3
2 Mixed ability with no more than TWO subjects setted	21(23.9)	18(20.2)	0	0	21	18	23.9	19.8
3 Mixed ability with no more than FOUR subjects setted	3 (3.4)	17(19.1)	0	0	3	17	3.3	18.7
4 Ability sets for MOST or ALL academic courses	0	25(28.1)	0	0	–	25	3.3	18.7
5 TWO or THREE ability bands with parallel classes	0	7(7.9)	0	0	–	7	–	7.7
6 Streaming for all academic subjects	0	1.1	0	0	–	1	–	1.1
7 Streaming for all classes and courses	0	0	0	0	–	–	–	–
Totals	88	89	2	2	90	91		

Progress towards a common course

In a powerful article published in *Forum* in the Spring of 1966, Peter Mauger, at that time headteacher of Nightingale County Secondary School in the London Borough of Redbridge, argued that non-streaming, though clearly important, *was not an end in itself*; and he was critical of those who were preoccupied with flexibility of grouping and changes in method to the exclusion of everything else. What was also needed, in his view, was 'a fundamental examination of the content of the secondary-school curriculum'. It was not enough, even in an unstreamed school, to teach children 'the same old subjects in the same old way'. School work must be relevant to the needs of the pupils, and must be seen by them to be relevant. Without relevance, the so-called flexible school would always be 'a floppy school, all flexed up and nowhere to go'. As far as Mauger was concerned, the traditional subject-based curriculum was both irrelevant to pupil needs and blatantly inadequate in the light of the continuing and rapid increase in the sum total of human knowledge:

Children cannot be expected – in any type of school – to see school work as relevant to their needs while their curriculum is fragmented into uncoordinated subjects. The subject-based curriculum, with syllabuses determined by external examination requirements, encourages didacticism and rigidity in teaching methods, passivity and acquiescence in the regurgitation of received truths by the pupil.... Moreover, the subject-based curriculum is clearly inadequate in view of the knowledge explosion.... The idea that our schools should remain content with equipping children with a body of knowledge is absurd and frightening. Tomorrow's adults will be faced with problems about the nature of which we can today have no conception. They will have to cope with the jobs not yet invented. They need a curriculum that will teach them to ask questions, to explore, to enquire, to recognise the nature of problems and how to solve them: a curriculum that they can see as an organic whole, related to their present and their future needs. The flexible, unstreamed comprehensive school is only a means, but an essential means, to that end.

(Mauger, 1966:61)

The evolution towards a common curriculum within comprehensive schools – pointing the way to 'a well-balanced general education for all at the secondary stage' – had been one of the themes explored in *New Trends in English Education*, a symposium edited by Brian Simon and published in 1957, where a number of practising teachers had outlined plans for implementing syllabuses which could be taught to all pupils. And an editorial in the journal *New Left Review*, published in the Autumn of 1961, had argued that the changeover to comprehensive schools at the secondary stage, with its goal of achieving an educated community, would be meaningless without the simultaneous introduction of a common curriculum for all pupils:

The goal of *an educated community* must be taken together with the concept of *a common curriculum*, for the one is the means to the other. We know a great deal about specialisation and individual levels of attainment: what we know next to nothing about is the common educational experience from which specialisation and attainment must grow; and what we have never so far attempted is to sort out, and then to advance, levels of attainment along a single educational graph. The common curriculum, then, should be seen as the foundation of the education of every child to the age of 16 – 'a working area' or grouping of facts, interpretations, skills and values, without which no man or woman can be an active, participating member of the community. Up to the present, such 'a working area in education' has been generally restricted to the skills of literacy and the three Rs. This is now dangerously limited. We have to extend this 'working area', if for no other reason then certainly at least to keep pace with the growth in complexity of technical civilisation, with the spread of democratic practices, and the multiplying means of communicating information, ideas and opinions. An education which does not fit the vast majority to cope with such changes is simply, in historical terms, not adapted to the way society is moving.

(New Left Review, 1961, **11**, 38–44)

The questionnaire sent to all comprehensive schools in England, Wales and Scotland in 1968 for the Benn/Simon report on the British comprehensive school reform asked whether all pupils aged 11–14 years pursued 'the same basic subjects, even if at a different pace or depth', without asking for a precise definition of the common course on offer[9]. Of the 606 schools in England and Wales answering this question, 488 (80.5%) operated a common course for all pupils in the first year. Of these, 235 (48%) maintained the common course for the 3 years, from 11 to 14; 145 (30%) for 2 years; and 87 (18%) for one year[10]. In Scotland, where pupils were recruited at 12, 53 schools (79% of the total) stated that they provided a common course, 22 for two years (41.5%) and 30 for the first year only (56.5%) (Benn and Simon, 1970:144)[11].

A specific problem which arose in connection with the common course was that of a second language. The 1968 survey showed that 97% of 11- and 12-plus comprehensive schools in Britain offered a foreign language in the first year (650 out of 673). But a considerable proportion of schools stating that they provided a common curriculum for all pupils did not actually provide a foreign language *for all pupils*[12].

Another related subject heading to early differentiation was Latin – a subject presenting particular problems for comprehensive schools. The evidence showed that Latin was taught in the early years of the school most generally only in those comprehensives which had developed from grammar schools – and here some form of selection was necessary because the subject was seldom, if ever, taught across the entire ability range[13]. Some schools realised that the teaching of Latin to a minority of pupils and the provision of a common curriculum were incompatible and that it might be preferable to postpone the introduction of the subject until the fifth or sixth form.

In the 1970s, a number of comprehensive schools and teachers began to take seriously the case for a common curriculum for all 5 years of secondary schooling (see Chapter 9); but as late as the period 1975–78, HM Inspectors of Schools found that only around 7% of the comprehensive schools included in their general survey of the secondary sector (15 out of 208 comprehensive schools) stated that they offered their pupils 'a wholly common curriculum in the first 3 years' (DES, 1979:14). The policy of a large number of the comprehensive schools was to keep the curriculum as broad as possible in the first, second and third years and avoid premature specialisation. But the vast majority also indicated that *at some stage* there was significant differentiation in the curriculum according to the sex and ability of the pupils.

It needs to be emphasised that this very low figure of 7% referred to all 3 years taken together and that, although detailed information was not available, sufficient evidence was forthcoming to suggest that common curricula generally gave way to differentiating strategies as the pupils got older. In the words of the HMI report: 'the limited evidence showed a tendency for the extent of differentiation in curricula to increase from the first year to the third year as the strengths and weaknesses of individual pupils become better known and their interests more apparent' (DES, 1979:16). At the same time, it is clear that the Inspectors were using a very strict definition of a common curriculum – making an interesting contrast with the earlier surveys of the 1960s which did not always take into account differentiation by sex, and, as we have seen, included in their lists of schools offering a common course those comprehensives which did *not* provide a modern foreign language for *all* their pupils.

The main areas of differentiation in lower-school provision highlighted in the 1979 survey concerned the teaching of modern languages and science to third-year pupils. Those in 'higher' streams were often given the opportunity to start one or more additional foreign languages – additional, that is, to French; while their 'less able' contemporaries were often encouraged to drop French altogether. Of the 192 comprehensive schools which supplied information for this part of the survey, 77 (40%) indicated that not all pupils were studying French in the third year. For those pupils who had been allowed to drop the subject alternative provision varied: about a third substituted French Studies or European Studies; some turned to an entirely unrelated subject (commerce was named in five schools, and an additional practical subject in 12); while many of the remainder used the time for further study of English and mathematics (DES, 1979:18).

Similarly, a select group of pupils in the third year might be studying separate physics, chemistry and biology; while the sciences on offer to the 'bottom' streams or sets could be general science, rural science or science incorporated into 'environmental studies'. And in many schools only the 'less able' were thought to profit from extended contact with the creative/aesthetic area of the curriculum (DES, 1979:17–19).

The responses to question 98 in our own survey (see Table 6.6) show that in Year 7, 93.4% of comprehensive schools provide a completely common curriculum for all pupils; and this percentage holds good for all types of school (11–18, 11–16, etc), in all parts of Britain and regardless of the nature of the school's catchment area. Where there is variety of provision at this stage in a small minority of schools, this largely refers to a degree of choice in the modern foreign languages on offer (to be discussed below).

As one might expect, there are a significant number of cases where the common curriculum is modified to permit a degree of differentiation as pupils progress through the school[14]. The percentage of schools providing a common course for all pupils has dropped from 93.4 for Year 7 to 78 for Year 8 (1002 schools out of a total of 1284 responding); and to 59.7 for Year 9 (734 schools out of 1229). As pupils get older in some comprehensives, they are given a degree of choice in academic subjects and even, in some cases in Year 9, in vocational options. By far the biggest area of choice lies in the provision of modern foreign languages – affecting 461 schools, or 37.5% of the total, in Year 9.

Table 6.6 Organisation of the curriculum at Key Stage 3 (Responses to question 98. Results are given in numbers of schools, with percentages in parentheses*.)

A   Completely common curriculum for all
B   Some choice in academic subjects
C   Some choice in vocational subjects
D   Some choice in arts or music
E   Some choice in sports
F: Some choice in languages

Year	A	B	C	D	E	F	Total Responding
7	1140(93.4)	26(2.1)	3(0.2)	7(0.6)	22(1.8)	96(7.9*)	1220
8/S1	1002(78.0)	107(8.3)	9(0.7)	16(1.2)	29(2.3)	271(21.1)	1284
9/S2	734(59.7)	233(19.0)	73(5.9)	79(6.4)	70(5.7)	461(37.5)	1229

*Strictly speaking, the percentage for A combined with the percentage for any other single letter should not exceed 100%, but it appears that a few schools have circled two mutually contradictory letters in error. It is, of course, possible for schools which have not selected A to circle various combinations of letters from B to F.

A modern foreign language is, of course, one of the foundation subjects for secondary schools in the National Curriculum. In the vast majority of schools, this means French, but it is clear from the answers to questions 102, 103 and 104 in our survey that a very large number of schools also provide a second or third foreign language for some or all of their pupils at some stage in the first 3 years[15]. Of 1353 schools responding to question 104, 1330 (98.3%) provide French for some or all of their pupils; 1002 German (74%); 304 Spanish (22.5%); 39 Italian (2.9%); 24 Russian (1.8%); 62 Welsh (4.6%); and 106 Latin (7.8%). Further analysis shows that of these 106 schools offering Latin, the vast majority (86 schools, 81% of the total) fall within categories B or C of question 27: taking their pupils from either private residential or owner-occupied housing (B) or a mix of council and private housing (C)[16]. Latin is still a subject posing particular problems for the comprehensive sector and is never taught across the entire ability range.

Question 100 in our survey asking schools to identify those subjects in the National Curriculum where provision was 'difficult' brought forth 200 responses, broken down in the following way, with some schools indicating more than one subject: English 7, mathematics 5, science 8, technology 54, a modern foreign language 32, religious education 115, history 10, geography 10, music 39, art 16 and physical education 18. Interestingly religious education figures prominently in the list (57.5% of responding schools), at a time when many teachers are debating how best to teach the subject in a society of many faiths and cultures and against the background of government preoccupation with the moral values associated with a particular interpretation of Christianity (see Tombs, 1994).

Information was also sought as to the status of the cross-curricular themes identified by the now disbanded National Curriculum Council (NCC, 1990) as essential components of a common entitlement curriculum. Table 6.7 shows the number and percentage of schools offering the cross-curricular themes as separate timetabled subjects or courses at Key Stage 3.

Table 6.7 Number (%) of schools offering cross-curricular themes as separate timetabled subjects or courses at Key Stage 3 (n = 486)

1	Economic and industrial understanding	105(21.6)
2	Careers education and guidance	336(69.1)
3	Health education	349(71.8)
4	Education for citizenship	153(31.5)
5	Environmental education	127(26.1)

Of 486 responding schools, over two-thirds offer both careers education and guidance and health education as separate time-tabled subjects. A total of 61 schools, (12.5% of those responding) include all five cross-curricular themes in the curriculum. Those schools which do not feature in the above list may have found a way of accommodating the themes within the curriculum by teaching them through existing subjects. Many schools are clearly determined that national curriculum requirements should not be allowed to deprive children of access to areas of experience that fall outside the Government's narrow framework.

Notes

1 The full text of this speech is reproduced in *Forum*, **7**(**3**), 79.

2 Strictly speaking, the proportion of schools using mixed – ability groupings for *all* pupils and in *all* subjects was just 4%; and this was also the figure arrived at by the NFER (National Foundation for Educational Research) using a somewhat different category system. Their data was gathered in 1965, and they were using a smaller sample of schools (331) (see Monks, 1968:103).

3 The author of the article in *Forum* from which this extract is taken was Headteacher of the Woodlands Comprehensive School for Boys in Coventry. The article was a detailed account of the relaxation of streaming that had taken place in the school over the previous two and a half years. The system of parallel forms referred to here would embrace pupils in the VRQ (Verbal Reasoning Quotient) range 90–130 plus. The article accepts that it may be necessary to place pupils with very low VRQs in a separate remedial class (see also Thompson, 1969, 1974).

4 Many teachers were thrown on to the defensive by political attacks on their classroom practice. The 1976–9 Callaghan administration in particular was anxious to discourage the relaxation of streaming and the adoption of so-called progressive teaching strategies in state schools (see Chitty, 1993).

5 The enquiry covered only those comprehensive schools with an age range of 11–12 to 16–18. For the purposes of the exercise, 'most subjects' meant that not more than *two* subjects were excluded from mixed ability organisation in the curriculum of any one year group. (For a detailed critique of the HMI approach to carrying out this enquiry, see Simon, 1979.)

6 In Scotland, mixed-ability groupings are very prominent in Year 8/SY1. This is discussed later in the chapter.

7 Over 200 teachers from a variety of comprehensive schools in the West Midlands were asked for their attitude towards Year 7 grouping policies in the period January to March 1995.

8 This figure now includes comprehensive schools in Scotland where pupils are recruited at 12.

9 The survey of London comprehensive schools published by the Inner London Education Authority in 1967 defined the 3-year general course then in operation in many of its schools as comprising all the normal subjects at this stage of the secondary course: 'English, mathematics, science, history, geography, art, music, drama, handicraft (for boys) or housecraft (for girls), religious education and physical education, generally with periods for games' (ILEA, 1967:59).

10 An additional nine schools reported that the common course was maintained for 4 years and five for a full 5 years (seven did not provide the necessary information).

11 One of the 53 schools answered incorrectly.

12 Of the 541 comprehensive schools in England, Wales and Scotland claiming to provide a common course for *all* their pupils, only 227 (42%) provided a foreign language for *all* their pupils (Benn and Simon, 1970:145).

13 The survey conducted by the Incorporated Association of Assistant Masters (IAAM) in 1967 found that three of the 30 schools surveyed introduced Latin

in the first year; four in the second. 'Where the school does not stream or set its pupils,' concludes the IAAM report, 'Latin is unlikely to be taught' (IAAM, 1967:65).

14 The original DES National Curriculum consultation document, published in July 1987, suggested that the core and foundation subjects of the National Curriculum would 'commonly take up 80–90% of the curriculum in schools where there is good practice' (DES, 1987:8).

15 The answers to 103 show that a second foreign language has a close rival in drama as a popular additional subject in the Key Stage 3 curriculum. Of 814 responding schools, it is offered by 697 (85.6% of the total).

16 A similar situation exists with regard to the provision of Russian. Of the 24 schools in our survey which offer this subject, 17 (just over 70%) fall within categories B or C of question 27.

7

Academic Policy, Curriculum and Assessment: 14 to 16 Years

Attitudes towards the organisation of upper-school courses: before ROSLA and after

In the years before the raising of the school leaving age to 16 in 1972–73, it was possible for pupils to leave school without embarking on a fifth year of secondary schooling[1]. Indeed, large numbers of pupils with the 'appropriate' dates of birth were able to leave school after completing only two terms in the fourth year[2]; and in the case of Leicestershire, with its two-tier system of secondary schools, pupils could not even move from the high school to the upper school at 14 unless they were prepared to commit themselves formally to at least 2 more years of schooling[3].

At the time of the Benn/Simon survey, the overall staying-on rate in England and Wales was 50%; the average staying-on rate in comprehensive schools in England and Wales in the survey itself was slightly higher, at 52%[4]. This meant that, in the typical comprehensive school of the late 1960s, just under half the pupils left school shortly after reaching the age of 15 (Benn and Simon, 1970:166).

In the early days of the comprehensive reform – and regardless of how many pupils stayed on for a full 5 years of secondary schooling – very few schools offered a common curriculum to all their pupils in all 5 years; and to do so in the upper school was thought by many to be neither practicable nor desirable. The fourth year (age 14–15) was the key point at which, according to Benn and Simon (1970:167): 'the differentiation of pupils, already under way in some schools through such techniques as streaming and setting, becomes actual and recognised in terms of differences in courses and direction.'

The comprehensive school was actually applauded by many on the grounds that it was often large enough to offer a wide array of courses and options to 14-year-old pupils. In his influential book *The Comprehensive School*, first published in 1963, Robin Pedley cited with approval the diversity of subjects and courses available to fourth-year pupils at a large mixed comprehensive school in South London with its 18 forms ranging from 4S and 4K for the scientists, down through 4N for the engineers and 4R with the emphasis on catering, to 4Y for the Easter leavers. Such provision, argued Pedley (1963:90) 'exceeds in diversity anything a normal grammar or "modern" school can offer'. And the 1966 ILEA survey of London comprehensive schools (published in 1967) reached the conclusion that 'a great deal of care is taken in most schools to ensure that the courses and variety of subjects on offer in the fourth and fifth years will, within the resources of the school, meet the needs of all the pupils and give each one the choice his (sic) interests and abilities require'. It was further claimed that many schools could offer such a wide variety of courses and such a large number of possible combinations of subjects that 'no two pupils need necessarily be following the same timetable' (ILEA, 1967:65).

The responses to question 24 in the 1968 Benn/Simon survey indicated the variety of methods used in organising the upper-school curriculum in 605 comprehensive schools in England, Wales and Scotland (Table 7.1). In this question schools were asked to indicate in which of three main ways their upper-school curriculum was arranged: by a system of required subjects, plus options; by a system of complete course choices; or by a system of completely free choice of subjects from a number of different option groups[5]. The category of 'complete course choices' was meant to indicate a structure comprising clearly differentiated courses (for example: academic, commercial, technical, general); while the first and third categories referred to systems based more on the principle of individualisation of programmes. An example of the first category would be a system where a limited number of subjects had to be studied by all pupils, but another five subject options could be chosen from the five groups of subjects. The third category carried the principle of individualisation furthest, since it required no principal subjects to be studied.

Table 7.1 Curriculum arrangements in comprehensive schools with 13–14 to 15–16 age group, England, Wales and Scotland, 1968*. Results are given in numbers of schools, with percentages in parentheses

Curriculum arrangements	Number	(%)
1. Required subjects plus options	420	(68.5)
2. Complete course choices	84	(13.5)
3. Free choice from option groups	53	(8.5)
4. Other systems (or combinations of above)	48	(8.0)
5. Unknown	8	(1.5)
Totals	613	(100)

* This appears as Table 10.1 in Benn and Simon, 1970:173.

The findings showed that the system of offering choices of complete courses was followed by nearly 14% of schools covering the 14–16 age range (84 schools out of 613). By far the largest number of schools (420 or 68.5% of the total) were using a system where pupils were presented with a very free choice of options, together with a limited core of required subjects (an example is given in Table 7.2). And a comparatively small number of schools (53, or nearly 9% of the total) claimed that their curriculum structure for the fourth and fifth years allowed a complete free-choice system based on option groups. Closer examination of the schools in this category, however, shows that, in reality, the free-choice system merged into the core-plus-options system described above. It seems clear that, even in this category, English and mathematics were required subjects for all pupils, with some schools requiring religious education (as a separate subject), 'careers' and physical education as well (Benn and Simon, 1970:179).

A complicating factor in all these upper-school arrangements was the co-existence of two parallel school examinations: the Ordinary Level GCE (General Certificate of Education) and the CSE (Certificate of Secondary Education)[6]. Despite official recognition of a grade 1 pass at CSE being equivalent to a GCE pass, the two examinations did not enjoy equal status, and it was not often thought desirable for GCE and CSE pupils to be taught together in the same classes. Table 7.2 shows that subjects which appeared in option columns on the timetable could be offered in some cases only for GCE, in others only at CSE and in some cases at both levels.

The school-leaving age was raised to 16 in 1972–73 during Margaret Thatcher's 4-year period as Conservative Education Secretary in the 1970–74 Heath administration, and what became known as 'ROSLA' might have encouraged schools and teachers to plan a common, unified 5-

year curriculum for *all* their pupils. But it seems clear that this did *not* immediately happen on a large scale.

Table 7.2 Subject pools for options in the fifth year in a large 11–18 comprehensive school*

1	2	3	4	5
French (18) o/c	History (23) o/c	Geography (23) o/c	Chemistry (30) o/c	Physics (20) o/c
Spanish (8) c	Typing(4) c	Chemistry (9) o	Physics (15) o/c	Biology (35) o/c
History (37) o/c	Technical	Biology (11) c	General	General
Geography (37) o/c	Drawing (8) o	Typing (8) c	Science (11) c	Science (14) c
	Metalwork (8) c	Scripture (6) c	Economics (4) o	Art (14) o/c
	Engineering (8) c	Art (14) o/c	Social	Typing (9) c
	Domestic	Technical	Studies (15) c	Accounts(8) c
	Science (24) o/c	Drawing (14) o/c	Music (9) c	
	Needlework (10) o/c	Domestic	Typing (9) c	
	Catering (7) c	Science (7) c	Accounts (7) c	
	Woodwork (8) o/c	Engineering (8) o		

o = GCE group only; c = CSE group only; o/c = GCE and CSE.
The figures in parentheses give a rough indication of the percentage of pupils choosing that subject in that column in a typical year. The columns do not include the required subjects which all pupils must study: English, mathematics, religious education, careers education and physical education.
* This appears as Table 10.2 in Benn and Simon (1970:178).

Four years after ROSLA, in a paper outlining the Labour Government's agenda for the 1977 Great Debate, DES civil servants argued that:

> Few could claim that a common curriculum exists in secondary schools.... Certainly current practice shows a fairly standard pattern of subjects in Years 1 to 3, moving to diversification by student choice in Years 4 to 7 in the majority of schools. In the first 2, and sometimes 3, years, all pupils are likely to be offered a common programme, with some modifications in the third year, particularly for the less able or the more able pupils.... In the fourth and fifth years, however, when the programme for most pupils covers some eight or nine subjects, the fixed points in the curriculum in current practice are likely to be no more than four: English, mathematics, religious education and physical education.
>
> (DES, 1977a:4)

The DES was itself seeking to establish 'generally accepted principles for the composition of the secondary curriculum for all pupils' (DES, 1977b:11), but it faced opposition from those teachers who valued the principles of choice and diversity with regard to the upper-school curriculum.

All the evidence suggests that the DES was indeed right (in its background paper for the Great Debate regional conferences) to single out the third year as a sort of transition period for many pupils (and this was touched upon in the last chapter). In *Framework for the Curriculum*, the report of an NFER study of the third-year curriculum in a number of West Midlands secondary schools carried out in the mid-1970s, Penelope Weston suggested that a common course was often seen as the one desirable goal which 'like virtue, all must be seen to be pursuing, whatever the context and circumstances of the school' (Weston, 1977:46). But, in reality, as she discovered in the course of her research, the unified approach barely survived for 2 years, and the third year was a sort of 'bridge', when the pretence of a common course was finally dropped and preparations were made for the examination-directed curriculum of the fourth and fifth years. The raising of the school leaving age to 16 could, in Weston's view, have been used as a marvellous opportunity to plan a unified 5-year curriculum for *all* comprehensive schools; instead, it had had the adverse effect of turning the third year into a time of decision-making and forward planning for *all* pupils. The pressure was there to promote differentiation in a number of key areas. In the words of one headteacher quoted in the study: 'The third-year curriculum is inevitably a compromise. Conflict between a common curriculum with stable primary groups and increased specialisation with the flexibility required is most acute in the third year' (Weston, 1977:82).

The 1979 HMI survey of secondary education showed that most comprehensive schools viewed an extension of the common curriculum into the fourth and fifth years as a quite unworkable proposition. They might talk in terms of a 'core curriculum' – the basic nucleus of subjects commonly held to be essential or actually required by law and usually consisting of English, mathematics, religious education, 'careers' and physical education – but this normally accounted for only about two-fifths of each pupil's timetable[7]. The work in the rest of the timetable would then be organised in one or other of a number of different ways.

Some comprehensive schools ran completely segregated courses or 'bands' each with its own specific examination objectives. Pupils might be asked to choose a given number of subjects within their particular course; but the system had obvious in-built inequalities, and for those taking CSEs only or no examinations at all, the choice could often be very restricted and heavily weighted towards the practical and the vocational. Subjects which were limited to particular bands were additional foreign languages (almost always reserved for the 'top band') and the separate sciences. The 'bottom' band might often be following a programme reminiscent of the 'special' courses for early leavers made available in many schools prior to the raising of the school-leaving age. A system of 'free' choice, on the other hand, enabled pupils to choose from a wide selection of subjects ostensibly open to all; and a rigid banding structure gave way to more flexible ability groupings geared to the different examinations. A third less common possibility – which perhaps came closest to the ideal of a common curriculum in Years 4 and 5 – was the Required Option system where pupils were expected to achieve a balanced diet by choosing at least one subject or course of study from each of the major disciplines within the curriculum: science, humanities, languages and design.

The inspectors concluded that the upper-school curriculum often involved a loss of balance and coherence:

> The organisation of options and courses in the fourth and fifth years is almost always complex and frequently necessitates compromise on the part of both pupils and school. Less able pupils are given in effect less real choice than other pupils. The examination courses they take are sometimes inappropriate and were not designed for the levels of ability for which they are now used. The more able pupils may be given opportunities to take additional languages and separate sciences, but may suffer from the loss of practical, aesthetic or humanities subjects and those courses devoted to aspects of personal and social education.... It seems clear that the introduction of options in the fourth and fifth years leads to the abandonment of some important subjects for some pupils and to insufficient breadth in some individual pupils' programmes.
>
> (DES, 1979:37)

Non-streaming and the common curriculum

It would be wrong to give the impression that throughout the 1970s, there were no effective challenges to the prevailing orthodoxy where the organisation of upper-school courses was concerned. A number of teachers and educationists were, in fact, beginning to make the case both for a common curriculum for *all* pupils throughout the secondary school, including the fourth and fifth years (now known as Years 10 and 11), and for a more flexible approach to pupil grouping at all stages of development. It should also be emphasised that all this went far beyond the thinking of the DES which tended to see the common curriculum in terms of an irreducible but limited core of compulsory subjects.

John White produced *Towards a Compulsory Curriculum* in 1973; but although the book provided a sound theoretical basis for an all-embracing, nationally imposed, compulsory curriculum, the proposal was seen by many as running counter to the English tradition of an education service that was centrally supported but locally administered.

At the same time, Denis Lawton was writing in terms of an integrated curriculum (1969) or a common culture individualised curriculum (1973), acknowledging his debt to the work of Broudy, Smith and Burnett in America (1964) and to the more accessible writings of Raymond Williams in this country (1958, 1961). Somewhat ironically, Lawton's notion of a 'common culture curriculum' was criticised by some on the Left at the end of the 1970s (see, for example, Ozolins, 1979; Robins and Cohen, 1978) for being an insidious means of justifying the continuing transmission of middle-class values, with all that that implied for the status of working-class culture. But this criticism of the common curriculum concept had already been touched upon (and refuted) by the Conservative MP Timothy Raison in an article published in *The Times* in February 1973:

> My conviction is that comprehensive schools must be committed to the transmission of our traditional culture and academic values, though certainly in a searching and fresh rather than stereotyped way.... When it comes to the point, it will not only be middle-class parents who take that view. There has always been a strong and admirable commitment among working-class parents that they, too, want the best for their children.... Moreover, at its extreme, there can be something halfway between insulting and defeatist in the idea of providing a *different* sort of culture for working-class children. Of course the style in which our civilisation and crafts should be conveyed to different children must vary with the circumstances. But the essence should be same.
>
> (*The Times*, 20 February 1973)

It was also at this time that a challenging and innovative version of a common curriculum was being devised by the so-called Curriculum Publications Group (or CPG) within Her Majesty's Inspectorate. And in a number of key texts (usually known as the HMI Red Books) published between 1977 and 1983 (DES, 1977c, 1981, 1983), HMI rejected the DES concept of a narrow subject-based core curriculum and argued instead for whole-school curriculum planning to be organised according to a checklist of eight 'areas of experience': the aesthetic and creative, the ethical, the linguistic, the mathematical, the physical, the scientific, the social and political, and the spiritual. For members of the Inspectorate, the chief concepts to be considered were those of *access* and *entitlement*: all pupils, regardless of ability, should have access to an 'entitlement curriculum' viewed as a broad synthesis of the vocational, the technical and the academic. There should certainly be no separation of pupils at 14 into 'academic sheep' and 'vocational goats'. Recognising the need to provide a clear and unequivocal statement of the distinctive HMI approach to curriculum construction, the last of the three Red Books, published in 1983, contained a succinct summary of the main conclusions reached by the Inspectorate after a decade or more of curriculum enquiry and debate:

> It seems to us essential that *all* pupils should be guaranteed a curriculum of a distinctive breadth and depth to which they should be *entitled*, irrespective of the type of school they attend or their level of ability or their social circumstances, and that the failure to provide such a curriculum is unacceptable.... The conviction has grown that all pupils are entitled to a broad compulsory common curriculum to the age of sixteen which introduces them to a range of experiences, makes them aware of the kind of society in which they are going to live and gives them the skills necessary to live in it. Any curriculum which fails to provide this balance and is overweighted in any particular direction, whether vocational, technical or academic, is to be seriously questioned. Any measures which restrict the access of all pupils to a wide-ranging curriculum or which focus too narrowly on specific skills are in direct conflict with the entitlement curriculum envisaged here.
>
> (DES, 1983:25, 26)

All of this exerted a profound influence on a small but growing group of teachers who were now beginning to write of their experiences in trying to implement a unified curriculum appropriate to an age of comprehensive primary and secondary schools (see, for example, Chitty, 1979, 1980; Clarke, 1979; Fulford, 1979). For these classroom practitioners, there was no justification for allowing common approaches to give way to differentiating strategies when pupils reached the age of 14. And in a number of powerful contributions to the debate, Maurice Holt (1969, 1976, 1978) from 1969 to 1977 headteacher of Sheredes School in Hertfordshire, sought to bring together the related issues of non-streaming and common curricula, particularly where the fourth and fifth years were concerned. Holt asked the question: 'Is unstreaming irrelevant?' And his answer was that we should be talking more about flexible grouping than about non-streaming or unstreaming. What was needed was a flexible school supporting a variety of grouping patterns. In Holt's view, the danger with an inadequately-prepared changeover to mixed-ability groupings was that too many individual teachers could remain isolated and struggle on with unsuitable material. Block timetabling, on the other hand, would facilitate a flexible approach to grouping. With sufficient numbers of teachers allocated to whole-year groups or half-year groups for each curriculum area, there was scope for a variety of different teaching and learning situations. It was possible to take account of the different skills of different teachers and to establish teams – both within and across subject boundaries – which would harness those skills most effectively to child-centred learning situations.

Such were the issues being debated by a minority of secondary-school teachers at the end of the 1970s. And, truth to tell, it was certainly only a minority. Persuasive though the arguments of Maurice Holt and others might be, they did not, it seems, prove sufficiently attractive for teachers responsible for upper-school programmes in comprehensive schools under increasing pressure from both politicians and the media to prove themselves as institutions with high academic standards. The need to achieve good results in the GCE and CSE examinations (replaced in 1986 by the new GCSE or General Certificate of Secondary Education) meant that even those schools which experimented with non-streamed groupings for academic subjects in the first 3 years were tempted to move over to various combinations of banding and setting for students following examination courses. And the emphasis by the 1979–90 Thatcher Government on the desirability of greater involvement by governors in the running of schools was also meant to act as a curb on progressive experimentation by teachers in grouping and allied policies.

The findings of our own survey reveal that by the fourth year (Year 10), the vast majority of comprehensive schools have abandoned mixed-ability teaching for all subjects. Table 7.3 shows that of the 1212 schools which responded to the relevant sections of question 99, 640 (52.8%) use ability sets for most or all academic courses in Year 10 and 11. And this percentage is remarkably consistent across the three main types of comprehensive schools catering for students at Key Stage 4: 54.2% of 11/12–18 schools, 51.5% of 11/12–16 schools and 52.9% of schools covering the 13–16/18 age range. Overall, only just over 3% of schools (38 in number) continue to operate mixed-ability classes for all pupils and in all subjects; while a further 35% (423) use mixed-ability groupings with up to four subjects setted. The number of schools now using various forms of streaming, setting and banding is 751 (62% of the total).

Table 7.4 shows the situation separately for Scotland where nearly 54% of schools use various forms of streaming, setting and banding.

Table 7.3 Years 10 and 11 upper-school groupings by type of comprehensive school in Britain 1993–94 (Results are given in numbers of schools, with percentages in parentheses; n = 1212.)

Method of grouping	11/12 to 18	11/12 to 16	13 – 16/18	14 – 18	Total number of schools	Percentage
1 Mixed ability for all subjects	15 (2.5)	22 (4.1)	1 (1.5)	–	38	3.1
2 Mixed ability, with no more than TWO subjects setted	55 (9.2)	41 (26.9)	6 (8.8)	3 (37.5)	105	8.7
3 Mixed ability, with no more than FOUR subjects setted	152 (25.3)	144 (26.9)	20 (29.4)	2 (25.0)	318	26.2
4 Ability sets for most or all academic courses	325 (54.2)	276 (51.5)	36 (52.9)	3 (37.5)	640	52.8
5 TWO or THREE ability bands with parallel classes	33 (5.5)	33 (6.2)	4 (5.9)	0 (0)	70	5.8
6 Streaming for all academic subjects but NOT for sport or drama	19 (3.2)	17 (3.2)	1 (1.5)	–	37	3.1
7 Streaming for all classes and courses	1 (0.2)	3 (0.6)	0 (0)		4	0.3
Total number of schools	600	536	68	8	1212	100.0

Table 7.4 Pupil Grouping by type of comprehensive school in Scotland S3 and S4 (Years 10 and 11) (Results are given in numbers of schools, with percentages in parentheses.)

Method of grouping	12–18	12–16	Total number of schools	Percentage
1 Mixed ability for all subjects	4 (4.5)	1 (50)	5	5.5%
2 Mixed ability with no more than TWO subjects setted	15 (16.9)	0	15	16.5%
3 Mixed ability with no more than FOUR subjects setted	21 (23.6)	1 (50)	22	24.2%
4 Ability sets for MOST or ALL academic courses	42 (47.2)	0	42	46.1%
5 TWO or THREE ability bands with parallel classes	6 (6.7)	0	6	6.6%
6 Streaming for all academic subjects	1 (1.1)	0	1	1.1%
7 Streaming for all classes and courses	0	0	0	
Totals	89	2	91	

Developments since 1988

It has been argued (see Chitty, 1992) that the curriculum proposals which constituted such an important part of the 1988 Education Reform Act represented a defeat for the thinking of two major groups: Her Majesty's Inspectorate and a faction within the Conservative Party of the 1980s that is often referred to as either the 'Industrial Trainers' or the 'Conservative Modernisers'[8].

HMI were concerned that the new National Curriculum had little in common with the common 'entitlement' curriculum for which they had been arguing since at least 1977. The original DES model of a limited 'core' of subjects at Key Stage 4 had, it is true, been modified over time to arrive at the new structure of 10 foundation subjects; but there was little or no evidence of a rational framework or coherent underpinning philosophy. As Peter Watkins, until 1991 Deputy Chief Executive of the National Curriculum Council, was to comment (in a lecture delivered at the University of Birmingham in November 1991):

> There is... one fundamental problem from which all others stem. The National Curriculum had no architect, only builders. Many people were surprised at the lack of sophistication in the original model: ten subjects, attainment targets and programmes of study defined in a few words in the 1987 Bill, that was all.
>
> (Watkins, 1993:73)

The repudiation of the thinking of the Conservative Modernisers was of a different order but no less significant. This group of prominent Conservatives and industrialists had become particularly influential while the late Keith Joseph was at the DES from 1981 to 1986. Led by David (now Lord) Young, their chief power-base was the Manpower Services Commission of which Young was chairperson between 1982 and 1984. Rejecting much that was taught in schools as both book-bound and irrelevant, their main aim was to see the secondary school curriculum – and particularly Years 4 and 5 – re-structured to prepare pupils for the 'world of work'. Their main achievement in the area of curriculum initiatives was probably the introduction of the Technical and Vocational Education Initiative (TVEI) in a number of carefully chosen schools and local authorities in the autumn of 1983. Unlike those Conservatives who made up the Thatcherite New Right, they had no time for the grammar-school tradition in this country and considered it to be largely responsible for Britain's long industrial decline. At the same time, there was nothing remotely egalitarian in their thinking: in their view, the secondary-school curriculum should be sharply differentiated to prepare pupils for the differing tasks they would perform in the modern capitalist economy. Their view of educational 'opportunity' was neatly summarised by Lord Young in an article in *The Times* in September 1985:

> My idea is that... there is a world in which 15% of our young go into higher education... roughly the same proportion as now. Another 30 to 35% will stay on after the age of 16 doing the TVEI, along with other courses, and ending up with a mixture of vocational and academic qualifications and skills. The remainder, about half, will simply move on to a 2-year Youth Training Scheme.
>
> (*The Times*, 4 September 1985)

The decline in the modernisers' influence in the late 1980s was due to a number of related factors. Employment prospects appeared to be improving and, paradoxically, there was therefore *less* need to be concerned about vocational education for older pupils in schools. It was difficult for the Manpower Services Commission to retain its enormous authority and influence once David Young was no longer its chairperson; and it lost a powerful ally when Keith Joseph was replaced by Kenneth Baker as Conservative Education Secretary in May 1986. From that date, the DES came increasingly under the influence of the Downing Street Policy Unit, headed until 1990 by Professor Brian Griffiths. The proponents of the so-called 'New Vocationalism' were losing ground to those members of the Radical Right who had always resented the MSC's interference in the education service and saw no virtue anyway in a vocationalised curriculum. The object now was to erect a hierarchical system of schooling subject both to market forces and to government by strict curriculum guidelines. As Jamieson and Watts pointed out in a *TES* article published at the end of 1987, the structure and content of the National Curriculum clearly represented something of a 'defeat' for the 'enterprise' lobby. Yet they concluded their paper by arguing that the battle was not necessarily lost if the lobby was 'prepared to fight its corner and to follow through the implications of its rhetoric' (*The Times Educational Supplement*, 18 December 1987).

In fact, the National Curriculum was still very much in its infancy when it became obvious, even to the Government, that Key Stage 4 could not survive in the form envisaged by Kenneth Baker and the civil servants of the DES. The last 2 years of compulsory schooling soon became the most problematic area of the Government's hastily-conceived curriculum plans. Many teachers complained that it was simply not possible to fit all 10 foundation subjects (and religious education), together with a number of cross-curricular themes, into a finite amount of curriculum time. Some talked of the risk of incurring pupil resentment and indiscipline. And as general economic prospects worsened, the argument re-surfaced that many of our problems would be solved if the secondary-school curriculum had a greater vocational content. In other words, the battle for the high policy ground was about to be fought all over again in the changed conditions of the early 1990s.

Speaking at the conference of the Society of Education Officers in London in January 1990, the then Education Secretary, John MacGregor (who had replaced Kenneth Baker the previous July), announced that he was reviewing the requirement that all schools should teach 14–16-year-olds all National Curriculum subjects 'for a reasonable time'. In looking at a 'wider range of options' for these older students, he revealed that he had asked vocational examination bodies such as the Business and Technician Education Council and the Royal Society of Arts to submit 'new qualifications for approval' (reported in *The Times Educational Supplement*, 2 February 1990).

At the end of July 1990, in a speech to the Professional Association of Teachers (PAT) Conference meeting in Nottingham, the Education Secretary signalled a further retreat on the Key Stage 4 arrangements by suggesting that some pupils could be allowed to 'drop' some subjects from the age of 14. The subjects most likely to become optional were art, music and physical education; but the position of history and geography could not be guaranteed. Mr MacGregor sought to assure his audience that the National Curriculum would remain intact up to the age of 14, but, after that, we could reach a point where pupils were obliged to take only five of the foundation subjects: the three core subjects of English, maths and science, together with technology and a modern foreign language. The Education Secretary admitted that Key Stage 4 was posing special problems for the Government:

> Essentially, the question is one of fit – how to achieve a broad balanced curriculum for all pupils without sacrificing worthwhile options.... There is a genuine dilemma here.
>
> (*The Guardian*, 1 August 1990)

Then in an interview with the education correspondent of the *Daily Telegraph* at the end of October 1990, Education Minister Tim Eggar announced that the Government had decided to encourage all secondary schools to develop a vocational alternative to the academic curriculum at Key Stage 4. In his view:

> Far too many children from 14 upwards are studying things which they and their teachers do not regard as appropriate.... We have to offer these youngsters the sort of vocational courses and qualifications that will make sense to them and encourage them to stay on in full-time education after the age of 16.

Schools, said Mr Eggar, would be encouraged to develop parallel 'academic' and 'vocational' streams, with the main objective being to enhance the general status of vocational qualifications:

> That is the main issue facing us in education. That is the area where we are so much weaker than Germany – not in turning out graduates, but in producing skilled workers and supervisors.... To achieve that, we must now have two parallel streams – the vocational and the academic – from half-way through secondary school, so that children can concentrate on what interests them.
>
> (*Daily Telegraph*, 30 October 1990)

Finally, Education Secretary Kenneth Clarke effectively abandoned Key Stage 4 of the National Curriculum in his speech to the North of England Education Conference meeting in Leeds in January 1991. Ignoring the advice of the National Curriculum Council that all 10 subjects of the National Curriculum should remain compulsory for all students to the age of 16, Clarke announced that only English, maths and science would remain 'sacrosanct' in the last 2 years of schooling. All students would still have to study technology and a modern language in addition to the 'core', but not necessarily to GCSE level. Of the remaining foundation subjects, students would study *either* history or geography, but art, music and physical education would become optional. In the words of the Education Secretary:

> I believe we should not impose on young people a rigid curriculum that leaves little scope for choice. By the age of 14, young people are beginning to look at what lies beyond compulsory schooling, whether in work or further study. We must harness that sense of anticipation if every pupil is to have the chance of developing to the full.
>
> (*Guardian*, 5 January 1991)

The Government's revised plans for 14–16-year-olds appeared to fit in neatly with new proposals for education and training at the post-16 stage. The White Paper *Education and Training for the 21st Century*, published in May 1991, set out the intention to establish a coherent framework of national vocational qualifications in schools and colleges to run alongside a strengthened 'A' and 'AS' level academic system. And it made it clear that vocational awarding bodies would be encouraged to develop a new range of examination courses for subjects both inside and outside the National Curriculum – or for combinations of them (DES, 1991:3, 19, 40).

As Peter Watkins pointed out in his 1991 Birmingham lecture, the Government's original proposals for Key Stage 4 certainly ensured that the upper-school curriculum would be more demanding and more rigorous and require the study of more subjects than hitherto; but that was in line with the practice of other countries and it would keep open a variety of 'routes into education post-16'. Now, according to Mr Watkins, the National Curriculum was, to all intents and purposes, 'dead beyond the end of Key Stage 3'. The vision had become a nightmare – but perhaps it was always simply 'too idealistic to be realisable'. Mr Watkins accepted that the Government was concerned to see a vocational element included for at least some pupils, though still harnessed to the National Curriculum; but he argued that the proposal was hedged around with ambiguity:

> There is doubt about whether the sort of qualifications hitherto provided by the vocational examining bodies are appropriate for schools, and whether they have the resources to offer them widely in any case. There is a danger that all this could mark a return to an academic route for the able and a vocational route for the less able.
>
> (Watkins, 1993:79)

It is fair to say that many regard the abandonment of Key Stage 4 as a retrograde step – even allowing for the inadequate nature of the original design. It is also true that the teaching profession is itself divided as to the desirability or otherwise of implementing a common curriculum through all the years of secondary schooling. This will have to be an important area of debate, involving issues of choice and diversity, as we approach the final years of the century.

It is certainly clear from the results of our own survey that in the years before what would have been the full (or modified) implementation of Key Stage 4, very few schools operated a genuinely common curriculum for all students beyond the age of 14. Table 7.5 shows that of the 1218 schools which responded to the relevant section of question 98, only 105, or (8.6%) provided a completely common curriculum for all students. Just over 90% provided some choice in academic subjects and nearly 50% in vocational subjects. Two-thirds of the responding schools were able to offer choice in languages.

Table 7.5 Curriculum arrangements at Key Stage 4, 1993–94

	Number of schools	(%)
A Completely common curriculum to all	105	(8.6)
B Some choice in academic subjects	1097	(90.1)
C Some choice in vocational subjects	604	(49.6)
D Some choice in arts or music	864	(70.9)
E Some choice in sports	505	(41.5)
F Some choice in languages	832	(68.3)
Total of responding schools	1218	

Looking at the same issue from a different perspective, the responses to question 106 (Table 7.6) show that in the period before the Dearing Review, to be discussed in the next section, many schools operated a comparatively limited core of compulsory subjects at Key Stage 4. Only English, maths and science figured as compulsory subjects in all schools for all pupils[9]. Of the remaining foundation subjects in the Government's original curriculum framework, only physical education (94.6% of schools), religious education (85.8%), technology (82.4%) and a modern foreign language (67.1%) stood a chance of being included in the common or core curriculum as separately timetabled subjects. Both history and geography as such appeared in the core of just over 15% of schools; art in 8.6% and music in just 6.8%.

Table 7.6 Subjects included in the 'common' or 'core' curriculum at Key Stage 4* before the period of the Dearing Review (n = 1199)

	Number of schools	(%)
A English	1199	(100)
B Mathematics	1199	(100)
C Sciences	1197	(99.8)
D A modern foreign language	805	(67.1)
E Technology	988	(82.4)
F History	182	(15.2)
G Geography	182	(15.2)
H Art	103	(8.6)
I Music	81	(6.8)
J Physical Education	1134	(94.6)
K Religious Education	1029	(85.8)

* This would refer to their inclusion as *separately timetabled* subjects.

With regard to language provision, 1169 (98.2% of the 1190 schools responding) provided French for some or all students; 990 (83.2%) German; 368 (31%) Spanish; 58 (4.9%) Italian; 33 (2.8%) Russian; 121

(10.2%) Latin; and 59 (4.9%) Welsh. Once again, the vast majority of schools offering Latin and/or Russian were those drawing their pupils from either a mix of council and private housing (category C in question 27) or mainly private residential or owner-occupied housing (category B).

With regard to cross-curricular themes at Key Stage 4, Table 7.7 shows the number and percentage of schools offering the themes as separate timetabled subjects or courses.

Table 7.7 Number (%) of schools offering cross-curricular themes as separate timetabled subjects or courses at Key Stage 4 (n = 628)

1 Economic and industrial understanding	186	(29.6)
2 Careers education and guidance	599	(95.3)
3 Health education	401	(63.8)
4 Education for citizenship	224	(35.6)
5 Environmental education	140	(22.3)

Once again, as with Key Stage 3, the most popular themes to be offered as separate timetabled subjects are careers education and guidance and health education, the former now occupying a prominent place in the curriculum. A total of 105 schools (16.7% of those responding) include all five themes in the curriculum.

The Dearing Review and its implications

In the event, Key Stage 4 never, of course, took the form envisaged by Kenneth Baker and his DES advisers. Realising by the Spring of 1993 that the framework for the National Curriculum and related testing arrangements could not survive in their existing form, the Major Government asked Sir Ron Dearing, chairperson-designate of the new School Curriculum and Assessment Authority (SCAA), to carry out a full-scale review of the National Curriculum and its assessment. One of the key issues outlined by Education Secretary John Patten in his remit letter of 7 April 1993 concerned 'the scope for slimming down the curriculum'. And in his Interim Report, published in August 1993, Sir Ron Dearing identified the structure of Key Stage 4 as a major issue for consultation in the second stage of the review. In the words of the report:

> ...should there be a modified approach to the curriculum from 14 to 16 to provide a smoother transition to study post-16 and to respond sensitively to the developing needs of all our young people?
>
> (NCC/SEAC, 1993:7)

By the time the final Dearing Report was published, in January 1994, there had already been a considerable slimming down of the proposals for Key Stage 4 contained within the original 1987 consultation document and many subjects had yet to make an appearance (Table 7.8).The Report itself proposed that the process of reduction and simplification should be accelerated, and media reports emphasised that the National Curriculum for Years 10 and 11 would now occupy students for only about 60% of the normal school week (Table 7.9). This, however, assumes that the majority of students will choose no more than the minimum statutory requirement. As Table 7.9 shows, the National Curriculum could, in fact, take up between 70 and 80% of the timetable if students follow a double course in science and full courses in technology and a modern foreign language.

Table 7.8 The National Curriculum at Key Stage 4: the situation in December 1993*

	Percentage of curriculum time
English	12.5
Mathematics	12.5
Science	12.5
(most students follow the recommended double course)	(20)
Technology (single subject or as part of a combined-subject course)	5 or 10
Modern foreign language (single subject or as part of a combined-subject course)	5 or 10
History and/or geography (single subject or as part of a combined-subject course)	10
Physical Education	5
Religious Education	5
Totals:	67.5 or 85.0

*This table of statutory requirements is taken from the final Report of the Dearing Review, (SCAA, 1994:41).

The final Dearing Report talked in terms of the abandonment of Key Stage 4 in its original form 'allowing greater scope for academic and vocational options'. It identified three broad pathways in post-16 education and training – the 'craft' or 'occupational' linked to NVQs; the 'vocational' linked to GNVQs; and the 'academic' leading to 'A' and 'AS' levels – and argued that development of these pathways had implications for students aged 14–16. In the words of the Report: 'it will be a particular challenge to establish how a vocational pathway which maintains a broad educational component might be developed at Key Stage 4 over the next few years as part of a 14–19 continuum' (SCAA, 1994:47). The Report then went on to recommend that the School Curriculum and Assessment Authority should be asked to work 'closely and urgently' with the National Council for Vocational Qualifications to identify whether various possibilities concerning GNVQs could be developed (SCAA, 1994:49).

Table 7.9 Two versions of the Dearing proposals at Key Stage 4

	1. Minimum requirement proposed percentages	2. Extended requirement proposed percentages
English	12.5	12.5
Mathematics	12.5	12.5
Science	12.5	20.0
Technology	5.0	10.0
Modern foreign language	5.0	10.0
Physical education	5.0	5.0
Religious education	5.0	5.0
Sex education and careers	2.5	5.0
Totals:	60.0	80.0

Column 1 would leave 40.0% of the timetable for other options; column 2 only 20.0%.

Addressing the Secondary Heads Association's annual conference meeting in Bournemouth in March 1994, Sir Ron Dearing announced that 14-year-old students would soon be able to study for qualifications in *five* vocational areas: manufacturing; art and design; health and social care; leisure and tourism; and business and finance (report in *The Financial Times*, 21 March 1994). And in December 1994, schools minister Eric Forth announced the names of the 118 schools which would be piloting three of the new 2-year GNVQ courses to be offered as alternatives to GCSE courses from September 1995. The GNVQ Part One would be offered at two levels: *foundation*, the equivalent to GCSEs below grade C; and *intermediate*, the equivalent to four GCSEs at grade C and above. Schools would receive £10,000 grants to pilot business or health and social care courses and £12,000 for manufacturing. Schools offering two subject areas would get £15,000 (or £17,000 if this included manufacturing), and £20,000 for offering all three subject areas (*Guardian*, 22 December 1994).

The Dearing Report received warm approval from teachers' leaders, politicians and media commentators when it first appeared in January 1994. More recently, however, concern has been expressed about the evolving shape of the upper-school curriculum, and the Dearing Review must bear much of the blame for the present confusion. It remains to be seen whether all 14-year-old students will be able to take a useful mixture of academic, practical and vocational subjects; or whether – and this seems more likely – the end-result of the new initiatives will be the virtual segregation of students at 14. Writing in *The Times Educational Supplement* in February 1995, John Dunford, vice-president of the SHA, argued that 'with no consensus to reflect and no philosophical foundation, the Dearing proposals are a fudge' and 'do little for the development of a coherent 14 to 19 curriculum'. He advocated delay of at least a year in implementing the recommendations in the Final Report. An RSA report published in the same month called for an end to the 'debilitating divide' between academic and vocational education (White, Pring and Brockington, 1995). And an article in *The Independent* in March 1995 by Sir Geoffrey Holland, formerly Permanent Secretary at the Department for Education, argued that we need to defeat 'the divide between the academic and the vocational which has so weakened our country' (Holland, 1995).

Of the 1186 schools responding to question 107 in our survey, 450 (38%) reported that they had already introduced vocational courses for some or all students in Years 10 and 11. In 77 schools (17.1% of the total), these were taken by all students in these years; 220 schools (48.9%) offered a vocational area as a single option open to all; and in 141 schools (31.3%) vocational subjects were used as a substantial option for students wanting an alternative to a full academic course. When asked for their views on the future development of vocational courses, a majority of schools (52.7% in Britain as a whole; 85.5% in Scotland) favoured the concept of an integrated upper-school curriculum with vocational and academic elements for all students. Of the remainder, 13.3% would opt for a self-contained vocational course alongside the academic one; and 34% favoured the idea of a vocational option within the National Curriculum. Nearly two-thirds of schools (64%) said that they planned to increase the vocational content of their curriculum in future years.

Examination performance

From the responses to question 112 in our questionnaire, we learn that in 11/12–18 schools, an average of 41.9% of students in Year 11 passed five or more GCSE examinations at Grades A to C/Standard Grade 1 to 3 in the academic year 1992–93. For 11/12–16 schools, the figure was 36.6%; for 13–16/18 schools, 38.3%; and for 14–18 schools, 36.7%. For Scotland alone, the figures were significantly higher: for 12–18 schools, 51.7%; for 12–16 schools, 70%.

In this same sample of schools, while there were clearly only small variations in achievement according to type of school in Britain as a whole, there were marked and significant variations according to type of catchment area (Table 7.10). And girls' schools achieved a higher percentage than either mixed or boys' schools: the figures were 39.3% for mixed schools; 33.8% for boys' schools, and 40.7% for girls' schools.

Table 7.10 Average percentage of students gaining five or more GCSE passes at Grades A–C or equivalent, according to type of catchment area[10]

School drawing most of their students from:	Percentage
A mainly council or housing association housing	23.2
B mainly private residential/owner occupied housing	52.1
C a mix of council and private housing	42.4
D mainly substandard accommodation	18.2
E a mix of council, private and substandard	31.6

Regardless of any other factors, a very high proportion of Year 11 students (94%) obtained at least one GCSE pass, and furthermore 81% obtained at least four GCSE passes (which is clearly a justification for the underlying philosophy of the new common examination system introduced in 1986). It is regrettable that among a number of groups in society only passes at grades A to C (the old 'O' level equivalent) are of real value.

Of the 1165 schools responding to question 113, only 141 (12%) said they regarded their schools' GCSE pass rate as a fair or adequate indicator to the public of their schools' academic worth. With regard to coursework, around half the schools (48%) said they retained coursework as a major element in most of their GCSE courses.

We have no evidence that GCSE results are significantly affected by the type of grouping chosen by a school or subject department; but from interviews conducted with heads and subject teachers, it seems clear that the use of mixed-ability or flexible groupings does have a favourable impact on the general ethos of the school. Mixed-ability teaching can therefore be advocated for its positive social effects in the knowledge that it makes no appreciable difference to a school's examination performance.

Notes:

1   This would be a fourth year in Scotland, where pupils were recruited at 12.
2   The situation was that if pupils were 15 by 2 February in the relevant year, they could leave school at the end of the spring term; if they were 15 *after* 2 February, they had to stay until the end of the summer term and complete 4 full years of secondary schooling.
3   There was early evidence that two-tier schemes tended to discriminate against

the children of working-class parents who were less likely than were their middle-class counterparts, to make the transition from the high school to the upper school. In the case of Leicestershire, for example, the 1964 staying-on (transfer) rate was 85% in middle-class Oadby and only 39% in the old industrial town of Hinckley (see Eggleston, 1965:17). In 1966, the Leicestershire Education Committee reached the important decision that when the school-leaving age was raised to 16, all pupils would automatically transfer from the high school to the upper school at the age of 14 (Elliot, 1970).

4 For all comprehensive schools in the 1968 survey (including Scotland's), it was 51%; for all those schools with sixth forms, it was 58%.

5 A fourth category enabled schools to describe either a totally different system or a combination of the three provided (Benn and Simon, 1970:398).

6 The single-subject GCE Ordinary Level examination had been introduced in 1951: CSE examinations were still in their infancy, pupils being entered for them for the first time in 1965.

7 The average proportion of time allocated to 'core' subjects in the comprehensive schools included in the HMI survey was 42% (DES, 1979:22).

8 Roger Dale uses the term 'Industrial Trainers' in his paper 'Thatcherism and Education' which first appeared in *Contemporary Education Policy* edited by John Ahier and Michael Flude and published in 1983. The label actually comes from Raymond Williams's well-known tri-partite division of nineteenth-century educational ideologies into 'public educators', 'industrial trainers' and 'old humanists', put forward in *The Long Revolution* published in 1961. Ken Jones prefers to use the term 'Conservative Modernisers' in his 1989 book *Right Turn*.

9 Strictly speaking, the proportion of schools including science in the common or core curriculum was 99.8%, but this may be our error in feeding the material into the database.

10 It is, of course, true that this table conceals as much as it reveals. Many schools situated in areas of extreme deprivation achieve remarkable success with their pupils – and in all manner of ways (see Chapter 2; and Searle, 1996).

8

Administration and Democratic Accountability

Schools and colleges that provide for all attainments are more difficult to run than are selective schools that concentrate on a limited attainment range or colleges specialising in a limited range of learning. It is not the size and it is not the strain. But, as an early comprehensive headteacher said, 'The complexity of organisation in a comprehensive school hardly begins to resemble that in other secondary schools' (Benn and Simon, 1970:246).

Most early comprehensive schools were run with the structure and organisation familiar to the post-war grammar or secondary modern schools – with extra staff 'added on' to match the greater pupil numbers. There was little understanding that the multiple tasks required to deal with a variety of needs, aspirations and programmes, often compounded by size, necessitated a very different form of organisation – at once more democratic but also far more systematic. The management task in the last 30 years has been to develop both the system and the democracy, and over the years many comprehensive schools and colleges have achieved this. Some, however, have developed the system without the democracy; and occasionally, the democracy without the system. Much more of a problem, a significant number have continued to try to run the new schools in the old schools' image.

During the early years of comprehensive reorganisation, discussion of management and administration was not to the fore. Those writing about comprehensive education – like Robin Pedley (1963) – concentrated on educational issues concerning the system as a whole. Early reports by teaching organisations or local authorities (IAAM, 1967; ILEA, 1967) were limited largely to their own concerns. The accounts of charismatic heads running successful schools – like Raymond King of Wandsworth (1958) or Margaret Miles of Mayfield (1968) – were not necessarily instructive about management tasks, however inspirational on values and policy.

For the first few years it was almost as if everyone believed that administrative and management tasks would take care of themselves, once the educational direction was clear. However, the first independent Enquiry warned of a simplistic approach to management tasks and argued for a higher priority for them (Benn and Simon, 1970: Chapter 14); while the NFER in its Second Report on comprehensive schools warned about lack of delegation of responsibility and of problems falling through nets (Monks, 1970).

The DES occasionally produced material about staffing or administration but little to show how badly UK comprehensives were staffed compared with comparable schools in other countries, particularly in terms of ancillary support. Scotland seemed to grasp the problem, however, and in the early 1970s the SED published guidance for reorganising schools recognising that merely doubling what the old separate schools had was not sufficient. For senior posts, for example, it laid down – ideally – five times as many in schools of 1500 compared with the old 600 size academy (SED, *The Structure of Promoted Posts*, 1971:19).

An earlier study from Edinburgh Corporation had listed all administrative tasks being done by teaching staff which it reckoned should be done by clerical, bursarial or secretarial staff. Anyone reading this list in the 1990s was reminded of how it was when teachers were expected to direct the work of janitorial staff, receive all visitors to the school, organise school meals, supervise all clerical staff, organise supplies, do the filing, typing and duplicating, and take part in medical inspections. The SED report concluded that the extra work required in a comprehensive school was 'justification for the employment of an administrative assistant' in addition to the school secretary. Defining this post, it drew an important new line for all comprehensive institutions by 'distinguishing between executive decisions requiring guidance on educational policy and other decisions, referring former to Head, dealing with latter'. Not without coincidence, this was the post most of the schools responding to an additional question in the first independent Enquiry, said they would request if the LEA could find the money (Benn and Simon, 1970:246).

Democratic decision-making

During these earlier years the schools which were doing most to promote discussion of management were those concerned about promoting democracy in the new schooling. They assumed that good organisation was dependent on good democracy, which meant ensuring that despite larger size, full staff meetings continued to take place, where regular voting decided issues as they arose. It meant admonition to heads to allow the full staff meeting to be 'the ultimate decision-making body' (Semmens, 1972:19). It meant heads seeing that all staff shared in all aspects of the administration, not leaving these to those at the top (Bunnell, 1972). But new tasks were constantly appearing. In one school heads of pastoral care took to meeting in turn in each other's homes to thrash out policy and problems; and eventually it became obvious that those with special responsibilities had to have their own separate meetings (Howe, 1991).

There began a period of breaking down administration into separate functions. The pastoral side became organised separately from the academic side and each of these was often subdivided further into age groups, where individual staff were involved in two capacities, one as form or year or house tutor, another as subject teacher in a department. Democracy was maintained by making sure everyone was invited to attend everyone else's meetings, especially where decisions were taken. Enthusiasm was high; but so was workload. In time it became evident that this way of running schools was a case of too many meetings chasing too little free time.

Streamlining was required, especially with regard to the numbers of departments, as many early comprehensive schools had a separate department for almost every subject, including, sometimes, one for woodwork and another for metalwork; one for history and another for geography. The average number was about 14 per school by 1968 (Benn and Simon, 1970:237). Amalgamating these into faculties or larger departments over the years has meant the pendulum moving the other way. In many schools by the early 1990s four or five curricular teams or mega-departments housed everything taught.

Before this, in the 1970s, as departments integrated into larger departments, and these tended sometimes to work independently, the new task became learning all over again how to manage the whole school as one. A new group of headteachers began working on school management that integrated organisational, care and educational structures. Certain university education departments – at Cardiff in Wales and Bristol University – began specialising in running schools and training senior staff for the task, the latter teaming up with Harlech TV to produce an imaginative series, *Heading for Change*. The text was by William Taylor, an educationist who did not think management was boring (Taylor, 1973; Weeks, 1986:128). These courses convinced many heads to move away from the happy-go-lucky 'word in the corridor' that often sufficed in a unifunctional school. Comprehensive schools had to recognise that their management style from now on was going to be closer to that of departmentally based colleges. As one ILEA inspector later put it, consultation in a comprehensive school 'implies...papers, published agendas, Minutes...and dissemination of information' (Felsenstein, 1987:73).

Formality of system did not necessarily mean formality of spirit, but the system had to be there. Many schools and colleges looked increasingly towards corporate industry for models of practice. Some schools took to this naturally, one headteacher putting it bluntly at a DES conference on comprehensive education in 1977, 'If this smacks of the Army, the Civil Service or ICI, then so be it' (DES, 1978). Others, however, doubted the efficacy of corporate industry's model as applied to education because it threatened the more democratic 'management method that enhances the confidence, participation and contribution of every member of the learning community' (Barker, 1986:70), the learning community model being 'incompatible with a strategy that seeks to describe tasks and objectives in order to check that everyone is following instructions with due urgency'; management's job was to 'encourage teachers and children to take responsibility for their activities to ensure that authority and power are distributed evenly throughout the system' (Barker, 1986:70).

The new seriousness about organisation could mean even more democratic management forms could be developed, opening the way for greater involvement of parents and teachers and students in the work of schools and colleges. But the experience of a certain few schools most deeply concerned with democratic practice did not always augur well. Although the efforts of each were always collective, they were often known by their headteacher's and school's name only: Michael Duane of Risinghill, London; R.F. MacKenzie of Summerhill, Aberdeen; Stewart Wilson of Sutton Centre, Nottinghamshire. Among them were several heads of Countesthorpe College in Leicestershire, which developed a well-known 'moot' model of decision making, a discussion/conflict assembly with particular success at reaching consensus that lasted (Evans, 1983; Watts, 1977).

The influence of these innovating schools was wide from the mid-1960s to the mid-1980s, but over this period something akin to media mob rule, linking arms with a disgruntled minority in each school, sometimes only a single person, also drummed up such public angst about their various innovations that one by one each was changed or shut down. Looking back from the early 1990s over what triggered the public fuss in each case was instructive. With Risinghill it was its decision to end the use of corporal punishment, taken by the whole school (but without consulting the local authority, the ILEA). By the 1990s the practice had been made illegal. With Sutton Centre it was sex and relationships education, which by the 1990s the Government wanted in every school (albeit tightly prescribed). But these were only the anecdotal event seized on for 'the story'; the thread that was common in all these cases – studied later by a Nottingham University team (Fletcher, Caron and Williams, 1985) – was organised opposition to their attempts to extend democracy and involve the whole school and all its staff – as well sometimes as the local community – in the running of their own education.

Some of those who chose to innovate in democracy were thus 'ring fenced' and the effect was to scare off many schools from continuing with management and administrative reform along democratic lines. Comprehensive schools were often branded as ultra-experimental, when most went on running on traditional lines. The education inside was traditional too, though the media often claimed that comprehensive schools were operating 'progressive' education – when no more than a handful was ever progressive in the stricter educational meaning of this word. On the contrary, many comprehensive schools and their heads harboured the utmost suspicion of both progressive education and much democratic management, choosing instead the good old-fashioned 'tight ship' with a captain very firmly in charge. Some were successful (Boyson, 1974; Dawson, 1981); others were not successful. Either way they were often represented as struggling against the tide, when, in fact, they were the tide.

After 1976, when the Labour (Callaghan) Government changed tack on comprehensive education and lost interest in an effective comprehensive system, the Centre for the Study of Comprehensive Schools, formed in 1980, renewed interest in management issues. The Centre had links with several multinational companies that helped finance it, many with go-ahead education sections anxious to help comprehensive schools. CSCS brought them together with individual schools already determined to move on and working quietly to promote good management practice within as democratic a framework as possible. But despite CSCS's work, disseminated through its journals and conferences, reports of comprehensive schools stuck in the grip of the old uni-functional grammar school continued to come in (Reynolds et al., 1987).

They were not just schools which 'stream' teachers as well as pupils and were thus 'unlikely to produce any sort of adequate response to the demands of comprehensivisation' (Ball, 1984a:23); they were schools still run autocratically with no collective decision-making, poor communications, goal confusion, only formal contact with parents, a grammar ethos with over-concentration on an academic few and under-concentration on the educational development of the larger middle ranges, as well as minimum concern all round for personal and social development.

To those still committed to change it was a case of teachers having to become much more involved in running of the schools (Reynolds *et al.*, 1987), while others, even those who had pioneered good management, began to doubt whether management education was really working all that well after all. By the 1980s education was overtaken by new problems like falling pupil numbers and economic difficulties which forced everyone to recognise how closely education was linked to a precarious world economic system that no one seemed able to predict or control. Money was less available for schools and colleges; work was increasingly unavailable for school leavers, even after they had gained qualifications. Nationally, a government was slowly centralising curriculum and assessment control at the centre, leaving 'the market' in charge.

Effective schools

Simultaneously, another movement was taking place that was destined to link old and new concerns. It was based on the studies in the late 1970s and early 1980s around the notion of the effective school (Rutter *et al.*, 1979). Its importance was that it matched organisational and management matters to criteria that were educationally based, not viewed in terms of numbers and cost. Ultimately, school effectiveness depended on clear leadership, the full involvement of staff, a structured day, a work-centred environment, consistency of staff practice, communication between teacher and taught, parental involvement and high expectation of pupils. Its various studies also showed the way 'boring' details were often crucial, and how each part of the jigsaw could reinforce, or frustrate, a good outcome. For example, 'haphazard' record keeping in one school was the difference between some understanding of a pupil's progress and none at all (Ball, 1981:312, notes 39 and 41). Material change alone was insufficient, for while reasonable physical plant was helpful, and so was free time to organise the paper-work, this was only because these extras made it more likely that staff could work together to achieve consistency in practice. Consensus was more important than additional facilities (Rutter et al., 1979:193–94) – all convenient conclusions in a period when funding was getting ever tighter.

Effective school research proliferated and continued right up through the early 1990s, not directly related to comprehensive education but usually conducted within comprehensive settings. However, it became increasingly complex, concerned to demonstrate why schools differed, how sub-groups within schools differed, and differed at different stages of education, and how social, behavioural and parental-support factors all interacted (Reynolds and Reid, 1985). The more researchers looked, the harder it was to get any unequivocal guide for practitioners in every situation. One practitioner, Anne Jones, then head of Cranford Community School, confirmed the helpfulness of such studies but believed their global view of school had something missing (Jones, 1987).

One perspective that was very obviously missing from most of these studies was any consideration of the overall education system in which schools were embedded and how this might condition effectiveness (much less how wider social conditions might do so). How could a comprehensive school thrive in an area where selection had never actually been ended? Nor was effectiveness judged in relation to national policy, particularly the democratic nature of the system. For just when the unique problems of running a comprehensive education system that involved almost all schools and colleges, was at last possible, schools and colleges were put out to the market and told to manage on their own. Just as structures were being forged to develop comprehensive education in the wake of selection, the necessary support of local government in the planning associated with this task of development was being compromised by reduction in its funding and removal of its freedom to operate. Just at that moment when selection could have been ended education acts were being passed that were encouraging it to return; while others were making sure that local and regional democracy deferred to decisions being taken at the centre of government.

Not that this was immediately understood. Some of the changes seemed to enhance democracy – like letting schools vote to opt out, or handing management to schools through LMS. Opting out's defects in relation to democracy were soon recognised but LEA comprehensive schools, initially glad to have more control over their own management, took longer to realise that LMS had its downside, removing much of the support previously supplied by local authorities, and inside schools taking away many senior staff to master new administrative tasks, particularly in relation to budgets. This was all at a time when cuts in public expenditure were being passed along the line through the LMS mechanism. Schools also realised that selection was creeping back (partly through the 'votes' of the opted out) and they were powerless to deal with it. Teachers were experiencing some loss of professional standing as assessment and curriculum tasks were taken over by politicians and their appointees, while their own national rights to bargain over pay and conditions were being drastically eroded. Democracy was almost a forgotten word.

The new managerialism

In the late 1980s and early 1990s, reeling from an avalanche of legislation, schools were giving priority to translating or re-translating directives from successive Secretaries of State – related to hotly contested curriculum and testing regimes. In both schools and colleges the new vocational education was being radically assayed, increasing workloads. Taking time out to get ahead on administrative tasks that unburdened staff, much less to relate them to institutional effectiveness, seemed itself like just another burden. The effective schools movement was almost overpowered by the wave washing in from marketisation, accompanied by a whole new generation of gurus from the world of business and marketing, ready to mesmerise schools and colleges with their thinking. Newly 'independent' colleges and locally 'managing' schools were now encouraged to see themselves as businesses requiring managerial change rather than democratic overhaul, pushed forward by teachers who had taken 'flight into management training' in the early 1980s (Ball, 1984b:236) as well as by those who had always assumed education was going to be about the new technology, despite the fact that language labs had come in and out in under a decade and at any given moment all schools and colleges had unused terminals sitting on desks awaiting initiatives to train those who should be using them.

The new managerialism, as it was sometimes called, was characterised by concentration on measurable tasks within a business framework of audit and control, where principals and heads and governors and senior managers set performance targets and monitored relentlessly. Such activity gradually began to usurp the old educationally-based effectiveness and replace it with cost effectiveness and value for money. The positive virtue of the new managerialism was that it was simple to understand by lay people because it involved reducing the concept of effectiveness of schools, colleges and local authorities to a few measurable indicators, including simplistic 'league table' scores based on the attainment of top pupils.

Many comprehensive schools and colleges throughout the UK tried to stick to the democratic practices compatible with their original quest to be effective, but competitive pressure increasingly forced them to sideline the task, as success became more about marketing than managing, more about league table ratings and performance indicators sponsored by the new OFSTED than about equal education for all. Changes were taking place in a world where staff development was being mixed up with staff redundancies; and support for schools in difficulties mixed up with public punishment for 'failing'. More crucial still, comprehensive education's own original goals could be seen as impeding success because these required everyone in the school to do well. By contrast, the new managerialism's 'league table' indicators required only *certain* pupils to do well. Thus schools praised by OFSTED for improvement were often those that had given priority to the 'higher ability pupils in years 10 and 11' with the implication that the work of the rest was rather less important. Schools began taking the new line of least resistance, deliberately concentrating on 'top' pupils' performance because education had become a survival game. At the same time increasing numbers of comprehensive schools and colleges grew uneasy about the relative neglect this implied for such large numbers of pupils and students, a neglect that had profound implications in view of declared goals about giving every individual's education equal time, equal resources, and above all, equal value.

During the 1990s schools and colleges increasingly measured away in the sure belief that everyone and everything would improve just because performance was being recorded. But the new managerialism was not a panacea. Not merely because it meant neglecting some pupils for others but because many important aspects of education could not be reduced to 'measurable' criteria. Learning and teaching were not commercial activities. Human beings were not commodities. Once again, these drawbacks were appreciated much more readily in Scotland because Scotland during this period was active in retaining its own collective independence, and in renewing its own collective democratic control. It thus retained a more critical view of the Government's privatisation and centralisation changes, perceived as part of the forces coming from 'south of the Border'.

In the field of local government, for example, Scottish observers were among the first to realise that the indicators strategy was 'not always appropriate to public service situations' because what a 'customer' wanted became determined by government not by the community; and because so often users did not get a chance to take part in service design (Fairley and

Paterson, 1995). A Citizens' Charter society, so the critique went, had the limitations of any centrally controlled and planned society with its own managed 'success targets', where the indicators could be quite inappropriate, especially those associated with punishment when targets are not met, or where they could constrain staff in a school or college to work to one target when 'everyone knows that to expend effort in other ways would be more beneficial' (Fairley and Paterson, 1995:14). But most important, privatising management led to obsession with management rather than with education. In one typical study, for example, only 8% of materials relating to performance indicators for secondary school self-evaluation were devoted to teaching, learning and assessment in the classroom; 92% were about policy making, planning and management outside it (Brown, 1992:11).

From Scotland also came warnings about the danger of treating performance indicators as neutral when they were not. All criteria by which success is judged represent the ideology of the group that created them and has the power to see they are used (EIS, 1994). Other ideologies will have other indicators.To decide between ideologies was thus a fundamental right for education users, especially those involved in comprehensive education, but it required more democratic accountability and more debate in the education system than were possible by the 1990s, when democratic accountability was exactly what was being progressively withdrawn. True accountability needed what Fairley and Paterson called 'democratically reflexive systems' where both institutions and local governments run as 'collegial models' rather than as 'managed' hierarchies. At bottom most of the criticism of the new managerialism was thus about democracy.

Reviving democracy

As funding got tougher in the 1980s and 1990s, some schools and colleges experienced democratic participation being squeezed out of their own workings – an optional extra at best, subversion at worst. In some cases formality substituted for system; in others hierarchy was imposed. The loss of staff morale through progressive diminution of teacher independence, matched by increasing 'independence' for governing bodies, was increasingly serious in some schools and colleges, though mitigated in others by continuing work on democratic decision-making and student-centred learning. For there was some revival of the democratic teaching methods that had been part of the early years of comprehensive education, linked to enquiry methods in science and other work (Peters, 1970). In the late 1980s democratic student-centred practices began to grow in classrooms, although in some schools these practices could be completely at odds with the way schools and systems were run themselves. Schools need to be organised in ways that allowed the logic of learning styles to flourish (Brandes and Ginnis, 1990). If teaching styles and management styles are at variance, the worst of both worlds could be the outcome.

Dissatisfaction with the increasing centralisation of educational control and government dictation of every phase and sphere of schooling, has paradoxically revived democracy as a goal not only within classroom teaching but also within the education system at large. A new Centre for Democracy was established in the UK in 1994 – not the old democracy that appeared so threatening to a nervous *ancien régime* in the DES who spoke of comprehensive education having to be curbed until certain students 'know their place once more', but a wider one that allies the individualism of the age with enlightened management techniques. The objective is to initiate democratic self-management of people by people themselves as part of 'a growing international consensus on the need for democratic government' (Harber, 1995:1). It shows itself in student-centred learning, picking apart the lockstep mentality of mass examining, making use of the new technology for enhanced learning that is firmly in the control of the learner. It also means forcing schools and colleges beyond the authoritarian model of organisation, encouraging democracy by practising it within institutions themselves, involving all staff in the process of developing their students and pupils by developing themselves as well.

The Movement for Democracy in education is another import from the USA, and some of its advocates quote British-based business gurus like London Business School lecturer, Charles Handy, who has declared so many UK schools to be depressing factories, concerned with academic specialist end-products rather than with the development of competent and intelligent human beings (Handy, 1984). Educating by involving those being educated, so precious to the early comprehensive school, was now back on the agenda, spurred by that original impulse to link organisation with democracy.

But comprehensive education would be highly taxed to re-ignite democracy in a system where unquestioning attitudes to learning were being fostered through 'national' controls on curriculum and testing and course construction, measurement everywhere enforced, and the market, rather than the community, controlling development of the system. In addition, comprehensive schools would find it hard to make progress in those areas where selection was entrenched or returning.

When a British Gas school-help team laid on a management training weekend for a comprehensive school in 1994 it found the school to be over-managed, hierarchically structured, and in need of 'flatter' organisation. No doubt this was true of many comprehensive schools staying safe with older head-as-helmsperson styles. No doubt this school and its staff learned new ways of working from the British Gas team that will benefit them a great deal in-house. But no amount of good management – or new facilities – can make up for the deficiencies that came from the place of this school in the system, for this was a school in a town that still operated an 11-plus to decide who went to its two prestigious state grammar schools.

Effective comprehensive schools can make just so much headway in ineffective selective systems; just as democratic schools can make just so much headway in systems where the schools and colleges are inherently unequally placed in law or unequally funded on principle. Effective teaching can make just so much headway in a system where all staff are not valued professionally, as they cannot be by those who systematically curtail their responsibilities for developing learning (like shutting down course work); or where education proceeds from an ideology of inequality, disguised as triumphant individualism. If communities wish to balance this with the effectiveness of co-operative relationships, changes in the system have to be contemplated. Those at the leading edge of criticism have thus recognised a major weakness in modern managerialism's over-concern with 'the isolated activity of individuals' as against the collective activity of those who are protective of the community and the wider society through a democratic process embedded in locally accountable government (Fairley and Paterson, 1995:24–25). That process was still missing in 1994.

Democracy in colleges

Ironically, it was cuts that governments began making in education at the behest of corporate finance, that began unifying staff and parents and communities in the early 1990s, to protest in ways not seen for some time. It led to a coalition which pitted schools and their governors against LEAs and ultimately against government itself. In comprehensive general colleges, however, the same funding issue – and legislative changes – were having a different outcome: pitting staff against college management, for the fruits of 'independence' for colleges were soured from the first by the remote and unaccountable structures of oversight and control that were brought in with quango management and market forces.

An Employers' Forum, largely representing employers' concerns, replaced the older, more democratic structure of public accountability, which had fostered staff and student involvement in college management, and community responsiveness of institutions. For nearly three decades comprehensive colleges had been exploring their own way towards effective, democratic management. Their administration year was based on their regular departmental cycles of meetings, augmented since the 1970s by academic boards, faculty boards, and course committees; and additionally by quarterly meetings of management team and staff representatives, including the trade unions.

However, in the earlier days of reorganisation many of these Further Education (FE) colleges were not ready for the co-operation that was coming their way,operating more as a collection of departments than a single entity. Operating under different regulations, they could seem very different from schools, and these differences sometimes made early co-operation difficult between further education and the sixth forms of schools or sixth form colleges, even when they shared the same site (Griffin, 1974).

Tertiary colleges, when they began being formed, ironed out a lot of the difficulty by legal changes combining the sixth forms and FE work into one working organisation, for the early tertiaries were consciously concerned with bringing together the two traditions in the way they married the student-centredness of the school with the flexible community remit of further education. In time this drive to integrate the routes and provide a coherent education meant taking issue with college organisation, particularly trying to temper the stark vertical organisation of the traditional FE college, based on its discrete departments. This was done by pioneering new horizontal organisation cutting right across them: developing whole college departments for languages work, for the library, for counselling, and for information technology, and more cross-college responsibility for senior management (Trebilcock, 1985). This two-way grid was sometimes called the matrix pattern and was said to have come from the US aerospace industry where 'two axes of organisation' had promoted much more efficient working. In the tertiary college the matrix was designed to unify, provide more corporate connections, and bring a sense of a single institution out of a multiplicity of strong departments with their own budgets and heads. It didn't always work – because departments had a way of remaining the main units – but it made improvements, and many FE colleges adopted it as well.

Other tertiary colleges were pioneering in the 1970s and 1980s in other ways, some becoming 'workers' co-operatives' where all managers were teachers and all teachers managers. Others became expanding community institutions, constantly advancing to meet needs as they occurred in the area, extending frontiers in ways that were every bit as potentially controversial as the democratic innovation in schools which had occasioned such hostility from the conservative media. Still today such institutions continue stressing the need for tertiary education to break the bonds of 16–19 and extend their work to every age group – with profoundly revolutionary implications.

Comprehensive and democratic experiments in further education drew little of the fire heaped on schools, since further education was not an area of concern for watchdogs of the New Right – until, of course, Keith Joseph became aware of the changes that were taking place in the 16–19 sector and began turning down tertiary college schemes.

In any event, the popular drive to tertiary development was halted, followed by the detachment of colleges from local oversight through the legislation of the late 1980s and early 1990s, where, along with schools, colleges were commanded to abide by the market and compete as businesses – not just with each other but with schools as well. As Frank Reeves wrote:

> Further education (was) transformed in less than 5 years from a local service run for a range of interests as a tripartite partnership between the local authority, business and colleges staff, student and community representatives, to one run locally by a majority business interest as part of a national scheme to improve business productivity and occupational skills.
> (Reeves, 1995:41–42)

A rather bleak profile of general FE colleges at this point was sketched in the first report of the quango given charge of the new regime (FEFC, 1994a). It makes sober reading when set next to the community role and democratic development of local education envisaged in the writing of the earlier enthusiasts. It was an audit of 'could do better': tutorial support for part-time students needs to be as good as for those going full-time, as indeed it should; colleges must talk more to schools, as they must; counselling for students needs to improve; more work needs doing on why students drop out. More rigour in GCSE and 'A' level because FE colleges compare badly with selective schools; staff in further education are still spending too much time on paper-work; too many FE college libraries are weak and ill stocked; decor is depressing and too many buildings are drab and tatty (FEFC, 1994).

Absent was any awareness that many of these faults were the direct result of government policy in the previous decades or a selective post-16 system that had downgraded FE colleges for years in relation to more prestigious schools; or of recent legislation which required the very responses which were being complained about. As a report on individual colleges, it carried no understanding of the way so many of these institutions were integral parts of all-through comprehensive systems in their own areas (just as OFSTED inspection reports on 11–16 schools of the period ignored the 'next stage' in the education of pupils in these schools). It showed no interest in the 16–19 context as a whole in which colleges were operating (in the middle of so many sixth forms of schools),where institutions were divided by both old selectivity and by new 'competitive' funding arrangements providing both schools and colleges with positive disincentives to co-operate or share. There was no awareness of the market-driven dynamic that had changed the nature of so many colleges from outward-looking organisations responding to the community, to inward-looking operations dominated by short-term employer-interests.

Also unrecognised was the concerted overloading of staff with new tasks but no new rewards, or the tearing-up of old agreements and the attempted enforcement of new without consent; or the funding anarchy with the impossible juggling of TEC and FEFC and FAS funds, credits, grants, fees, European money and HEFC money, in an arena deprived of the support and assistance that a locally or regionally elected body could give in solving so many of the problems being met, not least the co-operation between these colleges and schools.

Nor was there much awareness here or elsewhere that a comprehensive system of post-16 education was already developing within so many communities in 1994 (see Chapter 9) – in the same way that an early secondary comprehensive school movement was networking its way into existence by the early 1960s. Changes were taking place in response to demand, as more and more students from an ever-wider swathe of the population looked to the colleges for their education, as more and more sixth forms and sixth-form colleges were finding ways to co-operate in providing for the age group.

The colleges were set to become the lynchpin of a new generation's tertiary education. Anyone could see this – except, it seems, governments. At the time of our 1994 survey no more inadequate paragraph existed in government publications in relation to 16–19 education than the single paragraph in the publication, *Unfinished Business: Full-time Educational*

Courses for 16–19 Year olds, which was headed *Planning of Overall Provision for 16–19* (OFSTED, 1993). Its five sentences told readers that overall planning was needed, that LEAs used to have responsibility for this, but that colleges now operate individually, helped by funding agencies. There was nothing about planning and nothing about 16–19. The document was largely dominated by a single concern: to cut the drop-out rate for 'A'-level courses.

Planning for the age range was not only rudimentary, it was contradictory. Thus in the Deering Review of 16–19 qualifications of 1995, mention was made of the importance of 'a coherent post-16 system...to provide competition or collaboration' to serve society's needs (Dearing, 1995: para. 7.16). But which? Competition is what the market system enforces; collaboration is what has to be chosen consciously in opposition to the market. So far institutions that wish to collaborate have to act on their own – without any circular, without any government support, without any real public consciousness of the importance of the developments taking place. We found instances where even the governors of the relevant institutions had no idea such connections were being forged by the institutions they governed.

Governing colleges

Meanwhile, within the comprehensive colleges there was a widespread perception of a diminution in their democracy. The way colleges' governing bodies work today is a far cry from the system the 1968 Education Act and Circular 7/79 devised to give each college its own instrument within a system that eventually encouraged staff to be involved, and students too; as well as one that encouraged a close connection between institution and the neighbourhood. The 1970s saw local colleges with 'community sub-committees' of governing bodies, half college and half community represent-atives, looking at ways the college could be involved in developing the local area. But in the 1990s this had changed. As Woolhouse wrote in 1993, the leadership of FE colleges had been given to 'local business people' while 'other key local people' had been brushed aside (Woolhouse, 1993). No one could take the chair other than a director of a company; by 1994 college governors were 82% male, 97% white, and almost all businessmen (Betts, 1994), a grouping the FEFC calls 'broadly representative of local community interests' (FEFC, 1994a:7).

Those concerned with the reduction of local democracy regard FE colleges as one of the institutions most adversely affected, enduring a three-fold fall through government legislation in the late 1980s and early 1990s: 'a cut in the...size of the governing body, an increase in the employment interest set up as a self-perpetuating oligarchy, and a reduction in the influence of the LEA, this last ... the government's ...stated intention' (Reeves, 1995:37).

Another problem was the rise of the all-powerful subcommittee, where more and more power is devolved to small executive groups 'empowered to take decisions without the necessary further endorsement from the full governing body' (Finch, 1994). Inevitably, this encouraged some bodies to go too far. One college governing body was disbanded and publicly criticised for harbouring a small group of senior governors, an inner circle or clique which effectively takes over decision making from the main body.

The college cited was greatly affected by this event, a situation that could have been solved, some staff members believed, had there still been oversight from some democratically elected local or regional authority: 'There would have been a lot more accountability; there would have been places for us to go to get action before it reached that stage' (Waugh, 1995:11). More such transgressions are inevitable in a system where those working within it do not 'have...places...to go to'.

Accountability requires governing bodies to be elected with reference to the communities they serve and to whom they can be accountable through locally or regionally elected bodies. An appointed quango, which can never be voted out of office, has no incentive to exercise democratic oversight. By the mid-1990s, for example, the quango for further education had not enforced the rule that all governors of FE colleges declare their business interests, as required in law. The National Audit Office had to point out that of 153 FE colleges, only one governing body had a register of such interests. In some colleges (mainly CTCs) governing body seats were even on offer to appointees of any businesses that donated a set sum towards capital funding (*Guardian*, 18 May, 1993), hardly a feather in the cap of modern democratic practice.

But it is not only independent colleges and FE colleges with potential problems relating to democratic accountability. The Auditor General had 'severe misgivings' about the way the grant maintained schools' promotion office 'runs its financial affairs' as well as about the way some grant maintained school governors had discharged their duties – e.g. giving contracts at their schools to companies they themselves owned or to those owned by their families. There is the same potential for the same kind of problem in LEA schools or in any public service where institutions are encouraged to behave like competing businesses and where the mechanism for overseeing their activity is remote and ineffective.

By contrast, staff salaries and conditions in the further education sector in 1994 were policed intensively by the Employers' Forum, called by some a 'Frankenstein creation' because it has overseen a growth in administrative staff relative to teaching staff. On governing bodies teaching staff representation was also at a low ebb. By 1994 on average each body had but one elected staff member (and 10% had no staff member at all) – a 'voice crying in the wilderness'; only about a quarter of all colleges had even taken up their rights to elect a second staff member (Finch, 1994).

As the gap between management and managed grew, so too the gap between college and community became a problem to some of those working in the colleges – colleges which one lecturer called 'unhealthy ...complete autocracies...of absolute power' (Betts, 1994). In the same year a public group, Article 26, the watchdog organisation for accountability in education, observed that the market-driven incorporation of FE colleges is transforming them into increasingly closed societies that are not democratically responsible either to the public or their staff. This does not mean they cease to try to serve their communities; only that they serve certain sections of it a great deal more vigorously (with much improved public relations) than they do others. How long it will be before those not being served come to claim their inheritance, waits to be seen.

Student democracy

During the last 30 years there has also been a decline in the democratic participation of students in educational institutions, including comprehensive schools. In the 1960s and early 1970s, when student democracy was being more widely developed, comprehensive schools were among the first to have students as governors. Many more comprehensive schools also set up councils, to give students a say inside the school. In a few pioneering schools, students were involved alongside staff in all the committee structures (Watts, 1977).

But pupil democracy as it showed itself in the 1960s and 1970s diminished in the same way democratic organisation did, in part due to government hostility to student organisation in any part of the education system. The incipient school students' union was stamped out; schools councils were discouraged by established authority (Richardson, 1975). The participation and political activity of pupils and students acting on their own, publishing on their own, organising on their own was met by constant disapproval from large sections of the conservative media. By the 1980s there was much demoralisation among young people with the opportunities offered in a society where unemployment or low-paid work awaited so many of them, even those who had struggled to get qualified. During the 1980s a greater passivity overtook the student population when it came to democratic involvement at school, colleges or in universities. When governing bodies were reconstituted in the wake of opting out and LMS in the late 1980s, student governors in schools were omitted. Schools that still wanted them could have them as observers, but it was not the same as student membership being recognised as a legal right.

Ironically many of those in the government that omitted students from the governing structure championed student democracy abroad (in Poland or Czechoslovakia), and were anxious to inaugurate citizenship education. But trying to educate pupils formally about democracy (by having it as a subject at school) has a history of only limited success, partly because LEAs appointing councillors to undertake campaigns of political awareness aroused Conservative hostility (Weeks, 1986:156–58), partly because educating about democracy as a 'class subject' has not been altogether successful more generally. More fruitful than 'teaching' democracy in some academic context, was participating democratically in self-directed activity. This is what many comprehensive schools have always tried to encourage: giving students real decisions to make; often in relation to a student's own educational and training life, in anticipation of their taking over the management of their own learning. This was difficult to promote in the 1980s.

By the 1990s, according to articles in the 1994 community issue of *All-in Success* (the magazine of the Centre for the Study of Comprehensive Schools), much of the democratic activity visible in comprehensive schools was thus having to receive a helping hand from outside. In one case, Community Service Volunteers came in to the school to set up a Schools Council for the pupils, with a view to encouraging them to be active in the school, moving discussion beyond the quality of meals and the state of the toilets. In other cases democracy work had to be routed through the market mechanism with school-based schemes that revolved around giving pupils their own money to manage, or a chance to undertake some entrepreneurial activity. In one comprehensive school, some spending decisions have been devolved to house committees, where students receive a budgeted sum to plan a community event (like organising tree planting or promoting reading schemes to help younger pupils). In one London school students were encouraged to set up a 'crime watch' scheme in their neighbourhood, working with the police and the local community. In a west country school, a prefect system was revived by election through peer voting, and students sent on a one-day management-training course to learn to be 'responsible and supportive' to fellow students (not just to act as 'guard dogs' for the head) (McTaggart, 1994).

Were these activities too 'managed' to be real? Possibly to start with, but in time students encouraged to think and act for themselves, will do just that. In Sweden, where students have participated more fully in the democratic running of their schools and colleges for longer than in Britain, recent studies found students wanted to extend the area of their influence beyond decisions regarding school journeys and community projects, to decision making relating to their *own* education, e.g. on issues like homework and testing and curriculum design (Ekholm, 1994). Davies, in a suggested checklist that might be used internationally to test democracy in schools, gave prominence to students' 'participation in deciding the indicators of assessment' for their own learning (Davies, 1995:109).

Such developments in the UK seem unlikely; but the future may well be quite different. Centralisation, privatisation and marketisation may threaten democracy in both comprehensive schools and colleges. But they have not routed it. Today's education management has been galvanised by the need for tighter control of spending but it has not necessarily led to autocratic rule, nor has commoditisation always overshadowed educational objectives. There is more sophistication in the running of schools and colleges in terms of understanding the way curriculum and assessment and social aims work together, but when much of the jargon is stripped away the basic requirement that staff share a common perspective, so stressed by the early pioneers of comprehensive education, remains the first goal in many schools and colleges. As does the commitment to see that the educational needs of all pupils and students get the equal attention they deserve. To achieve either of these important goals will always require full participation in the decision-making of schools and colleges for learners and teachers alike, in a framework accountable to local or regional government. By the late twentieth century such participation had been diminished by many forces, including market ones, but it could be that in having to battle back to life against these forces, democracy will emerge all the stronger in the twenty-first century.

Management styles

Getting that shared perspective in comprehensive school or college is harder today with so many years of neglect by government of the needs of comprehensive education. The subtle reintroduction of selection and the many conflicting demands on schools and colleges in the wake of agendas of privatisation and marketisation, mean that goals held in common by all who work in comprehensive education cannot any longer be assumed. They have to be consciously embodied; or even re-embodied.

Some find their way into school development plans, and even into the ubiquitous 'mission statement' required for most institutions. We asked schools and colleges whether they had long-term development plans (question 66) and 95% said they did. This included 100% of the colleges and even 92% of the middle schools. One school that did not, however, wrote in the margin, 'What is this?'. What indeed? Schools and colleges need the time to think beyond the given day or term. Whether all take the chance offered by the development plan to agree common aims is another matter. In some cases, drawing it up was a very narrow exercise; it did not involve the whole school, as might once have been the case, but came down from the governors and senior management team with a request for approval. In other schools and colleges we saw evidence it had been used to concentrate minds that have grown lax or demoralised by conflicting commitments, and that it could force them to rethink their wishes for their common educational enterprise, even at the risk of revealing hidden rifts.

Before asking for a detailed description of working practices, the 1994 survey gave four decision-making models (question 68) and asked schools and colleges which was closest to their own style. Very few chose the last two, which involved the most democratic methods. One was putting all matters to a binding vote of either full staff or departments (advocated by early comprehensive schools) (question 68C). This was used by only 3.3% of schools or colleges in 1994. A parliamentary model, where an elected body of staff took decisions, accountable to the groups who had elected them (question 68D) was used by only 16.6%. Instead, the first two methods were favoured. The first on the list (question 68A), used by 83.5%, was the traditional method of having 'senior staff consulting all involved' – after which, it can be assumed, senior staff took the decisions in those schools or colleges using this as their only method: 25% of all the survey. The second most favoured (question 68B), used by 69.7%, was to put all major matters out for full discussion to departmental or staff meetings before a decision is made; 43% of all schools and colleges used a combination of these two methods.

The general outcome was to confirm the widespread practice of making decisions from the top after sending the matter into the school to be kicked around – in nearly one out of four cases without much public debate. For only the last three possibilities are really democratic in that they involve voting or a process of consultation conducted openly within a forum of peers, not by unspecified 'consultation' from senior management. The survey showed that those institutions most likely to be among the group which made decisions solely on the basis of 'consultations' were the colleges and the grant maintained schools.

A choice of only four decision-making models was perhaps narrow; one study gave eight levels, starting with the head as lone decision-maker and going down to an informal structure involving everyone (Caldwell and Spinks, 1988). There were certainly representatives of the first in the survey. Thus from one headteacher in 1994, 'working party recommends – I decide'; while a more facetious deputy elsewhere replied, 'The head decides and then everyone knows he's wrong'. These were two replies to the open-ended question (question 70), where those replying (283) represented a continuum that started with head-decides-all across to the informal school which spoke about 'random groups of staff who meet at sixes and sevens' and 'whole staff...common room meetings' to thrash matters out 'when required'.

Most schools and colleges, however, regardless of the extent of democratic decision-making, had extensive committee structures, the workings of which were also revealed by this same question (question 70). The majority described one dominant style, the following not being untypical: regular meetings of heads of department (or faculty or curriculum teams), of year (or house) heads, of the senior management team – the school's 'cabinet' – on top of full meetings of departments and of years, as well as meetings of standing school committees, in this case finance, curriculum and pastoral. The majority of replies offered much explanation of 'line' management with various senior and middle management stages, along with commitment to 'decision making at appropriate level of responsibility' with heads of faculty meetings taking place on top of meetings of senior faculty members and meetings of whole faculties or departments. All appeared to be 'hierarchically nested' in the layer above (Cuttance, 1985), with views conveyed upwards to heads and senior teams, decisions coming back down again.

There was a distinct second group of schools, however, not as large but just as clear, whose sketch was not a 'line' up and down but a circle; one school literally drew a circle, suggesting a roundtable where everyone had a place. No one was at the top or the bottom; issues for discussion or decision were passed around from wherever they had originated – from senior policy group to departments to year groups to PTA to Student Council to the Governors and back to whoever had sent the suggestion off in the first place. If it seemed appropriate, this group then initiated further action.

These two styles have often been charted and were most recently characterised by Birmingham City Council as models of education management that will either 'tend towards the hierarchical/autocratic' on the one hand or towards the 'consensual/democratic' on the other (Birmingham City Council, *Quality Development*, 1995:167). Some who responded to the survey suggested that most schools and colleges say they prefer the latter (or claim they have it) while actually practising the former. But it is probably the case that most take from each in varying combinations rather than stick rigidly to one. Sometimes a third style can be brought in. One head in 1994 spoke of having introduced 'Quaker business practice' to his school and several spoke of further additions to practice. For example, where isolation of any curriculum areas was perceived, there was an immediate setting up of 'cross curriculum teams' or 'cross subject groups' or 'cross dept/faculty teams'.

Replies also revealed several types of committee membership. The more democratic involved formal staff elections to all committees, not just to *ad hoc* working groups but to senior management teams, consultative committees and advisory bodies. Other schools or colleges used self-selection to fill these posts, staff volunteering – with all those who wanted to join a working group or committee made welcome. Another school had an 'open management' policy, where senior management team meetings could be attended by any member of staff, as was practised in the earliest days of comprehensive education. But workloads were such in 1994 that the invitation to be consulted – and to stand for election – was not always taken up. Lastly, there was a third, less democratic way of obtaining committee membership: where all posts on committees or working parties were filled by appointment of the head or principal.

So complex had some of these committee structures become, and so great the proliferation of working groups, that one school spoke for many in saying what was needed now was a 'clear decision-making policy that outlines who does what'. Another said, our aim is to reduce meetings to 'three main committees for staff: in this case, curriculum, resources, development'; in a third, it was to reduce to two, 'a finance/curriculum board and a pastoral board'. There was something familiar in these replies: the same drive for simplification that occurred 20 years ago. The wheel was passing through the same phase in its cycle, 'We are streamlining but trying not to lose democracy'.

Support staff

In its second Report the NFER found the all-through comprehensive schools averaged 29 non-teaching staff – at that time cleaning, cooking, grounds work, security, secretarial, medical, careers, media resources, librarians, and technicians – part time and full time (Monks, 1970:173). Today the same comparison cannot be made since so many are 'bought in' from outside (see below) and because some of these one-time 'support' workers would by 1994 have been teaching staff members. In addition, the numbers are likely to have grown.

From the start many comprehensive schools and colleges included support staff in their decision-making. The history of comprehensive education's early years was full of their efforts for the schools: the groundsperson who contributed to biology lessons in the greenhouse, the cleaner who trained the school choir, the school keeper who added golf to the sports curriculum and took charge of the students opting for it. When new school governing body regulations were redrawn in 1988, a support staff representative was not included. As with students, a special decision had to be made to include them.

A good way to gauge how widely democratic frameworks stretch was to ask whether support staff in schools and colleges were involved in the decision making arrangements they had just described (question 69); 69% of schools and colleges said they were, but a large number added by hand, 'Only when it concerned them' or 'on occasion only' or 'not on curriculum matters'. Such replies compromised democratic practice slightly, but the figures as they stood showed that already nearly a third of the schools and colleges leave support staff out completely from any decision making – near the percentage that did not have voting or peer-discussion for making major decisions within the school or college itself. Perhaps an indication that there is still some way to go.

New developments

Over and above the descriptions of decision making, question 70 and question 71 also gave a clear picture of three areas where administrative practice had changed in comprehensive education over the last 30 years. The first was the addition of the disposable administrative unit: the working party. Most of those answering had working parties, convened for specific tasks, usually disbanded when the task was over (though some stayed on): task groups, quality circles, action teams, advisory groups, and consultative committees. Areas covered were planning, guidance, qualifications, community relations, behaviour, equal opportunities, curriculum, resources, staff development, and new accommodation. One school had 18 policy advisory groups – all elected by staff.

Working parties mushroomed during the late 1980s during the period of the National Curriculum and related testing arguments, and carried on for OFSTED and FEFC inspections. A few were specifically set up to produce proposals for change but more were a reaction to something that had gone wrong; or had been instituted to keep pace with the changes raining in on staff, a temporary response to yet another demand from government or quango. Some schools and colleges used them creatively to innovate or develop the comprehensive education in their schools or colleges. In all too many instances, however, they were regarded as a necessary response to an unnecessary burden.

The second major change in administration was the involvement of governors in school decision making. Thirty years ago there would have been few joint staff and governor working parties to decide school policy on the curriculum or staffing; in 1994 many schools and colleges reported such joint groups and committees. They exemplified the growth of governor power in schools and colleges that resulted from the legal changes from the late 1980s – as well as the moves towards privatisation of education through LMS and opting out.

Increases in governors' powers, however, were not the same as extensions of the democratic process. In fact, they could be seen as compensation for the whittling away of local democratic accountability. Parent power, for example, was diminished locally because the democratic forum on which parents could prevail, the local authority, was being stripped of its powers; and central government was showing itself ever less likely to consult parents (or anyone else) before acting. Instead parents were given increased representation on individual governing bodies, to compensate. Similarly, staff in schools may have been disempowered – with ever less say in the curriculum they taught and the assessment of their pupils, or ever less power collectively to defend themselves. They too were given a place on individual governing bodies as compensation; not as many places as parents, but a voice all the same.

The composition of individual governing bodies, no matter how constituted, could not really compensate for increasing inability of democratically constituted machinery to make schools accountable directly to the community. Indeed, some saw the changes in governing bodies as designed to override local democracy; or, as one school inspector put it, a movement of control of schools from professionals to lay, with policy 'on the basis of rule determined by the interests of the few rather than the many' (Felsenstein, 1987:110). Local authorities looked after everyone; governors only after their own.

But even that is increasingly difficult. As oversight has been removed from professionals and given to lay people, the danger is not constant interference so much as overload of work leading to concentration of decision making in an ever smaller number of hands. It is not all governors' fault. These 350,000 men and women up and down the country are now 'snowed under' by what is required of them (Riley, 1994). They carry an ever-increasing load as conscientiously as possible, taking on the tasks which LEAs have been forced to drop through the same funding changes and marketisation that created LMS and opting out in the first place. They decide on spending, make staff appointments, check the fabric and installations, oversee computing systems and security, write policy papers on everything from setting to parental involvement, analyse examination figures, implement curriculum policies prompted by government directives, and deal with everything from the hiring of premises to redundancy of staff.

An MP reviewed these tasks for governors of grant maintained schools. Finding them all undertaken without assistance from local authorities' professional workers, as would formerly have been the case for many, and hearing that governors were not paid, asked the permanent secretary at the DfE in the early 1990s if this was 'a realistic attitude ... in view of the responsibilities that you are expecting of governors?' It is a question that is just as appropriate for LEA schools and further education colleges. An army of unpaid amateurs is now doing the work once done by paid professionals. The question is not so much how well it can be done, though this is important, but is there sufficient oversight being exercised to account to the totality of taxpayers for a public service run on their behalf with funding they – the community at large – has provided? These are not private schools or colleges funded by students' fees and old endowments. These are institutions within a public service run on behalf of everyone, paid for by everyone – yet 'run' by a very small number of people.

The sums are not small. Many secondary schools spend two million pounds a year; and a few colleges up to 30 million. These are large sums in a system where accountability to the taxpayer in so many instances is no longer direct, and where public accountability mechanisms have been so eroded. It is not so much that they will put their hands in the till as that they will take decisions without knowledge of consequences. In discharging their duties some governing bodies have access to expert advice and others do not.

The Public Accounts Committee heard what 'a high proportion' of opted-out schools have accountants on their governing bodies, a luxury the majority of LEA schools do not share. If schools need accountants, any equitable public service would provide them if those without are likely to be disadvantaged. The same, possibly, for those schools lucky enough to attract retired teachers or inspectors to their governing bodies who can undertake the painstaking work now required on curriculum matters, or on assessment, preparing value added tables, calculating class size in relation to time taught and other necessary reports governors are forced to produce. A few schools have a few governors who now spend 2 or 3 days a week working for schools. What of those schools which do not have governors prepared to do this? Several comprehensive schools in depressed areas complained to the survey that they are unable to 'attract' governors to do even the routine work; or of governors failing to attend well. And who could blame some, when they discover how much is expected of them as well as how powerless they really are?

Governing bodies began to realise their new powerlessness after the initial euphoria of LMS and 'independence' had worn off and increasing numbers were faced with cuts in funding and the unpleasant task of dismissing good teachers. In more and more localities (in addition to joining national governors organisations) governors took to meeting together in their own local forums to see what collective strength they might have. These developments can be seen as the re-invention of collective local democratic representation in the wake of the downgrading of local democracy, and parents' organisations too have moved in the same direction. However, not all governors or parents are connected to such new forums, and most of these new groups are not representative. They are also separated from democratically elected bodies. But with a huge unfilled vacuum in local democracy, such activity is unlikely to die away.

Governors' sub-committees

The third administrative change in 30 years is the proliferation of sub-committees on both college and school governing bodies. Many sub-committees take key decisions, which the main body simply rubber stamps. This can mean an ever smaller circle of individuals have the say and that some sub-committee members never get a balanced view of the school or college as a whole. This is particularly the case if the governor is involved in the financial decision making.

Financial issues played a major role in management and administration of schools and colleges after the late 1980s. The school or college year no longer hung on an educational cycle but on a cycle determined by its annual budget. In the new market-led education system the budget frequently expressed each school's or college's educational purpose rather than any collectively agreed educational statement or plan.

A set of questions in the 1994 survey asked about the range of governors' sub-committees, and where these related to finance, about administrative changes that had been made to enable schools and colleges to do the work that used to be done by professionals. Of eight possible subcommittees set out (question 71), the most common was that labelled Finance (question 71A); 90% of the governing bodies of schools and colleges in the survey had such a sub-committee. In addition, nearly half (49.1%) replying to question 76B[1], had taken on extra non-teaching staff to assist with finance and administration.

In other schools, however, the initiative to organise around the INSET and capitation budget at each level and within each section of the school, signified a system where staff democracy now translated into the staff's collective decision making around finance (as had been done at Countesthorpe in the early 1970s). In these schools decisions about finance were not left to bursars and senior managers or governors, but taken by staff collectively.

Fund-raising

The sub-committee fewest governors had was also financial: one devoted to fund-raising (question 71G). Only 6% of schools and colleges in 1994 had set one up – with the highest percentages in sixth form colleges and grant maintained schools (11% of each had such sub-committees). The 1994 survey also found that only three schools and colleges had taken on extra staff with the specific role of fund-raising (question 76C), although these might be increasing. In 1995 a grant maintained school (Edmonton, London) advertised two new posts specifically for the purpose of raising money to build a new department.

Whether officially embedded in the staffing or governing body structure, it was clear that fund-raising was going on perpetually in many of the schools and colleges in 1994, as whole sections of education seemed to be moving back to nineteenth century dependence on munificent benefactors. In the 1980s HMI reports first called attention to the worrying problem of schools' dependency on fund-raising for essentials like books or equipment. By 1990 at primary level well over £80 million a year was having to be raised by parents, companies and charity trusts, to keep schools going (Mountfield, 1991:42); all involving activity in a very 'cut throat world'. At secondary level, according to the Information Executive of the Educational Publishers Council, 50% of secondary schools were having to raise money for books; in some cases it was teachers' salaries for whom schools canvassed funds. Richer schools were raising more than poor ones and the gap between rich and poor schools was widening because of differing parental contributions (Chitty, 1989:178–79; Mountfield, 1991:51).

Since this kind of dependency, if carried too far within a state system, might mark the death of an equitable public service, the 1994 survey asked a number of questions about outside funding. First, how many schools were dependent on money raised by parents for either curricular or extra-curricular activity (question 64)? Just over 47% of the schools admitted that they depended upon money raised by parents and over half of these answered the next question (question 65) which asked what their funding had had to provide. Top of the list was provision and/or maintenance of the school minibus (346 schools); followed by purchase of PE and sports equipment (262); contribution towards the cost of school trips in both this country and abroad (160); support for the Library Fund (104) along with provision of essential school textbooks (68); purchase of computer software (64); contribution towards the cost of building and maintenance and repairs (45); and purchase of AVA equipment (17).

Eighty one schools spoke of asking parents to contribute towards the cost of musical instruments in mainstream music classes and many spoke movingly about the fact that fund-raising could not cover the gap here, especially for instrumental lessons outside the classroom. Only richer (or specialist) schools were offering such training to all; and inside many other schools only children from better-off homes were getting it because the parents had had to be asked to fund it personally. To try to ease the issue off the agenda, some schools were placing their music training out to private contracts with firms that sent in peripatetic staff for those who could pay. But some of these firms came under criticism for the poor pay and conditions they offered music teachers and for their directors' practice of awarding themselves large bonus payments (Wearn, 1995).

Parents were not the only source of extra funding coming into schools. If anything, parental contributions in many schools were minor compared with other sources. The 1994 survey, therefore, asked colleges and schools (apart from parental or student fund-raising) whether they were now dependent on any other outside funding for any extra-curricular or curricular activity (question 81). Many did not like the word 'depend' and disowned the idea that because they were raising or receiving extra money they were schools or colleges in greatest need. Institutions do not like to be seen as having to raise funds; they like to be seen as worthy of being granted them, an increasingly fine distinction.

Two hundred and ninety schools and colleges (19%) replied that they did depend on such money. Some were specialising schools (see below). Of the rest, those with higher than average proportions depending on such funding were tertiary and further education colleges, along with upper schools of 13/14–18 (27%), voluntary controlled schools (28%) and special agreement schools (46%). By contrast, a far lower percentage of opted out schools (8%) said they depended on such funding, as might be expected with schools that had so often received preferential public funding.

Schools and colleges were much more forthcoming about the activities being funded than about who was funding them; and only about a third gave information on the latter (with a greater proportion of colleges than schools willing to say). A substantial proportion (mostly colleges) enjoyed some funding from TECs or Industry Training Boards, sometimes along with private funding – e.g., the Engineering Council and a private sponsor for 'technology enhancement'. Another was helped by BT who loaned time on a satellite dish for a college weather studies course. Money sometimes came from local firms who used colleges for training – e.g., a catering conglomerate sponsored a catering course, and several local industries sponsored local business courses in colleges as part of industry link projects. TECs also gave to schools for work on 'income generation' or to help 'sponsor enterprise'; and to help set up vocational courses (see Chapter 9). Most of this money, then, was public money.

In schools fewer projects were funded by public money and more by big companies. Schools named BP (with their ACE programme, encouraging pupils to think about higher education); and BT (an IT project in one school, innovative curriculum development through 'Gemini' science in another, and a third, with Toyota, sponsoring Key Stage 4 science modules). Shell helped organise work experience in some schools, locally and in Europe; British Gas provided some business studies courses. One school said Rover funded its work, but not what was funded; another said it had funding for energy generation from a military aircraft firm but did not say which one. Exel helped start a girls' football team in one school. The Wellcome Foundation promoted a 'prospects programme' for Year 10 in another; in a third McDonald's sponsored books and helped in an attendance compact. A privatised water company and Rolls-Royce helped fund drama productions in a few schools.

Local businesses also gave to local schools: an 'activity day' in one, or work placements in a local supermarket. Local Rotarians sponsored a Duke of Edinburgh scheme; another firm gave personal organisers to all students in an office skills class; a third sponsored the careers section of the library and two more helped with careers conventions and careers education. One helped a school set up a learning resources centre. In another, the help was 'a confidential matter'.

Local businesses were also tapped by schools for funding they needed (rather than receiving funding for purposes decided by the donors): help with sporting activities: transport to matches or buying of kit ; help with music, sponsoring the school band, concerts and music teaching; and many schools were given help to provide awards and certificates and to promote prize days. Another significant number received help for the school's newspaper, yearbook or prospectus, either by firms advertising in it or paying part of the cost.

Lastly, there were ubiquitous trusts which sponsored 'computers' in several schools; and there were schools with access to their 'own' charitable trust money (e.g., several voluntary controlled schools had such access); an aided school had a special 'governors' trust'; a grant maintained school a 'trustees fund'. Several schools had access to one specifically named fund, and, more quaintly, one mentioned a course on 'raising aspirations' funded by an un-named 'private benefactor', who gave the school £7,500 for the purpose.

Leaving aside all education or training funded by money that came from the taxpayer (say, by way of the TEC), two features stand out in relation to much of the outside funding mentioned from private benefactors:

1. How market-oriented a large bulk of the sponsored study was. Apart from some funding related to science teaching, and the money that went to support cultural activity like drama productions or music, relatively few study areas other than entrepreneurial activity or business education benefited. Little funding went to encourage study related to the environment or health or transport or housing. Almost nothing was given for international issues like world poverty; or for the promotion of learning related to human rights; or animal rights; or for the study of peace; or for the promotion of democracy.

2. How often traditional activities were the ones promoted: prize days, cups, and certificates.

It is good that local firms and businesses are involved in schools and colleges, for this helps to cement local connections between groups committed to an area; but there are many other groups locally, including pensioners, environmental groups, trade unions, voluntary groups, and community groups who might also like to be committed to their local school or college and help it in some way. Is there any risk that connections with them will be less because they cannot spend a lot? When pupils and students are given their own free hand about what they themselves will raise money for, it is often for groups like these, not for McDonald's or the privatised water boards.

Firms that donate to schools get good publicity in return, and sometimes a chance, indirectly, to promote the future of private industry, or even their own niche. All their activity is accepted as non-political. Yet the message left behind is not always neutral. For example, several schools mentioned one supermarket giant's donated study pack, Siting A Supermarket (Mountfield, 1991:46). It clearly embodied a political argument, yet how many schools decided it needed a counter-balancing study pack (or lesson) putting the case for the high street's shops; or the case against green field developments for supermarkets? Support from outside donors is never truly value-free and problems are possible in a few cases – for example, where schools or colleges might question offers from firms in the forefront of world controversy (with weapons connections, image problems relating to working practices, or working in the meat or animal trade) but be unable to refuse because of financial need.

The third feature to stand out is how completely random were the activities being funded and how impossible it is to judge the value of most of them to the comprehensive system as a whole. How, for instance, to know which initiatives were so successful they might be worth extending to everyone, and which, frankly, have been a waste of someone's funds. How the educational community decides in this matter is an important democratic issue.

The variety, of course, was part of the charm; but the sting in the tail was that little of this funding was in perpetuity and most was for a single year. That is why the reply received from one school in 1994 was salutary: yes, we once had several sources of business sponsorship 'but recession has taken them away'. Firms also go into receivership; get taken over; change policies. Charities switch attention to more fashionable causes. Private benefactors choose someone else next time. Even those who support the charities have this word of warning for schools and colleges: 'public taxation remains the only certain and...most cost effective way of raising money on the scale required for public services' (Mountfield, 1991).

Earning money

Meanwhile, schools and colleges are being encouraged to operate like businesses themselves. In particular they are urged to capitalise on their assets: to 'sell' them to the community. It can mean offering school grounds for car parking if the school is situated in a shopping area; or renting out its swimming-pool or football pitch or assembly hall to local sporting associations or drama groups. This will always mean that the school cannot use its own facilities when they are being rented out and, secondly, that it cannot look upon them as open to the whole community (unless they can pay). Yet if schools and colleges are given limited budgets, can they afford to 'give away' facilities from which they could obtain funding? A new national concordat on these matters is long overdue; this too is a democratic issue.

There are, of course, other ways that schools have open to them in which to raise money: jumble sales, sponsored activities, fairs and bazaars. Many take advantage of these, the activities often being socially useful in the school as well. But not all schools can raise big money in this way, especially those in circumstances where local poverty levels are high. As evidence presented to the Education Committee of the House of Commons commented, 'Car boot sales require cars' (House of Commons, Education Committee, Minutes of Evidence, March 16, 1994, p.14, para 3.7[2]).

But was there any evidence that it was rich schools that raised a lot of money and poor schools that did not? The 1994 survey set £5,000 as a sum schools and colleges might raise if they were seriously taking up the activity of fund-raising, and asked how many raised this much or more (question 77). The answer was 57%, which means quite a lot of comprehensive schools and colleges are raising (or having to raise) quite a lot of money: possibly over £9 million a year nationally.

All types and age ranges of schools were over the £5,000 mark, those that were big and those that were small. There were differences, however, in location. Schools in inner cities or out in the countryside had lower percentages (52% and 45% respectively) than those in towns (71%). Schools serving council estates only reached 40% raising this sum, for often council estate schools have fewer 'local' businesses, while those drawing from substandard housing areas (reaching only 50%) may have more local businesses and residents who are themselves on the edge.

The social class of intake also made a difference in that a slightly smaller percentage of schools with working-class intakes (53%) reached the £5,000 mark than those serving middle-class areas (60%). Those with an equal social mix also reached 60%, once again showing the way 'mixing' can sometimes maintain the balance towards the higher end of any scale. The differences are not yet so great that we can conclude 'rich' schools serving 'rich' areas are being greatly advantaged. But the start of polarisation is there, and could grow if schools or colleges are made increasingly dependent on what they themselves have to raise.

Specialisation

'Specialisation' has many meanings. Today's blurred system can use it to mean grammar schools with 11-plus exams ('specialising' in academic education) as well as an FE college with a horticultural wing providing agricultural courses for the region. The first is not compatible with comprehensive education and is not specialisation; it is selection. The latter is specialisation compatible with comprehensive education if the rest of the college is available for courses normally offered in general further education for 16–19 and the specialist facility itself is open to all without attainment testing, even if some entrants first must take qualifying courses in the college. The route is provided.

What about the comprehensive schools that specialise in music or science or technology? If they select their entry overall on account of being specialist schools, they are no different from any other selective school. If they select those 'good at' the specialist subject but not others, they are semi-selective schools, many of which will rapidly become selective, for the law gives any specialising school certain rights regarding admissions overall that other schools do not have.

If, however, schools merely make a particular activity their speciality, hoping to attract parents or students or funding on account of it, and encourage all who enter the school to take part in the work, but keep their entry itself non-selective, they are a comprehensive school with a special facility or activity. This was always a development in comprehensive education. Wandsworth Comprehensive School in the 1960s, for example, had a celebrated boys' choir but there was no special entry test based on music, just a big drive to get the normal range of entrants interested in joining the choir once they had joined the school. In 1994 Upton by Chester School was a comprehensive with a well-developed music department (and many award winning students). Like Wandsworth School it was the comprehensive school for the area and no pupils were specially selected. By contrast, some 'music' comprehensives do select their music entry by academic attainment; they are semi-selective.

The distinction is crucial and its importance lies in the need to develop comprehensive schools and colleges as institutions for the area but at the same time having their own education hallmark. If the hallmark is linked with attainment or social selection, the enterprise is doomed as one that would extend choice to parents, as experience makes clear (OECD, 1994). The speciality has to be without regard to academic or social selection to succeed and there have been many of these over the years: schools that have Welsh in Wales; or Gaelic in Scotland or Arabic in London; or a special reputation in football or pigeon racing. In the 1994 survey there were schools and colleges that specialised in environmental projects that used solar energy; and several were managing their own nature reserves. Some received special funding for their work because they were so advanced in that field. But none was selecting its entries to the school (or for the speciality) because of it, though some parents or students were no doubt attracted because of it. This is what we should want comprehensives to be like, with activities that make them unique, but growing out of the enthusiasms of those working or learning in the school or college rather than because schools or colleges have been artificially designated schools that can select because they specialise.

Experiments in this field have been problematic even where the intention was to improve all schools by making each one a specialist school. Alternative schools, for example, had a temporary vogue in the USA in the 1970s and 1980s when attempts were made to raise standards in inner city schools, especially for minorities. The results were not always as expected. In some areas parents did not like schools with 'maths specialisation' because they wanted every school to have mathematics to a high level. Nor were they attracted to schools specialising in slow learners, even though the same school might also be designated as specialising in Spanish. Nor did vocational schools make headway, even when well equipped and aggressively sold. Parents liked the broad-based comprehensive schools specialising in a full range of learning, with high standards throughout in *each* field in *each* school. The specialist movement slowly disintegrated, unpopular special units closing or modifying, the rest reverting to full comprehensive schools, as citizens voted out those school boards that had brought them in, in favour of new 'back to basics' boards. Only a few survivors remain like a school for the 'performing arts!' or a Montessori nursery here or there.

In areas with magnet schools – a single school with superior specialist facilities as well as alternative study programmes – there was success for a small minority of schools so designated and for some of those students who used such schools; but not for the majority of other local schools who received no extra resources and took the left-over pupils. Inevitably, magnet schools too are now in decline in the USA. On the other hand, much innovation is going on inside American comprehensive schools individually, to develop alternative programmes and curricula – but only where they avoid the pitfalls of selection and polarisation within the system.

Artificial attempts to engineer specialisation rarely work in comprehensive education; specialisation has to be an integral part of the work and life of the school or college that underwrites the speciality, where those working in the schemes are working for the sake of the specialism, not to turn a school – stealthily – into one that commandeers extra resources or selective status by deciding to specialise. Ideally, every school or college should have several features which are special to itself; or groups of schools and colleges specialising units or programmes common to an area. Not enough do as yet, but the sooner selection masquerading as specialisation ends, the sooner genuine diversity and alternative approaches can flourish.

1994 survey

To get a clearer idea of the way comprehensive schools and colleges operated in this respect, the 1994 survey asked whether any undertook specialist activity that was backed by extra funding. Many asked questions like, 'What money would this be?' or, 'We assume government funding?'; but, of course, it could be outside funding that schools had found for themselves.

Just over 15% of schools and colleges (238) said they had such speciaiisation. Those most likely to be getting funding in respect of it were the colleges, a third of whom (44) were receiving funding for what they considered to be specialist work. Yet most were answering in relation to TEC funding or to Compact arrangements in their area with business organisations, or funding for vocational extension work, business centres, training assessors for GNVQ, or the provision of youth training. A number of colleges had received funding in relation to provision for special needs; or had work funded by City Challenge, or were receiving money from the European Social Fund as well as from the FEFC. The interpretation of 'specialisation' in colleges was rather too loose to be meaningful.

The picture that emerged for schools was different (once funding from The Technical and Vocational Education Initiative (TVEI), GEST, and English as a second Language (ESL) was set aside). Specialist funding was spread right around all types of schools; with voluntary controlled schools (at 20%) having the highest level. Thirty of the specialising schools and colleges were receiving special 'technology' funding from the government – presumably under the new initiative where schools bid for 'technology' status. Fifty more reported funding related to 'subjects', which included modern languages, music, Nuffield subjects, sports coaching, science, environmental studies, and art and design. Exactly how they 'specialised' was not spelled out; nor whether they were selective.

Are Special Needs really the same as specialising?

By far the largest number of comprehensive schools reporting 'specialising' work were those who reported work for Special Needs: two-thirds of those taking advantage of the offer to name the field in question 80. Their specialising included units for the hearing impaired, severe hearing impaired, partially sighted, visually impaired, dyslexia units, specific learning difficulties, moderate learning difficulties, SEN 'special resource area', area support centres, 21 places reserved for 'moderate' learning difficulty, '60 places for statemented pupils reserved', places 'reserved for pupils with physical difficulties', 'designated school for disability', 'designated school for statemented pupils', schools providing a speech unit, or 'behaviour support units', providing 'partnership reading centres', 'community literacy centres', 'access to learning for adults', 'gross language deficiency/able child groups', 'severe literacy facility' – and one with 'provision for the mentally handicapped'.

The picture of specialisation was startlingly one sided and immediately raised the question of whether Special Needs work was ever meant to be a specialisation rather than part of any normal comprehensive school's provision? Was it ever envisaged that particular comprehensive schools would be 'designated' as schools specialising in learning difficulties to the extent they were in the replies received to the 1994 survey?

Education cuts have made integration more difficult and some believe that the Conservative Government has used the introduction of the market to thwart the integration movement. The Spastics Society, for example, believe that Special Needs Education (SEN) was a system 'set up to fail' by being left to the market. There were inadequate resources to deal with integrating pupils and students and 52% of heads could not cope with their share of this work (*Education Guardian*, 25 May 1993). According to Tim Brighouse and Barry Taylor writing in 1986, 'Those with severe mental, emotional or physical disability should only be educated in the mainstream provided that provision can answer their individual needs at least as well as they are met in the most effective special unit, school or specially designed college course' (Brighouse and Taylor, 1986:103). Funding problems have grown more acute since.

It looked as if pressure did remain strong – not on selective schools but on comprehensive schools, the ones expected to do the coping. The 1994 survey suggests that certain mainstream comprehensive schools are being singled out to act as semi-special schools for certain categories of special need (while other comprehensive schools are left to develop without much special needs work), thus compromising that mainstream comprehensive system that so many parents of disabled pupils, and the disabled themselves, support and want to enter (IPPR, 1991). For if it is a case of some comprehensive schools increasingly asked to 'specialise' in SEN pupils, while others take few or none, in time it would turn back into the very system so many were trying to leave behind.

A further question on this issue in the 1994 survey showed most schools and colleges assumed the original system was still in place – at least in theory – for it asked whether they accepted pupils or students from special schools for integration (question 35) and 83% replied that they did, or would. But many added that they had none or had not been 'asked' to take any. But is it a question of being asked or is it not that parents choose schools they want? It looks very much in some areas like schools are remaining passive and LEAs are proactive, singling out particular comprehensive schools for SEN work rather than encouraging every comprehensive school to make itself available for its share of SEN pupils. Is this the inevitable other side of the coin from designating some 'specialising' comprehensive schools that select pupils by attainment?

With colleges it was different. All three types (with the exception of two sixth form colleges) accepted students coming from special schools. It was 17% of comprehensive schools that did not accept them. This was less than 3% of LEA schools compared with the rather high figure of 28% of grant maintained schools that did not accept such pupils. Likewise, 27% of schools drawing middle-class intakes did not; nor 25% drawing from private housing. Comprehensive schools having predominantly working-class intakes and drawing from areas of mixed or substandard housing, had percentages accepting SEN pupils that were well above the survey average. Was it a case again of those already over-burdened conditioned to accept more than their fair share, while those with the most favoured circumstances exercising their legal privilege to 'opt out' even of their fair share?

We do not know. But we do know that in comprehensive education it cannot be a case of only some schools being asked to undertake work for pupils and students with learning difficulties, while others are exempted (or asked to undertake work with high attaining pupils only). Comprehensive schools take all attainments, as most schools and colleges accept. Some have staff specially trained for SEN pupils; others take pride in training all their staff – through INSET work – in the requirements of Special Needs work. Mainstream schooling has to stay mainstream in order to fulfil its commitment to meeting Special Needs.

Personnel and staffing: More governors' sub-committees

After finance, the next most frequently formed governors' sub-committee in comprehensive schools and colleges was personnel (question 71B). This dealt with hiring and firing of staff and planning staff deployment; 84% of the schools replying to our survey had such a sub-committee.

Half the schools and colleges had also funded at least one new post for finance or administration (see page 316) but as it was non-teaching, it meant the same kind of shift taking place as in other 'marketised' public services: more administrators, fewer floor personnel. What was disappointing for comprehensive schools was that extra personnel to help in administrative work was what so many had always wanted (see page 290), and now they were being added at the expense of classroom teachers.

The 1994 survey also asked another closely allied question, whether schools and colleges had had to let experienced teachers go or fail to appoint new ones as the result of having to balance budgets (i.e., make cuts), thus reducing the staffing levels at their schools or colleges still further (question 76A). Of the 1234 schools and colleges replying to question 76 (79% of the survey), 24% had had to do so and several wrote in that the situation was going to be far worse from 1995 onwards.

Initial teacher training

While looking at the role of personnel in schools, the survey touched on recent changes in the way teachers are being prepared to teach, and whether schools had welcomed (rather than felt forced into) taking on the additional work involved in the initial training of teachers on their premises – as part of

Educational oversight: Lower priority for governors

Whereas the three sub-committees of finance, personnel and buildings relate in large part to work passed on to schools which LEAs would formerly have undertaken, the fourth most convened governors' subcommittee was at least directly related to education and was one schools would always have been concerned with: curriculum and assessment, dealing with what was learned and how well it was taught.

This is what most governors expect governing body work to be about. Yet not even two-thirds of schools and colleges had such a sub-committee. In fact, an almost identical percentage – 65% – also had an additional financial sub committee dealing solely with Pay (question 71H – specific issues of salaries and wages which LEAs also used to deal with). When it came to sub-committees on Attendance (which could include discipline, behaviour and pastoral life), less than half the governing bodies had them (47%). This lack of sub-committees on curriculum or pastoral care was not necessarily a measure of school disinterest, since it could mean that half the schools and colleges considered these matters without reference to governors.

Even so, 30 years ago governors of comprehensive schools and colleges would have had most of their time taken up with discussion of the educational direction of schools and colleges and matters related to student welfare or the quality of the teaching. Today most of their time is spent on the business of running an 'education business'. It is not necessarily a bad thing that the costing of education should be seen by those planning curricula and deciding staffing levels, but the extent to which time was taken by non-educational activity was very high.

The picture that emerged from many comprehensive schools and colleges in 1994 was of some trying to run themselves as educational establishments, others as businesses that happened to deal in education – and a third group trying to run as comprehensive educational establishments. Although more autonomy has come to schools and colleges, it is highly circumscribed in law and governed by directives from outside in respect of policy and procedures over which governors have little influence, no more than LEAs. Governors have little power to influence the local framework in which they operate. They can discuss selection going on in the area; they can do nothing about it. They can discuss being underfilled but not the policy behind their 'designated number'. They have no input into the way education is organised – even in their most immediate area. No business would ever accept operation under such unfavourable conditions.

Even if operating in comprehensive situations, much less time was spent in 1994 on governing bodies and in staffrooms talking about comprehensive education itself – its rationale, its needs, its values, and the way the particular school or college is working in respect of these. Discussion is about profit making, value for money, renting out, buying in, keeping up particular examination figures rather than whole-school attainments; these are the stuff of much school and college government today. Even where comprehensive concerns can be retained, there is a lengthening agenda of non-educational tasks in the way, all to be undertaken in conditions of greater financial stringency.

Increasingly, in situations of this kind, decisions were being undertaken by heads, principals, senior staff, and sometimes a few specific governors, without reference to the rest of the staff or occasionally to other governors; and certainly without reference to neighbouring schools and colleges. Overall development of the system proceeded without a locally or regionally accountable democratic body to oversee it and hold the ring. In matters of continuing reorganisation of the system – especially after 16 – it was the same story. Individual governing bodies acting individually cannot do this work on their own.

Each school and college needs its own body to champion its claims within the system, a factor sometimes lacking in the past. But equally, some of the work being undertaken by governors needs the support of local or regional government, in terms of routine tasks and provision of services that at present are not funded fully, if at all. They need this support within a democratically accountable system as part of a collective development locally, accountable to the community that actually pays for the education service. They need recourse to a democratically constituted body that also oversees the way the institutions work together with some commonly agreed criteria to judge success of development. Yet most rethinking of governing body work does not relate to any of these issues. Many governors are narrowly concerned with re-jigging their composition once again; and ignore as yet the larger democratic issue at stake, which many have recognised presents us with an urgent choice: 'to accept the market vision of accountability or to re-invent a civic version and an institutional framework to embody it' (Marquand, 1995; see also Ranson, 1996).

Local government services

The centre of accountability in education is the relationship of the school or college to its locally or regionally elected democracy. The drive to run everything from Whitehall, going on for more than a decade, has not been successful in undermining the attachment of schools and colleges to their local bodies. Some believe that local authorities still possess considerable power and influence within the system. As the 1994 survey showed, the majority of secondary comprehensive schools were still close to their LEAs, and still using their services and good offices (see Chapter 3).

This is not to say that several LEA powers are not better being exercised by schools and colleges themselves, as now happens. Or that new powers are not required to handle new problems. Only that it is at least arguable that too many have been removed from the democratically elected bodies for the good of the education service. It is also arguable that schools and colleges have been pressured too far into hiring private commercial contractors to undertake the provision of services which they themselves are able to organise in-house far more effectively, or, with the help of local authorities, could organise better in new, non-profit ways. There was something questionable about finding so many school and college governors and staff spending so much time during the year of the survey racking their brains to see how they could ensure that private profit-making companies could continue to make a profit from their institutions.

When we look at the manifold activities that schools and colleges must now administer and oversee, as well as at the essential services being hived off to privatised working, we encounter a very problematic area. Not because all such arrangements are unworkable but because experience varies so dramatically. Whether through Direct Service Organisations (DSOs) or completely privately contracted, the provision of services to education from outside can work really well; it can also be one of the most wasteful ways of spending hard-won funding, and involve schools in spectacular mis-expenditure, waste and inefficiency.

But who is overseeing the process carefully enough to decide and advise? Who can handle the misgivings about the private sector moving into certain of the areas of services for schools and colleges and especially about compulsory competitive tendering (CCT)? Although some schools believed such changes have helped to make systems more efficient – 'much smarter', said one – others have found that changes have undermined effectiveness and involved schools and colleges in complicated contract arrangements that have offered little improvement, and in some cases, downright deterioration. As is no wonder when surveying the commercial movement in this area. To make any profit from education – which is the motive of all the new private arrangements – little-fish firms have gone to the wall quite quickly and have been swallowed up by big fish, with increasing numbers in even bigger mergers (sliding into cartel operation in several areas) – with giant conglomerates mopping up meals, cleaning and overall facility management in one contract. None of this is unexpected in an economy driven by privatisation and the market. The question is, what are the alternative ways of operating?

Not all LEAs are sitting back and letting private contractors grab all the work. Many responded positively to the situations in which they found themselves, and moved ahead in many areas to new ways of operating: in Cambridgeshire personnel management trades as a limited company to which local schools belong – 'like club membership'. Waltham Forest has set up 'agencies' that trade with their schools (and with opted out schools, which, increasingly, are 'buying back into' LEA services). Some LEAs are delegating more of their budgets to schools so that schools can buy back services they provide – with LEAs acting to promote the role of schools as purchasers (Cordingly, 1994).

Although some authorities have lost a large portion of their personnel, they have reorganised into units (relating to services like meals, personnel, finance) which schools can now buy in, 'never priced higher than the money allowed to schools' (Condon, 1994). Other far seeing LEAs were planning services to further and higher education as well. Some schools were thinking in terms of organising services collectively, starting their own co-operatives. Many of these LEAs and schools do not regard the services bought and sold as 'privatised' arrangements, nor do the agencies regard themselves as operating in the private sector. They are competing against it, a new sort of public enterprise.

Survey 1994

So far there has been little in the way of opinion from schools and colleges about changes in respect of services. One set of questions (72) in the 1994 survey was designed to discover which services that LEAs traditionally had provided schools or colleges valued most. In view of widespread support for returning democratic accountability to local government in respect of the running and servicing of schools and colleges, this was an important question. A second set of questions (74) was designed to discover opinion about the quality of services being provided under any new arrangements schools and colleges had made.

Twelve local authority services were listed (question 72) and schools asked to say which they regarded as (a) essential, (b) appreciated, or (c) not essential. Very few rated any service as non-essential: but the highest 'not essential' rating was 30% for the library service. At the other end, only 3% regarded LEA legal services as non-essential.

The schools regarded the following advice as essential[3]:

- legal services (76%)
- payroll (69%)
- education welfare (68%)
- educational psychologist (61%)
- personnel support (52%)
- building and maintenance (49%)
- admissions appeals (45%)
- admissions (28%)
- staff training (35%)
- information technology support (31%)
- library (25%)
- central purchasing (20%)
- training governors (14%).

As can be seen, what schools consider essential varies a good deal. Governor training was regarded as least essential (several schools wrote additionally that they thought their own was poor); but legal, payroll, and the two pupil welfare services were supported so widely that it is difficult to envisage a policy where all schools are forced to organise them privately, or that if they did, they would be any better off. Some would be worse off, particularly schools with the most problems or where need for certain services is high.

It might be argued that those services thought least essential by schools could be given over to them to undertake, or be undertaken by schools collaborating, with the LEA only required to see that the service is undertaken and that all schools in the area have the chance to benefit, since private arrangements within or between schools would not necessarily guarantee this. This is an example of an area where the role of the LEA might change but not the service.

In other cases the LEA's role might have to be extended. One example is overseeing and approving capital expenditure above a certain sum. Schools may wish to install their own information technology systems or build new extensions, but the public interest and the taxpayer might question whether such expenditure decisions can be theirs alone. First, because expenditure is likely to be very high. Second, because experience already with public bodies wasting millions on privately contracted projects which no public body has overseen – e.g. Hospital Trusts with £30m computer systems that have to be scrapped – suggests some special public oversight is required on items of large expenditure. Yet with every passing day less and less public oversight is exercised in respect of spending in schools and colleges, not just 'independent' colleges or schools or GM schools, but in many operating under LMS. Everyone in every school or college has a private story of large sums spent where oversight was lax.

Misuse of funds is another hazard and the new devolved system also makes this much more likely. Already Select Committees, Audit Commission enquiries and Comptroller General inspections (from far-removed vantage points) have detected enough improper expenditure and questionable behaviour by governors in grant maintained schools and independent colleges, not to mention continual transgressions in TECs (see Chapter 9) for us to know that it is only a matter of time before such queries arise too in LEA schools operating under LMS. Locally or regionally elected bodies should have clearer roles as public watchdogs for all educational institutions in their areas. Not to run them, but to monitor their policies and decisions more closely in the public interest.

There is one more reason, even more important: where a decision has implications for the planning of the local service and affects other schools and colleges, the locally elected democratic body should be involved – with legislation or government policy to guide it. This is especially essential for the co-ordinated capital funding that will be essential to reorganise comprehensive education's next phase of 16–19 development, as well as for its earliest phase of pre-school development.

In the 1990s schools were able to 'save' current expenditure and spend it on capital building programmes they alone decided upon. Or they could decide to keep millions in the bank and not spend at all. It was also being proposed that some schools could borrow. New buildings, new works, even new schools, including in some areas new grammar schools, were all being suggested with no reference whatsoever to the needs of the area as a whole, the excess of places that already existed, much less to the wishes of all existing schools, parents and staff, and certainly not to rational public expenditure, let alone the development of a coherent national educational policy[4].

As more schools and colleges collaborate, seeking to end their isolation in the imposed competitive market, some publicly accountable forum for discussion and decisions about 'new projects' must be made available – if only to ensure that public money is going to serve the widest range of needs in any area in the most cost-effective way. The elected authority's duty would be to ensure consultation and agreement about building and development as part of normal planning responsibility to maximise use, reduce duplication, rationalise services, provide a coherent system, and to serve all institutions equitably. At present no such forum exists and no such criteria exist. It is one of the greatest defects of the market system.

Affordable services of quality

At the same time there should also be more leeway for schools and colleges – as well as local authorities – to provide their own services and organise their own labour forces to compete with services privately provided. Local or regional authorities should be empowered to organise services for schools and colleges, and encouraged to be as enterprising as possible. The lowest bid should not be the only criterion, for everyone knows a firm can bid lowest by employing fewer people to do the work than are needed. In every area of the country schools and colleges are experiencing problems because laws do not also require considerations of quality to be taken into account in the same way as cost for contracts of services. There is also the issue of contract compliance with fair wages and non-discrimination; as well as freedom for all those working in services to education to be represented by trade unions, who will in turn take a hand in training the workforce. Taking these factors into account will produce better services in the end.

To give some idea of what comprehensive school practice was in 1994, and what schools' and colleges' views were about quality, we asked how many had contracted with private contractors for eight types of service: cleaning, care of grounds, meals provision, buildings maintenance, personnel, payroll, insurance and security. It was evident from some writing-in that some schools assumed 'buying in' from the LEA's own DSO was buying privately. This does not affect their opinion of services, however.

Schools and colleges opted for the following services from 'outside':

- grounds care (919 schools, 59%)
- cleaning (896, 57%)
- meals (781, 51%)
- routine building care (776, 50%)
- security (328 or 21%)
- insurance (335 or 21%)
- payroll services (214 or 14%)
- personnel services (83 or 5%).

The institutions most likely to use these services overall were the grant maintained schools and the colleges; at the lower end of services least often bought (payroll, personnel, and insurance) 79%, 77%, and 64% respectively of tertiary colleges, FE colleges and grant maintained schools were using them.

Were schools and colleges that have bought in satisfied with the privatised or newly provided services when comparing them to the services formerly provided? Again, caution is needed in interpreting the total figures since write-in comment showed that once again schools were confused about the status of in-house staff who had 'won' contracts as private suppliers and services from LEA-backed providers. What is common to those replying, however, is that they had changed systems in respect of these services in one way or another. Any confusion would not affect their opinion of the present services compared with those of the past.

Schools and colleges were asked to fill in a grid for each service to say whether it was (a) better than under the old regime, (b) the same, or (c) worse. For over half the services (meals, cleaning, grounds, personnel, payroll) only a minority thought there had been improvement – with cleaning, grounds, and meals showing large percentages that believed they were no better or actually worse. Such a finding is important because of the inability of contracted-out services to build in essential features relating to both job-satisfaction and user-satisfaction in the way locally or in-house provision can (Fairley and Paterson, 1995). These are features that cannot be reduced to 'measurable' criteria no matter how tightly performance targets or specifications are set.

The quality of cleaning was especially condemned and it is instructive that some private schools advertising their wares in competition with state education, make a special point of mentioning along with 'high academic standards', the provision of 'clean, well-maintained buildings'. Several comprehensive schools spoke of wishing to take cleaning back in-house and hire their own staff. Struck by the 'rock-bottom' wages being offered to the contracted cleaners, they believed higher wages and better working conditions, with genuine training, would bring better results. They were often prevented from taking action by laws requiring them to put such services out to competitive tender. Several schools, however, have taken work back in-house where the numbers to be employed are small, e.g., some have taken back groundswork from private contractors by employing their own full-time groundsperson, and report not only large savings but better maintenance. School meals drew some unfavourable comments as well, as they have in the national press with letters like 'wait in lines...in grotty hall...to buy...nutritionally poor snack food...eat standing in playground or perched at a table without cutlery, water...or plates'[5]. Nevertheless, the range of new departures being pioneered in relation to meals and snacks and drinks services in schools and colleges must mean some will emerge as models for improvement.

Good service

The services which over 50% of schools and colleges believed were as good as or better than those provided formerly were building maintenance (60%), insurance (58%) and security (57%). The freedom to get that broken window mended without having to send triplicate forms to the architects' department is by now a stereotyped reply, but it was a long-overdue release for many schools and colleges. All the more unfortunate that now that the freedom has come, the funds are being cut.

Schools and colleges were also asked whether there were any further services (not listed in question 73) they bought in from private contractors (question 75): 128 wrote in additions (with some of the same confusion between non-profit services set up by LEAs and profit-making services from outside), including architects and building advisers, subject inspectors, psychologists, functions catering, refuse collecting and security services, the last the most often mentioned (even though security had already been covered in question 73). Possibly, it was a new area of security not previously covered. With over £50 million a year being lost in public spending on schools through fire and theft, where two-thirds of schools believe school staff should be trained in security and crime prevention (DfE, *Statistical Bulletin*, 4/93), this is a fertile field for 'bought in' assistance.

After security came services related to provision of IT, and there was additional mention of equipment maintenance, appliance testing, auditing, banking, window cleaning, travel arrangements – right down to sanitary towel collection and insect riddance. One college had hired a service to provide a workplace nursery and another hired a firm to provide management for a fitness facility.

One area the 1994 survey did not ask about but which several mentioned was transport. There seemed to be great confusion and many haphazard arrangements about the provision of transport to schools, especially in countryside areas, not to mention some dissatisfaction. One secondary school student was compelled to write to the local press to draw an authority's attention to the inadequacy of arrangements where pupils on buses had to 'sit on floors, stand up, sit three to a seat...even in the luggage compartments'.

Another area where schools wrote comments was on the diminishing advisory services from LEAs and the unaffordability of private consultants for important areas where advice was needed. Stewart Sutherland (Chief Inspector of Schools), cross-questioned by the Education Committee of the House of Commons, said he had 'noticed a reduction in the number of advisory teachers' and that 'private agencies are...beginning to offer support services'. But when asked if the private buying was making up for the loss by LEA staff reductions, he was unable to say whether 'this is complementary to a sufficient extent' (House of Commons Education Committee, 1994). Nor can anyone else.

Services to schools and colleges is an area of fast-moving development, with success coming where least expected, and easy pickings (previously assumed by the private sector) not as easy as first imagined.

Collaboration

Organising a comprehensive system has become increasingly difficult as schools have opted out and comprehensive colleges have been removed from local systems to 'independence' under quango oversight. But schools and colleges still persevere to develop common policy. This was a finding that the survey confirmed. Development of the system is going ahead, but only unofficially. In Somerset, for instance, making use of the network built up locally by TVEI co-operation, a group of secondary schools formed themselves into a consortium to co-ordinate their admissions policies, press releases and open days, and minimise the lethal effects of what they saw as the cut-throat competition that LMS had encouraged. While 'not denying competition...can benefit...the cause of state comprehensive education', one of their headteachers said, there was a real need to counteract the tendency of 'running down others' (Morris, P., 1994). So schools got together. It seemed remarkable that in such an inhospitable climate so many schools and colleges have organised collaborative work in this way. There is no agency to encourage it; no government or LEA to fund it; and no policy to guide it. Yet it grows, a development of potential importance, designed primarily to provide students with a better course offering through the more effective deployment of combined resources. (See Chapter 9.)

The 1994 survey wanted to know just how many schools and colleges collaborated in the provision of education. We did not expect to find more than a minority involved in this work, bearing in mind the difficulties schools and colleges had experienced during the 1960s and 1970s in running even one joint course, let alone full-scale consortia. In 1994, however, the scene had changed. The enquiry discovered that nearly two-thirds of the schools and colleges were collaborating (question 83, 68.7%) – a remarkably high figure.

Although upper schools, tertiary and FE colleges were the most likely to be involved, in no type or age range of school was collaboration under 50%. There were larger proportions of schools collaborating in the middle of cities than in villages, as was to be expected. In terms of ability of the top 20%, however, collaborating and non-collaborating institutions were nearly identical in the percentages they attracted; in terms of the social classes, a slightly larger percentage with working-class intakes (66%) were collaborating than institutions with middle-class intakes (60%). Schools and colleges drawing from private residential areas were the least likely to collaborate (only 57% did so) while those drawing from areas with substandard housing were the most likely (82%).

At first sight this suggests most collaboration might have been in respect of schools and colleges anxious to develop vocational courses, but this was not the case. Question 85 showed that three-quarters of the schools and colleges collaborating were doing so in respect of academic study (74.5%), with nearly as many working together to provide cultural and sporting activity (72.5%). Only a small minority of collaboration in 1994 was for vocational education (12.7%), although this is a figure we can expect to see increase in the years to come, since by 2000 almost every school with a sixth form aiming to educate the whole age group (by offering the full vocational range) will be collaborating with at least one other institution.

How were they collaborating?

The 995 schools and colleges which confirmed they were collaborating were asked to be specific about the form of such collaboration (question 84). Only 3.4% were exchanging staff only; only 5.3 % were exchanging students only in an informal arrangement. Most of the rest were in formal consortia – 38% part of a consortium where pupils and staff were exchanged between the collaborating schools or colleges, while 53% were part of a consortium where in addition the partnership ran jointly organised courses. That so large a group of schools and colleges in the survey were part of formal consortia was surprising because consortia in comprehensive education have a chequered history. Again and again in the last 30 years they would be started with high hopes but then peter out, usually due to timetable problems. Yet in 1994,when the conditions were even more unfavourable than in the days when it was only a case of concentrating a different modern language in each school in the group, and when schools and colleges were separated by such wide legal and funding mechanisms, consortia were gaining ground (see Chapter 9 for a more detailed discussion).

Not for the first time in comprehensive education's history, schools and colleges were moving ahead of governments, signalling needed development. What is missing is that capacity within the public education service, properly accountable in a democratic system of government, to assist and monitor these and other changes so clearly required. Developing this democratic accountability – for a whole range of reasons in a whole range of educational activities – is as important as developing comprehensive education itself.

Notes

1 Seventy-nine per cent of all schools and colleges replied to question 76.
2 The evidence was taken from the *Memorandum Submitted by the Hackney Education Authority.*
3 Eighty-eight per cent of all schools answered questions in this section.
4 One such proposal was for a new grammar school in Milton Keynes from Buckinghamshire County Council, 1994; another was for a taxpayer-funded direct-grant fee-paying selective school, proposed by Kensington and Chelsea Council, 1995.
5 Letter to the *Guardian* from Nicole Bechirian, 28 June, 1994. This was with reference to schools in Kingston LEA.

9

Comprehensive Education for the 16 to 19 Age Group

Over the last 30 years the drive for comprehensive education has transformed the early years of secondary education. The tide reached the 16–19 age group by the late 1980s and gave cause for optimism that the UK might well see comprehensive secondary education finally established by the twenty-first century, possibly even before it begins. It would not be too soon.

At first sight, however, the 16–19 sector in 1994 looked as unreformed as it had for much of the twentieth century. An academic track for the minority still operated separately from all occupationally related learning, and much of the latter remained little known to most staff and students in schools. Despite a drive to codify vocational courses, there was still a lack of coherence in the system of qualifications, and curricular selection was still entrenched. The divide between schooling and further education, and between different types of schools, was still wide, exacerbated by a minefield of new funding bodies with conflicting remits, supporting all the old institutional and structural divisions – and new ones. Comprehensive education's unified system seemed a long way off.

But it was much nearer than it had been in 1965, although few at that earlier time were aware of how great the divisions were at 16–19. The largest group of students were in schools, usually studying full time and enjoying 'comprehensive education' on traditional 'A'-level courses. A second group of young people, most working for vocational qualifications related to their jobs in FE colleges, were not generally considered part of 'comprehensive education', and nationally their courses and achievements were not recorded with the same care.

The largest group were those who had left education altogether, many at 15 without any qualifications and most without any intention of returning. The education system had made clear it had little more to offer them. At that time there were jobs for those who were unskilled and better ones for those with 'O' level or 'O' grade education. The future education of these young people, including those few destined for training on the job, was not considered to be part of comprehensive reform either, and there was even less information about their learning experiences between 16 and 19 than about those working for vocational qualifications in colleges.

Yet in a considerable number of industrial countries at this time almost all these young people would have been staying on in mainstream comprehensive education until they were 17 or 18, the great majority obtaining a common qualification achieved through a combination of academic, vocational or work-related study within a common learning system. Such societies had already realised that without such extended education not only did these students have little future but neither did the society.

In the last 30 years almost all industrialised countries have come to the same conclusion and developed comprehensive systems (see Chapter 2) – varied in nature, but common in principle and unified in organisation. In Sweden there are 16–19 colleges with a choice of over 20 different lines of study around a common core; in France there are half a dozen baccalaureate programmes within a system of common schools; in the USA there is a common high school offering an elective system of courses organised in a unified modular system with common credit accumulation. Even though some students always drop out before they complete the full programme in these countries, both the course and the final award are intended for everyone in the age group.

In Britain there has never been a common system for this age group, nor a common institution, nor a common course structure, nor a common award; much less a post-16 education that was fully integrated with the earlier years or one that allowed vocational and academic education to count equally. Quite simply, education was not intended for everyone in Britain; and it was not until 1992 that even 50% in England stayed on in full-time education past the legal leaving age of 16 (DfE, *Statistical Bulletin*, No. 11/94).

It was no wonder that Britain's target in 1994 for the year 2000 was regarded with scepticism: 50% to reach two 'A' levels or vocational equivalent (assuming an equivalent was agreed). A comprehensive culture had not been pursued, and there was not even a popular name for this target, or even for the last 2 years of 'secondary education for all' itself. Some still called them the sixth form; others Years 12 and 13. In colleges they were the 16/17 and 17/18 age groups; in Scotland, standards 5 and 6.

For quite a sizeable number none of these applied: young people were 'on a scheme' or studying under the 21 (later 16) hour rule.

Yet at the start of the reform in 1965 everyone expected a change in the way education after 16 would be organised, to render it capable of absorbing the massive growth expected through the 1970s and beyond (Benn and Simon, 1970). As previous chapters have shown, that growth came at a much slower pace than anticipated (see pages 88–89). They show why Britain has not bettered its place much in the industrialised nations' league table of continuing participation in education over the last 30 years; and why it has become known internationally for having an 'early selection/low participation' model of education (Spours, 1993:84).

Basically, while successive British governments may have been actively trying to increase participation, they have not dealt with selection, the other half of the equation. From 1976 the strategy after 16 has been to make changes in the education and training of the majority but to leave the academic élite's education largely untouched. Reform therefore has not dealt with a divided curricular system, it has merely concerned itself with adding new programmes to the 'non-academic' side of the scales – what Raffe called the characteristically English solution to reform 'of creating yet another stream' (Raffe, 1993:65) and what Spours calls the capacity of the English system 'to absorb change by simply adding initiatives and thereby increasing complexity and confusion' (Spours, 1993:147) – actually avoiding real radical change.

Pressure to end divisions after 1965

Yet the pressure for 16–19 change was present from the start of the reform in 1965 despite the fact that the reform concentrated upon ending institutional selection at age 11 or 12 rather than tackling curricular and assessment divisions at these ages. Divisions at that time were characterised by GCE 'O' level for the top 20% , CSE for the next 40%, and most significantly, for the 'bottom 40%' (as the third level was often called) no attainment objective at all. After the 1976 Great Debate had blamed the 'bottom 40%' (and their schools) for lacking basic educational skills, the government of the day still did not act to implement a common curriculum and assessment system that might have helped remedy the problem. Instead improvement concentrated on yet more separate programmes for the 'bottom 40%', which later translated into separate training schemes after 16.

Dividing young people further and institutionalising new curricular selection was exactly the opposite of what comprehensive education should have been trying to do. This is why, earlier, during the 1970s and early 1980s, countless comprehensive schools had simply taken matters into their own hands by entering all their pupils for one or other of the two examination courses, doing away with the 'bottom 40%' in practice. This pressure ended in 1986 with the establishment of the single GCSE, a common assessment and course system for the 14–16 age group as a whole. This was a significant step in secondary comprehensive reform for it was after this that numbers staying on in full-time education started to rise appreciably (see OFSTED/Audit Commission, 1993:22; and DfE, *Statistical Bulletin*, No. 10/94: Figure 1).

It was also when pressure began to be exerted on the deeply ingrained curriculum divisions of the system after the age of 16, with their hierarchy of assessment and a jungle of qualifications. By contrast to most other countries with only one academic qualification at the end of secondary education (and some with no national testing at all), Britain still retained national examination hurdles at both 16 and 18 (and in the 1980s introduced national tests at 7,11, and 14 as well). Both exams and tests ranked students in a clear hierarchy of attainment, while yet another hierarchy was added in the early 1990s when league 'tables' were used to rank their schools and colleges as well.

The ranking was not based on what all students achieved (as it would have been in a comprehensive system where all who get any final award are counted). Ranking was on the percentages achieving the minimal first stage of university entrance in certain academic combinations: five GCSE A–C or five O Grade 1–3 in Scotland. This was essentially the same marker as had been used since the nineteenth century, and one that less than half the students in England had achieved by 16 in 1994 in any case (and only just over half in Scotland). Not only were achievements at other levels less important but attainment other than norm-referenced examinations scores were not counted in 'league tables', which also excluded academic success in vocational qualifications at any age.

To the lower-ranked 16 year olds and the lower ranked schools, whose achievements did not count in the same way, no matter how much achievement any one had in any of a dozen other ways, such grading systems acted to reinforce failure just as much as to spur further improvement, especially when schools begin concentrating on those students likely to pass at the magic five-or-more levels, giving less attention to those achieving 1–4 levels. In the 1990s attainment in these latter levels began to decline in some schools, including in half of those which OFSTED singled out for particular improvement in their five or more scores. In 1994 young people in Britain not only continued to leave education earlier than in other countries (see Chapter 1), they continued to drop out of courses on a massive scale (OFSTED/Audit Commission, 1993).

Even more discouraging at the 30 year stage were the plans for the future of the 16–19 age group, outlined by the chairperson of the Government's main curriculum body. Instead of ending divisions his document proposed a three-way split between an academic path linked to 'A' levels, a vocational path linked to vocational qualifications (including the new GNVQ) and a training path linked to training qualifications like NVQ (SCAA, 1994). Since it had been recognised for years that after 16 'the main instrument of selection is the curriculum itself' (Flower, 1983:19), it meant that 16-plus selection was to remain.

Even if 'A' level and Higher examinations were later updated, as was likely, there would still be a tripartite system. Such a system might have made sense in the late 1960s and early 1970s as a stage on the way to comprehensive reform, but it was wholly inadequate for a modern nation heading into the twenty-first century, when, almost everywhere else in the industrial world by this time, academic and vocational learning had been integrated within a single system, and assessment was mostly organised in unified systems of courses and credits that provided the flexibility and progression required. Almost everywhere else institutional integration had taken place as well, along with rational replanning of the age group's education, and in many other countries there was also a far higher investment in training and retraining. Most understood that although employers play their part, the main contribution has to come from governments.

It was not as if there were no voices raised in Britain for many of the changes other societies had already made. By 1994 almost every interested body, official and unofficial, had by then proposed similar radical changes for 14/16–19. Save for Conservative far-right think-tanks (the main sources of government policy at that time), most of the proposals recognised the difficulties listed above and sought to overcome them. In varying degrees and with varying emphases, all suggested some form of integration of vocational and academic education, as well as a reorganisation of curricular pathways to ensure coherence through a unified system of transferable credit and assessment. Most had tougher policies to get investment in training from employers. All stressed the importance of securing higher levels of participation in full-time education. Some were strictly concerned with economic performance; others more interested in radical social change. But even where proposals come from quite opposite corners of the political spectrum, what would have struck any reader was not how they differed but how much they had in common.

There is thus a basis for a new consensus for this age group, and good reason to explore an integrated and unified 16–19 system that would achieve some of the goals that so many have identified as necessary. These include curricular and assessment reform – as well as institutional reorganisation to deliver learning coherently and ensure maximum choice within the system. It is also worth assessing new forms of democratic oversight to make learning more responsive to society's wider (and longer term) needs. Instead of tying the system so closely to employers' short-term requirements by leaving all regulation and decision-making to 'the market', it is worth discussing whether there should be a return to some form of rational planning that is democratically accountable to the community as a whole. Lastly, many believe it is well worth getting agreement to expand the determinants of educational progress beyond the limited markers of 'excellence' currently in 'league table' use.

However, all such changes would require moving on from the strategy pursued by governments for almost 20 years: continual change that never dared touch the basic system – what Woolhouse has so aptly characterised as a policy of 'reform built on the failure to reform' (Woolhouse, 1993:224). Had there been real reform, the 16–19 system in 1993 would not have merited OFSTED's conclusion using words appropriate for any year of the previous 30: 'there is no general consensus about what full-time education for 16–19 year olds should include', adding a reflection of the Senior Chief Inspector from 1990 that 'a broad sixth form curriculum underpinned by a sound rationale is still quite rare' (OFSTED/Audit Commission, 1993:38). That such conclusions can be made against a backdrop of 20 years' rhetoric about developing ever higher levels of achievement within a coherent and updated system fit for the twenty-first century, is a measure of how far there is to go to achieve a 16–19 system on a par with other societies – let alone move towards that long-term vision of comprehensive education so many had in mind in 1965.

The aim of this chapter is to look at the 16–19 age group across the board, examining in detail the way its institutions operate individually and collectively in a wide variety of situations – to assess how far comprehensive education has come and how far it has to go in terms of developing a unified public service capable of developing all types of intelligence and many varieties of learning, coherently organised within a democratically accountable framework.

348

The 16–19 system over 30 years: A confined reform

The 1965 comprehensive reform, as we have seen, chose to approach comprehensive education institutionally. There was no question of changing the curriculum or the assessment system in place at the time and because there was not, the all-through school based on the grammar school became the preferred model. This meant that the reform was committed to the institution of the 'sixth form' in England and Wales and to the higher standard years in Scotland.

These school years housed the external examinations that had set the standards for attainment of the nation's academic élite and it was only natural that early comprehensive all-through and upper schools (whose full 1994 survey profiles are given in Chapter 3) started off trying to prove themselves in respect of 'A' level and Higher Certificate results. Passes were announced with pride, particularly those from students who had failed the 11-plus earlier or who came from backgrounds where no one in the family had ever stayed beyond the leaving age (see, for example, King, 1962; Pedley, 1963). Thus the main divide between the selective and non-selective system for this age group at this time was not so much the courses being followed as the different social and economic origins of many of the students. For a while this difference carried on to higher education, for those entering universities from comprehensive sixth forms included a greater percentage of students from working-class backgrounds than did entries from grammar or private schools (Neave, 1975).

As time went on, however, and the numbers of comprehensive schools increased, along with their numbers entering universities, the social origins and attainment levels of those staying on to their sixth form for 'A' level work began moving nearer to those of students in the sixth forms in other types of state schools. By 1980 rises in working class numbers to universities were no longer detectable (Venning, 1983). By the 1990s, although greater percentages of initial entrants obtained 'A' level passes 7 years later in academically selective schools than in comprehensive ones (and greater proportions in sixth forms than in FE colleges), once GCSE scores had been matched, there was no difference in 'A' level achievement between selective, comprehensive, private, or FE-based education in academic performance (Audit Commission, 1991; OFSTED/Audit Commission, 1993:32–33).

Quite early on it was obvious that – given comparable *intakes* – comprehensive institutions' capacity to match 'standards' from élite schools and colleges was not the problem when it came to doing something about Britain's continuing low percentages qualifying after 16 (though attempts to prove otherwise continued to be made – see Chapter 2). The problem was confining academic attainment to one course and confining this one course to ultra-narrow early specialisation and forcing it upon a minority of students, some as early as 13 or 14. Such a system could stretch only a limited number of capabilities in a limited number of students; but its monopoly on standards meant that many other types of intelligence (and a whole range of alternative capabilities) were neglected for decades in the age group as a whole. Comprehensive education was not being developed at this age, no matter how many 'A' level students were being added to the nation's totals as a result of ending selection at the age of 11 or 12.

The new sixth and other attempts at reform

Governments made several weak attempts at reform of these narrow academic courses during the 30 years after 1965, most aiming to 'broaden' the range of subjects which academic students studied after 16. Some reforms – like the N and F Levels – were proposed as early as the late 1960s; they failed to get accepted. So too did a similar reform – Q and F – proposed in the late 1970s. Later, recommendations from committees that governments had set up – the McFarlane Committee of 1980 and the Higginson Committee in 1988 – were also ignored, though the proposals from all of them were far from radical. Even proposals for widening made as late as 1989 by the government's own standing committee on curriculum and assessment, SEAC, were left to lie on the table. Except for A/S levels, which could be seen as strengthening rather than changing 'A' levels, no change had been made in this main academic qualification for this age group since 1951.

Never had an examination so widely criticised been so long retained. One reason was undoubtedly the failure of comprehensive reform after 1965 to challenge a system that permitted 'standards' for 16–19 to depend upon a single course taken by a small minority. Élite criticism of the comprehensive idea forced comprehensive schools to collude with the system because 'A' levels were one way they could establish their own academic credibility in a political world where this was continually being challenged. Thus comprehensive educators continued to support 'A' levels even when it was clear that the dominance of external exams for a minority was preventing the development of 16–19 education for the majority, comprehensive or otherwise (CCCS, 1981).

Even stronger support for 'A' levels all these years came from the private sector and the selective state sector because 'standards' so available to an élite minority helped them retain their own privileged positions within the national system. Their opposition to change in this one examination – and particularly the opposition of the major public schools – was deeply entrenched and highly influential, particularly on Margaret Thatcher in the late 1980s (see Kerr, 1992; Richardson, 1993:3–7, 14, 22).

Failure to reform the academic course not only delayed necessary national educational development at specific historical moments, it also created social contradictions in the developing comprehensive schools' own sixth forms. For the 'sixth form' was a descendant of the public schools. Up to the late 1960s even the sixth forms of grammar schools were seen as mere 'popular' grafting on to 'an institution born of an aristocratic tradition' (Neave, 1975:26). Along with other élite hallmarks such as close links to older universities, subject mindedness, and intellectual discipleship (all of which comprehensive education eventually went on to challenge), one of the main features of the sixth was its social responsibility for 'leadership formation' (Neave, 1975:6). This was not in relation to younger pupils but to society at large; for the public school of the nineteenth century set itself consciously to train the nation's leaders. In the twentieth century many grammar schools continued to harbour such aspirations about their own mission, but such a social purpose went counter to the democratic nature of most comprehensive schools, where contemporaries saw each other as political equals, and did not look at the world in terms of leaders and led.

On both social and educational grounds, therefore, many comprehensive schools tried radically to adapt their sixth forms, building on that democratic impulse to widen both its entry and its academic offering, in the hopes of persuading the majority to continue their education in a 'new sixth' , as it came to be called. All kinds of approaches were tried, including the chance to retake 'O' levels or to translate their CSE passes into an 'O' level by retaking the same subject in the 'better' exam. Occasionally, it was taking new 'O' levels, sometimes combined with a single 'A' level rather than the standard two or three. There were a few non-exam courses – such as office skills – and for a while there was also the Certificate of Extended Education (CEE), a paler 'A' level, intended for the continuing CSE student. The CEE never attracted large numbers and the government let it die in the 1980s, intending to replace it with the SPVE, its early version of an omnibus vocational course[1].

The triumph of the new sixth was that many students who would otherwise have left after 16 undoubtedly were encouraged to stay on, some to gain extra qualifications, and others just to improve their general education. But the number of new sixth formers was never high and accommodating them did not always mix the education of the sixth; in some areas, it stratified its organisation instead (Weeks, 1986:95–96). It also meant two decades went by when pressure was diverted from the comprehensive objective after 16: to transform the 'lower sixth for some' into a 'sixth year for *all*'. It was part of the price paid by the decision in 1965 to limit comprehensive reform to schools and to approach it institutionally rather than planning for the age group as a whole, where curricular and assessment issues could have been tackled from the start in both schools and colleges.

The rise of the comprehensive colleges and the campaign on the curriculum

The sixth form in the comprehensive school also had another drawback, evident from the start: how to ensure large enough student numbers to run a 'viable' number of 'A' levels in any one school, and thus prevent gross diversion of teacher time at the expense of larger sized classes in the lower years (see Chapter 3). The isolated sixth form in the all-through school never fully succeeded in overcoming this problem and by 1979 only a third were over the minimum size the Secretary of State had laid down as viable (DES, 1978: Appendix I). The problem continued through the 1980s and into the 1990s.

At the start of the reform in 1965 some of those in the further education sector had already foreseen the predicament of the isolated small sixth form (Mumford, 1965, 1972). For this reason the sixth form college was proposed, serving several 11–16 schools. It was originally opposed by élitists because a school simply formed to rationalise 'A' level provision was not in the grammar school or public school tradition of character formation and social leadership. Nor was a limited 2-year school necessarily satisfying for these colleges themselves, or always as economic as assumed. For all these reasons some local government officers had already suggested fusing sixth forms and further education as a way of 'retaining the principle of comprehensive education at substantially less cost' (Alexander, 1969; quoted in Terry, 1987:13, note 7).

Sixth form colleges developed quickly and were popular (see Chapter 3 for their history and 1994 survey profile), and it seemed logical to many to form links with local further education for the sake of their many students attracted to learning other than offered by 'A' levels; and thereafter, in increasing numbers, even more logical to become tertiary colleges themselves by joining forces with local further education in a new formal organisation (see Chapter 3). A quick canvass by the University of Southampton of sixth form colleges being planned in 1972 showed that over half were already either planned to link formally with FE colleges or to develop as full tertiary colleges (Lynch, 1972) rather than stay as mere "A' level academies', the nickname they had already acquired by 1970.

In the 1970s all types of comprehensive colleges thus began to grow in number and to transform the approach to the 16–19 sector – but none so fully as the tertiary college, formed specifically to promote the development of comprehensive education rather than just rationalise 'A' level (like the sixth form college) or offer a limited range of work-related qualifications (like many FE colleges at the time). The tertiary college had a specific curricular objective related to its development within comprehensive education: to unite academic and vocational education (see Chapter 3 for their survey profile in 1994).

Because it had a specific comprehensive objective, the tertiary college's growth was accompanied by a sustained critique of the isolated sixth form in the all-through school. It was the only institution which could criticise the comprehensive sixth form. The sixth form college was too closely based on it; and the traditional FE college of those days usually saw itself as complementary, not yet a rival. But the new tertiary college could question the sixth form rationale because it was the only institution formed especially to provide for the whole age group – offering 'A' levels like the schools,but also general vocational education, both full-time and part-time, along with work-related education; and in several instances also developing further programmes for adults or the local community.

The tertiary voices were not always tactful in their critique of the sixth, nor did they concentrate on obvious points like the great economies to be made and the wider range of studies available by going 'tertiary'. They pointed up the defects of sixth forms attached to schools from an ideological and educational perspective, concentrating on the narrow academic objective (largely based on 'A' levels). Many sixth forms in schools were just becoming university entrance institutions, excluding 3/4 of the 16–19 age group and not in the least comprehensive (Terry, 1987:5). Even the 'New Sixth' was criticised for its CSE conversions and 'O' level retaking, which tertiary colleges claimed showed a 'staggering lack of success' (Terry, 1987:5). Instead of wasting a year re-taking academic exams with little improved grades, students could have achieved a meaningful qualification in some other useful field in the tertiary college.

There was some truth in the claim, for few of those retaking GCE 'O' level examinations after 16 plus ever showed substantial improvement. Research as recently as 1991 showed there continues to be a problem in relation to GCSE taken after 16 plus (OFSTED, 1993:34–35) and evidence about private crammers taking pupils from all types of sixth forms, suggested that retaking 'A' levels with them can sometimes be equally unproductive (Samurez-Smith, 1994).

There was also the important matter of student preference. During the 1970s research and experience alike confirmed that the break at 16, followed by a switch to a college, was popular with students from both comprehensive and grammar schools. Many preferred the adult atmosphere and the mixed student body (especially if they had come from a single sex school). They were more satisfied with their 16–19 courses than their contemporaries were in the sixth forms of schools they had left (Briault and Smith, 1980; Dean et al., 1979). Socially the colleges were more advanced and some educators supported tertiary colleges specifically for their capacity to help students experience democratic practice in education appropriate to their status as young adults in a way schools do not allow (Wymer, 1975).

These views began to trickle down to schools, with some significant rule changes after the 1970s. As the 1994 survey showed earlier, although the wearing of uniforms has increased as a practice in comprehensive schools' early years (Chapter 5), the relaxation of uniform requirements for sixth form students has also increased. In many sixth forms in schools there are more privileges, relaxed attendance rules, and as much separation from younger years as can be managed, promoting further departures from traditional sixth form practice.

By the start of the 1980s the tertiary idea (as distinct from the institution) had established a dominance within the comprehensive field as the 'pattern' of the future, particularly in terms of a new curricular approach to the integration of 16–19 learning. Those in tertiary colleges had a wide view of the age group and its needs, and some were already arguing for equivalence of qualifications, compatibility of courses, unified progression routes, transferable credits, a common core of skills including computer literacy, and the involvement of students (including all trainees on YTS) in the planning and design of their own progress inside the education system. Their courses were designed to 'reduce the automatic presumption in favour of the established academic, rather than technologically and socially relevant, disciplines when the choice is made at 16' (Moseley, 1983:27).

Reinforcing the old divisions and digging new ground: The 1980s and 1990s

Plans for tertiary developments were being drawn up by a wide range of local authorities for submission to the Secretary of State by the early 1980s. By 1982 the tertiary pattern had become the favoured form of reorganisation in both Labour Party and Liberal Party policies. Although Conservatives had been returned to government in 1979, they were not totally hostile because tertiary organisation had always been able to show that it was the most cost-effective arrangement for the age group and, as it happened, most tertiary colleges were being developed in Conservative controlled authorities. Although the first few years saw a few tertiary schemes win approval, the political wind changed direction by the time the Secretary of State was Keith Joseph. Tertiary schemes began being refused, despite the fact that most were continuing to be submitted from traditionally conservative areas like Gloucestershire and Salisbury (Ball, 1984a:16–17; Terry, 1987; Weeks, 1986:27). This series of refusals of tertiary college plans from a string of local authorities had far greater influence in setting back 16–19 comprehensive education than most realised at the time.

Joseph was a fellow of All Souls, operating very much in the mould of his mentor, Warden John Sparrow, whose *Black Paper* contribution in March 1969 (Sparrow, 1969:66) had stressed his doubts about the extent to which universities should 'lower the intellectual standard they demand on matriculation in order to make admission easier for candidates who have not had the specialised training provided by the sixth forms of Public Schools'. For both Joseph and Sparrow, even grammar schools were still on trial as institutions of excellence. It was unthinkable that comprehensive schools should do other than also keep on emulating public school sixth form practice in the hopes of one day being accepted as well.

Thus did the grammar tradition (which was really the public school tradition) greatly influence the development of comprehensive education in its upper secondary years: on the one hand, giving it the necessary academic status to survive in an élitist system that continued to show it hostility, but on the other keeping it selective and narrow for decades and blocking that development of a new 16–19 tertiary system in the UK that most comparable industrial countries had already undertaken.

The fact that institutional change remained difficult, however, did not impede continued agitation for curricular and assessment reform. If few of the education secretaries of the 1980s, but particularly Joseph, had any understanding of the 16–19 education reform required for a modern education system, Conservatives connected to the world of industry had a broader understanding of what was needed to compete in the modern world. None, however, dared take on the sixth form élite and many compromised by choosing Germany's system as a model, for Germany was the odd country out in terms of ending academic selection (see Chapter 2), which, however, was only possible because for over 100 years it had developed a parallel technological élite. The UK had never been prepared to back a rival to the classically oriented sixth form tradition, and if, by the 1980s, the CTC was supposed to achieve this, the plan was soon revealed as grossly miscalculated. It was another development more appropriate to 1945 than 1985, as most industrialists indicated by refusing to fund these colleges when requested (see pages 137–38).

The policies that moved matters on most were those directed across the board at comprehensive education's development like GCSE reform in 1986; and, coming from the Department of Employment rather than the Department of Education, certain vocational initiatives. Most government ministers did not really appreciate the way TVEI, for example, was used to forward comprehensive curriculum goals in a few areas rather than, as they supposed, 'technical' education for those not destined for All Souls. But neither also did many in comprehensive education. The advent of training schemes and the development of work-related education in the wake of rising unemployment in the 1980s often reinforced divisions within the comprehensive schools and it was only a minority that continued to experiment with a comprehensive approach to 16–19 or to TVEI or, later, to develop competence-based assessment in the context of a wider comprehensive initiative from 14 to 19.

Despite the work of this significant comprehensive minority, the goal of an integrated 16–19 sector fell progressively from view as successive Conservative governments made a point of reinforcing 'A' level and strengthening school sixth forms in the name of 'standards', with opted-out schools a key part of the strategy. Their creation promoted the proliferation of small sixth forms (opt-out status often awarded to schools which LEAs wanted to close because their sixth forms were too small). Such a policy was pursued knowing full well such schools were a costly alternative, especially where class sizes were also small, confirmed later by examination of 'A' level teaching costs at various post-16 institutions (OFSTED/Audit Commission, 1993:48–49). One of the Audit Commission's researchers put it bluntly to MP s later : the small sixth in the small school 'is not an economic teaching unit'. What is more, 'it must be repermutating its resources from more junior age groups'[2]. Younger years in secondary education were getting less in situations having to maintain small sixth forms (or small 'A' level teaching groups). The vast majority of sixth form classes still had less than 20 students,and a third had less than 10 – all at a time when class sizes for younger age groups were beginning to grow in size.

Another drawback of the 'gold standard' policy was that almost all schools with sixth forms still had better funding for the years up to 16 than schools without sixth forms, because having 'A' level classes meant a school was more favoured in staffing overall, a manifestly unjust position for the 40% of secondary schools that had no sixth forms. A comprehensive education system should be organised to give each age range comparable funding in its own right.

For all these reasons and many more, during the 1980s the tertiary colleges were particularly active despite the fact that their growth in numbers had been curtailed and they were in an increasingly ambiguous position, sometimes picked out in statistics and research as distinct institutions, sometimes subsumed as part of further education. In one research study comparing the 'broadening' work of schools as against colleges, even though it had been the tertiary college more than any other which had made a point of developing broadening work, tertiary colleges were inexplicably excluded (OFSTED/Audit Commission, 1993:17, 32/33), inevitably sending the message that they were not important enough to look at separately.

However, the attempt to downgrade the tertiary college failed and the main reason was that FE colleges themselves continued to develop in an increasingly 'tertiary' direction. Of all the institutions originally involved in comprehensive provision for the 16–19 age group, the general further education college was probably the one that developed most over the 30 years from 1965 (see Chapter 3 for general profile in 1994 survey). Yet it is the one whose work and potential is still the least well known to so many who concern themselves traditionally with 'A' level education in schools, including those in comprehensive schools.

Comprehensive schools and comprehensive colleges: Changing relations

In the 1960s, FE colleges were there largely to provide 'package' courses for early leavers – in hairdressing or motor mechanics (although some comprehensive schools had links with them). These did not prosper because the aim of the all-through school in those days was to shed such links and become self-contained in their post-16 offering. After 1972 the move was to distance comprehensive schools from further education, particularly in areas like London (Weeks, 1986). Nationally, teachers and sixth formers and their parents often looked down upon the work with which further education was most often associated, including both general studies and vocational education (Dean *et al.*, 1979), for there were fears that links with further education or adopting too much vocational education would lower the status of the comprehensive schools' sixth forms.

In the 1980s, when youth training schemes were being introduced, there was widespread concern in comprehensive schools that 'training' was always in opposition to education, rather than part of it. For years governments underwrote this academic apartheid by taking less interest in what 16 and 17 year olds were doing in the further education sector or in work-related education, in marked contrast to the interest shown in such education in American, far Eastern and most European education systems (Smithers and Robinson, 1991).

But changes were already underway, begun in the early 1970s, when FE colleges became increasingly important through providing full-time commercial and technical courses for school leavers. This provision grew rapidly alongside the original tradition of part-time specialised courses run for local employers. Paradoxically, the 1980s saw an increase in the colleges' 'academic' courses, for during that decade there was a certain amount of conflict with the MSC, the organisation which was given the role of developing youth training schemes and the new work-related learning. It often liaised directly with employers, cutting out the colleges. One FE principal saw this as preferring 'to see the education service playing a minor role' (Pratley, 1983:25). Paradoxically, this spurred the colleges to expand their offering, which this same principal characterised as 'good for those who know what they want and want what they know we provide' but not so good for those who were not yet sure what they want or sure what FE provided (Pratley, 1983:26).

Increasingly, the FE colleges began to let young people know what they had and to approach a greater range of 16-year-old students in a much more individual way. They added to their courses, not just their full-time technical and business qualifications but in the 1970s they built up their 'O' levels and in the 1980s, their 'A' levels. By 1994 it was clear that many general FE colleges considered themselves to be providing comprehensive education for their area's 16–19 group in the same way comprehensive schools' sixth forms and sixth form colleges did – often with a far greater range of learning to offer.

Over 30 years the gap between those coming from sixth forms at 18 and those from FE colleges has progressively narrowed. From the 1980s onwards anecdotal evidence of qualified leavers from schools (and even higher education) who failed to find work, enhanced the status of institutions providing qualifications on vocational courses, particularly related to technological employment. Recessions and the steady loss of employment prospects for young people raised the status of the FE college because what it was seen to offer was employment related. This was aided by propaganda for various youth training schemes during the 1980s, for while the schemes may have been disappointing, the message about updating general skills that can transfer to new jobs, had taken hold widely.

Problems of selectivity and progression at 16–19

When training initiatives tapered off and the MSC was disbanded by the 1990s, colleges were given a major new role in developing the new GNVQ and NVQ work and privatisation gave them an incentive to 'market' themselves more aggressively to students in the 16–19 sector. This brought many back into conflict with sixth forms. For schools, meanwhile, were being encouraged to develop GNVQ courses and to be aggressive themselves. The competitive, privatised 'market' system relied on pitting institutions against each other, when the obvious answer was to pool the developments taking place. Thus college 'independence' also postponed reorganisation on comprehensive lines.

It also increased one of the least attractive aspects of further education, outlined earlier in the 1980s as the tendency to indulge in 'an abuse of counselling' by persuading new students into courses which the colleges themselves happen to run rather than pressing for the means to negotiate the right course for students individually (Pratley, 1983). In a market system few institutions advise students to go elsewhere and while market competition continues to decide entry, this kind of abuse will continue; and not only in colleges. Schools also abuse their counselling responsibilities – sometimes stacking the brochures for the local FE colleges in the cupboard and never handing them out, to make sure students stay with them. Occasional assurances are given nationally that this information is widely available but the market system militates against open choice because all institutions stand to lose substantial funding if real choice is exercised. Only a common system, where courses are jointly run as a public service, can offer this.

Choice was not the only problem. In a competitive free-for-all polarisation becomes a problem and selection creeps back and the more it does the greater the danger that performance-related pay and league tables will make 'teachers less willing to work with less promising students' and render 'institutions serving such students ... doubly disadvantaged' (OFSTED/Audit Commission, 1993:62).What hangs in the balance is how far many sixth forms and colleges can fight being ring-fenced as the 'secondary moderns' of the 16–19 sector because others in the area are selecting or specialising or concentrating solely on academic courses.

League tables and competition in schools are moving education in this direction, and now tables have started in the colleges. Even with value added, tables strengthen hierarchy in an unreformed system, especially when combined with 'value for money' drives. Where 'value added' work on 'A' level entrants dominates the analysis , for example, the pressure in future will be to make sure students are shifted from academic to vocational study and from higher to lower level courses. Ostensibly the motivation is to reduce dropping out, but conclusions between the lines (and sometimes on them) were that only those with GCSE grades A or B should enter any 'A' level course as a general rule in any institution (OFSTED/Audit Commission, 1993:14, 23–34. See also Audit Commission, 1991).

This is a ruling that would seriously curb further education's 'A' level work (and the work of many comprehensive school sixth forms) as well impede the free choice of students. It is a rationalising exercise in the name of 16–19 development that is reminiscent of conclusions which education ministry officials reached in 1945 when they recommended restricting entry to grammar schools as a way of providing for post-war expansion (see page 6). Once official time is spent finding reasons why those with academic aspirations have to be discouraged from pursuing them (rather than offering a means to do so by reorganising the curriculum and assessment or restructuring the institutional framework), it is an indication that all so-called 'reforms' being instituted are not only inadequate, they are dangerously short-sighted.

Another drawback to a selective, 'market' system is the disadvantage for those 40% of comprehensive schools that have no sixth forms. For as yet it is only in a minority of areas that general further education colleges (or tertiary or sixth form colleges) are organised as integral parts of an all-through comprehensive system in relation to 11–16 schools individually in the same area (see Chapter 3). 'Independence' has made such organisation all but impossible for many, as the FEFC does not perceive FE colleges as integral parts of all-through education which starts in schools, but as isolated and competing institutions. In its first report only one example of collaboration between schools and colleges is given, a temporary arrangement for engineering study (FEFC, 1994: para. 51). There is nothing about co-operation between schools and colleges other than a statement that the links between FE colleges and schools are 'often cordial' (while elsewhere acknowledging this is not always so). There is nothing about the role of colleges or sixth form/college consortia in providing the all-through experience from early secondary years to 19 for schools ending at 16. Nor in most inspection reports on 11–16 schools is there any assessment of 'ongoing' provision after 16 for their leavers. National reports have almost nothing to say about *system* coherence across the 14/16–19 years.

Recent changes as part of the new 'independence' and market orientation have not only risked pouring FE colleges into a secondary modern mould, they have seriously disrupted the democratic development of colleges themselves by tending to restrict so many to a 'business' remit rather than encouraging an independent community role (see Chapter 8). The Charter for Further Education puts emphasis on 'employers' and top businessmen as if they were first-class citizens and all others second-class.

Against these developments are those that have been going on for 30 years in quite another direction, where all institutions in the 16–19 age group are converging in a communal spirit, spurred by a wish to provide comprehensively for the whole age group. FE colleges have developed both more 'A' level work and more vocational work for 16–19 but they have also developed upwards to degree level – by franchising the first year (or two) of degree courses in co-operation with local universities. A few colleges may be so advanced they are about to be incorporated into universities; while at the other end some are still providers of quite restricted occupational courses to local industry. The majority in the middle are developing as mainstays of a comprehensive 16–19 sector, broadly based and offering a wide range of learning.

But not every area in the country has such a college as yet. The task in future is to ensure that after 16 all have access to such a range of learning, so that in time there would be a network of comprehensive colleges spanning the country, well placed to co-operate with the sixth forms of their areas in providing fully for the 16–19 age group in a new tertiary system (see also Chapter 3).

Work-related education, the third tradition

Further and Tertiary Education colleges are also pivotal for having the closest relationship to that third group of young people that comprehensive education from 16–19 includes: those whose education is part time or related specifically to their job or profession.

Schools and colleges developing comprehensive education may be able to envisage vocational and academic education within the same institution, even their integration in a new curriculum and assessment system, but the majority are not yet thinking in terms of accommodating occupationally-related education – or job training – into the 'comprehensive' canon for 16–19. Or, if they are, not on the same terms or in the same system. Yet no comprehensive education for this age group could be complete without their full inclusion and without the inclusion of those in the age group studying part time, whether their learning is related to work or not.

Part-time students and trainees are not a small group. Throughout the 1980s the numbers of young people on training schemes roughly equalled the numbers of their contemporaries in the sixth forms of schools. The number studying part-time on their own initiative in this age group was claimed as a 'quiet revolution' and estimated by the mid-1990s to be nearing 150,000 (Finn, 1995). A greater number have been moving to full-time education and this is a trend to be encouraged. But for the foreseeable future some will be studying on their own or working at jobs already secured and learning in colleges on certain days of the week only; others will always opt (or be forced) to be trained on the job, including those on schemes without promise (or even hope) of a job. Those undertaking education on their own initiative at this age and beyond will also probably increase in number. Yet if they were unemployed in 1994, they were forbidden to study more than 21 hours (later reduced to 16) or lose their benefit, surely one of the restrictions that will shame this era in future eyes almost more than any other.

Those trying to study part-time saw themselves as particularly second class. Yet the future of education will belong to the part-time student as much as to the full-timer. After 18 part-time numbers will grow, as people learn to take their education in stages through life, accumulating their learning as it is needed, regardless of profession or trade (Robinson, 1986, 1994). Meanwhile, it is a struggle to make sure part-time learners command the same level of teaching care for the hours they are learning and the same access to the same facilities as those studying full-time. At the time of the 1994 survey there were many indications that their education was not equal in many of these respects (see, for example, FEFC, 1994a: para. 57).

The rise of 'training' education

The spotlight first fell on 'trainees' when a Labour government began shaming schools for not producing students with basic skills in 1976, partly in response to media clamour to deal with so-called declining standards. In the event standards turned out not to have declined but this did not prevent comprehensive schools being used as scapegoats for other national failures, like those of employers (Finegold, 1993:42). Compared with other countries there had not been much improvement in the quality and extent of the training employers managed to provide for both youth and adults.

But the system too had its failures, for too many students were still confined to that sector of secondary education where no effective learning targets or qualifications had ever been set officially: the 'bottom 40%'. As many now realise, the real blame should have been shared between the still unreformed curriculum and assessment system (despite comprehensive reorganisation) and those employers still unable to carry their share of training – not to mention an economic system that could not provide work for everyone. As the state of the economy clarified from the late 1970s onwards, unemployment (at first thought to be temporary) turned out to be a permanent structural feature of 'advanced' societies, resulting from the restructuring of the world economy, as western and global-national corporations began to take advantage of world development and its lower labour costs. This was an altogether bigger crisis and one to which education as a whole has not yet fully responded.

Meanwhile, in the late 1970s and 1980s, governments responded in the short term by introducing schemes of 'training', including those for 16 year olds. These schemes were originally endorsed by trade unions and employers alike, and welcomed at a time when all were encouraged to believe unemployment was only temporary. Work on the development of new transferable skills, usable throughout life, had seemed highly promising and good standards in this respect were built in to several early training schemes. Even more important, a promising sketch of future developments, linking these with far-reaching changes in the education of the whole 16-plus age group, was available from the Further Education Unit in the positive and far-seeing document, *A Basis for Choice*, published in 1979.

But the FEU principles were not applied comprehensively, they were applied selectively. They were applied to those in vocational education only, including increasing numbers of training schemes emerging that were highly flawed in both principle and in practice. The best known was the Youth Training Scheme (YTS) supposedly developing learning through work and knowledge-based qualifications, but often deteriorating into dead-end, low-level general jobbing. The best of YTS (representing only a fraction of schemes) were still the training schemes run by the big corporations which had their own in-house programmes, where entry could be even more selective than the 11-plus in the schools system. Many such schemes merely reproduced the characteristics of the old apprenticeship so dominated by young white males from skilled working-class backgrounds (a profile seen later in the 1990s in some of the 'modern apprenticeship' programmes).

Every sort of concession and bribe was offered to employers, to get them interested in providing high level programmes (and work to follow) for young people, but without much success. Even had there been work available, the schemes were a pre-comprehensive-education solution to post-16 education that pandered to the traditional British employer's long history of looking at training as a burden and not as an investment (Coopers and Lybrand, *A Challenge to Complacency*, 1985). Employers with short-term outlooks saw youth training schemes as a chance to get free labour rather than a chance to train their future workforce, and successive governments made it all too easy for them to do so. The lucky youngsters were those hand picked by employers taking a longer view, who saw training as a chance to improve society's share of skilled workers as well as the status and skills of their own workforce. But there were not many such employers. In 1994 less than half the larger employers with over 500 workers, and only 6% employing less than 50, were offering NVQ training for any age group (FEFC, 1994a:58).

The pre-comprehensive training schemes had other troubles as well. Racism was prompting calls for monitoring of black trainees (CRE, 1984) in the same way as there were calls for monitoring of streaming or setting in schools, to see if black young people were being 'disproportionately allocated' to any streams, courses or schemes 'which do not serve to provide for their realistic aspirations' (Duncan, 1986).

Sexism was another pitfall, for young women in work-related education during the 1980s were often herded into stereotyped occupational 'families' within a narrow range of 'female' caring and service work (see also Blackman and Holland, 1990; Brown et al., 1985; Weiner, 1985). This was in sharp contrast to the way 'academic' girls in schools at this time were competing increasingly well with boys, passing them by in achievements at several levels and enlarging the areas of learning where they felt free to compete. However, academic improvement in schools was disproportionately found in middle-class girls' performances, while, needless to say, the numbers of young people from middle-class backgrounds on training schemes – boys or girls, black or white – was small. In some ways it could be said that young people on youth schemes were a mirror-image of those on 'A' level courses at the other end of the 16–19 spectrum.

Dead ending in the 1990s

Gradually young people and their families became disillusioned with training schemes, increasingly entered as the only way to survive at 16, since measures had been taken to withdraw benefits and lower allowances for those who did not wish to take up dead-end schemes. Despite some bright islands of good practice, overall it was a 'crude experiment in social engineering' to discipline the workforce for the market (Finn, 1983). Hence the continuing education of a large number of young people became entangled disastrously with government policy to drive down wages, drive up profits, and undermine workforce bargaining so that jobs could be replaced by new technology. Training policy also involved attacks on the financial autonomy of local authorities, the privatising of public services, the freeing of employers from legislative constraints (like those relating to safety and most of the race and sex discrimination acts) and the 'pricing of the young back to work' by ensuring that by the time they were adults they would be thoroughly conditioned to accept intermittent work at low pay (since it was all employers could offer them). In short, the majority of young people on training schemes perceived themselves to be exploited rather than advanced. Very few thought of the experience as education.

The public education service initially entered into the cause of improving work-related education for students outside the 'academic' courses, but as the 1980s continued, deep scepticism followed. For a start, public education had to mark time as governments gave an increasing number of contracts for 16–19 education and training to private agencies, many with 'questionable educational and financial credentials', rather than build up courses of quality in public colleges. A training scheme in a private agency was 'cheaper than its education-based alternatives', which appealed to the government, as did the fact that it was 'shifting the balance of the resources (and) control towards employers and away from the public services in the post-compulsory sector' (Evans, 1991:58).

However, success even in the modest YTS venture required private industry to do the work 'voluntarily' and by 1990 it had been acknowledged even in parliamentary committees that voluntarism had failed once again (see Richardson, 1993:20). YTS was run down and from

1991 replaced by Youth Training, where places for new trainees were progressively cut from 389,000 in 1988 to about 275,000 in 1993. Eventually, the firm guarantee of a place on a training scheme for every school leaver who wanted one (long promised by the government) was not able to be met – a broken promise that occasioned little mainstream comment. It is interesting to speculate what might have been the reaction if thousands of young people with GCSE passes had suddenly been told that there were not enough 'A' level courses in the system to offer them a place.

As youth training schemes contracted, in 1989 the CBI's Task Force argued for the idea of training credits, a pre-emptive strike against any attempt by governments to require employers to pay a training levy. The Conservative Government then launched the 'voucher' into the education system in yet another attempt to get employers moving by using trainees' 'choice' as a catalyst. By the mid-1990s take-up of training credits by the school leavers was slow and the scheme's profile was low (see pages 78–79) – basically because the system still offered nothing for young people to choose from, its purchasing power illusory (Unwin, 1993) in a market-led system where employers picked trainees not trainees' education and training.

The 'bottom 40%'-approach remained and was underlined by the totally divided curriculum and assessment system that still prevailed from 16 to 19. Occupationally related education was being offered only to the 'least able and articulate' school leavers, that group of students which occupied that end of the 16–19 spectrum where the pitfalls of a system with so many selective hurdles still seemed the most pronounced. Britain's 16–19 education system at the time of the 1994 survey was still as one observer had characterised it earlier, one which ensured 'independence and creativity for the upper strata; passivity, dependency and conformity for the lower' (quoted in Evans, 1991:59).

In the year of the survey thousands of young people of 16–19 had no jobs, no training, no income, no education. Yet they were as much a part of the 16–19 age group as the same-age students who were earning qualifications in schools or colleges or learning skills on the job. Possibly, they are comprehensive education's most exacting test, for comprehensive reform of the 16–19 sector will not be successfully completed until these young people are offered inclusion within the system on the same terms as anyone else, with the same rights, the same quality of oversight, and the same facilities and standards applied to their learning.

This is why all oversight and all resources relating to education for the 16–19 age group should be shifted back to the public education service as soon as possible – with all funding for work-related education transferred to local or regional education budgets (from TECs and LECs) so that work-related learning can be overseen by the democratically elected. TECs and LECs, meanwhile, can either be wound up, as many have suggested, or be left to concentrate upon the 'E' for 'enterprise' of their title, which many of them would prefer. This move would permit the learning of all 16 and 17 year olds to be unified within a single comprehensive system. Only when all learning for the age group is administered as one can everyone in the age group perceive their own learning as having equal value within the system.

Curriculum and assessment reform, 16–19. Qualifications: the cure

If the Government was standing still in 1994 over long-term curriculum and assessment reform for comprehensive education, it was by no means standing still in the short term. Since the late 1980s it had been making changes to boost participation within the system, including enlarging the number and nature of higher education institutions – in the hope that increasing numbers would stay in the system and proceed to degree-level work. At the other end of the spectrum, having disciplined the workforce to its satisfaction, it seemed readier to accept the advice of its industrial wing that education-led change should have priority over low-level training schemes when it came to the supply side of work-related education.

Within a short time the government suggested it had found the answer: qualifications. Qualifications were to be the cure because everyone wanted them and everyone should now be able to have them in the secondary system – as passports to higher education, the professions, and to jobs.

When, nearly 30 years earlier, Sweden began organising work-related education for young people from 16 to 19, it set up a Royal Commission (reporting in 1974) which eventually led to special local committees to organise the new learning: each one composed of LEA representatives, employers, trade unions, and teachers, making sure work-related education related to general education preparation up to 19, and fitted well into the new modularised post-16 curriculum in the comprehensive education system being developed at the same time.

Britain's approach was very different. First came the introduction of its version of the USA's private industry councils (PICs) – to be called TECs and in Scotland, LECs – but without the comprehensive college system that was the essential support of the American Councils' work. Not only was there no comprehensive system in the UK at this age as yet, there was not even a coherent system of vocational qualifications. Earlier training programmes of the 1980s had been heavily criticised for their divorce from academic education. Governments had been warned to avoid further changes 'not embracing all in a single framework' (Farley, 1986:149).

Second, therefore, came this new framework, created at lightning speed by revamping vocational qualifications, asking existing awarding bodies to work together so that courses like business education from the City and Guilds (CGLI), the Royal Society of Arts (RSA), or the Business and Technical Education Council (BTEC) could be converted into a single new course. Occupational fields without existing awards – like tourism and leisure – would have new courses created for them. All vocational qualifications, new and old, would be whittled down to two: the National Vocational Qualification (NVQ; SVQ in Scotland), which was occupationally specific, and designed to be obtained mainly in the workplace, and the GNVQ (SNVQ in Scotland), described as 'a new type of vocational qualification for such young people' as 'want to stay in education full time after 16 but are not ready to commit themselves to a specific occupation' (OFSTED, 1993:16) .

This OFSTED description was a typically negative way of describing what – in a comprehensive reform – could have been a positive and major aspect of a many-faceted drive to develop the talents of the whole age group. But at least there was a hint at progression, for the new system was to have several levels, ranging from basic pre-GCSE standard up to degree level equivalent. Even if the equivalence was questionable, this provision fulfilled one of the main criteria of any comprehensive curriculum: to have a coherent route upwards covering all levels of attainment.

Integrating learning

The success of the change was put in instant doubt by the failure to integrate the new qualifications with existing academic education. Although Scotland was already working on integrating Highers, 'A' levels were omitted from the new framework in England. There was no attempt (as in other countries) to undertake a comprehensive reform of curriculum and assessment for the age group as a whole, or to eliminate separate tracks and early specialisation; or to reorganise the system institutionally on comprehensive lines after 16 to eliminate selection at 16 plus.

This was not a single new framework of qualifications for the age group, as comprehensive education would have required; it was merely the reorganisation of existing vocational qualifications, 'raising the esteem of vocational education within the existing dual track' (Richardson, 1993:19) or, as others put it, just another attempt to 'reproduce (the) different and divisive traditions' of schools and colleges (Spours, 1993:81). This was simply a 'new way of separating higher and lower ability pupils'; and in the long run the negative relationships of a divided qualifications system, fragmented and competing institutions, and low level demands from a weakened labour market, threatened still to keep Britain trapped in a low-achievement, low-skill system. The NVQ in particular was merely reinforcing 'the low skills equilibrium' of the UK by being used as a means to absorb existing qualifications (Spours, 1993), 'the centralisation of power to remedy market failure' (Finegold, 1993:49).

There were endless implementation difficulties relating to the quality and nature of the new qualifications, already set out in Chapter 2, including doubts about lack of quality, choice, and coherence; and about failure to encourage 'cognitive competence' on the new NVQ courses. To these were added fears about inadequate development of core skills, poor funding, slow take-up, high drop-out, weak monitoring, inconsistency in GNVQ assessment across centres and a host of other accreditation problems (see pages 69–77). These included endless doubts about equivalence and whether GNVQ level 2 was equal to four or five GCSEs and if so, at A–G or A–C (see OFSTED, 1993:35/36); or what was required to start on level 3 or advanced courses, for if it took a year longer for a vocational student to reach university entrance level qualifications, was this really equivalent? Research suggested most university admissions tutors were also confused or doubtful about GNVQ[3] and the gloomiest outlook from critics was that 'students will continue to fail in droves' (Spours, 1993:168).

To compound the difficulties, the new structure was rushed into being with only nominal consultations (though this was not unusual for Conservative governments at this time), the plan being for problems to be ironed out once courses had started. Many of them have been ironed out (albeit by loading extra work on to already hard-pressed lecturers in colleges and teachers in schools), but much deeper faults were then revealed, including continuing failure, inherent in any market approach, to commit the nation to 'institutional collaboration to ensure a range of progression routes is available to students' (Spours, 1993:168). This concern was bad enough but another was even more ominous, even if it took longer to emerge. It involved the development of the capacity for critical enquiry in those who are in work-related learning, the essence of education. Support for such development was noticed to be ominously absent from most of the emerging vocational courses by one critic after another who saw no attempt to encourage (or even allow) students to look at their vocation or profession in any social or economic context at all, summarised as 'the increasing trend to expunge critical analysis of contemporary society from vocational education' (Green and Rikowski, 1995). If anything would set the qualifications cure on a course to ultimate failure (and render it incompatible with comprehensive education's principles as well as thoroughly unattractive to higher education) it would be locating vocational learning in some kind of thought-compound, failing to accord its learners the academic freedom those on 'academic' courses have always enjoyed.

The root of the difficulty was that the 'reform' was not really a reform; it was a new exercise in parallelism rather than an integration of academic and vocational study within a single system. It was a mechanistic half-way stage, comparable to the introduction of CSE in 1964 at 14-plus, where 'equivalence' was only at Grade 1 to GCE 'O' level rather than through a unified curriculum and assessment system. It was also comparable to the introduction of SCOTVEC NC modules in 1984, a successful experiment whose major fault was recognised in good time in Scotland and need not have been repeated in England and Wales: the failure to integrate it with the academic course and the increasing limitations this imposed on course coherence for the entire age group (Raffe, 1993:63). Yet repeat it the new plan did in England, proposing new vocational qualifications to run alongside the old academic course (or whatever replaces it) for the indefinite future, despite the certain knowledge that everyday pressure to integrate vocational and academic study will increase in the same way it did on the CSE/'O' level system for all 20 years of its existence.

Nevertheless, GNVQs and NVQs were a meaningful change. However inadequate and problematic and narrow – and many were all three – the response was dramatic in both schools and colleges and signified real change. Thousands of students took to them at once, as they once did to CSEs, revealing the enormous vacuum that the education system had concealed for so long through its obsession with the narrow, subject-centred 'A' level course as the only academic discipline worthy of the name for this age group.

One of the outcomes of the change will be increased pressure for full comprehensive development after 16, if only because it has increased fears that a new two-tier arrangement was being developed, triggered by the old promise of 'parity of esteem' made in several speeches by Prime Minister John Major in 1992. He used the very words used on behalf of secondary modern schools in 1945, the CSE in 1964, and comprehensive schools in areas with coexisting grammar schools at every stage ever since. The track record of the phrase was poor and dented the impact of the simultaneous suggestion that there should be a single new over-arching diploma given to all who completed courses at 18.

Pressure for assessment change over 30 years

One reason two-tier systems failed before 16 was because they could not take account of radical changes taking place in the system overall, not only in curriculum and institutional reorganisation but in assessment practice as well. The introduction of vocational changes after 16 in the early 1990s increased pressure for reform of assessment, another pressure that had accompanied comprehensive education from the start.

Pressure began modestly in the 1970s, for example, when a few schools experimented with records of personal achievement, approaches to learning that encouraged students to record all activities in which they were proficient, not just their 'marks' in a few external exams. One of the earliest experiments of achievement-based learning was on behalf of pupils excluded from academic courses in schools in Swindon. It was called a Record of Personal Achievement (RPA) and was developed in Swindon's Curriculum Study and Development Centre, where it systematically set out 'to give the pupil an incentive of the kind given to academic pupils by an examination'. It was intended to 'show what the pupils has achieved in various fields of activity' – both in and out of school, a wholly 'new qualification' based on personal qualities and capabilities (Stansbury, 1971:16).

Nowadays such Records of Personal Achievement are more sophisticated and the principle has developed further – for example, in the Youth Award Scheme in 1994 there were over 1,200 schools and colleges with over 80,000 students working on various levels of achievement offered by the Award Scheme Development and Accreditation Network (ASDAN). These involved awards from 14 to 18 in fields like health, the environment, sport, home management, world of work, community and the expressive arts. Such a programme offers radical new routes to raising levels of achievement; and not just for students. For 'classroom teachers and lecturers ... it offers ... the opportunity to draw on their own experience and judgement in designing and implementing programmes of activities ... at a time when some feel their very professionalism is under critical scrutiny' (Crombie White *et al.*, 1995:20).

In the 1990s developing the academic side of such courses offered the same kind of freedom found by many teachers in the Mode III CSE work, where course work was first developed. Course work was one of the most positive changes of the decade in terms of raising standards (perversely curtailed by a Conservative government as a threat to 'standards' in the early nineties). Such work would continue to be an essential part of the 16–19 curriculum in any fully developed comprehensive system, even though nationally the Record of Achievement folios, when they came into being in the UK in 1991, were often limited in practice to those at lower attainment levels.

Like so many other reforms introduced in the wake of comprehensive education, the new assessment was never intended to be confined to one group; achievement-based change was intended to free *all* students from the narrow over-academicism of the nineteenth century, which still lingered on in too many twentieth century school programmes. Its 'formative in function' approach – based on doing rather than factual recall – had some of its roots in the work of those trying to reform the secondary curriculum in the United States in the 1960s, where educators like Jerome Bruner and his colleagues had become concerned for students across the whole attainment range imprisoned by 'academic skills' and turned off by the academic curriculum's incapacity to move on from tight, subject-based teaching that required knowledge 'committed to memory and tested by the usual means' (Bruner, 1970:12).

Bruner's conclusions led him to distinguish between 'something that one "knows about" and something "one knows how to"', an earlier version of the debate that developed in Britain in the 1990s in relation to vocational competence between criterion and norm-referenced learning (see Chapter 2). Bruner too was concerned to encourage testing by 'competence' but within traditional academic, subject-based learning, in order to move such teaching away from merely memorising facts. In physics, for example, facts about physics were intrinsically meaningless; study should move towards the idea of 'doing physics' instead. In 1995 the authors of the RSA proposals for 14–19 used much the same phrase when making their own distinction between 'the "knowing that" of theoretical knowledge as against the "knowing how" of practical knowledge', while arguing the same point in relation to reform of the curriculum and assessment system in the UK: that there can no longer be any 'justification for the proposed dualism between the academic and vocational' when it comes to curriculum design for 16–19 (Crombie White *et al.*, 1995: para. 1.4).

'Doing physics is what physics instruction should be about', wrote Bruner, because teaching at all levels should be about how 'to make the subject your own ... part of your own thinking – whether physics, history (or) ways of looking at painting' (Bruner, 1970:15). It is about 'competence as the objective of education', about problem solving, enabling young people to 'operate ... upon the world' not only by motor skills in learning to operate a computer but 'operate in a parallel fashion upon that world as it is encoded in language and other more specialised symbol systems' common in all the academic disciplines. Learning to be competent in operating upon the world is what makes learning meaningful, 'not the assurance that some day you will make more money or have more prestige'. It gives students at all levels an objective for their learning and is not confined to those selected for high-flying work. This being so, a system of counselling is needed to make sure 'that the learner knows what he is up to and that he has some hand in choosing the goal' because, above all, 'learning IS individual, no matter how many pupils there are per teacher' (Bruner, 1970).

Other significant pressures for change
In time new thinking of this kind spread through the system in Britain, with special relevance for the older secondary years, looking for ways to integrate vocational education with existing academic methods. One such development was sparked by TVEI, that rare Conservative initiative that did not seek to direct how funding would be spent, but left it to schools and colleges to innovate. Schools with no ideas used it predictably to fund lower stream work for those not destined for academic routes; but a few enlightened ones used it for innovations they had long been planning in respect of everyone's education. One was the Wessex Project (building on GCSE with a 60% core and four modules) that ran from 1987 to 1993 (Rainbow, 1993). Although originally a development for 14–16, it was soon obvious it was just as relevant for 16–19, a development which would be 'satisfying, varied and marketable ... not institution-dependent' and one that would 'not ... rigidly track students into specialisms or narrowly vocational programmes' (Plaskow, 1989).

The 16–19 model was developed when five LEAs co-operated in

modularising 'A' level with core and integration of vocational and academic education, incorporating NVQs. The work promoted continuous assessment and autonomy in learning. But its developers were forced to conclude that no further progress could be made because 'a national framework for credit accumulation and transfer' is required first, so there could be 'true parity of esteem' and full development of this new form of education (Rainbow, 1993:92, 95, 99). Elements from this experiment influenced a number of reform proposals in several think-tanks, including the IPPR and the RSA, where the translation of academic and vocational education into modular formats had the common progression and accreditation that characterises so many proposals for change. But TVEI funding ended and Wessex work was put on hold. Like the tertiary college in the institutional field, it was an important initiative that was mothballed – simply because official encouragement for the comprehensive reform had lapsed.

Many comprehensive schools, therefore, in the absence of any national lead, inevitably accepted that their work at 16–19 in the 1980s and early 1990s, was to strive to excel within the narrow range of options set out in the divided framework still prevailing. They tried to follow the political leaders' exhortation on standards and dedicated themselves to the competitive model of schooling with the aim of bringing more of their pupils up to GCSE five A–C standard, and thereafter building up better percentage pass rates at 'A' level. These were the 'important' qualifications, made all the more important by becoming the criteria for ranking in the new league tables. Some comprehensive schools also welcomed opting out in a world where, 'frankly ... competition is the name of the game and the school which rejects the notion is unlikely to survive' (Halls-Dickerson, 1989:27). Others, having resisted 'market competition' as inimical to a comprehensive purpose, reluctantly entered the 'results fray' to escape censure (Barker, 1995).

Most comprehensive schools were willing to look at vocational education but only as a separate alternative to 'A' levels. Nevertheless, once any school begins running vocational courses alongside academic ones, issues that require resolution begin presenting themselves. It was the same with schools that established links with industry during the 1980s, providing areas of work-related learning. For this link, forged between education and the world of work, fuelled another important development for comprehensive education, one which had not been present in the 1960s or most of 1970s. In fact, until the Great Debate work experience was seen as rather squalid. It was mainly with the start of the Schools

Council Industry Project in 1981 in 26 LEAs and the work of the Centre for the Study of Comprehensive Schools (with finance from industry setting up more links, including 14 with teacher education colleges), that the issue of work itself finally got a foothold in the education of the upper years of secondary education.

Transforming learning: further proposals from comprehensive experience

All these changes that had been taking place within the comprehensive world (despite the hierarchy of institutions and divisions in curriculum and assessment) not only continued to encourage a mix and match of vocational and academic subjects in the later 1980s and 1990s, they continued to spur new developments in integration from 16 to 19 that could unify the learning of the whole age group, and lead to the transformation of learning itself.

Their antecedents had been around for some time. For example, some groups had long worked on the idea of a common 'core' of learning, wherein programmes could be developed within the academic curriculum itself, expanding to include everyone in the age group. Others started inside the new vocational initiatives with a view to expanding these common elements for both the general education sections of colleges and related training schemes, as well as in the sixth forms of schools. Many common core proposals in the early 1980s were designed to deal imaginatively and rigorously with transferable skills and IT training, English, maths, and social and personal education for everyone after 16 (Mitchell, 1983; Warwick, 1983). Some made these 'cores' part of the New Sixth, others introduced them through progressive TVEI work which set up modules to be applied across the curriculum from English to social studies to mathematics to business studies (Green and Poat, 1983).

In schools and colleges that pursued the 'core' idea, in-house courses were developed for everyone in the year group. One, developed in a sixth form college, dealt with civic rights, the media, money, and personal relationships, all being essential matters, claimed its headteacher, 'too important for any student ... in a free society to be allowed to neglect' (Warwick, 1983). Within FE colleges one general education practitioner advanced a model for a post-16 'general education' core that included study skills, IT, basic maths and language work, basic science (to teach scientific method), practice in democratic procedures and decision making (like formal debating), media education, basic economics and labour process theory, including an understanding of trade unions, as well as anti-racist and anti-sexist education (Waugh, 1989).

In the 1980s other comprehensive schools were experimenting with additional single courses in the sixth year of education, to be taken by everyone, whether they were on academic or vocational routes. The City and Guilds 365 was sometimes used(Mitchell, 1983); so was the General Education A/S level. Equally important were new approaches through 'negotiated' learning and counselling and self directed study, regardless of whether the study was in common or not, and regardless of whether individual students were 'academic' or 'vocational' (distinctions that were found to be increasingly meaningless by an increasing number of schools and colleges developing common courses or cores).

The idea of a core continues to have resonance with the 'core' developments for the new vocational education (NCC, 1990; NCVQ, 1990) and the many 'supplementary studies' which 16–19 institutions continue to offer for those on academic courses (and which are reckoned to add 15% cost to most 16 plus budgets (OFSTED, 1993:18, 39)). But the core idea is now itself divided into academic and vocational sides, and until a decision to integrate academic and vocational education is made, the idea of a 'core' for the age group as a whole will continue to mark time.

Convergence of institutional styles

During the two decades before 1994 institutions also began to reassess their administration styles in preparation for the future integration of the 16–19 age group in a more comprehensive direction. This meant that sixth forms and FE colleges were converging even where there was no formal liaison.

One Head of Sixth Form Studies thought this had been inevitable since 1974, the date when the colleges started up commercial, services-related qualifications courses on a full-time basis, and accelerated when they began enlarging their own 'O' and 'A' level work. They would soon be doing all that schools would be doing, once they had learned to develop some of the values schools had. These were seen as coming from schools as learning institutions defined as a community (*Gemeinschaft*) with 'relationships that were intimate, affective, enduring, voluntary and essentially moral'. Schools in turn soon saw they would profit by developing those strengths more common to the FE colleges, which saw themselves as an institution defined as an 'association' (*Gesellschaft*), where relationships were voluntary, partial, contractual and instrumental' (Green, 1989:20).

The convergence was set to continue because increasingly school teachers were 'having to practise seeing their own subject specialisms as means to a vocational end'; while on the other hand, FE colleges lecturers were having to develop more 'individualised and student-centred' provision for their own learners, including encouragement of their skills of critical enquiry, traditionally confined to those on academic courses.

No matter which of the many traditions is examined in relation to 16–19 education, we can see the way new curriculum initiatives, institutional development, and methods of assessment – all previously separated within a divided system – became increasingly closely interwoven during the 30 years of comprehensive reform after 1965.

Whether we look at change from the point of view of schools or of colleges or of academic education or work-related education, a major recasting of the curriculum and assessment system is not only desirable, it is already taking place informally. The unifying thread is once more 'common' development – the 'same for all' in the sense that it would have a curriculum organised on common principles, a system organised with common pathways and assessment organised with common criteria – and the education of everyone valued equally.

Work – the last selective barrier

The next stage of the Government's cure by qualifications for 16–19 has yet to be produced – dealing with 'A' levels (and in Scotland, finalising the new Highers) and the way these will relate to vocational courses. Whatever the relationship turns out to be, it will end up forcing further reforms in access, progression, certification and transfer – away from a divided system and towards a more common one, away from selection, tracking and separation and towards unified learning where differentiation by individual needs and aspirations can be accommodated without traditional 'selective' practices.

The problem for those supporting comprehensive education is that while divisions may be opposed, there has not been general agreement about the changes that would serve best, especially where it comes to the relationship of academic and work-related courses. The issue has never had the chance to be fully debated; the Great Debate launched in 1976 has never really taken place. Indeed, comprehensive educators were often separated after this time, where, simply because of its exploitative nature and low-level quality, some saw most work-related education and training as a lesser form of education, or some sort of secondary modern stream that was opposed to 'real' comprehensive sixth form work. Many taking this view were the keenest supporters of comprehensive education, yet ignorant of work-related traditions outside the sixth form. As Ken Jones wrote in 1983, 'the left has taken too little notice of work related education'.

At the same time, others, no less committed to full comprehensive education for this age group, were hunting avidly within YTS developments for initiatives that could be used as a base to develop new forms of learning for all – as well as exploring new forms of intelligence that the existing system has ignored. They were often ignorant of the problems developing within the sixth forms of schools. Slowly, however, contacts were made and numbers grew who saw the way the two worlds would have to be integrated, and the changes that would have to take place as a result of bringing together learning that was knowledge based and 'knowing what' – with learning that was based on competence and 'knowing how'.

The segregation of work-related education in the 1980s

In the early 1980s the groups already trying for this synthesis were small but none the less enthusiastic about the 'great achievement' this new approach to learning represented, where 'for the first time ... the unity of education and training is formally acknowledged and the world of work is part of the scheme of things' (Kaufman, 1984). What such educators deplored about the new approach, however, was the way the government of the day had implemented the principles solely in relation to the narrow youth training programmes rather than applying it to the education of the whole age group. They deplored the fact that 'the strengthening of the vocational element is ... being seen in the narrow sense of job preparation rather than preparation for adult life and the world of work' for *everyone* (Kaufman, 1984). They wanted it education-led, not employer-led. They saw the comprehensive approach hijacked; they also saw it subject to commercial competition, so that learning was no longer about improving the quality of life and reorienting society but was given narrow aims instead, dictated by employers' short-term interests.

These complaints about narrowness of vision and experience were a mirror image of those already given for 'A' level at the other end of the 16–19 qualifications system by many who had no knowledge of vocational education but who had long believed 'A' level study was too narrow and too specialist to survive. Those in a position to see both ends, such as Fred Flower, principal of Kingsway College of Further Education, were the most stringent critics of the proposals for vocational education. Flower had taken one look at YTS and declared, 'This is never going to work' because a training scheme, no matter how good, serves but one section of the age group: 'It cuts them off and is in turn cut off from the rest of 16 to 19' (Flower, 1983:21).

Along with others, Flower was particularly distressed that the landmark work, *A Basis for Choice* (FEU, 1979) had been so traduced. This had developed the ideas of transferable skills and guidance, where a common core was coherently explored and proposals made for carefully structured, modular learning, backed by a clear pedagogy for post-school education. The Further Education Unit had set out clearly the way education could be restructured to cover a range of levels of performance for 'anyone thought able to benefit', but the impact of its work was thoroughly blunted by being translated into a narrow vocational certificate which specifically excluded 'those who have the potential to take two or more 'A' levels' as well as those who might need 'remedial help'. It had been devised as a guide to transform the education of the whole age group (and, as such, had close affinities to the HMI work on areas of curriculum entitlement for the 11–16 age group that was going on at the time) but was not subsequently used for this purpose. The same could be said about *A Basis for Credit* 10 years later (FEU, 1992). By the 1990s for some, the drive to widen the forms of assessment had picked up much more momentum and had moved beyond credit accumulation and transfer in a unified modular system. Some were now arguing that the whole basis of assessment had to change:

> so long as achievement is based on the learner's ranking in relation to the norm rather than their capacity in relation to agreed criteria, obstacles will remain to prevent...achievement...by all but a small elite of learners.
>
> (Morris, 1993:129)

The future of work
Those at both ends of the 16–19 education system deplored the failure of formal reforms to acknowledge the need for a unified system and an integrated curriculum, accompanied by integrated assessment arrangements that enabled all forms of intelligence and attainment to be recorded and promoted. However, economic forces and the requirements of the roller-coaster economy – now insisting on new approaches to work itself – ironically ensured that the issue of 'work' would not be segregated from education, as it had been in the past, particularly the learning of the so-called 'academic' student. Nor could it be confined to providing meaningful schemes for trainees, for it applied to everyone going through education, all of whom will eventually go into work and all of whom will

relate their learning to their work in some way – not just at 16–19 but throughout their lives. The prospects for integrating education have been revolutionised by admitting work to the equation, no longer just occupational training for the less academic but educating everyone to do the tasks required to run their societies, to make what these need, to provide their services, and to further cultural development in all its forms.

Thus a major contribution of the 16–19 sector, so central to comprehensive education reform, is in denting that last great selective barrier, the one that selects for work. The same economic and social changes that are widening the gap between rich and poor are also changing irrevocably the division between the 'thinking classes' who monopolise the professions and the rest of the workforce. In the short term, prospects for the poor and for vocational learners may seem bleak but access in the long term could dramatically improve – partly under the impact of the new technology that makes information available to all, partly through pressure for more open learning systems that makes learning more accessible, and partly through economic demand upskilling the economy. These changes will take place even if the 'reformation of social classes and the restructuring of work organisations and the state (are) ... accelerating economic decline' (Ainley, 1995:54).

For the first time in almost two centuries there is the possibility of our society reshaping itself democratically because there is the possibility of reshaping work itself. The changes in 16–19 education and the expansion of further and higher education in Britain 'may present itself as professionalisation of the proletariat but in the reality of education without jobs and hyper-inflation of qualifications it is really a proletarianisation of the professions' (Ainley, 1995). Thus 'expansion is ... unstoppable' regardless of what governments do. The twenty-first century should see comprehensive education followed in time by comprehensive work.

A new tertiary system: Institutional reform

Qualifications are vital but they are not the sole cure. New methods of assessment are required but they are only as good as the curriculum which they accompany. And there is still the matter of institutional reorganisation.

At the start of the reform in 1965 changes for the 16–19 age group were postulated as 'some form of integration for this age group, whether by means of co-operation between institutions specialising in different objectives, joint working and possibly joint control, or through the development of a single institution for all' (Benn and Simon, 1970:307). By 1994, as we have already seen, reform for this age group was oriented towards curricular and assessment changes and ignored institutions, the very reverse of what had happened in 1965.

As history has shown, however, reform of one part without the rest, rarely lasts. So whether the future organisation of learning for the older secondary years is reorganised into a modified tripartite system with new bridges where 'broadly defined vocational ... and broadly defined academic should interrelate in a way which is not stratified or selective of certain groups of learners' (RSA, 1995:37), or whether it is more radically organised along baccalaureate style pathways (IPPR, 1990), or eventually develops into a fully integrated and common system – it will still be necessary to reform institutionally. Whether the 16-plus external exam hurdle is abolished, subsumed within an internal assessment system, or made part of a new single system from 14 to 18, remains to be decided. But whatever is decided, it will be necessary to reform the delivery of learning.

Developments since 1965 have gradually brought institutions with 16–19 education closer, working towards a common understanding of what might be required in a unified system. This development slowed in the 20 years before 1994 as a result of policies implemented by governments hostile to continuing reorganisation on comprehensive lines, and anxious to privatise the education service by having competing institutions. But such a strategy can only be a delaying tactic. Growth of a comprehensive system continues and renews itself, as it has throughout history. In the 1960s Hadow reforms were still being completed (Hainsworth, 1986). In the twenty-first century 16-plus reforms will still be being finalised while post-18 changes take the limelight.

Meanwhile, a conflict of sorts characterises the 16–19 sector. On the one hand is the 'market' with its proliferating small sixth forms, adding immeasurably to the cost of it all; the blight on rational planning; and the endless legal status difficulties and wasteful funding arrangements resulting from the proliferation of funding agencies. A market free-for-all as the sole determinant of a great national education service is inadequate and inefficient at any level, let alone from 16 to 19. For in the market system individual students are constantly short changed. Some may be in comprehensive schools that concentrate largely on 'A' levels, with far less care for their majority not choosing this academic path. Since these are the schools most praised for high 'league table' standing, there is scant incentive to concentrate upon all pupils equally. On the other hand, some schools that try to develop both 'A'-level and vocational education find increased inability to provide a full range of the latter (another outcome of schools' small size relative to colleges). Even those that do, as in Scotland, cannot any longer tolerate the destructive effects of 'parallelism' between vocational and academic courses and are determined to press on to greater integration (see pages 68–69, 164–168).

Countering this drive is pressure to keep numbers up. Not by providing an equitable public service through access to the full range of courses normally available for this age group, as comprehensive education requires, but by pitting institution against institution. As a result, in too many areas students are denied a real choice. In others the full range does not yet exist because there are gaps and the *system* for this age group has no capacity to 'fill the gaps'. Meanwhile some courses are too full, others too empty and many students lack access to the 'specialising' facilities jealously preserved by favoured institutions exercising 'selection'.

However, two features of the 16–19 comprehensive education at the end of the twentieth century are firmly fixed: very few institutions offer the full range of study that will by the twenty-first century be regarded as the range normally provided for the age group; and secondly, very few institutions will be willing to be restricted to providing one 'type' of education alone, or one level of qualification alone. The majority want to be able to develop a variety of education in their 16–19 years, and to provide for as wide a section of the age group as possible. Since no one institution can offer everything, and so many have already shown themselves more than willing to club together to make the necessary provision (see pages 339–41 and 445–57), the latter option seems the only promising course, provided that:

- schools and colleges are assisted and funded in the task;
- legislation allows students to have access to the full range of learning available regardless of where they started at the age of 11 or 12; and
- institutions co-operating are not penalised for the fluctuating numbers that the regulation of such a public service in the interests of greater access, choice and meeting of their community's needs would require.

As the 1994 survey shows, it is too late to decide that FE colleges will specialise in vocational and schools in academic study, since so many of both have both already – even though levels and range in each can vary dramatically from institution to institution and area to area. The extent of the integration that has already taken place makes it impossible now to turn back. Some form of tertiary system has to be organised, where institutions are not penalised financially for co-operating within local or regional developments within the principles of development that each school or college has itself agreed to, with programmes for students that are reasonably convenient and programmes for institutions that are reasonably broadly based, various and balanced. Whatever else the 'market' can do, it cannot undertake any of this. But it can seriously impede what is required by forcing 16–19 institutions to specialise, others to go without, and the system as a whole to polarise.

Reorganisation of the system: The undiscussed development

Little has been agreed about the structure of the 16–19 tertiary 'system'. The subject has hardly even been discussed during the whole of the comprehensive reform years. As Finegold points out, throughout these years governments have failed to 'develop a single, coherent national policy structure focused on the needs of all 16–19 year olds' (Finegold, 1993:52). Governments failed to do so long before the present government acted to prevent any further reorganisation by refusing comprehensive tertiary schemes or by initiating privatisation and market competition. Both the government and the DES at the end of the 1970s were singularly bereft of ideas for the development of the comprehensive system after 16 (see, for example, DES, 1978). This probably rightly reflected local government exhaustion at planning activity, for Ranson later suggested that one of the reasons that we are seeing a 'rigid ... re-emergence at 16 of tripartite education' was that local authorities in the 1980s shrank from the task of going through reorganisation again as they had to do in the 1960s and 1970s (Ranson, 1986:7).

But all this was before local authorities were emasculated through LMS and opting out and before co-operative development was disrupted by competitive and irrational market organisation of the system, including the removal of colleges from localities by making them 'independent' and isolated. It was before schools were loaded with the tasks LEAs had to relinquish and before even essential, minimal local planning was disowned. All this was before a Secretary of State or a quango was given power to intervene without warning anywhere at all and where each institution was forced to be theoretically at war with every other, competing for dwindling resources (unless one of the favoured few). It was before the proliferation of small sixth forms was encouraged and before sixth forms and FE colleges withheld information to keep students from knowing what the other provided.

By 1990 even the Senior Chief Inspector for Schools in the DES discreetly mentioned a lack of national guidance on many of these matters (DES, 1990:5) while more outspoken commentators put it down to a lack of political courage: 'the major political parties have ducked the issue to date, perhaps mindful of the impact on electoral fortunes' (Kerr, 1992:53). But electoral expectations change and some have suggested it is time to knock heads together over the integration of vocational and academic education (Whiteside, 1992:20), while others have been speaking out about the need for a mass reorganisation on tertiary lines ... every authority required to plan a full range of options – in schools and FE colleges – and make them available to all students.

As the twenty-first century approaches, and so many of the rushed policies of the 1980s are coming to be questioned, such a policy for 16–19, far from damaging electoral fortunes in the UK, would most certainly enhance them. With every passing year the case for reorganisation of the 16–19 stage is making itself, as increasing problems arise within a completely unreformed institutional structure fractured by divisions and differentiated funding, dominated by uneconomic sixth forms, private sector training agencies and a general further education sector wherein all schools and colleges must compete (though their wish is often to co-operate). The great mass of individual sixth forms attached to schools, most of which will be developing vocational education, will be increasingly less well funded and protected compared with the few 'high league table' sixth forms, even while the majority take refuge in sensible co-operative schemes and consortia. But with no national help or recognition, these arrangements are hard to sustain. On top of all this, 120 private enterprise councils (TECs and LECs) and several large funding quangos, each operating on different criteria and with wildly different approaches to education, will receive funding and be empowered to intervene in the work of schools and colleges, while the local education authorities have less power (and funding) to help protect or service local systems effectively. Overlooking the age group will also be 165 lead bodies from industry able to input to much vocational education – not to mention several examination boards and national qualifications councils, and dozens of awarding bodies.

Instead of getting simpler, the 16–19 system is even more of a jungle than ever. Vocational qualifications may be being simplified, but institutional arrangements are becoming ever more complex, and the system ever more selective. The competition that is supposed to fuel development isn't real competition, for it is heavily controlled and

because this is already happening. It is not whether part-timers are to be included everywhere, since an increasing number of schools and colleges are including them. It is whether the public education service after 16 will be rationally planned with equity in admissions and funding, agreed between institutions locally and regionally, and whether there will be equal attention to the needs of *all* learners, regardless of courses and future careers. In short, whether the service is comprehensive or not.

As yet no one is discussing comprehensive reorganisation for the 16–19 age group, possibly for fear it would mean ending the sixth form, but why should it be a threat to co-ordinate what any one sixth form provides with the work of other 16–19 institutions, to make up a tertiary system for each area? Co-ordination would be based on some common agreement between all institutions – under guidelines that would require each to provide a reasonable spread of work and have a reasonable spread of students as well as to offer a minimum level of educational and vocational and work-related learning. At most it would mean some sixth forms would have vocational courses added, or greater sharing with local colleges or other sixth forms; while others had additional academic courses. Each institution would remain itself but it would cease to be a self-contained competitor to every other, becoming instead part of a wider network providing for Years 12 and 13.

In practice the great majority of students in schools would remain where they started, but a significant minority would be free to choose elsewhere or share studies between two venues; and, most important, large numbers in comprehensive schools without sixth forms would have their prospects dramatically improved by requiring LEAs or boards to organise direct links to a tertiary college, FE or sixth form college for all of them, where liaison can start from the age of 13 onwards (as it does in areas where such organisation is already in place) and with their years up to 16 funded as 'all through' institutions are funded for the same years. That such schools have been allowed to stay in inequitable positions *vis-à-vis* all-through schools for 30 years – given the huge percentage of the young people attending them – with no action taken or even proposed for their development along the lines suggested, is one of the least creditable aspects of English education over the last 30 years.

Such a change, however, requires formal reorganisation planning, as do other changes already discussed. But what of the equally important task of providing for the growth of a system which we cannot yet chart? To accommodate whatever pattern of study or combination of qualifications will be required in future for any 'single' new qualification or laid down by university departments or professions or trades for entry to their courses, or by employers for entry to jobs, including jobs not yet created in fields not yet known? What about accommodation for learners increasingly willing to undertake their own learning more autonomously, where institutions are resource bases, advice centres and providers of assessment services rather than custodial mentors? Or those who need support every step of the way? The system has to be kept flexible to provide for everyone's needs and prevented from degenerating into divisive and inefficient selectivity.

The idea that any of this can be done by a Secretary of State in Whitehall or a collection of remote quangos trying to interact with each other, is not realistic. These are matters for local or regional planning – albeit under national guidelines. The work being done now by government on 16–19 (and mirrored by documents like *Unfinished business*) is going in the wrong direction. It is a narrow, academic exercise that concentrates on reducing waste in courses, most particularly 'A' level, without regard to the rest of the system. Present work on 'value added' is also heading in the wrong direction when used to measure post-16 'A' level performance related to GCSE scores earlier. Value added is a useful tool, perhaps, when used within a school or college, but for comparative purposes its use for rating institutions by attainment at entry is a patronising procedure akin to ensuring homeless hostels will always be the 'equal' of five star hotels because some very clever statisticians have devised a way to make them look fairly judged within the same system. Such work diverts us from the task of finding high standard education for everyone, getting rid of unequal offering and giving everyone a choice from the same full range of learning throughout their lives.

Measuring standards is a vital part of education but 'league tables' as presently constituted are devices for reinforcing hierarchy and increasing polarisation among institutions which are inherently unequal to start with. Our efforts should be directed to equalising the institutions within a new tertiary system according to criteria that maximise student choice and provide a balanced course provision in each institution – along with incentives to meet the whole community's educational needs. Only this approach will ensure the rational spending that will enable a far greater percentage of the age group to achieve high standards of learning. Not to mention ensuring that by the age of 19 students will be so committed to learning, they will want to return to it repeatedly during their lives.

Progressive development of a new tertiary system
Circular 10/65 in 1965 was based on a half dozen forms of reorganisation, all operating before it was issued. Today there are equally as many forms of reorganisation of the post-16 (or 14-19) system competing for our attention.

Reorganisation in this sense was much further along in 1994 than it was in 1965, however little this has been officially acknowledged. Some models had been operating for years. Coventry, for example, has long had a system where all 11–18 schools are community units in their upper years, providing full-time, part-time and adult education and training after 16 for the locality – its 16-plus centres a 'concept' as much as a building, but guaranteeing access, the preparation of personal development planning for each student, as well as careers advice (D'Hooghe, 1983). The Coventry model, however – like all others – exists in a system with as yet little coherence overall.

Of more recent origin are systems where towns (or a section of large cities) pool their sixth forms so that students can move between them. In other authorities some of the most successful departures are those on a very small scale, where only one department in a school co-operates with one department in a college; or are organised as single sixth form centres linking only a handful of schools. All such arrangements are flexible but they often change from year to year, and most, of course, are once again only partial, including those operating in areas with well-established grammar schools and opted-out schools running alongside. No tertiary system could work unless all publicly funded institutions were co-operating equally. That said, such co-operation for a grammar school today would involve a good deal less upheaval than the incorporation of grammar schools into comprehensive reorganisation in the 1960s or 1970s.

Very little research into the advantages and disadvantages of these arrangements has ever been undertaken, yet they increase steadily in importance. For example, more and more colleges are being called upon by schools, especially as GNVQ grows, to help them develop vocational courses. Some colleges, encouraged by the 'market' mentality, look upon the work as a money spinner and their charges to schools can sometimes impose so great a cost that a school has to curtail its own vocational development.

A 'market' solution to co-operation is not the same as expanding the system to offer the age group as a whole a full education. This is a job for a public education service, publicly organised and democratically overseen.

But it was never a search for a perfect institution; it was rather a search for a sound tertiary system, and a common tertiary educational culture in which all participate.

The principles for the new system are relatively simple: integration of the curriculum; a common assessment and accreditation system; and full progression for all within a common framework. In terms of institutional organisation there would be no selection for institutions individually but each (by mutual negotiation under the auspices of the local or regional authority) would have as full a range of study and students as possible. No one institution could offer every course and qualification, but together all could offer that other essential of comprehensive education: all that is normally expected for the age range as a whole. To these must be added the duty of the service to accommodate part timers on an equal basis with full timers, and, as time continues, to be open to adults of all ages as well.

Ensuring that every area of the country had an effective tertiary system (as well as increasing the numbers of effective schools or colleges, a quite different objective) would not happen overnight. There are too many 'holes' in provision and too much inequality in the system to reorganise instantly. But with electorally accountable bodies given the duty to undertake the work, it could be accomplished in a lot less than the 30 years it took the 11–16 years in British schools to end selection and achieve comprehensive-compatible curricula and assessment.

It would involve developing most general FE colleges to 'network' the country, each college allied to the local sixth forms of schools or sixth form colleges. More and more FE colleges would become tertiary colleges but even without this development the system could be built around sixth forms and FE colleges working co-operatively. What counts would be a common tertiary administration where courses would be available within the network to learners wherever based.

The FE colleges would benefit by the expertise many schools already have in 'A' level work and some new courses of vocational education, while colleges in turn would add their expertise in vocational and academic fields, as well as their much greater experience dealing with those already at work and studying part time. The FE colleges have experience second to none in dealing with that link between education and employment, yet for nearly two decades Britain has insisted it turn to employers to get work-related learning off the ground. It is time to realise, as John Woolhouse remarked about most other industrial nations, that 'it is the colleges rather than work-based training facilities which are seen as the powerhouses of educational advance for this age group' (Woolhouse, 1993:247).

social background of students as upon the prior attainment levels of those who enter. As with comprehensive schools overall, polarisation at 16–19 is increasing – with more institutions joining either end of the continuum each year, reducing the numbers in the middle that stand the best chance of developing comprehensively.

The chances of change in a more comprehensive direction in 1994, however, were much better than those in 1965, as a more detailed examination of the dynamics of practices within the 16–19 system will show.

1994 Survey

The institutions that made up the responding population in the 16–19 age group are set out in Table 9.2. They included just over half (54%) of the institutions participating in the survey. Although most were schools, more of the students in this age group in the survey were in colleges than in schools.

Overall in the UK for the 16–18 age group (including both full- and part-time day students) government figures showed the colleges had 53% of students with schools having only 47% (*Education Statistics for the UK,* 1994: Table 20(22)). For full time only and in England only (but for 1991–92), OFSTED registered 52% in schools and 48% colleges for Year 12 with the position reversing by Year 13, when colleges had the majority (OFSTED, 1993: Exhibit 3, p. 12).

Table 9.1 shows that colleges held a bare majority of full-time students at 16 by 1993–94, the year of the survey.

Survey proportions were roughly in line with national figures, once private education was removed, a population that accounted for only 9% of the total for England and Wales – just about the same percentage as attended opted-out schools in the same year (Table 9.1) – quite a contrast to the early days of comprehensive reorganisation when students in private schools accounted for a very large proportion of those studying full time at 16 plus. In 1968, for example, they were nearly a quarter of all those on 'A' level courses (*DES Statistics,* England and Wales, 1968, Vol. 1, Table 26). In 1994 – because of the growth of comprehensive education and the rise in staying on, but particularly because vocational education and education in FE colleges was now included in all statistical accounts of education for this age group – the proportion of students in private settings as a percentage of the total has declined markedly.

Table 9.2: Number (%) of schools and colleges with students in the 16–19 age group in the survey, 1994

Institution	No.	(%)
All through	626	75
13/14–18 upper schools	77	9
Sixth-form colleges	37	4
Tertiary colleges	24	3
FE colleges	75	9
Total	839	100

The different types of state supported comprehensive schools and colleges in the 1994 survey are set out in Table 9.2.

Earlier chapters gave findings relating to the different types of comprehensive schools and colleges, including those with students in the 16–19 age group, and Chapter 3 gave profiles for each type of school and college. The first part of this chapter gave the history of comprehensive reform in this age group over the 30 years before the survey, making the case for bringing the whole age group together under one administration within a unified system in order to end education and training arrangements divided into such inflexible, outmoded and over-specialised pathways. As increasing numbers of institutions provide a wider range of learning and pressure to integrate curricular pathways and divided assessment systems grows, so too does pressure to unify the system institutionally in some way.

This section looks at the 16–19 years across the board through the 2 years that make it up: the 12th and 13th years of education, still often called the sixth form, and in Scotland Standards 5 and 6. For those in training and in most of the colleges they are simply the years covering age 16/17 and age 17/18.

16–19 in schools and 16–19 in colleges – some general findings, 1994

One of the first enquiries people make is how different types of comprehensive institutions compare with each other for this age group. This information is given in Table A6 related to their different contexts and characteristics and a range of indicators.

Although sixth forms in comprehensive schools of 11–18 are often lumped together with those from comprehensive upper schools of 13/14 to 18, as Table A6 shows, there were differences between them. For example, on the indicator of size of Years 12 and 13, the average size of the upper schools was much larger (241 against 152). Upper schools also had higher average numbers entering for two or more 'A' levels and the 14–18 schools a slightly higher average of numbers entered for BTEC National, two more of the indicators used in the table. The 14–18 schools had the high 'A' level grade point average of 13.4 (as against 12.7 for the survey as a whole). They also had 100% sending at least 31% of their second year students to universities, compared with only 82% and 84% of all-through and 13–18 schools respectively.

The all-through schools, however, had higher percentages entering for two or more 'A' levels; and both types of upper schools had smaller average numbers entering degree courses with vocational qualifications than the all-through schools, though in the year of the survey the numbers taking these qualifications at level 3 were as yet too small to draw any real conclusions. What can be deduced, however, is that for both BTEC National and GNVQ advanced qualifications, the tertiary and FE colleges outstrip schools in numbers entering and qualifying, as might be expected given their head start in the provision of vocational courses. The average number of vocational students a year accepted in 1994 on degree level courses from the 1994 survey comprehensive colleges was 60. We would expect schools (with smaller year groups at 16 and 17) to have lower numbers but the highest average for any type of school was 5, while 14–18 schools (with comparatively large year groups) as yet had only one per school.

Comparing schools of differing legal status, the sixth forms of voluntary controlled comprehensive schools had the highest average number entering a degree course with vocational qualifications – as well as 100% of schools sending at least 31% to degree level courses (compared with 90.6% of grant maintained schools and 79.5% of LEA schools). On the other hand, voluntary controlled (along with special agreement) comprehensive schools had the lowest rates of staying on from the 5th year to the sixth form: only 51% (compared, say, with 58% for grant maintained schools). This is an odd finding for the voluntary controlled category, which had the highest percentage of schools with predominantly middle class intakes (Table A5) and a very high percentage of its upper sixth taking two or more 'A' levels: at nearly 90%, the highest for any comprehensive school type in the Survey (Table A6).

Without looking a great deal more closely it is not possible to say whether the differences noted could illustrate the choice to be made between larger *numbers* getting qualifications on both academic and vocational courses (a comprehensive goal) and higher *rates* passing examinations (expressed as a percentage of those entering who pass), a more selective goal. In recent years league-table pressure within a market-driven system has increased pressure on schools to go for the latter, even at the expense of fewer qualifying overall.

Such pressure to maximise attainment at the five GCSE (A–C) level (the score that counts in league tables) has already led to a drop in the numbers of pupils achieving exam success overall in GCSE, even as percentages getting passes at the five GCSE level increase. Forty per cent of the schools commended by OFSTED in 1995 for improving GCSE league table scores showed drops in percentages achieving fewer than five passes on other GCSE scores (C. Bell, Article 26, 5/2/95, 26/7/95; *TES* 6/10/95).

Another set of findings from the 1994 survey (given earlier in Chapter 4) bears on another choice to be made: between running vocational and academic qualifications and how far to expand the former in the school sixth form. This is illustrated by differences observed between girls' and boys' comprehensive schools in the survey (see pages 122–24). Tables A5 and A6 show that at 16-plus GCSE attainment was higher in girls' comprehensive schools than in boys' but that after 16 positions reversed, with boys' comprehensive schools having a higher 'A' level grade point average at 13.8 than the girls at 11.6.

In looking for an explanation for this difference, what the girls' comprehensives had can be seen (in Table A6) to be higher percentages staying on and higher numbers and percentages on vocational courses (and of those students who were on vocational courses, a higher percentage achieving success). Girls' schools also had almost three times the average percentage of students attached to the school on a part-time or day-release basis than did boys' comprehensive school sixth forms. Taken together, all this suggests girls' comprehensives aim for a more 'comprehensive' policy of maximum numbers of passes in the widest range of courses after 16 (while more boys' schools may give a greater priority to 'A' level provision and high 'A' level pass rates).

The comprehensive colleges

Concentrating on 'A' levels at the expense of a wide range of study was also characteristic of the sixth form college. The 1994 survey shows such colleges were far more selective institutions academically than many have assumed. Their 'A' level point score (at 13.9) was the highest of any comprehensive institution serving the 16–19 age group (Table A6), though the difference in the survey was not as great as it was nationally.

Being larger than any sixth form in a school, sixth form colleges naturally had higher average numbers of students entering two or more 'A' levels – 278 a year – when compared with the all-through schools' 54. It is easy to see why the sixth form college found favour with administrators and why élitists who called for it to be banned in the 1970s as a threat to standards are now so silent. Its university entry record was equally good in the 1994 survey with 100% sending at least 31% on degree courses in the year of the survey.

However, the sixth form college of 1994 was less accommodating to vocational learning than many individual sixth form colleges had always claimed to be in writing over the years and less so than many sixth forms in all-through schools. An average of only 10 students a year from sixth form colleges were entering BTEC National or City and Guilds National level qualifications compared with an average of 315 from colleges as a whole (and 435 from the further education colleges) (Table A6).

We would expect FE colleges, as multi-purpose colleges, to be offering a greater range of courses than the sixth form colleges, but not necessarily that schools' sixth forms would also be doing so. Yet in 1994 with the exception of the Special Agreement schools, all types of comprehensive schools had over double the sixth form colleges' percentages taking GNVQ in those institutions where they were offered (Table A8). For those entering students in BTEC or City and Guilds National qualifications, sixth form colleges had only 3% of their Year 13 entering compared with the general FE colleges 69%, the grant maintained schools' 18% , and 21% for LEA comprehensives (Table A6).

The sixth form college also had an average of only one student per college entering university through BTEC/GNVQ or NVQ compared with a survey average of 13 and an FE average of 100. Both all-through and upper schools had greater numbers (see Table A6), despite their smaller size and the fact that over 90% of sixth form colleges in the 1994 survey claimed a relationship with the local TEC (question 134) compared with less than half of the all-through comprehensive schools (Table A6). This picture of a limited offering in vocational preparation for sixth form colleges was confirmed in an HMI 16–19 research project, which showed such work to be largely confined to 1-year courses (OFSTED, 1993:17).

A selective divide?

This rather restricted development is certainly not the way many sixth form colleges were planning to develop in the 1970s and at first sight we might be tempted to say that such colleges were now the grammar schools of the 16–19 sector. Certainly their intakes set them apart from other comprehensive institutions with over half having intakes that were predominantly middle class (Table A5) compared with a survey average of only 26% with middle-class intakes – and to an average of only 17% for FE colleges. Even more telling, sixth form colleges were very selective with 67% in the top 20% of the attainment range – compared with FE colleges with 13% and a survey average of 18.0%. Their concentration on 'A' levels with 78% of 17 year olds entered for two or more compares with the FE colleges' 27%. In the sixth form colleges 100% sent at least 31% of this year to degree level study compared with only 34% of the FE colleges doing so.

These figures combined indicate the way sixth form colleges have moved in recent years that suggest they could have retreated somewhat to their "A' level academy' past. Although moving away from diversity and choice would hardly be a deliberate policy for most such colleges, for just as likely a cause is the continuing failure to develop the education as a whole for the age group along comprehensive lines. Instead of the development of a spread of courses to match the wide range of interests and types of intelligences in the age group, offered in each school or college (by pooling of resources within each area), we have a competitive 'market' driven by 'league table' competition between isolated centres of learning where 'excellence' is determined by pass rates and in one type of qualification alone.

But this trend to greater concentration on academic courses and possibly greater selectivity is not exclusive to sixth form colleges. A substantial number of school sixth forms in the 1994 survey gave every indication of being 'selective' in the sense of concentrating upon 'A' level, setting selective entry hurdles, and failing to develop vocational qualifications. Inevitably, this has meant a growing number of schools and colleges battling to avoid development as the 'secondary moderns' of the 16–19 sector.

Most are resisting this pressure, particularly the tertiary colleges, which, as we saw in Chapter 3, always aimed to provide the breadth and coherence that came with uniting general further education work with that of the "A' level academies'. Within the 1994 survey tertiary colleges were holding their own in this respect by their midway position between the sixth form colleges and general FE colleges relative to a number of indicators (see Table A6). The tertiary college had a social class intake that placed it between that of the sixth form colleges and the general FE colleges (see Table A5) and an attainment intake that did the same: with 25.7% in the top 20% compared with FE colleges with 13.1% and sixth form colleges with 57.8%.Tertiary colleges also had average numbers higher than the survey average for BTEC and GNVQ students accepted on university courses, while also maintaining a creditable percentage of 72.2% sending over 30% of students in the 17–18 year to degree courses.

Much more detailed analysis of the many figures relating to all the colleges would be needed (with agreement about criteria) before tertiary colleges could be termed 'best buy' from the point of view of providing genuine comprehensive opportunity for the 16–19 age group as a whole, although at first sight it looked as if it did so in 1994. However, there is nothing a tertiary college does that schools' sixth forms and FE colleges might not do as well, if they worked together in a properly organised and coherent tertiary system.

Staying on

A good measure of how any education system is doing has always been how many stayed on after the law allows them to leave. Many features in British education in the twentieth century conspired to promote early leaving, particularly the selective divisions within the system. Comprehensive education was expected to increase numbers staying on. But, as we have seen, the rise has been slow, even though in the earliest days – and especially in all-through schools – several studies showed a higher staying-on rate for students in comprehensive schools than prevailed nationally (King, 1962; Robertson, 1977).

But not all young people were in all-through schools. Where the system had a break coinciding with the legal age of leaving, the picture was different. In the first Independent Enquiry of 1968 staying-on rates were found to be lowest in the comprehensive schools without sixth forms (and highest in upper schools of 13/14–18). It also turned out staying on was much affected by where schools were and what kind of intakes they had. Thus, for example, staying on rates were higher in suburban areas than in inner city schools (Benn and Simon, 1970: Table 9.3, p.152; Tables A1, A2, pp.372, 373).

Other influences on staying-on figures in the earlier days were the policies schools adopted about entry to the sixth form: open to all or open only if a certain level of attainment had already been reached? In some areas – particularly Wales and Scotland – a minimum number of 'O' level (or O grade) passes for entry to the sixth (or to a certificate course in Scotland) was the rule (Benn and Simon, 1970:190). Staying-on rates tended to be lower in such areas (in Scotland particularly) but in England policies were less restrictive. Many comprehensive schools allowed any student to pass to the sixth form who chose to do so and as a consequence schools with sixth forms having an open entry policy often had higher staying-on rates – as well as more students with passes in 'A' level examinations.

Apart from the raising of the school leaving age in 1972 – with legally enforced staying on – most national increases in staying-on rates have been due to changes in the curriculum and assessment system. Studies in the 1980s found that what influenced staying on most was social class and qualifications students had obtained by the age of 16. That qualifications mattered is shown by the rise in staying on after the introduction of a 'comprehensive' examination and assessment system after 1986 when the GCSE replaced the divided system of GCE/CSE, and in Scotland after the introduction of SCOTVEC curriculum reforms in 1984.

In the 1990s with the addition of more vocational courses (and less hope of work at 16) there has been a continued rise in staying on past 16. In 1992–93 (the year from which most survey figures would have come) the rate in England for full-time students was 70%, an 18% increase over 1989 (DfE, *Statistical Bulletin*, 11/94).

Staying on versus going on

The 1994 survey did not provide any comparable figures, choosing instead to look at the going-on rates for 11–16 schools and the staying-on rates within all-through schools and upper schools (both relating to the 1992–93 academic year).

The going-on rate of 63% (Table A5) was a figure for which there is no national equivalent, for it was only for schools that ended at 16. They were asked to record the known intentions of all leavers going on to both local colleges and to the sixth forms of other schools (question 115). Its accuracy is hard to be sure about because of differences in the way schools follow up their students. Even allowing for this, what was interesting was that this figure was higher than the staying-on rate for students inside all-through schools, which was 56% – again a figure with no national equivalent since it related only to students staying on to their own sixth forms and did not include students who left to attend colleges. Nor can the difference of 7% between the two rates be said to represent that percentage who left all-through schools for FE, again because so few schools as yet have accurate and thorough follow-up figures for their own leavers, but also because of factors relating to differential entry to further education.

The value of the two staying-on rates in the survey was to enable a comparison between schools operating in a variety of contexts in respect of continuing on to 16–19 education. As can be seen in Table A5, the highest staying-on rates were in Scotland: 70.5%, a figure likely to be more accurate than any for England because all Scotland's comprehensive schools were all-through schools and very few students leave schools at this age to go to colleges. In fact, the survey figure fell between the two rates given by the SOED for Scotland for 1994: 76% staying on in to S5 and 67% of S5 staying beyond Christmas[6].

Scotland had reversed its position from lowest staying on in the first independent Enquiry of 1968 to the highest in 1994 and there can be little doubt that this was due largely both to the fact that it was the most fully comprehensively reorganised area of the UK; and, secondly, to the introduction of SCOTVEC vocational qualifications in 1984 – 10 years before the rest of the UK started serious vocational education in schools (see pages 167–71).

The lowest staying on in the 1994 survey was in Northern Ireland (where caution is required owing to its small number of comprehensive schools in the survey) but hardly unexpected in view of its being the least comprehensively reorganised area of the UK. As Table A5 shows, staying-on rates were higher than survey average in UK comprehensive schools in the following groups: comprehensive schools situated in the countryside and villages, those serving mainly private housing estates, those within the London area; and in girls' comprehensive schools (which also had the highest rate of 'going on' from 11–16 schools of 72%). Staying on was lower in voluntary controlled and special agreement comprehensive schools, in schools serving council estates and in schools drawing from areas with substandard housing.

In previous chapters we have already seen that both predominantly middle-class composition of schools and high attendance rates were related to both high staying on and going on (see pages 188, 220–21). Staying on may also have been affected by whether students had an 'all-through' path to 18 already organised within the local system, with support and advice along the way – as against a system stopping at 16 with no particular 16–19 institution attached to the school as its 'next stage'.

Staying on was complicated in 1994 because although rates were rising dramatically, so were rates of dropping out. The same student who is recorded in national figures as staying on may well have dropped out a month later. Dropping out by 1994 had reached rates of between 30% and 40% on 'A' level and GNVQ courses and suggested that a large percentage of students post-16 were dissatisfied with the courses available to them. High failure and drop-out rates were found at 16–19 both in sixth forms in schools and in all kinds of colleges (OFSTED, 1993: exhibit 6, page 24). It was sometimes linked to types of courses (like engineering), but there was no link between dropping out of 'A' level and any one type of school or college – private, state, comprehensive, or selective (OFSTED, 1993). All that can be said about it is that it cost a lot wherever it occurred: £330 million for state schools and colleges in 1992 (OFSTED, 1993:60).

Staying on figures can give us some facts to go on but since schools and colleges and local areas differ so widely in the information and encouragement they provide their pupils from age 13 or 14 (when staying on first begins to be considered), and since institutions and governments are still so casual in the records they keep about those who proceed to continuing education or to training at 16, including those who drop out, it is very unlikely that a true comprehensive picture of staying on will be obtained until the 16–19 age group as a whole is monitored much more closely by a single agency charged with its comprehensive development.

Admissions policies and practices: The 16–19 years

Admissions policies to comprehensive education at 16 plus can often be as important as admission at 11 or 12 or 13. Yet not only is far less information given out about 16 plus admissions procedures, but little research has been undertaken in respect of them.

Admission after 16 to comprehensive education has been subjected to years of conflicting pressures between those anxious to increase numbers staying on and those anxious to keep exam pass rates high. The latter has resulted in pressure on some students to move to less-prestigious institutions or courses, now augmented by pressure to select for entry to 'A' level to cut down drop-out rates and move more students to other courses. This is proving difficult in a 'market' system where schools and colleges generally try to retain students, having to persuade them that what is on offer, however limited, is what they want. Even students who are unfortunately placed and drop out later, bring in good money meanwhile; there is little incentive to chase them away.

The whole basis upon which 16–19 education presently rests is thus inherently unstable and the practices and policies of comprehensive schools and colleges in relation to admissions reflect this position. In a genuine comprehensive system, where variety of education matched variety of interests and competence – and first-class guidance was available to everyone – selection would be unnecessary. But with the continuing failure to reorganise the curriculum and assessment system for 16–19, combined with league table pressure, selection remains and polarisation between institutions at 16–19 is inevitable.

History of admissions policies at 16 plus

In the first independent enquiry of 1968 16-plus entry questions applied almost entirely to sixth forms and upper standards in schools, since colleges were not considered part of comprehensive education. The main finding was that 68% of comprehensive schools allowed entry to the sixth form without specific 'O' level passes (Benn and Simon, 1970: Table 11.1, p.189). The general view – in the words of a teachers' group writing at the time – was that 'if you are old enough, you are good enough' (IAAM, 1967:98). Comprehensive education did not turn students away. Yet even at this time a third of the comprehensive schools were 'selecting' at 16 plus by imposing qualifications for entry to the sixth form.

During the 1960s and early 1970s, this spirit of 'all welcome' fuelled the expansion of the 'new' sixth, despite the fact that the narrow 'A' level education (the main course available) was quite unable to meet the needs of so many and despite the fact that the imposition of prior requirements for entry to 'A' level continued to operate in some comprehensive schools, including those with 'open' sixth forms. In 1981 Ball found that a supposedly open sixth form required Grade B passes for 'A' level courses, its 'open' part only relating to non-academic courses or retakes; half the girls in the lower sixth were on courses other than 'A' level (Ball, 1981:160).

By the 1990s the emphasis was once again on rationing places on academic courses like 'A' level, to keep pass rates high for 'league table' purposes, and to reduce drop out. Hence the OFSTED pressure on both schools and colleges to restrict 'A' level courses to students who have obtained A or B grades in GCSE. In effect, to tighten academic selection, possibly along the lines pursued in City Technology Colleges, where students seeking transfer to their own sixth forms are subject to 'rigorous selection'. Institutions that do not select or which have lower entry requirements have lower status – even though they often offer a greater range of students a greater chance to get a greater range of qualifications, as well as the chance to pursue education for its own sake, a feature of the system that has virtually disappeared in many schools and colleges.

The lower entry requirements for FE colleges are the outcome of many years whereby these colleges provided opportunities for students 'selective' sixth forms did not necessarily want. Today, however, with the need to hang on to students (in order not to lose funding) fewer schools would be encouraging their students to move. According to HMI research in the early 1990s, most schools do not tell their 14–16 students about post-16 opportunities elsewhere and only one-fifth arrange for them to visit other venues (OFSTED, 1993:42).

But instead of dealing with this situation by proposing an extension of the comprehensive principle so that all students' aspirations and pathways are provided for by long overdue institutional and curricular reform – and records kept of everyone's progress – there is a crackdown on high drop-out rates for the higher level courses alone. Such action achieves very little in terms of positive outcomes for young people for whom no alternative is available that matches their educational aspirations.

1994 admissions: The sixth form of schools

The 1994 survey had two questions which gave information about admissions policies to the colleges (questions 119–120) and four about admissions to the sixth year in all-through schools (questions 115–118).

Both schools and colleges had already answered general questions on admissions (question 19) which gave initial information about their policies, particularly in relation to the geographical spread of students and criteria used for priority at entry (see Chapter 4). Here the emphasis is on entry to the 16–19 age group and how this is organised within the comprehensive system.

We start with schools with their own sixth forms – both all-through and upper schools – and policy for admitting to the 12th year or sixth form. Question 116 set out five alternative methods, starting with automatic entry and ending with the setting of tests. Results are given in Table 9.3.

Table 9.3: All-through comprehensive schools – admissions to Year 12*

Policy	Percentage of all-through schools using this policy	'A' level score
A Automatic entry	43.7	12.6
B Informal selection by staff views of suitability for courses chosen	56.9	12.8
C Minimum GCSE/Standard Grade passes	34.2	13.5
D GCSE/Standard Grade passes only for subjects to be studied	8.4	13.5
E Selection by tests	0.1	18.0

*Total number of schools: 675, omitting schools in Scotland.

The figure of only 43.7% giving automatic entry above represents a less liberal entry policy today over 30 years ago when it was 68%; although the figure of 34.2% requiring minimum passes, representing an informal form of selection, shows this requirement was near the same level as prevailed in 1968: 32% (Benn and Simon, 1970: Table 11.1, p.189). What has changed is the majority using some form of counselling or advice for students, operating their own 'informal selection', as the question implied. Without further analysis it would be hard to say whether this amounts to helpful counselling to determine wishes and awareness of alternatives (compatible with comprehensive practice) or well-meaning manipulation and selection by past attainment (with or without direction to courses students may not wish to take), possibly with a view to ensuring 'league table' figures stay high by admitting to 'A' level or Highers courses only those students likely to keep figures high.

A few schools combined methods in what could seem like a contradictory system – e.g. 9.6% used automatic entry combined with informal selection through counselling, and 29 schools had automatic entry combined with minimum GCSE passes. The contradictions could be resolved (as they were later with college courses) by realising different departments or subjects could have their own entry requirements.

Of the all-through schools giving information about their admissions in Table 9.3, 625 also gave information about their average 'A' level point scores. Table 9.3 shows the averages for schools using each admissions policy.

Interpreting information in the light of the several cautions relating to examinations (see Appendix II, Note B), we see that schools using methods requiring minimum exam passes for entry have higher average 'A' level scores, although not so much higher than schools using other methods, as to be conclusive. This caution is reinforced by the finding that schools using automatic entry alone (uncombined with any other method) had a higher score than schools also using informal teacher guidance. On the other hand, schools that used GCSE requirements (C) as their only method had the highest score of 15.5, though their numbers were few (46).

Entrants from outside to comprehensive schools' Year 12 (S5)

All-through schools were also asked (question 117) whether they had a policy of accepting 16-plus students coming from other schools, and whether students came from other schools with or without sixth forms of their own.

In the 1960s poaching from one sixth form to another was rare and transfers were mostly in respect of official 'mushroom' sixth forms that set themselves up to receive students from comprehensive schools without sixth forms. In Scotland such schemes were also common because higher certificate courses were only available in certain schools at that time, a situation that no longer exists.

By 1994 the transfer culture was pervasive and 96.9% of all-through schools said it was their policy to accept pupils applying to come in from other schools after the leaving age, regardless of where they came from. That said, most had very few such students – 59% fewer than five (question 118A), including those with none at all. The percentage of LEA schools in this category was 62%, while that of grant maintained schools was only 45% , suggesting the latter may have been attracting sixth form entrants at a slightly greater rate. Even so, most of the remaining 41% of schools (those attracting more than five entrants from outside) still took in fewer than 20 students each (question 118B).

There were, however, a small number of schools (10% of the total, most of which were LEA schools) with more than 20 pupils entering at 16 (Question 18 C and D), including 19 schools with more than 50 (Question 18D). If sixth forms in schools in these two categories were playing the same role as the 'mushroom' schools of the late 1960s (Benn and Simon, 1970: Table 5.2, p.72), the percentage of schools acting as 'mushroom' schools in 1994 had more than doubled.

Admissions to the colleges

At first sight colleges seemed more open than schools in their admissions, but on looking closer, their policies could also be quite complicated and often contradictory.

As we saw earlier, most of the FE and tertiary colleges in the 1994 survey did not recognise the concept 'full' that was applied to schools (question 12). Only sixth form colleges accepted it and gave returns showing 66% were full (considerably higher than the survey average of 40%). Judging from their results and their attainment percentages at intake, some of these colleges could well have entry arrangements that aim to attract the highest attainers rather than a cross-section of the age group.

Tertiary and FE colleges, on the other hand, often mentioned that it was their policy not to turn anyone away – 'We fit them in as best we can'. Nor did they start selecting when entry reached a standard number, for they had no such number. On the contrary, they often considered expanding to let students in. But this was only to the college as a whole. When it came to 'A'-level or GNVQ advanced or NVQ level 3 courses, many colleges did set limits (see below).

In answers to question 19 about general policy of admissions (discussed on page 212 in respect of schools – which 86% of comprehensive colleges also answered) very few colleges considered entry in relation to zoning, medical factors, denomination, nearness or siblings. On the other hand, a third gave priority to those from 'feeder' comprehensives. About one in five (22.8%) used information from tests and exams when admitting; and 34.2% relied on staff opinion about suitability of students for the courses. But by far the largest number (84.2%) said entry was based on the capacity of the college to provide the course of study desired.

Question 119 asked about admissions policies that related specifically to comprehensive colleges, repeating some questions already asked in question 19. Almost all colleges gave information (Table 9.4).

Table 9. 4 Admissions policies used by comprehensive colleges at 16 plus, 1994

Criteria used	Number (%) of colleges		'A' level average score
A Entirely open access	78	(62.9)	11.8
B Open access but differs according to departments	35	(28.2)	10.1
C Priority to students from feeder schools	28	(22.6)	13.5
D Priority to students from the area	15	(13.2)	13.4
E Informal selection – staff opinion	40	(32.3)	10.6
F Minimum number of GCSE Standard Grade passes	60	(48.3)	10.5
G GCSE/Standard Grade passes for subjects studied	25	(20.1)	10.4
H Tests	22	(17.7)	9.7

Total number responding to question: 124.
'A' level average for all colleges in survey was 11.4.

A far larger proportion of colleges claimed to be entirely open access in these answers than the 46% answering 'first come, first served' in answer to question 19 earlier; and a smaller proportion mentioned priority to feeder schools – in both cases possibly because the percentage answering the second question was higher. About the same percentage as in question 19 claimed staff opinion about suitability counted most. But over a quarter refined the reply by saying policies differed according to departments within the college.

Only about half the colleges claimed they had a requirement of a minimum number of GCSE passes – a far cry from the nearly universal practice in this respect claimed by the FEFC's Inspector's Report on colleges in England for the year of the survey, which suggested that almost every college had a 4 or 5 GCSE minimum for entry – at least to 'A' level courses (FEFC, 1994a:55). The FEFC Report concluded with approval of such evidence of 'increasing selectivity' at entry to courses in this age group as being 'in the students' best interest'. It was a course the government favours for several reasons, including cutting losses due to non-completion.

However, this strategy is not a simple matter for several reasons. First, because in a competitive 'market' many colleges prefer to keep courses full (for the funding) and secondly, because any who accept the need to select can experience conflict between the 'counselling' of those guarding entry and the 'choice' made by many students. And not only students. FE colleges in particular are showing more awareness now of parental approval in the race to win entrants – with brochures advertising special parents' evenings and visits to see 'A' level courses (the only ones usually open for parents' inspection). Counselling may have been improved, but as noted by the FEFC Inspector, parents resist counselling if it means having their children turned away from high-status 'A' levels to courses regarded as less prestigious (FEFC, 1994a). From experience in schools it would be middle-class parents whose children get admitted anyway or those from working-class backgrounds who know how to dig their feet in over education matters (Ball, 1981), while students likely to be 'persuaded' in colleges as well as in schools are those without such additional support for their choices or with little knowledge of the system. While the present divided curriculum remains with an 'all-academic' versus an 'all-vocational' choice, this problem will remain.

The relation of college admission systems and 'A' level scores was somewhat the reverse of that for the school sixth form in that the highest 'A' level point scores (Table 9.4) were not associated with policies requiring minimum GCSE passes or GCSE passes for the subject to be studied; nor with prior testing (which actually had the lowest 'A' level scores) nor with selection by staff opinion about the students' suitability. As the table shows, they went with admissions policies giving priority to students from feeder schools or living in the area.

This suggests that having 'selective' criteria at this 16-plus entry point might not be as helpful in securing good outcomes and less dropping out as having the continuity and planning that is possible in a coherent 'all-through' comprehensive scheme where colleges are formally linked to local schools. It means students have a chance to plan their courses long before admission in the light of awareness of the range of courses from which they can choose, while colleges get to know students' strengths and weaknesses before they arrive (often beginning liaison with them in the third year) – by contrast to other colleges where students are first met when they turn up for registration in September.

In this connection it is interesting that OFSTED inspectors found 'disturbing' lack of liaison generally between colleges and the lower years of the schools students came from as well as between sixth forms in schools and their own lower years (OFSTED, 1993:27).

Additional entry criteria to colleges

Question 120 asked for any additional criteria colleges used to be written in and several colleges stressed the 'open access' nature of the college, explaining that the seemingly contradictory policy of open entry plus requirements for individual courses was because courses were so various. It was noticeable, however, that the main courses mentioned where requirements were in force were 'A' level and GNVQ advanced or NVQ level 3.

The problem of requiring specific passes for GNVQ entry was even more difficult than for 'A' level, for the evidence of a link between non-completion of vocational courses and previous GCSE scores is less clear than it is for 'A' level (OFSTED, 1993: Exhibit 9:26). Attainment of a vocational qualification is only 'weakly correlated with prior GCSE attainment' and not strong enough to justify using GCSE ' as the baseline for measuring progress in a value added approach' (OFSTED, 1993:36). In that case, it seems hard to justify using these qualifications to decide entry to vocational courses at all.

Extra writing-in on behalf of sixth form colleges suggested admissions were often according to vacancies in subjects individually (sometimes even in subjects sets), though several such colleges were also anxious to make it clear that places were filled first from our 'partner schools' and only then was there 'open competition for the last 200 places'. In other colleges access was 'entirely open' to those who lived locally, and only filled competitively for those from outside the area. We could not quantify it, but additional comment suggested movement towards closer links with surrounding 'feeder' schools was increasingly being considered.

FE and tertiary colleges were more systematic in processing entrants, especially those colleges that were very large. Applications often went directly to those running courses, who accepted them if the student was well qualified or tried to find them another course if they were not. As one college put it, this is a process of 'application, reference, interviews, induction on the probability of following the course successfully'; or 'interview, preferences, existing qualifications, and tests'. A few spoke of 'suitability for the course' but many more (having sometimes looked at Records of Achievement) admitted students by their 'ability to benefit' and their possession of an 'acceptable attitude' and 'commitment to work'.

Inevitably, much of the process was not really apparent. Methods could be compatible with a comprehensive remit to provide for everyone; on the other hand, they could be selective in ways that did not show. 'Acceptable attitude' begs many questions – acceptable to whom?

These same comments apply equally to schools screening for sixth form entry, a process getting more rigorous in some schools, as 'league tables' put on the pressure to relinquish the comprehensive criterion of 'open access'. Nevertheless, many schools and colleges seemed anxious to try to keep open access – at least as a general rule. Much more of a problem to them was having a wide enough range of courses to provide for the whole age group.

On one point, however, colleges did differ from schools: in relation to students from minority groups. Earlier sections gave information from the 1994 survey about percentages of students not having English as their first language (Chapter 4) and Table A5 shows that somewhat larger percentages of colleges had such students in large numbers than did schools (equally in all three types of college). This would seem to confirm recently published research showing higher percentages of black and other ethnic minority students attend FE colleges than do white students of the same age or gender. Pakistani and Bangladeshi women, for example, are five time more likely than white women to attend FE, and Afro-Caribbeans twice as likely. It also chimes with findings in other countries about local comprehensive colleges.

That comprehensive colleges in the UK are possibly more congenial to minorities than are the sixth forms of the schools, is a fact that might possibly concern more schools with sixth forms than it seemed to do in 1994.

Transfers from private education to comprehensive schools and colleges

In the past there has been discussion about pupils switching to comprehensive education from private schooling, but not much hard evidence. Anecdotal information suggests that transfers are made by students weary of single-sex or boarding life or where parents prefer not to pay the heavy fees for 'A' level teaching when it is offered free in a local college with an increasingly good reputation. Private schools might say that some of these transfers were presenting disciplinary problems.

Both schools and colleges with 16–19 students were asked about post-16 entry from the private school sector (question 121) and almost all replied: 61% had such entrants, although in most numbers were less than 5% of those coming into the school or college. Only 7.4% had over 5%, though six had over 30%. Those most likely to have entrants from private schools were the sixth form colleges, 97.2% of whom had them, and the grant maintained schools with 71.7%. The percentage for LEA schools was 47.8%.

Size: 16–19 age group in schools and colleges

The size of groups in the 16–19 age range in comprehensive education has been a subject of debate since 1965 and long before (see Chapter 3). Tables A5 and A6 give extensive information about the average sizes of different types of comprehensive schools and colleges overall, as well as sizes separately for Year 12 (age 16–17 or S5) and Year 13 (age 17–18 or S6).

The colleges were larger, as would be expected, but just how much larger often comes as a shock – especially if we look at Year 12 on its own. Nationally in the 1994 survey the average size of this one year in the comprehensive colleges was 692 compared with 91 in the all-through comprehensive schools of the UK. This difference is becoming increasingly significant as increasing numbers stay on, and as education diversifies at this age.

Taking both Years 12 and 13 together (the 'sixth form'), the upper comprehensive schools of 13/14 to 18 had the largest size. The 14–18's average of 281 for the two years was considerably larger than the all-through school sixth form of 152. Of schools with different legal status, the largest sixth form was the voluntary controlled with 198, followed by the grant maintained and LEA schools not significantly different (167 and 159 respectively). None of the school types, however, came remotely near the averages for the colleges for the two years: the sixth form college with 865, the FE college with 1400, and the tertiary college with 1658.

Some school types had quite small sixth form averages, particularly single-sex schools with boys at 135 and girls at 138 (question 122a and b). This represents a considerable change over 30 years earlier when it was boys' schools that had the largest sixth forms (Benn and Simon, 1970: Table 17.3, p.287). Another type of comprehensive with a smaller than average sixth form in 1994 was that in the village or countryside with only 142.

Such dramatic differences were problem enough when there was only 'A' level study to worry about – as at the start of comprehensive education. But today there is a growing range of vocational courses that will soon be properly counted as essential to a fully comprehensive curriculum offering for this age range. When curriculum reform takes place and vocational and academic courses are either integrated or more regularly combined, the problem will escalate rather than end. Unless a common tertiary system is organised, few schools with small sixth forms are going to be able to stay 'comprehensive'. This will be their fate whether they specialise in 'A' levels and seek to select or whether they increasingly offer vocational courses or try to combine the two. It is true of colleges as well: some are not yet able to provide the comprehensive range that students would expect to have on offer in a fully comprehensive system, particularly academic courses in languages.

Table A9 shows the problem and the solution at a glance by looking specifically at the way the single Year 12 population in the UK divides with reference to institutional size. At one end are hundreds of schools with fewer than 100 pupils in the year and at the other end are a relatively small number of colleges – each with at least 500 students in the same year.

The size range of schools and colleges for Year 12 was wide ranging as well as polarised. One college had over 2000 in this single year while one school had under 5. There were small clusters at each end with 8% (mostly colleges) having over 500 in this one year; while at the other end, another 8% (including 104 schools) had 50 or less.Overall 51% of schools with 16–19 years had less than 100 in Year 12. These were not always schools in remote places; some were being 'run down', others just starting up. Regardless, there was hardly the same opportunity for those staying on compared with schools and colleges with larger numbers.

Throughout the history of comprehensive education there has always been a substantial number of schools with sixth forms which were considered less than viable (viability being calculated in relation to 'A' level). In the first days of comprehensive reorganisation the minimum size was 40 pupils for the two years (Benn and Simon, 1970:127). In the late 1970s it was raised but still substantial numbers of comprehensive schools were under the minimum size named (Briault and Smith, 1980:27). By the mid-1980s Keith Joseph decreed a minimum of 150 overall despite large numbers still under this size (and a contradictory government policy of creating more small sixth forms as a way of protecting an élite, selective academic sixth form).

By the mid-1990s the Audit Commission and OFSTED presented figures about numbers in schools and showed just how many sixth forms were uneconomic in size, both overall and in classes as taught: 54 comprehensive schools in the 1994 survey had sixth forms with less than 75 students (7.6% of all schools with sixth forms), the size of sixth form where standard courses cost up to four times as much to teach as those where total numbers are over 250. Many more sixth forms would have had subject range limited and a shortage of accommodation to run vocational education.

By Year 13 the size problem was worse, particularly in schools. For many in Year 12 had only been retaking 'O' levels or enrolled on 1-year courses. Table A6 shows that by Year 13 there was a dramatic drop in average numbers in all types of comprehensive school. For example, LEA schools had a drop of over 34% between the 12th and 13th years. The average Year 13 size for comprehensive colleges, meanwhile, was 536.

The survey (question 122C) also asked about students in the age range of 18–19 (Year 14) traditionally associated with students preparing for Oxbridge entry in the 'third year sixth' but nowadays just as likely to be those retaking exams. Of the schools in the 1994 survey, 402 had students of 18–19. The average size of this year in schools was only nine students.

A comprehensive equal opportunity

What was striking in the 20 years previous to 1994 was that there were no criteria about providing equal education for all or comparable opportunities or the same choice for everyone at this age regardless of the school in which a student has started out or of the area in which he or she lived; and regardless of the institution which (often by chance) he or she entered at 11 plus or 16 plus.

Were reorganisation along comprehensive lines to resume, then the system would be judged by whether it provides for the whole age group all that is 'normally available' in institutions serving the age range – as happened at the age of 11 in 1965. By this test comprehensive education is still very under-developed in the UK after the age of 16. Indeed, as OFSTED stated, 'there is no consensus about what full-time education for 16–19 year olds should include'.

The problem is that if all sixth forms are to be capable of offering even a minimum range of study at this level – to include the 14 'A' levels from question 138 (see below), plus at least one further foreign language, and possibly half a dozen GNVQ courses up through level 3/advanced – and all classes were to be of viable size, this would mean a sixth form overall of at least 250. Yet less than 10% of the survey schools in 1994 had sixth forms of this size and although two-thirds of the colleges did, they did not necessarily provide a full range of courses, if only because at present there is no recognised 'full range of courses' normally offered at 16 plus against which to judge systems locally (or institutions individually) concerning even the minimum spread of 'A' levels and GNVQs that should be on offer, much less other qualifications of importance.

Once such a range is determined officially (or perceived in popular opinion), there are only two ways to ensure equal access for students: either to fund every school and college to provide every course that is 'normally available' or detach the funding from individual students and instead fund institutions on the basis of what each provides, organising all institutions in an area to contribute courses to a common tertiary pool.

Though many schools will expand, there is no way most will increase in size five times over. There is no way that colleges can admit all those currently in the sixth forms. Every school and college has to remain. Table A9 shows why the only way comprehensive reorganisation will work is for individual colleges to form a network of tertiary education around the country and for individual sixth forms to form a network around the colleges: the two networks becoming a new national tertiary system (a development that schools and colleges are already beginning to make on their own – see page 455).

Size and academic results

Meanwhile, the race for enlargement on the basis of selective entry is distorting the system, for as 'full' schools start to select and then enlarge, and 'empty' schools contract and fall in size, selectivity at both 11 and 16 encourages the system to polarise between large schools with 'better' results and smaller schools with 'worse'. In the 1994 survey the differences were as yet not very great (Table 9.5) but they highlighted a disturbing trend.

Table 9.5 1994 survey. Averages for selected examinations by size of comprehensive schools (colleges omitted)

Size	Percentage with 5 GCSE A–C (O-grade 1–3)	'A' level point score*
1 under 600	36.4	12.0
2 600–900	37.2	12.0
3 900–1200	40.8	13.1
4 1200 and over	44.4	13.9

* Scottish schools omitted.

At first sight it looks like the larger the size, the better the results but the picture is not so simple. As Table A6 shows, although it is true that some types of comprehensive school with high 'A' level grade scores (like voluntary controlled schools, sixth form colleges, and 14–18 schools) had far larger Years 12 and 13 than the survey average, there were also several types with smaller than average numbers that also had high 'A' level scores (like boys' and Church of England comprehensives). Selectivity at intake (either at 11 or 16, social or academic) may be a factor in some of these schools but it is unlikely to be in all of them. Where it is, however, for every comprehensive school or college that 'selects', two or three others are left to take those who were not selected. Numbers fall. As numbers fall, polarisation increases, risking the divided system that comprehensive education was introduced to end in the first place.

As Chapters 3 and 4 and Tables A5 and A6 show clearly, for both GCSE and 'A' level, there is enough disparity already in the system, where, taking only 'A' level, grade point averages can differ a great deal according to legal status, context and intakes – with lower scores found for schools in large cities, on council estates and in schools serving housing areas that included substandard housing, while higher scores were associated with comprehensive schools serving private housing areas or those that drew the majority of their intake from middle-class homes.

The problem is that both five GCSE A–C and 'A' level point scores are 'selective' criteria: they measure only a minority of the age group. League tables, based on them, will thus reflect factors like social class and attainment intakes just as much as the 'excellence' of the school, for measures of league table success are so limited they are incompatible with comprehensive education. Some schools with the lower 'scores' were actually more successful than those with higher scores – when other factors were fed into the equation (even using these limited 'league table' exam criteria). Early exercises in 'value added' assessment, for example, (taking into account measured attainment at intake to schools) showed that ranks were dramatically rearranged (Hugill, 1994). When the results of an NFER project measuring exam outcome against measured attainment at intake for a sample of schools nationwide was published, some local authorities found it necessary to place non-selective LEA comprehensive schools higher than selective or GM schools[7].

But there was a further objection to the 'success' criteria used in league tables. They are based on one academic exam each at 16 and 18, the GCSE and the GCE 'A' level (Ordinary level and Higher in Scotland). These are not measures that are compatible with assessment of comprehensive education, which should be judged on **all** results and **all** forms of assessment for **all** types of qualifications pupils and students have obtained in **all** institutions. If league table status were to depend on 'comprehensive' criteria where all results were aggregated for all routes, at 16–19 there is no doubt that a different concept of excellence would be forwarded – which was 'comprehensive' in scope. Bearing this in mind, it is no surprise that the 1994 survey found that 88% of schools and colleges do not believe league table criteria at present give a fair or meaningful picture of any school's or college's achievement, including their academic achievements (see Chapter 7).

The national '12th year' in the UK

In previous sections of the book we have discussed the way sixth forms in schools and colleges with 16–19 groups differed in their organisation and intake as institutions within a comprehensive system. This section looks more closely at education across the single age group of year 12 (age 16–17, lower sixth, S5) in schools and colleges in the UK. Such a picture is difficult to get from official statistics because information for schools and colleges is so often given separately for each country as well as for each type of school, and separately again for schools as against colleges. Rarely is the single year group examined as one, especially from the perspective of comprehensive education.

Spread of academic and vocational offering

In comprehensive education both the spread and balance of what is on offer is important. The 1994 survey asked schools and colleges to set out the courses they offered, and in the case of 'A' level and Highers also the subjects. It also asked about examination courses, including entries and pass rates. Information for the 'national 12th year' is set out in the following tables and in Tables A6 and A8.

Only a few schools or colleges at either end of the spectrum make no attempt (for whatever reason) to offer at least two different kinds of courses. For example, a few sixth forms offered no 'A' level courses at all. Instead, 100% took a vocational course or GCSE retakes; in another it was A/S levels offered rather than 'A' levels. It could be said that such institutions denied students the chance to pursue specific subjects to the depth that was offered in neighbouring schools or colleges. At the other end were 23 comprehensive schools with high 'league table' ratings which offered their students only 'A' level courses after 16 and no others at all. Those who wanted to consolidate previous attainment or whose talents would have been forwarded by courses leading to other qualifications, were similarly denied any chance for continuing education.

Both sets of schools could be regarded as incompatible with comprehensive education and were unlike the vast majority of schools and colleges with students in the 16–19 age group, which offered a combination of 'A' level (Highers) and other work. Nevertheless the offerings could differ both in breadth and variety. Comprehensive education's development having lapsed, we have no way to judge which pass muster as 'comprehensive' because we have no criteria for that all-important feature of a comprehensive system: deciding what should be 'normally available to all' for this age group from which to choose.

This is one of the reforms that is urgently required. For any system should have a policy about what should be available in the last years of secondary education. It should also be concerned that individual students coming up to 16 have this full range of study available from which to choose and that each can find a combination of learning that suits their own interests and type of intelligence – if not in the schools where they started, at least in an institution with which the school has formal and continuing arrangements for further progression. In the present divided system (with everyone competing against everyone else) this is not possible. First, because too many schools and colleges lack a complete range; second, because too many students in schools are unaware of what is on offer in schools and colleges outside their own; and third, because co-operative ventures to provide for everyone are embryonic and nowhere receive official encouragement. For along with agreement on the range that should 'normally be available' for the age group, there is also the need in a public education service to be sure a democratically constituted body has the duty to oversee the development of institutional comprehensive provision to make it available.

Courses offered in 1994

Table 9.6 sets out 17 different courses often offered to Year 12 (age 16–17) in schools and colleges serving the 16–19 age range in the UK in 1994. It gives both the numbers of schools and colleges offering them in the survey as well as the average percentage taking the courses in the schools and colleges where they were offered.

Eighty per cent of schools and colleges eligible to answer this question gave replies (question 123), a lower response rate than for most questions in the survey, possibly because the information required extra calculations which not all schools and colleges had to hand (or had time to perform). For this reason figures need to be read with caution.

Table 9.6 Courses and qualifications offered in Year 12 in UK comprehensive schools and colleges (n=670), 1994

The courses offered	No. giving information	Average percentage within the school or college enrolled on the course
GCE 'A' levels	589	62.1
GCE A/S levels	364	14.5
Higher Grade	76	71.8
SCOTVEC	75	69.0
Certificate of 6th Year Studies	57	16.1
First BTEC	137	15.8
National BTEC	127	17.5
GCSE Mature	249	20.7
HND/HNC	28	9.6
City and Guilds	146	20.6
RSA	191	15.0
NVQ	79	13.8
SVQ	11	11.5
GNVQ	274	21.9
GSVQ	19	14.3
CPVE/DOVE	58	29.4
International Baccalaureate	5	11.6

Although Table 9.6 gives only an approximate idea of the way courses in the first year of 'staying on' were distributed in the UK, it was not possible to show the range of courses schools and colleges of different types were able to offer. However, from answers to a later question (138), which had a 95% response rate, it was possible to determine that almost all schools and colleges in England provided 'A' levels and in Scotland almost all provided Highers and SCOTVEC. With the rest of the courses the numbers of institutions offering them is much lower because some courses were more often centred in colleges than in schools.

Where 'A' level courses were offered, the average percentage in the UK Year 12 in the survey taking the course was just under two-thirds (62%)

– with the percentage in Scots schools on the academic Highers higher at 71%. When colleges are included, and by way of very rough comparison, national statistics (England only) for 1994 for Year 12 show 50% on 'A' or AS level studies in full-time education, with 40% on vocational courses, the remaining 10% on courses like GCSE (DfE, *Statistical Bulletin*, No. 10/94: para. 2). At 17 (Year 13), a third of those remaining in full-time study in England were on 'A' level courses and a fifth on vocational courses.

GNVQ was the most widely offered course in the survey outside 'A' levels (omitting Scotland), and 46% of the schools and colleges with 16–19 students answering this question offered it. Just as important, where they were offered, GNVQ courses were taken by a greater proportion of the year group inside each institution than any other course after 'A' levels (and the omnibus vocational course – DOVE – although this latter, as the table shows, was offered by very few institutions overall). GNVQ courses will increase in number because many of the other vocational courses listed in the table in 1994 as BTEC, RSA, or City and Guilds, were being converted to the GNVQ system.

In the absence of any further change to the system, we could look forward to seeing GNVQ relate to 'A' level as SCOTVEC courses relate to Highers in this table, where 10 years after their introduction not only are much the same numbers of schools offering them as offer Highers but the same percentages inside the schools and colleges are taking them up as take Highers. Which means that most students would be combining academic and vocational courses in Year 12, as happened in 1994 in Scotland, putting Scotland yet another important step further along the road to comprehensive curriculum development than the rest of the UK.

The other course offered by a substantial number of institutions and with a fifth of all students taking it where it is offered, was GCSE Mature. It is, however, a course whose numbers are declining rapidly at this age, having halved during the 10 years prior to the 1994 survey (DfE, *Statistical Bulletin*, No. 7/94). How far this decline continues depends upon the success of GN/SVQ and N/SVQ, and on decisions yet to be made in respect of 'A' level and Highers and what replaces them.

Considering that NVQ and SVQ were courses designed for the workplace (and in any case were only just launched in 1994) higher percentages than might have been predicted were already opting for them where they were being run in comprehensive schools or colleges.

School or college?

Table 9.7 shows the way courses set out in question 123 divided between schools and colleges offering the courses already named. Colleges were more likely to run vocational courses than schools. For example, only 10% of schools offered BTEC national courses in 1993–94, but nearly half the colleges did. That said, however, the table shows there is no cut and dried division between schools which offer the academic courses and colleges vocational. Most offer both. However, what is also evident is that the distribution of courses is hardly uniform. Which means that in the system as a whole what any student finds on offer in his or her area is a matter of potluck – hardly the principle upon which a comprehensive system from 16 to 19 should operate at the start of the twenty-first century.

Table 9.7 Division of courses named in question 123 between comprehensive schools and colleges (percentages being run in each sector) (omitting Scotland and 'A' levels)

	Schools	Colleges
BTEC (first)	14	32
BTEC (nat)	10	43
GCSE Mature	27	47
HND/HNC	0.7	17
City and Guilds	13	38
RSA	19	43
NVQ	5	32
GNVQ	30	44
CPVE/DOVE	7	5
International Baccalaureate	(4 schools)	(1 college)

Additional courses offered

Table 9.6 did not list the full range of courses available in the national Year 12 by any means; and in question 124 schools and colleges were invited to write in any additional courses they offered. Several colleges claimed there were too many to name and the space given on the form was inadequate. Nevertheless, about a quarter of those replying to question 123 added further information.

Several listed courses already named but described their own special use of them – like a foundation course using GCSE mature – in one case 'as a fresh start' for the age group made up of GCSE subjects none had studied before. Twenty-one mentioned their own foundation course using the general Diploma of Vocational Education (DOVE) as a core: every student staying on to the sixth did the course. Other courses mentioned were the Youth Award Scheme, the Certificate of Further Studies and the Oxford University Certificate for the Development of the Under 5s. Two institutions were running the Technological Baccalaureate. Most of those mentioned above were schools.

Additional courses (more likely to be run by colleges) were: a girls-only foundation English course; courses in road safety for learner-drivers; in hairdressing, motor vehicle maintenance, and in Japanese. Access courses were popular for Year 12, including one special preparation course for the uniformed services. Others were more general, preparing students for entry to both vocational and academic qualifications courses (GCSE, 'A' level or GNVQ at various levels). In two colleges 10% of those enrolled were on access courses of various kinds. Many colleges also had courses called Basic Maths or Basic English for students wanting a fresh start at this or any age.

There was also a wide range of professional qualifications run by the colleges (some probably for the post-18 age group more than those who were aged 16), including those for dental technicians, nursery nurses, secretaries, and legal executives. There were courses in childcare, English as a second language, and sports. The qualifications offered seemed legion[8].

Lastly, there were in-house courses of a general nature unrelated to any qualification – mainly to develop students personally and to assist their general learning or prepare them to profit from professional training. Hardly any related to requests from employers; they were the colleges' own response to perceived educational needs.

'A' Levels and Highers

One of the marks of a comprehensive education is that each school or college has a reasonable range of education appropriate to each age range in the 'going' qualifications of the day. In earlier decades for the national Year 12 this meant merely a reasonable range of 'A' levels or Highers. Today the full offering has to be much larger, but the range of 'A' levels and Highers is still a central feature of any comprehensive system.

Question 138 listed 14 of the most commonly offered subjects at 'A' level/Higher Grade and asked schools and colleges to say which they offered in 1994. Almost all schools and colleges with students in the 16–19 age range responded to this question – in marked contrast to question 123. It was clear that detailed information about 'academic' subjects is still more likely to be at the fingertips than information for other types of learning.

With certain exceptions (given below) most schools and colleges provide a full range of 'standard' academic subjects: English, French, art, history, physics, geography, chemistry, biology, and mathematics – with slightly more schools than colleges providing each at the level of 90% and over. 'A' level/Higher mathematics was the most universally offered – by 98% of all schools and colleges.

However, some subjects on the list were below 90% in either schools or colleges or both. In colleges the subject that fared worst was music 'A' level with only 62% able to provide it. Colleges also found it harder to provide German 'A' level (only 75% did so) as well as Geography (only 79%). Otherwise, all the other subjects were provided by over 80% of colleges, while English, art, history, physics, chemistry, biology, and mathematics were provided by over 90%. Psychology, sociology and economics were also provided by over 90% of colleges.

By contrast schools did not provide the last three subjects to the same degree, particularly psychology, which was only on offer in 32% of school sixth forms, while only 60% offered sociology and 76% economics. Schools, like colleges, also had trouble offering music (only 78% did) and only 79% had German, but all the other subjects (biology, chemistry, physics, history, French, geography, English, art, and mathematics) were offered by over 95%. These figures suggest that colleges made psychology, sociology and economics their special subjects, with over 90% providing 'A' levels in these fields. These are subjects which continue to be very popular with students from 16 to 19, particularly social science and sociology.

Scotland's offering was more traditional. For example, only three schools in the survey offered psychology or sociology at Higher grade, although 54% offered economics. Except for German (offered by only 76% of Scottish comprehensive schools) all other subjects in the list were offered at Higher level by 95% or more.

All 14 subjects – traditional and non-traditional – were provided by 137 institutions, including 75% of Tertiary colleges, 70% of sixth form colleges and 25% of FE colleges. By contrast only 9% of LEA sixth forms (and the same percentage of grant maintained sixth forms) were able to do so.

Extra 'A' levels and Highers

This was not the end of the story by any means, for many schools and colleges offered additional 'A' levels or Higher Grade examinations not listed among the 14. In fact, 43 extra subjects were named in written answers to question 139 – of which the most popular addition was business studies (202 ran it) followed by technology and design (154), and computing (140). The remainder are listed in Note 9 (p.459).

Again, colleges were those likely to have the widest range of extra 'A' level courses, particularly the sixth form and tertiary colleges, simply because concentration of numbers made this possible. But when academic courses are reorganised (with or without integration with vocational) and comprehensive development moves towards a unified tertiary system, all these courses could be offered in each area and made available to many more, even if some are on offer in only one or two institutions. Only tertiary reorganisation will make this possible, however.

'A' level attainment

Table A6 gives information about percentages of each 17–18 year age group entering for two or more 'A' levels (see below for Scotland) as well as the grade point averages for all types of comprehensive schools and colleges in all types of contexts. These results need to be read with caution because only 80% (594) out of the total possible gave their 'A' level results in answer to question 140a (for colleges, only 67%) and because percentages entered for two or more 'A' levels were calculated as percentages of year numbers for a year later than the year in which the examinations were taken. (See also Appendix II, Note B for further information on 'A' level and Highers statistics.)

Overall, Table A6 shows that on average 65% of the students in Year 13 (17–18) were entered for two or more 'A' levels. The percentages for sixth forms in schools was generally higher than for colleges – with all-through comprehensive schools having the highest figure at 89% and FE colleges the lowest at 27%.

The spread of those entering for 'A' level showed the usual extremes. At one end there were 23 (mostly colleges) that entered 300 or more students for two or more 'A' levels, while at the other 61 (mostly schools) entered 20 or fewer. Just over half, however, (311) entered at least 55 candidates for two or more 'A' levels.

Some individual results

Overall comparisons between 1994 survey results for 'A' level and Highers and results nationally are given in Appendix II, where generally we see that for both exams survey results were slightly lower than national ones at this level in contrast to GCSE (SCE O grade) results which were slightly higher. Possible reasons to account for these differences are given in Appendix II.

This Appendix also discusses reasons for one other difference found at

'A' level, and that was a lower 'A' level grade point average for grant maintained (GM) schools than for LEA county schools: 11.9 compared with 13.1, the reverse of the national statistics for the same year, where grant maintained schools' scores were higher than national averages at 15.7 (DfE, *Statistical Bulletin*, No. 7/94: Table 10).

The most likely explanation is that the GM schools appearing in the 1994 survey (declaring themselves comprehensive) are somewhat different from many of those GM schools not taking part, including the substantial number (76) in the survey year which were official grammar schools, as well as others which must have been quite selective – to account for the GM national score. Whatever the explanation, when we remove the GM schools from the comprehensive schools' national score in England, we get a survey average for 'A' level (including Wales and Northern Ireland) of 13.1, not that much lower than the national figure for comprehensive schools in England of 13.6 (DfE, *Statistical Bulletin*, No. 7/94).

At the same time, some schools replying to the 1994 survey had very selective sixth forms – some because they restricted their work to 'A' level, others because their intakes at age 11 were selective (shown by their attainment levels of the top 20% , their higher than average middle-class intakes, their GCSE results, or all three). The GM schools were well represented but this group of schools also included aided, voluntary controlled and LEA comprehensive schools – some with 'A' level averages higher than the national averages for LEA grammar schools' or private schools' figures for the same year. Some were schools of ancient lineage, though others were established in the 1960s and 1970s.

Any impartial observer would say that were such schools to insist they were selective (or to call themselves grammar schools) few would contradict them. Yet all chose to class themselves as comprehensives, and by taking part in the 1994 survey made it clear that this was the status they chose in a positive way. Their numbers are more than is generally realised by some of those conducting both sides of the education debate at the top, though their definition of comprehensive differs drastically from that used in most schools, where a representative spread of attainment is expected. In these schools, there is a less than representative spread of pupils with average (and particularly below average) attainment – possibly, 'token' numbers only.

'A' level differences between institutions with 16–19 students

The high grade point averages (and percentages entering for two or more

'A' levels) for voluntary comprehensives with controlled status compared with all other types of voluntary comprehensive school (Table A6) was one example of differences that showed up. 14–18 comprehensive schools also had higher than survey average figures. Previous pages in this book have already discussed the differences that showed up for mixed and single-sex schools at this level (see pages 122–24), while Chapters 3 and 4 discuss 'A' level differences related to different legal status and different geographical and social contexts.

Despite the differences observable within the comprehensive field, and despite the far larger differences that seem to be apparent in scores between comprehensives and selective schools or between comprehensive schools and comprehensive colleges, when it comes to actual performance at 'A' level, almost all research to date shows no one type of institution has any superiority. For example, when looking at 'value added', as OFSTED calls the improvement that a school or college makes on the GCSE scores with which students started 'A' level courses, a round-up of research to 1993 'found that no single type of institution appeared markedly more effective at 'A' levels than the others' (OFSTED, 1993: para. 33, p.32) with the possible exception of the upper tier comprehensives with a 13–18 age range (although this was found in only one study (OFSTED, 1993: para. 89)). There was also no clear link between size of 16–19 years and value added (OFSTED, 1993: Exhibit 1.6, p.34) – an interesting finding in relation to the 1994 survey's apparent linking of large size and 'good results' (see Table 9.5).

What accounts for most of the differences in league-table results is the social and attainment intake to any institution, precisely the information which is never given in any league table.

Although the 'A' level is a different kind of examination from the GCSE, the same associations of 'results' with different intakes and contexts repeat themselves (as Table A6 shows): higher percentages from schools serving private housing areas or countryside and village and lower ones where schools serve council estates or large cities or sub-standard housing; or, as analysed elsewhere, better results where comprehensive schools have middle-class intakes irrespective of what type they are or, particularly where comprehensive schools have mixed intakes, with no grammar schools competing in their vicinity. Differences were also shown for 'A' level scores relating to schools having high and low percentages of free dinners and high and low attendance rates.

It will take more sophisticated analysis to show which factor correlates most closely to 'A' level entry numbers and grade point averages in the

1994 survey. What makes results interesting at this initial stage of analysis is that although overall findings may not bring many surprises, a reasonable number of individual schools and colleges achieve outside the levels that would be expected of them – both less well as well as much better than expected. These possibly deserve their own special analysis, particularly those achieving really well in the most 'unfavourable' of conditions.

Other academic courses

A/S levels were introduced nationally in order to add breadth to everyone's Year 12 study but this is not working out as planned with only one A/S to every 14 'A' levels being run and 'still insufficiently used' to broaden courses (OFSTED, 1993: p.38). Some say they are used mainly to give certain students the edge in Oxbridge entry (Spours, 1993:154). But to others using them for university entrance, 'They're a total failure ... they just don't open any doors' (*TES*, 19 August, 1994).

If the picture as reflected in Table 9.6 is in any way representative, only 61% of comprehensive institutions (omitting Scotland) offered them in Year 12 and within the schools and colleges that did run them, only an average of 14.6% took them. Nevertheless, they were one of the most popular examinations used in combination with other courses in 'combination' programmes chosen by students in comprehensive schools and colleges.

International Baccalaureate

The International Baccalaureate (IB), a UNESCO-sponsored qualification born at the International School in Geneva in 1967, was widely promoted at the time in the UK by liberal educationalists like ADC Peterson and by 1994 was in use in some 62 countries (Leggate, 1993).

The IB is an academic course that requires three 'major' subjects and three 'minor' ones to be studied – and is thus a wider form of 'A' levels, where its main asset is that it has less specialisation. But because it requires so many subjects and is rather expensive to run, the number of institutions offering it in any country is small, and its main providers in the UK seem to be private and selective schools.

In the 1994 survey only four schools and one college were running the IB in the comprehensive sector, and although this may seem a tiny number, proportionately it is not much less than what might be expected given the very low percentages taking the course inside any of the participating countries. In 1992, for example, a total of only 28 institutions in the UK offered it (Leggate, 1993).

Vocational qualifications

If we look back at the earlier years of comprehensive education, many schools had vocational courses: commercial, technical, agricultural and pre-nursing, some run in collaboration with colleges, some initiated in the school. They were often called 'link courses' and were run exclusively in the 5th year for those who had to stay on but were not sitting GCE or CSE examinations.There were few vocational courses after 16 in schools, although sometimes RSA, Pitmans or City and Guilds courses were started by schools that wanted to encourage more pupils to stay on who would not be taking 'A' levels, but who needed more than 'O' level retakes (Benn and Simon, 1970:196–98).

After 1972 and the raising of the school leaving age, 5th year vocational courses were gradually eliminated as a sign of comprehensive education's determination to prove itself in terms of 'results' in selective academic examinations like 'O' level, CSE and 'A' level. This led many schools to process an ever increasing number of pupils into 'academic' studies before 16 and afterwards into 'A' levels or retaking 'O' levels. Later this same anti-vocational pressure was being put on certain schools by the 'league table' requirements based exclusively on five GCSE A–C or two-plus 'A' levels, taking no account of vocational qualifications or other forms of learning that might also be open to them. The thinking still prevailed among some schools (and parents) that vocational courses are a sign of low league table status or working-class students.

Slowly the numbers of these schools and parents began to shrink, as vocational qualifications were progressively introduced into schools after 1989 as additions to, rather than substitutes for, 'A' level. Colleges have increased their own range through GNVQ/NVQ reorganisation, but they have also increased their 'A' level work. It is obvious these two drives will create a certain amount of tension between academic and vocational education in the 16–19 sector, as well as between institutions, even within institutions, possibly even within departments. But precisely because such tension threatens polarisation, it also increases the pressure for unification of the 16–19 system and for integration of the academic and vocational curriculum and for some form of common assessment.

'A' level equivalent vocational courses

Information in the 1994 survey pertained to the 1992–93 academic year, when GNVQ was only just starting up and many comprehensive schools and colleges were still rather confused about its levels and equivalences. Not enough with completed GNVQ advanced or NVQ level 3 courses were available for study. The 1994 survey, therefore, looked at progress in vocational provision and achievement through those entered for both BTEC and City and Guilds courses leading to qualification at national level, the already accepted equivalent to two 'A' levels. These included the average numbers entered for these qualifications per institution and the percentage entering who achieved them. Table A6 sets out the survey's findings.

No comparisons are possible to figures nationally for reasons given in Appendix II, Note B, but internal comparisons can be made within the survey population, where the numbers of institutions giving information for national level qualifications in BTEC or City and Guilds was 175 (question 140b) – just over one in five of the survey's schools and colleges with 16–19 students (if Scotland is omitted)[10].

As Table A6 shows, the average number of students entering per institution where the national level was run was 94 and the percentage achieving the qualification was 76%. This covered a huge difference between FE and tertiary colleges on the one hand and the sixth forms of schools (along with sixth form colleges) on the other – both in terms of numbers entering and percentages qualifying. Even with sixth form colleges included (with success rates for this qualification lower than the survey average) the colleges as a whole had higher success rates at 83% achieving the qualification than any of the schools (with tertiary colleges and FE colleges having very high rates at 90% and 86% respectively).

Other comprehensive schools and colleges with high percentages passing (though the average numbers entering may have been small and the numbers of schools running the courses may have been few) were girls' schools, special agreement schools, 14–18 schools, and voluntary controlled comprehensives. The latter achieved 100% success rates, as did all institutions running these courses which answered from the Channel Islands, Isle of Man and SCEA.

BTEC and City and Guilds National awards are marks of distinction for any school or college with students in the 16–19 age range. Many of their courses will in future be converted to GNVQ awards (the process going on during the year of the 1994 survey), but that is no excuse for an education system that has ignored excellence of academic achievement in this type of work-related learning when it comes to 'rating' institutions as good, bad or indifferent in the so-called league tables. Such tables are as backward as the pre-twentieth-century notions of excellence that only counted scholarship in the classical languages, philosophy or mathematics as real learning, ignoring attainment in many fields of natural science or in languages people actually spoke and read. Developing comprehensive education is about a great deal more than merely ending selection; it is also about enlarging learning and extending excellence itself. Despite the prominence of 'standards' in party-political programmes, national notions of excellence in education are still very simplistic, and largely selective academically.

Vocational education – which fields?

GNVQs (SNVQ in Scotland) were launched in 1992 in the expectation that 4 years later at least three levels of qualifications would be available (and five eventually, though not necessarily in all institutions or even in any one). In the year of the survey five were already running including business, manufacturing, health and social care, leisure and tourism, art and design; and three more were being piloted in science, construction/built environment and catering – with more to follow. Each course was also to have core skills in IT, numeracy and communications.

Despite the controversial introduction and the many disagreements attending the creation of these courses (see Chapter 2), by the year of the 1994 survey GNVQ courses were spreading in comprehensive schools and colleges where 82,000 students in the 16–19 age range were already taking them in 1400 institutions nationally (NCVQ, 1994:13) – probably about 40% of comprehensive schools and colleges.

GNVQ raised important questions for comprehensive schools and colleges in terms not only of whether to run GNVQ courses, but in which fields and at what levels. Some qualifications would be closed to schools because they lack specialist facilities, e.g. for engineering (Huddleston, 1993). This means most schools were unable to contemplate most GNVQ fields, including construction, built environment, catering, and engineering. However, any classroom can be turned into an 'office' for business or for tourist transactions. Thus business studies and tourism became the GNVQ qualifications so many offered – meaning these were all many students would have had on offer.

The FEFC Report for 1994 confirmed that business studies had the highest enrolments that year in the further education sector for this qualification, again raising the issue of how many were choosing the field because they were interested or because it was the main course available? It also raises the question about the future entrants to work in the rest of the occupational fields, where courses were harder or more expensive to run and staff.

To help shed some light on this issue (and after having asked about vocational courses generally in questions 123 and 124), the 1994 survey also asked all schools and colleges which were providing courses leading to qualifications in BTEC or GNVQ (SCOTVEC or SNVQ in Scotland) to give some indication of the range of courses they offered, including the individual courses/titles (question 125). Some of the larger FE colleges quite rightly protested that the space allowed would not permit a full list. 'You must be joking!', wrote one, thinking we were after every unit being offered, while another sent a brochure with 800 listed, to make the point. Many Scottish schools sent their full lists of SCOTVEC modules.

Nevertheless, a reasonably large number of schools and colleges (459) gave information about the vocational areas in which they were running courses, especially those leading to qualifications in GNVQ and BTEC. The results were inevitably impressionistic (since some listed every course and others gave general categories) but answers give some insights into the spread of provision being offered as the 'vocational explosion' was getting under way, particularly in schools.

The information is given in Note 11 (p.459), with the outcome quite dramatic in terms of the domination of the field in both schools and colleges by relatively few fields of learning, including leisure and tourism or health/caring, but particularly by business studies, which topped the list by a wide margin, variously set out as Business and Finance, Business Administration, or Business Studies, depending on the qualification and the level at which it was offered. In GNVQ the domination was at all levels: pre-vocational up to 'A' level equivalent and beyond, and from foundation level up to national level for BTEC. The BTEC Business First also comprised a large percentage of the courses at level one. Colleges often had business courses at all three levels, but it was rare for schools to have them at more than two.

National figures suggest 40% of those choosing GNVQ chose business studies in the survey year (NCVQ, 1994) and two-thirds of those enrolled on NVQs were on those 'providing business services' or 'goods and services' (FEFC, 1994a:58). Nationally, it was almost as if as one business shut down, a new business studies course was set up.

Many of the students taking these business courses were young women, since 'business studies' has long been associated with girls' vocational work in comprehensive education (Felsenstein, 1987:29; Marsh, 1986). The FEFC also specified health and community caring GNVQs as those showing heavy imbalance towards women (FEFC, 1994a:10–11). Such feedback suggests that the sex-stereotyping so associated with occupational training in the 1980s (see pages 121, 363) might be continuing in vocational education in the 1990s.

There are also problems for GNVQ as well in dealing with high drop-out rates, inappropriate use of resources (or lack of them altogether), especially where part-time students are concerned, and very poor records for job placement after many courses. It is too early to say what kind of jobs students were getting after leaving schools and colleges at 17 or 18 – say, with qualifications in business or health or caring fields. There is obviously a worry that the credibility of qualifications will be threatened if too many gaining qualifications, especially at levels below 3 – both GNVQ or NVQ – end up with the same menial, poorly-paid or part-time work they could have got without taking them. Especially if it turned out there were greater chances for work after other types of vocational courses (which far fewer schools and colleges were running) or that despite the good publicity offered when GNVQ qualified students were first offered university places, the university entry rate turned out to be poor from such courses. In 1994 stories of numbers entering university clashed with research suggesting difficulties in achieving progression (or work) in several vocational fields (FEFC, 1994a:10–11; Young, 1994).

But it is not just about whether qualifications will enhance chances in the jobs market, or whether they were what students really wanted to learn, but also about what society needed. No one anywhere seems to be in charge of ensuring that courses are developed in rough approximation to national, local or regional needs, let alone those of society in the future.

The vocational/academic balance

The CPVE was phased out in the year of our survey, replaced by DOVE (Diploma of Vocational Education), both courses having their origin in attempts to replace the CEE in the early 1980s[1] and having since inherited some of the pedagogic features of the old CGLI and BTEC Foundation Awards. A few schools in the 1994 survey used DOVE rather imaginatively, as a start on a common core for all students in Year 12. But others used it for the lower achievers, previewing a darker future. Many fear at pre-GCSE level it will simply become a 14-plus GNVQ course, possibly integrated with PSHE (Spours, 1993: 158–59), ear-marked for those pre-judged unlikely to obtain many GCSEs – a course run in the poorest schools in the poorest areas. This form of curricular selection starting at 14 is what is incompatible with a comprehensive curriculum (see Chapter 7).

After 16 there are other balance problems. Table A6 breaks down enrolment and attainment in selected academic and vocational courses during the national Year 12, giving us a chance to see the way schools and colleges performed in both academic and vocational fields, and which comprehensive types were associated with high vocational attainment. It shows what was already evident in Scotland in relation to SCOTVEC certificate courses (see pages 170–71): comprehensive schools and colleges less likely to rate highly in these limited academic 'league table' indicators of achievement, were often likely to achieve well by indicators relating to vocational qualifications.

For example, Table A5 shows that there are lower average percentages of the 16–19 age group taking 'A' levels in schools in large cities, on council estates, or where schools draw from sub-standard housing, but that comprehensive schools or colleges in these situations had far higher than survey averages taking GNVQ (and Table A6 shows the same for numbers entering BTEC at national level). Where schools drawing from private housing were running national level vocational qualifications, for example, only 25% were entering these vocational courses. Where schools served council estates, 54% were entering (Table A6).

But it was not a question of polarisation between schools that are vocational and those that are academic. As Scotland's figures show, once the vocational qualification is well entrenched (as it has been for 10 years), the balance after 16 changes in the direction of an increasing number of leavers with both types of qualification. In Scotland the balance was 24% gaining three or more Highers and 38% three or more SCOTVEC modules (Table A6). Scotland's columns also show that in certain situations the balance towards vocational qualifications is likely to be greater still: e.g. on council estate comprehensives the balance was 16% to 44%. The same trend was already evident south of the border. Where BTEC National was being run, council estate comprehensive schools had higher average numbers on such courses than on 'A' levels. So did the 1994 survey for all institutions where the two were run together: 94 entering for BTEC and City and Guilds National as against 83 for two or more 'A' levels.

The future

All this speaks well for both the vocational qualifications and the institutions offering them but it raises the problem of the majority of 16–19 venues that do not as yet run both types of courses at this level, and the polarisation both within and between schools. Another problem is whether a divide is developing not so much between schools and colleges as between vocational and academic courses in certain types of schools or colleges (or in those serving specific populations in certain social conditions). A divide that encourages those with 'higher' level courses to be selective and limit themselves to students with better qualifying grades while others are steered elsewhere, is not a situation comprehensive education can sustain in the long run. But the present system's dynamic, controlled by the market rather than by any form of educational planning, naturally pushes in this selective direction.

It is a division that would be against the conscious development of the 16–19 years in most schools and colleges. Comprehensive education has gone far enough to ensure that any attempt to divide education at this age between 'academic' students to the schools, for example, and 'vocational' to the colleges, would be very hard to accomplish. As would a divide between some schools specialising in 'A' levels and academic study while others did the GNVQ. Most schools and colleges wish to provide a range of types of education (including both vocational and academic) and the popular development of the 16–19 sector is moving in the direction of greater balance in this respect. But keeping this balance is much more difficult than it should be at this stage in the late twentieth century.

At college level there is already a divide. Where national level qualifications (in BTEC or CGLI) were on offer in tertiary colleges, the average number entering in 1993 per college was 279. With sixth form colleges the average was only 10 (less than the average for schools which had much smaller numbers in Year 13). It may be argued that the sixth form colleges had an average of 278 entering for two or more 'A' levels in the same year but so does the tertiary college: in fact, almost the same average of 272. Thus in terms of providing **both** academic and vocational education to a high level by the Year 13, tertiary colleges stand out as the best balanced.

Increasing numbers of schools will be providing vocational qualifications – just as increasing numbers of colleges will be providing academic ones. Every type of 16–19 institution will wish to have both sets of students making their way upwards to degree level or going on to further professional learning or to work, and can do so, provided destructive polarisation can be avoided. The competitive nature of 16–19 education, combined with a crackdown on dropping out, could mean a gradual return to selection – in defiance of the development most institutions would want.

Selective sixth forms that do not provide for vocational study will find their numbers dropping if there is any sort of curricular integration reform. So, although the 1994 survey can show some worrying divisions opening up within the comprehensive sector, it can also point to parallel developments which are acting to close other longer standing divisions. The movement to divide 16–19 education by schools versus colleges or by academic versus vocational or by higher versus lower prior attainment, though currently being fostered assiduously, is being met head on by the continuing development of institutions which are committed to providing comprehensively. It is not a question of which will win but how long the contest has to go on before proper comprehensive development of the 16–19 sector takes place.

Scotland

Scotland offered a better balance between vocational and academic qualifications and it also offered it in almost every school – unlike the rest of the UK, where only certain schools as yet had any real choice in this respect.

Of those replying to question 123 from Scotland all offered Highers and almost all offered SCOTVEC modules. In addition 74% ran the Certificate of Sixth Form Studies, 22% the GSVQ and 10% the SVQ.

Information on the range of Highers has already been given (see pages 169–70) and the range of SCOTVEC NC modules was impossible to document since the number of such modules is so great. The average number per survey school giving information was 55 per school (each usually 40 hours of study). Unlike the GNVQ for England and Wales, which was strictly vocational, SCOTVEC modules covered both academic and vocational fields: not just technology but also mathematics, not just physical education but also chemistry, not just home economics but also history, although a large number of those taking the modules took them in the arts, caring services, technology, business studies and sports studies. They were distinguished from Highers by criterion-referenced testing and by practical application of knowledge.

The popularity of these short vocational courses, introduced only in

1984, has been phenomenal. Although designed for further education originally, the real growth has been in schools (Raffe, 1993). This took place alongside growth in numbers taking Highers, now nearly half the school population (as against one-third taking 'A' levels in England); 81% of schools with H grade in the survey had 50% or more in the school taking them, by contrast to schools in the survey offering 'A' levels, where only 66% had more than 50% taking such courses. In eight Scottish schools 100% did Highers; and in 15, 100% did SCOTVEC modules.

Results – Scotland

Of the 91 schools, 84 gave their results for the percentage of the S4 roll gaining three or more Highers (A–C) (question 141a): 77 had 10% or more gaining this qualification, while 34 had 25% or more and 6 had 50% or more. As Table A6 shows, the average was 24.1% for survey schools (see Appendix II, Note B for comparison with national figures from the SOED for that year).

Sixty-seven schools gave their results for percentages of students on the S5/S6 roll gaining 3 or more SCOTVEC modules: with 65 of these having 10% or more gaining the qualifications, 52 having 25% or more and 20 50% or more. The average percentage for the survey as a whole (question 141B) was 38.2% (Table A6).

Highers and SCOTVEC attainment differed in Scots schools and colleges in relation to the schools' location and intakes, these factors having already been explored in relation to Highers in Chapter 4 (see page 169). Chapter 4 also included results in Highers examinations analysed in relation to social class of intakes and level of attainment at entry to its schools. The main findings (apart from the association of higher levels of middle class and attainment intakes with higher percentages achieving the Highers qualification) was, as already said, that in those situations where schools did rather less well than the survey average at achieving three or more Highers, they often did better than the Scottish average in obtaining SCOTVEC modules. No Scottish schools had succumbed to being 'SCOTVEC schools' rather than 'Highers' schools, however.

GSVQ, Certificate of Sixth Form Studies and SVQ

The rest of the courses available in Scottish schools and colleges at this age trail considerably in terms of popularity, as shown in Table 9.6 – with the Certificate of Sixth Form Studies leading the pack. About three-quarters of those schools and colleges replying offered this course and an average of

16% in the schools took it, often students in S6 who are headed for university and who want to improve their study skills.

GSVQ and SVQ have lower numbers of schools running them than was the case with GNVQ in England and Wales – and only time will tell the way these will 'mesh' with the NC modules. In the four FE colleges which replied SCOTVEC was offered and so was SVQ and Certificate of Sixth Form Studies. GSVQ was offered in three.

Ironically, it is the SCOTVEC success story which is now fuelling discontent in Scotland's educational community, where so many want to end the segregation between academic and vocational courses and achieve some integration within a system where academic success in vocational qualifications 'counts' in the same way (e.g. for higher education entry) and is assessed in a common system. The Howie Commission revealed many favoured a new system that would somehow combine vocational and academic elements within a single system of assessment (but not in the type of 'two-track solution that government ... envisaged for England and Wales' (Raffe, 1993:64)). The latest government proposals do not meet the challenge, being essentially still divided: 'the solution ... of yet another stream is ... characteristically English' (Raffe, 1993:65). Many Scottish educators are equally unhappy about the continuing exclusion of young people at 16 on YT schemes quite outside education, subject to employers' short-term needs. Although it is far ahead with its mixing of academic and vocational, Scotland has learned the hard way that in the present system academic and vocational 'do not mix on equal terms' (Raffe, 1993:63). Equalising these terms is thus Scotland's continuing task.

Work-related education

Day-release and part-time study

So far we have looked at students in 16–19 comprehensive education who are attending full time. But the extent to which comprehensive schools and colleges have accommodated part-time study for this age group is just as much a measure of their fully comprehensive status. Many schools find it hard to accept that once legal compulsion to stay in education ends, part-time learning becomes a very significant part of education.

In the 1990s most schools could envisage coping with new qualifications and assessment that combine academic and vocational learning, even integrating the two, but far fewer were ready as yet to deal with the young person who is not a full-time student at 16 – let alone with one in occupationally related learning in a workplace, though the majority of schools and colleges are increasingly involved in linking education with the workplace, even if only for the 'work experience' week. Yet almost all predictions about the future show that in time, as comprehensive education pushes beyond the 'school' barrier and in to lifelong learning, part-time learning (along with short spells of full time) will become the standard mode of education, the heart of comprehensive experience.

Some colleges too find part-time study hard to accommodate, although day-release courses for those at work are set to increase. As for providing occupationally specific education, as Tables 9.6 and 9.7 show, numbers of schools and colleges as yet providing for qualifications of NVQ and SVQ are small: 79 schools and colleges out of the total answering (13.4%) in England and Wales; with 11 in Scotland. Within the colleges where such courses were offered only 14% (and 12% in Scotland) were taking them. But the qualification itself had only just begun, and had faced enormous criticism and difficulties because of an inadequate introduction by government. Its future could be quite different.

Question 132 asked specifically about work-release students and part-timers who came to school or college for certain periods from training courses like YT: 788 schools and colleges gave information with 20.3% of those replying having such students. Tertiary colleges had the most (78%) but only 6% of the sixth form colleges had such students. By contrast, all-through schools had double this percentage: 12% (Table A6). Of those giving information, 137 were able to say what percentage of the Year 12 these groups represented (question 133), showing that three-quarters had under a quarter of their students released from work or training. 21%, however, had over 50%. Scotland's record was yet again in advance of the rest of Britain: 33% of the schools and colleges in the 1994 survey had students studying on day-release.

But part-time students were not just those on day-release programmes. They could also be students who were working in jobs with no training or not working and not on any scheme but who nevertheless wanted to continue learning. Recent estimates suggest that the totality of part-time numbers in this category, studying for whatever reason, could be as high as 150,000 (Finn, 1995). The 1994 survey therefore also asked about any part-timers on any courses (question 128); 764 replied and those with such students were 27%. The difference made by adding general part-time students to specific day-release percentages, was thus 7%. Not a definitive figure in any way but one that suggests the category may be larger than previously assumed.

Again colleges were more involved than schools in providing for part-timers which included those without specific day-release programmes. Whereas only 13% of 11-18 schools and 19% of upper-tier comprehensive schools had any students enrolled part-time after 16, 74% of the colleges did (with tertiary colleges at 87% followed by FE colleges with 79% and sixth form colleges with 51% – a contrast with the small percentage of sixth form colleges having day-release students). Schools other than LEA schools had negligible numbers (including only 2% of aided and 4% of GM comprehensives with any part-time students after 16).

That only one in four comprehensive schools and colleges have part-time students of whatever kind, may not seem like a large number and possibly it is all that could have been expected in 1994, but for a properly functioning comprehensive system that will be extended to provide education for life-long learning, it should be 100% – at least until the whole of the national Year 12 stays on full time.

Relationship of schools and colleges with TECs and LECs

One reason the part-timer students were remote from 16–19 education is that so many still came under the auspices of the segregated, privatised Training and Enterprise Councils (TECS – LECs in Scotland). Divorcing education and training has never been satisfactory and it is doubly unsatisfactory for those only just 16, for even though they may be on 'schemes', they are still young people of secondary education age, still learning. That they may be learning in the workplace makes no difference. They are finishing their secondary education, and like the rest of their contemporaries their learning should be overseen within the same system, where they enjoy the same rights and where they have the chance to extend their choices. This objective will never be accomplished while they are isolated in 'schemes' run by private companies like TECs.

Not that TECs are even uniform in the way they run themselves. Some take a big hand in setting up vocational education and overseeing schemes and courses, others do very little. Some are successful in this work; a lot are failures in this work, in large part because it is a task they are ill-equipped to accomplish. In the end it is up to the employers whether they succeed, and TECs' powers are very limited in relation to employers. Previous sections have dealt with TECs or LECs as part of the education structure and discussed doubts about their capacity to organise work-related education, especially for this age group (see pages 16–17, 77–79).

One measure of any success for TECs and LECs would be establishing contact with every single school and college having students of 16–19, since they are charged with the responsibility of training schemes, can promote vocational education courses (both NVQ and GNVQ) and have been given vast sums of public money to do both. It is not only important to learn how this money was distributed, what decisions are taken about what shall be funded and what and who takes them, it is also important to know how many actually have any relationship with the schools and colleges where the main educational input to their work would be bound to be located.

Yet the survey discovered (question 134) that only just over half the schools and colleges with a 16–19 age group had any relationship with their local LEC or TEC. This was usually but not always in the form of a contract to deliver training for the TEC, although some mentioned former schemes only: 'Our LEA scheme was TEC funded but no longer receives any funding'. Breaking replies down further (see Table A6) showed that 95% of colleges had TEC relationships compared with only 47% of all-through schools. The two upper-tier comprehensive schools had very different profiles here with 76% of 13–18 schools having TEC relationships compared with only 25% of those with a 14–18 age range. Others with contacts at percentages significantly lower than the survey average were boys' comprehensive schools (27%), Catholic comprehensives (37%), and schools drawing mainly from council estates (42%).

But it was not only having some relationship (including access to funding), it was also having a relationship that was meaningful educationally. Question 135 asked the 441 schools and colleges that had a relationship to write in what it was: 350 specified the kind of contact they had but the largest group giving information was not about learning programmes or training initiatives but about the interchange of bodies sitting on mutual boards and quangos. Thus 60 schools said their relationship was headteachers sitting on TEC boards; while many colleges replied that they had TEC/LEC chief executives sitting on their own governing bodies. Both schools and colleges also cited occasional representation on TEC committees, education forums, vocational consortia, liaison groups, and strategic planning bodies.

It was impossible to say how full involvement was, how often liaison took place, or how fully the parties contributed to any planning or decision making. Even those institutions that gave very specific information (e.g. 'Eight college principals meeting 2–3 times annually with the TEC') only talked about the arrangements they made to meet, not what they did when they met.

Some, however, did specify the outcomes of contact: 60 with business links through education-business partnerships; over 50 with funding for initiatives like Youth Training, European Enterprise, work experience, funding for work placements and generalised contracts for training provision, including work accrediting training providers for NVQ. There was also funding for a diverse array of projects: 'to encourage staying on'; for 'our enterprise Bureau'; 'for the progression project'; 'staff shadowing project'; and 'for flexible learning projects'.

A few cited TEC funding for straight education, e.g. one for 'A' level RE; another for adult education courses. Some were related to the years before 16: 'For KS4 work,' for a '14–16 engineering course' as well as those for 16-plus courses, which could, of course have included GNVQ development. Only 10 schools or colleges mentioned GNVQs specifically, however, although a further 12 cited training credits (or skills seekers) programmes. Ten cited TVEI or post-TVEI; 14 mentioned funding received for careers work (in relation to libraries, conventions, departmental support); and 20 funding for compacts.

The relationship with TECS or LECS may have seemed lacking any rationale (as it did) simply because there is not as yet any standardised way of making reference to specific funding activities of TECs, or because the scope and nature of activity was so various. But chaotic it did seem when viewed overall,as other researchers have already noted. Several schools commented that they did not know how to influence a TEC and others that they did not know how decisions were made in TECS and LECS. One school wrote, 'It's a mystery'; and another, referring to a contract that had been made: 'attempted it but little commitment from employers'. In the end, that was the key to most TEC work. And it was often missing.

What comes over is success one moment, failure the next; but over and above this, absence of TEC involvement in many schools. Even when present, involvement seemed almost a matter of chance, with schools viewing funding as windfalls from some unseen benefactor (a word occasionally used) rather than the chief conduit of public funding from taxpayers designed for work-related education for this age group. TEC relationships were more business-like with colleges, but colleges also treated the funding as fortuitous: 'Support for college work ... let's us do some BTEC'.

There was no sense of having a right to such funding; no pattern to the funding given; no principle for educational involvement discernible (or at any rate conveyed by most respondents). Just a chequerboard of experiments. Viewing it overall (and reading pages of testimony) made a

powerful case for bringing expenditure in relation to ages 16–17 and 17-
–18 into far greater local accountability through normal democratic
channels to develop coherent work-related education across the age group,
to use funds cost-effectively, and above all, to ensure that those in work-
related education receive as much support and as wide a range of choices
in their learning as any others in the same age group.

It was very hard to believe in a mechanism where accountability was so
remote from the institutions or workplaces, made clear when Michael
Portillo as Secretary of Employment was pressed on the point of lack of
accountability. He dismissed it in a single statement: 'TECs are private
companies ... accountable to me' (quoted in *The Training and Enterprise
Journal*, Vol. 3, no. 1, 1995). With training and education now within the
same department, education-led work on this aspect of comprehensive
secondary education can at least be undertaken without delay.

Moving on

The last set of survey questions in the 16–19 section relates to the way
students at the end of secondary education move on to further study or
work-related education or to work, or possibly to take time off for some
special bit of enterprise like travel or voluntary activity.

Traditionally, figures about this aspect of education have been limited
to reciting the university entrance figures of sixth forms of schools,
starting with the percentage who achieved Oxbridge entry. Until recently
information for the rest of the age group was sparse or non-existent and
this was the case at the start of comprehensive reform in 1965 in relation
to leavers from further education and many schools. It was still far from
complete 30 years on, yet it is self-evident that no 16–19 education
system is comprehensive where interest in, and support for, the
continuing education or employment of students does not apply equally
to everyone.

Compacts

Helping the majority to move on is now a major part of the activity of
those developing comprehensive education after 16, particularly since
there has been a (very belated) national recognition that ideally everyone
needs to stay on in learning until they are 18. Still to come is the same
recognition that after 18 continuing education is going to be a near

universal activity in the twenty-first century, but recognition of this too is becoming more widespread.

Developing this incentive is difficult in our 'advanced' societies where so many factors conspire to turn students away from education and where the practice of keeping large percentages out of work on a permanent basis is now a normal (and to some even an essential) feature of a capitalist economic system. Many see no hope for justice without changing the system, while others believe that the system can work only by persuading as many people as possible to stay on in learning longer, and to acquire the habit of continually updating their skills and knowledge in the hope that this will make everyone employable in the economy of the future.

'Compacts' were a new form of arrangement that were supposed to help in this process of moving students on and equipping them for taking responsibility for their learning. In 1994 they were made – sometimes with a company, sometimes with a college or university – for particular pupils or groups of students within a school or college who agreed to fulfil certain conditions – like attendance or course completion or qualification gain – in return for rights: like the promise of work experience (or more rarely, work) or of interviews for work and/or places reserved on further and higher education courses.

The idea originated in the USA where large companies attached themselves to schools in their (often disadvantaged) factory outlet areas and encouraged pupils there to achieve well, usually in return for a promise to consider them for a job in the company. Supporters of such schemes see the compact as the benevolent and disinterested involvement of corporations trying to raise local standards and help develop their future workforce. To others, such schemes are seen as companies trying to cherry-pick the best of the local talent to their own advantage, as well as engage in useful public relations generally. For these reasons doubters have nicknamed the initiative 'Con-pact'.

When compacts relate to attainment at the end of secondary education, they are seen as a way of offering progression for students from schools to higher education qualifications, giving them the incentive to get their qualifications so as to be able to continue with learning. Universities make the offers to students and some say it is not all that disinterested either, for higher education can use compacts to encourage as wide a trawl of talent as possible for themselves or as a way of making sure less favoured courses (or institutions) keep filled. Occasionally compacts have been used by prestigious institutions to achieve wider intakes, seen by some as merely lowering their standards. Thus did the *Daily Mail* wage war against an admissions system at several Oxbridge colleges seeking to enlist a wider intake from comprehensive schools (*Daily Mail*, 19 June, 1978) in the face of continuing disinclination of comprehensive students to choose these older universities.

A typical compact for students interested in post-school employment involves 'a bargain struck between student, their schools, colleges and local employers' where the student is required to put in 90% attendance, undertake work experience, complete course work on time, participate in building up an official Record of Achievement, and often undertake extra-curricular work. In return he or she is offered the guarantee of a job interview (though not necessarily a job) by the employer and, increasingly, by the school or colleges, training to NVQ level 2 standard. Some compacts are pre-16; some are post 16, when the pledge may involve training to GNVQ advanced or NVQ level 3 (Jessup, 1993:139).

TECs can also oversee compacts by pledging funds to provide courses of a specific nature, often involving several groups in a single community working on the same project. Several colleges and a few schools in the 1994 Survey described their compact courses in detail and were very enthusiastic about some of them – like the Derby Community Heritage project. Others declared themselves uninterested in the idea.

Question 136 asked schools and colleges in the 1994 survey whether they had compact arrangements of any kind: 33% said that they did (52% of colleges and 29% of the schools). Question 137 asked for written-in information about the kind of compacts; 145 gave such information.

The answers divided between compacts for pre-16 and those for 16 plus, those for pre-16 sometimes being for specific groups (e.g. 'KS4 for pupils who are school avoiders') but in other cases for every student in Year 10. Its promise usually related to providing work experience, or help with job interviews; sometimes arranged through TECs and education/business partnerships, sometimes 'arranged on an LEA basis'. However, because TECs are not contiguous with LEAs, some schools were on two compacts from two different TECs. Others, it must be presumed, fell through the net.

A few schools organised their own compacts with individual local employers outside TEC auspices, a practice much more common at the 16 plus stage. These were often compacts between tertiary and sixth form colleges with specific students in local schools before the age of 16, where pupils would be fulfilling conditions set down in terms of attendance and courses/work completed. Sometimes it was only one school with one college in relation to only one course – like a BTEC first level technology course. In others, as one sixth form college put it, the arrangement was that the college pledged itself to be open 'to all Compact graduates'.

The practice raised issues about rights of pupils in feeder schools attached to colleges, for while it can be made a condition that students coming from schools can enter certain courses only if they have complied with their conditions of entry, fulfilling compacts as such should not be made a condition for progressing to the next stage of education. Compacts are there to provide incentive, and cannot be used as sanctions against students exercising their normal rights, one of which must surely be to refuse a compact arrangement if the student chooses to do so or to choose to continue education whether or not a compact has been fulfilled.

Higher education compacts

The other type of compact seen in survey schools and colleges – very different from those described previously – was one made with the 'neighbourhood' university (usually one within commuting distance), where, having fulfilled certain criteria in terms of examinations and course work completed, entry to a designated university course was assured. Altogether 20 such schemes were described in detail by respondents to this question, naming universities in Scotland, Wales, and several parts of England. In England those most frequently named were the universities of Surrey and Wolverhampton.

In one case it was a relationship between a tertiary college and a local university in respect of one specific course in management studies. In some cases the compact was general, but as with many compacts, support is most often bestowed on those students thought unlikely to progress upwards without positive reinforcement. One comprehensive college put it thus: it is about 'Higher Education entry for students of non-traditional backgrounds'. As might be expected from the origins of the scheme, those schools and colleges in the 1994 survey most likely to have compacts were those serving the widest range of intakes. The type of comprehensive institution most likely to have a compact was the tertiary college (96% had them), while that least likely to have one was the grant maintained school (only 17% did).

Where compacts work well, they have many lessons to teach, particularly about providing incentives. But the schemes have to deliver something which is valued by students and this is not always the case, particularly those related to outside companies' offers before the age of 16. Compacts relying on TECs also require funding, not always assured, as employers' support is so fickle. Funding arrangements were liable to crash or change targets. As one school put it, 'Our LEA scheme was TEC funded but no longer receives any funding'. The comprehensive school that had received visits from local business leaders who 'helped out in the school' on a regular basis, did not know now whether this would continue owing to difficulties the company was having; while another reported that it now had 'a much reduced Compact with little employer participation' because the employer, so crucial a part of these arrangements, had lost all interest.

Once again, opportunity in education is left to chance or to the whim of employers and their own short-term interests. The funding of continuing education at the 16–19 level for young people of 16 and 17 is too important to be a matter of chance, subject to 'market' whims. It should be there as a matter of right. Above all, expenditure decisions in the public domain (like some of those made in respect of compacts, many underwritten with public funds) should be (as they presently are not) subject to normal local or regional democratic accountability and oversight.

Degree level study: colleges and universities

Generally speaking, the record of comprehensive schools sending students to universities has been good.

Although comprehensive schools did not get their fair share of high attaining (and middle-class) intakes in the early years of comprehensive reorganisation (a situation which still continues for some), the numbers passing through the comprehensive sixth forms to universities began to grow rapidly after 1965. As early as 1970, 25% of students entering British universities from maintained schools were already from comprehensive schools (Neave, 1975:14). Moreover, with the exception of Oxbridge, they entered a good spread of universities. Their numbers have gone on increasing and today the vast majority of university students in Britain have been educated in comprehensive schools and colleges.

Far fewer criticisms have been made against comprehensive schools on this score (than, say, on examination results), possibly because concentration upon the students likely to enter universities has always been a feature of comprehensive education (and a source of criticism from some who believe such students have commandeered far too great a share of resources compared with others). If anything, the criticism has been the other way around from some universities: not enough comprehensive students wanted to come to them. This was particularly so in the case of Oxbridge, owing to the long war of attrition against comprehensive education from the *Black Paper* élitists and their supporters, so many Oxbridge based, which included such well-publicised campaigns as that of all Oxford University college principals writing to the *Oxford Times* (2 February, 1976) to denounce the sixth forms of comprehensive education.

This reputation of Oxbridge hostility to comprehensive students, whether real or imagined, combined with Oxbridge's convoluted entry requirements, meant large numbers of comprehensive school staff and parents (very few of whom had any Oxbridge connection anyway) decided in those crucial early years to fix their sights on the rest of the university population instead. Many in the comprehensive school world saw Oxbridge as the domain of the public school entrant in any case, likely to be socially uncongenial as well as certain to require special coaching within the secondary regime, which many early comprehensive schools condemned out of hand, including both teachers and pupils (Peston, 1979).

There was a further factor as well and that was the tendency, as time went on, for comprehensive schools to establish links with universities within their own regions: Welsh with Welsh, Scottish with Scottish, Northern with Northern. This became known as the 'neighbourhood university' development, and, ironically, many of those comprehensive schools that established special Oxbridge links were schools in the general vicinity of these universities as well.

For some Oxbridge colleges, therefore, far from it having been a case of graduates from comprehensive schools and colleges having to fight to obtain their fair share of places in competition with students from private and grammar schools, it became a case of trying to win the support of comprehensive schools and their students and staff in order to increase their own entries from such schools. Universities too like to think they take in a cross-section; and if they are thinking in terms of public funding, none likes to be peopled entirely by entries from public schools.

Certain colleges worked hard in this respect. For example, during the 1970s, Alan Bilsborough, admissions tutor for Kings College, Cambridge, had built up Kings' comprehensive numbers by 1979 to one-third of all entrants – at a time when many Oxbridge colleges still had minuscule percentages, particularly of girls, from comprehensives. Kings worked out its own special compact with comprehensive students whereby if they obtained the 'A' level grades required, they could bypass the complex Oxbridge entry and interview process and gain automatic admission (in the same way as students were admitted to all non-Oxbridge universities). As Bilsborough wrote at the time, he found comprehensive students far wider ranging in their interests than those from selective schools, often showing a greater 'breadth of enquiry' in their work; and often 'far more enterprising in extra curricular activities' than students he regularly saw coming from his own 'rather jaded' old grammar school (Bilsborough, 1979). Others also found such students more 'individualistic' as well and one found them more likely to be concerned with 'social equity' than peers from selective and public schools (Weinberg, 1972).

As comprehensive school numbers entering universities expanded, as they continued to do throughout the 1980s, much more worrying was the prospect of being left without work after obtaining the degree, a fear that led many students and staff to look more favourably upon qualifications that were directly related to work – such as the BTEC national – or degrees that combined work and study, often sponsored by employers. But these were changes all sixth forms were undergoing during the 1980s and 1990s. Thus the differences between sixth forms in comprehensive schools and those in selective schools grew less and less. When it came to 'A' level students in 1994, in many cases it would have been hard to spot the difference – with respect to interests, activities, achievements, or even backgrounds – between students in some comprehensive schools and those in grammar schools. This is an argument some make for continuing grammar separation but which, of course, can be used equally well to argue the case for ending selection.

The big difference between selective and non-selective 16–19 education that still remains, however, is that of the relationship of those on the academic course with that 70% of the age group not taking 'A' levels (or the 50% not taking Highers). Those in many comprehensive schools and colleges who may be university-bound, are still studying and working alongside peers whose interests and intelligence are expressed through different qualifications and measures of achievement from those still required for entering degree level study through the traditional academic route.

Attitudes to different forms of intelligence are changing, however, not just generally but specifically in relation to higher level education. For example, since the early 1990s the way has been smoothed for vocational students to enter degree level study more easily along with increasing numbers of mature students, with a variety of 'prior learning' achievements. As vocational courses continue to develop and as pressure to integrate them with academic study increases, the prospect for school sixth forms will become increasingly problematic where they are exclusively tied to the academic course.

Prior links: 'old person' networks in the neighbourhood university

Comprehensive schools and colleges continued to develop their links with local and regional universities and colleges during the 1970s and 1980s – sometimes through compacts, but often through other forms of association as well. The 'old person' networks of comprehensive education can be fairly extensive, even if not constructed on the same lines as in grammar schools and private schools. As hinted earlier, they are often more along geographical than social or professional background lines.

Question 144 asked comprehensive schools or colleges with 16–19 students whether they had links of any kind with any universities in Britain (e.g. where group visits for prospective entrants were organised); 71.3% had them. Those most likely to have them were the colleges, with 90% of FE colleges having them and 81% of sixth form colleges. By contrast only 66% of LEA schools with sixth forms had them, and only 55% of grant maintained schools or 25% of special agreement schools. But were the links regional or national? Question145 asked those with links, and the replies were as follows

A links to universities in own region   286

B links to some universities in own region, some outside   237

C links to universities only outside own region   16

Just over half had their links entirely in their own region, while only 16 had links entirely outside it. The phenomenon of the 'neighbourhood university', suspected in the 1970s, seems to be here to stay.

Progress to higher education

Table 9.8 breaks down the numbers of comprehensive schools and colleges with students accepted on degree courses in the year of the survey, a question 86% of all schools and colleges with students in the 16–19 age range answered in respect of their Year 13 (2nd year sixth/S6/17–18 year group). The figures are given in numbers of schools in each of the percentage ranges asked for in question 142. Next to each range are the average scores for those within the category for both five GCSE (A–C) and 'A' level grade average.

Table 9. 8 Comprehensive schools and colleges (n=714) with students in 16–19 age range accepted on degree courses (1992–93, 1994 survey)

Percentages accepted from the school or college	Numbers	Five GCSE (A–C) average*	'A' level score average†
10 or less	34	20.2	7.0
11–20	42	36.3	8.3
21–30	63	39.0	10.5
31–50	113	39.5	11.4
51–75	281	43.7	13.2
Over 75	181	45.4	14.5

*Including O grade (1–3) Scotland. Survey average 39.3.
†Omitting Highers, Scotland. Survey average 12.7.

Where more than 50% of the 16–19 age group proceeded to universities, as we see, averages for GCSE and 'A' levels were higher than survey averages. Schools sending between 20% and 50% of the year group had average GCSE scores (though 'A' level scores were less than average – see Appendix II, Note B).

Looking at the social class composition of schools and colleges, Survey findings showed that although the percentages of the schools and colleges having predominantly middle-class intakes rose at each percentile, in no one percentile were middle-class schools the majority.

Put another way, of all schools and colleges in the survey having students in the 16–19 age range that had intakes that were predominantly working class (question 36A, C), the percentages with one or more students accepted for university was 84.1%, while for all with intakes predominantly middle class (question 36BD) it was 92.2% – higher, but not so much higher that anyone can say working-class comprehensive schools in 1994 were not succeeding very well at this level. In fact, showing far less of a difference than many would have predicted.

Differences within the community of comprehensive schools and colleges

Nevertheless, as Table A6 shows in more detail, there were some differences in moving students to degree courses between the various types of comprehensive schools and colleges, and between those with differing intakes situated in different contexts.

The criterion chosen for comparison was having at least 31% or over accepted for degree level courses (question 142C, E, or F), on the grounds that 32% of 17–18 year olds in the UK obtained at least one 'A' level or H grade pass in the year before the survey (HMSO, *Education Statistics for the United Kingdom*, 1993:2). The survey average for achieving this target of 31% or more was 80.5% for all schools and colleges.

Table A6 shows what factors might be associated with differences in the percentages achieving the target. For example, the target of 31% or more was reached by 100% of the sixth form colleges and 100% of the 14–18 upper schools, but by only 77% of comprehensives in the countryside, 72% of tertiary colleges and 43% of FE colleges. It was reached by 92% of schools and colleges drawing mainly from private housing but by only 67% of those in large cities, and by only 44% of schools drawing intakes mainly from council estates. The factors accounting for differences here could be attainment at intake, size, social mix or demographic location. No doubt a fuller analysis of the exact relationships between any of these (and many other) factors and the percentages sent on degree courses would be able to pinpoint more exactly which factors were closely associated with university entrance. One finding that was very tentatively made was that schools' and colleges' league-table results at GCSE and 'A' level could vary a great deal even within the same percentiles.

'A' Level specialisation or wide spread of qualifications?

There were interesting differences between schools that were developing vocational qualifications alongside 'A' level and those that were not doing so to any very great extent. One reason the 'league table' criterion of percentage pass rates at 'A' level is so misleading is that it tends to give higher placement to the latter, even though the former may actually be graduating higher numbers of students with qualifications overall , including more with 'A' level qualifications. If a third of your age group is working for professional, academic or vocational qualifications related to work or further professional training (rather than for 'A' levels and a degree course), then naturally percentages of the total age group going on to degrees will be less than in a sixth form that restricted its work to 'A' level study. The latter's sixth form may be very small and thus send fewer students and possibly none at all succeeding in other forms of learning or gaining other types of qualification, but it will have higher percentages entering 'A' level (or higher rates passing). It is because tables reward this selective policy relating to the work of less than a third of the age group over policies that may be more comprehensive and serve the education of a far wider section of the age group, that they are so unsuitable as markers of success for a comprehensive system at 16–19. In a comprehensive system the achievements of all students have to be counted, and criteria overall have to take into account numbers and percentages in the age group as a whole reaching their goals, not just those on one type of course for one type of examination.

One good example of the inadequacy of 'league table' measures of success that use 'A' levels (or Highers in Scotland) is that this fails to register those students qualifying for universities through vocational learning. Question 143 asked the 714 schools or colleges which had had students accepted for universities, how many of this number had been qualified by BTEC, SCOTVEC, GSVQ or GNVQ rather than 'A' levels or Highers; 97 schools and colleges – or 13.5% – had had such students accepted, 78 with five or more accepted, and 16 with 100 or more – inevitably most from the colleges, as Table A6 shows.

Table A6 records that entry through this qualification was on average overall already 13 students per year per comprehensive institution running these qualifications, although numbers were very low in both sixth form colleges and in schools' sixth forms compared with those, for example, in the tertiary colleges at 58 per college, and FE colleges with 100. But every type of comprehensive school was already involved, and even if their numbers were small as yet, this is an alternative route that is set to grow. The future lies in the direction of provision of both academic and vocational learning, and of increasing numbers entering universities having qualified through academic attainment in work-related learning – as well as by other forms of attainment such as are used in 'accredited prior learning'. A criterion of success that ignores all these developments is not only inadequate, it is a reinforcement of the selective past at the expense of the comprehensive future.

Keeping track of leavers

Theoretically schools and colleges should have records of those who leave at 16 as well as those who enter Year 12 of education, and what happens to them after they too leave. Such information is vital to the planning of any institution's own education. But record keeping in many schools and colleges is poor and follow-up is all too often patchy and ineffective (OFSTED, 1993:27, 32).

It is also selective. The 1994 survey showed that most of the schools and colleges with 16–19 students knew to a specific percentage how many went to universities but that far fewer had kept records relating to other leavers, including those going to study at various levels in further education. This may have been all too typical of British education in the twentieth century, but it is hardly adequate for comprehensive education in the twenty-first. Goals set well in to the twenty-first century do not yet envisage the majority of leavers entering university immediately after school – or even further education – but most assume almost everyone will return to education at some point in their lives.

Keeping records does not just benefit the education industry or schools and colleges individually (as well as give a good impression to the public), it is reassuring for students to know that their subsequent progress is of interest to the public education service. But such reassurance is likely in a comprehensive system only if every student's subsequent destination is sought and the information valued, however different destinations may be. The days should be fast drawing to a close when one destination mattered more than others.

The survey suggested comprehensive schools and colleges have much ground to cover in reaching this particular form of equal valuing. For replies to records kept about students other than those going to universities (question 146), including numbers going on to jobs, training and further education, showed only 63% of schools and colleges kept any records at all. The most likely to do so (and to publish the most informative information about what students went on to do) were the comprehensive colleges – only 17% of whom kept no records. Schools were less likely to do so, the least likely being special agreement and aided schools (with 75% and 42% keeping no records respectively).

Of those schools and colleges keeping records, only 265 kept records of who had gone on to full- or part-time courses in further education *below* degree level; and only 160 had records of those who had gone on training courses (question 147). One of the marks of élite schools has always been to lend a helping hand to 'old boys' and 'old girls' in later life. Comprehensive schools and colleges must learn to do the same for all those who stay to the end of their courses (and in return possibly find themselves supported by former students in the same way). This is one of the tasks that local authorities, with the help of careers' services, could oversee.

Institutional collaboration and curricular integration

So far this chapter has looked at schools and colleges individually. Working together is just as important, yet the ways of working together are not even a statistic that is collected nationally or officially, though the 1994 survey found such practice to be widespread. As already recorded two out of every three schools and colleges in the survey already co-operated in some way in their work (see pages 339–41). In this section we look at collaboration specifically in relation to the 16–19 year age group.

Combining qualifications

It is not just about institutions refusing to live by market rules of isolation and competition and deciding to co-operate with others. It is also that within institutions, possibly even aided and abetted by the collaboration, students are refusing to live within the system's imposed curricular pathways, refusing to take 'orthodox' courses that divide them into 'academic' versus 'vocational', or theoretical versus practical, and opting instead for a mix. In both cases the trends illustrate movement 'on the ground' as opposed to change imposed from above, and provide indicators for the future curriculum organisation as well as for the structural development of comprehensive education.

Previous curriculum questions were about courses that institutions offered individually and about the range of individual courses and qualifications made available within each school or college. But what about students who wanted to combine courses – who were unhappy, for example, with having to choose at the early age of 16 whether they would be entirely academic or entirely vocational, so often suggested as normal practice?

Being able to combine is not just about having wider subject spread or making sure academic students have both arts and science subjects; or even about recognising those in vocationally related learning as equal learners. It is also about each individual's right to pursue interests in theoretical, abstract and practical ways with some chance of an integrated understanding. It is about having different aspects of one's own intelligence nurtured and assessed, for in the twenty-first century more than one type of intelligence will be required by students within the world of work and in their own future development in life.

The traditional UK model is everyone on a single course at any age. At age 16 plus in 1994 this often meant either academic or vocational. Studying an 'A' level language together with a vocational course was unusual, and often a course had to be specially devised. Yet what more natural than to pursue Spanish 'A' level along with tourism and leisure studies? Or learning music if on a YT scheme? Several institutions and educationalists have looked at unusual mixes and found demand for them to be high, like BTEC and 'A' levels or business with sociology (Burgess,

1993:102-3, 108). Certain institutions have pioneered combined-learning in a conscious way – such as the Gloucester College of Arts and Technology which developed a basic curriculum for a 'common first year' at 16 that obviates the usual division. In another area where curriculum combining was being developed it was sold to students with the motto: 'Don't choose: do both' (Burgess, 1993).

One project started in London in 1991 specialising in 'unified curriculum projects' within a single sixth form centre (Morris, 1993), involved a compact partnership between employers and educators that motivated learners through a link with the London University Institute of Education (as suggested in *A Basis for Credit*, 1992). The course provided modularised learning across a network of post-16-providers – with different credit accumulations for different purposes fixed in relation to agreed criteria rather than 'ranking in relation to the norm' and including work-related education. As with combining vocational and academic education, the curriculum conjunction that ensued produced change in assessment and course structure, and ultimately also in institutional relationships.

The subjects and courses combined
Question 126 asked about combining courses in ways the system did not normally sanction. It asked about students who chose 'elements' from two or more of the courses listed in question 123 or 124 to make up their own individual courses – and about the way schools and colleges assisted them in this practice.

Just about half (49.9%) of the schools and colleges which had supplied information in answer to question 123 said they already had as many as 20% of the Year 12 combining the courses listed in question 123 in this way; a third said they had 50% or more and 31 schools and colleges had all students taking a combination of courses or elements of courses during this Year 12 as a matter of school or college policy. The figures suggest that in almost every sixth form or college there will probably be students who combine in the ways suggested. In other words, combining across the curriculum is common practice.

Two hundred and sixty gave additional information about what they combined (question 127). A few years earlier the answer would probably have been 'A' levels and AS levels, and although many were taking this still (especially in 11–18 schools), only 67 said this was their most popular. Another combination that might have been chosen earlier (especially in the

(22), information technology (14), catering (including hotels, cooking, home economics) (11), performance arts (8), art (7), media studies (7), computing (9), construction (including furniture) (6), childcare/nursery (4), built environment (including housing studies) (3), information services (2), social science, photography (3), agriculture (2).

12 Other combinations reported were 'A' level combined with certificated vocational studies (like DOVE/CLAIT); GCLI combined with GCSE; RSA combined with GNVQ/BTEC/CGLI; NVQ combined with BTEC; GCSE and DOVE; DOVE and Certificate of Sixth Year Studies; and several 'A' level courses courses where computing, IT and word processing had been organised for everyone in the group.

13 For example, see the proposals of the Council for Industry and Higher Education, *A Wider Spectrum of Opportunities*, 1995.

10

Conclusions and Recommendations

This book has tried to compare the comprehensive education we have with the comprehensive education we *could* have – based on the long historical view that the world at large has been moving towards a more democratic and inclusive education system, involving more of each age group opting to remain in education to a later stage of life, from the end of the seventeenth century.

History – and the experience of much of the rest of the advanced industrial world – have made the case for continuing to extend comprehensive education. Its principles have won increasing support in Britain over the last 30 years and now command the approval of the great majority of the population[1]. If attempts to re-create selection are designed to return to a system of rationing opportunity based on judgements made at the end of the primary stage, they are mere self-defeating delaying tactics. They could, however, have beneficial offshoots if they force us to debate matters like admissions systems, increasingly corrupted in certain areas; and much more important, if they force the question of whether 'grammar education' is itself any longer a worthy goal, even for 'selected' pupils.

The one conclusion to jump out of any review of the last 30 years – re-affirmed in one research project after another, as well as in individual and collective experience – is that the main brake on educational development in Britain has been trying to hold on too long to the inappropriate ways of the past, not any attempt to change too quickly. Thus most considered criticism of comprehensive reform has been that it has changed education too little, not that it has changed education too much.

One fault regularly stressed was the retention of a narrow education designed for a minority, within a system intended to develop *everyone*. Grammar education not only cannot serve everyone; it is now dangerously specialised and over-theoretical even for the minority supposed to be suited to it, especially after 16. Pressure for reform applies regardless of the social or political changes people might want to see in the future. Critics from all quarters question Britain's continuing divided approach and believe its approach is outdated in terms of developing the multiplicity of talents and the many forms of intelligence now required in society, including for the so-called high-fliers. Described historically as 'vocational education for monks', grammar education lacks relevance in a modern democracy where all vocations require flexible, wide-ranging and demanding preparation of a quite different kind.

Since Britain has effectively and irrevocably changed to a comprehensive system, it is time to concentrate on comprehensive excellence. It is time to develop comprehensive-compatible criteria that enable us to judge progress; and to debate the direction we wish comprehensive education to take. It is particularly destructive to be debating the past over and over again when there are many alternative paths that can be chosen for comprehensive education. Those with differing concerns and priorities should be arguing them out in the only arena where they can be realistically advocated or realised.

We hope the findings and recommendations in this book – some of which are summarised in this chapter – will assist in this process.

The change in attitudes to the majority

A first important conclusion is that comprehensive education has drastically reshaped our attitude to the majority's education after childhood. In 1965 Britain had an officially sponsored divide between a selective sector for the few and a non-selective sector for the majority who were systematically labelled as failures, officially deemed 'less able', publicly considered less needful of qualifications, and therefore asked to do with less funding and support. The prevailing view was that none of the 11-plus 'failures' required a full secondary education and certainly very little further learning after leaving school. It is shocking to realise how little was *expected* of the majority in terms of educational development after the end of childhood only 30 years ago, and how little was provided; and to remember that it was society at large, including all political parties, that had these low expectations; it was not a few teachers in certain classrooms, as it became fashionable later to claim.

In 1965 comprehensive education was tentatively inaugurated, having been pressed by a determined band of educators from the 1930s in Britain (and already being developed in most advanced industrialised countries elsewhere in the world). It has revolutionised society's expectations in that most people now support the idea of everyone having the same broad educational experiences up to 14 or 16 and the same choices after. Ironically, it is the critics of comprehensive education who have changed their line most. Few (no matter how élitist) are willing any longer, as most were when the reform began, to write off the majority of young people as ineducable after 14 or 15 – positively better off without further learning. It is now understood by all but the most die-hard that unless the great majority can be induced to remain in education to strive for qualifications, acquire skills and develop a wide range of intelligences as well as cultivate the habit of continuous learning, the nation's status and society's well-being in all the ways that affect everyone in the society will not be forwarded. After 30 years of official comprehensive education (retrograde 'league tables' and media editors' obsessions notwithstanding) it is accepted that educational standards are no longer about what the 'top' people or 'top' schools do, as they were such a short time ago – they are about what every pupil and every student does in every school and college.

There is thus a new context in which those arguing against comprehensive education are having to make their case: a context that *accepts* the validity of a comprehensive education and realises that the old divided system cannot be resurrected. Governments can require testing to make 11-plus scores available – but they cannot compel the education community to use such testing for selection rather than for monitoring comprehensive development. They can give legal 'permission' to select but whether schools act on it depends not upon governments any longer but upon schools, parents, teachers and communities. This book shows that there has been a battery of legislative 'permissions to select' enacted since 1979; but it also shows that most have been unsuccessful, and that many schools and colleges which could have been selecting in 1994 chose not to do so.

Even those few areas that still continue with the old 11 plus are being increasingly forced to recognise the strong views of primary and secondary schools around them who believe their own educational efforts are harmed by a neighbour's unilateral selection. They have good reason for their views. One of our most telling findings was the educationally depressing effect that the remaining grammar schools had upon the comprehensive schools in their own vicinities in 1994: distorting their intakes (with fewer high attaining pupils and unrepresentative social mixes), lowering their numbers and staying-on rates and depressing their examination results: e.g., 29% with five GCSE A–C compared with 48% for a matched group of comprehensive schools which had no 'competition' from grammar schools and who attributed their success specifically to this factor.

Progress overall – reasons for optimism

This finding may be alarming but it is important to remember that the percentage of comprehensive schools suffering in this way in 1994 was immeasurably smaller than it was in the 1960s – only 14% of our total compared with over 50% in our previous survey of 1968. Likewise, even the most vigorous efforts of the 1980s to reintroduce selection nationally have only produced about a 1% increase in the officially selective population in national statistics. However, as most now recognise, it is unofficial – or 'hidden' – selection that poses an equally great problem. We have presented some evidence that 'hidden' forms of selection were present in a larger way in 1994 than they were 30 years earlier. Thus campaigns to return to selection may have positive as well as negative aspects in that they help to bring more of the 'hidden' selection in to the light of day.

For selection can never be a matter for 'private' decision by individual schools or colleges, nor an issue which governments can delegate to individual schools set up to bypass local democracy, because selection affects *all* schools in a community, even when only one school selects. The selective school's parents and staff might vote for selection, but local communities, given the chance to choose between having four successful non-selective schools as against one 'very successful' selective institution (accompanied by one that is struggling and two that are under-par) might choose the first option – provided the decision is put to them. One of the biggest problems in recent years is the extent to which an erosion of democratic accountability (through such procedures as opting out and quango decision-making) has prevented such questions from being put. It is not only comprehensive education that needs to be further developed; it is democracy itself .

When considering progress, it is also important to remember that attainment selection by schools and colleges in 1994 did not have the drastic impact on individual children or schools that it did 30 years ago when it was accompanied by internal selection for a 'grammar' versus a secondary modern curriculum, processed by a divided assessment system. It took an outrageous length of time to accomplish – and ironically was introduced by a Conservative rather than a Labour government – but by 1994 the principle of a single curriculum system and common assessment up to 14/16 had largely been won. Most pupils have a chance to experience a curriculum in common with their peers, whatever the degree of selection in the area. Selection in 1994 did not render comprehensive education impossible or deny it to parents and children; what it did do, however, wherever it was taking place, was decrease comprehensive education's *effectiveness for the majority* – and in some cases, severely depress outcomes in neighbouring schools.

Common curriculum and learning in mixed-ability situations

Along with ending selection, moving towards a more common curriculum was also one of the features that characterised a comprehensive education at the earlier secondary stage. In our 1968 research we found many comprehensive schools were trying to implement such a curriculum – all pupils with the same learning programme in any one school, though not necessarily a uniform one throughout the country. 30 years on, a common curriculum was still the most favoured approach in comprehensive schools, used by just over 50% in the first year of secondary schools. Most of those that did not use it in 1994 or failed to keep it up through Years 8 and 9, were not choosing a divided curriculum but adding an extra subject or two for some (but not all). A second language was the most common addition (though numbers taking it were often very small).

The National Curriculum in some ways reinforced the 'common curriculum' approach, but in others subjected it to a rigid interpretation. We found the vast majority of comprehensive schools have managed to widen it with additional common learning for all pupils, the most popular extra additions being drama and careers education.

To some, another feature of a comprehensive approach was mixed-ability grouping for learning, where instead of pre-determining the educational outcome for each pupil by assigning each to a stream based on previous attainment, activities and teaching took place in groups where attainments were mixed. We found mixed ability practice has also grown over the last 30 years in the first year of secondary education, especially in Scotland. Overall in Britain in 1994 streaming and broad banding were very much a minority choice when students started out their secondary comprehensive education, and were used by only 14% of schools.

But though most used mixed ability for social and physical education and for drama throughout school life, our survey showed it was not retained throughout secondary education in most schools for more 'academic' subjects. Rather, it was progressively modified after this first year by the setting of particular subjects like mathematics and languages into differentiated groups based on attainment. Both the numbers of learning areas to which setting was applied and the numbers of schools using setting in any form, increased in each successive year. The overall picture was very much one of mixed ability modified by setting up through Year 9, with grouping by GCSE courses thereafter increasing 'setted' practices. Less than 1% of schools used mixed ability for all subjects for all years up to age 16.

Although grouping by 1994 was thus a new amalgam of mixed ability with setting, it was nevertheless possible to divide schools into those that were largely streamed or with most subjects in ability 'sets' in the early secondary years and those that were generally mixed ability (with no more than four subjects set at any time). One could then see if there was any relationship between these two broad approaches and the 'academic results' of the two groups later (albeit judged only in 'league table' terms of five GCSE A-C, 'A' level point scores and percentages going to universities). Analysis showed that the type of grouping policy used made no difference for any of these factors. That it did not, however, was a positive finding because it leaves the way open for many to consider pupil grouping in terms of the social cohesion of schools. In contrast to no definitive academic advantages found in research for streaming over many years, research has found on several occasions that mixed ability was associated with schools that were often more socially successful or easier to run.

16 plus selection

After 16 there was selection as well, much more pronounced than we had expected to find. But the form it took was as much curricular as institutional – as much segregation between 'academic' and 'vocational' courses as between selective and non-selective schools or colleges. Ending attainment selection will not be enough to cure curricular selection; only reforming the curriculum and assessment system overall from 14 to 18 will do so.

This is why in addition to recommending an end to selection by attainment as a feature of admissions at any stage, we also support an end to the segregation of academic and vocational education throughout the secondary stage, but particularly after 16. There are several ways this could be done (already outlined in a wide variety of proposals from the nation's 'policy community', as it has come to be known) and we have no preferences. However, change would probably have to be based on some form of modularisation of all existing courses and their inclusion within a common framework of assessment and accreditation, possibly initially from 16 to 19 and then in time from 14 to 19 – with a 16 plus examination eliminated eventually in favour of a single award for everyone at 18. But this is a matter for debate, which should by now have become one of the main debates in national educational life. We would also favour an extension of criterion-referenced testing for the new curriculum, possibly even the elimination of norm-referenced testing entirely as another step to encouraging successful learning in every field. This is another of the questions which needs debating.

Within schools and colleges we would be in favour of every student having both academic and vocational modules in their programmes from the age of 14, as well as a common core from 16 to 19 around which students could construct their own individual learning. Our 1994 survey found that having a required core within each school or college at each stage from 14 onwards – with options grouped in such a way as to provide a reasonably balanced course for each student – was still the most preferred form of organising learning in the middle and later years of the secondary course, just as it was 30 years ago. The content of that core and the nature of that balance, however, were subject to wide interpretation and should also be subjects for discussion on a far wider scale.

But first, support the comprehensive principle

These necessary debates have little chance of occurring in any constructive way (despite the widespread support for most of the changes from all points in the political compass and both sides of industry, which our research has documented) unless there is at the same time open and unequivocal support from government and society for the comprehensive principle of equal value for each and every individual's learning and some attention to the matter of equalising outcomes. There has to be the prospect of equity in the treatment of all schools, colleges and local communities: with a fair and universally accepted system of monitoring educational improvement, none of which can be developed effectively until support is given to the principle that education, however diverse, should be entirely free from barriers based on prior judgements about who is 'capable' of learning.

For along with reasons to feel optimistic about comprehensive education, we also found a severe and debilitating contradiction at the heart of the majority's education over the last 30 years in Britain. On the one hand, governments were ostensibly supporting the comprehensive education to which most schools and colleges were progressively becoming committed; while at the same time they were either failing to support it adequately or working hard to undermine its principles and practices, and in some cases repeatedly making it clear they had no confidence in education that did not pre-judge an individual's worth or facilitate an escalation of enclaves for the favoured few.

In both government and national media circles there so often was (and still is) no understanding of the widespread *support* that the comprehensive principle enjoys among the majority. Not necessarily support for the stereotyped model of an anonymous inner city secondary school, still carried in the heads of opponents – but for the educational approach embodied in a system that assumes every single human being is educable and that given the right support and opportunities, and a diversity of goals that develop the full range of human intelligence, we are all capable of reaching the highest standards.

Whether individuals develop their potential, and whether communities are treated equally, depends upon the individual and collective support received from families and society at large. We do not discount these wider social or political factors or the need to work on them as hard as we work on the education system itself. That this project has not been about the relationship of education to society in this wider way, does not mean we do not consider the way education interacts with social and economic change supremely important. It means only that we believe comprehensive education – to which we confine ourselves – is an educational reform, not a social experiment.

The majority's opinion

Yet within Britain's educational community, including those charged with the task of running comprehensive schools and colleges, it is precisely this general educational support that so many find to be missing, including a declared respect for the values and principles upon which a comprehensive educational approach is based.

The last question in our 1994 survey asked those running Britain's schools and colleges what single factor (apart from better funding) holds the key to improvement of their school or college and to the future of comprehensive education (question 148). A summary of answers is given in Note 2 (p.491) and includes a number of specific reforms or changes schools and colleges would like to see, but at a deeper level almost all replies were about recognition of the national comprehensive commitment that is required first and foremost if Britain is to develop successfully in its educational life.

These 1500 practitioners said, in effect:

- Free us (from constant *un*constructive criticism and *in*effective interference in our work).
- Unburden us from inconsequential changes that take up our time and energy and prevent us from the major tasks of educating.
- Protect and develop a public education service rather than subject education to constant threats to privatise and commercialise.
- Support the form of education society has asked us to develop: non-selective, co-operative, equitable, innovative and well funded enough to deliver high standards everywhere rather than continue to augment opportunities for already-favoured groups at the expense of the majority.
- Above all, respect the majority belief in the comprehensive principle.

Ninety per cent of all pupils and students in schools and colleges up to 19 – funded by public money – are in comprehensive institutions, according to official government statistics. All governments for 30 years have broadcast each rise in this percentage as a positive accomplishment. What kind of a society then spends so much time trying to undermine the education system upon which almost all its population actually depends, while declaring its commitment to the welfare and educational development of these very same pupils and students and their parents? If we want to know what is holding up educational development in Britain, it is not comprehensive education and it is not the failure to have selection, it is this debilitating and long-standing contradiction that lies at the heart of the education system.

Against the odds: progress over the 30 years

The evidence in this book shows that although the national failure to go one way or the other has held up comprehensive education in Britain, it has not stopped it developing. Comprehensive education is advancing year by year in most of its aspects. Even in Northern Ireland the ground is shifting as increasing numbers boycott the official 11 plus.

In terms of range of attainment entering comprehensive schools and colleges overall in Britain, we found comprehensive education has become *more* comprehensive over 30 years, not *less*. In 1968 5% of the top 20% of the attainment range was missing from comprehensive schools; in 1994 it was only 2%. An improvement rate of only 1% a decade may not seem like great progress but in terms of capturing those percentage heights that account for so many of the qualifications at all higher levels, it certainly is.

So too is the growth in support from all sections of society. In 1965 almost no comprehensive institutions would have been predominantly middle class in intake, let alone mostly so. In 1994 over one in four were mixed but predominantly middle class. Much more important, with the possible exception of comprehensives in certain large cities and those serving large housing complexes, the majority were socially mixed individually, whether 'working' or 'middle' by a slight margin – only a minority being 'one class'. Comprehensive schools and colleges – primary, secondary and tertiary – are the most representative schools in British history, possibly the only 'one nation' educational institutions there have ever been with the exception of some of the earliest grammar schools in the seventeenth century.

For this reason comprehensive schools and colleges are well supported in their communities. This includes those schools that pundits and powers-that-be decide are 'failing', as attempts to close such schools over the last 15 years have so often confirmed. Supporting a school or college wherever it is, even at the cost of prolonged planning to improve it, would seem almost always better than robbing a neighbourhood of an educational resource or punishing it for being poor, which is how such events can appear to people locally. Where, on the other hand, schools and colleges have to be closed because they are unsafe or redundant, let the community (including the local educational community of schools and colleges acting together) play a major part in discussing and deciding local or regional educational developments. One of the really sad consequences of the privatisation of colleges and the opting out of institutions, is that their collective role in the community has been so diminished. Somehow, this situation has to be reversed.

For communities care about their comprehensive schools and colleges, and that includes the local media, where education is always an important issue. Opinion among schools and colleges in the 1994 survey may have been that most of the national media were hostile to comprehensive education (as evidence incontrovertibly suggests), but when it came to their own experience (and almost all had had media attention in the previous year, mostly from *local* press and broadcasting) 82% had found media attention supportive.

Scotland's significance

In looking at which areas of Britain were furthest ahead in developing comprehensive education, the area in front is Scotland. The 1994 survey found Scotland was not only 100% comprehensive but with the best academic results (at a level that could be compared nationally: five O grade 1-3, the equivalent of five GCSE A–C): 52% compared with schools in England with 38.4% . It also had the highest percentages staying on in all-through schools partly because almost all its schools are all-through as well as because it started including vocational education nearly 10 years before the rest of Britain. Its record for achieving vocational qualifications cannot be directly compared, but 38% of its survey schools had students gaining at least three or more vocational qualifications.

Yet government policy in Scotland has also been to try to undermine the comprehensive system – through the imposition of opting out, specialisation, privatisation and engineered 'placement' enrolment. There have also been attempts to retain separate tracks for vocational and academic education, when (after a decade of running the two in parallel) most Scots in education have made it clear they want to see these two types of education integrated in some way in the upper standards of schools. Scotland is thus by no means free from problems. However, if evidence is needed to show that the more comprehensive a school system is, the better it does in terms of some of the 'standards' that those opposing comprehensive education so often use, Britain has good evidence in Scotland.

Comprehensive colleges

Another of the survey's findings was the success of the comprehensive colleges throughout Britain: sixth form, tertiary, and general FE colleges, a large number now an integral part of comprehensive education's 'all-through' path in any area. In general, they also had the widest range of courses available after 16, including often the widest range of 'A' levels. Those who still think comprehensive education is only about schools (or only about children) are in danger of missing some of the most important developments of the last 30 years, and the key to most development for the next 30.

Mixed versus single sex

In the survey all the colleges were mixed sex, and so were all Scots schools and all middle schools; for another finding was the extent to which since 1965 mixed schooling has continued to grow everywhere in Britain. Only 7% of the survey schools were single sex. Surprisingly, they were distinguished as much, if not more, by the way they differed from each other than by the way either differed from mixed schools. Although both boys' and girls' schools were more likely to be full than mixed schools (in September, 1993) and both had marginally lower levels of attainment at entry, as well as a smaller average size, it was girls' schools that were often different from boys' or mixed. The proportion of their schools with working-class majorities was higher than either boys' or mixed and they had higher percentages of students entitled to free school meals, and very much higher percentages where students did not have English as the first language. The percentages of their schools that were in poor repair was much higher as well. Yet these girls' comprehensive schools had more students staying on in education and their five GCSE A–C score of 41% was better than the boys' figure (and slightly better than the mixed); and compared with boys' schools, their sixth forms had three times the average numbers sitting for the main (national level) vocational qualification and over twice as high a percentage succeeding.

Boys' schools up to 16 lagged in 'league table' terms (where their five GCSE A–C score was only 34%), but at the post-16 stage reversed the position (with an 'A' level point score of 13.8 compared with the girls' of 11.8). However, they had smaller percentages having students on vocational courses or having compacts or any relationship with local TECs – all of which suggested less concentration on vocational education. Why the two sets of schools should have been different in these ways is hard to say, though it is often observed (wherever there is a choice of single-sex education) that many parents (particularly of girls from certain Christian churches, minority groups and the Muslim faith) prefer their girls to go to girls' schools but want their boys to go to mixed ones.

Equal opportunities

We have few recommendations for single-sex schools – except to continue to collaborate with others in providing a full range of learning, and possibly, for boys' schools to follow girls more closely in providing more vocational work – though we have recommendations for both single-sex and mixed schools when it comes to equal opportunities. For one of the survey's disturbing findings was that work in schools and colleges on equal opportunities had lapsed generally, despite the fact that most schools said they had equal opportunities policies and rules about racial or sexual harassment – as well as policies to fund games kit or uniform for children from families who could not afford them.

What they did not have was much positive action or much monitoring of their own educational practices such as participation in school events or examination outcomes in relation to gender, race or social background. Only 28% were monitoring pupil grouping overall, for example, and only 10% in relation to social class. Social background was the factor least monitored in relation to institutional and educational practices (despite the presence in each school of basic information like percentages qualifying for free meals). This was followed by race. Although not every school had black, Asian or other ethnic and minority group members in substantial numbers, a third had at least one group present in percentages over 5%, and most would have had one or two individual members.

We found that gender watching was the most likely form of equal opportunities work to be taking place – more for girls than for boys, however, and certainly not universal. Many schools wrote on their forms that they knew they were not monitoring for equal opportunities as they should, or were just about to tackle the issue, prevented from doing so by excessive workloads in recent years. In others there was a policy of class and race and gender 'blindness', which seemed to say 'because we take no notice, we cannot be accused of discrimination'.

Monitoring could be a task which local or regional authorities help schools to undertake in future, where it could include as well as race, class and gender, disability and pupils who do not have English as a first language. We found 16% of schools and colleges had more than 5% without English as a first language, and some had percentages over 50%; and that colleges had higher percentages than schools. All these figures should be available to those planning the balance of intakes to education in any area, as well as to the public.

Harmonisation

Both the major denominations are committed to comprehensive education and have larger percentages of their total school numbers comprehensive than does the non-denominational sector. Overall church schools were not more 'selective' at entry, though they were more likely to be full in the survey year than were non-denominational schools. Both Church of England and Roman Catholic comprehensive schools also had higher than survey average scores in the 'league table' marker of five GCSE A–C (46% and 42% respectively) – though not always the highest scores after 16 plus.

The two main denominations differed in their class composition (over two in five Church of England comprehensives having middle-class majorities, while Catholic schools were more working class than the survey average); and church schools as a whole had fewer pupils who did not have English as a first language than did county-LEA schools.

An interesting finding in respect of church schools was that although 60% reserved most of their places for their own faiths in 1994, the same percentage also welcomed Christians of any faith – with a third glad to accept local pupils regardless of faith and/or from other major world faiths. In some cases the minority was already substantial. We support an extension of these developments – what one Catholic publication called defining church schools as a service to the community with a specific religious ethos, but not limited to any specific denomination. We also support further harmonisation of schools' legal status (which would include all voluntary schools and GM schools, whether denominational or not) in relation to funding, staffing regulations and admissions. This would include ending the requirement that aided schools find 15% of their capital costs. A comprehensive system does not need to perpetuate the divisions of pre-comprehensive days, especially when recent legal changes like LMS have made the original reasons for differential funding redundant.

The survey found differences among voluntary schools themselves and between voluntary schools and LEA schools. Voluntary controlled schools – half of which had previously been grammar schools (compared with the survey average of only a quarter with a grammar background) – had marginally more selective intakes, higher percentages with middle-class intakes than survey schools generally, and a higher average percentage for five GCSEs A–C – a profile not unlike that of the GM comprehensive schools, at least up to age 16. At 'A' level, however, the voluntary controlled schools did better than did GM schools on certain markers, including 'A' level point scores and percentages entering 'A' level courses.

All three school types – LEA, GM, and voluntary controlled – along with voluntary aided comprehensives, whose profile often lay between the voluntary controlled and the LEA school, had equally good records for students entering and passing vocational qualifications (at 'national' level). Surprisingly, most were more advanced in this respect than were the sixth-form colleges, which were found to have less vocational education – with an average as yet, for example, of only one student per college accepted on a degree course with a vocational qualification. Overall sixth-form colleges were the most selective in attainment terms of all the institutions in the survey (and the most middle class).

Sixth-form colleges were highly successful and turned out to be a great deal more like the "A' level academies' they were in the 1960s and less like the all-purpose institutions so many claimed they were hoping to become in the 1980s. This raises the question of whether this development might not also have applied to many sixth forms in 1994, especially those that were concentrating on 'A' levels – and not yet developing vocational education, and whether these developments could have reflected 'league table' pressure rather than conscious changes in policy.

Special agreement comprehensive schools are few in number and had only small numbers in the survey. They seemed to have a profile rather different from those of other voluntary schools: many were quite small in themselves with smaller than average sixth forms and with results at GCSE and 'A' level slightly below survey averages. On the other hand, they were leading the way in collaborating with other schools and colleges in enlarging their range of courses.

The position of GM schools was not entirely what some might have expected, since a good number gave evidence of commitment to remaining comprehensive. They were more likely to be full at intake in the September of the survey and their scores of five GCSE A–C were higher than those in LEA schools. However, after-16 GM results were not as good as those in LEA schools on criteria like 'A' level point scores; and not as high as GM results in *national* figures at either GCSE or 'A' level. These findings suggested that GM schools committed to comprehensive education and taking part in the survey could be rather different from those not taking part – and that many of the latter must be very selective indeed to produce the GM figures in national statistics. Since 14% of their national total were officially grammar schools in the year of the survey, it seems likely.

Though GM comprehensive schools were less distinctive than anticipated, they did show quite a few differences in relation to both LEA and (most) voluntary schools in the 1994 survey – differences that would lead them in rather a different direction over time. Their average attainment level on entry was higher than that for LEA schools and so were percentages of schools with middle-class intakes. They had smaller percentages of schools with very high levels of pupils eligible for free meals and they were less likely than LEA schools to accept pupils from special schools or share premises with community groups (but more likely to accept pupils transferring from private education). Far fewer operated admissions policies based on nearness, catchment or feeder school criteria, the three methods adopted by most schools in the UK in 1994 (all three of which had increased in popularity since the 1960s). A lot of GM admissions were based on 'governors' selection' or 'personal' factors – with criteria that were not always very clear.

For reasons mainly to do with the alienation of GM schools from their local community of schools (and the destructive potentialities of a 'parallel system' of increasingly selective schools being developed nationally), we concluded that the legal position should not remain as it is and that the harmonisation changes spoken of above should include measures that would enable GM schools to resume membership of their local school communities once more – to take part with all other schools locally in determining the development of education in each area.

A new role for local authorities

This would not entail drastic change for most GM comprehensive schools – or for voluntary schools – for in most ways these schools would run their own show in the way that they do now. It might not even disturb intake patterns, for despite widespread attempts to get schools to select from far afield in recent years (and break their 'neighbourhood' connections) the survey found that nearly 80% of all comprehensive schools were still neighbourhood schools in the sense that their intakes came from their own area or within their own LEA (rather than from outside either). This included just over half the GM schools (as well as almost all schools in Scotland, the area with the most neighbourhood based education). Contrary to what might have been expected, however, the areas where comprehensive schools were the least neighbourhood based were the big cities.

A further finding was that when it came to organising admissions, most comprehensive schools co-operated in some way with their local authority (or kept in touch with their plans), while half left admissions for LEAs entirely to arrange. This strengthens the case for bringing all admissions under the auspices of the LEA (or after 16, possibly a regional authority) though a new system would be rather different compared with the 1960s owing to the advent of LMS. It has been largely accepted that schools and colleges would individually retain their local (or independent) management of budgets, staff appointments, internal organisation and ethos. It is only where decisions impinge inevitably on the well-being or organisation of other institutions that the local authority is required – not to dictate, but to oversee solutions agreeable to all concerned.

The LEA would not be asked to undertake the task of deciding itself, as used to be the case. It would instead have the duty to convene local schools and colleges for specific purposes – like coming to agreement about admissions, or planning closures and new institutional development. Its duty here might be a legal requirement to have regard to such factors as the all-through progression for pupils in the area between schools at various stages – as well as to balanced attainment intakes in respect of each school, or to the rational operation of the system generally, but these should be subject to agreement by all schools and colleges in any area.

Another specific change, which would bring the UK into line with most other countries (and end the admissions anarchy and uncertainty in a system where no UK child has any right to enter any school) is to agree by the same process a 'school of right' for each stage of the school system for all pupils. A legal right to a named school would give all parents a choice of a known school which their child had a right to enter (a significant increase in parental rights over the present position where there are no rights to enter any school, even if it lies next door) and, in time, a college of right for older students and young adults.

The current right to state a preference would also remain (if the school named was not accepted) and schools would have to accept students in the same way (provided none whose school-of-right it was, was displaced). In fact, with these two rights in operation, and selection gone as well, parents' 'choice' would be much wider than at present, since they could apply to any school, including those previously closed to majority application. More important, parents could be assured (as many cannot be now) that the system under which their applications would be considered, was conducted in accordance with publicly agreed rules accepted by all schools, and always operated openly and fairly under the auspices of an electorally accountable body (as is not always the case at present).

Having schools themselves discuss and agree admissions criteria and fix schools of right – under the auspices of the democratically elected body – not only holds out the best chance of getting agreement on these difficult matters, including helping the odd selective school progressively to widen its attainment intake, and the currently disadvantaged school to improve its situation, it also offers some possibility of rationalising the system and reducing the unseemly waste of millions of pounds each year on providing excess places in the system, simply to ensure favoured schools are 'filled'.

Monitoring development

For one of the survey's most surprising findings was that 60% of schools are undersubscribed, including over a third of the GM schools and voluntary schools, and those drawing exclusively from areas of private housing (where comprehensive schools had many advantages). Clearly, it was not a question of 'unfilled' schools only being those rejected by parents: among those unfilled were large numbers of schools and colleges with the best academic results and the best attendance records in any area. For many schools the problem was over-inflated standard numbers, along with a national system manipulating 'parental choice' as a substitute for selection through the mechanism of over-provision. This problem cannot be resolved by national or local governments alone (both of which have failed to tackle the problem for years). However, it might be solved jointly by all schools and colleges in each area being required by law to reach agreement between themselves on numbers of pupils and students and their distribution within the local community of schools and colleges – under the good offices of a democratically accountable body, whether local authority or regional authority, any of their sub-committees, or some newly formed electoral unit.

With this relatively simple set of changes, there would be no need for any wholesale comprehensive reorganisation, as there was in 1965, but there would be a need for close monitoring of intakes and outcomes that could chart progress towards specific goals over time – for example, towards generally balanced intakes to all schools. Parents and students need to be assured that they are not being faced with continuing 'hidden' practices that could so easily disadvantage their children. For the picture of comprehensive education in 1994 was not one with most schools comfortably balanced already in terms of attainment intake – either free from being selective themselves or free from being the victim of someone else's selection (the two so often going together). Instead there was a continuum from less than comprehensive through comfortably comprehensive to quite selective, a significant change from a clear-cut division of 1965.

The continuum had a little over a quarter of schools and colleges comprehensive in attainment terms (having between 15% and 25% of the top 20% of the attainment range). At one end of the continuum were about 15–20% of schools that were semi-selective with far more than their fair share of high attaining pupils, and a few with intakes indistinguishable from grammar schools. These naturally played a part in shaping the intakes to some of the 40–50% of schools at the other end which had intakes below 11% of the top 20% of attainment, and some below 5%.

How big a part the schools at one end played in unbalancing the intakes at the other cannot be said exactly, for schools' intake levels can also vary naturally according to their geographic area or the type of housing or social class groupings from which they draw. But just because there will always be some imbalance in some areas is no reason to insist on increasing it where it does not have to exist. For whatever reason, the overall picture of comprehensive education in Britain in 1994 was, as the survey showed, one where a core of comprehensive schools was being whittled away at either end – a process that has been observed only in the last 15 years. This process has to be reversed if a healthy education system is to be maintained, and progress towards this goal should become a matter the public is informed about in a regular way.

Disadvantage

Monitoring of the state of educational plant – and publication of these 'results' – might also be considered, for a third of the schools and colleges said they needed major repairs or refurbishment before they could function effectively. The survey also found that most schools and colleges with new arrangements under compulsory, competitive tendering (CCT) for meals and cleaning and groundskeeping services, believed standards in these services were no better or actually worse than before CCT. On the other hand, when it came to carrying out repairs and building work in schools and colleges, most thought today's arrangements were an improvement over the previous system.

In 1994 it was 'upkeep' issues and those related to the services schools were running (or buying in) that eclipsed issues like purpose building and split sites which had loomed so large in the comprehensive schools of the 1960s. The survey found no differences in any important aspect of education or organisation between split-site and one-site institutions, while those that were not purpose built were, if anything, slightly more favoured in some respects than those which were. It makes the cynic suspect that some of the old arguments around these issues (like 'botched' schemes) had sometimes been delaying tactics.

Nor was large size the bogey it was even 10 years ago. Since engineered enrolment took over after 1986 and some favoured schools were given leave to enlarge, large size has been more of a bonus than a defect; and the survey produced some tentative evidence that the bigger the school the better the results (albeit in league table terms). After those years of denigrating the comprehensive institutions for their large size, it is now the small comprehensives (that the anti-comprehensive minority once claimed were so necessary) that are more likely to be shunned or accused of 'failing'.

A deeper look at comprehensive schools in the 1990s, however, showed that disadvantage, though generally diffused, was not a matter of size or legal status or age range but was related to a few rather precise educational factors. These factors were concentrated in certain schools, and have led to pressure to end the present system of funding schools on the principle of 'poll-tax egalitarianism' and instead take account of needs that some schools (or areas) have but others do not. In this respect the survey provided information on schools that had high levels of pupils with particular characteristics that might make education more difficult in one institution than in another. These included schools with very high levels of pupils not having English as a first language or those having very high turnover – but even more important was that much smaller number of schools where two or more of these disadvantages applied at once. Special new measures specifically directed for extra *educational* support in these situations (to make sure English is learned quickly, for example) would seem to make much better sense than harassment over external exam figures in relation to criteria of 'failing' or 'succeeding'. To pass exams in the English language you first need a good command of the English language.

Another approach to exclusions is needed as well, difficult though it is to decide the most effective way of dealing with that 8–10% of pupils who reject what the system has to offer or the way it is being offered (a level surprisingly similar in most industrial countries), including those whose behaviour is too disruptive to tolerate. Some say this minority may be increasing today through the 'dropping' of pupils who are likely to damage a school's 'league table' standing. Whatever the reason to exclude, the practice is growing. We found that over the course of the single year before 1994, there had been a 10% rise in exclusions and a 20% rise in expulsions. These are practices that could be monitored locally and published in information tables – both pupils removed and pupils accepted, for it sometimes turns out some schools do all the excluding while others are forced to do all the accepting, an inequity that should be addressed.

Attendance rates of schools showed very wide variations. Just under one in five had rates of less than 90% with over a quarter having them over 95%. Previous research suggesting rates were linked to the social and demographic background of pupils seemed to be confirmed as well as earlier research suggesting that good attendance figures declined somewhat as students got older or as you moved northwards, for attendance figures were relatively poorer in Scotland than elsewhere. But this was not true of Northern Ireland, which had the best attendance figures (though the number of comprehensive institutions were as yet very few).

School and college life

In terms of the social organisation of schools, a big change was detected over the 30 years involving the casting aside of the house system (borrowed from private education) as the main form of organisation and so popular in the 1960s. By 1994 it had very largely given way to internal social and pastoral organisation based on year groups. During the earliest secondary years in 1994, uniform was almost universal; with only 10% requiring none at all, although over two in five required it only for main garments and/or excused those who were older from wearing it. Half the comprehensive schools had prefect systems, while parent teacher associations were the most popular form of parental organisation. Inside schools, the form of sanction for pupil offences most often used was calling a meeting with parents.

Parents were very unimpressed with the government's new statutory requirement for governors to meet with parents, with over half the survey schools reporting they had had no more than 20 parents at this particular meeting in the previous year. This was in schools where parents played a very active part in school life, including in the raising of extra funds. Parental fund raising was nearly universal but it did cause anxiety, as nearly half the schools claimed they were already depending on parental money to meet both curricular and extra-curricular needs. They were worried particularly where it was necessary for certain school lessons (like music) and 19% of schools and colleges said they depended on money from other sources, including trusts and business. When it came to fund raising, the middle-class schools and colleges raised somewhat more than the working class; and schools serving private housing areas more than those serving council estates. Not particularly unexpected news, but underlining warnings that although it was not at this stage yet, funding for schools might one day become inequitable in ways that no democratic country could accept.

This might also include funding given to schools to 'specialise'. In 1994, 15% of comprehensive schools and colleges said they were specialising and receiving extra money. However, there seemed to be a division between comprehensive schools given extra to concentrate on academic subjects like maths or technology or music and those given funding to specialise in meeting Special Educational Needs (SEN) like dyslexia or slow learning. Those who expect all comprehensive schools and colleges to assist with integration might be discouraged to find that in some areas policy seemed to be to allocate special needs work to certain comprehensive schools alone rather than assume each will shoulder its own share of such work. A quarter of the survey schools had SEN pupils that represented more than 20% of their intakes.

Once you send the 'gifted' in any one field to one comprehensive school and SEN pupils to another, you have yet another form of selection. Yet schools and colleges *should* be places where specialisation goes on – in all kinds of fields and activities (as it did in many schools and colleges in the survey). The ways, however, should arise from the individual traditions and enthusiasms of schools or colleges, and their teachers and students, not from artificially imposed selectivity programmes for either end of the attainment scale. Provided social or academic or racial selection is ruled out, all schools should be encouraged to have their own 'hallmark' education – but each should also be able to look after the needs of pupils at every point along the attainment scale.

The next stage of reorganisation: 16–19

The system up to 16, although it urgently requires national support, monitoring and a return to democratic oversight of its general development along comprehensive lines, does not require reorganisation of its schools as it did in 1965. Where reorganisation is required in the system in the 1990s is after 16. As most of the education 'policy community' realises, this next stage will require radical rethinking about curriculum and assessment for everyone. The government recognised this at the end of the 1980s with its drastic drive to increase vocational education and introduce criterion-referenced assessment.

The start was not well handled and consequently alienated even many of those well disposed to an upgrading of work-related learning. It alienated others because it was made without any attempt to include 'academic' education or to consider institutional change, particularly in relation to the plethora of small, uneconomic, isolated sixth forms that continue to increase. These have always been the Achilles' heel of comprehensive education and their situation is now growing more acute as vocational education grows and schools have to provide a full range of vocational courses as well as a full range of academic courses.

Unless there is continued comprehensive development we will continue leaving many students of this age with restricted choices at 15 plus. With the survey showing an average of only 92 students in all-through schools in Year 12 (the lower sixth), while colleges had an average of 692 for that same year group, it really is an issue of no contest in terms of the future organisation of the system in respect of one of the essential features of comprehensive education (now largely solved before the age of 16): the capacity to make available to everyone all that is normally available in curriculum and qualifications for the age group as a whole. Schools and colleges will have to join forces in new tertiary systems which can organise the pooling of school and college work for each area.

An even earlier task is to link certain schools to colleges in a more formal way. For even though comprehensive schools converged in size over the 30 years – with more now around the 900–1000 mark (and fewer very small or very large), the all-through schools (other than in Scotland) have declined as a proportion of the total. After 16 the majority of students are now in colleges, not schools; and in 1994 two out of every five schools ended at 16.

The survey found that some of these short-course schools continued to be disadvantaged in areas where they were not part of an organised 'all through' arrangement linking them formally to a sixth form college or tertiary college in the area. Thus one start on improving standards could be to organise these links with specific colleges (or, temporarily, the large sixth forms of schools with a good mix of vocational and academic education). One sign of need in this respect is that the percentage of mushroom schools (offering sixth forms to schools ending at 16) has more than doubled since 1968.

Admissions systems at 16 seem to attract less concern nationally than admissions at 11 or 12 plus, though their implications are just as important, particularly the drive (consequent on retaining 'A' level so long beyond its natural life) to reduce numbers opting for academic courses and divert them elsewhere. Although the percentages of all-through schools requiring specific numbers of (GCSE) passes for sixth-form entry has not changed much since 1968, percentages of schools with open admissions policies at 16 plus (where no pre-existing qualification is required to continue education) has gone down from 68% to 44%. The new admissions practice that takes up the space between open entry and prior passes is the use of 'counselling' for entry both to schools' sixth forms and to colleges' courses.

We were unable to determine all that was involved in counselling but there was some evidence of the polarisation of institutions after 16 – in the form of quite selective sixth form colleges which, like the sixth forms of some comprehensive schools, were identified mostly with 'A' level work (and not yet equally with vocational education) and the non-selective FE colleges, which, despite having developed rapidly in a comprehensive direction in the last 30 years, were still having to do battle with local 'sixth forms' in a competitive, market system relating to 'A' level students. The tertiary college stood in between these two poles, the most 'comprehensive' in attainment intake and social mix of the three college types, providing overall as wide an 'A' level offering in the basic subjects as the sixth-form colleges (and sending on good numbers to degree courses) while also providing an equally wide range of vocational courses, including courses for students who were on day release or studying only part time.

Not every area can yet have a tertiary college (though the general FE college in many areas now operates in a tertiary role for the 16–19 age group) but schools and colleges with students from 16 to 19 in every area could be helped to collaborate formally in a new tertiary system (by the same means as schools would be brought together to agree development) – with local or regional authorities having a duty to secure agreement from participating institutions on the balance of courses for the area and for each institution. There should also be agreement on admissions so that all young people at 16 have access to all that is normally provided for the age range, and given what so many presently lack in a 'market' system: a real choice. Funding for courses at this age would be better based on the nature and number of the courses institutions run than on the body count each happens to capture in its net.

Integrating vocational and academic education

The second reform required, the integration of vocational and academic education itself (together with a unified and coherent qualifications system), is one that has been far more widely discussed in Britain (especially in Scotland where almost every school runs both types of education and wants to bring them into closer alliance). Overall in 1994 38% of schools already had a vocational course by 14 plus and most were planning more; after 16 almost all colleges had both types of education and an increasing number of schools were beginning the same dual development. In addition, opinion among most schools and colleges in the survey favoured some form of change in the 16–19 curriculum, with a third voting for full integration of academic and vocational education after 16.

Meanwhile, as we found, most schools and colleges were trying to widen their offering by enabling students to 'combine' courses intended to be taken separately, e.g. 'A' levels and GNVQ. A third had more than half their 16–19 students combining. Even more important, in an education system supposedly run on 'market' lines where each school and college was supposed to be competing from a position of isolation, the 1994 survey found that two out of three of all comprehensive institutions were in fact co-operating in some way with other schools and colleges at some point in their work during the secondary stage. Many were in formal consortia, others in one-to-one exchanges – with co-operation in academic, vocational and cultural/sporting provision. After the age of 16 over a third said they had at least one major full-time course that was being provided only because they were collaborating.

All this is taking place without any formal requirement from governments national or local, without any planning or policy guidance – simply because it is recognised that such co-operative effort is what will provide progression and extend choice for students and develop education itself. These changes now taking place 'on the ground' in the 16–19 system cry out for some tertiary commission to guide national change within a framework that will assist rational development institutionally as part of the drive to reduce division and increase internal coherence and progression from 14 to 18 in curriculum and assessment. The question is not whether this will take place, but how long must the system wait for it to happen in some co-ordinated way?

When it does, the role of the elected authority would not be one of making decisions and sending plans, as in former times, but of convening and presiding over the full group of institutions in any one area or region

– and securing agreement under national guidelines. One duty might be to have regard to the need for an 'all through' education in terms of pathways through the institutional and curricular systems; another, to give all schools and colleges balanced programmes of work.

Included in this would be the development of work-related education and training up to the age of 18, where young people should have the same rights of democratic oversight and appeal as those in full-time education. It is quite impossible to develop any coherent system that looks to a goal of the whole age group in education up to 18, when such a large slice of young people's learning is handed over to private companies controlled by employers' short-term interests. The track record of the TECs and LECs is anything but spectacular in relation to education and the survey found that in 1994 half the schools and colleges with 16–19 students had no contact with them at all. It is time all funding for the under-19s was restored to locally or regionally elected bodies, with a requirement to integrate their continued learning of those in work-related education with that of their peers within the schools and colleges, in co-operation with employers. A quarter of all comprehensive schools and colleges in 1994 had part-time students already.

Those bodies organising work-related learning in each region, and undertaking the work of setting payment, conditions, placements and meeting educational needs, should also be democratically based, no longer dominated by employers and their appointees – with representatives from all interested parties, including trade unions and professional bodies, teachers and lecturers, members of the community and voluntary bodies, and most important, representatives elected by students and trainees themselves. After 16 students should also have some formal place in the democratic government of institutions where they are studying – and, eventually, a great deal more say over their own work and the nature and design of the courses they are taking.

Moving on

When it came to keeping track of part-time students and those moving on to work (or looking for work) schools' and colleges' record keeping systems were not particularly impressive. Only 62% were keeping any records of student progress after leaving – even for those going to courses in full-time further education (though colleges were far better than schools). Only university entrance was well documented – with all institutions able to provide exact percentages of students in their last year accepted on degree courses the previous year: 81% had had at least 31% or more accepted on a degree course, including (where such courses were run) a survey average of 13 per institution having qualified in BTEC, GNVQ or NVQ.

Though middle-class schools and colleges sending students to degree courses had higher than average ('league table') scores for GCSE and 'A' level than did working-class schools, there was not a great difference between the two groups overall in terms of those institutions able to send students to universities: 84% of working class ones as against 92% middle class. Most schools and colleges were also able to provide a full standard range of 'A' level and Higher grade subjects – but there were exceptions in areas like music 'A' level, which only about three-quarters of schools could manage; and although almost all schools and colleges offered French, a quarter could not always provide another modern European language in addition. Nor were schools as likely to provide popular subjects like social studies, psychology and economics in the way colleges could.

Standards

As we have indicated throughout, the issue of standards is narrowly interpreted in schools and colleges in 1994, and over-reliant on measures that apply to the attainment of a minority rather than the majority. The 'league table' approach has been an exercise in ranking the minority, not one designed to raise standards overall; and for this reason did not carry the confidence of the majority of comprehensive schools and colleges in 1994, where only 12% of survey schools and colleges thought currently published 'league table' figures represented their own school's or college's academic achievements adequately.

Standards need re-interpreting in a way that is compatible with comprehensive education, while methods of motivating schools and students require criteria that judge schools and colleges on their total success, involving a much wider range of achievements than is currently part of the assessment of progress. We have to find ways to demonstrate success in comprehensive terms that use all forms of qualifications and testing in relation to all types of achievement and intelligence rather than to one limited form of intelligence or one set of qualifications. We also need to uncouple testing from selection. To assist in this, while governments monitor nationally, schools and colleges could be given more freedom to set their own tests for all kinds of purposes – possibly selected from an approved national bank, as has been common practice in Scotland for some time. They should also be freer to undertake their own assessment in relation to their own courses.

The inspection system for both schools and colleges is cumbersome, prolonged and costly without being universally helpful to schools and colleges or to pupils and students. What is required are more frequent (but far less prolonged and formal) 'inspections' in a system that encourages schools to ask for help from a range of bodies licensed to assist, rather than a system that discourages schools and colleges from admitting that help is required while they wait for long spells before receiving feedback. Our survey turned up schools – not large in number but very much in need of immediate assistance – where for various reasons it was plain OFSTED would find it difficult to assist. We could see others, basking in high 'league table' acclaim for their good work for a minority of students, unaware that the needs of a substantial minority (or even a majority) were not being fully met.

Community

Encouraging greater connection between schools and their neighbourhoods is important, since the whole community pays for education, not just parents and students and current governors. Yet we found rather low percentages of schools and even lower ones of colleges sharing their premises with local groups or agencies (like the Youth Service or pensioners or the local drama club). The objective in the 1990s seemed to be to sit on such facilities as 'private' holdings and leave them under-used, or to hire out as much as possible at commercial rates. While the latter was understandable in times of financial cutting, it is hardly acceptable that educational institutions should be removed from public use altogether. Possibly it is time to organise a new concordat (as the 1994 Act did) whereby a percentage of all letting-time for educational facilities and premises must be at 'peppercorn' rates for a range of community groups and local individuals who could not afford the commercial fees that could be charged at all other times.

Whether these arrangements are best done by institutions individually or by local authorities should be debated, for the survey discovered schools' administrative tasks and the work of governors to be very much more onerous than in the early days of comprehensive education. While there is general agreement to continue giving schools and colleges leave to run their own affairs, set their own approach, and hire their own staff, there is also evidence that for certain tasks further support or oversight for schools and colleges might be necessary – either because it would relieve burdens or because decisions that impact on local provision as a whole need to be considered in a wider light.

While returning to a situation of schools and colleges acting jointly to provide a public education service, there is also every case for allowing staff in classrooms and lecturers in colleges much more scope for devising and assessing the courses they teach. For example, there is no reason why the use of 'course work', so widely accepted as increasing commitment and raising standards of work by students, should become a classroom practice prime ministers decide about (rather than teachers and schools). If it helps raise standards, it will be continued somehow. Thus even though schools were ordered to cut this practice back severely in the early 1990s, almost half the schools in the 1994 survey said it was still a 'major' element in their school's learning.

There is also no reason why schools and colleges should be required to hold full-scale assemblies daily rather than when they believe such meetings would be useful, even less to require that they be religious in character (in one specific way). Many schools will wish to continue with religious assemblies and should be free to do so, but others should be freed to develop other forms of collective activity.

The teaching of religion (particularly one major world faith in schools where the majority are not of that faith) is another legal requirement long past usefulness, although most schools would wish to continue teaching *about* religion within their own common curriculum; and in today's world it would seem an elementary necessity if 'religious literacy' levels are to be raised. In 1994, however, comprehensive schools reported that religion as presently required (followed by technology) was the subject schools had most difficulty in providing for their pupils.

Democracy

At the bottom of many of the suggestions we make for improvement are wider democratic issues – usually related to the level at which decisions are best taken in the system: the classroom, the institution, the local authority or central government. Over the past 20 years the drift has been away from the former and towards the latter, and it needs to be gradually reversed. Those involved in comprehensive education need to know their own efforts can effect change and improvement. At present so many believe both are out of their hands in a system where self-reliance and democracy have been whittled away, and education handed over to unaccountable bodies and appointed individuals – under remote and often bureaucratic centralised control, whose task is to hand down edicts.

To justify this shift to the Centre, the efforts of teachers and lecturers in particular have often been belittled, and their freedom to make decisions regarding their own work and its assessment (or their own conditions) reduced. Why should 'local management' of schools and 'independence' of colleges be considered a healthy innovation but not local management or independence of classrooms and courses? To justify the reduction of spending that goes with the shift, governing bodies of schools and colleges, along with senior staff, are being loaded with work few are trained to manage effectively, having to give more time to financial and administrative tasks with less time for considering teaching and learning in its widest sense, or to practise democracy itself. In 25% of schools and colleges in 1994, policy decisions were taken by the principals or heads and their inner circle without staff necessarily voting or meeting to give their own separate opinion; and a third of comprehensive schools and colleges do not include any support staff in their institutional decision making. Most schools have student councils, which we were glad to learn, but how many are run entirely by students rather than for them?

As well as renewing democratic activity within educational practice, some way to renew local and regional democratic accountability also needs to be found, where elected bodies can relate to schools and colleges on a new basis, reversing changes that have undermined their positive role to monitor, assist and service – but without going back to the paternalist and interventionist styles of the past. Their main job should be to have general oversight with few (albeit important) essential duties that new legislation should define most carefully. At the same time they should be freed to compete in providing non-profit services to education at all levels, and encouraged to become entrepreneurial in new ways, including interacting with parents, unemployed people, adult students and various other important constituencies within their community.

Comprehensive education also needs to enlist more research to meet its specific needs, particularly to monitor and assess its development according to comprehensive goals rather than selective ones, and to make more information available about the working of education at all levels – from central government subsidies to individual schools' outcomes. The Centre for the Study of Comprehensive Schools is a body that could be enlarged to tackle some of this work, as well as looking at some of education's longest standing problems. It might find better ways, for example, of dealing with disadvantaged schools, previously tackled by a special centre which the Conservatives abolished in 1979 when its work had hardly started. Other work might focus on urban areas or rural areas or council estates; or upon ways that private education enjoying taxpayers' support could contribute to the wider community's educational development, replacing that host of ill-fated subsidies and 'assistance' that have been depriving comprehensive education of funding and support for decades.

What needs reviving most is the idea of a public education service – a service that is there to serve society as a whole, under the control of society as a whole rather than a segregated host of institutions driven by 'the market' and the forces of privatisation, which inevitably means domination by special interest groups and dictation by central government. Publicly-funded education is a collective, community task – not a series of individual, private races. It is about developing the widest range of human potential through a democratically accountable system.

In 1961 Raymond Williams looked ahead to a more comprehensive education in this wider sense, not merely at the removal of obvious obstacles – though this is important, especially those that curtail opportunity through pre-judgement of worth by 'inherited' intelligence or wealth or social status. He said,

> The privileges and barriers of an inherited kind will in any case go down. It is only a question of whether we replace them by the free play of the market, or by a public education designed to express and create values of an educated democracy and a common culture.
>
> (Williams, 1961:176).

That is still the question that faces us as we head for the twenty-first century; and comprehensive education – in all its many forms – is still the answer.

Notes

1   30 years ago the principle of fully comprehensive education was supported by about a quarter of the population and opposed by about a quarter – with the rest undecided. By 1996 the principle of educating at secondary stage, whereby everyone goes to schools designed for all abilities, was endorsed by 65% of the population while 27% still favoured a system where some schools cater for the 'able' and others for the remainder – with only 7% now unable to give a view (ICM poll, results given in the *Guardian*, 7 February, 1996).

2   A number of headteachers and principals chose to answer this question at great length and their

responses were often surprising and idiosyncratic; but, that said, a set of recurring themes may be detected which tell us a good deal about the problems facing comprehensive institutions.

One in four identified a need for greater stability, less interference from central government and greater autonomy for schools. These were seen to be related factors that prevented comprehensive schools and colleges from concentrating on the quality of the learning process. A large number of replies were not specific, but 47 identified curriculum stability, and another large group referred to legislative stability. One head spoke for many when he implored the government to 'stop messing about with crazy ideological schemes'; and another asked simply for 'peace to get on with the job'.

Just under 20% wanted a change of government policy or governmental attitudes towards state education; and, of these, 44 wanted a change of government as the main solution. One looked forward to 'the appointment of an education secretary who was prepared to listen to...teachers instead of systematically undermining them' (possibly one who found difficulty coping with John Patten, who was Secretary of State at the time). One wanted to see 'greater co-operation between government and the education sector with..some humility from the former'. Calls came for the 'abandonment of market forces' and several for a government 'that actually believes in state education'.

Staffing was of concern to a significant group of those replying, particularly the need for more ancillary and support staff (a perennial need identified over 30 years). As many as 23 headteachers identified low staff morale and self-esteem as the major issues requiring to be tackled.

Another group identified selection as the key issue; and only three replies suggested selection might have any positive aspects. The main request was for the abolition of all selection without further discussion; but 54 elaborated by asking specifically for the abolition of grammar schools and City Technology Colleges and grant maintained status, with all schools brought back under local authority control. One summed it up by asking for 'a return to co-operation...rather than competition'.

Of those who asked for curriculum stability only two wanted to see the National Curriculum abandoned; but many felt it should be more coherent and relevant with less built-in diversity in the revised Key Stage 4. Of those who referred specifically to the 'vocational curriculum' half wanted vocational courses to enjoy parity of esteem, and the other half believed it was important to have a fully integrated curriculum from 11 to 16 with elements of both types of learning for all pupils. Fifteen wanted the abolition of 'raw' league table scores and the requirement that information be presented only in the context of value added assessments.

About a third of the colleges asked for 'tertiary education' to be given priority and called for a major overhaul of 16-plus and 'A' levels. Here again, it was felt there should be closer integration of academic and vocational options.

As one might expect, a genuine concern to see comprehensive education succeed was at the heart of the majority of replies. One asked for 'a re-recognition that inner city comprehensive schools need help and support, not punishment'; another, an end to the 'avoidance of the use of "comprehensive" as a dirty word'. These would agree with one headteacher who yearned for 'positive government and media support for comprehensive schools'. The answers clearly showed that comprehensive schools and colleges long for the day when their achievements are acknowledged and they cease to be the butt of ill-informed comments from media gurus and politicians of all parties.

Appendix I: The Survey

The information in this book is based on a questionnaire survey carried out between March and May in the academic year 1993–94. The Questionnaire is printed on pp.521–38.

Our first objective was to make sure we contacted all categories of secondary schools and general education colleges likely to qualify as institutions providing comprehensive education according to our definition: schools for all levels of attainment where admission is without academic selection, or open access general colleges acting as one of the main providers of education for the 16–19 age range in the area (see Questionnaire, Part I, Note 1, page 522).

The first problem was that there was no list of schools and colleges classed as comprehensive, as there had been for the first Independent Enquiry nearly 30 years earlier (the Benn/Simon survey) when a partial one was provided by the DES and a full one by the Comprehensive Schools Committee. National lists of comprehensive schools were abandoned in the 1970s, even by voluntary organisations. The numbers simply grew too large.

It was not possible to collect names from local lists either (e.g. in Yearbooks), for schools changing to comprehensive status sometimes kept their old names (including a few keeping the name 'grammar school'), while a number of local authorities, following leads by successive governments, began to blur distinctions by calling all schools 'secondary' or 'high schools' without indicating which were selective. Recent 'league table' lists provided by the mass media contain too many omissions or errors of designation to be reliable.

Further decisions were whether to include middle schools, sometimes classed in government statistics as comprehensive, sometimes not; and schools formerly listed under maintained secondary but now grant maintained, which the government classifies as maintained for UK wide statistics but as grant maintained for examination statistics. We decided to include middle schools covering some of the secondary years (9–13 in age range), assumed to be comprehensive in the same way primary schools are. Some grant maintained schools, however, are grammar schools, and their inclusion would not have been appropriate; many others, however, are comprehensive and should be included. The problem is that no list shows which is which by name.

The colleges were an even bigger challenge, since the 'FE' sector is so diverse and contains a fair number of colleges that are specialist (e.g., for agriculture or drama) or do not cater for the age group under 19. Until 1992 sixth-form college statistics were included with secondary schools but after this date all colleges were segregated from secondary schools for statistical purposes, even those closely aligned with secondary schools in comprehensive 'all-through' arrangements. They were incorporated instead in the FEFC-funded sector in England and under equivalent quango structures in Wales, Scotland and Northern Ireland. Numbers had to be obtained from each area.

For all these reasons and to be sure of reaching all institutions, we simply mailed to all schools and colleges taking pupils and students between 9 and 19 in the UK and relied on schools and colleges to define themselves according to our criteria. The final mailing thus comprised 4835 secondary schools, (including 420 middle schools and 338 grant-maintained schools) and 570 further education colleges, including 58 tertiary and 116 sixth-form colleges[1].

The first task: eliminating ineligible responders

Most of those not eligible for the survey (e.g., grammar schools, specialist further education colleges) eliminated themselves by not replying. The next step was to eliminate schools and colleges that had replied but were still not eligible, a task the first three questions in the survey were designed to accomplish. The first asked respondents to state whether they were comprehensive or not within the Enquiry's definition. To double check, all who responded 'No' were asked to say what their status was by checking one of four options in question 2.

Those checking any of the first three options in question 2 were all eliminated, since by identifying themselves as fee-paying schools, grammar schools or secondary modern schools, they were not eligible. The survey made it clear that at this stage they had completed the questionnaire.

Those defining themselves under the fourth option question 2 as schools comprehensive for some but selective for others, could remain in the survey if they had answered "yes" to question 1. Six had done so but those who answered "No" were eliminated.

Profile of those excluded

Altogether 267 were eliminated, including 241 who had nevertheless completed questionnaires. These latter were analysed separately and presented the following picture:

- 68 self-defined as grammar schools (question 2A)
- 1 self-defined as feepaying (question 2B)
- 103 self-defined as non-selective but not comprehensive (question 2C)
- 55 not replying to one or other of the first two questions (including some giving reasons in the write-in section of question 3)

Of the 56 which gave information on their status, 29 were schools classed as county, 4 voluntary aided, and 9 as grant maintained. Their average size of 777 was smaller than that of institutions included in the survey (893) and they had a higher average intake of the top 20% of the attainment range (24% compared with 18%). When analysed further it could be seen that the mixed schools and colleges had attainment intakes (18.5%) very near the survey average and a full analysis showed them to be very little different from some of those saying they were comprehensive. But having said they were not, they were ruled out. Many of the single-sex schools were self-defined as selective grammar schools (many in Northern Ireland). All schools defining themselves as grammar schools were ruled out.

Among the 55 institutions answering 'no' to question 1 which did not reply to question 2 were schools writing in their reasons in question 3. In almost every case it was clear where they belonged; most queries arose because respondents had not read the notes attached to question 1. They were eliminated or included as appropriate, including a group of about 20 schools eliminated who were unable to answer 'Yes' to question 1 because the presence of selective schools in their areas meant they were not operating as comprehensive schools in practice. Since by definition these might have been comprehensive schools in unfavourable circumstances, their absence from the final survey might have contributed marginally to factors making the survey less representative of schools in the most difficult circumstances (see below).

Also in this 241 were three sixth-form colleges. All were well established and possibly had become so selective that it was impossible for them to claim to be comprehensive – even though they resembled some of the sixth-form colleges that remained in. A few FE colleges, and two tertiary colleges, also answered that they were not comprehensive; however, we could detect no difference between these and those that said they were.

A last group of institutions we eliminated ourselves, regardless of what they had answered to questions 1 or 2. These included those who had answered too few questions overall to give a complete picture of their school or college. Two institutions answered twice; their most complete response was the one included.

General comments from respondents on the questionnaire

None of the schools and colleges that replied to our mailing queried our definition of 'comprehensive'. Several schools and colleges phoned before replying, almost always to ask if we were independent as claimed, most wanting assurance we were nothing to do with the government, or were not an agency commissioned by any government department or quango.

Some took the time to comment on the survey itself by letter in addition to filling in the questionnaire. Most expressed gratitude that interest was being taken at last in comprehensive education, but two expressed doubts about the length of the questionnaire, saying that institutions would not give considered answers to so many questions (one had its own questionnaire eliminated under incomplete response).

The questionnaire had clearly been very time-consuming. In telephone follow-ups we found that was the main reason for non-response. The survey reached schools in the middle of one of the most over-burdened periods of secondary history; and at a time when questionnaires were getting increasingly common. Several said they receive a new one every day, so had to say no to all of them; luckily many said that for ours they were making an exception.

A few Scots respondents pointed out the way some of the questions assumed 'English' answers but on the whole most Scots schools and colleges were generously uncritical of any bias of this kind.

A few FE college principals were critical of the restricted nature of the enquiry, limited as it was to the years 16–19 and not asking in more detail (or with more sophistication) about the work of colleges as a whole, or about the choice and levels of qualifications. They also complained about the restricted space allowed for writing in the additional courses or qualifications (or levels of qualifications) they were providing – all part of a larger observation that the survey was more oriented to schools and sixth-form colleges than to FE colleges, particularly those that were very large. All but one of the six who criticised the survey were principals of very large colleges. One said he was making the survey a subject of study in a course looking at information gathering in order to see how a survey might give a fuller picture of the life and work of that particular college for all the ages it served.

On the other hand, several schools complimented us on the questionnaire, and one said that it had been made the basis for a staff review of the school's working practices. We were grateful to all of them, critical and complimentary, for taking the time to answer in full, as they all did.

Minimum and maximum response rates

This mailing was over five times larger than for the Benn/Simon survey of 1968. The questionnaire was almost five times longer and far more detailed with 20 pages and 148 questions, some questions requiring up to 30 replies (compared with the first survey's 6 pages with 28 questions). We knew the original response rate of 81% was impossible, not only because of the longer length but also because the enthusiasm of schools and colleges for change in 1994 had been dampened by the endless 'reforms' of the 1980s and early 1990s in an atmosphere perceived by many to be hostile to the comprehensive principle. But we hoped we could get enough responses to be able to set up a representative sample of schools and colleges to be used for this report as well as for further research, available to comprehensive schools and colleges and those working in their interests.

In the event, the volume of replies was sufficient to use all the returns as a reasonably representative picture of comprehensive education in 1994, even though it was clear that data were more representative for some areas and categories than others: 1827 returns were received, 33.8% of the total mailing of 5405 (a mailing response, not a response rate).

As set out above, 267 schools and colleges were eliminated for various reasons and the final total of included schools and colleges was 1560. It is hard to express this as a total percentage of all comprehensive schools and colleges that *could* have replied, since (for the reasons given above and others added below) we cannot know the comprehensive total exactly. However, we have attempted an approximate assessment in the following paragraphs. This depends in part upon official statistics for numbers of comprehensive schools and colleges, however, which are not always consistent, since some of the schools listed as maintained/comprehensive in certain tables are clearly shown to be selective in other tables or in additional data.

For numbers of comprehensive schools in the UK in 1993–94,

information came from several sources (HMSO, *Education Statistics for the United Kingdom*, 1993 and 1994; DfE, *Statistics of Education, Schools in England*, 1993 and 1994; *Statistics of Education and Training in Wales*, 1994; *Scottish Office Educational Statistical Bulletin* DEN/B1/1994/2; and *Northern Ireland Annual Abstract of Statistics*, 1994).

These showed (actual or predicted) that for England in the educational year of our survey middle schools deemed secondary and comprehensive secondary schools came to 3284 or 90.5% of state secondary schools. In Wales the 225 comprehensive (and middle) schools were 97% of all state secondary schools and in Scotland the 408 comprehensives were 100% of them. In Northern Ireland 70 schools (43% of secondary schools) were grammar schools, the rest classed as secondary, with no comprehensive schools listed (though some chose to identify themselves as such for our survey). For the Channel Islands, Isle of Man and Services Children's Education Authority (SCEA) we identified separately another 15 (though a slightly higher number responded and qualified).

Minimum response rates

This came to 3932 comprehensive schools in the UK and the 1994 survey schools (1424) are 36.2% of this total. This, however, is a minimum rate of response, because it is quite possible that national totals over-estimate schools that were comprehensive by our definition and which should not be included in the total from which this response rate is calculated (for the reasons given above and below).

For example, some of the comprehensive schools listed as non-selective in government statistics (LEA, voluntary and GM) were in fact operating selectively in 1994. The only reliable evidence we had on this point, however, was in respect of grant maintained schools, where earlier research had found that nearly one third were practising some form of selection for entry (Bush *et al.*, 1993:95), though this would not have been uniform. However, if one third of GM schools are eliminated from the UK year total (see above), the survey's UK response rate for schools would rise to 38%.

The response rate for English comprehensive schools in our survey (including middle schools) was 37.2%. When middle schools were removed it was 37.7%. Removing a third of all GM schools brought the response rate for English schools up to 39.9%. Removing both middle schools and selective GM schools would bring it to over 40%.

Breaking responses down by regions (but not adjusting for selectivity as in the previous paragraphs)[2], the survey's response rates were 30.9% for

Greater London, 33.9% for the metropolitan boroughs and 41.0% for the English counties. Removing selective GM schools from the total would result in higher response rates in all categories; removing schools of other legal status that also selected at entry, including those selecting partially, would raise them still further. But at this point the criterion for 'comprehensive' becomes problematic since we do not know the exact numbers of schools which are selecting on a partial basis and even the survey had no agreed criterion for comprehensive status in relation to partial selection (other than the school's own declaration of comprehensive intent).

The fact that there is such difficulty in determining an exact response rate (owing to differing types of selection as well as to different totals of 'comprehensive' schools in different DfE statistics) illustrates one of the main points our survey tried to make: that selection in 1994 was not only 'hidden' in all sorts of ways, even in official statistics, but without some national agrement over the legal definition of comprehensive education it was becoming increasingly difficult to define for statistical purposes.

An additional problem in survey statistics themselves with regard to regional categories (question 25) was that school and college numbers were calculated on definitions given in question 4, where analysis showed that 143 institutions had not replied or had replied incorrectly – probably because of uncertainty over their own legal status (see also pages 124–26). Since they had all replied to many other questions, including question 6 (asking their age range), these 143 were re-analysed 'by hand' and allocated to their appropriate category for the survey totals (see Table A2). However, they were not always included in analysis where totals were based on responses to question 4; and thus would not have been included in regional figures. Some of the three English categories may thus have had higher response rates than those given here.

Even if they were higher, rates for the large cities would probably not rise to the levels of the counties. Other survey data (see Chapter 4) suggests that comprehensives in the large cities in all parts of the UK are under-represented, as they were in the first independent enquiry (Benn/Simon survey) of 1968 and in the NFER's three-stage investigation of comprehensive schools from 1968 to 1972[3]. Greater problems with local disadvantage and larger numbers of coexisting selective schools caused some city schools to be over-pressed, leaving little time for the extra work of responding to questionnaires. Reasons for London's lower figure still could include excessive attention from researchers and the national media (compared with comprehensive schools in other areas). Many London-based schools felt beleaguered by over-exposure (as well as by continuing biased comment).

Colleges

The response rate for colleges overall was a little lower than for schools, possibly because FE colleges are not yet used to thinking of themselves as 'comprehensive' institutions – whatever definition is used.

There were 570 colleges mailed. But it was even more difficult to distinguish which ones of these were comprehensive by our definition and arrive at a total from which to calculate a response rate. Some official statistics, such as those giving examination results (*Statistical Bulletin* 7/94, 1994, Table 9, for example) identify sixth-form colleges' and 'other' FE sector populations separately, but no population figures are given for tertiary colleges; and no numbers of institutions are given for any of these groups. In *Education Statistics for the UK*, 1994, Table 22, for example (which sets out courses followed after 16), only two types of institution are given for the age group: schools and FE sector establishments.

The *Education Yearbook 1994*, however, gave a list of 58 tertiary colleges in England and Wales, as provided by the Tertiary College Association. And the FEFC *Annual Report, 1994* gave a total of 116 sixth-form colleges. Based on these figures our response rate for sixth-form colleges was 32.7% (37 out of 113) and for tertiary colleges 41.3% (24 out of the 58).

Finding a total for FE colleges was more difficult for reasons already given. The FEFC *Annual Report, 1994* (FEFC, 1994b), distinguished a list of 287 general (as opposed to specialist) FE colleges in England, including those classed as tertiary above. Twenty more were removed that we considered were really specialist or not serving the whole age group, and 111 sixth-form colleges were added. This gave an approximate total of 378 possible general education comprehensive colleges for England. The survey numbers of colleges in England (117) were 31.2% of this total.

For the other regions of the UK, using the *Yearbook's* figures for Wales, Scotland, and Northern Ireland, we drew up a total of 102 FE colleges that we identified as general in nature (28 Wales, 44 in Scotland, 25 in Northern Ireland, and 5 in other areas but not making final deductions for those that might be too specialist to include). This gives a 20% response rate for colleges outside England. Adding these to the England total gives a total of colleges of 473. The 136 colleges in our survey were 28.7% of this total.

Four hundred and seventy three colleges added to 3932 schools make a possible total of comprehensive institutions of 4405 that might have responded – even though this almost certainly overestimates the total that is comprehensive even by our definition. Our 1560 used in the survey is 35.4% of this total, but since the national total probably includes a number of schools and colleges that none would class as comprehensive for a variety of reasons and a number of others whose comprehensive status would be disputed, this is a minimum response rate. What the maximum rate for the survey might be is hard to say for all the reasons already given, many concerning one of the central issues considered by the survey: do official national statistics any longer accurately represent the real extent of selectivity in the comprehensive system?

National coverage

The extent of our 1994 survey's coverage was an easier question to answer, since every single Local Education Authority in England and Wales is represented in the survey by schools or colleges or both, as is every single Educational Region of Scotland and every single Education and Library Board in Northern Ireland. Represented also are the Channel Islands, the Isle of Man and the majority of schools run by the Services Children's Education Authority (SCEA).

We are satisfied that the information we make available, while it must be read in certain parts with caution for the reasons given above and below, gives a reasonably reliable general picture of comprehensive education in Britain from 9 to 19 years at the time of the 30 year anniversary of the official start of secondary comprehensive education in Britain.

Notes

1 The Local Schools Information Service made the number of GM schools for this year 507. The difference was that our total was for the year just ended, theirs for the school year just starting. All GM schools would have been covered in the survey, even if under their old legal status. For statistical purposes in calculating GM schools that could be selective, the LSI total is used, since it gives the national total for the survey year.

2 This total of comprehensive schools broken down for the London boroughs, metropolitan boroughs, and non-metropolitan counties was supplied by the DfE in 1995 from a special list of comprehensive schools. It was its latest at time of publication and was for 1992–93, but total numbers amounted to a difference between this year and the next (compared with totals available in other national statistics) of only nine schools. The DfE list included GM schools but not middle schools. Comparable survey rates given in the text also omitted middle schools but included GM schools and did not make clear whether selective GM schools had been omitted or not.

3   See Benn and Simon, 1970: Appendix 1, pp.515–16 for data about its own survey and that of the NFER on this point. The first independent enquiry – like that in 1994 – also had lower response rates from Scotland (Benn and Simon, 1970:515).

Appendix II: Some Notes on Education Indicators (as used in the 1994 survey and its appendix tables)

Note A

Throughout the book a range of indicators is used to compare comprehensive schools and colleges of different types. They were included because they have featured prominently in the history of the comprehensive reform or because they are of interest to the general public and to educators. Each is considered at the appropriate place in the text – and additional data about some are included in the appendix tables that follow.

Some, like the socio-economic background of intakes, feature in social research generally. Others, like percentages relating to students without English as their first language, feature in general educational research. Still others, like the percentage of intakes in the top 20% of the attainment range, are more specific to research related to comprehensive education. All are indicators that apply universally to both schools and colleges and their use is explained in the text.

Other indicators apply only to schools or only to colleges and are also explained in the text. These include attendance percentages and the level of free dinners taken, generally used only for schools; or those like percentages studying on day release, more applicable to colleges.

Some indicators are common to both schools and colleges but not necessarily to every age range. These include external examination figures for GCSE or SCE O grade, 'A' level or Higher grade, G(S)NVQ, BTEC, and N(S)VQ. Almost all are partial indicators only. Unless combined with other forms of assessment and examinations, none, used alone, forms a reliable indicator of the totality of achievement in any comprehensive school or college, let alone an adequate indicator of comprehensive education's wider educational achievement (a view strongly supported by the schools and colleges taking part in the survey – see Chapter 7).

Use and misuse of education 'indicators'

Several indicators named in previous paragraphs or used in the survey have been recommended for use in relation to interpretation of a school's or college's examination scores or other aspects of its work in a 'value added' context; and while some may well throw light upon performance that helps to give a fairer picture, none should be used to suggest any one type of comprehensive in any one situation is inherently less capable of success than any other.

This applies particularly to percentages of black, Asian or other minority ethnic or national groups in schools and colleges (about which the survey also enquired), as these can so easily become 'value subtracted' indicators, even if this use is unintended. We looked at such groups as ones that can often culturally enhance the experience of comprehensive education – but not as indicators directly related to educational performance.

The same applies to other types of intakes (including low/high attainment or working/middle class). Comprehensive education requires admissions policies that permit intakes to be as balanced as possible in relation to all these factors in any local area or region, but it is important to accept that schools or colleges whose natural, locally balanced intakes include high or low levels of any such groups, are as capable of success as any other.

The same applies to pupils with special educational needs, their presence sometimes creating another negative indicator in 'value added' work. We regard them as part of the normal full range of attainment that would be present in any comprehensive school or college – just as we would expect to find some pupils with rather special capabilities. It is only when numbers of pupils in any of these groups in any one institution (or set of institutions) rise far above or fall far below local or regional norms that there is reason to consider adjustments that achieve a fairer balance.

Guide to survey findings

Some survey findings are set out in the appendix tables that follow while others are set out in the text itself. When findings are given where there is no table, reference is made to the question number in the survey itself. In all findings, unless otherwise stated, percentages given relate to the totals of those schools and colleges answering the question, not the total of all schools and colleges of the type or group, but data always relates to answers where at least 90% of those eligible have replied to the question concerned. Where the answering-total is less than 90%, this is always indicated in the text or in notes attached to it.

Where information in the text is not given on the same basis as it is in the printed tables or in the appendix (e.g. where categories might be collapsed), this is also indicated.

Note B: examination results

Examination statistics used in this survey illustrate differences within the survey population of schools and colleges and in many cases between their policies as well – e.g., how far they have extended their courses leading to vocational qualifications in addition to those examinations used for ranking in 'league tables'.

Caution should be exercised in comparing survey figures to those given nationally in HMSO or DfE or SOED official statistics for the survey year because examination statistics in the survey apply generally to the academic year 1992–93 and not to the year of the survey; and because the response rates for examination questions in the survey were not always over the 90% level we have set for our data (see above). Only 86% of schools gave figures for five GCSE A–C, for example, and only 80% gave them for 'A' level grade point averages, a fact that may partly account for some of the differences noted in 'A' level figures between the survey's results and those given nationally (see below).

Other reasons for caution include the fact that survey questions sometimes asked for information in a slightly different form from that used in national statistics and because although some examination statistics in the survey are given individually by countries (e.g. England, Scotland), others are given for the UK as a whole. Similarly, while some survey institutions are singled out for separate findings (GM or LEA or Aided schools, for example) many of our tables give findings, including examination results, for all types of comprehensive schools in the same figure; and after 16, some include both schools and colleges in the same figure.

GCSE and O Grade

The survey makes use of the 'league table' figures of five GCSE passes A–C (or O Grade 1–3) as well as 'A' level grade point averages, average passes for three or more Highers and for SCOTVEC certificate exams, and pass rates for BTEC – not because we believe they give anything more than partial information (usually about a minority of students in the secondary years), but because they are currently widely understood and thus help to show differences within the survey population.

Caution should be exercised in comparing survey figures to figures nationally, since (even when all adjustments are made) comparisons require exactly the same types of school or college to be included in both sets. Even where the match seems close – as, for example, in the following comparison (as percentages) for five GCSE A–C results for England's three types of local authorities in 1992–93 – it has to be remembered that the DfE figures are for all maintained schools (and would include LEA grammar schools), while the survey figures are for comprehensive schools only.

	DfE figures (from Table 3, DfE Bulletin 7/94)	1994 survey (from Table A5)
Greater London	34.3	34.7
Metropolitan Districts	32.9	31.6
Shire Counties	41.1	41.3

The DfE figure for five GCSE A–C for all schools in England in 1992–93 was 41.2% but that included all private schools, all GM schools, and all grammar schools as well as comprehensive schools and cannot be compared with the 1994 survey figure for all schools of 39.3% which was for comprehensive schools alone (but which also included those in Wales and Scotland). Looking at figures for England-only for that year, the DfE average for comprehensive schools was 36.4% (DfE, *Statistical Bulletin* 7/94, Table 1) while the England-only average for all comprehensive schools in the survey was 38.4% (for county-LEA schools, 38.0% – Table A5).

Again, although these figures seem comparable, closer analysis shows that the survey figures are generally somewhat higher than national figures. In some tables this can be accounted for by the fact that figures include results from Scotland and GM schools, but where populations are roughly comparable and survey figures are still higher, a contributing factor could be that survey schools and colleges were less representative of schools and colleges in difficult circumstances (see above and Chapter 4). Another could be the nature of the GCSE performance in relation to self-declared comprehensive schools (see below).

GM comprehensive schools' results for five GCSE A–C, by contrast, although higher than the survey average, were lower than their figures in national statistics: 43.3 against a national figure of 45.3. This may be accounted for in part by the fact that the schools in the survey were from the comprehensive end of the GM continuum and that some of those not responding to the survey (from the other end) were highly selective, including the 76 officially designated as grammar schools (DfE, *Statistics of Education, Schools in England 1994*, Table 128). Other reasons that might account for differences are given in the text (see page 141).

GCSE attainment at less than five GCSE A–C

The 1994 survey average for achieving at least one GCSE A-F/G was 94.0% (see Table A7), which compared with a national average for comprehensive schools in England in the same year of 94.1% (DfE, *Statistical Bulletin 7/94*: Table 1). Again, figures are not strictly comparable because the survey figure was for the UK as a whole, but even so the comparison suggests that the survey population might be representative enough for Table A7's breakdown of information related to this attainment level (and to that for four GCSE) to be meaningful in relation to the various categories shown.

'A' levels and post-16 qualifications

At 'A' level, instead of schools and colleges in the survey having higher figures than national statistics, they had slightly lower average scores for certain indicators, one of which was the 'A' level grade point average. This was especially the case for the GM schools. In the 1994 survey their score was 11.9 compared with a national figure for GM schools in the same year of 15.7 (DfE, *Statistical Bulletin 7/94*: Table 10). This suggests once again that those GM schools not responding contained a lot of schools with highly selective sixth forms; which seems quite likely given that we know that in England the GM sector in the survey year contained a far higher percentage of grammar schools (at 14% of the GM total) than did the LEA sector (with 5%) (DfE, *Statistics of Education, Schools in England 1994*, Table 128).

This difference is not reflected in national DfE statistics, however, where distinction is made between results from comprehensive schools and grammar schools in the LEA sector but not in the GM sector (DfE, *Statistical Bulletin 7/94*: Table 10). Just as important, of course, is that this 14% of GM grammar schools represents only those GM schools *officially* selecting; it does not cover any that may be unofficially selecting or partially selective.

The 'A' level grade point average for comprehensive schools for the year in national statistics in England (DfE, *Statistical Bulletin 7/94*, Table 10) was 13.6 (not including GM schools and sixth-form colleges), only slightly higher than the average for English comprehensive schools in the survey (not including GM schools or any of the colleges) at 13.1. The difference may not be significant. Nevertheless it is interesting to speculate on a possible feature of examination results as revealed in the survey: higher than 'national' averages for the first external examination and lower for the second, and whether this could possibly be related to the different nature of the two examinations in relation to comprehensive goals.

The GCSE (and SCE O grade) are 'comprehensive' examinations: everyone is encouraged to sit them and achieve at least one pass. Keen comprehensive schools (such as responded to the survey) would always try to maximise results and enter as many as possible. 'A' level, on the other hand, is a selective exam. Only a minority are expected to enter and even fewer to succeed. Some schools concerned with 'league table' scores may limit numbers to ensure high pass rates; others may be more interested in the numbers getting passes. If schools allow all who wish to enter 'A' level and Higher exam courses to do so (as survey results seem to confirm is not an unusual practice), then pass rates and point scores risk being lower than when only those pupils likely to get good scores are allowed to enter. If a greater percentage of comprehensive schools and colleges in the 1994 survey than nationally pursued a policy of 'all may enter who wish', this might have adversely affected 'A' level grade point averages and 'league table' pass rates – even though it might also have resulted in more actual passes for students.

As for percentages that attempted two or more 'A' levels, this too could be affected by the policies of the schools and colleges, particularly in relation to GNVQ and BTEC courses. Schools and colleges that run both academic and vocational qualifications were likely to have smaller percentages of their total numbers taking 'A' levels but could have had large numbers and percentages gaining vocational qualifications, and possibly gaining more qualifications overall. 'League table' ranking would not reflect any such achievements.

When it came to colleges' examination figures for 'A' level grade point averages, Table A6 shows scores to be 13.9, 12.0 and 8.8 for sixth-form colleges, tertiary colleges and FE colleges respectively – compared with national figures of 14.7 for sixth-form colleges and 10.1 for all other FE colleges combined (DfE, *Statistical Bulletin* 7/94, Table 1). No national figures were given for tertiary colleges separately in government statistics, but survey figures for all three types of college in relation to several indicators, however, suggest that tertiary colleges' results could be distinctive enough to justify recording them separately in all national statistics.

That sixth-form colleges responding to the survey had lower scores than sixth-form colleges nationally suggests that among those colleges not responding were many that were more selective than those taking part, though the difference was not as great as with GM sixth forms.

Scotland

Scotland's percentage for five Standard O grade (1–3) passes was 52.0% of its S4 roll for the 1994 survey and that for three or more Higher passes was 24.1%. The figures for Scotland from the Scottish Office for that same year (92/3) were 50.8% for five or more Standard passes (1–3) and for three or more Higher passes 28.5% (*Scottish School Leavers and their Qualifications 1982/3 to 1992/3*, Edn/E2/1994/9).

The same phenomenon as seemed to characterise the rest of the UK is also suggested in Scotland: first level qualifications slightly higher than the national average while figures for Highers were lower. It is likely that the same factors given above and below to account for the differences might also apply to Scotland.

Conclusion – examination figures

Although there were differences between survey figures and national figures owing to the different populations of schools included in various categories (making comparison on a like-with-like basis difficult) and although it was necessary to exercise caution because the percentages of schools and colleges giving examination figures were not as high as their replies for most other questions to the survey, it is possible to say that most examination figures from the 1994 survey, where directly comparable, tend to confirm that the population of survey schools and colleges was broadly representative of the majority of comprehensive schools and colleges in Britain.

Data note

All data were analysed using a relational data base. Names of all schools and colleges participating were held on a separate list and none is identifiable in the survey data. Anonymity was guaranteed and no schools or colleges are identified in the survey findings or in any discussion of the findings. Names of schools and colleges used in the text are those that have been given out in publications, reported in the public media or issued by schools and colleges themselves.

Our objective in this book was to set out the main findings of our survey. We presented base-line data only and made no attempt to apply any sophisticated analysis, leaving it to readers to exercise the usual caution in interpreting figures in certain situations – e.g. where numbers of schools in certain sub-categories were particularly small. We realise there is scope for further analysis, and further studies are planned.

Appendix Tables

Table A1 Legal status of comprehensive schools and colleges

Status	Number (%)
County	1006 (64.5)
Voluntary aided	102 (6.5)
Voluntary controlled	45 (2.9)
Special agreement	13 (0.8)
Grant maintained	127 (8.1)
Sixth-form college	37 (2.4)
Tertiary college	24 (1.5)
FE college	75 (4.8)
No response	131 (8.4)
Total	1560 (100)

Table A2 Age range of comprehensive schools and colleges

Age (years)	Number (%)
11–18	626 (40.1)
11–16	564 (36.2)
13–16	1 (0.1)
13–18	69 (4.4)
14–18	8 (0.5)
9–13	137 (8.8)
11–14	19 (1.2)
16–19+	136 (8.7)
Total	1560 (100)

Table A3 Comprehensive schools and colleges by region

Region	Number (%)
England: London Boroughs	128 (8.2)
England: Metropolitan Boroughs	289 (18.5)
England: Counties	930 (59.6)
Wales	78 (5.0)
Scotland	95 (6.1)
Northern Ireland	12 (0.8)
Channel Islands, Isle of Man, SCEA	20 (1.3)
Unknown	8 (0.5)
Total	1560 (100)

Table A4 Grouping used in comprehensive schools (Key Stage 3), 1994. Results are given as numbers, with percentages in parentheses

Year 7					
Method of grouping	*11/12–18*	*11/12–16*	*9–13*	*11–14*	*Total*
Mixed ability for all subjects	316 (57.2)	254 (48.6)	38 (29.7)	8 (47.1)	616 (50.5)
Mixed ability, with no more than two subjects setted	128 (23.2)	124 (23.7)	44 (34.4)	3 (17.6)	299 (24.5)
Mixed ability, with no more than four subjects setted	31 (5.6)	41 (7.8)	31 (24.2)	4 (23.5)	107 (8.8)
Ability sets for most or all academic courses	33 (6.0)	50 (9.6)	7 (5.5)	1 (5.9)	91 (7.5)
Two or three ability bands	40 (7.2)	44 (8.4)	7 (5.5)	0 (0)	91 (7.5)
Streaming for all academic subjects except sport, drama and art	2 (0.4)	8 (1.5)	0 (0)	1 (5.9)	11 (0.9)
Streaming for all classes and courses	2 (0.4)	2 (0.4)	1 (0.8)	0 (0)	5 (0.4)
Total	552 (100)	523 (100)	128 (100)	17 (100)	1220 (100)

Year 8					
Method of grouping	*11/12–18*	*11/12–16*	*9–13*	*11–14*	*Total*
Mixed ability for all subjects	125 (21.0)	57 (10.6)	28 (21.9)	6 (31.6)	216 (16.8)
Mixed ability, with no more than two subjects setted	201 (33.7)	177 (32.8)	42 (32.8)	3 (15.8)	423 (33.0)
Mixed ability, with no more than four subjects setted	127 (21.3)	131 (24.3)	40 (31.3)	7 (36.8)	305 (23.8)
Ability sets for most or all academic courses	92 (15.4)	102 (18.9)	8 (6.3)	2 (10.5)	204 (15.9)
Two or three ability bands	47 (7.9)	60 (11.1)	8 (6.3)	0 (0)	115 (9.0)
Streaming for all academic subjects except sport, drama and art	2 (0.3)	9 (1.7)	0 (0)	1 (5.3)	12 (0.9)
Streaming for all classes and courses	2 (0.3)	4 (0.7)	2 (1.6)	0 (0)	8 (0.6)
Total	596 (100)	540 (100)	128 (100)	19 (100)	1283 (100)

Year 9					
Method of grouping	*11/12–18*	*11/12–16*	*9–13*	*11–14*	*Total*
Mixed ability for all subjects	46 (7.7)	29 (5.3)	3 (4.5)	2 (11.1)	80 (6.5)
Mixed ability, with no more than two subjects setted	111 (18.5)	97 (17.8)	14 (20.9)	3 (16.7)	225 (18.3)
Mixed ability, with no more than four subjects setted	207 (34.5)	194 (35.6)	22 (32.8)	9 (50.0)	432 (35.1)
Ability sets for most or all academic courses	173 (28.8)	147 (27.0)	19 (28.4)	3 (16.7)	342 (27.8)
Two or three ability bands	56 (9.3)	65 (11.9)	9 (13.4)	0 (0)	130 (10.6)
Streaming for all academic subjects except sport, drama and art	6 (1.0)	9 (1.7)	0 (0)	1 (5.6)	16 (1.3)
Streaming for all classes and courses	1 (0.2)	4 (0.7)	0 (0)	0 (0)	5 (0.4)
Total	600 (100)	545 (100)	67 (100)	18 (100)	1230 (100)

Table A5 All schools and colleges

Category of school/college	a	b	c	d	e	f
Average for survey	893	18.0	33.2	39.8	18.1	61.0
County (LEA)	832	16.6	34.1	34.5	21.2	64.2
Voluntary aided	766	18.1	28.7	64.0	15.2	63.4
Voluntary controlled	837	19.0	33.3	40.0	11.4	44.4
Special agreement	660	17.8	16.7	38.5	7.7	69.2
Grant maintained	911	18.5	26.4	62.9	10.3	49.6
Sixth-form college	887	57.8	16.7	65.6	2.9	27.0
Tertiary college	1860	25.7	30.4	–	–	62.5
FE college	1891	13.1	32.2	–	–	64.4
11–18	974	18.6	35.4	45.0	14.0	55.0
11–16	763	15.4	27.9	37.7	27.4	70.9
13–18	921	16.6	38.2	43.3	9.0	60.9
14–18	992	22.4	50.0	37.5	0.0	50.0
9–13	419	15.9	45.3	25.4	14.9	59.0
11–14	496	19.0	47.4	10.5	5.3	42.1
All colleges	1587	31.9	27.7	–	–	52.7
Mixed	896	18.2	34.0	38.2	16.9	60.8
Girls	806	16.4	20.4	67.9	42.3	68.5
Boys	802	16.7	17.1	64.7	25.7	60.0
Roman Catholic	723	17.1	32.8	58.0	18.6	71.1
Church of England	801	18.0	31.8	57.6	10.9	45.5
Large city	965	13.6	30.3	44.4	65.6	89.8
Town	940	17.8	32.3	35.8	13.1	62.6
Suburban area	914	18.5	34.0	46.7	15.4	57.1
Village or countryside	642	21.5	36.4	30.0	2.8	44.5
Council estate	757	8.6	46.1	15.5	63.5	99.0
Private housing	951	26.4	33.1	63.5	1.3	9.7
Council and private	872	19.6	32.2	40.9	6.3	58.7
Substandard	785	9.8	11.1	22.2	88.9	100
Council, private and substandard	976	13.5	29.4	32.8	31.8	83.9
England: London Boroughs	1016	16.0	27.0	65.4	35.8	68.0
England: Metropolitan Districts	950	14.5	28.5	42.7	36.4	73.1
England: Counties	882	19.1	30.4	37.8	10.6	54.7
Wales	978	20.5	45.5	37.8	14.9	67.1
Scotland	718	17.7	67.7	21.7	18.9	68.1
Northern Ireland	689	17.7	45.5	27.3	–	72.7
Channel Islands, Isle of Man and SCEA	450	26.6	65.0	23.5	–	75.0

a = Average size of school/college
b = Percentage of intake estimated to be in top 20% of attainment range
c = Percentage of schools/colleges which were purpose built
d = Percentage of schools/colleges with first year of entry full in September 1993
e = Percentage of schools/colleges in which more than 30% of students qualify for free school meals
f = Percentage of schools/colleges in which the majority of the intake is working class
g = Percentage of schools/colleges in which the majority of the intake is middle class
h = Percentage of schools/colleges in which the attendance rate was more than 95%

g	h	i	j	k	l	m	n	o	p
26.4	28.8	19.3	16.4	24.7	62.7	56.1	39.3	21.5	71.2
24.7	25.9	21.9	17.1	25.8	61.6	55.5	38.0	19.5	69.9
25.7	36.6	12.9	13.1	15.7	65.7	57.3	42.3	2.9	65.4
35.6	48.9	11.1	4.7	13.3	68.5	51.3	41.5	9.1	56.5
15.4	23.1	7.7	0.0	23.1	58.5	49.5	36.9	15.4	100
33.9	41.3	7.1	17.9	23.8	68.0	57.7	43.3	16.7	59.2
56.8	18.8	21.9	25.0	13.5	–	–	–	75.0	72.2
20.8	–	–	29.2	25.0	–	–	–	82.4	86.4
16.9	–	–	23.3	38.7	–	–	–	77.8	91.4
31.0	29.1	17.0	15.9	27.7	–	56.3	41.9	19.1	67.5
20.7	24.9	25.8	16.5	24.0	64.0	–	36.7	19.5	–
23.2	18.8	20.3	20.6	17.6	–	55.2	38.3	20.3	75.6
25.0	0.0	37.5	12.5	0.0	–	54.3	36.8	12.5	75.0
26.9	54.8	0.7	10.3	14.8	–	–	–	0.7	–
31.6	63.2	0.0	5.3	10.5	–	–	–	0.0	–
29.8	–	–	25.8	30.4	–	–	–	75.9	86.2
26.7	28.3	21.1	14.3	24.0	62.4	55.6	39.3	21.7	70.8
18.5	20.4	25.9	60.4	42.6	72.3	63.6	40.7	20.6	76.7
28.6	28.6	20.0	34.3	22.9	51.9	58.7	33.8	11.4	73.9
17.4	25.4	15.3	10.2	19.8	65.2	55.8	42.1	6.6	73.4
42.4	50.8	6.2	14.3	15.2	65.6	55.7	45.5	6.1	57.6
5.4	8.0	58.3	54.2	39.5	56.1	53.1	24.2	45.9	79.3
24.2	27.2	19.5	9.0	19.3	61.1	54.6	39.9	22.7	74.1
30.8	27.8	19.2	17.3	29.1	63.7	56.3	39.8	19.6	67.7
37.7	46.1	4.1	4.8	17.5	68.7	62.6	47.5	5.4	61.7
0.5	6.7	62.6	19.6	32.8	49.3	50.1	23.2	29.2	73.8
82.2	56.0	3.5	7.4	19.9	72.9	61.1	52.1	10.8	61.4
24.0	30.6	10.0	10.4	21.0	66.0	56.0	42.4	17.1	72.4
0.0	5.9	64.7	66.7	33.3	51.5	–	18.2	58.8	100
3.9	10.7	39.9	37.1	34.4	59.1	54.4	32.1	36.8	75.0
18.8	18.7	33.3	60.8	35.4	69.8	61.1	34.7	41.1	65.3
18.0	15.5	34.9	28.2	37.4	54.5	51.2	31.8	26.6	73.1
32.2	34.4	13.7	7.8	18.7	64.5	53.3	41.3	17.3	72.2
17.1	19.1	38.2	20.5	29.5	67.3	56.6	37.2	23.7	66.7
18.0	13.0	30.4	2.2	28.4	73.6	70.5	52.0	17.4	73.6
9.1	41.7	8.3	0.0	36.4	23.3	43.7	35.7	25.0	83.3
5.0	45.0	5.0	3.2	10.0	58.0	52.3	51.4	20.0	60.0

i = Percentage of schools/colleges in which the attendance rate was less than 90%
j = Percentage of schools/colleges in which 5% or more of students do not have English as a first language
k = Percentage of schools/colleges needing major repairs/refurbishment to function effectively
l = Percentage of students continuing education post-16 in schools ending at 16
m = Percentage of students staying on after 16 (in all-through schools)
n = Percentage of students passing five GCSEs (Grade A–C) or five Standard Grade (1–3) 1992–3
o = Percentage of schools/colleges in which the student turnover is at least one per week
p = Percentage of schools/colleges collaborating with other schools/colleges

Table A7 GCSE/Standard Grade (1992–93)

Category of school/college	Percentage of 15/16 year group obtaining at least one GCSE grade A–G or Standard Grade 1–6	Percentage of 15/16 year group obtaining at least four GCSEs grade A–G or Standard Grade 1–6
Average for survey	94.0	81.0
County (LEA)	93.6	80.0
Voluntary aided	95.7	83.8
Voluntary controlled	96.1	84.8
Special agreement	93.6	83.0
Grant maintained	94.4	86.0
11–18	94.5	82.9
11–16	93.2	79.0
13–18	95.2	81.6
14–18	95.1	80.0
Mixed	94.1	81.3
Girls	93.1	79.1
Boys	92.4	76.4
Roman Catholic	94.9	82.9
Church of England	96.6	87.2
Large city	87.3	68.3
Town	94.7	82.1
Suburban area	93.8	81.3
Village or countryside	97.0	86.7
Council estate	88.6	71.8
Private housing	97.3	87.7
Council and private	95.2	83.1
Substandard	83.6	63.5
Council, private and substandard	92.2	77.4
England: London Boroughs	92.2	80.3
England: Metropolitan Districts	90.8	74.2
England: Counties	95.1	83.0
Wales	91.3	73.1
Scotland	96.3	88.1
Northern Ireland	92.0	84.7
Channel Islands, Isle of Man and SCEA	96.6	91.8

Table A8 Percentage of 16/17 age group enrolled (Year 12/Lower Sixth) in academic and vocational courses in institutions where these courses are offered

Category of school/college	'A' levels	GNVQ
Average for survey	62.1	21.9
County (LEA)	65.2	24.0
Voluntary aided	63.1	24.8
Voluntary controlled	73.5	21.1
Special agreement	59.8	10.0
Grant maintained	64.4	25.6
Sixth-form college	65.4	10.3
Tertiary college	27.9	11.9
FE college	21.3	13.2
11–18	66.4	24.3
13–18	57.4	25.7
14–18	63.0	28.3
All colleges	40.5	11.8
Mixed	61.9	21.8
Girls	61.7	22.4
Boys	67.3	21.7
Roman Catholic	59.7	24.5
Church of England	70.3	22.8
Large city	45.2	23.7
Town	62.4	22.6
Suburban area	64.6	20.4
Village or countryside	68.6	21.3
Council estate	45.2	30.7
Private housing	72.8	15.3
Council and private	64.8	19.8
Substandard	24.0	15.0
Council, private and substandard	49.9	28.0
England: London Boroughs	55.7	20.1
England: Metropolitan Districts	56.4	25.0
England: Counties	65.3	20.1
Wales	62.8	25.8
Northern Ireland	43.5	43.3
Channel Islands, Isle of Man and SCEA	58.7	17.5

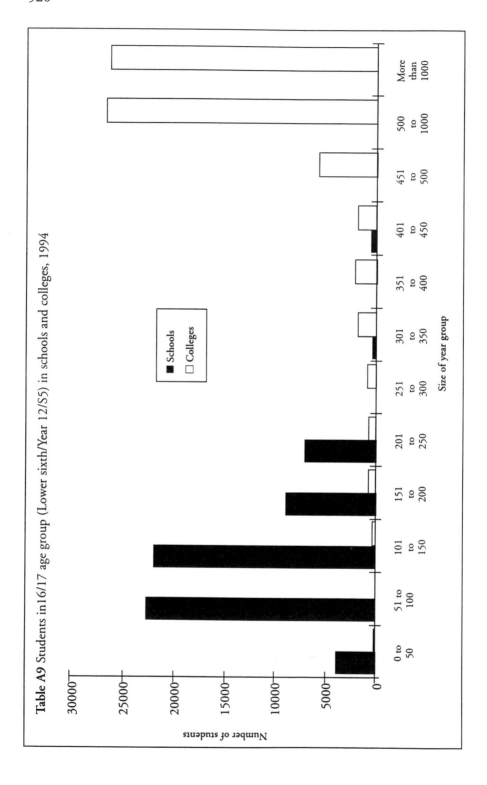

Table A9 Students in 16/17 age group (Lower sixth/Year 12/S5) in schools and colleges, 1994

Survey Questionnaire: Comprehensive Education in Britain. Independent National Enquiry, 1994

NAME of school or college

_____

ADDRESS

_____

_____

_____

NO SCHOOL OR COLLEGE WILL BE IDENTIFIED IN ANY PUBLISHED DATA.
Where an institution might be named   e.g. as one pioneering in a certain field, written permission will be obtained first.
If you would like to be notified of this Survey's published results, please tick this box ☐

Instructions for marking:

For Yes/No and lettered options, please CIRCLE the appropriate word or letter to the right of each question or option column

For all other questions, please WRITE the number or information requested in the space provided.

ALL institutions: please answer questions in Part I (those without pupils under 16 omit starred questions).

Schools with a sixth form and all colleges (tertiary, sixth form, and further education): please ALSO answer Part II.

Unless information is only available for 1992/3, please give all information in respect of the school/college year 1993/4.

Any school or college wishing to make additional comments, please do so at the end of the questionnaire.

Thank you for your help.

PART I

Questions for all schools and colleges. Colleges without pupils under 16 to omit starred questions

Section 1: Institutional type and admissions

1. Is your school or college a comprehensive school/college? *(see note 1 below) (please circle the appropriate word)* Yes/No

2. If you answered 'No' to Question 1, how would you define your school or college *(Please circle one letter only)*

A designated grammar school *(see note 2)*	A
A fee-paying school/college with or without assisted places	B
A non-selective school/college but not comprehensive *(see note 3)*	C
A partially selective school/college *(see note 4)*	D

3. If you were unable to circle a letter in Q2, how would you define your school/college?

   _____

   If you circled A, B, or C in answer to Question 2, you have completed the questionnaire. Please return in the envelope provided. Thank you.

4. What is your school's/college's legal status? *(please circle letter to the right of the appropriate reply)*

Local Education Authority maintained		FEFC funded as a	
County	A	Sixth Form College	G
Voluntary aided	B	Tertiary College	H
Voluntary controlled	C	Further Education College	I
Special Agreement	D	Community College	J
Grant Maintained	E		
City Technology College	F		

5. If you circled none of the letters in Q4, how would you class your school or college?

   _____

6. What age range does your school/college cover? *(please circle appropriate letter)*

11/12 to 18	A	9/10/11 to 13/14	E
11/12 to 16	B	16–18	F
13/14 to 16	C	16 through to adults	G
13/14 to 18	D		

7. What is your school's/college's standard number or designated site? *(please give number)*

   _____

8. Was your school/college purpose-built as a comprehensive school or as a tertiary/sixth form college? *(please circle appropriate word)* Yes/No

Note 1: Regardless of the name of your school, are all levels of attainment and all pupils/students admitted without academic selection?
If you are a college, are you open access, or one of the main providers of 16–19 education for your area?
Note 2: Admission restricted to pupils or students of above average academic attainment.
Note 3: Designated for pupils or students of average or below average attainment (e.g. a secondary modern school).
Note 4: Admission by academic attainment for some pupils or students but not for others.

9. If your answer to Q8 was 'No', was your school/college *(please circle the letter to the right of the appropriate reply)*

formerly a grammar school/senior secondary (with or without additions)	A
formerly a secondary modern school/junior secondary (with or without additions)	B
reorganised as a comprehensive school/college from a combination of grammar school(s) and other secondary schools	C
reorganised as a comprehensive school/college from a combination of secondary modern or other secondary schools	D
built as/or reorganised from an adult or further education college	E

10. With respect to admissions, does your school/college *(please circle the letter to the right of the appropriate reply)*

leave decisions to the LEA according to its set criteria	A
share decisions with the LEA according to its set criteria	B
make your own admissions decisions, having regard to LEA guidelines as well as your own criteria	C
Undertake your own admissions according to your own criteria	D

11. If you were unable to circle any letter in Q10, state briefly your admissions procedure

_____

12. At the start of your school/college year in August/September 1993 was your school's first year of entry full? *(please circle appropriate word)* Yes/No
(If yes, move to Q16)

13. If you answered 'No' to Q12, was under-subscription of pupils/students by *(please circle appropriate letter)*

fewer than 5   A   6 to 30   B   31 to 50   C   more than 50   D

14. If you ringed any of the letters in Q13 above, which factors might account for under-subscription? *(please circle as many letters as might apply)*
Presence in the area

of grammar or selective school(s)	A	falling population in the area	E
of 'special status' comprehensive school(s) (e.g. GM, CTC, 'magnet', or some LEA or aided)	B	poor public image	F
		unfavourable placing in league tables	G
of private schools with assisted places	C	location in rundown or inaccessible neighbourhood	H
of private schools without assisted places	D	excess places in schools/colleges in the area	I

15. If you circled no letters in Q14 or wish to cite additional reasons, please specify

_____

16. If 'Yes' to Q12, was last September's entry oversubscribed by *(please circle letter)*
1 to 5   A   6 to 30   B   31 to 49   C   More than 50   D

17. If you ringed any of the letters in Q16, which factors might account for over-subscription *(please circle as many letters as might apply)*
Absence from the area

of grammar or selective school(s)	A	good public image	E
of 'special status' comprehensive		favourable placing in league tables	F

school(s) (e.g. GM, CTC, 'magnet', or some LEA or aided)	B	location in 'pleasant' or affluent neighbourhood	G
of private schools with assisted places	C	shortage of places in schools/colleges in the area	H
of private schools without assisted places	D		

18. If you circled no letters in Q17 or wish to add additional reasons, please specify

---

19. Which factor(s) below are used to decide which pupils/students are admitted to your school/college in the event of over-subscription? *(please circle as many letters as apply)*

first come, first enrolled	A
nearness of home to school/college	B
coming from liaising/feeder primary or secondary schools	C
living in zone designated by LEA for admission	D
siblings already in the school	E
special medical/personal factors	F
information from tests/exams (LEA, national or set by you)	G
information about behaviour, including attendance record	H
staff opinion about pupils'/students' suitability for school's/college's traditions or curriculum	I
denominational membership	J
capacity of school/college to provide the course of study desired	K

20. If you operate any admissions criteria additional to those listed in Q19, please state

---

21. Is your school/college *(please circle one letter)*

mixed	A	girls only	B	boys only	C

22. Is your school/college *(please circle one letter)*

non-denominational	A	Jewish	D
Roman Catholic	B	Methodist	E
Church of England	C	dual denominational	F

If you circled A in Q22 above, please move to Section 2, Q25

23. If you circled any letter from B to F in Q22, does your admissions policy *(please circle as many letters as apply)*

reserve most or all of your places for pupils/students of your own denomination	A
welcome applications from practising Christian pupils/students from other denominations	B
welcome applications from pupils/students practising other major world faiths	C
welcome pupils/students regardless of religious practice, belief or denomination	D
welcome pupils/students from the immediate area in addition to any of the above	E

24. Approximately what percentage of your pupils/students are from other than the school's/college's denomination? *(please circle the appropriate letter)*

5% or less	A	between 36% and 50%	D
between 6% and 20%	B	between 51% and 75%	E
between 21% and 35%	C	over 75%	F

Section 2: Location and intake

25. What is the name of the Local Education Authority in which your school or college is located – whether or not your school/college is maintained by it or run independently? *(please write name)*

26. Where is your school or college situated? *(please circle the appropriate letter)*

in the middle of a large city (200,000+)	A
in a town (5,000 to 200,000)	B
in a suburban area (or outskirts of a town or city)	C
in a village (under 5,000) and/or surrounding countryside	D

27. From what kind of housing does your school/college draw most of its pupils/students? *(please circle the appropriate letter)*

mainly council or housing association housing	A
mainly private residential or owner-occupied housing	B
a mix of council and private housing	C
mainly substandard accommodation (including rented, private, council, or bed and breakfast)	D
a mix of council, private, and substandard	E

28. Approximately how many primary/secondary schools regularly send at least 10 pupils/students to your school/college *(please circle appropriate letter)*

None	A	11–15 schools	D
1–4 schools	B	16–25 schools	E
5–10 schools	C	Over 25 schools	F

29. What liaison does your school/college have with the majority of schools cited in Q28? *(please circle any that might apply)*

only as required	A	weekly contact	D
a yearly meeting	B	familiarisation visits for pupils/students	E
meetings at least once a term	C	exchange of teaching staff	F

30. Does your school/college draw 5% or more of its population from any of the following ethnic or geographic groups (regardless of where pupils/students were born)? *(please circle as many as might apply)*

Afro-caribbean	A	South American	E
Indian/Pakistani/Bangladeshi	B	Australian/North American	F
Chinese/Southeast Asian	C	European (East and West)	G
Middle Eastern/North African	D	Irish	H

31. Approximately what percentage of your school's/college's roll do NOT have English as a first language (regardless of where they were born)? *(please circle the appropriate letter)*

5% or less	A	between 31% and 50%	D
between 6% and15%	B	over 50%	E
between 16% and 30%	C		

32. If you ringed any letter from B to E in Q31 above, do you consider your resources adequate for teaching English to the students designated? Yes/No

33. Are the majority of pupils/students in your school/college *(please circle the appropriate letter)*

from the school's/college's local area or LEA   A

from its local area but with a substantial minority from outside the LEA and/or local neighbourhood   B

from outside and inside your local neighbourhood and/or LEA in about equal measure   C

mostly from outside the local area or LEA   D

34. What percentage of your latest intake do you estimate to be in the top 20% of the attainment range *(please write percentage)*   _____%

35. Does your school/college accept pupils/students from special schools for integration?

    YES/NO

36. From your knowledge of the parental occupations of your pupils/students, do you consider your school'/college's intake to be *(please circle the appropriate letter)*

mostly working class   A

mostly middle class   B

a mix but probably more working class than middle class   C

a mix but probably more middle class than working class   D

drawn equally from both middle class and working class   E

37. Is your school or college on *(please circle the appropriate letter)*

one site   A   two sites   B   three sites   C   more than three sites   D

38. What is your rate of pupil/student turnover – in terms of the number of pupils/students entering or leaving between the start and end of the academic tear? *(please circle the appropriate letter)*

an average of at least one a day	A	between three and ten a term	D
an average of three a week	B	fewer than ten a year	E
an average of one a week	C		

39. What was your school's/college's attendance rate during 1992/93? *(please circle the appropriate letter)*

above 95%   A   between 90% and 95%   B   below 90%   C

40. According to your administrative records, what percentage of your pupils/students qualify for free meals? *(please circle the appropriate letter)*

5% or less	A	between 31% and 50%	D
between 6% and 15%	B	over 50%	E
between 16% and 30%	C		

Section 3: Social and pastoral policy

41. Which of the following policies does your school/college have regarding pupil/student dress? *(please circle any letters that might apply)*

full uniform required with/without named suppliers	A	no uniform but an agreed dress code	D
uniform for main garments only	B	free choice of dress	E
older pupils/students excused uniform	C		

42. What method(s) of discipline does your school/college use for infraction of its rules? *(please circle as many letters as might apply)*

on report	A	suspension for a stated period	F
detention during breaks or after hours	B	removal to separate unit (on or off site)	
extra academic, practical or physical work	C	for a stated period	G
removal of privileges	D	indefinite removal to a separate unit	H
interview with parents or guardian	E	expulsion	I

43. How many pupils/students had to be excluded in the last two academic years from your school/college? *(please write the number for each year in each of the three categories)*

	91/2	92/3
temporarily (e.g. 2 days to 2 weeks)	_____	_____
temporarily, pending enquiry	_____	_____
permanently	_____	_____

44. Did your school/college take in excluded pupils/students from other schools/colleges in the last academic year? *(please circle the appropriate word)*　　　　　YES/NO

45. If you answered 'Yes' to Q44, were these numbers? *(please circle one letter)*

higher than those excluded from your own school/college	A
lower	B
about the same	C

46. Does your school/college have an Equal Opportunities policy? *(please circle the appropriate word)*　　　　　YES/NO

47. If your school or college has pupils/students from ethnic groups in its intake, do you have a policy for, or monitoring of, these groups in relation to *(please circle as many letters as might apply)*

attainment/examinations	A	your grouping policy for teaching	D
course choices and options	B	your teaching practices	E
participation in school/college events and activities	C	dealing with racial harassment	F

48. If you have developed any further policy in relation to ethnic groups, please specify

_____

49. In relation to the different socio-economic groups represented in the school/college, do you have any of the following? *(please circle as many as might apply)*

a policy for supporting pupils/students from lower income homes for activities where financial contributions are required
(e.g. trips, music lessons)　　　A
a policy for monitoring socio-economic groups in relation to

attainment/examinations	B	your grouping policy for teaching	E
course choices and options	C	your teaching practices	F
participation in school/college events and activities	D		

50. If you have developed any further policy for equalising the opportunity of pupils/students of differing socio-economic status, please specify

_____

51. If your school/college is mixed, do you have a policy for, or monitoring of, gender in

relation to *(please circle as many as might apply)*

attainment/exams	A	participation in school events and activities	E
course choices	B	dealing with sexual harassment	F
your group policy for teaching	C	classes/courses restricted to one sex only	G
your teaching practices	D		

52. If you circled option G in Q51 above, please specify the course(s) or subject(s)

_____

53. If you have developed any further gender policy, please specify

_____

_____

54. Is your school's/college's social/pastoral organisation by *(please circle as many as might apply)*

sites	A	registration/tutor forms	G
lower and upper school	B	mixed age groups	H
departments (or 'schools')	C	friendship groups	I
courses	D	teaching groups	J
houses	E	guidance structure	K
years	F		

55. Does your school/college have pupils/students with SEN (Special Educational Needs) **with** statements? YES/NO

56. Does your school/college have pupils/students with special educational needs but **without** statements? YES/NO

57. With regard to the pupil /students mentioned in Q55 and Q56, are resources generally adequate to meet their needs? YES/NO

58. What percentage of your school/college population (with and without statements) do you estimate to have special educational needs? *(please write percentage)* _____%

59. Do some or all pupils/students have any of the following? *(please circle any letters that might apply)*

a students' association	A	societies run by themselves	D
a students' union	B	an elected students' council run by themselves	E
a prefect system	C	the right to elect observers/governors to the governing body	F

60. Does your school/college have any adult students (over 21) enrolled in the same classes as pupils between 14 and 18? YES/NO

*61. If you are a school do parents have *(please specify as many as might apply)*

no organisation	A	a school/community liaison body	E
a parents' organisation	B	a fund-raising committee	F
a parent/teacher organisation	C	a role in classroom support	G
a parent/teacher/pupil organisation	D		

*62. If parents are involved in additional activities not included in Q61 above, please specify

_____

*63. Approximately how many parents attended the last statutory yearly meeting of parents and governors? *(please write in the number)* _____

*64. Does your school depend for any of its curricular or extra-curricular activities on money raised by parents? *(please circle the appropriate word)* YES/NO

*65. If you answered 'Yes' to Q64, please name the activities

_____

Section 4: Management and administration

66. Does your school/college have a long term Development Plan?
(please circle the appropriate word) YES/NO

67. Is the physical fabric of your school/college *(please circle the appropriate word)*
generally in good repair and state of decoration   A
needing minor repairs or redecoration, but otherwise sound   B
needing major improvements/repairs/refurbishment to function effectively   C

68. With respect to staff participation in the decision-making process of your school/college, is this undertaken by *(please circle as many letters as might apply)*
senior staff consulting all involved   A
putting all major matters to departmental/full staff meetings for discussion before decision is made   B
putting all major matters to a binding vote of departmental/full staff meetings   C
delegating decision-making to a body elected by staff to represent them and report back   D

69. Are support staff included in the decision-making arrangements cited in Q68 above? *(please circle the appropriate word)* YES/NO

70. If your school/college has forms of decision-making additional to those listed in Q68, please specify

_____

71. Does your school/college governing body/board have executive subcommittees with oversight of any of the following? *(please circle as many letters as might apply)*

finance	A	premises/accommodation	E
personnel and appointments	B	admissions	F
discipline and attendance	C	fund-raising	G
curriculum and assessment	D	pay and remuneration	H

72. If you are LEA-maintained, which services provided by the LEA do you consider

essential   A   appreciated   B   not essential   C

Please circle one of the above letters (A, B, or C) next to each of the following options

training for staff (e.g. INSET)	A B C	processing admissions	A B C
building and maintainence		dealing with admissions appeals	A B C
(architects and contractors services)	A B C	payroll services	A B C
legal and insurance services	A B C	information technology support	A B C
central purchasing	A B C	educational psychology service	A B C
educational welfare services	A B C	personnel support and advice	A B C
school library services	A B C	training for governors	A B C

73. Do private contractors provide any of the following services at your school/college? *(please circle as many letters as might apply)*

preparation and service of meals	A	security services	E
cleaning on the premises	B	payroll service	F
caring for grounds/gardens	C	personnel	G
routine maintenance and repairs to buildings	D	insurance or legal services	H

74. With regard to services ringed in Q73 above, do contractors give *(please circle as many letters from Q73 as apply to the three options below)*

1. better service than when managed by LEA/in-house staff   A B C D E F G H
2. about the same service   A B C D E F G H
3. inferior service   A B C D E F G H

75. If there are further services undertaken by private contractors, please specify

---

76. Since assuming LMS/GM/CTC/developed/independent status, has your school/college *(please circle any letters that apply)*

had to release, or failed to fill any vacancies for, teaching staff in order to keep within budget?　　　　　　　　　　　　　　　　　　　　　　　　　　　　　　　　A
hired additional non-teaching staff to assist with financial or management tasks?　　　B
engaged professional help for fund-raising　　　　　　　　　　　　　　　　　　　C

77. Does your school or college earn at least £5,000 a year from outside lettings/commercial activities? *(please circle the appropriate word)*　　　　　　　　　　　　　　　YES/NO

78. In respect of proposals for training of PGCE/B.Ed students in schools, would your school/college *(please circle the appropriate letter)*

welcome it as a desirable activity　　　　　　　　　　　　　　　　　　　　　　A
welcome it, provided that financial and staff support are adequate　　　　　　　　　B
welcome it in some departments but not in others　　　　　　　　　　　　　　　C
prefer not to accept the extra work　　　　　　　　　　　　　　　　　　　　　D
disagree with it in principle　　　　　　　　　　　　　　　　　　　　　　　　E

79. Does your school or college specialise (or plan to specialise) in any field which is recognised by special funding? *(please circle the appropriate word)*　　　　　　　　　YES/NO

80. If you answered 'Yes' to Q79 above, please name the field

---

81. Does your school/college depend for any of its curricular or extra curricular activities or facilities on money from sponsors (e.g. local business, national companies) *(please circle the appropriate word)*　　　　　　　　　　　　　　　　　　　　　　　　　　YES/NO

82. If you answered 'Yes' to Q81, please name the activities/courses and those funding them

---

83. Does your school/college collaborate with any other local school/college in its work? *(please circle the appropriate word)*　　　　　　　　　　　　　　　　　　　　YES/NO

84. If you answered 'Yes' to Q83, is this collaboration *(please circle as many letters as might apply)*
by exchange of staff　　　　　　A　by running jointly organised courses　　　　　E
by exchange of pupils/students B　by formal cooperation in a consortium arrangement F

85. If you circled any of the letters in Q84, is this collaboration in respect of *(please circle as many letters as might apply)*

academic courses　　A　　　　vocational courses　B　　　　cultural and sporting activities　C

86. Excluding commercial lettings, does your school/college share its premises with any of the following public services or users? *(please circle as many letters as might apply)*

Youth Service	A	Library Service	E
Careers Service	B	pensioners clubs	F
Adult Education	C	disabled groups	G
community, sports, cultural or religious groups	D	Community Medical Service	H

87. Has your school/college received any special publicity during the last year in the local or national media?　　　　　　　　　　　　　　　　　　　　　　　　　　　　YES/NO

88. If you answered 'Yes' to Q87, in the school's/college's general opinion was this publicity considered to have been *(please circle as many letters as might apply)*

| supportive | A | unhelpful | C | mixed in nature | E |
| informative | B | misleading | D | | |

Section 5: Academic policy, curriculum and assessment

89. How often each year do parents/students receive written reports on academic progress? *(please circle the letter that applies)*

    twice a term   A   once a term   B   twice a year C   once a year D

90. Do the reports mentioned in Q89 indicate progress by *(please circle as many letters as apply)*

written comment	A
written comment combined with interview	B
numerical or letter grades for attainment in subject/course/activity	C
numerical or letter grades for effort in subject/course/activity	D
numerical standing in class/group	E
results of tests (your own or other)	F
information on attendance and punctuality	G
pupils'/students' self-assessment	H
parental assessment	I

91. Does your school have a system of Records of Achievement? *(please circle the word that applies)*   YES/NO

92. If 'Yes' to Q91, is it *(please circle the letter that applies)*

nationally based   A   locally based (e.g. through LEA)   B   school based   C

93. Does your school or college make special arrangements for pupils/students of exceptional attainment? *(please circle the appropriate word)*   YES/NO

94. If you answered 'Yes' to Q93, is this by *(please circle any letters that might apply)*

extra assistance in the mainstream classroom		support for outside visits or courses	D
by subject teachers	A	support for extra tuition/coaching	E
by learning support staff	B	express sets for some subjects	F
by cooperative/team teaching	C	an express stream for all classes	G

95. With regard to pupils/students needing learning support or with SEN statements, is this provided by *(please circle any letters that might apply)*

extra assistance in the mainstream classroom		part-time withdrawal for teaching	D
by subject teachers	A	separate classes for some academic work	E
by learning support staff	B	separate classes for all academic work	F
by cooperative/team teaching	C	support for outside visits or courses	G
		support for extra tuition/coaching	H

96. Have you provided a programme of sex education for pupils/students at any time since 1986?   YES/NO

97. If you answered 'Yes' to Q96, has this programme been provided *(please circle as many letters as might apply)*

within National Curriculum (e.g. science)	A
by tutors in tutorial time	B
by teachers providing a programme of personal and social education	C
by outside specialist teachers	D
by in-house staff specially trained	E
by in-house staff without special training	F

If you are a tertiary, further education or sixth form college, please move to Part II, Q115.

*98. In terms of the six forms of organising the curriculum lettered below,

completely common to all	A
some choice in	
academic subjects	B
vocational subjects	C
arts or music	D
sports	E
languages	F

how is your school organised in each of the following years? (*please circle any of the above option letters that apply next to each year below*)

1. the first year/year 7	A	B	C	D	E	F
2. the second year/year 8/S1	A	B	C	D	E	F
3. the third year/year 9/S2	A	B	C	D	E	F
4. the fourth year/year 10/S3	A	B	C	D	E	F
5. the fifth year/year 11/S4	A	B	C	D	E	F

*99. In terms of the seven forms of grouping for teaching purposes lettered below,

mixed ability for all subjects	A
mixed ability classes with no more than 2 subjects taught in ability sets	B
mixed ability classes with no more than 4 subjects taught in ability sets	C
ability sets for most or all academic courses	D
2 or 3 broad ability bands with parallel classes	E
classes streamed by overall attainment for all academic subjects but not	
for sport/drama/art	F
streamed for all classes and courses	G

How is your school grouped for each of the following years? (*please circle any of the above option letters that apply to each year below*)

1. in the first year/year 7	A	B	C	D	E	F	G
2. in the second year/year 8/S1	A	B	C	D	E	F	G
3. in the third year/year 9/S2	A	B	C	D	E	F	G
4. in the fourth year/year 10/S3	A	B	C	D	E	F	G
5. in the fifth year/year 11/S4	A	B	C	D	E	F	G

*100. At Key Stage 3 (S1 + S2), which of the following subjects, if any, do you find it difficult to include in your school's curriculum? (*please circle any of the letters that apply*)

1. English	A	7. history	G
2. mathematics	B	8. geography	H
3. science	C	9. music	I
4. technology	D	10. art	J
5. foreign language	E	11. physical education	K
6. religious education	F		

*101. Which of the following, if any, do you offer at Key Stage 3 (S1 + S2), as separate time-tabled subjects or courses? (*please circle any of the letters that apply*)

	KS3 (S1 + S2)	KS4 (S3 + S4)
1. economic and industrial understanding	A	A
2. careers education and guidance	B	B
3. health education	C	C
4. education for citizenship	D	D
5. environmental education	E	E

*102. At Key Stage 3 (years 7 to 9/S1 + S2) does your school offer any subjects additional to the National Curriculum (e.g. media studies, drama)? *(please circle the appropriate word)*

YES/NO

*103. If you answered 'Yes' to Q102, could you please name the subject(s) below?

---

*104. In respect of languages offered in Key Stage 3 (years 7–9/S1 +S2) and Key Stage 4 (years 10–11/S3 + S4) can you circle the language letter offered at each stage (and in brackets circle whether it is taken by some pupils or by all pupils)

	KS3	KS4
1. French	A (some/all)	A (some/all)
2. German	B (some/all)	B (some/all)
3. Spanish	C (some/all)	C (some/all)
4. Italian	D (some/all)	D (some/all)
5. Russian	E (some/all)	E (some/all)
6. Latin	F (some/all)	F (some/all)
7. Welsh	G (some/all)	G (some/all)
8. Gaelic	H (some/all)	H (some/all)
9. Urdu	I (some/all)	I (some/all)
10. Arabic (modern or classical)	J (some/all)	J (some/all)
11. Bengali	K (some/all)	K (some/all)
12. Punjabi	L (some/all)	L (some/all)
13. Hindi	M (some/all)	M (some/all)
14. Gujerati	N (some/all)	N (some/all)

*105. If you offer any additional languages, please specify the language, the stage, and whether for some or all pupils

---

If you are a 9/10/11 to 13/14 school, you have completed the questionnaire except for Q148 on the last page. Thank you for your cooperation.

*106. Which of the following subjects are included in your school's 'common' or 'core' curriculum for ALL pupils in years 10–11/Key Stage 4/S3 + S4? *(please circle as many of the letters as apply)*

1. English	A	7. geography	G
2. mathematics	B	8. art	H
3. science	C	9. music	I
4. a modern foreign language	D	10. physical education	J
5. technology	E	11. religious education	K
6. history	F		

*107. Have you introduced any vocational courses for pupils in years 10–11/Key Stage 4/S3 + S4? *(please circle appropriate word)* YES/NO

*108. If you answered 'Yes' to Q107, are these taken *(please circle the letter that applies)*

by all pupils in these years	A
as a single option open to all	B
as a substantial option for pupils wanting an alternative to a full academic course	C

*109. As regards future development in years 10–11/Key Stage 4/S3 + S4, would staff at your school generally favour

a self-contained vocational course alongside the academic one	A
a vocational option within the National Curriculum	B
an integrated curriculum with vocational and academic elements for all pupils	C

*110. Does your school plan to increase the vocational content of its curriculum in years 10–11/Key Stage 4/S3 + S4? *(please circle appropriate word)* YES/NO

*111. How many GCSE/Standard Grade courses in your school retain course work as a major element?

      none A   a few B   half C   most D   all E

*112. What percentage of your 5th year/year 11/S4? *(please give percentage)*

1. passed at least one GCSE exam at grades A–F/Standard Grade 1–6? _____%

2. passed at least 4 GCSE exam at grades A–F/Standard Grade 1–6? _____%

3. passed five or more GCSE exam at grades A–C/Standard Grade 1–3? _____%

4. passed five or more GCSE exam at grades A–C/Standard Grade 1–3 (including English, maths, science, and a foreign language? _____%

*113. Does your school regard the single figure given in answer to 3 in Q112 to be an adequate indicator to the public of its academic achievements? YES/NO

*114. If you do not have a sixth form, approximately what percentage of your pupils transferred to sixth forms/12th years/years S5 + S6/colleges elsewhere to continue their education? _____ %

If your school has no pupils beyond the age of 16 (5th year/year 11/S4) you have completed the questionnaire – except for Q148 on the last page.

Thank you very much for your help.

Part II

Questions for schools and colleges with students aged 16 and over.

115. If you are an all-through school, what percentage of your 5th year/year 11/S4 stayed on to your 6th form/12th/S5 year? *(please give percentage)* _____ %

116. If you are an all-through school, how do students enter your sixth form/S5 + S6 from inside the school? *(please circle the letters that apply)*

automatically	A
by informal selection according to staff opinion about suitability for courses for which students have applied	B
by showing a minimum number of GCSE/Standard Grade passes or passes at specific levels	C
by showing GCSE/Standard Grade passes for only those subjects to be studied	D
after sitting in-house (or other) tests	E

117. If you are an all-through school, do you accept students from other schools at 16? YES/NO

118. If you answered 'Yes' to Q117, how many students from outside were accepted into your sixth form/S5 last September?

5or fewer   A   between 6 and 20   B   between 21 and 50   C   over 50   D

119. If you are a sixth form college, tertiary or further education college, what are your admissions criteria? *(please circle as many letters as might apply)*

entirely open access	A
generally open access but policy can differ between departments ('schools')	B
priority to students from feeder secondary schools	C
priority to students living in the area	D
informal selection according to staff opinion about suitability for courses for which students have applied	E
a minimum number of GCSE/Standard Grade passes or passes at specific levels	F
GCSE/Standard Grade passes for only those subjects to be studied	G
in-house (or other) tests	H

120. Do you have any criteria additional to those mentioned in Q119? *(if so, please specify)*

_____

121. Approximately what percentage of students enter your school or college from feepaying schools?

none	A	between 16% and 30%	D
no more than 5%	B	over 30%	E
between 6% and 15%	C		

122. How many students are in each of the following years? *(please write the number in the space provided)*

a. first year sixth/year 12/S5/ages 16/17 _____

b. second year sixth/year 13/S6/ages 17/18 _____

c. if a school, third year sixth _____

123. Which of the following courses does your school/college provide for its 16/17 age group (year 12, S5) – and next to it, approximately what percentage of the year is enrolled? *(please circle any letters that apply and write in percentage)*

GCE A levels	A	_____	%
A/S levels	B	_____	%
Higher Grades	C	_____	%
SCOTVEC	D	_____	%
Certificate of Sixth Year Studies	E	_____	%
First BTEC	F	_____	%
National BTEC	G	_____	%
GCSE Mature	H	_____	%
HND/HNC	I	_____	%
City and Guilds	J	_____	%
RSA	K	_____	%
NVQ	L	_____	%
SVQ	M	_____	%
GNVQ	N	_____	%
GSVQ	O	_____	%
CPVE/DOVE	P	_____	%
International Baccalaureate	Q	_____	%

124. If you offer courses additional to those named in Q123, please specify

_____

125. If you ringed BTEC, SCOTVEC, GNVQ or GSVQ in Q123, please list all the individual courses/titles offered

_____

126. Approximately what percentage of students combine elements from two or more of the courses named in Q123? *(please give percentage)* _____ %

127. In respect of any combination cited in Q126 above, which are taken most often *(please specify)*

_____

128. Do any of the courses listed in Q123 and Q124 have students enrolled who are studying part-time only? *(please circle the appropriate word)*   YES/NO

129. Are some of the courses listed in Q123 and Q124 available only through collaboration with other institutions? *(please circle the appropriate word)*   YES/NO

130. If you answered 'Yes' to Q129 above, please specify

_____

131. As regards future development for ages 16/17/18, would staff at your school/college generally favour *(please circle the letter that applies)*

retaining A level/Higher Grade and a separate vocational path	A
widening A level but retaining a separate vocational path	B
more opportunity to combine A level/Higher Grade with vocational options	C
integrating academic and vocational courses within a single new qualification	D
integrating academic and vocational courses within a single new qualification, including a common core for everyone	E

132. Are any of your 16/17 year old students on a work training course (e.g. YT) or release from work/work experience/apprentice training? *(please circle the appropriate word)*   YES/NO

133. If you answered 'Yes' to Q132, approximately what percentage of the 16/17 year group do they represent? *(please give percentage)*   _____ %

134. Does your school/college have any direct relationship with your area's TEC/LEC? YES/NO

135. If you answered 'Yes' to Q134, please specify

_____

136. Are you part of a COMPACT scheme in your area? *(please circle the appropriate word)*   YES/NO

137. If you answered 'Yes' to Q136, please specify

_____

138. Please indicate which of the following subjects at A level/Higher Grade are currently being offered at your school/college *(please circle all letters that apply)*

1. English Literature	A	8. music	H
2. geography	B	9. physics	I
3. French	C	10. chemistry	J
4. German	D	11. biology	K
5. art	E	12. mathematics	L
6. psychology	F	13. sociology	M
7. history	G	14. economics	N

139. Please list any additional A levels/Higher Grade subjects being taken this current academic year

_____

140. If you are a school/college in England or Wales, how many candidates

a. entered for 2 or more A levels last year and what was their average point score? *(please write a number and score in spaces provided)*

number _____   average _____

b. entered for BTEC National and/or City and Guilds National and what percentage achieved qualifications? *(please write number and percentage)*

number _____   _____%

141. If you are a school/college in Scotland, what percentage of your S4 roll

a. gained 3 or more Higher Grades (A–C) *(please write percentage)*

_____%

b. gained 3 or more SCOTVEC modules (% of S5/S6 roll)? *(please write percentage)*

_____%

142. What percentage of the 2nd year sixth/year 13/S6/17–18 year old students were accepted last year on a degree course (full or part time)? *(please circle the letter that applies)*

10% or less	A	between 31% and 50%	D
between 11% and 20%	B	between 51% and 75%	E
between 21% and 30%	C	over75%	F

143. Please state the number of students within the category ringed in Q142 who were on BTEC, SCOTVEC, GNVQ or GSVQ courses

_____

144. Does your sixth form/college/S5 & S6 have any special links with higher education institutions (e.g. group visits for prospective entrants)? *(please circle the appropriate word)* YES/NO

145. If 'Yes' to Q144, are these institutions mainly *(please circle letter that applies)*
    in your own region (e.g. Wales, NW England) A
    some in your region, some outside it B
    all from outside your region C

146. Do you keep follow-up records of your students after they leave? YES/NO

147. If 'Yes' to Q146. please attach a copy of your record for 1992/3 or give percentages of students who left for the following destinations insofar as you know them *(please write the figures in the spaces provided)*
    a. to look for jobs or sign on _____%
    b. to take up a job already offered _____%
    c. to go on a training scheme _____%
    d. to enroll full time or part time on a college course (below degree-level) _____%
    e. without giving information about their future intentions _____%

148. Apart from improved funding, is there any one factor that you would identify as holding the key to your school's/college's future development or to the successful future development of comprehensive education?

_____

If you wish to make additional comments, please name your school/college clearly on any extra sheets. Thank you.

Caroline Benn
Clyde Chitty

We are very grateful to you for completing this questionnaire. Please return it in the envelope provided.

Bibliography

Ahier, J. and Flude, M. (eds) (1983) *Contemporary Education Policy*. London: Croom Helm.

Ainley, P. (1995) 'Democratising higher education'. In Harber, C. (ed.) *Developing Democratic Education*. Ticknall: Education Now Books, 53–90.

Allen, M. and Waugh, C. (1995) *14–19: Towards a Saner System*. Sheffield: General Educator Press.

Althusser, L. (1971) 'Ideology and ideological state apparatuses.' In *Lenin and Philosophy and Other Essays* London: New Left Books, pp. 123–73.

Armstrong, M. (1970) 'The case for small comprehensive schools', *Where*, July, 100–102.

Aronowitz, S. and Giroux, H. (1991 *Post-Modern Education: Politics, Culture and Social Criticism*. Minneapolis: University of Minnesota Press.

Association for Comprehensive Education (1991) *The Transfer Market: Selection for Secondary Education in Northern Ireland 1947-1991*. Lisburn: ASE, June.

Audit Commission (1991) *'Two B's Or Not? Schools' and Colleges' A Level Performance*. London: Audit Commission.

Bailey, B. (1994) 'Developing community links', *All-In Success*, 5, (3). Northampton: Centre for the Study of Comprehensive Schools.

Ball, S.J. (1981) *Beachside Comprehensive: A Case Study of Secondary Schooling*. Cambridge: Cambridge University Press.

Ball, S.J. (1984a) 'Introduction: comprehensives in crisis.' In Ball, S.J. (ed.) *Comprehensive Schooling: A Reader*. Lewes: Falmer Press, 1–26.

Ball, S.J. (1984b) 'Becoming a comprehensive? Facing up to falling rolls.' In Ball, S.J. (ed.) *Comprehensive Schooling: A Reader*. Lewes: Falmer Press, 227–46.

Ball, S.J. and Green, A.G. (eds) (1983) *Progress and Inequality in Comprehensive Education*. London: Routledge.

Barker Lunn, J. (1969) 'Some problems involved in comparative investigations of different types of schools.' In Ingenkamp, K. (ed.) *Methods for the Evaluation of Comprehensive Schools*. Basel.

Barker, B. (1984) 'Is TVEI compatible with comprehensive principles?', *Comprehensive Education*, 48, 12.

Barker, B. (1986) *Rescuing the Comprehensive Experience*. Milton Keynes: Open University Press.

Barker, B. (1995) 'Driven by fear into the results fray', *The Times Educational Supplement*, 24 February.

Batley, R., O'Brien, O. and Parris, H. (1970) *Going Comprehensive: Educational Policy-Making in Two County Boroughs*. London: Routledge and Kegan Paul.

Baxter, J. (1995) 'Mixed ability.' In Goodwyn, A. (ed.) *English and Ability*. London: David Fulton Publishers, 28–46.

Bell, D. (1994) 'Small local School Boards are at the heart of educational democracy in the USA', *Education*, 25 February.

Bellaby, P. (1977) *The Sociology of Comprehensive Schooling*. London: Methuen.

Benn, C. (1970a) 'Allocation methods in the comprehensive system', *Comprehensive Education*, 15 (Summer), 29–35.

Benn, C. (1970b) 'Examination results from fifteen comprehensive schools in 1970', *Comprehensive Education*, 16 (Autumn), 8–11.

540

Benn, C. (1971a) 'Short course comprehensives', *Comprehensive Education*, **18** (Summer), 9–18.

Benn, C. (1971b) 'Linked primary and secondary schools', *Comprehensive Education*, **17** (Spring), 26–28.

Benn, C. (1972) 'How comprehensive is our secondary education?', *London Educational Review*, Journal of the University of London Institute of Education, 1(2).

Benn, C. (1975) 'Social class and secondary education', *Comprehensive Education*, **29** (Spring), 18–22.

Benn, C. (1979) 'Oxbridge entry and comprehensive education', *Comprehensive Education*, **40** (Summer), 11–12.

Benn, C. (1980) 'Comprehensive School Reform and the 1945 Labour Government', *History Workshop Journal,* **10**. London: Lawrence and Wishart.

Benn, C. (1982) 'The myth of giftedness', *Forum*, **24**(2), Spring, 50–52.

Benn, C. (1986) *All Faiths in All Schools.* London: Socialist Education Association.

Benn, C. (1990) 'The public price of private education and privatization', *Forum*, **32** (3), 68–73.

Benn, C. (1992) *Keir Hardie.* London: Hutchinson.

Benn, C. and Fairley, J. (eds) (1986) *Challenging the MSC: On Jobs, Education and Training.* London: Pluto Press.

Benn, C. and Simon, B. (1970) *Half Way There: Report on the British Comprehensive School Reform.* London: McGraw-Hill.

Benn, C. and Simon, B. (1972) *Half Way There: Report on the British Comprehensive School Reform.* (2nd edn.) Harmondsworth: Penguin.

Best, R., Ribbins, P., Jarvis, C. and Oddy, D. (1983) *Education and Care: The Study of a School and its Pastoral Organisation.* London: Heinemann Educational Books.

Betts, D. (1994) 'Calling colleges to account', *NATFHE Journal,* Summer.

Bilsborough, A. (1979) 'A view of comprehensive education from an Oxbridge college', *Comprehensive Education*, **40** (Summer), 18–21.

Blackman, S. and Holland, J. (1989 'Equal opportunities in education and training', *Comprehensive Education*, 2(1), 19.

Blezard, D. (1985) 'The community dimension'. In Janes, F. *et al.* (eds) *Going Tertiary.* Yeovil: Tertiary College Association, 71–76.

Bourdieu, P. and Passeron, J.C. (1977) *Reproduction in Education, Society and Culture.* London: Sage.

Bourne, J., Bridges, L. and Searle, C. (1994) *Outcast England: How Schools Exclude Black Children.* London: Institute of Race Relations.

Bowles, S. and Gintis, H. (1976) *Schooling in Capitalist America: Educational Reform and the Contradictions of Economic Life.* London: Routledge and Kegan Paul.

Boycott, O. and MacCann, P. (1992) 'Kicking together', *The Guardian*, 30 June.

Boyson, R. (1969a) 'The right to choose', *Education*, 18 July; 29 August.

Boyson, R. (1969b) 'The essential conditions for the success of a comprehensive school'. In Cox, C.B. and Dyson, A.E. (eds) *Black Paper Two: The Crisis in Education.* London: Critical Quarterly Society, 57–62.

Boyson, R. (1974) *Oversubscribed: The Story of Highbury Grove School.* London: Ward Lock Publications.

Boyson, R. (1995) *Speaking My Mind.* London: Peter Owen.

Brandes, D. and Ginnis, P. (1990) *The Student Centered School.* Hemel Hempstead: Simon & Schuster.

Briault, E. and Smith, T. (1980) *Falling Rolls in Secondary Schools.* Slough: NFER.

Bridges, L. (1994) 'Exclusions: how did we get here?' In Bourne, J., Bridges, L. and Searle, C. (eds) *Outcast England: How Schools Exclude Black Children*. London: Institute of Race Relations.

Bridges, R.T. (1987) *Grammar Schools Survey*. Birmingham: King Edward's School.

Brighouse, T. and Taylor, B. (1986) 'Equal opportunities and special needs'. In Ranson, S., Taylor, B. and Brighouse, T. (eds) *The Revolution in Education and Training*. Harlow: Longman, 101–107.

Broudy, H.S., Smith, B.O. and Burnett, J.T. (1964) *Democracy and Excellence in American Secondary Education*. Chicago: Rand McNally.

Brown, H. *et al.* (1985) *Class of 84*. London: Fawcett Society and the National Joint Committee of Working Women's Organisations.

Brown, S. (1992) 'Raising standards: factors influencing the effectiveness of innovations'. In Brown, S. and McPherson, A. (eds) *Critical Reflections on Curriculum Policy*. Edinburgh: Scottish Council for Research in Education.

Bruner, J. (1970) 'The relevance of skill or the skill of relevance'. In *Education in the Seventies*. London: Encyclopaedia Britannica International Ltd.

Bullivant, A. (1971) 'The neighbourhood comprehensive school', *Comprehensive Education*, 18 (Summer), 27–31.

Bullivant, B. (1977/78) 'Parental choice and its dangers', *Comprehensive Education*, 37 (Winter), 22–24.

Bunnell, W.S. (1972) 'Comeback: school democracy', *Comprehensive Education*, 20 (Spring), 17–18.

Bunting, M. (1994) 'The Abandoned Generation', *Guardian*, 1 June.

Burgess, M. (1993) 'Linking BTEC and A/AS Levels'. In Richardson, W., Woolhouse, J. and Finegold, D. (eds). *The Reform of Post-Sixteen Education and Training in England and Wales*. Harlow: Longman, 101–109.

Burgess, R.G. (1983) *Experiencing Comprehensive Education: A Study of Bishop McGregor School*. London: Methuen.

Burstall, E. (1995) 'Set to make a comeback', *The Times Educational Supplement*, 27 January.

Bush, T., Coleman, M. and Glover, D. (1993) *Managing Autonomous Schools: The Grant-Maintained Experience*. London: Paul Chapman Publishing.

Butler, R.A. (1952) *Yearbook of Education, 1952*. London: HMSO.

Caldwell, B.J. and Spinks, J.M. (1988) *The Self-Managing School*. Lewes: Falmer Press.

Carlen, P. *et al.* (1992) *Truancy*. Milton Keynes: Open University Press.

Carnoy, M. (1974) *Education as Cultural Imperialism*. New York: David McKay.

Carspecken, P. (1985) 'Community action and community schooling: the campaign to save Croxteth Comprehensive'. In Walford, G. (ed.) *Schooling in Turmoil*. London: Croom Helm, 107–36.

Carspecken, P. and Miller, H. (1983) 'Parental choice and community control: the case of Croxteth Comprehensive'. In Wolpe, A. and Donald, J. (eds) *Is There Anyone Here From Education?* London: Pluto Press, 154–61.

Catholic Media Office (Department of Christian Doctrine of the Catholic Church) (1984) *Learning From Diversity: A Challenge for Catholic Education. Working Party Report*. London: Catholic Media Office.

CBI (Confederation of British Industry) (1989) *Towards a Skills Revolution – A Youth Charter*. London: CBI, July.

CCCS (Centre for Contemporary Cultural Studies) (1981) *Unpopular Education: Schooling and Social Democracy in England Since 1944*. London: Hutchinson.

CCE (Campaign for Comprehensive Education) (1980) *Comprehensive Education Away From Home. A Report on Boarding and Residential Education*. London: CCE.

CGLI (City and Guilds of London Institute) (1993) *GNVQ Handbook*. London: CGLI.

Chetwynd, H.R. (1960) *Comprehensive School: The Story of Woodberry Down*. London: Routledge and Kegan Paul.

Chitty, C. (1969) 'Non-streaming in comprehensives: a review', *Comprehensive Education*, 12, 2–9

Chitty, C. (1970) 'The house system in the comprehensive school', *Secondary Education*, 1(1) 6–9.

Chitty, C. (1979) 'The common curriculum', *Forum*, 21 (2), 61–5.

Chitty, C. (1980) 'Freedom of choice and the common curriculum', *Forum*, 22(3), 73–76.

Chitty, C. (1987a) 'The commodification of education', *Forum*, 29, (3) 66–69.

Chitty, C. (ed.) (1987b) *Redefining the Comprehensive Experience*. Bedford Way Papers, No. 32. London: Institute of Education, University of London.

Chitty, C. (1989a) 'City Technology Colleges: a strategy for élitism', *Forum*, 31 (2), 37–40.

Chitty, C. (1989b) *Towards A New Education System: The Victory of the New Right?* Lewes: Falmer Press.

Chitty, C. (ed.) (1991a) *Post-16 Education: Studies in Access and Achievement*. London: Kogan Page.

Chitty, C. (ed.) (1991b) *Changing the Future: Redprint for Education (The Hillcole Group)*. London: Tufnell Press.

Chitty, C. (1992a) 'Key Stage Four: the National Curriculum abandoned?', *Forum*, 34(2), 38–40.

Chitty, C. (1992b) *The Education System Transformed*. Manchester: Baseline Books.

Chitty, C. (1993a) 'Great Debate or great betrayal?', *Education Today and Tomorrow*, 44(3), 9–11.

Chitty, C. (ed.) (1993b) *The National Curriculum: Is it Working?* Harlow: Longman.

Chitty, C. (1994) 'Sex, lies and indoctrination', *Forum*, 36(1), 15–17.

Chitty, C. (1995) 'The price of ignorance', *Forum*, 37(1), 18–20.

Chitty, C. and mac an Ghaill, M. (1995) *Reconstruction of a Discourse*. University of Birmingham: Educational Review Publications. Headline Series 4.

Chitty, C. and Simon, B. (1993) *Education Answers Back: Critical Responses to Government Policy*. London: Lawrence and Wishart.

Church of England (1984) *A Future in Partnership*. London: National Society.

Clarke, F. (1940) *Education and Social Change: An English Interpretation*. London: Sheldon Press.

Clarke, J. and Willis, P. (1984) 'Introduction'. In Bates, I. *et al.* (eds) *Schooling for the Dole? The New Vocationalism*. London: Macmillan, 1–16.

Clarke, M. (1979) 'A core-curriculum for the primary school', *Forum*, 21(2), 45–48.

Clegg, A. (1969) 'Admissions to Comprehensive Schools', *Education*, 22 August (Letter).

Clifford, P. and Heath, A. (1984) 'Selection does make a difference', *Oxford Review of Education*, 10(1), 85–97.

Clwyd, A. (1995) *Illegal Employment of Children*. London: House of Commons Report.

Cole, R. (1964) *Comprehensive Schools in Action*. London: Oldbourne.

Commission for Racial Equality (1984) *Racial Equality and the Youth Training Scheme*. London: CRE.

Commission for Racial Equality (1992) *Secondary School Admissions: Hertfordshire County Council Formal Investigation* (Report). London: CRE.

Conant, J.B. (1967) *The Comprehensive High School: A Second Report to Interested Citizens*. New York and London: McGraw-Hill.

Condon, J. (1994) 'Life in the service sector', *The Guardian*, 2 August.

Council for Industry and Higher Education (1995) *A Wider Spectrum of Opportunities*.

London: CIHE.

Cordingley, P. (1994) 'A framework for managing choices'. In Riley, K. (ed.) *Quality in Education: The Challenge for LEAs*. London: Local Government Management Board.

Cornell, R. *et al.* (1982) *Making The Difference*. Sydney: Allen and Unwin.

Croall, J. (1993) 'Rocky road to integration', *The Guardian*, 14 September.

Crombie White, R., Pring, R. and Brockington, D. (1995) *14 to 19 Education and Training: Implementing a Unified System of Learning*. London: RSA.

Cuttance, P. (1985) 'Frameworks for research on the effectiveness of schooling'. In Reynolds, D. (ed.) *Studying School Effectiveness*. Lewes: Falmer Press, 13–28.

Cuttance, P. (1992) 'Evaluating the effectiveness of schools'. In Reynolds, D. and Cuttance, P. (eds) *School Effectiveness: Research, Policy and Practice*. London: Cassell.

D'Hooghe, D. (1983) 'View from the combined system', *Comprehensive Education*, 45/46, 30–32.

Dale, R. (1983) 'Thatcherism and education'. In Ahier, J. and Flude, M. (eds) *Contemporary Education Policy*. London: Croom Helm, 223–55.

Dale, R.R. (1974) *Mixed or Single Sex?* Vol. 3. London: Routledge.

Daunt, P. (1975) *Comprehensive Values*. London: Heinemann Educational.

Davies, L. (1984) 'Gender and comprehensive schooling'. In Ball, S.J. (ed.) *Comprehensive Schooling: A Reader*. Lewes: Falmer Press, 47–65.

Davies, L. (1995) 'International indicators of democratic schools'. In Harber, C. (ed.) *Developing Democratic Education*. Ticknall: Education Now Books, 106–15.

Dawson, P. (1981) *Making a Comprehensive Work: The Road from Bomb Alley*. Oxford: Basil Blackwell.

DE (Department of Employment) (1994) *Effective Training Delivery: Youth Credits – Learning From Experience* (Developing Good Practice Series). London: DE.

DE (Department of Employment) (1995) *Financial Controls in Training and Enterprise Councils in England: A Report by the Comptroller and Auditor General*. London: DE.

Dean, J., Bradley, K., Choppin, B. and Vincent, D. (1979) *The Sixth Form and its Alternatives*. Slough: NFER.

Dean, J. and Choppin, B. (1977) *Educational Provision: 16–19*. Slough: NFER.

Deegan, W. (1991) 'Continuing education and the young adult: the community college experience in the USA'. In Evans, K. and Haffenden, I. (eds) *Education for Young Adults: International Perspectives*. London: Routledge, 44–53.

Denscombe, M. (1984) 'Control, controversy and the comprehensive school'. In Ball, S.J. (ed.) *Comprehensive Schooling: A Reader*. Lewes: Falmer, 133–54.

Denton, C. and Postlethwaite, K. (1984) 'The incidence and effective identification of pupils with high ability in comprehensive schools', *Oxford Review of Education*, 10(1), 99–113.

DES (Department of Education and Science) (1965) *The Organisation of Secondary Education*. Circular 10/65. London: HMSO.

DES (Department of Education and Science) (1966) *Middle Schools*. Building Bulletin No. 35. London: HMSO.

DES (Department of Education and Science) (1968) *Comprehensive Schools From Existing Buildings*. London: HMSO.

DES (Department of Education and Science) (1977a) *Educating Our Children: Four Subjects for Debate*. A Background Paper for the Regional Conferences, February and March 1977. London: HMSO.

DES (Department of Education and Science) (1977b) *Education in Schools: A Consultative Document* (Cmnd. 6869) (Green Paper). London: HMSO.

DES (Department of Education and Science) (1977c) *Curriculum 11–16 (HMI Red Book One)*. London: HMSO.

DES (Department of Education and Science) (1978) *Comprehensive Education: Report of a Conference held at the Invitation of the Secretary of State for Education and Science at the University of York 16th–17th December, 1977.* London: HMSO.

DES (Department of Education and Science) (1978b) *Mixed Ability Work in Comprehensive Schools: A Discussion Paper by a Working Party of Her Majesty's Inspectorate.* HMI Series: Matters for Discussion, 6. London: HMSO.

DES (Department of Education and Science) (1979) *Aspects of Secondary Education in England: A Survey by HM Inspectors of Schools.* London: HMSO.

DES (Department of Education and Science) (1980) *Examinations 16–18* (Macfarlane Report). London: HMSO.

DES (Department of Education and Science) (1981) *Curriculum 11-16: A Review of Progress (HMI Red Book Two).* London: HMSO.

DES (Department of Education and Science) (1983) *Curriculum 11–16: Towards a Statement of Entitlement: Curricular Reappraisal in Action.* London: HMSO.

DES (Department of Education and Science) (1987) *The National Curriculum 5–16: A Consultation Document.* London: DES.

DES (Department of Education and Science) (1988) *Advancing A Levels* (Higginson Report). London: HMSO.

DES (Department of Education and Science) (1991) *Education and Training for the 21st Century,* Vol. 1 (Cmnd.1536). London: HMSO.

De Witt, K. (1994) 'Let my people go – out of town', *New York Times,* reprinted in the *Guardian,* 18 August.

DfE (Department for Education) (1994a) Circular 7/94. London: HMSO.

DfE (Department for Education) (1994b) *Statistics of Education: Schools in England.* London: DfE.

DfE (Department for Education) (1995) *Statistics of Education: Schools in England.* London: DfE.

Docking, J.W. (1980) *Control and Discipline in Schools.* London: Harper and Row.

Donaghy, T. (1971) 'Northern Ireland's comprehensive schools', *Comprehensive Education,* **18** (Summer), 20–24.

Donald, J. (1990) 'Interesting times', *Critical Social Policy,* **9,** (3), 39–55.

Donald, J. (1992) *Sentimental Education.* London: Verso.

Douglas, J.W.B. (1964) *The Home and The School: A Study of Ability and Attainment in the Primary School.* London: MacGibbon and Kee.

Dummett, A. and McNeal, J. (1981) *Race and Church Schools.* London: the Runnymede Trust.

Duncan, C. (1986) 'Racism in education, training and employment'. In Ranson, S., Taylor, B. and Brighouse, T. (eds) *The Revolution in Education and Training.* Harlow: Longman, 109–120.

Dunford, J. (1995) 'A circle yet to be squared', *The Times Educational Supplement,* 10 February.

Edwards, T.,Fitz, J. and Whitty, G. (1989) *The State and Private Education: An Evaluation of the Assisted Places Scheme.* Lewes: Falmer Press.

Eggleston, J. (1965) 'How comprehensive is the Leicestershire Plan?', *New Society,* 25 March, 17.

EIS (Educational Institute of Scotland) (1994) *Higher Still.* Edinburgh: EIS.

Ekholm, M. (1994) 'The international context'. In Riley, K. (ed.) *Quality in Education: The Challenge for LEAs.* London: Local Government Management Board.

Elliott, B. (1970) 'The implementation of the Leicestershire Plan', *Forum,* 12(3), 76–78.

Evans, B. (1983) 'Countesthorpe College, Leicester'. In Moon, B. (ed.) *Comprehensive Schools: Challenge and Change.* Slough: NFER-Nelson, 5–32.

Evans, K. (1991) 'Vocational preparation in the United Kingdom: policy trends in education and training for young adults'. In Evans, K. and Haffenden, I. (eds) *Education for Young Adults: International Perspectives*. London: Routledge, 54–66.

Evans, K. and Haffenden, I. (eds) (1991) *Education for Young Adults: International Perspectives*. London: Routledge.

Fairbairn, A.N. (ed.) (1980) *The Leicestershire Plan*. London: Heinemann.

Fairley, J. (1994) 'The Worst Part of Breaking Up', *TES* (Scotland), 9 December.

Fairley, J. (1995) *A New Agenda for Local Government* (Public Lecture). Aberdeen: Centre for Public Policy and Management, Robert Gordon University.

Fairley, J. and Paterson, L. (1995) 'Scottish education and the New Managerialism', *Scottish Education Review*, 27(1), 13–36.

Farley, M. (1986) 'Examinations post–16: the need for radical reform'. In Ranson, S., Taylor, B. and Brighouse, T. (eds) *The Revolution in Education and Training*. Harlow: Longman, 141–51.

FEFC (Further Education Funding Council) (1994a) *Quality and Standards in Further Education in England: Chief Inspector's Annual Report, 1993/94*. London: FEFC.

FEFC (Further Education Funding Council) (1994b) *Annual Report*. London: FEFC.

FEFC (Further Education Funding Council) (1995) *Quality and Standards in Further Education in England: Chief Inspector's Annual Report, 1994/95*. London: FEFC.

Felsenstein, D. (1987) *Comprehensive Achievement*. London: Hodder and Stoughton.

Fenwick, I.G.K. (1976) *The Comprehensive School 1944-1970: The Politics of Secondary School Reorganisation*. London: Methuen.

FEU (Further Education Unit) (1979) *A Basis for Choice*. London: FEU.

FEU (Further Education Unit) (1992) *A Basis for Credit*. London: FEU.

Finch, W. (1994) 'Life on the Board', *NATFHE Journal*, Summer.

Finegold, D. (1993) 'The emerging post-16 system: analysis and critique'. In Richardson, W., Woolhouse, J. and Finegold, D. (eds) *The Reform of Post-Sixteen Education and Training in England and Wales*. Harlow: Longman, 38–53.

Finn, D. (1984) 'The Manpower Services Commission and the Youth Training Scheme', *Comprehensive Education*, 48, 6–9.

Finn, D. (1987) *Training Without Jobs: New Deals and Broken Promises*. London: Macmillan.

Finn, D. (1995) 'Job Seekers' Allowance and the 16-hour Rule'. *Working Brief 66* (July/August). London: Unemployment Unit and Youthaid.

Firth, G.C. (1963) *Comprehensive Schools in Coventry and Elsewhere*. Coventry: Coventry Education Committee.

Fiske, D. (1979) *Falling Numbers in Secondary Schools*. Sheffield: Sheffield City Polytechnic.

Fletcher, C., Caron, M. and Williams, W. (1985) *Schools On Trial: The Trials of Democratic Comprehensives*. Milton Keynes: Open University Press.

Floud, J.E., Halsey, A.H. and Martin, F.M. (1956) *Social Class and Educational Opportunity*. London: Heinemann.

Flower, F. (1983) 'Overview: analysis and problems', *Comprehensive Education*, 45/46, 18–21.

Flower, F. (1984) 'Common assessment', *Comprehensive Education*, 47, 14–15.

Fogelman, K. (1984) 'Problems in comparing examination attainment in selective and comprehensive secondary schools', *Oxford Review of Education*, 10(1), 33–43.

Ford, J. (1968) 'Comprehensive schools as social dividers', *New Society*, 10 October.

Ford, J. (1969) *Social Class and the Comprehensive School*. London: Routledge and Kegan Paul.

Fulford, C. (1979) 'A small comprehensive', *Forum*, 21(2), 65–8.

Galloway, D. *et al.* (1982) *Schools and Disruptive Pupils*. London: Longman.

Gane, V. (1985) 'A Head's view'. In Janes, F. *et al.* (eds) *Going Tertiary*. Yeovil: Tertiary College Association.

Gay, J. (1983) *The Debate About Church Schools*. Abingdon: Culham College.

546

Goldstein, H. (1984) 'The methodology of school comparisons', *Oxford Review of Education*, 10(1), 69–74.

Gray, J. (1995) 'Labour's struggle to avoid class war', *The Guardian*, 10 August.

Gray, J., Jesson, D. and Jones, B. (1984) 'Predicting differences in examination results between different local education authorities: does school organisation matter?', *Oxford Review of Education*, 10(1), 45–68.

Gray, J., McPherson, A.F. and Raffe, D. (1983) *Reconstruction in Secondary Education: Theory, Myth and Practice Since the War*. London: Routledge.

Green, A. (1990) *Education and State Formation: The Rise of Education Systems in England, France and the USA*. London: Macmillan.

Green, A. and Rikowski, G. (1995) 'Post-compulsory education and training for the 21st century', *Forum*, 37(3), 68–70.

Green, A.G. (1988) 'Introduction and overview: choice, progress and inequality'. In Green, A.G. and Ball, S.J. (eds) *Progress and Inequality in Comprehensive Education*. London: Routledge, 1–22.

Green, A.G. (1991) 'Magnet schools: not so attractive after all?' *Forum*, 33(2), 38–41.

Green, P. (1989) 'Sixth forms versus further education: overcoming the separation', *Comprehensive Education*, 2, (1), 20.

Green, P. and Poat, D. (1984) 'Some issues raised by TVEI in one school', *Comprehensive Education*, 48, 13–16.

Griffin, P.G.E. (1974) 'Darlington's divide', *Comprehensive Education*, 28 (Autumn), 22–23.

Grosvenor, I. (1995) 'Race, racism and black exclusion', *Forum*, 37(3).

Hainsworth, G. (1986) 'Planning the education system in Manchester'. In Ranson, S.,Taylor, B. and Brighouse, T. (eds) *The Revolution in Education and Training*. Harlow: Longman, 11–22.

Halls-Dickerson, P. (1989) 'Comprehensive education: surviving in the modern world', *Comprehensive Education*, 2(1), 27.

Halsall, E. (1968) 'The small comprehensive – flexible and open-ended?', *Comprehensive Education*, 8, (Spring), 7–9.

Halsall, E. (1973) *The Comprehensive School: Guidelines for the Reorganisation of Secondary Education*. Oxford: Pergamon Press.

Halsall, E. (ed.) (1970) *Becoming Comprehensive: Case Histories*. Oxford: Pergamon Press.

Handy, C. (1984) *Taken For Granted? Looking at Schools as Organisations*. Harlow: Longman.

Handy, C. (1994) *The Empty Raincoat*. London: Hutchinson.

Handy, C. and Aitken, R. (1986) *Understanding Schools as Organisations*. Harmondsworth: Penguin.

Harber, C. (1995) 'Democratic education and the international agenda'. In Harber, C. (ed.) *Developing Democratic Education*. Ticknall: Education Now Books, 1–19.

Harber, C. (ed) (1995) *Developing Democratic Education*. Ticknall: Education Now Books.

Hargreaves, D.H. (1967) *Social Relations in a Secondary School*. London: Routledge and Kegan Paul.

Hargreaves, D.H. (1982) *The Challenge for the Comprehensive School: Culture, Curriculum and Community*. London: Routledge and Kegan Paul.

Hargreaves, D.H. (1994) *The Mosaic of Learning: Schools and Teachers for the Next Century*. London: DEMOS Publications.

Heath, A. (1984) 'In defence of comprehensive schools in Oxford', *Review of Education*, 10(1), 115–123.

Hill, D. (1991) 'What's left in teacher education: teacher education, the Radical Left and policy proposals for the 1990s'. In Chitty, C. (ed.) *Changing the Future: Redprint for Education* (the

Hillcole Group). London: The Tufnell Press.

HMSO (1994) *Value for Money at Grant Maintained Schools: A Review of Performance. A Report by the Controller and Auditor General.* London: HMSO.

Holland, G. (1985) 'An MSC perspective'. In Watts, A. (ed.) *Education and Training 14–18: Policy and Practice.* Cambridge: NICEC.

Holland, G. (1986) 'Training young people for the future'. In Ranson, S., Taylor, B. and Brighouse, T. (eds) *The Revolution in Education and Training.* Harlow: Longman, 31–40.

Holland, G. (1995) 'A piggy bank for knowledge', *The Independent*, 20 March.

Holt, M. (1969) 'Is unstreaming irrelevant?', *Forum*, 11(2), 58–60.

Holt, M. (1976) 'Non-streaming and the common curriculum', *Forum*, 18(2), 55–57.

Holt, M. (1978) *The Common Curriculum: Its Structure and Style in the Comprehensive School.* London: Routledge and Kegan Paul.

Howe, D. (1971) 'Staff participation in comprehensive schools: Kingston-upon-Hull', *Comprehensive Education*, 17 (Spring), 23–24.

Huddlestone, P. (1993) 'Delivering the new 16–19 curriculum in FE colleges'. In Richardson, W., Woolhouse, J. and Finegold, D. (eds) *The Reform of Post-Sixteen Education and Training in England and Wales.* Harlow: Longman, 172–85.

Hugill, B. (1994) 'Tables turned on top schools', *The Observer*, 20 March.

Humanist Society (1975) *Objective, Fair and Balanced.* London: the Humanist Society.

Husen, T. and Boalt, G. (1968) *Educational Research and Educational Change: the Case of Sweden.* Stockholm: Almqvist and Wiksell; New York: John Wiley.

Hustler, D., Brighouse, T. and Rudduck, J. (eds) (1995) *Heeding Heads: Secondary Heads and Educational Commentators in Dialogue.* London: David Fulton Publishers.

Hutton, W. (1995) *The State We're In.* London: Jonathan Cape.

IAAM (Incorporated Association of Assistant Masters) (1967) *Teaching in Comprehensive Schools: A Second Report.* Cambridge: Cambridge University Press.

ILEA (Inner London Education Authority) (1967) *London Comprehensive Schools 1966.* London: ILEA.

ILEA (Inner London Education Authority) (1973) *Headteachers' Statement. A Stab in the Back.* London: ILEA.

Illich, I. (1971a) *Deschooling Society.* New York: Harper and Row.

Illich, I. (1971b) *Celebration of Awareness: A Call for Institutional Revolution.* Harmondsworth: Penguin.

Ingenkamp, K. (ed.) (1969) *Methods for the Evaluation of Comprehensive Schools.* Basel.

IPPR (Institute for Public Policy Research) (1990) *A British Baccalaureat: Ending the Division between Education and Training.* London: IPPR.

IPPR (Institute for Public Policy Research) (1993) *Education: A Different Version: An Alternative White Paper.* London: IPPR.

James, E. (1951) *Education and Leadership.* London: Harrap.

Jamieson, I. and Watts, T. (1987) 'Squeezing out enterprise', *The Times Educational Supplement*, 18 December.

Janes, F. *et al.* (eds) (1985) *Going Tertiary.* Yeovil: Tertiary Colleges Association.

Jessup, G. (1993) 'Towards a coherent post 16 qualifications framework: the role of GNVQs'. In Richardson, W., Woolhouse, J. and Finegold, D. (eds) *The Reform of Post-Sixteen Education and Training in England and Wales.* Harlow: Longman, 131–45.

Jones, A. (1987) *Leadership for Tomorrow's Schools.* Oxford: Basil Blackwell.

Jones, K. (1983) *Beyond Progressive Education.* London: Macmillan.

Jones, K. (1989) *Right Turn: The Conservative Revolution in Education.* London: Hutchinson Radius.

Jones-Davies, C. and Cave, R.G. (eds) (1976) *The Disruptive Pupil in the Secondary School.* London: Ward Lock.

Judd, J. (1994) 'Excluded pupils condemn school's selection lottery', *The Independent*, 11 May.

Kaufman, M. (1984) 'YTS and TVEI: hopes or threats?', *Comprehensive Education*, 48, 4.

Kent County Council (1978) *Education Vouchers in Kent.* Kent: Kent County Council.

Kerr, D. (1992) 'The academic curriculum – reforms resisted'. In Whiteside, T. *et al.* (eds) *16–19 Changes in Education and Training.* London: David Fulton Publishers, 42–54.

King, E. (1991) 'International perspectives on youth, development and education: a case study of China'. In Evans, K. and Haffenden, I. (eds) *Education for Young Adults: International Perspectives.* London: Routledge, 141–52.

King, H.R. (1958) 'The London School Plan: the present stage', *Forum*, 1(1), 6–9.

King, R. (1970) 'Short course neighbourhood comprehensive schools: an LEA case study', conducted by The University of Exeter, *Educational Review*, 26(2).

Labour Party (1982) *Learning for Life.* London: the Labour Party.

Labour Party (1994) *Opening Doors to a Learning Society: A Policy Statement on Education.* London: the Labour Party

Labour Party (1995) *Diversity and Excellence: A New Partnership for Schools.* London: the Labour Party.

Lacey, C. (1970) *Hightown Grammar: The School as a Social System.* Manchester: Manchester University Press.

Lacey, C. (1974) 'Destreaming in a "pressured" academic environment'. In Eggleston, J. (ed.) *Contemporary Research in the Sociology of Education.* London: Methuen.

Lacey, C. (1984) 'Selective and non-selective schooling: real or mythical comparisons?' *Oxford Review of Education*, 10(1), 75–84.

Lambert, R. (1966) *The State and Boarding Education.* London: Methuen.

Lang, P. (1994) 'Trying, but could do better'. In Lang, P., Best, R. and Lichtenberg, A. (eds) *Caring for Children; International Perspectives on Pastoral Care and PSE.* London: Cassell, 26–41.

Lang, P., Best, R. and Lichtenberg, A. (eds) (1994) *Caring for Children; International Perspectives on Pastoral Care and PSE.* London: Cassell.

Laslett, R. (1977) 'Disruptive and violent pupils: the facts and the fallacies', *Educational Review*, 29(3), 152–62.

Lawton, D. (1969) 'The idea of an integrated curriculum', *University of London Institute of Education Bulletin, New Series*, 19 (Autumn), 5–12.

Lawton, D. (1973) *Social Change, Educational Theory and Curriculum Planning.* Sevenoaks: Hodder and Stoughton.

Lawton, D. (1980) *The Politics of the School Curriculum.* London: Routledge and Kegan Paul.

LCC (London County Council) (1961) *London Comprehensive Schools: A Survey of Sixteen Schools.* London: LCC.

Leggate, P. (1993) 'The International Baccalaureat'. In Richardson, W., Woolhouse, J. and Finegold, D. (eds) *The Reform of Post-Sixteen Education and Training in England and Wales.* Harlow: Longman, 110–18.

Lewis, B.R. (1971) 'Transfer in Rotherham', *Comprehensive Education*, 17, 30–32.

Little, A. (1973) 'The bogus comprehensive', *Where*, No. 79.

LMNI (Labour Movement National Inquiry) (1987) *Report of the National Labour Movement Inquiry into Youth Unemployment and Training* (by Caroline Benn, John Eversley and Diana Holland). Birmingham: Trade Union Resources Centre (TURC).

Lovey, J., Docking, J. and Evans, R. (1993) *Exclusion From School: Provision for Disaffection at Key Stage Four.* London: David Fulton Publishers.

Lucas, N. (1995) 'Challenges facing teacher education: a view from a post-16 perspective', *Forum*, **37**(1), 11–13.

Lynch, J. (1972) 'Sixth Form College planning', *Comprehensive Education*, **21** (Summer), 17–19.

McAdam, N. (1994) 'Ulster's parents call for an end to 11-plus', *The Times Educational Supplement*, 11 November.

McAdam, N. (1995) 'Religious divide costs £35m', *The Times Educational Supplement*, 10 February.

McCarthy, E.E. (1968) 'The comprehensive myth', *Forum*, **11**(1), 25–27.

Macintosh, H. (1983) 'View from an external examiner', *Comprehensive Education*, **45/46**, 7–8.

Mackenzie, R.F. (1970) *State School*. Harmondsworth: Penguin.

Mackinnon, D. and Statham, J. with Hales, M. (1995) *Education in the UK: Facts and Figures*. London: Hodder and Stoughton, in association with the Open University.

Maclaggan, I. (1994) 'Youth Credits: Pilots Prove Ineffective', *Working Brief* (October/November). London: Unemployment Unit and Youthaid.

McPherson, A. and Willms, J.D. (1987) *Equalisation and improvement: The Efffect of Comprehensive Reorganisation in Scotland*. Edinburgh: Centre for Educational Sociology, University of Edinburgh.

McPherson, A. and Willms, J.D. (1988) 'Comprehensive schooling is better and fairer', *Forum*, **30**(2), 39–41.

McTaggart, M. (1994) 'Flashman is out', *The Times Educational Supplement*, 26 August.

Maden, M. (1995) 'Against all the odds', *The Times Educational Supplement*, 17 March.

Makins, V. (1985) 'The full course', *The Times Educational Supplement*, 26 July.

Marks, J. and Cox, C. (1984) 'Educational attainment in secondary schools', *Oxford Review of Education*, **10**(1), 7–31.

Marks, J., Cox, C. and Pomian-Srzednicki, M. (1983) *Standards in English Schools*. London: National Council for Educational Standards

Marsh, S. (1986) 'Women and the MSC'. In Benn, C. and Fairley, J. (eds) *Challenging the MSC on Jobs, Education and Training*. London: Pluto Press, 153–177.

Marquand, D. (1995) 'Vision wanted', the *Guardian*, 18 September.

Marsden, D. (1969) 'Which comprehensive principle?', *Comprehensive Education*, **13** (Autumn), 2–5.

Marsland, D. (1991) 'Trends in youth education and development, East and West'. In Evans, K. and Haffenden, I. (eds) *Education for Young Adults: International Perspectives*. London: Routledge, 28–43.

Mason, M. (1990) 'Special educational needs: just another label'. In Rieser, R. and Mason, M. (eds) *Disability Equality in the Classroom: A Human Rights Issue*. London: ILEA, 88–90.

Maude, A. (1969) 'The egalitarian threat'. In Cox, C.B. and Dyson, A.E. (eds) *Fight for Education: A Black Paper*. London: Critical Quarterly Society, 7–9.

Mauger, P. (1966) 'The flexible school', *Forum*, **8**(2), 60–61.

Maycock, M. (1978) *The Church of England Wants to Buy an Ealing Comprehensive: Why This is a National Issue*. London: Ealing High Schools Defence Campaign.

Maynard Potts, E.W. (c. 1970) *Defending Voluntary Grammar Schools*. London: National Education Association.

Measor, L. and Woods, P. (1984) *Identity and Culture: The Sociology of Pupil Transfer*. Milton Keynes: Open University Press.

Measor, L. and Woods, P. (1984b) *Changing Schools: Pupil Perspectives on Transfer to a Comprehensive*. Milton Keynes: Open University Press.

Meighan, R. (1988) *Flexi-Schooling*. Ticknall: Education Now Books.

Meighan, R. (1995) *Free Thinkers' Pocket Directory to the Educational Universe*. Nottingham: Educational Heretics Press.

Midwinter, E. (1971) 'The school and the community', *Comprehensive Education*, **18** (Summer), 31–36.

Miles, M. (1968) *Comprehensive Schooling: Problems and Perspectives*. Harlow: Longman.

Ministry of Education (1945) *The Nation's Schools: Their Plans and Purposes*. Pamphlet No. 1. London: HMSO.

Ministry of Education (1947) *Organisation of Secondary Education* (Circular 144). London: HMSO.

Ministry of Education (1959) *Fifteen To Eighteen* (The Crowther Report). London: HMSO.

Mitchell, P. (1983) 'View from the all-through school', *Comprehensive Education*, **45/46**, 22–23.

Monks, T.G. (1968) *Comprehensive Education in England and Wales. A Survey of Schools and their Organisation*. Slough: NFER.

Monks, T.G. (ed.) (1970) *Comprehensive Education in Action*. Slough: NFER.

Moon, B. (ed.) (1983) *Comprehensive Schools: Challenge and Change*, Slough: NFER/Nelson.

Morris, A. (1993) 'Towards a unified 16 plus curriculum'. In Richardson, W., Woolhouse, J. and Finegold, D. (eds) *The Reform of Post-Sixteen Education and Training in England and Wales*. Harlow: Longman, 119–30.

Morris, P. (1994) 'A local challenge to competitive pressure', *All-In Success*, 5(3).

Morris, R. (1994) *The Functions and Roles of Local Education Authorities*. Slough: Education Management Information Exchange (EMIE).

Morrish, I. (1970) *Education Since 1800*. London: Unwin.

Mortimore, P., Sammons, P., Stoll, L., Lewis, D. and Ecob, R. (1988) *School Matters: The Junior Years*. Wells: Open Books.

Moseley, P. (1983) 'View from the tertiary college', *Comprehensive Education*, **45/46**, 27–29.

Mountfield, A. (1991) *State Schools: A Suitable Case for Charity?* London: Directory of Social Change.

MSF (Union of Manufacturing, Science and Finance) (1994) *Why NVQs Need To Be Re-Assessed and Revised: Education and Policy Statement*. London: MSF.

Mumford, D.E. (1972) 'Unified 16–19', *Comprehensive Education*, **20**, 25–26.

Munn, P. (1995) 'Teacher involvement in curriculum policy in Scotland', *Educational Review*, 47(2), 209–17.

National Commission on Education (1993) *Learning to Succeed: A Radical Look at Education Today and a Strategy for the Future*. London: Heinemann.

NCC (National Curriculum Council) (1990) *Curriculum Guidance 3: The Whole Curriculum*. York: NCC.

NCC/SEAC (1993) *The National Curriculum and its Assessment: An Interim Report*. York: NCC/London: SEAC.

NCSS (National Council of Social Service) (1976) *Charity Law and Voluntary Organisations: A Report of an Enquiry under the Chairmanship of Lord Goodman*. London: National Council of Social Service.

Neave, G. (1970) 'Comprehensive schools in Berlin', *Comprehensive Education*, **15** (Summer), 21–23.

Neave, G. (1972) 'The Comprehensive Sixth', *Comprehensive Education*, **20** (Spring), 26–27.

Neave, G. (1975) *How They Fared: The Impact of the Comprehensive School upon the University*. London: Routledge and Kegan Paul.

NFER (National Foundation for Education Research) (1993) *Evaluation of the Second Year of Training Credits: Final Report*. Slough: NFER.

Norton, R. (ed.) (1994) *The Future of Education and Qualification in Youth and Community Work and the Irrelevance of NVQs*. Sheffield: The Community and Youth Workers' Union Education and Training Committee.

NUT (National Union of Teachers) (1958) *Inside the Comprehensive School*. London: Schoolmaster Publishing Company.

NUT (National Union of Teachers) (1993) *Comprehensives or Co-Existence*. London: NUT.

O'Connell, P.J. (1970) 'Sir Richard of Chichester School, London'. In Halsall, E. (ed.) *Becoming Comprehensive*. Oxford: Pergamon Press.

O'Connor, M. (1977) *Your Child's Comprehensive School*. London: Pan Books.

O'Connor, M. (1987) *Ruskin Ten Years On*. Contributions, 11. York: Centre for the Study of Comprehensive Schools, 2–10.

O'Keefe, D. (1992) *Truancy in English Secondary Schools*. London: University of North London Truancy Unit.

OECD (Organisation for Economic Cooperation and Development) (1994) *School: A Matter of Choice*. London: HMSO.

OFSTED (1993) *Unfinished Business: Full-time Educational Courses for 16–19 Year Olds: A Study by the Audit Commission and HMI*. Local Government Report No. 2. London: HMSO.

Orfield, G. (1993) *The Growth of Segregation in American Schools*. Report: National School Boards Association.

Osborne, G.S. (1968) *Scottish and English Schools: A Comparative Study of the Past Fifty Years*. London: Longman.

Owen, D. (1994) *Analysis of Ethnic Minorities in Further Education*, an Equal Opportunities Commission Report. Coventry: University of Warwick.

Owen, J. (1970) 'A 16–19 solution', *Education*, 27 March.

Ozolins, U. (1979) 'Lawton's refutation of a working-class curriculum'. In Johnson, L. and Ozolins, U. (eds) *Melbourne Working Papers*. Melbourne: University of Melbourne.

Palmer, J. (1974) 'Is this really comprehensive?', *Comprehensive Education*, 28 (Autumn), 24–25.

Passmore, B. and Durham, M. (1984) 'Eleven-plus plans come under parental fire', *The Times Educational Supplement*, 15 June.

Paterson, L. (1996) 'Liberation or control: what are the Scottish educational traditions of the twentieth century?'. In Devine, T. and Finlay, R. (eds) *Scotland in the Twentieth Century*. Edinburgh: Edinburgh University Press.

Pedley, R. (1963) *The Comprehensive School*. Harmondsworth: Penguin Books.

Pedley, R.R. (1969) 'Comprehensive disaster'. In Cox, C.B. and Dyson, A.E.(eds) *Fight for Education: A Black Paper*. London: Critical Quarterly Society, 45–48.

Peston, M. (1971) 'Address to the 1971 North of England Education Conference', *Comprehensive Education*, 17 (Spring), 3.

Peston, R. (1979) 'Unfair Oxbridge: a student's view', *Comprehensive Education*, 40 (Summer), 13.

Peters, R.S. (ed.) (1976) *The Role of the Head*. London: Routledge.

Pike, N. (1994) 'Not a sensible use of funds', *The Times Educational Supplement*, 26 August.

Plaskow, M. (1989) 'The case for a comprehensive curriculum from 16 to 19', *Comprehensive Education*, 2(1), 21.

Pluckrose, H. and Wilby, P. (eds) (1979) *The Condition of English Schooling*. Harmondsworth: Penguin.

Postlethwaite, K. and Denton, C. (1978) *Streams for the Future? The Long-term Effects of Early Streaming and Non-streaming: The Final Report of the Banbury Enquiry*. Banbury: Pubansco Publications.

Potter, G.H. (1969) 'Parental choice', *Education*, 8 August.

Potter, I. (1994) 'Gas Works in school', *All-In Success*, 6(1).

Pratley, B. (1983) 'View from the further education college', *Comprehensive Education*, 45/46, 25–26.

Pring, R. (1983) *Privatisation in Education*. London: RICE (Right to a Comprehensive Education), February.

Raffe, D. (1989) 'The Scottish Action Plan: a comprehensive system in the making for 16-plus', *Comprehensive Education*, 2(1), 23.

Raffe, D. (1993) 'The changing Scottish scene: implications for south of the border'. In Richardson, W., Woolhouse, J. and Finegold, D. (eds) *The Reform of Post-Sixteen Education and Training in England and Wales*. Harlow: Longman, 54–73.

Rainbow, B. (1993) 'Modular A and AS levels: the Wessex Project'. In Richardson, W., Woolhouse, J. and Finegold, D. (eds) *The Reform of Post-Sixteen Education and Training in England and Wales*. Harlow: Longman, 87–100.

Ranson, S. (1984) 'Towards a tertiary tripartism: new codes of social control and the 17-plus'. In Broadfoot, P. (ed.) *Selection, Certification and Control: Social Issues in Educational Assessment*. Lewes: Falmer Press, 221–44.

Ranson, S. (1996) 'Local democracy for education', *Forum*, 38(1), 11–13.

Ranson, S., Taylor, B. and Brighouse, T. (eds) (1986) *The Revolution in Education and Training*. Harlow: Longman.

Reed, J. (1961 edn) *Ten Days That Shook the World*. London: Lawrence and Wishart.

Reeves, F. (1995) 'The Modernity of Further Education', *Education Now*, Bilston College.

Reeves, F. (1995b) 'Democratising further education'. In Harber, C. (ed.) *Developing Democratic Education*. Ticknall: Education Now Books, 36–43.

Reid, I. (1990) *Social Class Differences in Britain* (3rd edn.). London: Fontana.

Reynolds, D. (ed.) (1985) *Studying School Effectiveness*. Lewes: Falmer Press.

Reynolds, D. and Reid, K. (1985) 'The second stage: towards a reconceptualisation of theory and methodology in school effectiveness'. In Reynolds, D. (ed.) *Studying School Effectiveness*. Lewes: Falmer Press.

Reynolds, D., Sullivan, M. and Murgatroyd, S. (1987) *The Comprehensive Experiment: A Comparison of the Selective and Non-selective Systems*. Lewes: Falmer Press.

Richardson, E. (1975) *Authority and Organisation in the Secondary School*. London and Basingstoke: Macmillan Educational.

Richardson, W., Woolhouse, J. and Finegold, D. (eds) (1993) *The Reform of Post-Sixteen Education and Training in England and Wales*. Harlow: Longman.

Rieser, R. and Mason, M. (eds) (1990) *Disability Equality in the Classroom: A Human Rights Issue*. London: ILEA.

Robertson, T.S. (1977) 'Pupil progress in ten comprehensive schools', *Comprehensive Education*, 36 (Summer), 8–19.

Robins, D. and Cohen, P. (1978) *Knuckle Sandwich: Growing Up in the Working-Class City*. Harmondsworth: Penguin.

Robinson, E. (1986) 'The MSC and adult education'.In Benn, C. and Fairley, J. (eds) *Challenging the MSC on Jobs, Education and Training*. London: Pluto Press, 123–33.

Robinson, E. (1994) 'Politics and curriculum', *Forum*, 36, (2) 50–52.

Rogers, M. (1992) *Opting Out: Choice and the Future of Schools*. London: Lawrence and Wishart.

Ross, J.M., Bunton, W.J., Evison, P. and Robertson, T.S. (1972) *A Critical Appraisal of Comprehensive Education*. Slough: NFER.

Rowe, A. (1970) 'An answer to Dennis Marsden', *Comprehensive Education*, 14 (Spring), 8–10.

Rubinstein, D. (1979) 'Ellen Wilkinson re-considered', *History Workshop Journal*, 7.

Rubinstein, D. and Simon, B. (1973) *The Evolution of the Comprehensive School 1926-1972*. London: Routledge and Kegan Paul.

Rutter, M., Maughan, B., Mortimore, P. and Ouston, J. (1979) *Fifteen Thousand Hours: Secondary Schools and their Effects on Children*. London: Open Books.

Saumerez-Smith, J. (1994) 'Crammers fail to make the grade', *The Sunday Telegraph*, 20 March.

Sayer, C. (1989) 'The importance of a post-16 plan', *Comprehensive Education*, 2 (1), 17.

SCAA (School Curriculum and Assessment Authority) (1994) *The National Curriculum and its Assessment: Final Report*. London: SCAA.

SEA (Socialist Education Association) (1981) *The Dual System of Voluntary and County Schools: First Report*. Manchester: SEA.

Searle, C. (1994a) 'The culture of exclusion'. In Bourne, J., Bridges, L. and Searle, C. (eds) *Outcast England*. London: Institute of Race Relations, 17–28.

Searle, C. (1994b) 'Strengths and struggles', *Teaching London Kids*, No. 27.

Searle, C. (1996) 'A different achievement: excellence in the inner city', *Forum*, 38 (1), 17–20.

Secular Society (1984) *Say No to Denominational Schools*. London: the Secular Society.

SED (Scottish Education Department) (1971) *The Structure of Promoted Posts in Secondary Schools*. Edinburgh: SED.

Semmens, G.C. (1972) 'Comeback:school democracy', *Comprehensive Education*, 20 (Spring), 18–19.

Sharp, J. (1973) *Open School: The Experience of 1964–1970 at Wyndham School, Egremont, Cumberland*. London: Dent.

Shrosbree, C. (1988) *The Public Schools and Private Education: The Clarendon Commission 1861–1864 and the Public Schools Act*. Manchester: Manchester University Press.

Simmons, H. (1971) 'Examination results', *Comprehensive Education*, 17 (Spring), 8–9.

Simmons, H.W. and Morgan, R. (1969) *Inside a Comprehensive School*. Brighton: Clifton Books.

Simon, B. (1953) *Intelligence Testing and the Comprehensive School*. London: Methuen.

Simon, B. (ed.) (1957) *New Trends in English Education*. London: MacGibbon and Kee.

Simon, B. (1966) 'The neighbourhood school', *Comprehensive Education*, 4 (Autumn), 4–8.

Simon, B. (1970a) 'Egalitarianism versus education', *Comprehensive Education*, 14 (Spring), 6–8.

Simon, B. (1970b) 'Streaming and the comprehensive school', *Secondary Education*, 1 (1), 3–5.

Simon, B. (1979) 'HMIs and mixed ability', *Forum*, 21, (2), 53–55.

Simon, B. (1991) *Education and the Social Order, 1940-1990*. London: Lawrence and Wishart.

Simon, B. (1994) *The State and Educational Change: Essays in the History of Education and Pedagogy*. London: Lawrence and Wishart.

Simon, B. (1996) 'IQ redivivus, or the return of selection', *Forum*, 38 (1), 4–7.

Simon, B. and Chitty, C. (1993) *SOS: Save Our Schools*. London: Lawrence and Wishart.

Slinn, R. (1983) 'View from a researcher on profiles', *Comprehensive Education*, 45/46, 9–10.

Smithers, A. and Robinson, P. (1991) *Beyond Compulsory Education*. London: Council for Industry and Higher Education.

Smout, T.C. (1986) *A Century of the Scottish People, 1830–1950*. London: Collins.

SOED (Scottish Office Education Department) (1992) *Upper Secondary Education in Scotland: Report of the Committee to Review Curriculum and Examinations in the Fifth and Sixth Years of Secondary Education in Scotland* (Howie Report). London: HMSO.

Sparrow, J. (1969) 'Egalitarianism and an academic elite'. In Cox, C.B. and Dyson, A.E. (eds) *Fight for Education: A Black Paper*. London: Critical Quarterly Society, 64–66.

Spours, K. (1993) 'The recent background to qualifications reform in England and Wales' and

'Analysis: the reform of qualifications within a divided system'. In Richardson, W., Woolhouse, J. and Finegold, D. (eds) *The Reform of Post-Sixteen Education and Training in England and Wales*. Harlow: Longman 76–86 and 146–170.

SSEC (Secondary School Examinations Council) (1943) *Curriculum and Examinations in Secondary Schools* (The Norwood Report). London: HMSO.

STABIS (State Boarding Information Service) (1993) *Directory of Maintained Boarding Schools*. London: STABIS.

Stansbury, D.R. (1971) 'R.P.A: a new qualification', *Comprehensive Education*, 17 (Spring), 11–13.

Steedman, J. (1980) *Progress in Secondary Schools*. London: National Children's Bureau.

Steedman, J. (1983) *Examination Results in Selective and Non-selective Secondary Schools*. London: National Children's Bureau.

Stewart, T. (1972) 'Coexistence and creaming: Birmingham's double standard', *Comprehensive Education*, 20 (Spring), 7–8.

Svensson, N.E. (1962) *Ability Grouping and Scholastic Achievement: Report of a five year follow-up study in Stockholm*. Stockholm: Almqvist and Wiksell.

Szamuely, T. (1969) 'Comprehensive inequality'. In Cox, C.B. and Dyson, A.E. (eds) *Black Paper Two: The Crisis in Education*. London: Critical Quarterly Society, 48–56.

Tawney, R.H. (1922) *Secondary Education For All: A Policy for Labour*. London: George Allen and Unwin.

Taylor, B. (1971) 'The Newcastle experience', *Comprehensive Education*, 17 (Spring), 29–30.

Taylor, M. and Garson, Y. (1982) *Schooling in the Middle Years*. Stoke-on-Trent: Trentham Books.

Taylor, W. (1973) *Heading For Change*. London: Routledge and Kegan Paul.

Terry, D. (1987) *The Tertiary College: Assuring Our Future*. Milton Keynes: Open University Press.

Thewlis, J. (1988) 'Progress and the radical educational press'. In Green, A.G. and Ball, S.J. (eds) *Progress and Inequality in Comprehensive Education*. London: Routledge, 247–68.

Thompson, D. (1965) 'Towards an unstreamed comprehensive school', *Forum*, 7(3), 82–89.

Thompson, D. (1969) 'An experiment in unstreaming', *Forum*, 11(2), 56–7.

Thompson, D. (1974) 'Non-streaming did make a difference', *Forum*, 16(2), 45–49.

Thomson, G. (1929) *A Modern Philosophy of Education*. London: Allen and Unwin.

Thornbury, R. (1978) *The Changing Urban School*. London: Methuen.

Tombs, D. (1994) 'The New Right and RE', *Forum*, 36, (3), 85–86.

Toogood, P. (1984) *The Head's Tale*. Telford: Dialogue Publications.

Travers, T. (1976) 'Academic results and Comprehensives', *Comprehensive Education*, 32 (Spring), 14–19.

Trebilcock, R. (1985) 'A matrix structure'. In Janes, F. *et al.* (eds) *Going Tertiary*. Yeovil: Tertiary College Association, 91–101.

Unwin, L. (1993) 'Training Credits: the pilot doomed to succeed'. In Richardson, W., Woolhouse, J. and Finegold, D. (eds) *The Reform of Post-Sixteen Education and Training in England and Wales*. Harlow: Longman, 205–223.

Venning, P. (1980a) 'A level absolutes', *The Times Educational Supplement*, 18 January.

Venning, P. (1980b) 'Overloading the system', *The Times Educational Supplement*, 21 October.

Venning, P. (1983) 'The mystery of the vanishing students', *The Times Educational Supplement*, 31 October.

Vernon, P.E. (ed.) (1957) *Secondary School Selection*. London: Methuen.

Walford, G. (1990) *Privatisation and Privilege in Education*. London: Routledge.

Walford, G. (1992) 'Privatisation in education', *Forum*, 34 (4).

Walford, G. (ed.) (1985) *Schooling in Turmoil*. London: Croom Helm.

Walters, L. (1994) 'Brown v Board of Education – A report on racial segregation', *The Christian Science Monitor*, 16 May.

Warwick, D. (1983) 'View from the sixth form college', *Comprehensive Education*, 45/46, 24.

Watkins, P. (1993) 'The National Curriculum: an agenda for the nineties'. In Chitty, C. and Simon, B. (eds) *Education Answers Back: Critical Responses to Government Policy.* London: Lawrence and Wishart, 70–84.

Watts, J. (ed.) (1977) *The Countesthorpe Experience: The First Five Years.* London: George Allen and Unwin.

Waugh, C. (1989) 'Empowering the majority after 16', *Comprehensive Education*, 2(1), 22.

Waugh, C. (1995) 'Interview with practitioners', *General Educator*, 33.

Wearn, B. (1995) 'Peripatetic music teachers and the lethal cocktail'. In *Some Educational Issues of 1995.* London: Council for Educational Advance.

Webb, S. (1908) 'Secondary education'. In Binns, H.B. (ed.) *A Century of Education.* London: Dent, 284–96.

Weeks, A. (1983) *London Comprehensive Schools in 1982.* Twickenham: St Mary's College (unpublished research report).

Weeks, A. (1986) *Comprehensive Schools: Past, Present and Future.* London: Methuen.

Weinberg, A. (1972) 'Comprehensive school leavers in the community', *Comprehensive Education*, 20 (Spring), 20–21.

Weiner, G. (ed.) (1985) *Just a Bunch of Girls.* Milton Keynes: Open University Press.

Weston, P. (1977) *Framework for the Curriculum: A Study in Secondary Schooling.* Slough: NFER.

Weston, R. (1991) *Schools of Thought: Hampshire Architecture 1974–1991.* Winchester: Hampshire County Council.

Whalley, G.E. (1970) 'Guided parental choice', *Trends in Education*, 18, 28–34.

White, J. (1973) *Towards a Compulsory Curriculum.* London: Routledge and Kegan Paul.

Whiteside, T., Sutton, A. and Everton, T. (eds) (1992) *16-19: Changes in Education and Training.* London: David Fulton.

Wilby, P. (1979) 'Streaming and standards'. In Pluckrose, H. and Wilby, P. (eds) *The Condition of English Schooling.* Harmondsworth: Penguin.

Williams, P. and Murphy, T. (1979, updated 1984) 'The Dual System: End it or Mend it'. *Teaching London Kids*, Nos. 14 and 22.

Williams, R. (1958) *Culture and Society.* London: Chatto and Windus.

Williams, R. (1961) *The Long Revolution.* Harmondsworth: Penguin Books.

Willis, P. (1977) *Learning To Labour: How Working-Class Kids get Working-Class Jobs.* Aldershot: Saxon House.

Woodley, A. (1976) 'Academic results and comprehensives', *Comprehensive Education*, 32 (Spring), 11–13.

Woolhouse, J. (1993) 'Towards a world-class system'. In Richardson, W., Woolhouse, J. and Finegold, D. (eds) *The Reform of Post-Sixteen Education and Training in England and Wales.* Harlow: Longman.

World Bank (1993) *Social Indicators of Development.* London: John Hopkins Press.

Wright, N. (1977) *Progress in Education: A Review of Schooling in England and Wales.* London: Croom Helm.

Wymer, I.K. (1975) 'Power Partnership', *The New Schoolmaster*, 52, 1.

Young, S. (1994) 'GNVQs beat path to degrees', *The Times Educational Supplement*, 26 August.

Index